PHILIP'S
WORLD
ATLAS

CHANCELLOR
PRESS

Text: Richard Widdows
Picture Acknowledgement: page 16, Tony Stone Images

Previously published in 2000 by Chancellor Press
as Philip's School Atlas

This 2001 edition published
by Chancellor Press, an imprint of Bounty Books,
a division of Octopus Publishing Group Ltd,
2-4 Heron Quays, London E14 4JP

Copyright © 2000 Octopus Publishing Group Ltd
Maps and index © 2000 George Philip Ltd
Cartography by Philip's

ISBN 0 75370 436 6

A CIP catalogue record for this book is available
from the British Library.

Produced by Toppan Printing Co., (H.K.) Ltd.
Printed in Hong Kong

Contents

● The Physical Earth

The Earth in Motion	4–5	Shaping the Landscape	10–11
Oceans	6–7	Climate	12–13
The Unstable Earth	8–9	Water and Vegetation	14–15

● Maps

General Reference	1	Arabia and the Horn of Africa	32
The World: Political	2–3	The Near East	33
Arctic Ocean	4	Northern Africa	34–35
Antarctica	5	Central and Southern Africa	36–37
Scandinavia	6–7	Australia and Oceania: Physical and Political	38
England and Wales	8–9	New Zealand	39
The British Isles	10	Western Australia	40–41
Netherlands, Belgium and Luxembourg	11	Eastern Australia	42–43
Middle Europe	12–13	Pacific Ocean	44–45
France	14	Canada	46–47
Spain and Portugal	15	Eastern Canada	48–49
Italy and the Balkan States	16–17	Western Canada	50–51
Eastern Europe and Turkey	18–19	Eastern United States	52–53
Russia and Central Asia	20–21	Middle United States	54–55
Japan	22–23	Western United States	56–57
China and Korea	24–25	Mexico	58–59
Indonesia and the Philippines	26–27	Central America and the West Indies	60–61
South Asia	28–29	South America – North	62–63
The Middle East	30–31	South America – South	64

● Index

65–112

The Earth in Motion

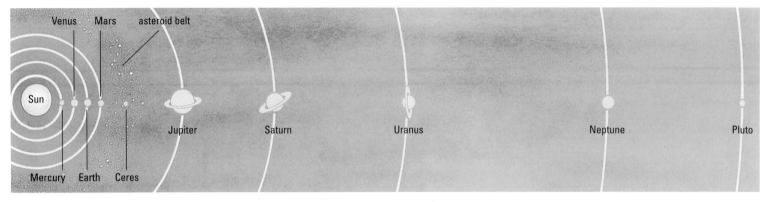

Venus   Mars   asteroid belt

Sun

Jupiter   Saturn   Uranus   Neptune   Pluto

Mercury   Earth   Ceres

● The solar system

A tiny part of one of the billions of galaxies (collections of stars) that make up the universe, the solar system lies about 27,000 light-years from the centre of our own galaxy, "the Milky Way". At least 4,700 million years old – and possibly far more – it comprises a central sun with nine planets revolving around it, attracted by its strong gravitational pull *(above)*.

The Sun's diameter is 109 times that of Earth's 12,756 kilometres, and the temperature at its core – caused by continuous fusions of hydrogen into helium – is estimated to be 15,000°C. The Sun accounts for almost 99.9% of the total mass of the solar system (Jupiter contains most of the remainder), and is its only source of light and heat.

By composition as well as distance, the planets divide neatly into two groups: an inner system of four small solid planets, and an outer system of four huge gas giants. Between the two groups lies a scattering of asteroids, perhaps as many as 40,000. The ninth and smallest planet, Pluto (discovered only in 1930), appears to be a rocky world of the "inner" type.

All the planets orbit the sun in the same direction and almost in the same plane. Only Mercury and Pluto follow paths that deviate noticeably from a circular one. Near perihelion (its closest approach to the Sun) Pluto actually passes inside the orbit of Neptune, a situation that last occurred between 1983 and 1999.

● Time

Year The time taken by the Earth to revolve around the Sun, or 365.24 days.
Month The approximate time taken by the Moon to revolve around the Earth; the 12 months of the year in fact vary from 28 (29 in a Leap Year) to 31 days.
Week An artificial period of 7 days; unlike days, months and years, it is not based on astronomical time.
Day The time taken by the Earth to complete one rotation on its axis.
Hour One day comprises 24 hours, which are usually divided into hours AM (*ante meridiem*, or before noon) and PM (*post meridiem*, or after noon), though timetables use the 24-hour system from midnight to midnight.

● The seasons

The Earth revolves around the Sun once a year, always "tilted" an angle of 66½°. In June *(far left)*, the northern hemisphere is tilted towards the Sun, and as a result it receives more hours of sunshine during a day and enjoys its warmest season, summer. By December the Earth has rotated halfway round the Sun, so that the southern hemisphere is now tilted towards the sun and has its warmest season, while the hemisphere that is tilted away from the Sun has its coldest season, winter.

On 21 June the Sun is directly overhead at the Tropic of Cancer (23½°N), representing midsummer in the northern hemisphere; midsummer in the southern hemisphere occurs on 21 December, when the Sun is directly overhead at the Tropic of Capricorn (23½°S). These are the solstices; the equinox occur in spring and autumn.

Northern Spring Equinox

Southern Autumn Equinox

Equinox is one of the two times in the year when day and night are of equal length due to the Sun being overhead at the Equator.

Northern Summer Solstice

Northern Winter Solstice

21 March

21 June   SUN   **21 December**

Southern Winter Solstice

Southern Summer Solstice

21 September

Southern Spring Equinox

Northern Spring Equinox

Solstice is one of the two times in the year when the Sun is overhead at one of the Tropics 23½° north or south of the Equator.

● Day and night

The Sun appears to "rise" in the east, reach its highest point at noon, and then "set" in the west, to be followed by night. In reality it is not the Sun that is moving but the Earth, rotating ("spinning" on its axis) from west to east. Due to the tilting of the Earth, the length of day and night varies from place to place and month to month *(left)*.

At the summer solstice in the northern hemisphere (21 June), the area inside the Arctic Circle has total daylight and the area inside the Antarctic Circle has total darkness. The opposite occurs at the winter solstice on 21 December. At latitude 50° the length of day and night varies from about 16 hours to about 8 hours; at latitude 30° it varies from about 14 to 10 hours; at the Equator, the length of day and night are almost equal all year round.

The Earth rotates through 360° in one day, and moves 15° every hour. As a result the world is divided into 24 official time zones *(right)*, each centred on lines of longitude at 15° intervals. The Greenwich meridian lies at the centre of the "first" zone.

21 June   21 December

N. Pole: 24 hours daylight

N. Pole: 24 hours darkness
10½ hours daylight

N

N

SUN'S RAYS

12 hours daylight 0°

13½ hours daylight

13½ hours daylight

0° 12 hours daylight

10½ hours daylight

S. Pole: 24 hours darkness

S. Pole: 24 hours daylight

S

S

The Moon

The Moon rotates more slowly than the Earth, making one complete turn on its axis in just over 27 days. Since this corresponds to its period of revolution around the Earth, the Moon always presents the same hemisphere to us on Earth, and we never see "the dark side".

The interval between one full Moon and the next (and thus also between two new Moons) is about 29½ days – a lunar month. The apparent changes in the shape of the Moon are caused by its changing position in relation to the Earth (right); like the planets, the Moon produces no light of its own and shines only by reflecting the rays of the Sun.

Distance from Earth The Moon orbits the Earth at a mean distance of 384,199 kilometres, at an average speed of 3,683 kilometres per hour in relation to the Earth.
Size and mass The average diameter of the Moon is 3,475 kilometres. It is 400 times smaller than the Sun but about 400 times closer to the Earth, so we see them as the same size. The Moon has a mass of about $1/81$ that of Earth, and its surface gravity is one-sixth that of Earth.
Visibility Only 59% of the Moon's surface is directly visible from Earth; reflected light takes 1.25 seconds to reach Earth – compared to 8 minutes 27.3 seconds for light from the Sun.
Temperature With the Sun overhead the temperature on the lunar equator can reach 117.2°C, and at night it can sink to -162.7°C.

Tides

The daily rise and fall of the ocean's tides are the result of the gravitational pull of the Moon and that of the Sun, though the effect of the latter is less than half that of the Moon. The effect is greatest on the hemisphere of the Earth facing the Moon and causes a tidal "bulge".

When lunar and solar forces pull together, with Sun, Earth and Moon in line (near new and full Moons), higher spring tides and lower low tides occur, creating a greater tidal range; when lunar and solar forces are least coincidental, with the Moon and Sun at an angle (near the Moon's first and third quarters) "neap tides" occur, which have a small tidal range.

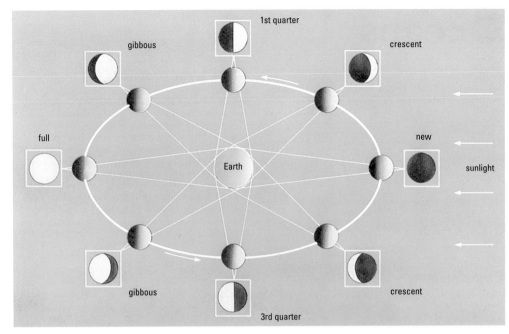

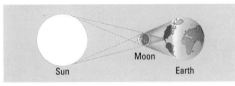

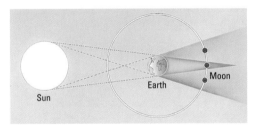

A solar eclipse (left) occurs when the Moon passes between the Sun and the Earth. It will cause a partial eclipse of the Sun if the Earth passes through the Moon's outer shadow, or a total eclipse if the inner cone shadow crosses the Earth's surface. A total solar eclipse was visible in many parts of the northern hemisphere in the summer of 1999.

In a lunar eclipse (left) the Earth's shadow crosses the Moon and, as with the solar version, provides either a partial or total eclipse. Eclipses do not occur every month because of the 5° difference between the plane of the Moon's orbit and the plane in which the Earth moves. In the 1990s, for example, only 14 eclipses were possible – seven partial and seven total – and each was visible only from certain parts of the world which vary with every eclipse. The same period witnessed 13 solar eclipses, six partial (or annular) and seven total.

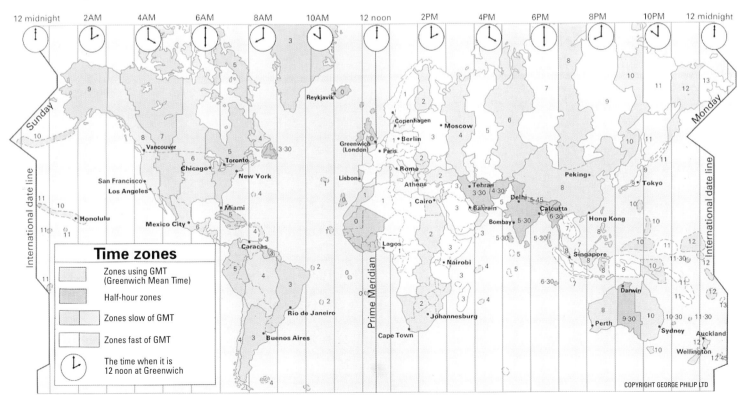

Oceans

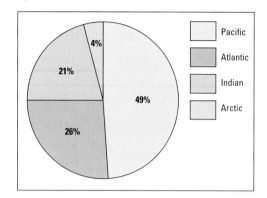

- Pacific
- Atlantic
- Indian
- Arctic

4%
21%
49%
26%

● The great oceans

The Earth is a watery planet: almost 71% of its surface is covered by its oceans and seas. This great liquid cloak gives our planet its characteristic and beautiful blue appearance from space, and is one of the two obvious differences between the Earth and its two near-neighbours, Venus and Mars. The other difference is the presence of life – and the two are closely linked.

In a strict geographical sense the Earth has only three oceans – Atlantic, Indian and Pacific. The legendary "Seven Seas" would require these to be divided at the Equator and the addition of the smaller Arctic Ocean. Geographers do not recognise the Antarctic Ocean (much less the "Southern Ocean") as a separate entity.

Over 360 million sq km of the Earth's surface area are covered by oceans and seas, with the Pacific accounting for nearly 36% of the total.

Winter in Northern Hemisphere

Ocean currents

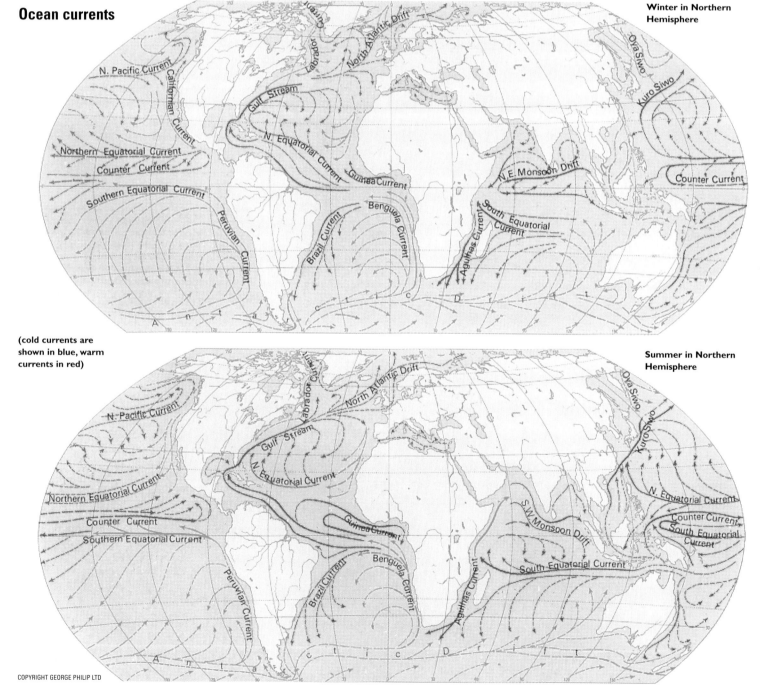

(cold currents are shown in blue, warm currents in red)

Summer in Northern Hemisphere

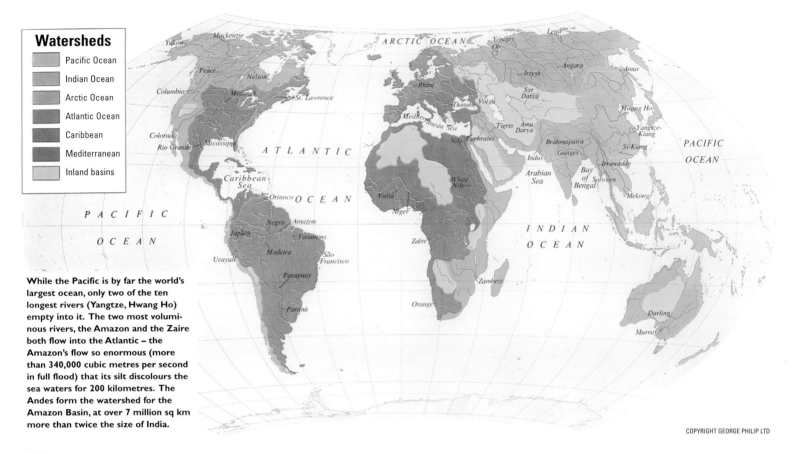

Watersheds

- Pacific Ocean
- Indian Ocean
- Arctic Ocean
- Atlantic Ocean
- Caribbean
- Mediterranean
- Inland basins

While the Pacific is by far the world's largest ocean, only two of the ten longest rivers (Yangtze, Hwang Ho) empty into it. The two most voluminous rivers, the Amazon and the Zaire both flow into the Atlantic – the Amazon's flow so enormous (more than 340,000 cubic metres per second in full flood) that its silt discolours the sea waters for 200 kilometres. The Andes form the watershed for the Amazon Basin, at over 7 million sq km more than twice the size of India.

The ocean currents

Moving immense quantities of energy as well as billions of tonnes of water every hour, the ocean currents (*left*) are a vital part of the heat engine that drives the Earth's climate. The currents are produced by a twofold mechanism: at the surface winds push masses of water before them, while in the deeper ocean variations in density cause slow vertical movements.

The pattern of circulation of the major surface currents is determined by the displacement caused by the Earth's rotation. The deflection is most obvious near the Equator, where the Earth's surface is spinning eastwards at 1,700 kilometres per hour; currents moving towards the polar regions are "curved" clockwise in the northern hemisphere and anti-clockwise in the southern hemisphere.

The result of this displacement (known as the Coriolis Effect) is a system of spinning circles called gyres (*below*). The Coriolis Effect piles water up on the left of each gyre, creating a narrow, fast-moving flow that is matched by a slower, broader returning current on the right.

North and south of the Equator, the fastest currents are located in the west and east respectively. In each case, warm water moves from the Equator and cold water returns to it. Cold currents often bring an upwelling of nutrients, supporting the world's most economically important fisheries; the Peruvian Current is an example.

It is this upwelling that is suppressed by El Niño, the phenomenon caused by the eastward movement of warm water from the western Pacific, thus depriving the fishing areas of nutrients. In an El Niño year the water is warmed by as much as 7°C, disturbing the tropical atmospheric circulation and causing climatic havoc in areas thousands of kilometres away – including heavy rainfall in the USA, rainforest fires in south-east Asia and drought in Australia.

Depending on the prevailing winds, some currents on or near the Equator may reverse their direction in the course of a year – a seasonal variation on which Asian monsoon rains depend. If the reversal fails, it can mean disaster for millions of people on the Indian subcontinent.

While the depths of the major oceans are not far apart (*below*), the sea-floor is no more uniform than the surface of the continents, featuring plains, hills, mid-ocean ridges and seamounts (underwater volcanoes). Trenches also slice dramatically into the Earth's crust – especially in the Pacific, where eight trenches reach down more than the height of Everest. Life is scarce in the deep ocean, but a few organisms have been found, even in the abysmal darkness of the great trenches.

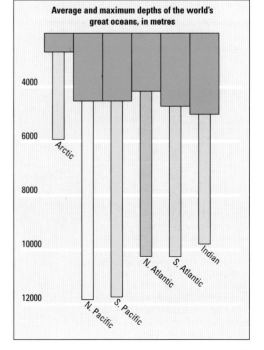

Average and maximum depths of the world's great oceans, in metres

NORTH
Arctic

Atlantic Ocean

SOUTH
Antarctic

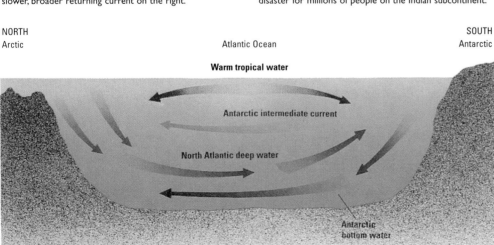

Warm tropical water

Antarctic intermediate current

North Atlantic deep water

Antarctic bottom water

7

The Unstable Earth

● Profile of the Earth

While the origin of the Earth is still open to debate, the most widely accepted theory is that it was formed 4,700 billion years ago – and possibly far more, from a solar cloud consisting mainly of hydrogen. The cloud condensed, forming the planets.

The lighter elements floated to the surface of the Earth, where they cooled to form a crust, but the inner material remained hot and molten. Although the first rocks were formed over 3,500 billion years ago, the Earth's surface has been constantly altered – from inside as well as outside forces – ever since.

The brittle, low-density crust accounts for only 1.5% of the Earth's volume. The rigid upper mantle extends to about 1,000 km, below which is a more viscous mantle 1,900 km thick. The molten outer core is 2,100 km thick, and a liquid transition zone about 5,000 km below the surface separates it from the solid inner core, a sphere 2,700 km across where rock is three times as dense as in the crust. The temperature here is probably about 5,000°C.

● The moving continents

The migration of the continents is a feature which, as far as we know, is unique to the planet Earth. The jigsaw puzzle fit of the coastlines on each side of the Atlantic Ocean led the German meteorologist Alfred Wegener to propose his theory of continental drift at the beginning of the 20th century (right). The theory suggests that an ancient super-continent, which he called Pangaea, once incorporated all the land masses and gradually split up to form the continents we see today.

Geological evidence that the continents once formed a single land mass is provided by distinctive rock formations that can be assembled into continuous belts when South America and Africa are lined up next to each other. There are also the processes of mountain building, notably India "colliding" with Asia and crumpling up sediments to form the Himalayas. Distribution of some plants and animals in the past, as well as ancient climatic zones, can only be explained by the theory of continental drift. There is nothing to suggest the process will not continue.

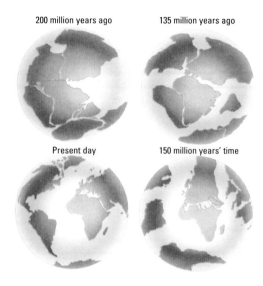

200 million years ago   135 million years ago

Present day   150 million years' time

● Plate tectonics

The original debate about continental drift was a prelude to a more radical idea developed since the 1960s: plate tectonics. The basic theory is that the Earth's crust is made up of a series of rigid plates (left) which float on a soft layer of the mantle, and are moved about by continental convection currents within the Earth's interior. These plates diverge and converge along margins marked by seismic (earthquake) activity. Plates diverge from mid-ocean ridges, where molten lava pushes upwards and forces the plates apart; converging plates form trenches or mountain ranges.

● Earthquakes

Earthquakes are a series of rapid vibrations originating from the slipping or faulting parts of the Earth's crust, when stresses build to breaking point. They usually occur at depths varying from 8 to 30 kilometres.

The magnitude of earthquakes is rated according to the Richter or the Mercalli scale. The former measures absolute earthquake power with mathematical precision, each step representing a tenfold increase in shockwave amplitude, and in theory there is no upper limit. Based on observed effects, Mercalli is more meaningful, ranging from I (recorded by seismologists) to XII (total destruction).

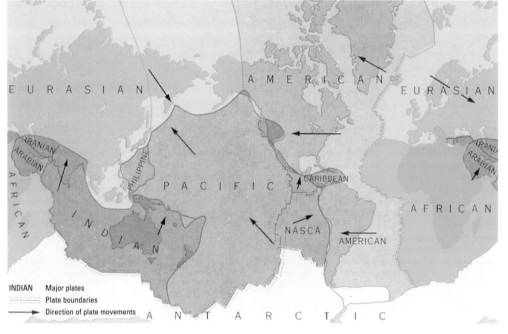

EURASIAN   AMERICAN   EURASIAN

IRANIAN   ARABIAN   PHILIPPINE   CARIBBEAN   ARABIAN

AFRICAN   PACIFIC   AFRICAN

INDIAN   NASCA   AMERICAN

ANTARCTIC

INDIAN Major plates

.... Plate boundaries

⟶ Direction of plate movements

Earthquakes

■ Major earthquake zones

■ Areas experiencing frequent earthquakes

The highest magnitude recorded on the Richter scale is 8.9, on 2 March 1933, for a quake that killed 2,990 people in Japan. The most devastating earthquake ever affected three provinces of central China, on 2 February 1556, when it is believed that about 830,000 people perished. The highest toll in modern times was at Tangshan, eastern China, on 28 July 1976: the original figure of over 655,000 deaths has since been twice revised to stand at 242,000.

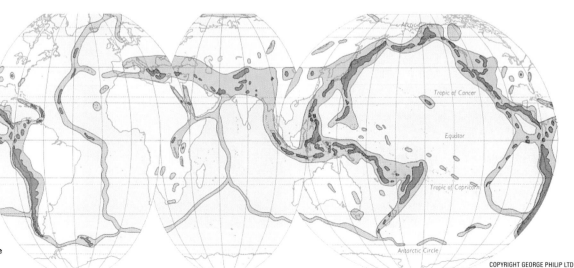

Arctic Circle

Tropic of Cancer

Equator

Tropic of Capricorn

Antarctic Circle

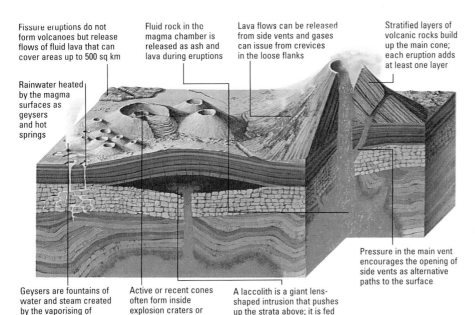

Fissure eruptions do not form volcanoes but release flows of fluid lava that can cover areas up to 500 sq km

Fluid rock in the magma chamber is released as ash and lava during eruptions

Lava flows can be released from side vents and gases can issue from crevices in the loose flanks

Stratified layers of volcanic rocks build up the main cone; each eruption adds at least one layer

Rainwater heated by the magma surfaces as geysers and hot springs

Geysers are fountains of water and steam created by the vaporising of ground waters.

Active or recent cones often form inside explosion craters or crater-shaped calderas

A laccolith is a giant lens-shaped intrusion that pushes up the strata above; it is fed from the magma chamber

Pressure in the main vent encourages the opening of side vents as alternative paths to the surface

Volcanic eruptions take various forms. Fissure eruptions [1] release the most basic and runny lava; in Hawaiian eruptions [2] the lava is less fluid and produces

low cones; Vulcanian eruptions [3] are more violent and eject solid lava; Stombolian eruptions [4] blow out incandescent material; in the Peléean type [5]

a blocked vent is cleared explosively; and a Plinian eruption [6] is a continuous blast of gas that rises to immense heights.

● Volcanoes

Volcanoes occur when hot liquefied rock beneath the Earth's crust is pushed up by pressure to the surface as molten lava. They are found in places where the crust is weak – the mid-ocean ridges and their continental continuations, and along the collision edges of crustal plates. Some volcanoes erupt in an explosive way, throwing out rocks and ash, while others are effusive and lava flows out of the vent. There are examples, such as Mount Fuji in Japan, which are both.

An accumulation of lava and cinders creates cones of various sizes and shapes. As a result of many eruptions over centuries, for example, Mount Etna in Sicily has a circumference of more than 120 kilometres. Craters at rest are often filled by a lake – and the mudflow caused by an eruption can be as destructive as a lava flow and, because of its speed, even more lethal.

Despite the increasingly sophisticated technololgy available volcanoes – like earthquakes – remain both dramatic and unpredictable. In 1991 Mount Pinatubo, located 100 kilometres north of the Philippines capital Manila, suddenly burst into life without warning after lying dormant for no fewer than six centuries.

Most of the world's active volcanoes are located in a belt round the Pacific Ocean, on the edge of the Pacific crustal plate, called the "Ring of Fire" – a circle of fear that threatens over 400 million people. However, the soils formed by the weathering of volcanic rocks are usually

exceptionally fertile, and despite the dangers large numbers of people have always lived in the shadows of volcanoes.

Indonesia has the greatest concentration with 90, 12 of which are active. The 1815 eruption of Tambora in Indonesia ranks as the greatest volcanic disaster in history: 10,000 people were killed by the eruption itself, and over 80,000 more died later of disease and starvation.

Climatologists believe that volcanic ash, if ejected high into the atmosphere, can influence temperature and weather conditions generally over a massive area and for several years afterwards. It has been estimated that the 1991 eruption of Mount Pinatubo in the Philippines threw up more than 20 million tonnes of dust and ash over 30 kilometres into the atmosphere, and it is widely believed that this accelerated the depletion of the ozone layer over large parts of the globe.

There are far more volcanoes on the sea-floor than on the land, however. Known as seamounts, they exist because the oceanic crust is thin and easily pierced by the underlying magma. The Pacific alone is thought to have more than 10,000 underwater volcanoes above 3,000 metres high.

The Hawaiian volcanoes were caused by hotspots in the Earth's mantle, which gave rise to a string of volcanoes as the crust moved slowly over them. Mount Loa, on Hawaii itself, is the world's largest active volcano, measuring 120 kilometres long and 50 kilometres wide; of its total volume, more than 84% is below sea level.

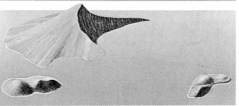

Situated in the Sunda Strait of Indonesia, west of Java, Krakatau (above) was a small volcanic island which had been inactive for over 200 years when, in August 1883, two-thirds of it was destroyed by a violent natural explosion. The eruption was so powerful that the resulting tidal wave killed 36,000 people, and tremors were felt as far away as Australia.

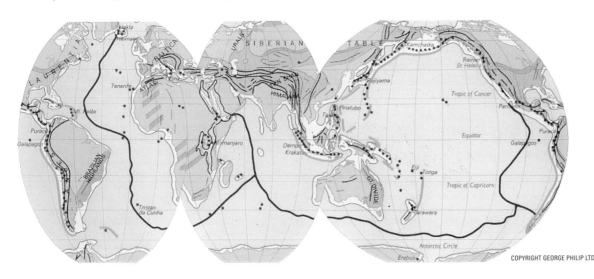

Volcanoes

˙	Volcanoes
▬	Sea floor spreading centre
	Ocean trench
	Continental shelf

Structure

	Pre-Cambrian
	Caledonian folding
	Hercynian folding
	Tertiary folding
	Great Rift Valley
// ||	Main trend lines

Of the 850 volcanoes to produce recorded eruptions, nearly three-quarters lie in the "Ring of Fire" that surrounds the Pacific Ocean on the edge of the Pacific plate.

Shaping the Landscape

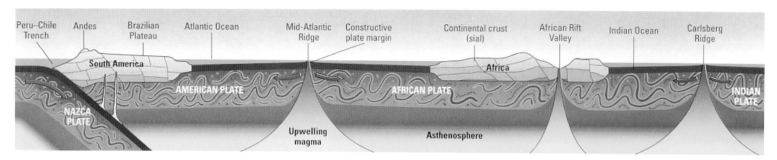

● Sea-floor spreading

The vast ridges that divide the Earth beneath the world's oceans mark the boundaries between tectonic plates that are gradually moving in opposite directions. As the plates shift apart (above), molten magma rises from the mantle to seal the rift and the sea-floor spreads towards the land masses. The rate of spreading has been calculated at about 40mm a year in the North Atlantic Ocean.

Near the ocean shore, underwater volcanoes mark the lines where the continental rise begins. As the plates meet, much of the denser oceanic crust dips beneath the continental plate and melts back to the magma.

● Mountain building

Mountains are formed when pressures on the Earth's crust become so intense that the surface buckles or cracks. This happens where oceanic crust is subducted by continental crust, or where two tectonic plates collide: the Rockies, Andes, Alps, Urals and Himalayas all resulted from such impacts. These are known as fold mountains because they were formed by the compression of the rocks, forcing the surface to bend and fold like a crumpled rug.

The other main mountain-building process occurs when the crust fractures to create faults, allowing rock to be forced upwards in large blocks; or when the pressure of magma inside the crust forces the surface to bulge into a dome, or erupts to form a volcano. Large mountain ranges may well reveal a combination of these features.

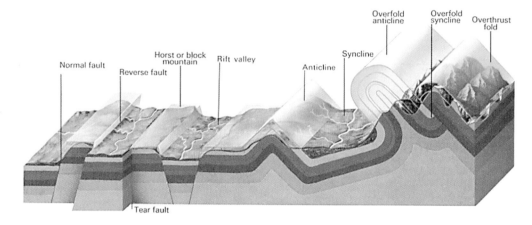

Faults occur where the crust is being stretched or compressed so violently that the rock strata breaks (above). A normal fault results when vertical movement causes the surface to break apart, while compression causes a reverse fault. Horizontal movement causes shearing, known as a tear or strike-slip fault. When the rock breaks in two places, the central block may be pushed up in a horst, or sink in a rift valley. Folds occur when rock strata are squeezed and compressed (above right). Layers bending up form an anticline, those bending down form a syncline.

● Agents of erosion

Destruction of the landscape, however, begins as soon as it is formed. Wind, ice, water and sea, the main agents of erosion, maintain a constant assault that even the hardest rocks cannot withstand. Mountain peaks may dwindle by only a few millimetres a year, but if they are not uplifted by further movements of the Earth's crust they will eventually disappear. Over millions of years, even great mountain ranges can be reduced to a low rugged landscape.

Water is the most powerful destroyer: it has been estimated that 100 billion tonnes of rock are washed into the oceans each year. Three Asian rivers alone account for a fifth of this total – the Hwang Ho in China, and the Ganges and the Brahmaputra in Bangladesh.

When water freezes, its volume increases by about 9%, and no rock is strong enough to resist this pressure. Where water has penetrated fissures or seeped into softer rock, a freeze followed by a thaw may result in rockfalls or earthslides, creating major destruction in minutes.

Over much longer periods, acidity in rain water breaks down the chemical composition of porous rocks such as limestone, eating away the rock to form deep caves and tunnels. Chemical decomposition also occurs in river beds and glacier valleys, hastening the process of mechanical erosion.

Like the sea, rivers and glaciers generate much of their effect through abrasion, pounding or tearing the land with the debris they carry. Yet as well as destroying existing landforms they also create new ones, many of them spectacular. Prominent examples are the vast deltas of the Mississippi and the Nile, the rock arches and stacks off the south coast of Australia, and the deep fjords cut by glaciers in British Columbia, Norway and New Zealand.

While landscapes evolve from a "young" mountainous stage, through a "mature" hilly stage to an "old age" of lowland plain, this long-term cycle of erosion is subject to interruption by a number of crucial factors, including the effects of plate tectonics and climate change.

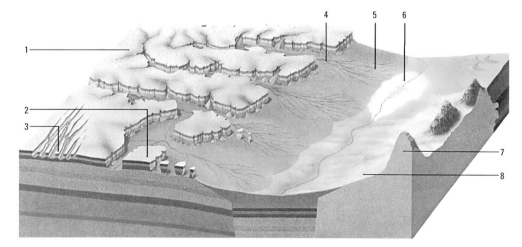

The topography of a desert is characterised by the relative absence of the chemical weathering associated with water, and most erosion takes place mechanically through wind abrasion and the effect of heat.

Mesas [1] are large flat-topped areas with steep sides, while the butte [2] is an isolated version of it. Elongated in the direction of the wind, yardangs [3] comprise tabular masses of resistant rock resting on undercut pillars of softer material. Alluvial fans [5] are pebble-mounds deposited in desert deltas by flash floods, usually at the end of a wadi [4]. A saltpan [6] is a temporary lake of brackish water also formed by flash floods. An inselberg [7] is an isolated hill rising from the plain, and a pediment [8] is an inclining rock surface.

● Shaping forces: ice

Many of the world's most dramatic landscapes have been carved by ice-sheets and glaciers. During the ice ages of the Pleistocene Epoch (over 10,000 years ago) up to a third of the land surface was glaciated; even today a tenth is covered in ice – the vast majority locked up in vast ice-sheets and ice-caps. The world's largest ice-sheet covers most of Antarctica and is up to 4,800 metres thick. It is extremely slow moving – unlike valley glaciers, which can move at rates of between a few centimetres and several metres a day.

Valley glaciers are found in mountainous regions throughout the world, except Australia. In the relatively short geological time scale of the recent ice ages, glaciers accomplished far more carving of the topography than rivers and wind. They are formed from compressed snow, called névé, accumulating in a valley head or cirque. Slowly the glacier moves downhill *(right)*, scraping away debris from the mountains and valleys through which it passes. The debris, or moraine, adds to the abrasive power of the ice. The sediments are transported by the ice to the edge of the glacier, where they are deposited or carried away by meltwater streams.

● Shaping forces: rivers

From their origins as small upland rills and streams channelling rainfall, or as springs releasing water that has seeped into the ground, all rivers are incessantly at work cutting and shaping the landscape on their way to the sea *(right)*.

In highland regions flow may be rapid and turbulent, pounding rocks to cut deep gorges and V-shaped valleys through softer rocks, or tumble as waterfalls over harder ones. Rocks and pebbles move along the bed by saltation (bouncing) or traction (rolling), while lighter sediments are carried in suspension or dissolved in solution.

As they reach more gentle slopes, rivers release some of the pebbles and heavier sediments they have carried downstream, flow more slowly and broaden out. Levées or ridges are raised along their banks by the deposition of mud and sand during floods. In lowland plains the river drifts into meanders, depositing layers of sediment, especially on the inside of bends where the flow is weakest. As the river reaches the sea it deposits its remaining load, and estuaries are formed where the tidal currents are strong enough to remove them; if not, the debris creates a delta.

● Shaping forces: the sea

Under the constant assault from tides and currents, wind and waves, coastlines *(right)* change faster than most landscape features, both by erosion and by the building up of sand and pebbles carried by the sea. In severe storms, giant waves pound the shoreline with rocks and boulders; but even in much quieter conditions, the sea steadily erodes cliffs and headlands, creating new features in the form of sand dunes, spits and salt marshes. Beaches, where sand and shingle have been deposited, form a buffer zone between the erosive power of the waves and the coast. Because it is composed of loose materials, a beach can rapidly adapt its shape to changes in wave energy.

Where the coastline is formed from soft rocks such as sandstones, debris may fall evenly and be carried away by currents from shelving beaches. In areas with harder rock, the waves may cut steep cliffs and wave-cut platforms; eroded debris is deposited as a terrace. Bays are formed when sections of soft rock are carved away between headlands of harder rock. These are then battered by waves from both sides, until the headlands are eventually reduced to rock arches and stacks.

A number of factors affect the rate of erosion in coastal environments. These vary from rock type and structure, beach width and supply of beach materials to the more complex fluid dynamics of the waves, namely the breaking point, steepness and length of fetch.

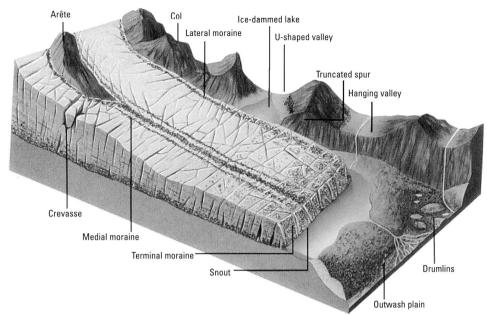

Arête · Col · Lateral moraine · Ice-dammed lake · U-shaped valley · Truncated spur · Hanging valley · Crevasse · Medial moraine · Terminal moraine · Snout · Drumlins · Outwash plain

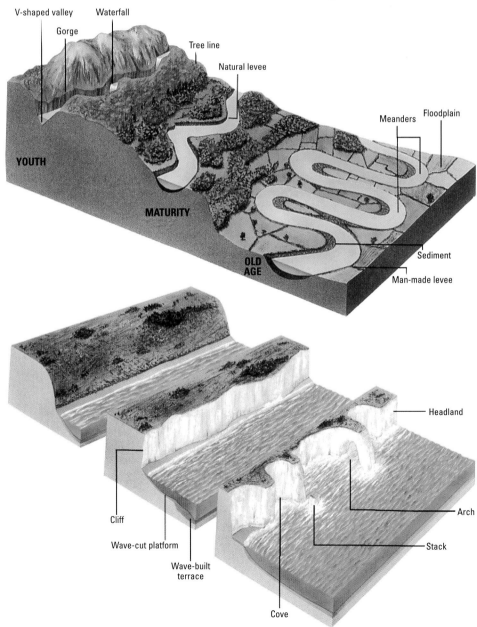

V-shaped valley · Gorge · Waterfall · Tree line · Natural levee · Meanders · Floodplain · YOUTH · MATURITY · OLD AGE · Sediment · Man-made levee · Headland · Cliff · Wave-cut platform · Wave-built terrace · Cove · Arch · Stack

Climate

Climatic zones

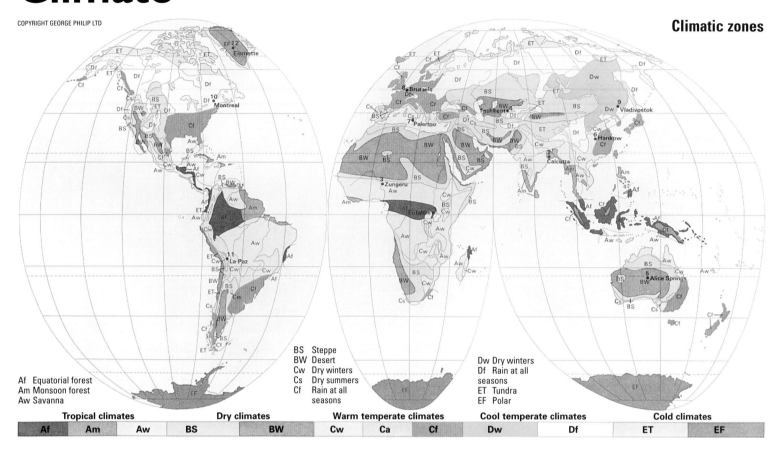

Af Equatorial forest
Am Monsoon forest
Aw Savanna

BS Steppe
BW Desert
Cw Dry winters
Cs Dry summers
Cf Rain at all
      seasons

Dw Dry winters
Df Rain at all
seasons
ET Tundra
EF Polar

Tropical climates			Dry climates		Warm temperate climates			Cool temperate climates		Cold climates	
Af	Am	Aw	BS	BW	Cw	Ca	Cf	Dw	Df	ET	EF

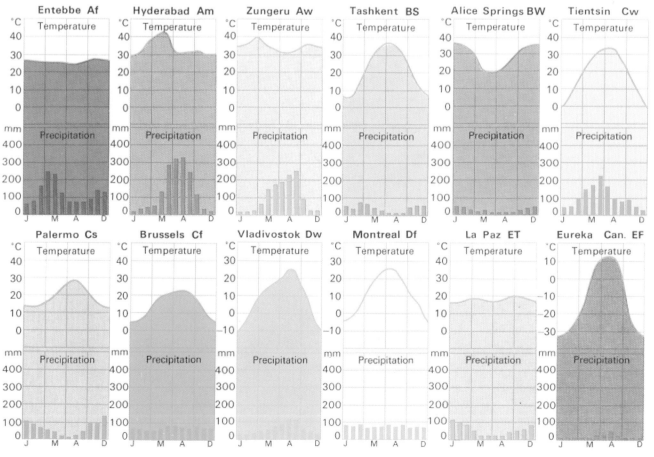

Entebbe Af — Temperature — Precipitation
Hyderabad Am — Temperature — Precipitation
Zungeru Aw — Temperature — Precipitation
Tashkent BS — Temperature — Precipitation
Alice Springs BW — Temperature — Precipitation
Tientsin Cw — Temperature — Precipitation
Palermo Cs — Temperature — Precipitation
Brussels Cf — Temperature — Precipitation
Vladivostok Dw — Temperature — Precipitation
Montreal Df — Temperature — Precipitation
La Paz ET — Temperature — Precipitation
Eureka Can. EF — Temperature — Precipitation

CLIMATE TERMS

Cyclone Violent storm called hurricane in N. America, typhoon in Far East

Depression Area of low pressure

Frost Dew when air temperature falls below freezing point

Hail Frozen rain

Humidity Amount of moisture in air

Isobar Line on map connecting places of equal pressure

Isotherm Line connecting places of equal temperatutre

Precipitation Measurable rain, snow, sleet or hail

Rain Precipitation of liquid particles with diameter larger than 0.5mm

Sleet Partially melted snow

Snow Formed when water vapour condenses below freezing point

Tornado Severe funnel-shaped storm that twists as hot air spins vertically; a waterspout at sea

● Definition of climate

Climate is weather in the long term – the seasonal pattern of hot and cold, wet and dry, averaged over time (usually 30 years). At the simplest level, it is caused by the uneven heating of the Earth. Surplus heat at the Equator passes towards the poles, levelling out the energy differential. Its passage is marked by a ceaseless churning of the atmosphere and the oceans, further agitated by the Earth's daily spin and the motion it imparts to moving air and water.

The heat's means of transport – by winds and ocean currents, by the continual evaporation and recondensation of water molecules – is the weather itself. There are four basic types of climate, each of which can be further sub-divided: tropical, desert (dry), temperate and polar.

● Climate records

Temperature
Highest recorded shade temperature: Al Aziziyah, Libya, 58°C [136.4°F], 13 September 1922.

Highest mean annual temperature: Dallol, Ethiopia, 34.4°C [94°F], 1960–66.

Longest heatwave: Marble Bar, W. Australia, 162 days over 38°C [100°F], 23 October 1923 to 7 April 1924.

Lowest recorded temperature (outside poles): Verkhoyansk, Siberia, -68°C [-90°F], 6 February 1933.

Lowest mean annual temperature: Plateau Station, Antarctica, -56.6°C [-72.0°F].

Precipitation
Longest drought: Calama, N. Chile, no recorded rainfall in 400 years to 1971.

Wettest place (12 months): Cherrapunji, Meghalaya, N. E. India, 26,470 mm [1,040 in], August 1860 to August 1861; Cherrapunji also holds the record for the most rainfall in one month: 2,930 mm [115 in], July 1861.

Wettest place (average): Mawdsynram, India, mean annual rainfall 11,873 mm [467.4 in].

Wettest place (24 hours): Cilaos, Réunion, Indian Ocean, 1,870 mm [73.6 in], 15–16 March 1952.

Heaviest hailstones: Gopalganj, Bangladesh, up to 1.02 kg [2.25 lb], 14 April 1986 (killed 92 people)

Heaviest snowfall (continuous): Bessans, Savoie, France, 1,730 mm [68 in] in 19 hours, 5–6 April 1969.

Heaviest snowfall (season/year): Paradise Ranger Station, Mt Rainier, Washington, USA, 31,102 mm [1,224.5 in], 19 February 1971 to 18 February 1972.

Pressure and winds
Highest barometric pressure: Agata, Siberia (at 262 m [862 ft] altitude), 1,083.8 millibars, 31 December 1968.

Lowest barometric pressure: Typhoon Tip, Guam, Pacific Ocean, 870 millibars, 12 October 1979.

Highest recorded wind speed: Mt Washington, New Hampshire, USA, 371 km/h [231 mph], 12 April 1934; this is three times as strong as hurricane force on the Beaufort Scale.

Windiest place: Commonwealth Bay, Antarctica, where gales frequently reach over 320 km/h [200 mph].

Conversions
°C = (°F -32) x ⁵/₉; °F = (°C x ⁹/₅) + 32; 0°C = 32°F
1 mm = 0.0394 in (100 mm = 3.94 in); 1 in = 25.4 mm

Temperature

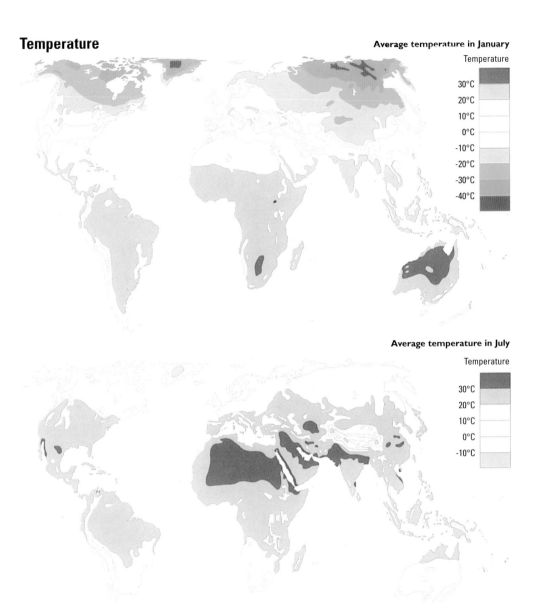

Average temperature in January

Temperature

- 30°C
- 20°C
- 10°C
- 0°C
- -10°C
- -20°C
- -30°C
- -40°C

Average temperature in July

Temperature

- 30°C
- 20°C
- 10°C
- 0°C
- -10°C

Rainfall

Average annual precipitation

- 3,000mm
- 2,000mm
- 1,000mm
- 500mm
- 250mm

Water and Vegetation

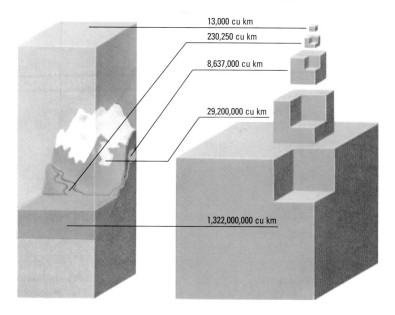

13,000 cu km

230,250 cu km

8,637,000 cu km

29,200,000 cu km

1,322,000,000 cu km

The total water supply of the world (*left*) is estimated to be about 1,360,000,000 cubic kilometres, and some 97% of it is accounted for by the oceans. Of the total water on land more than 75% is frozen in ice-sheets and glaciers, as in Greenland and Antarctica. Most of the rest, about 22%, is water collected below the Earth's surface and called ground water. Comparatively small quantities are in lakes and rivers (0.017% of the total), while water vapour represents only 0.001%. Without this, however, there would be no life on land.

The water of life

Fresh water is essential to all life on Earth, from the humblest bacterium to the most advanced technological society. Yet freshwater resources form a minute fraction of the Earth's 1.36 billion cubic kilometres of water: most human needs must be met from the 2,000 cubic kilometres circulating in rivers at any one time.

Agriculture accounts for huge quantities: without large-scale irrigation, most of the world's people would starve. Since fresh water is just as essential for most industrial processes, the combination of growing population and advancing industry has put supplies under increasing strain.

Fortunately water is seldom used up: the planet's water cycle circulates it with efficiency, at least on a global scale. More locally, however, human activity can cause severe shortages: water for industry and agriculture is being withdrawn from many river basins and underground aquifers faster than natural recirculation can replace it.

The demand for water has led to tensions between nations as supplies are diverted or horded. Both Iraq and Syria, for example, have protested at Turkey's dam-building programme, which they claim drastically reduces the flow of the Tigris and Euphrates rivers.

The water cycle

Oceanic water is salty and unsuitable for drinking or farming. In some desert regions, where fresh sources are in short supply, seawater is desalinated to make fresh water, but most of the world is constantly supplied with fresh water by the natural process of the water or hydrological cycle (*left*), which relies on the action of two factors: gravity and the Sun's heat.

Over the oceans, which cover almost 71% of the Earth's surface, the Sun's heat causes evaporation. Water vapour rises on air currents and winds; some of this vapour condenses and returns directly to the oceans as rain, but because of the circulation of the atmosphere, air bearing large amounts of water vapour is carried over land, where it falls as rain or snow.

Much of this precipitation is quickly re-evaporated by the Sun. Some soaks into the soil, where it is absorbed by plants and partly returned to the air through transpiration; some flows over the land surface as run-off, which flows into streams and rivers; and some rain and melted snow seeps through the soil into the rocks beneath. All the water that does not return directly to the atmosphere gradually returns to the sea to complete the water cycle.

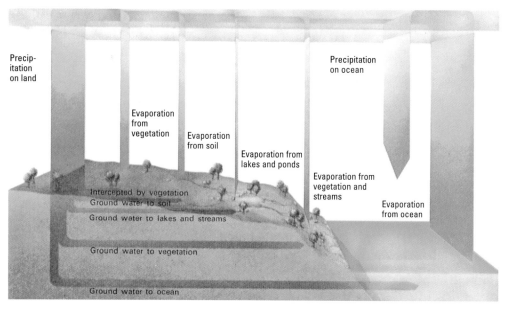

Precipitation on land

Evaporation from vegetation

Evaporation from soil

Evaporation from lakes and ponds

Precipitation on ocean

Evaporation from vegetation and streams

Evaporation from ocean

Intercepted by vegetation
Ground water to soil

Ground water to lakes and streams

Ground water to vegetation

Ground water to ocean

The lowest level of the water-table, reached at the driest time of year, is called the permanent water-table, and wells must be drilled to this level if they are to supply water throughout the year. In artesian wells (*right*) water is forced to the surface by hydrostatic pressure.

The water-table [1] in the confined acquifer [2] lies near the top of the dipping layers. A well [4] drilled through the top impervious layer [3] is not an artesian well because the head of hydrostatic pressure [6] is not sufficient to force water to the surface. In such wells the water must be pumped or drawn to the surface.

The top of an artesian well [5] lies below the level of the head of hydrostatic pressure and so water gushes to the surface. Artesian springs [8] may occur along joints or faults [7] where the head of hydrostatic pressure is sufficient to force the water up along the fault. Areas with artesian wells, such as the Great Basin of Australia, are called artesian basins. In the London and Paris artesian basins, the water has been so heavily tapped that the water level has dropped below the level of the well heads.

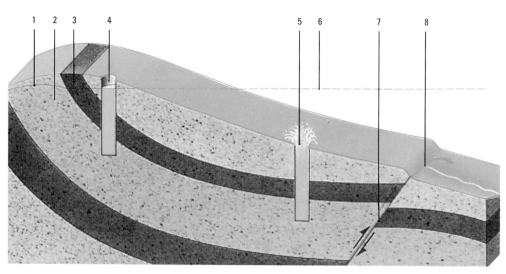

1 2 3 4   5 6   7   8

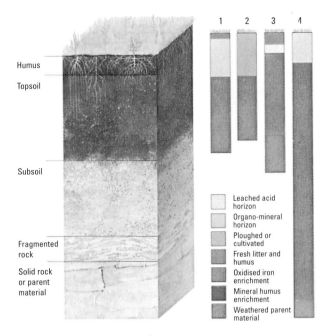

Humus
Topsoil
Subsoil
Fragmented rock
Solid rock or parent material

Leached acid horizon
Organo-mineral horizon
Ploughed or cultivated
Fresh litter and humus
Oxidised iron enrichment
Mineral humus enrichment
Weathered parent material

Profile 1 (*left*) is of acid brown earth found in temperate climates – this one on sandy rock – and 2 is a cultivated brown earth of the same climatic region. Grey leached podzol [3] is typical of wet, cool climates – for example, the taiga in Russia – while oxisol [4], a thick red soil containing iron compounds, is found in humid, tropical lands where chemical and biological activity are both high.

The composition and colour of a soil (*right*) identifies it to a pedologist. This tundra soil [1] has a dark, peaty surface. Light-coloured desert soil [2] is coarse and poor in organic matter. Chestnut-brown soil [3] and chernozem [4] – the Russian for "black earth" – are humus-rich grassland soils typical of the central Asian steppes and prairies of North America. The reddish, leached latosol [5] of tropical savannas has a very thin but rich humus layer. Podzolic soils [6,7,8,9] are typical of northern climates where rainfall is heavy but evaporation is slow.

● The living soil

The whole structure of life on Earth, with its enormous diversity of plant and animal types, is utterly dependent on a mantle of soil which is rich in moisture and nutrients.

Soil is a result of all the processes of physical and chemical weathering on the barren, underlying rock mass of the Earth that it covers, and varies in depth from a few centimetres to several metres. The depth of soil is measured either by the distance to which plants send down

their roots or by the depth of soil directly influencing their systems. In some places only a very thin layer is necessary to support life.

Formation of soil is the result of the interaction of five major elements – the parent rock, land relief, time, climate and decay. However, by far the most single important factor in the development of soil is climate, with water essential to all chemical and biological change in soil.

The map below illustrates the natural "climax" vegetation of a region, as dictated by its climate and typography. In the vast majority of cases, however, human agricultural activity has drastically altered the pattern of vegetation. Western Europe, for example, lost most of its broadleaf forest many centuries ago, and in other areas irrigation has gradually turned natural semi-desert into productive land.

Natural vegetation

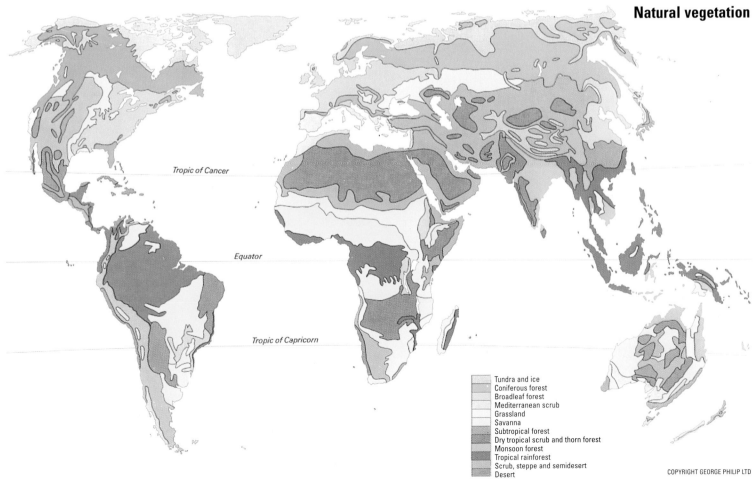

Tropic of Cancer
Equator
Tropic of Capricorn

Tundra and ice
Coniferous forest
Broadleaf forest
Mediterranean scrub
Grassland
Savanna
Subtropical forest
Dry tropical scrub and thorn forest
Monsoon forest
Tropical rainforest
Scrub, steppe and semidesert
Desert

WORLD MAPS

─ SETTLEMENTS ─

■ PARIS   ■ Berne   ◉ Livorno   ◎ Brugge   ◎ Algeciras   ○ Frejus   ○ Oberammergau   ○ Thira

Settlement symbols and type styles vary according to the scale of each map and indicate the importance
of towns on the map rather than specific population figures

∴   Ruins or Archæological Sites   Wells in Desert

─ ADMINISTRATION ─

─── International Boundaries	National Parks	Administrative Area Names
─ ─ ─ International Boundaries (Undefined or Disputed)	Country Names NICARAGUA	KENT CALABRIA
········ Internal Boundaries		

International boundaries show the *de facto* situation where there are rival claims to territory

─ COMMUNICATIONS ─

─── Principal Roads	⊕ Airfields	─── Other Railways
─── Other Roads	─── Principal Railways	─┼─ ─ ┼─ Railway Tunnels
─┼─ ─ ┼─ Road Tunnels	─ ─ ─ Railways Under Construction	·········· Principal Canals
⋈ Passes		

─ PHYSICAL FEATURES ─

─── Perennial Streams	Intermittent Lakes	▲ 8848 Elevations in metres
─ ─ ─ Intermittent Streams	Swamps and Marshes	▼ 8500 Sea Depths in metres
Perennial Lakes	Permanent Ice and Glaciers	*1134* Height of Lake Surface Above Sea Level in metres

Projection: *Hammer Equal Area*

Hanoi ● Capital Cities

COPYRIGHT GEORGE PHILIP LTD.

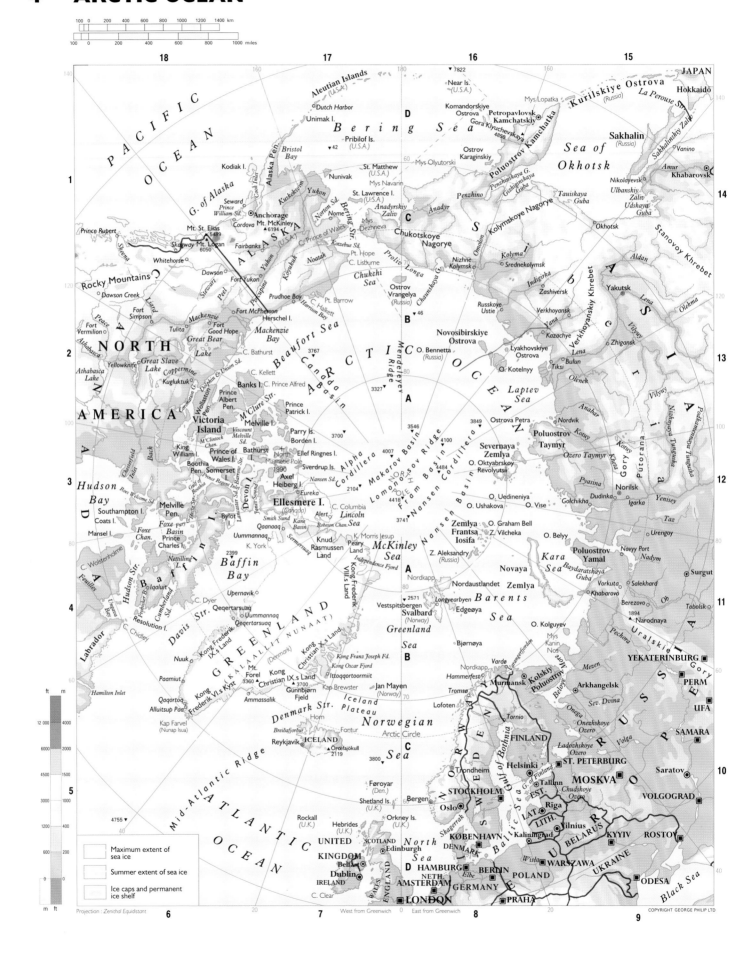

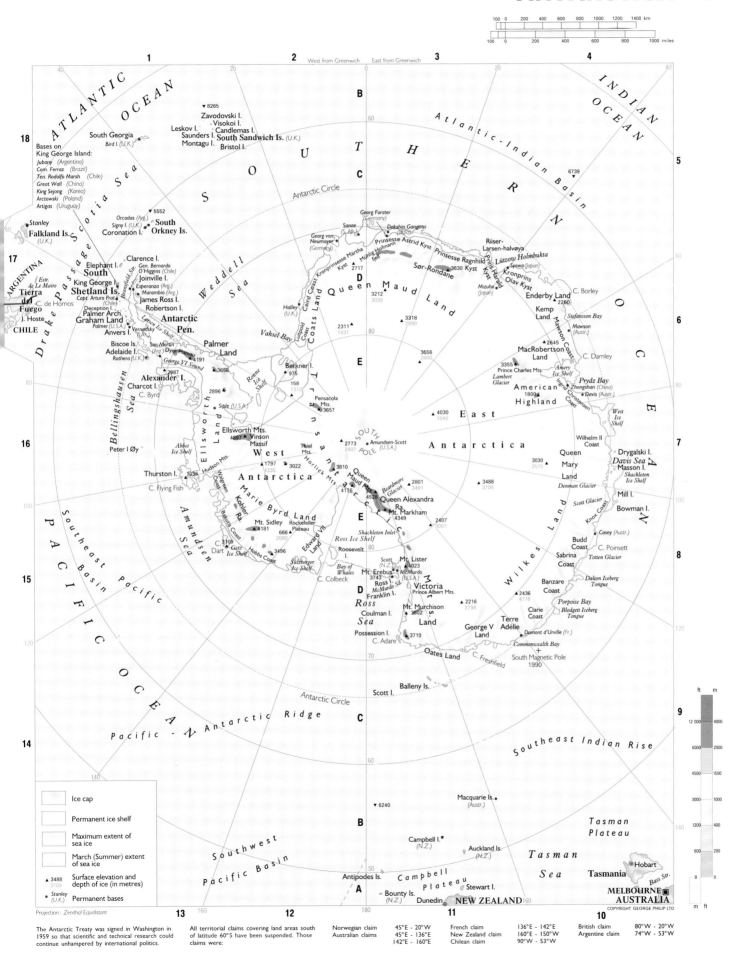

100 0 200 400 600 800 1000 1200 1400 km
100 0 200 400 600 800 1000 miles

1   West from Greenwich   East from Greenwich   3   4

ATLANTIC   OCEAN
INDIAN   OCEAN

▼ 8265

18   Zavodovski I.
      Visokoi I.
Leskov I.   Candlemas I.
Saunders I.   South Sandwich Is. (U.K.)
Montagu I.   Bristol I.

South Georgia
Bird I. (U.K.)

Atlantic-Indian Basin

S O U T H E R N

Bases on
King George Island:
Jubany   (Argentina)
Com. Ferraz   (Brazil)
Ten. Rodolfo Marsh (Chile)
Great Wall (China)
King Sejong (Korea)
Arctowski (Poland)
Artigas (Uruguay)

6739 ▲

S C O T I A

Antarctic Circle

▲ 5552
Orcadas (Arg.)
Signy I. (U.K.)   South
Coronation I.   Orkney Is.

Stanley
Falkland Is.
(U.K.)

Georg Forster
(Germany)
Sanae   Dakshin Gangotri
(S. Afr.)   (India)
Georg von
Neumayer
(Germany)   Prinsesse Astrid Kyst
Prinsesse Martha   Mühlig Hofmann
Kyst   2717 ▲
Prinsesse Ragnhild
Kyst
Sør-Rondane
Riiser-
Larsen-halvøya
3630 Kyst   Lützow Holmbukta
Kronprins   Syowa (Japan)
Olav Kyst
Mizuho   Kronprins
(Japan)

17   ARGENTINA   Clarence I.
      Elephant I.
Estr.   South   Gen. Bernardo
de Le Maire   King George   O'Higgins (Chile)
Tierra   Shetland Is.   Joinville I.
del   Capt. Arturo Prat (Chile)   Esperanza (Arg.)
Fuego   Deception I.   Marambio (Arg.)
I. Hoste   Palmer Arch.   James Ross I.
CHILE   Graham Land   Robertson I.
Palmer (U.S.A.)   Antarctic
Anvers I.   Pen.
Vernadsky
(U.K.)
San Martín
Biscoe Is.   (Arg.)
Adelaide I.
Rothera (U.K.)

Queen   Maud   Land
Enderby Land
C. Borley
2280
Kemp
Land   Stefansson Bay
Mawson
(Austr.)

3212 ▲
3039

3318 ▲
2990

2311 ▲
1431

Vahsel Bay

Halley
(U.K.)

Berkner I.
975
158
1312

George VI Sound
2987 ▲   4191 ▲
3658 ▲

Alexander I.
Charcot I.
C. Byrd

2896 ▲

3556 ▲
2600

3355 ▲
MacRobertson
Land   C. Darnley
2645 ▲
Prince Charles Mts.
Lambert
Glacier   Amery
Ice Shelf   Prydz Bay
Zhongshan (China)
1800 ▲   Davis (Austr.)
American
Highland   Ingrid
Christensen
Coast

16   Bellingshausen
      Sea
Peter I Øy

Pensacola
Mts.
3657 ▲

4030 ▲
1040

East
2773 ▲   Antarctica

West
Ice
Shelf

Abbot
Ice Shelf   Ellsworth Mts.
4897 ▲ Vinson
Massif
4335   Thiel
Mts.   Amundsen-Scott
(U.S.A.)
2407

SOUTH
POLE

Wilhelm II
Coast
3030 ▲
2570   Queen
Mary
Land   Drygalski I.
Davis Sea
Masson I.
Shackleton
Ice Shelf

Thurston I.
1036

1797 ▲   3022 ▲

Horlick Mts.
3810 ▲

West   Antarctica
Queen
Maud Mts.
4176 ▲

3488 ▲
3700

Denman Glacier
Scott Glacier   Mill I.
Knox Coast   Bowman I.

C. Flying Fish

Hudson Mts.
Walgreen
Coast   Marie Byrd Land
Koller
Ra.
Bakutis Coast   Mt. Sidley   Rockefeller
4181 ▲   Plateau
666 ▲
2080

Beardmore
Glacier   2801 ▲
2491
4528 ▲   Queen Alexandra
Ra.
Mt. Markham
4349 ▲
2407 ▲
3087

Budd
Coast   Casey (Austr.)
Sabrina
Coast   C. Poinsett
Totten Glacier

15   PACIFIC   OCEAN
      Southeast   Pacific
      Basin

3109 ▲
Dart   Getz
Ice Shelf   3496 ▲

Salzburger
Ice Shelf   Edward VII
Land   Roosevelt
I.   Shackleton Inlet
Ross Ice Shelf

Bay of
Whales
C. Colbeck   Mt. Erebus
3743 ▲
Ross
McMurdo Sd.
Franklin I.

Scott   Mt. Lister
(N.Z.)   4023 ▲
McMurdo
(U.S.A.)   Victoria
Prince Albert Mts.

Banzare
Coast
Dalton Iceberg
Tongue
2436 ▲
Clarie   Porpoise Bay
Coast   Blodgett Iceberg
Tongue

Mt. Murchison
3502 ▲   Land

2216 ▲
2798

George V
Land   Terre
Adélie
Dumont d'Urville (Fr.)

Ross
Coulman I.
Sea

Possession I.
C. Adare   3719 ▲

Oates Land   Commonwealth Bay
C. Freshfield   South Magnetic Pole
1990

14   Pacific-Antarctic   Ridge

Antarctic Circle

Balleny Is.

Scott I.

Southeast Indian Rise

▼ 6240   Macquarie Is.
(Austr.)

Tasman
Plateau

Southwest
Pacific Basin   Campbell I.
(N.Z.)   Auckland Is.
(N.Z.)   Tasman
Sea   Tasmania   Hobart
Bass Str.

Ice cap

Permanent ice shelf

Maximum extent of
sea ice

March (Summer) extent
of sea ice

▲ 3488   Surface elevation and
3700   depth of ice (in metres)

• Stanley
(U.K.)   Permanent bases

Antipodes Is.
Bounty Is.
(N.Z.)   Campbell
Plateau   Stewart I.
Dunedin   NEW ZEALAND

MELBOURNE
AUSTRALIA
COPYRIGHT GEORGE PHILIP LTD

ft   m
12 000   4000
6000   2000
4500   1500
3000   1000
1200   400
600   200
0   0
m   ft

Projection : Zenithal Equidistant

13   12   180   11   10

All territorial claims covering land areas south
of latitude 60°S have been suspended. Those
claims were:

Norwegian claim	45°E - 20°W	
Australian claims	45°E - 136°E	
	142°E - 160°E	
French claim	136°E - 142°E	
New Zealand claim	160°E - 150°W	
Chilean claim	90°W - 53°W	
British claim	80°W - 20°W	
Argentine claim	74°W - 53°W	

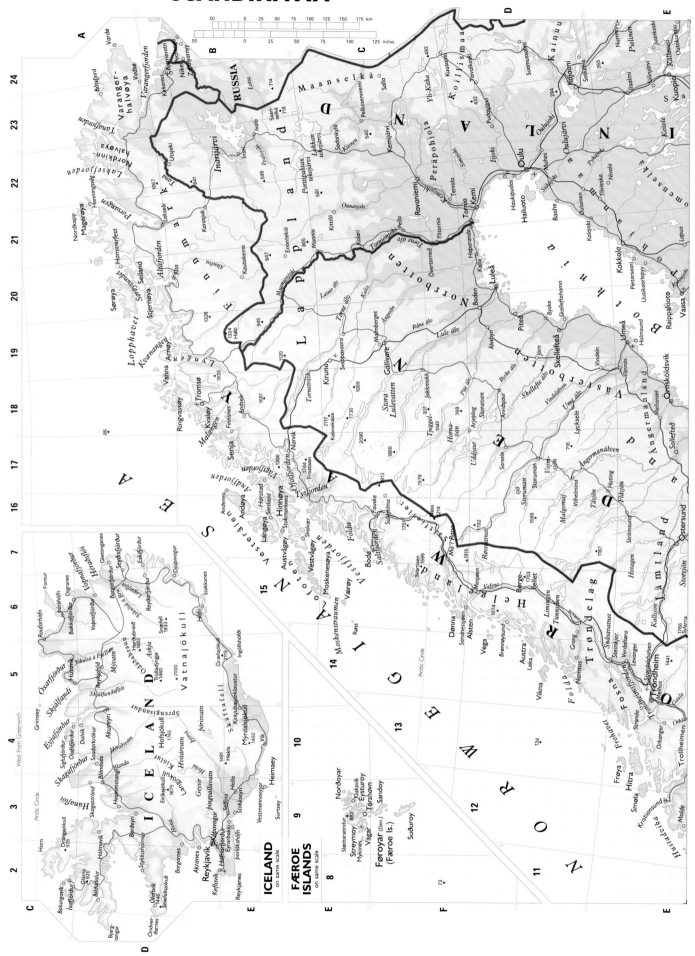

SCANDINAVIA

RUSSIA

ICELAND
on same scale

FÆROE ISLANDS
on same scale

Føroyar (Den.)
(Faroe Is.)

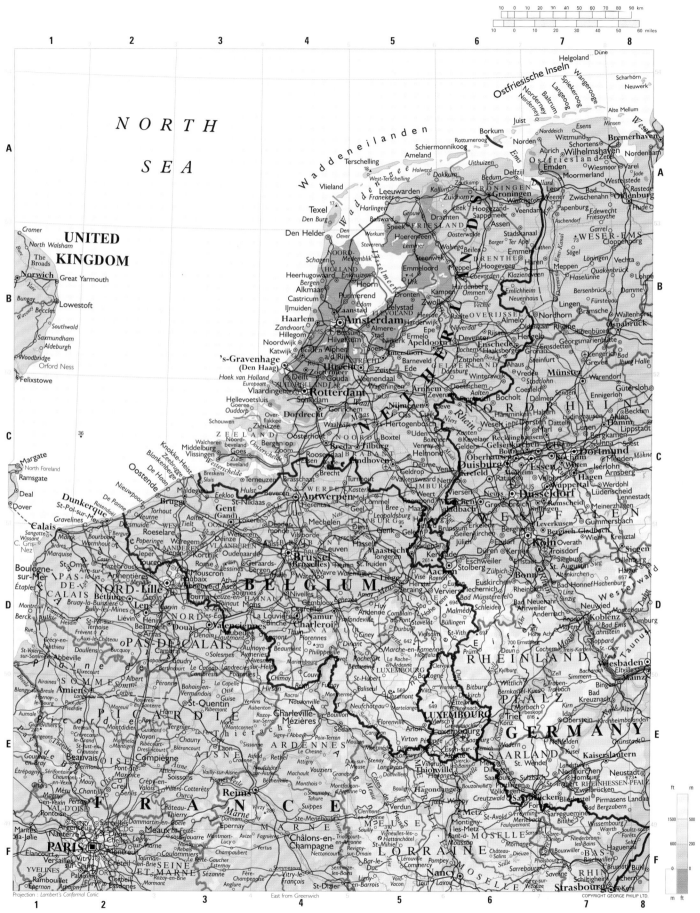

Projection : Lambert's Conformal Conic

East from Greenwich

COPYRIGHT GEORGE PHILIP LTD.

Underlined towns give their name to the
administrative area in which they stand.

East from Greenwich

COPYRIGHT GEORGE PHILIP LTD.

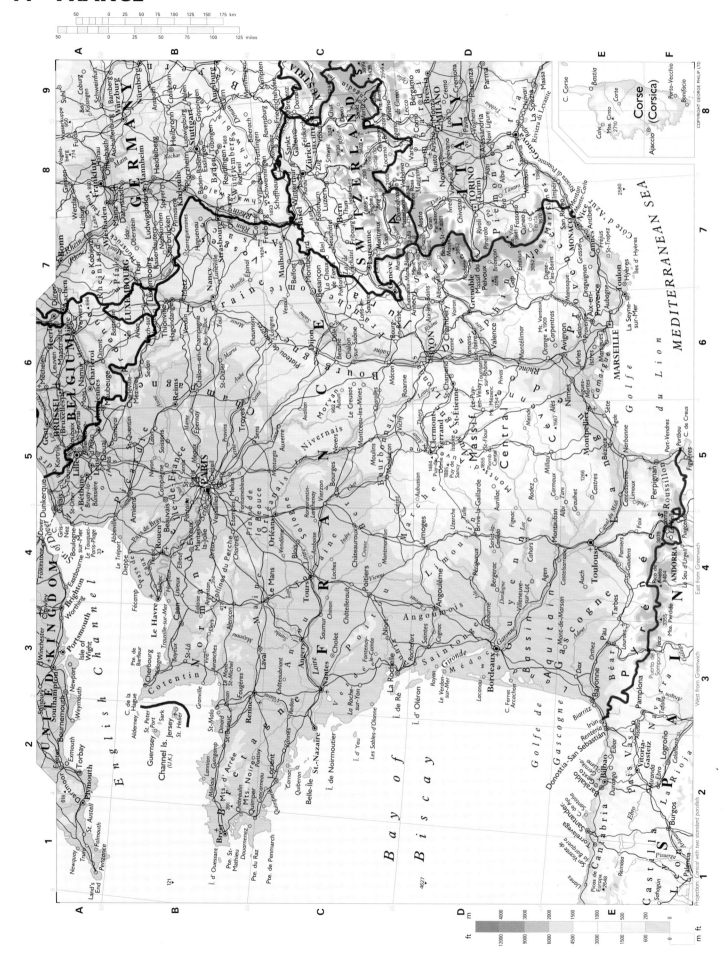

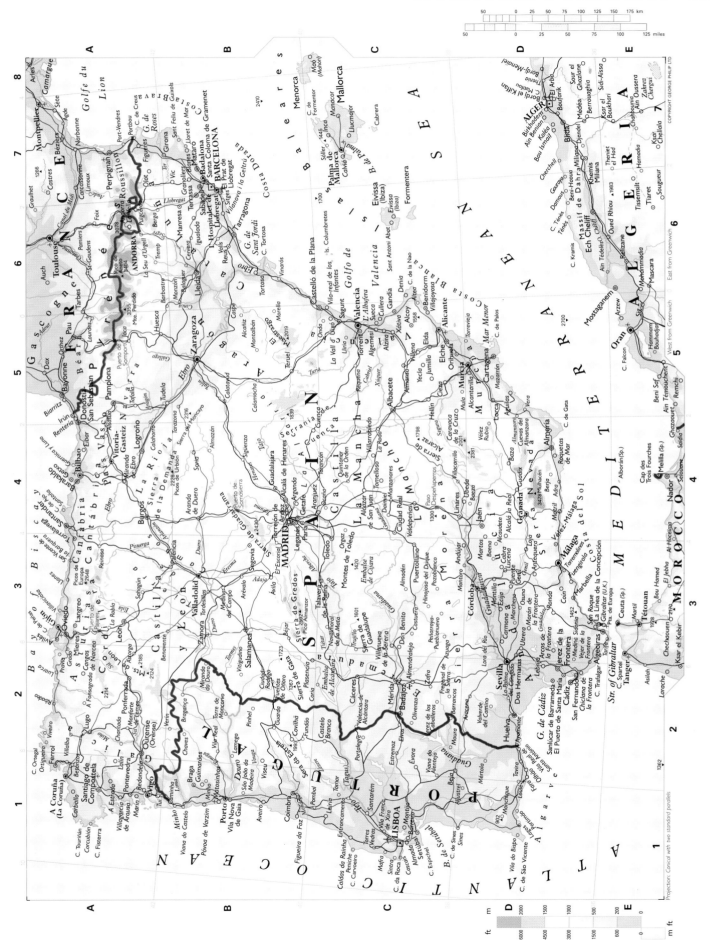

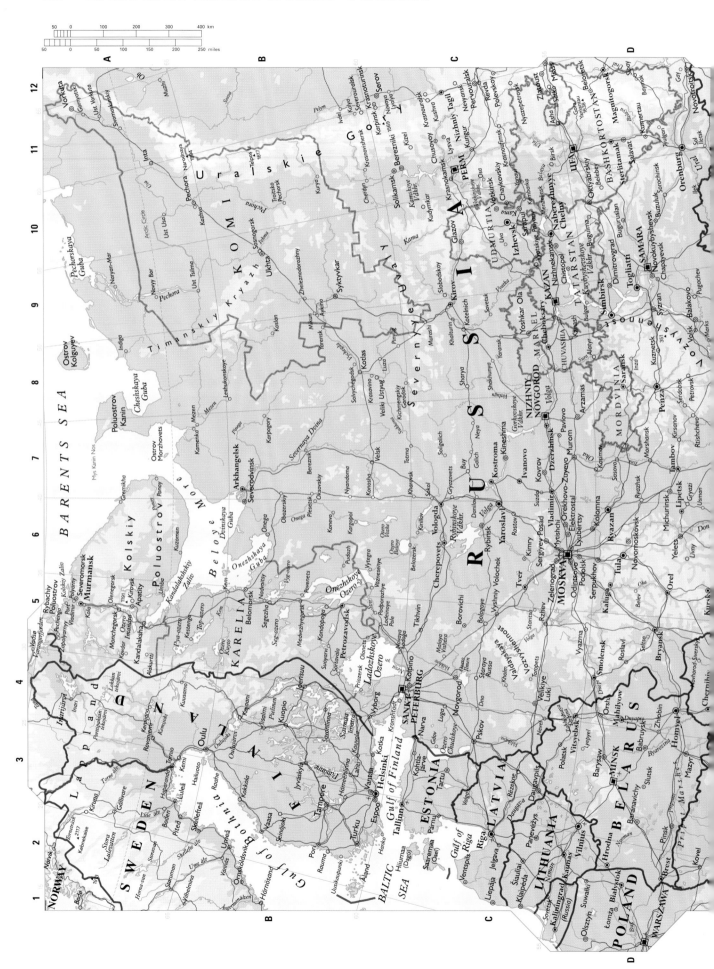

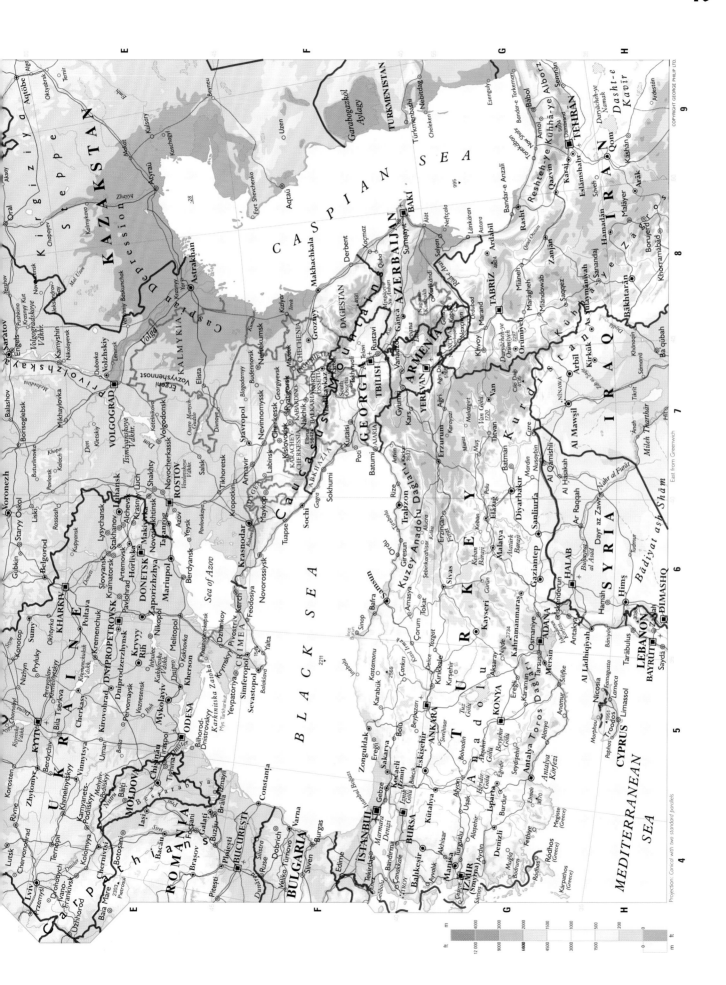

East from Greenwich

Projection: Conical with two standard parallels

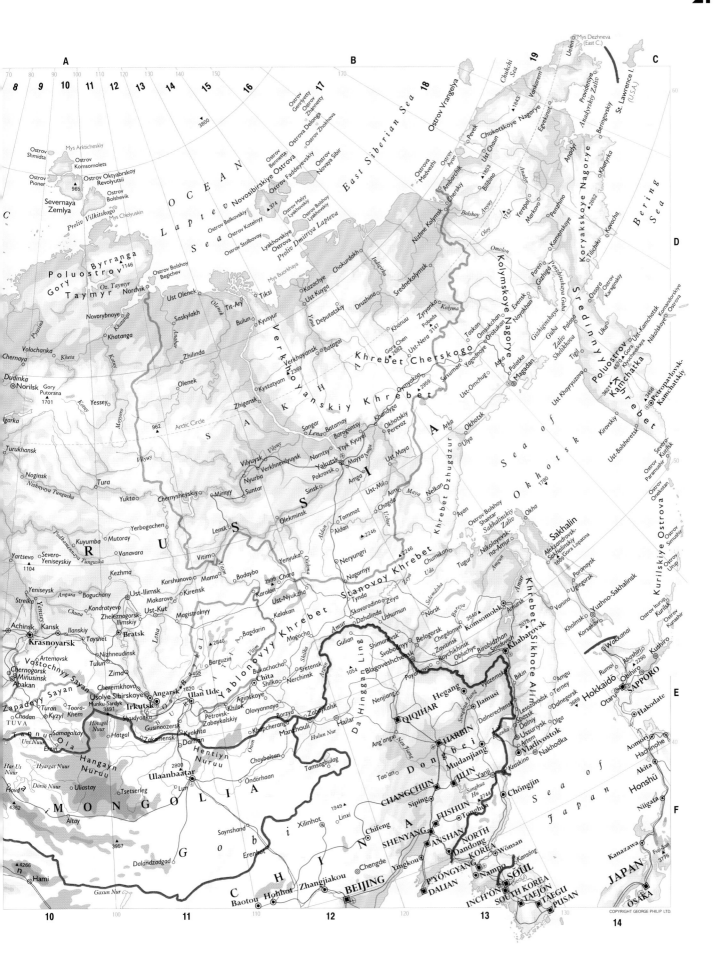

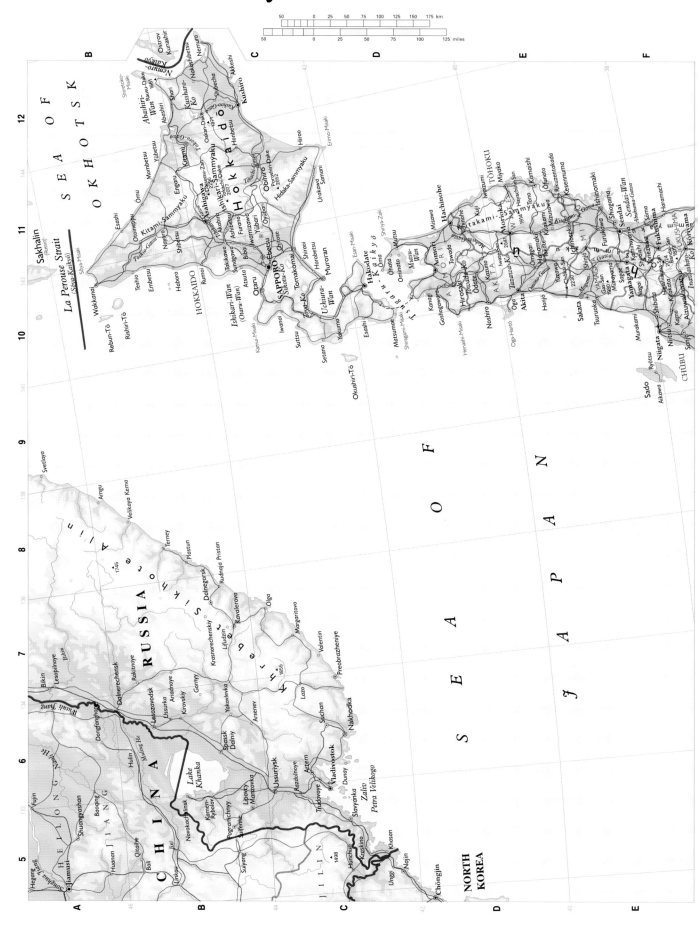

SEA OF OKHOTSK

SEA OF JAPAN

RUSSIA

CHINA

NORTH KOREA

HOKKAIDŌ

SAPPORO

TŌHOKU

CHŪBU

Sakhalin

La Perouse Strait
(Sōya-Kaikyō)

Lake Khanka

Vladivostok

Sikhote Alin

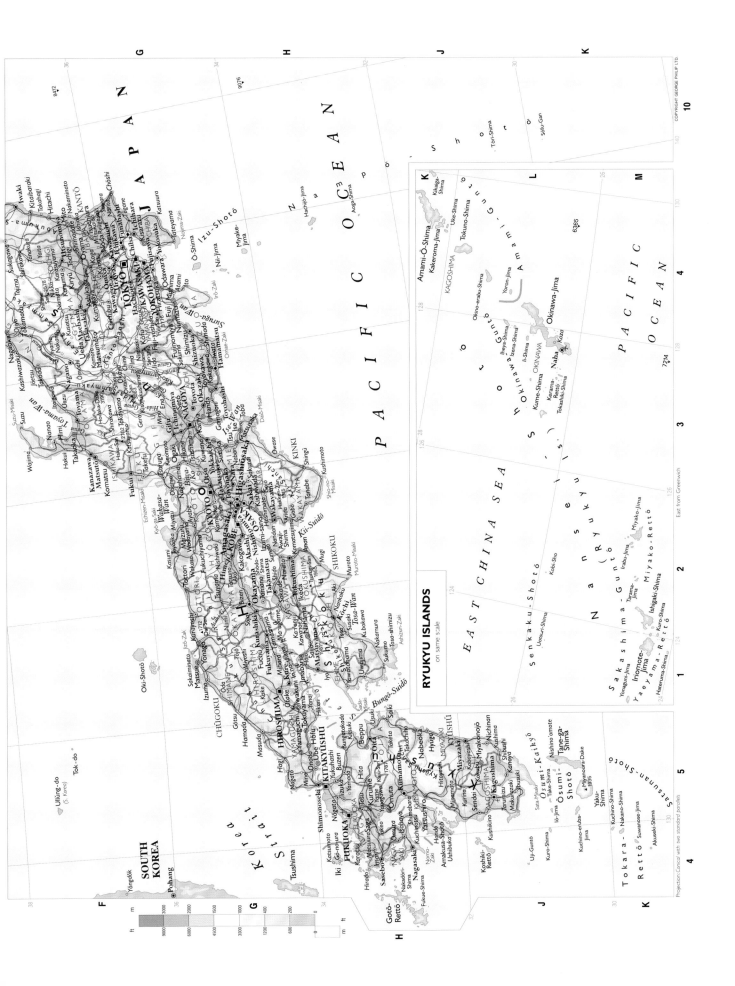

RYUKYU ISLANDS
on same scale

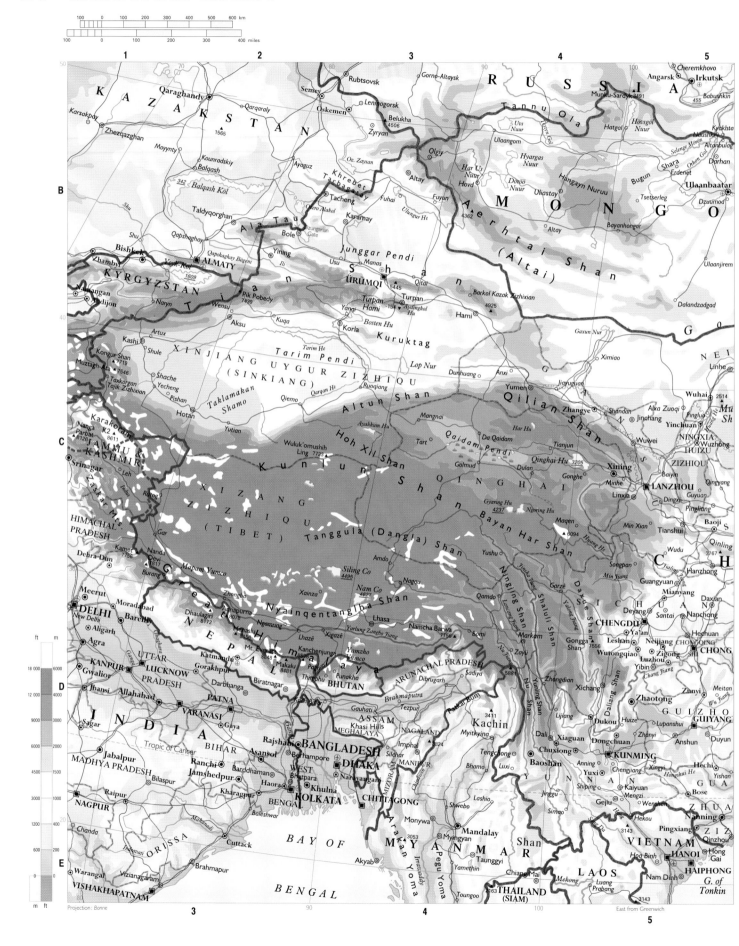

100 0 100 200 300 400 500 600 km
100 0 100 200 300 400 miles

Projection: Bonne

East from Greenwich

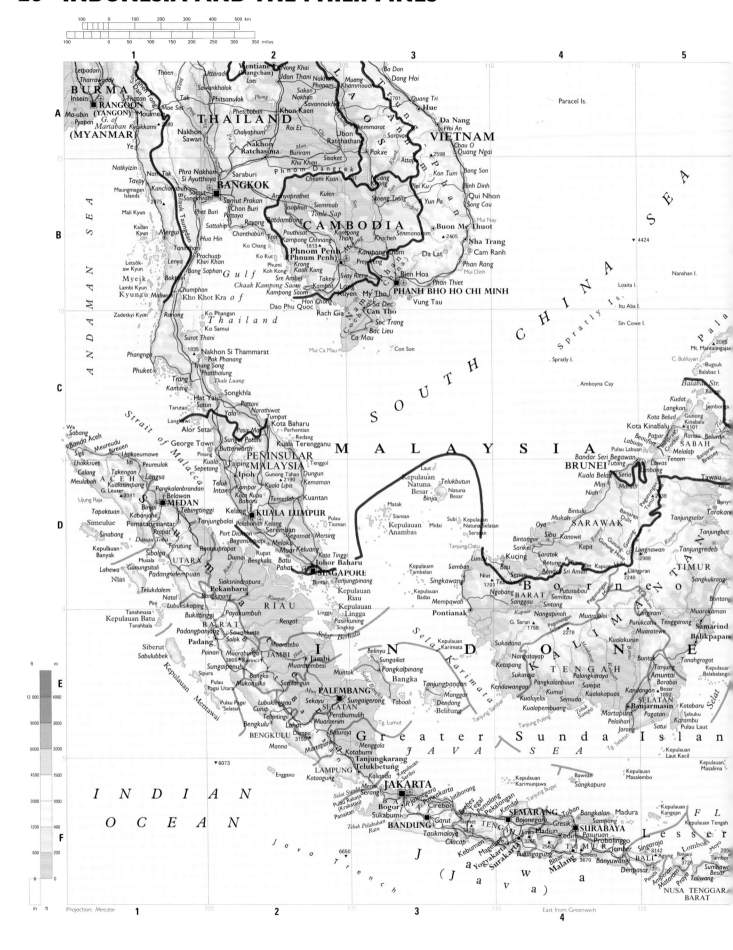

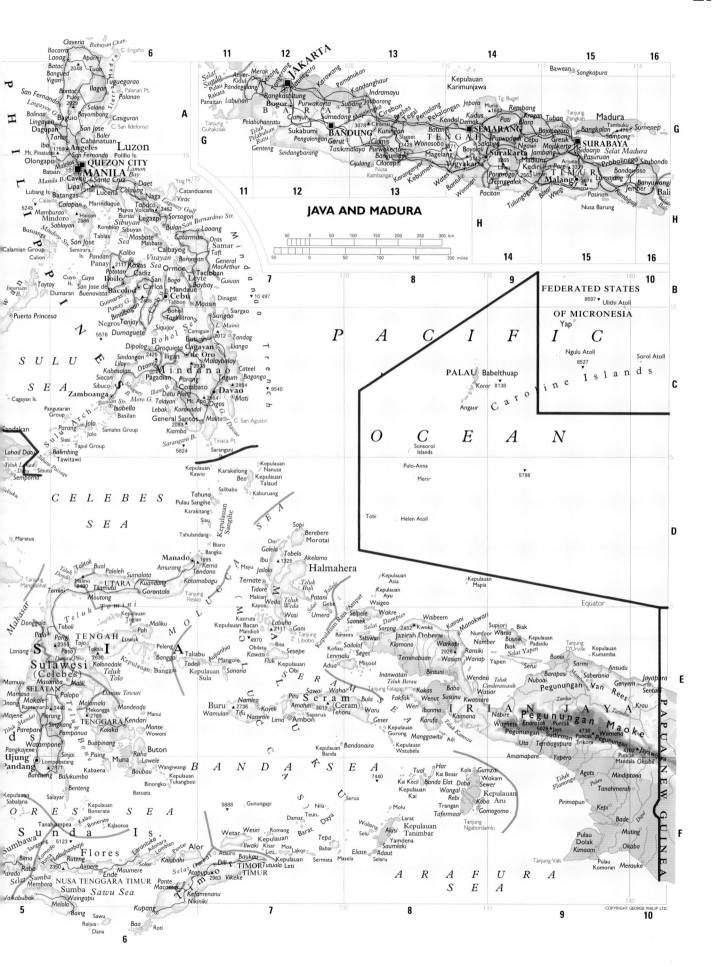

JAVA AND MADURA

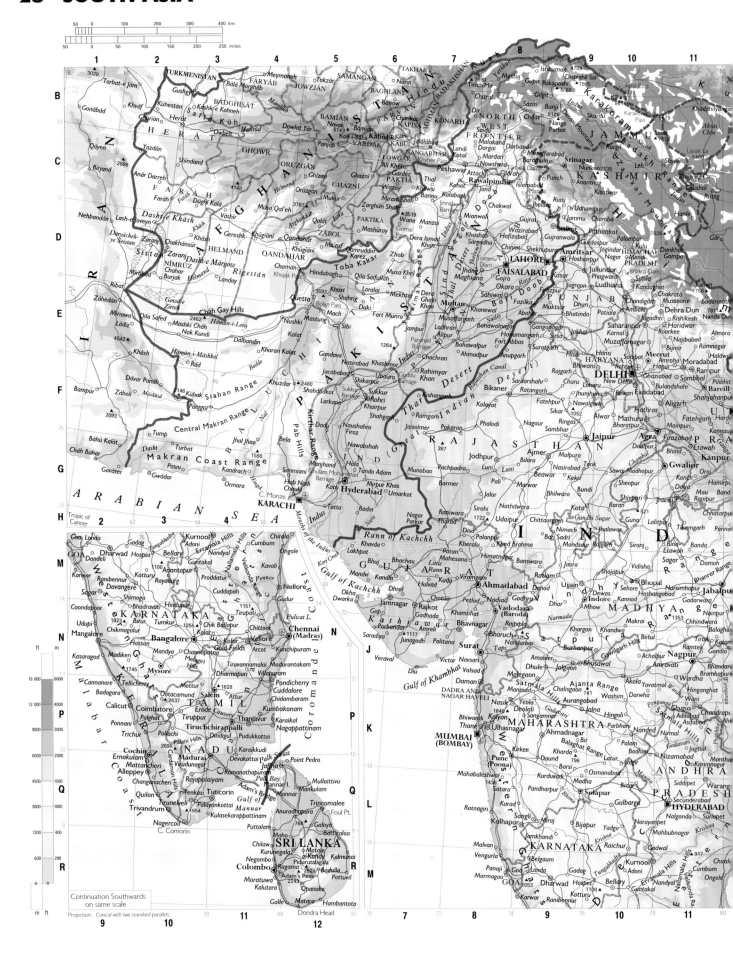

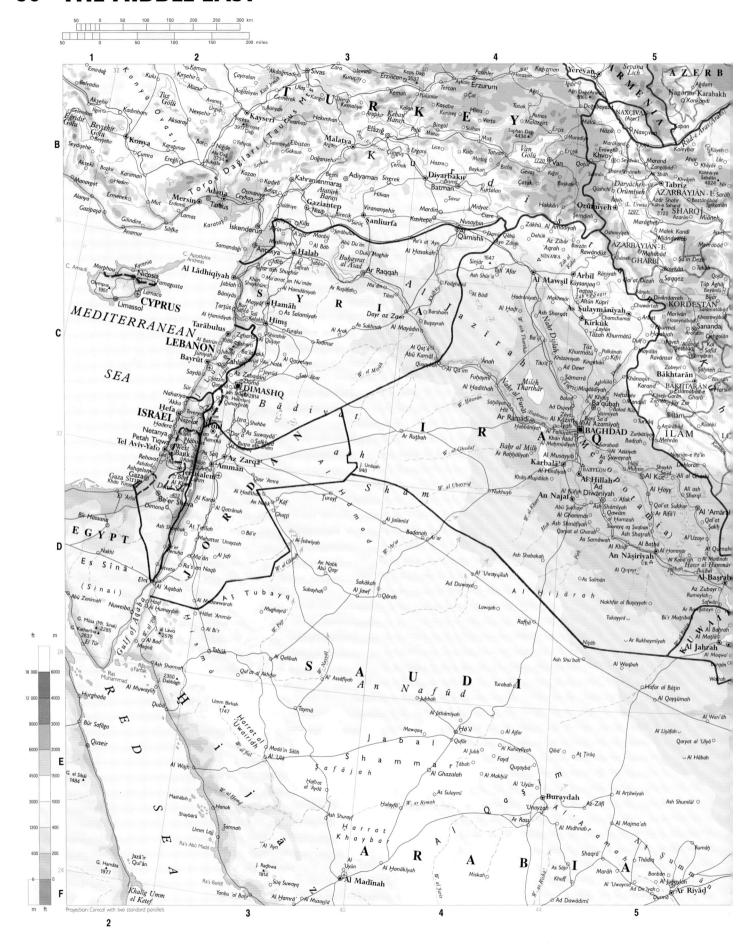

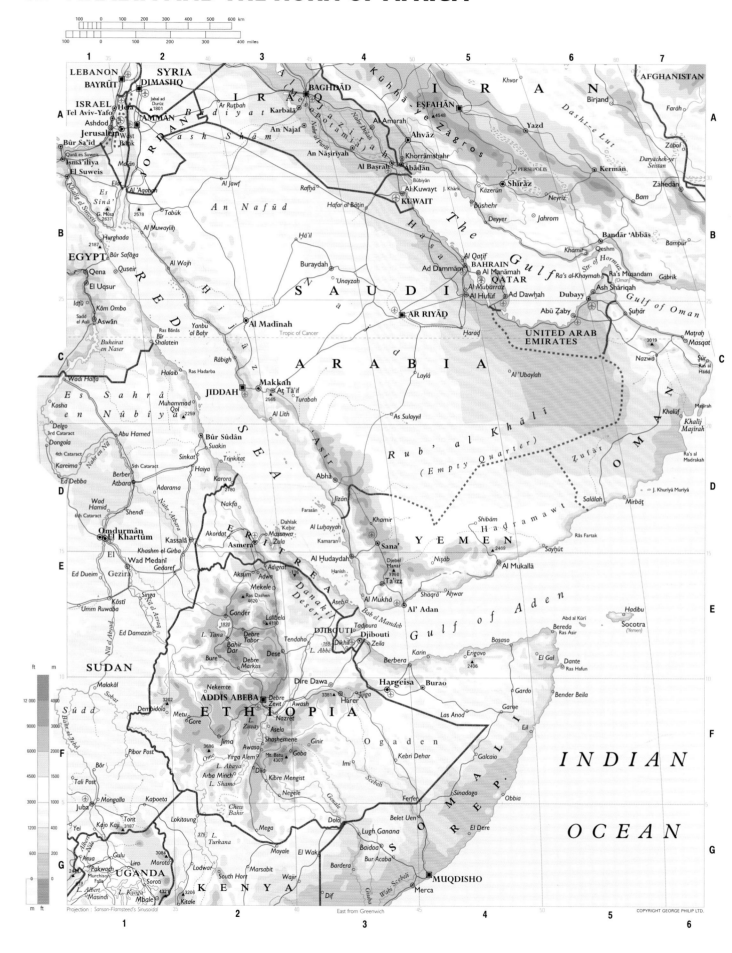

CYPRUS

Paphos
Episkopi
Episkopi Bay
Limassol
Akrotiri Bay
C. Gata

M E D I T E R R A N E A N

S E A

LEBANON

BAYRŪT
(Beirut)

SYRIA

Tarābulus
(Tripoli)
ASH SHAMĀL

DIMASHQ
(Damascus)

AL JANŪB

Golan Heights

ISRAEL

HAMERKAZ

Tel Aviv-Yafo
Bat Yam

West Bank

Jerusalem
(Al Quds)

Gaza Strip

JORDAN

'AMMĀN

Az Zarqā

HADAROM

Hanegev

E G Y P T

S Î N Î

E S   S î n â '
(Sinai)

Gebel el Tîh

Shibh Jazîrat Sînā'

SAUDI

ARABIA

Gulf of Aqaba

Bûr Sa'îd (Port Said)

El Suweis
(Suez)

1974 Cease Fire Lines

ft   m
9000   3000
6000   2000
4500   1500
3000   1000
1200   400
600   200
0   0
m   ft

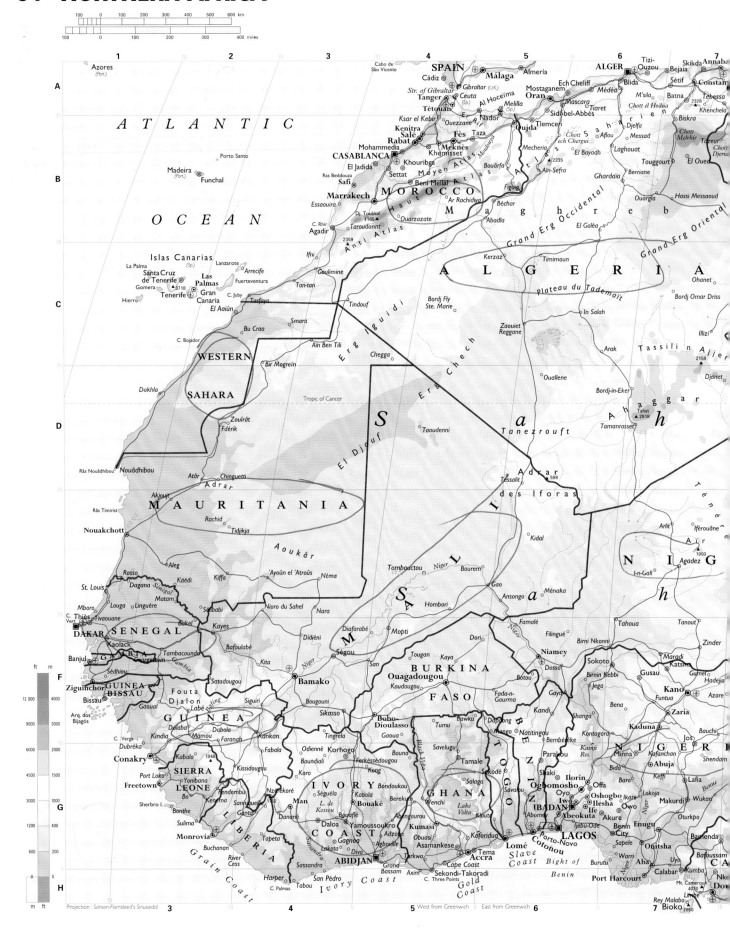

A T L A N T I C

O C E A N

SPAIN

Azores *(Port.)*

Porto Santo

Madeira *(Port.)* Funchal

Islas Canarias *(Sp.)*

La Palma
Santa Cruz
de Tenerife
Gomera Tenerife Gran
Hierro Canaria
Las
Palmas
Lanzarote
Arrecife
Fuerteventura

Cabo de
São Vicente Cádiz **Málaga** Almería

Str. of Gibraltar Gibraltar *(U.K.)*
Ceuta *(Sp.)* Al Hoceïma
Tanger Tétouan Melilla *(Sp.)* Mostaganem Oran
Ksar el Kebir Ouezzane Nador Sidi-bel-Abbès
Kenitra Taza **Oujda** Tlemcen
Salé **Fès**
Rabat **Meknès** Mecheria
Mohammedia Khemisset
CASABLANCA El Jadida Khouribga Moyen Atlas
Ras Beddouza Settat
Safi Beni Mellal Bouârfa Figuig
Marrakech **MOROCCO** Ar Rachidiya
Essaouira Dj. Toubkal Ouarzazate Abadla
C. Rhir 4165 ▲ Taroudannt 2359 ▲
Agadir Anti Atlas

ALGER Tizi- Skikda Annaba
Ouzou Bejaia
Ech Cheliff Blida Sétif Constan
Médéa Batna Tébessa
M'sila Chott el Hodna 2328 ▲ Khenchela
Mascara Tiaret Biskra
Chott ech Chergui Djelfa Chott
Aflou Messad Melrhir
El Bayadh Laghouat Chott
 Aïn-Sefra Ghardaïa Berriane Djerid
2235 ▲ El Goléa Ouargla Hassi Messaoud
Béchar Grand Erg Occidental Touggourt El Oued
Grand Erg Oriental

ALGERIA

Kerzaz Timimoun
Plateau du Tademaït Ohanet
In Salah Bordj Omar Driss
Bordj Fly
Ste. Marie Arak Illizi
Zaouiet Tassili n Ajjer
Reggane 2158 ▲
Ouallene Djanet
Bordj-in-Eker
A h a g g a r
Tamanrasset Tahat
▲ 2918

WESTERN

SAHARA

Dakhla

Ifni
Goulimine
Tan-tan

El Aaiún Smara Tindouf
Bu Craa
C. Bojador Bir Mogreïn
Chegga
Aïn Ben Tili

Tropic of Cancer

Zouîrât
Fdérik

S A H A R A

Taoudenni

Adrar
des Iforas
Tessalit ▲ 698

Ras Nouâdhibou Nouâdhibou
Atâr Chinguetti El Djouf

Adrar

Akjoujt

Ras Timiris

MAURITANIA Rachid Aoukâr
Tidjikja

Nouakchott

Aleg Kiffa 'Ayoûn el 'Atroûs Néma
Rosso Kaédi
St. Louis Dagana Senegal
Mboro Louga Linguère Séribabi Nioro du Sahel Nara
C. Thiès Tivaouane Bakel
C. Vert Kayes
DAKAR **SENEGAL** Kaolack Bafoulabé Kita
Banjul Georgetown Gambia
GAMBIA Sédhiou Gambia Satadougou
Ziguinchor **GUINEA** Fouta Labé Siguiri
Bissau **BISSAU** Djalon
Gaoual Dabola Kankan
Arq. dos **GUINEA** Dalaba Fabala
Bijagós Dubréka Mamou Faranah
C. Verga Kindia 1948 ▲ Odienné Korhogo
Kabala Kissidougou Boundiali
Conakry Port Loka **SIERRA** Séguéla Ferkéssédougou
Kabala **LEONE** Yonibana Nzérékoré Kong
Freetown Bo Kenema Man L. de Bouaké
Sherbro I. Bonthe Sanniquellie Kossou
Sulima Ganta **IVORY** Bouaflé
Monrovia **LIBERIA** Tapeta Danané **COAST** Yamoussoukro
Buchanan Daloa Gagnoa Adzopé
River Sassandra Divo Agboville
Cess Lakota
Harper San Pédro **ABIDJAN**
Tabou Grand
C. Palmas Ivory Coast Bassam
Grain Coast Sekondi-Takoradi
Gold C. Three Points
Coast

Bir Mogreïn

Nema

Tombouctou Niger Bourem
Gao Arlit
Ansongo Ménaka Aïr
Kidal ▲ 1900
Hombori A z a w a d
Famalé I-n-Gall
Diafarabé Mopti Dori Filingué Agadez
M A S I N A Tougan Kaya Botou Dosso Birni Nkonni
Ségou San **Niamey** **NIGER**
Didiéni **Bamako** **BURKINA** Gaya Sokoto Maradi Zinder
Nara **Ouagadougou** **FASO** Birnin Kebbi Gusau Katsina
Koudougou Fada-n- Jega Gumel
Bougouni Gourma Kandi Bena Funtua Hadejia
Sikasso Tumu Mango Natitingou Kontagora Zaria Azare
Bobo- Bawku Dapaong **Kano**
Dioulasso Shanga Bauchi
Gaoua Savelugu Bembéréké Kaduna
Tingréla Salaga Parakou Minna Jos Shendam
Tamale Kainji Kafanchan
Black Volta Res. **Abuja**
Bondoukou Sokodé Keffi Lafia
Berekum Lake Savalou **Ilorin** Baro Lokoja
GHANA Wenchi Volta Savé Offa Ikare Makurdi Wukari
Kumasi Kintampo Oshogbo Benue
Obuasi Koforidua **Ogbomosho** Ilesha
Asamankese **IBADAN** Ife Akure Benin Enugu
Tema Iwo **NIGER** City Onitsha Bamenda
Kloutse Ijebu-Ode Sapele
Abomey Lomé Porto-Novo **LAGOS** Warri
Accra Cotonou Aba Bafoussam
Cape Coast Slave Bight of Uyo CA
Axim Coast Benin Port Harcourt Calabar Nko
Bioko Mt. Cameroun Do
4070 ▲ Limbe
Rey Malabo Bioko 2850 ▲

F o u t a
D j a l o n

S A H E L

B E N I N

T O G O

Projection: Sanson-Flamsteed's Sinusoidal

West from Greenwich East from Greenwich

ft m
12 000 4000
9000 3000
6000 2000
4500 1500
3000 1000
1200 400
600 200
0
m ft

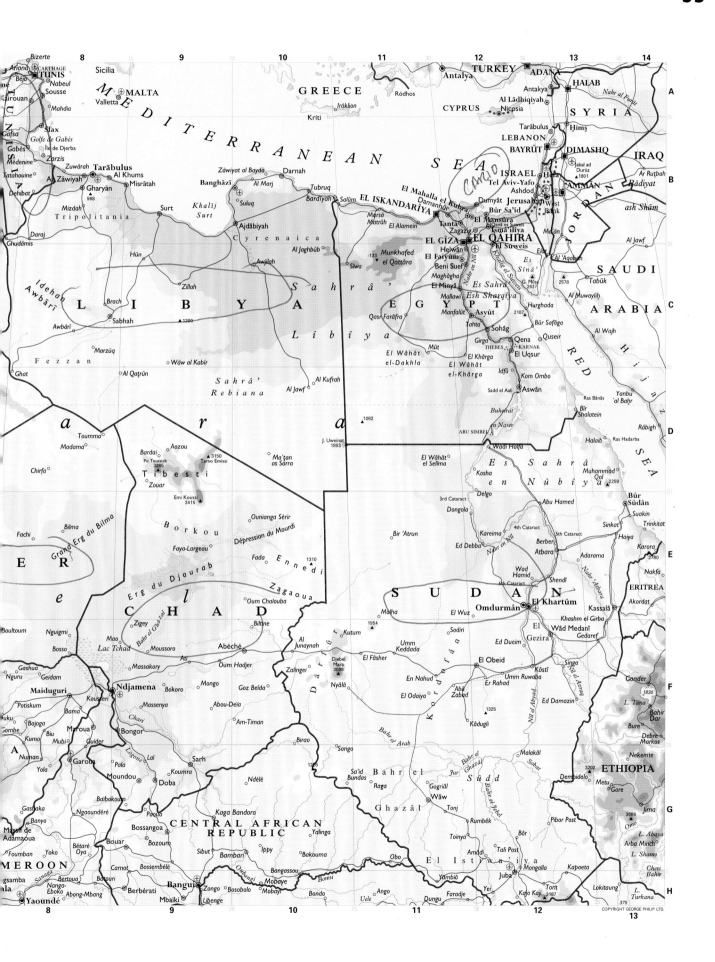

Bizerte
Ariana
CARTHAGE
Tunis
Beja
Nabeul
Sousse
Kairouan
Mahdia
Sfax
Gafsa
Golfe de Gabès
Île de Djerba
Gabès
Médenine
Zarzis
Tatahouine
Zuwārah **Tarābulus**
Dehibat
Zāwiyah
Al Khums
Gharyān
968
Mizdah
Misrātah
Daraj
Tripolitania
Ghudāmis
Hūn
Surt
Surt
Khalīj
Surt

MALTA
Valletta
Sicilia

GREECE
Iráklion
Kríti
Ródhos

Zāwiyat al Baydā
Darnah
Banghāzī
Al Marj
Suluq
Tubruq
Bardīyah
Salūm

TURKEY
ADANA
Antalya
HALAB
Antakya
SYRIA
CYPRUS
Al Lādhiqiyah
Nicosia
Tarābulus
Himş
LEBANON
BAYRŪT
DIMASHQ
IRAQ
ISRAEL
Tel Aviv-Yafo
AMMAN
 Badiyat
Ashdod
Dumyât
Jerusalem
West Bank
ash Shām

M E D I T E R R A N E A N   S E A

Zāwiyat al Baydā
Ajdābiyah
Cyrenaica
Al Jaghbūb
Awjilah
Zillah

EGYPT

El Mahalla el Kubra
Damanhûr
EL ISKANDARIYA
Marsā
Matrûh
El Alamein
Tanta
Zagazig
EL GĪZA
EL QAHIRA
Helwân
El Faiyûm
Beni Suef
El Minyâ
Mallawi
Manfalût
Es Sahrâ
Esh Sharqīya
Asyût
Tahta
Sohâg
Girga
Qena
El Khârga
El Uqsur
KARNAK
THEBES
Mût

Siwa
-133
Munkhafed
el Qattâra

Si
na
il
iy
a

El Suweis
Elat
Al 'Aqabah
Es
Sinâ
G. Mûsa
2637
Tabūk
Al Muwayliḥ
Hurghada
Bûr Safâga
Quseir
Al Wajh

SAUDI
ARABIA

Sahrâ'
Lîbîya

LIBYA

Idehan
Awbārī
Brach
Sabhah
Awbārī
1200
Marzūq

Fezzan

El Wâhât
el-Dakhla
El Wâhât
el-Khârga

Idfū
Kom Ombo
Sadd el Aali
Aswân

HIJA
Z

Ras Bânas
Yanbu
'al Baḥr

Ghat
Waw al Kabīr

Sahrâ'
Rebiana

Al Qatrūn
Al Kufrah
Al Jawf

1082

RED
SEA

Buḥeirat
en Naser

Bîr
Shalatein
Râbigh

J. Uweinat
1893

ABU SIMBEL

Wadi Halfa
Halaib
Ras Hadarba

Toummo
Madama
Bardai
Aozou
Pic Toussidé
3265
Tarso Emissi
3150
Tibesti
Zouar
Emi Koussi
3415

Ma'tan
as Sarra

El Wâhât
el Selima

Es   Sahrâ
en   Nûbîya

Kosha
Delgo
3rd Cataract
Dongola
Abu Hamed

Muhammad
Qol
2259

Bûr
Sûdân

Chirfa

a

r

a

Ouninga Sérir
Dépression du Mourdi
Fada
Ennedi
1310
Zagaoua

Borkou
Faya-Largeau

Bir 'Atrun

Kareima
4th Cataract
Delgo
Ed Debba
Berber
Atbara
5th Cataract

Suakin
Sinkat
Trinkitat
Haiya
Karora
2780

ERITREA
Nakfa
Akordat

Fachi
Bilma
Grand Erg du Bilma

ER

e

Erg du Djourab
Oum Chalouba
Biltine

Zigey
Bahr el Gha-zal

Malha

Wad
Hamid
Shendi
6th Cataract

SUDAN

El Wuz
Omdurmân
El Khartûm
Khashm el Girba
Kassalâ

Adarama

Gedaref

Boultoum
Nguigmi
Bosso
Gashua
Nguru
Geidam
Maiduguri
Potiskum
Bajoga
Biu
Mubi
Numan
Yola

Mao
Lac Tchad
Moussoro
Abéché
Ati
Massakory
Am-Timan

CHAD

1954
Kutum
Al
Junaynah
Zalingei
Djebel
Mara
3088
Nyâlâ

Darfûr

Sodiri
Umm
Keddada
El Fâsher
En Nahud
El Odaiya
Abû
Zabad

Kordofân

El Obeid
Umm Ruwaba
Er Rahad

Kôstî
El Dueim
Ed Dueim

El
Gezira
Wâd Medanî
Singa
Nil el Azraq

Gonder
1830
L. Tana
Bahir
Dar
Bure
Debre
Markos
Nekemte

ETHIOPIA

Kousseri
Ndjamena
Bokoro
Mongo
Goz Beïda
Massenya
Maroua
Guider
Bongor
Laï
Sarh
Koumra

Chari
Logone

Bama
Kurno
Garoua
Pala
Moundou
Doba
Ndélé

Birao
Songo
Bahr el Arab
Raga
Wâw
Gogrial
Tonj
Rumbek
Toinya
Amâdi
Tali Post
Bôr
Pibor Post

Nil el Abyad
Malakâl
Sobat
Kâdugli
1325
Ed Damazin

Metu
Gore
Dembidolo
3202

3686
Jima
L. Abaya
Arba Minch
L. Shamo

Baïbokoum
Bétaré
Oya
CENTRAL AFRICAN
REPUBLIC
Bossangoa
Bouar
Bozoum
Kaga Bandoro
Yalinga
Ippy
Bakouma
Sibut
Bambari
Bossembélé

Bahr   el

Ghazâl

Sa'id
Bundas

Jur

Bahr el
Ghazâl

Bahr el Jebel

Sudd

El Istywa'îya

Mongalla
Juba
Kapoeta

3187
Torit
Lokitaung
L.
Turkana

Foumban
Yoko
Banyo
Ngaoundéré
Paoua
Bouca

Bétaré
Oya
Batouri
Berbérati
Carnot
Nola
Bozoum

Nanga-
Eboko
Abong-Mbang

Bangui
Zongo
Bosobolo
Libenge
Mbaïki
Mobaye
Bondo
Ango
Bosolo
Bomu
Uele
Dungu
Faradje
Kajo Kaji
Yeï
Yambio

MEROON
Sanaga
Yaoundé

375

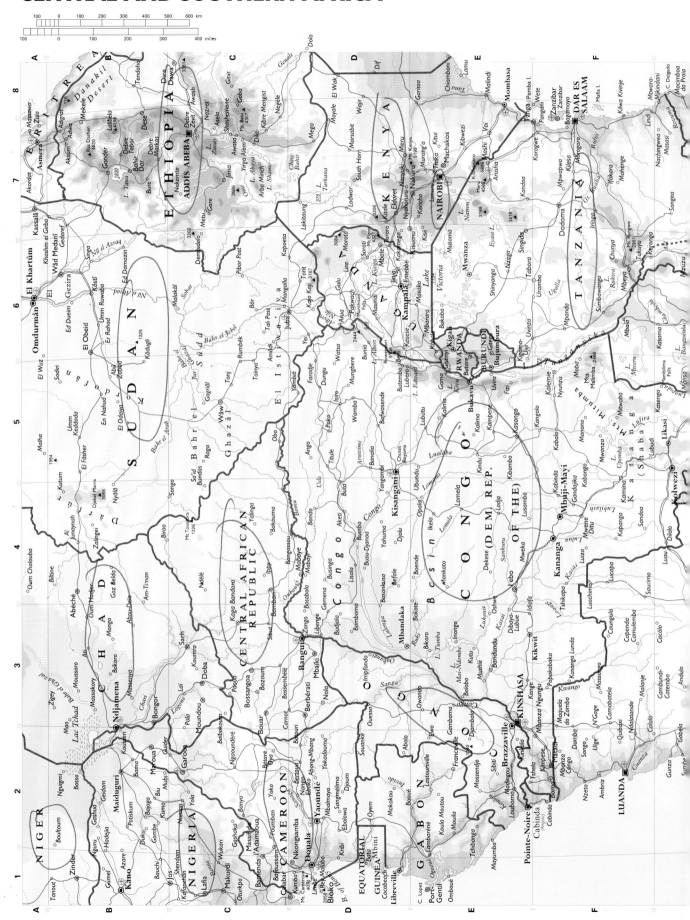

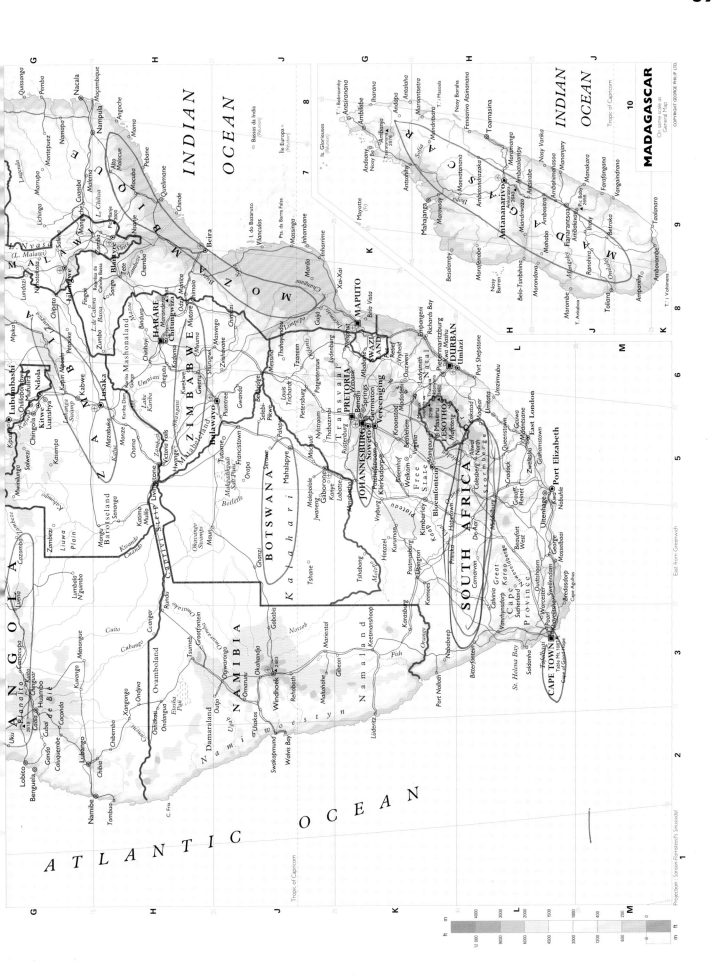

MADAGASCAR
On same scale as
General Map

COPYRIGHT GEORGE PHILIP LTD.

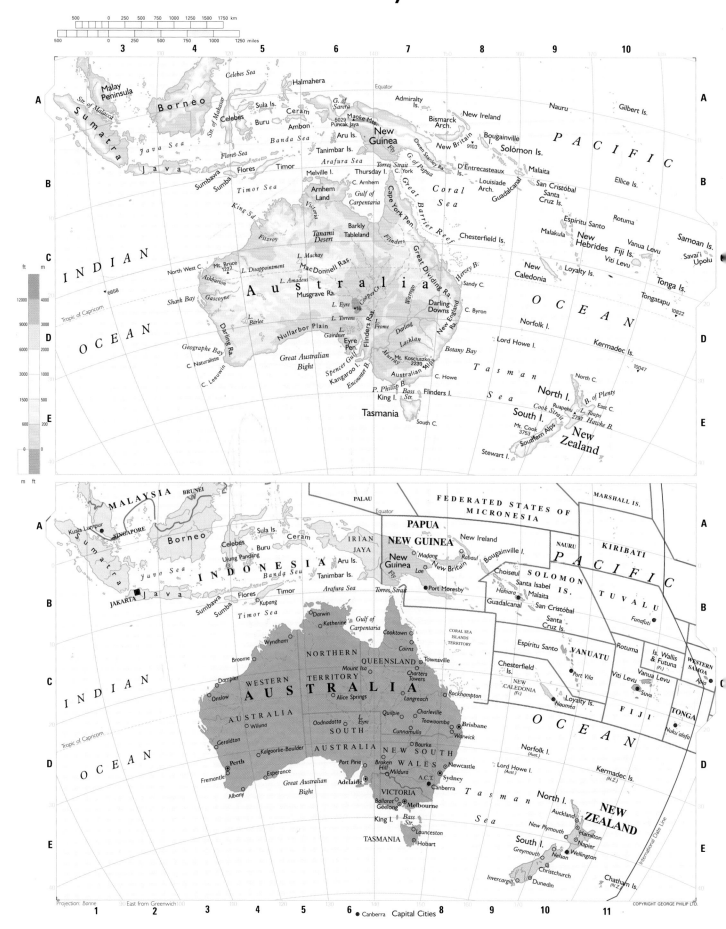

Projection: Bonne   East from Greenwich

● Canberra Capital Cities

COPYRIGHT GEORGE PHILIP LTD.

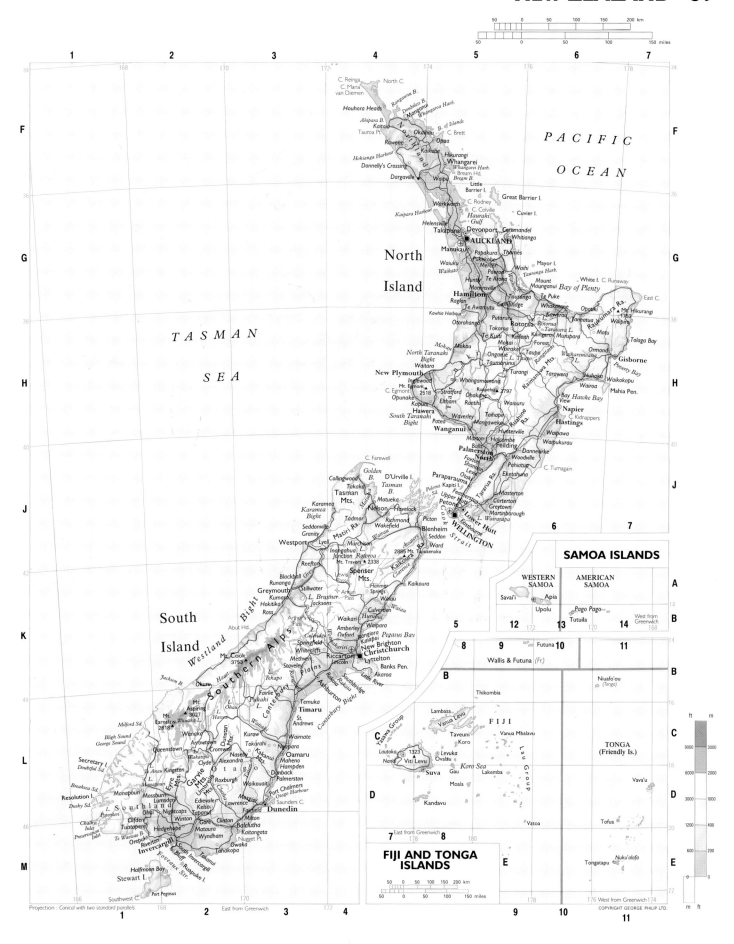

PACIFIC

OCEAN

North

Island

TASMAN

SEA

South

Island

Westland Bight

Southern Alps

WELLINGTON

Christchurch

Dunedin

Invercargill

Stewart I.

SAMOA ISLANDS

WESTERN
SAMOA

AMERICAN
SAMOA

Savai'i

Apia

Upolu

Pago Pago
Tutuila

West from
Greenwich

Wallis & Futuna (Fr.)

Niuafo'ou
(Tonga)

Thikombia

FIJI

Vanua Levu

Vanua Mbalavu

Lambasa

Taveuni
Koro

TONGA
(Friendly Is.)

Yasawa Group

Lautoka

Nandi

Viti Levu

Levuka
Ovalau

Suva

Gau

Koro Sea

Lakemba

Lau Group

Vava'u

Moala

Kandavu

Tofua

Vatoa

**FIJI AND TONGA
ISLANDS**

Tongatapu

Nuku'alofa

East from Greenwich

West from Greenwich

COPYRIGHT GEORGE PHILIP LTD.

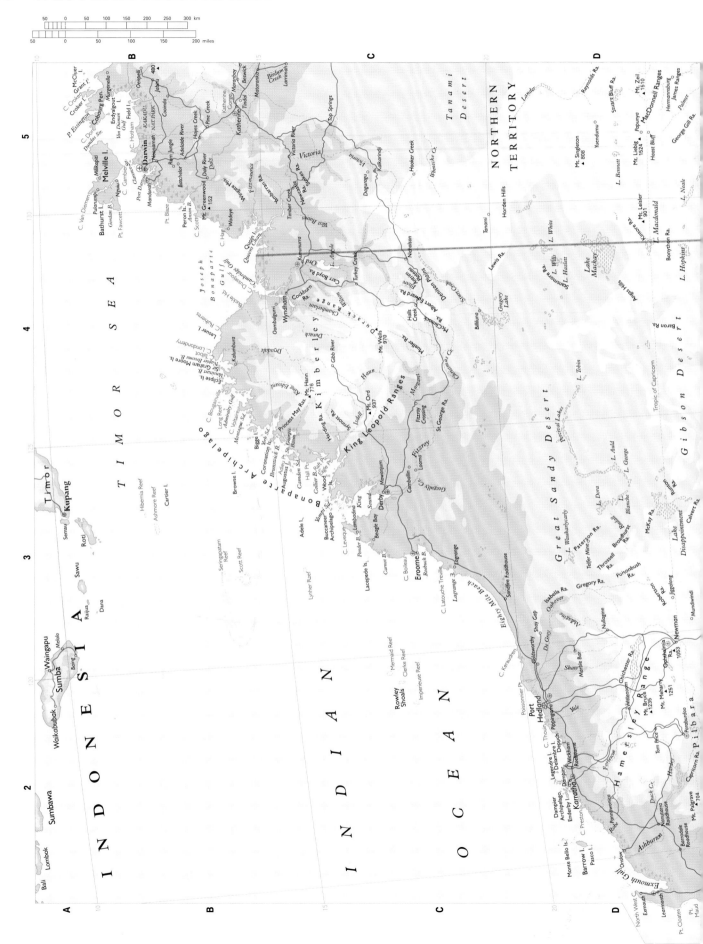

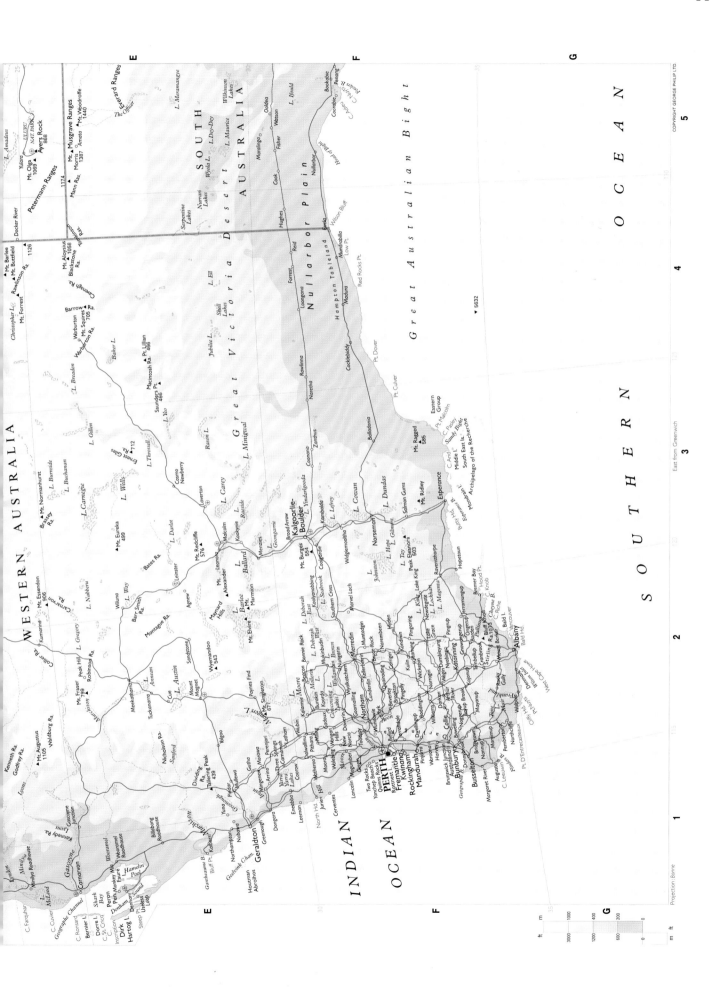

WESTERN AUSTRALIA

SOUTH AUSTRALIA

Great Victoria Desert

Nullarbor Plain

Hampton Tableland

Great Australian Bight

SOUTHERN OCEAN

INDIAN OCEAN

PERTH

Fremantle
Rockingham
Mandurah
Bunbury
Busselton

Geraldton

Carnarvon

Albany

Esperance

Kalgoorlie-Boulder

Norseman

Everard Ranges

Musgrave Ranges

Petermann Ranges

Ayers Rock 868

Mt. Olga 1069

Mt. Woodroffe 1440

Mt. Bruce

Projection: Bonne

East from Greenwich

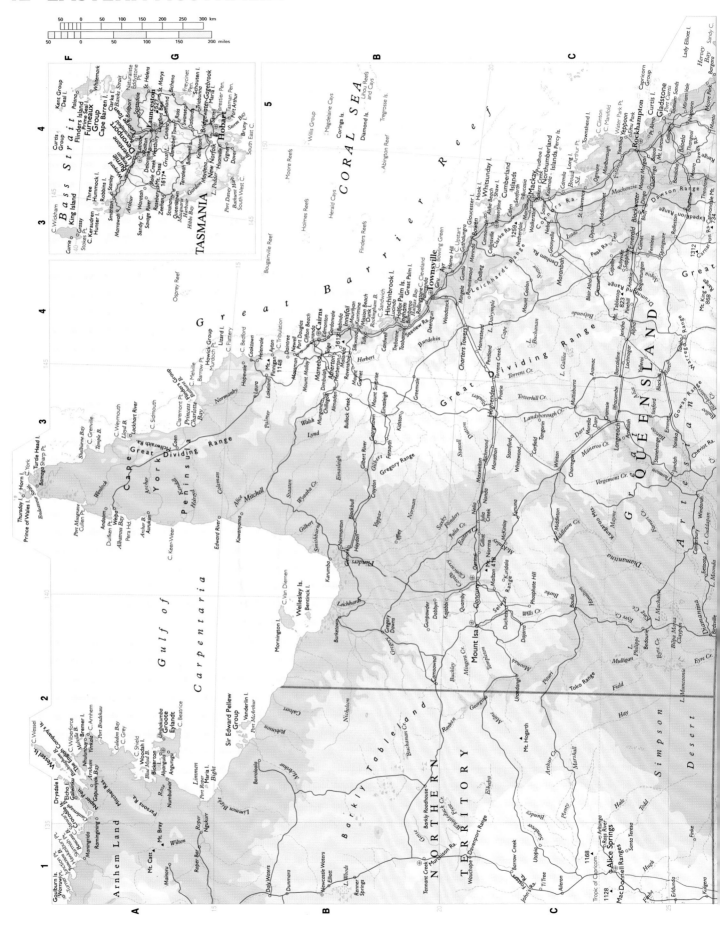

TASMANIA

C. Wickham
Currie
Grassy
King Island
Stokes Pt.
C. Keraudren
Hunter I.
Three
Hummock I.
Robbins I.
Smithton
Stanley
Marrawah
Woolnorth
Sandy C.
Waratah
Savage River
Strahan
Macquarie
Harbour
Hibbs Bay
Arthur
Zeehan
Rosebery
1617
Mt. Ossa
Queenstown
Gordon R.
L. Pedder
Port Davey
South West C.
Kent Group
Deal I.
Flinders Island
Palana
Cape Barren I.
Group
Furneaux
Group
Burnie
Devonport
Penguin
Ulverstone
Latrobe
Deloraine
Westbury
Launceston
4527
Longford Ben
Great
Lake
Bothwell
Hamilton
New Norfolk
Hobart
Huonville
Cygnet
Dover
Huon R.
Bruny I.
South East C.
Tasman Pen.
Port Arthur
Sorell
Maria I.
Triabunna
Tasman Pen.
Forester Pen.
Bridgewater
Brighton
Campbell Town
Ross
Tunbridge
Oatlands
Kempton
Swansea
Freycinet
Pen.
Schouten I.
Maria I.
Bicheno
St. Marys
Scamander
St. Helens
Eddystone Pt.
Georges Bay
Bridport
Scottsdale
Gladstone
Naturaliste Pt.
Whitemark
Banks Strait
Prime Seal I.
Clarke I.

Bass Strait

CORAL SEA
Willis Group
Magdelaine Cays
Coringa Is.
Diamond Is.
Tregrosse Is.
Moore Reefs
Abington Reef
Herald Cays
Holmes Reefs
Flinders Reefs
Bougainville Reef
Osprey Reef
Lihou Reefs
and Cays

Great Barrier Reef

Lady Elliott I.
Harvey Bay
Sandy C.
Bundaberg
Capricorn
Group
Port Curtis
Gladstone
Curtis I.
Miriam Vale
Bustard Hd.
Monto

Lucinda
Halifax Bay
Palm Is.
Great Palm I.
Hinchinbrook I.
Ingham
Halifax
Cardwell
Tully
Mission Beach
Dunk I.
Innisfail
Babinda
Gordonvale
Cairns
3612
Edmonton
Yarrabah
Green I.
Kuranda
Mareeba
Atherton
Herberton
Ravenshoe
Malanda
Millaa Millaa
Mossman
Port Douglas
Mowbray
Clifton Beach
Daintree
C. Tribulation
Cooktown
Helenvale
Ayton
Bloomfield
Lakeland
Laura
Hopevale
C. Bedford
C. Flattery
Lizard I.
Howick Group
C. Melville
Barrow Pt.
Murdoch Pt.
Princess
Charlotte
Bay
Claremont Pt.
Cape Weymouth
Lockhart River
Lloyd B.
C. Sidmouth
C. Direction
C. Grenville
Temple B.
Shelburne Bay
Orford Ness
C. York
Horn I.
Prince of Wales I.
Thursday I.
Bamaga
Sharp Pt.
Turtle Head I.
Jardine R.
Escape R.
Newcastle B.

Cape
York
Peninsula
McIlwraith Ra.
Coen
Archer R.
Kendall
Holroyd
Port Stewart
Port Musgrave
Cullen Pt.
Mapoon
Andoom
Weipa
Duifken Pt.
Albatross Bay
Pera Hd.
Aurukun
Archer B.
C. Keer-Weer
Edward River
Kowanyama
Mitchell
Nassau
Staaten
Gilbert
Smithburn
Inkerman

Gulf of
Carpentaria

Mornington I.
Wellesley Is.
Bentinck I.
Sweers I.
C. Van Diemen
Karumba
Normanton
Burketown
Leichhardt
Gregory Downs
Escott
Albert
Nicholson
Gregory
Lawn Hill
Camooweal
Urandangi

Wessel Is.
C. Wessel
Elcho I.
C. Newald
Milingimbi
Cape Stewart
C. Shield
Woodah I.
Bickerton I.
Groote
Eylandt
Angurugu
Umbakumba
Blue Mud B.
C. Barrow
C. Arnhem
Gove Pen.
Nhulunbuy
Yirrkala
Port Bradshaw
C. Grey
Caledon Bay
Rose
Numbulwar
Roper Bar
Ngukurr
Roper
Port Roper
Limmen
Bight
C. Beatrice
Maria I.
Bing Bong
Port McArthur
Sir Edward Pellew
Group
Vanderlin I.
Centre I.
Robinson
Wollogorang
McArthur
Borroloola
Cox
Calvert
Seigal
Creek
Tawallah
Mt. Isa
Cloncurry
Duchess
Dajarra
Selwyn
Kuridala
Malbon
Ballara
Mary Kathleen
Quamby
Corella
Kajabbi
Gunpowder
Dobbyn

Goulburn Is.
Warruwi
Maningrida
Arnhem Land
Mt. Catt
Mt. Bray
Wilton
Mainoru
Dajarra

NORTHERN
TERRITORY
Roper River
Mataranka
Elsey
Hodgson Downs
Dunmarra
Daly Waters
Newcastle Waters
Elliott
Renner
Springs
Tennant Creek
Wauchope
Murchison Ra.
Barkly Roadhouse
L. Woods
Powell Creek
Helen Springs
Brunette Downs
Alroy Downs
Anthony Lagoon
Alexandria
Avon Downs

Barkly Tableland

Ranken
Buchanan
Austral Downs
Lake Nash
Georgina
Urandangi
Tobermory
Marqua
Sandover
Ammaroo
Hart
Bundey
Plenty
Jervois
Arltunga
Ross River
1168
Alice Springs
1128
Wauchope
MacDonnell Ranges
Santa Teresa
Hale
Todd
Finke
Hugh
John
Alice
Ti Tree
Murray Downs
Barrow Creek
Harts Range
Ooratippra
Alcoota
Bond Springs
Erldunda
Kulgera

Simpson
Desert
Field
Toko Range
Hay
Marshall
Mulligan
Pituri
Mt. Hogarth
Buckley
Mingera Cr.
Lucy Cr.
Eyre Cr.
Diamantina
Bedourie
Cuttaburra
Eyre Cr.
Betoota
L. Machattie
L. Caroline
Monkira
Morney
Haddon Cr.
Kaliduwarry
Birdsville
Clifton Hills
Pandie Pandie
L. Mumpie
Eyre Cr.
Goyder Lagoon
L. Mionie

QUEENSLAND

Great
Dividing
Range

Great
Artesian
Basin

Townsville
C. Cleveland
Cape Bowling Green
C. Upstart
Home Hill
Ayr
Bowen
Gloucester I.
Gumlu
Merinda
Guthalungra
Proserpine
Airlie Beach
Cannonvale
Shaw I.
Hook I.
Whitsunday I.
Cumberland
Islands
Mackay
Sarina
Carmila
Koumala
Flaggy Rock
C. Palmerston
Ilbilbie
Clairview
St. Lawrence
Broad Sound
Long I.
Duke Is.
Northumberland
Islands
Islands Percy Is.
Marlborough
Ogmore
Yeppoon
Byfield
Rockhampton
Mt. Larcom
Biloela
Thangool
Mt. Morgan
Cawarral
Emu Park
Keppel Sands
Capricorn
Group
Water Park Pt.
Cape Capricorn
Curtis I.
Agnes Water

Charters Towers
Macrossan
Mingela
Ravenswood
Pentland
Homestead
Torrens Cr.
Torrens Creek
Prairie
Hughenden
Richmond
Maxwelton
Julia Creek
McKinlay
Kynuna
Nelia
Oorindi
Marathon
Tangorin
Corfield
Stamford
Winton
Vindex
Opalton
Cork
Middleton
Boulia
Springvale
Bladensburg
Mayne
Kaross
Carandotta
Roxborough
Glenormiston
Diamantina Lakes
Davenport Downs
Sandringham
Durrie
Springvale

Collinsville
Glenden
Mt. Coolon
Nebo
Moranbah
Dysart
Blair Athol
Clermont
Capella
Emerald
Blackwater
Dingo
Duaringa
Baralaba
Moura
Theodore
Cracow
Eidsvold
Mundubbera
Gayndah
Biggenden
Childers
Maryborough
Tiaro
Gympie

Belyando
Cape
Laglan
Lake Galilee
Jericho
Barcaldine
Alpha
Aramac
Muttaburra
Longreach
Isisford
Ilfracombe
Yaraka
Jundah
Windorah
Stonehenge
Barcoo
Blackall
Tambo
Augathella
Springsure
Rolleston
Bauhinia
Springsure
Comet
Rubyvale
Sapphire
Anakie
Gracemere
1312
Carnarvon Range
Carnarvon National Park
Expedition Range
Dawson Range
Dawson
Gogango
Westwood
Dululu
Mt. Scoria
Callide
Dawes Range
Kroombit

Georgina
Mt. Isa
Cloncurry
Kuridala
Boulia
Bedourie

Great Dividing Range
Great Barrier Reef
B a r r i e r
R e e f

Croydon
Georgetown
Forsayth
Einasleigh
Mt. Surprise
Greenvale
Lynd
Gilbert River
Gilberton
Kidston
Valley of Lagoons
Oak Park
Reedy Brook
Wrotham Park
Chillagoe
Almaden
Dimbulah
Mungana
Bullock Creek

Staaten
Wynoka Cr.
Alice
Hann
Coleman
Palmer
Walsh
Lynd
Mitchell
Tate R.
Gilbert
Norman
Flinders
Cloncurry
Leichhardt
Gregory Range
Selwyn Range
Saxby
Williams R.
Eastern Cr.
Julia Cr.
Flinders

Blackbull
Dunbar
Inverleigh
Iffley
Donors Hill
Augustus Downs
Armraynald
Floraville
Punjaub
Talawanta
Lorraine
Planet Downs
Wills Cr.
Burke
Phosphate Hill

Woolgar
Maxwelton
Richmond

Hann
Laura
Lakeland
Hopevale
Cooktown

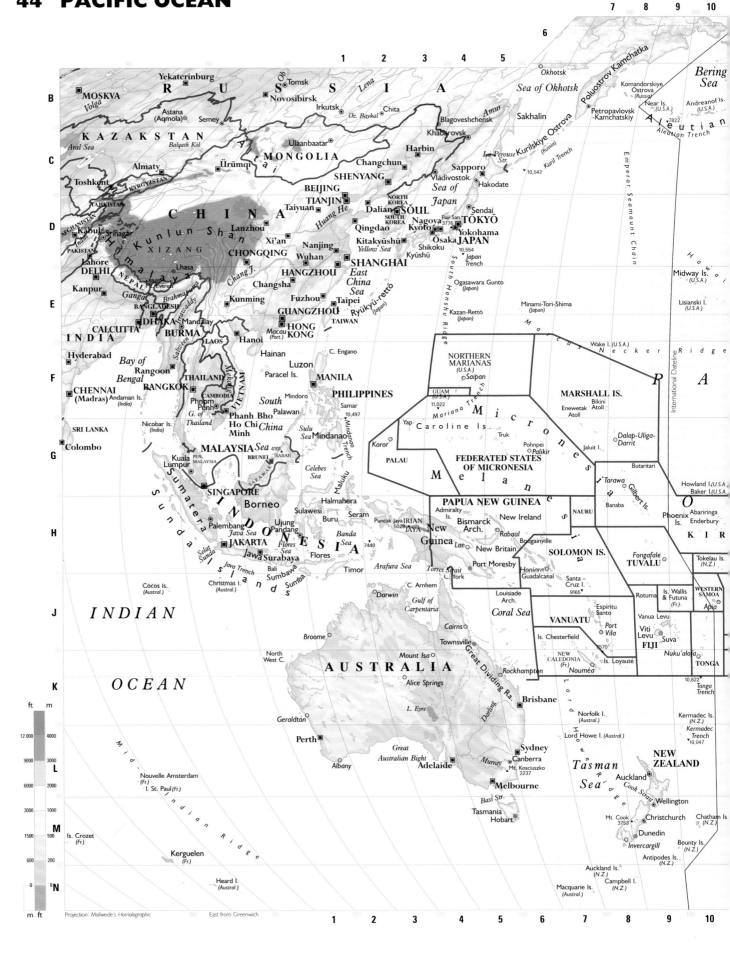

11 12 13 14

Arctic Circle

15

ALASKA
(U.S.A.)
Anchorage
5959

Bristol Bay Juneau

Gulf of Alaska

16 17 18 19 20

Prince of Wales I.
(U.S.A.) *Prince Rupert*
Queen Charlotte Is.
(Canada)

C A N A D A

Edmonton

L. Winnipeg

Newfoundland

B

Vancouver Calgary Regina Winnipeg
Vancouver I. Victoria
Seattle
Portland

St. Lawrence

Québec
St. John's

N O R T H

C

L. Superior

Minneapolis
Boise
L. Huron
L. Michigan Toronto Ottawa Boston
Detroit Buffalo

Montréal

Salt Lake
City
Denver
Sacramento
4418

C. Mendocino

6741

CHICAGO Pittsburgh
L. Erie
Kansas City St. Louis Cincinnati
UNITED STATES

NEW YORK CITY
PHILADELPHIA
Baltimore
Washington D.C.

A T L A N T I C

D

SAN FRANCISCO

Oklahoma City Memphis
Appalachian Mts.
Atlanta
C. Hatteras

Bermuda
(U.K.)

LOS ANGELES
San Diego
Guadalupe
(Mex.)

Phoenix
Dallas
Houston
San Antonio
New
Orleans
Jacksonville

Sargasso Sea

Ciudad
Juárez

Gulf of Mexico Miami
Monterrey

BAHAMAS

O C E A N

E

Tropic of Cancer

Honolulu
Oahu
HAWAIIAN IS.
4205
(U.S.A.)
Hawaii

Johnston I.
(U.S.A.)

C

I F I C

C. San Lucas

Guadalajara

MEXICO
5700
Puebla
Acapulco

La Habana
West Indies
Canal de Yucatan
Mérida

9200

C U B A
7680
HAITI DOMINICAN REP.
JAMAICA Kingston Leeward
PUERTO Is.
RICO
(U.S.A.)

F

BELIZE

Caribbean Sea

North West Christmas

Is. Revilla Gigedo
(Mex.)

GUATEMALA
Guatemala
San Salvador
EL SALVADOR
HONDURAS

O

I. Clipperton
(Fr.)

NICARAGUA
Managua

BARBADOS
Windward Is.

Barranquilla
Maracaibo

P

Palmyra Is.
(U.S.A.)

Teraina
Tabuaeran
Kiritimati

Ridge

Jarvis I.
(U.S.A.)

Equator

COSTA
RICA
San José
Colón Panamá
PANAMA

Caracas
Orinoco

VENEZUELA

G

I. del Coco
(Costa Rica)
Medellín
I. de Malpelo
(Colombia)

Bogotá
Cali
COLOMBIA

C E A N

Galápagos
(Ecuador)

Quito
ECUADOR
Amazonas

I B A ⊃ T I

Malden I.
Starbuck I.

Guayaquil
Iquitos
C. Paliñas

BRAZIL

H

Tongareva
Pukapuka Manihiki

Caroline I.
Vostok I.
Flint I.

Is. Marquises

Trujillo

6369

PERU

AMER.
SAMOA
(U.S.A.)

Suwarrow Is
Is. de la
Société Tahiti
Papeete

Is. Tuamotu

LIMA
Cuzco
L. Titicaca

Nevada Ancohuma
6550

J

Niue
(N.Z.)

Cook Is.
(N.Z.)

FRENCH POLYNESIA

Arequipa
6866
Peru-
Arica

La Paz
BOLIVIA

Rarotonga

Is. Tubuai

Mururoa

Tropic of Capricorn

Iquique
Chile

PARAGUAY

Ducie I.

Antofagasta
8050
Trench

Asunción

San Miguel
de Tucumán

K

Pitcairn I.
(U.K.)
Rapa

Sala-y-Gómez
(Chile)

San Felix
(Chile)
San Ambrosio
(Chile)

I. de Pascua
(Chile)

Pôrto
Alegre

Córdoba
Arch. de
Juan Fernández
(Chile)

Aconcagua
6960
Valparaíso Rosario

URUGUAY
Montevideo

L

SANTIAGO
Concepción

BUENOS
AIRES
Río de la Plata

ARGENTINA

Chile Rise

SOUTH

M

Pacific-Antarctic Ridge

6212

ATLANTIC

Punta Arenas
Est. de Magallanes
Tierra del Fuego
C. de Hornos

Falkland Is.
(U.K.)

South Georgia
(U.K.)

OCEAN

N

11 12 13 14 15 16 17 18 19 20

West from Greenwich COPYRIGHT GEORGE PHILIP LTD.

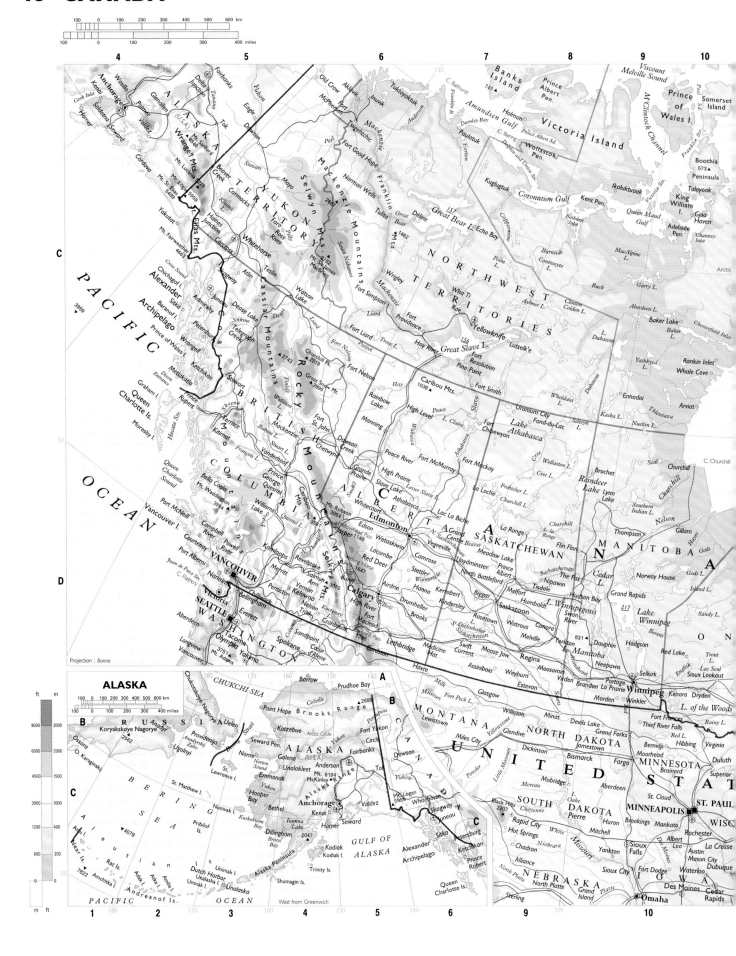

Projection : Bonne

ALASKA

West from Greenwich

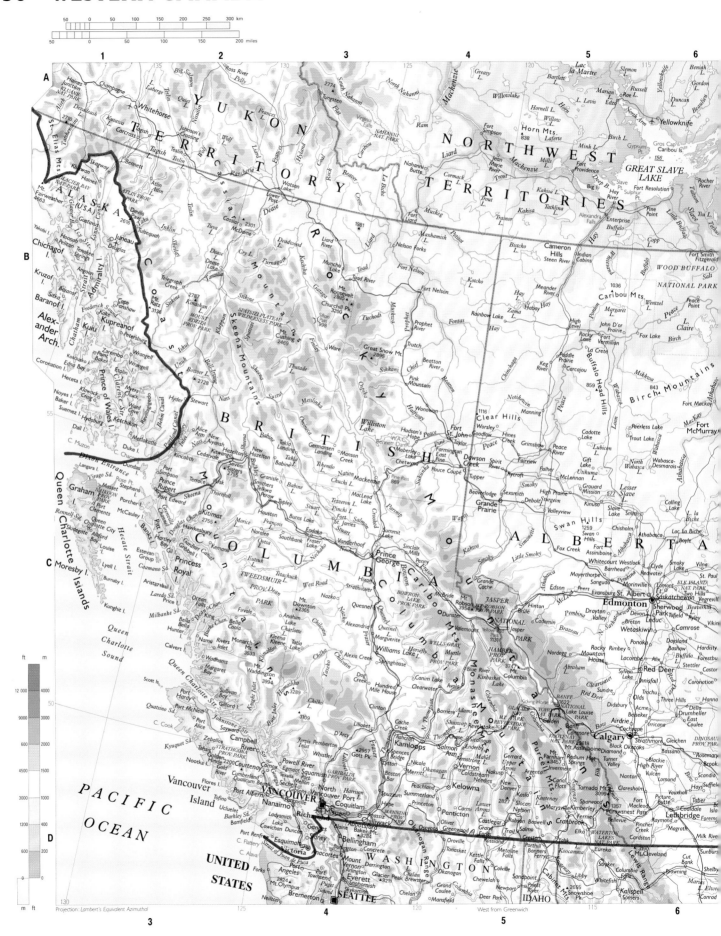

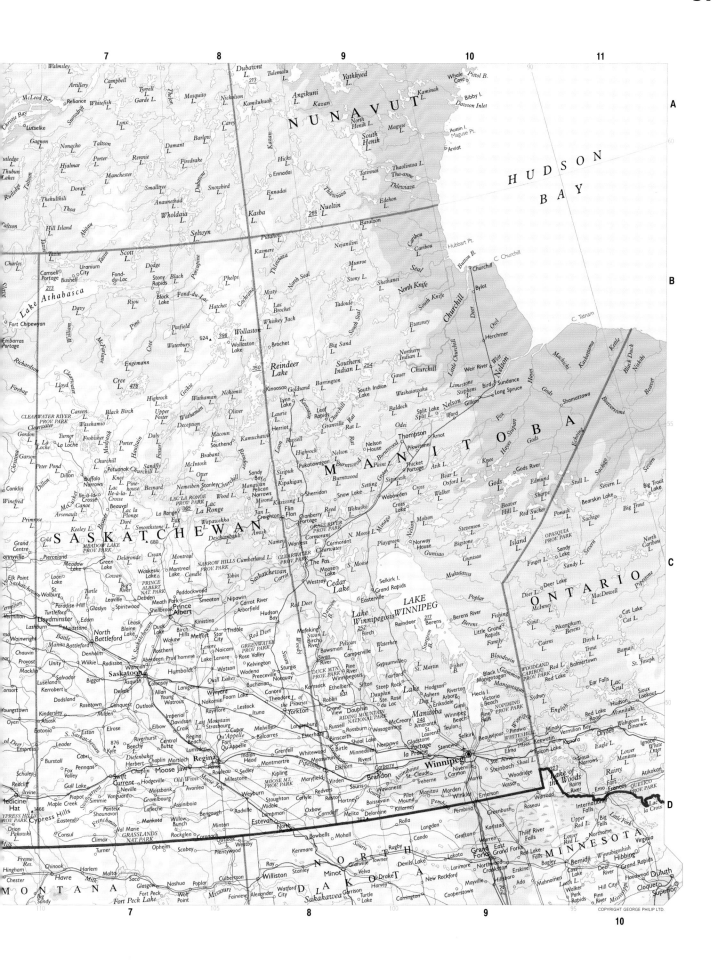

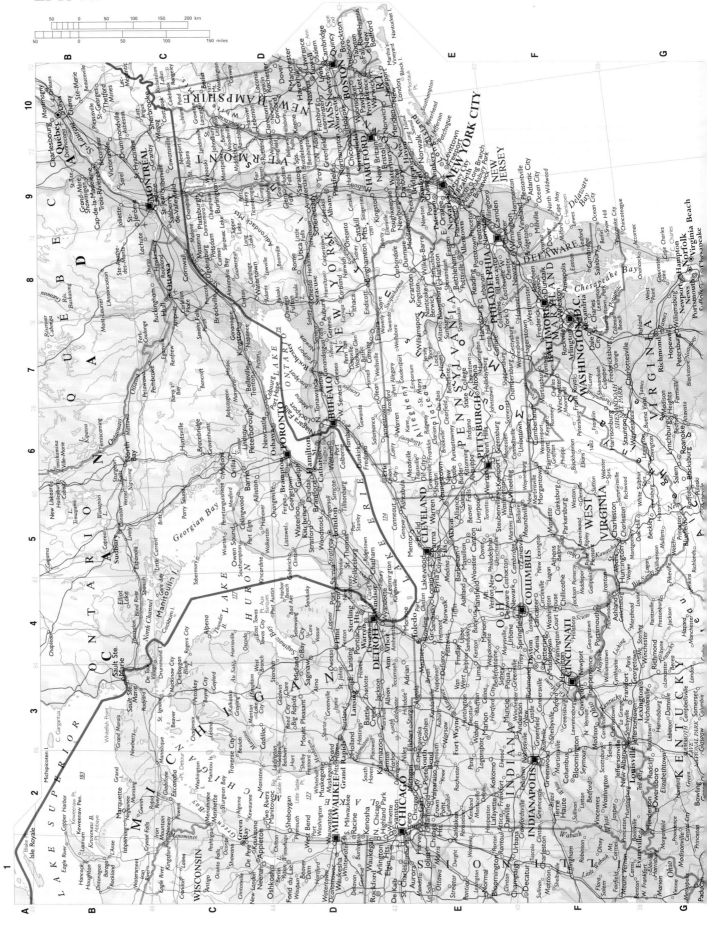

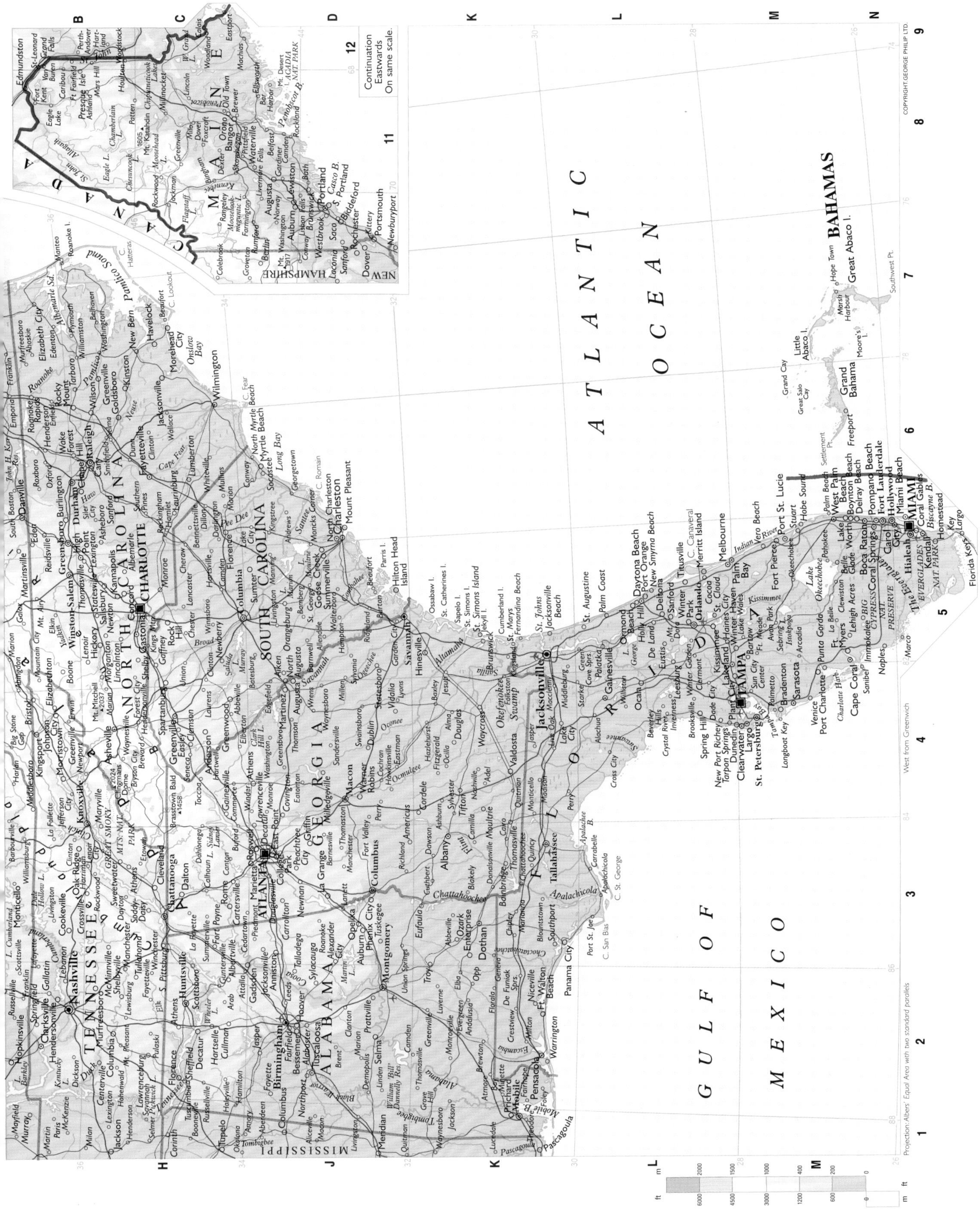

MAINE

CANADA

NEW HAMPSHIRE

Continuation Eastwards On same scale.

ATLANTIC OCEAN

BAHAMAS

Great Abaco I.

Grand Bahama

TENNESSEE

NORTH CAROLINA

SOUTH CAROLINA

GEORGIA

ALABAMA

MISSISSIPPI

FLORIDA

GULF OF MEXICO

ATLANTA

CHARLOTTE

Nashville

Birmingham

Montgomery

Jacksonville

TAMPA

MIAMI

Florida Keys

EVERGLADES NAT. PARK

BIG CYPRESS NAT. PRESERVE

Projection: Albers' Equal Area with two standard parallels

West from Greenwich

COPYRIGHT GEORGE PHILIP LTD.

ft   m
6000
4500
3000
1500 2000
1200 400
600   200
0   0
m   ft

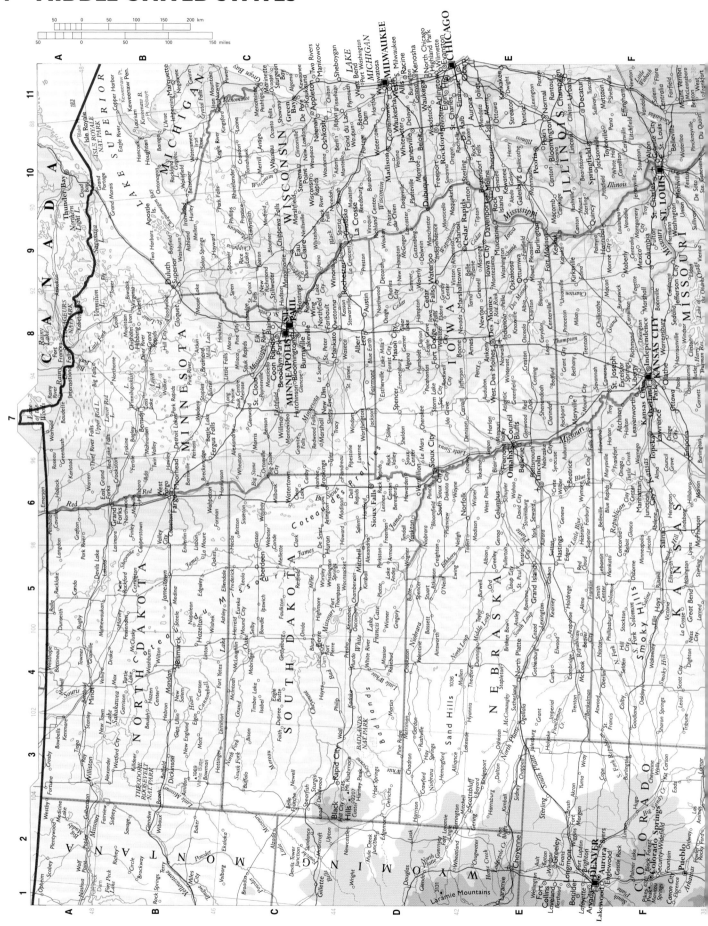

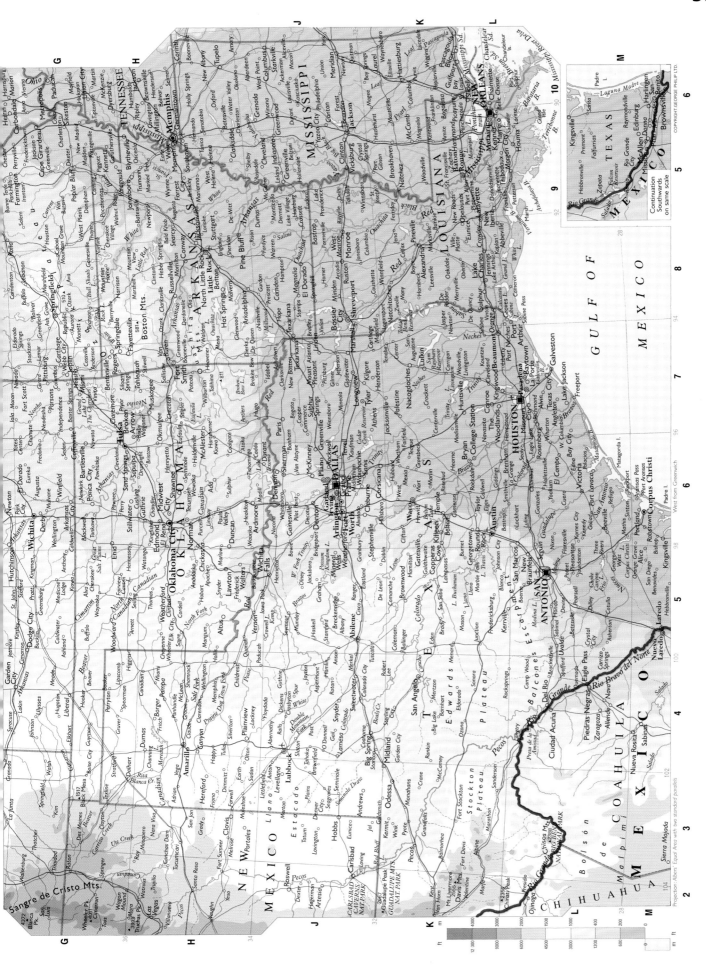

Projection: Albers' Equal Area with two standard parallels

West from Greenwich

AMAS

A T L A N T I C

Tropic of Cancer

O C E A N

Arthur's Town
The Bight
Cat I.
San Salvador I.
Conception I.
Rum Cay
Long I.
Sandy Cay
Clarence Town
Samana Cay
Crooked I.
Plana Cays
Albert Town
Snug Corner
Mayaguana I.
Acklins I.
Mira por vos Cay
Cay Verde
Hogsty Reef
Little Inagua I.
Caicos Is.
Turks & Caicos (U.K.)
Turks Is.
Cay Santa Domingo
Lake Rosa
Great Inagua I.
Matthew Town
Banes
Antilla
Mayari
Moa
Baracoa
Pta. de Maisi
Î. de la Tortue
Monte Cristi
LA ISABELA
Santiago de los Cabelleros
Puerto Rico Trench
Guantanamo
Paso de los Vientos (Windward Passage)
Cap-Haïtien
Puerto Plata
San Francisco de Macorís
Milwaukee Deep 9200
Jean Rabel
Port-de-Paix
Fort Liberté
La Vega
Nagua
Samana
Cap-à-Foux
G. de la Gonâve
Gonaïves
Cord. Central
Sánchez
Sabana de la Mar
Anegada
Virgin Is. (U.K.)
Sombrero (U.K.)
St-Marc
Hinche
3175
Hato Mayor
Virgin Gorda
Road Town
Anguilla (U.K.)
Jérémie
Î. de la Gonâve
HAITI
DOMINICAN REP.
San Pedro de Macorís
Higüey
C. Engaño
Bayamón
SAN JUAN
Carolina
Arecibo
St. Thomas
Tortola
Virgin Is. (U.S.A.)
St.-Martin (Fr.)
St. Maarten (Neth.)
St.-Barthélemy (Fr.)
Navassa I. (U.S.A.)
Dame Marie
PORT-AU-PRINCE
San Juan
L. Enriquillo
Azua
Bani
San Cristóbal
SANTO DOMINGO
La Romana
B. de Yuma
Mayagüez
Ponce
Fajardo
Caguas
Charlotte Amalie
Christiansted
Saba (Neth.)
St. Eustatius (Neth.)
Barbuda
C. Carcasse
Massif de la Hotte
Petit Goâve
2280
Pedernales
Barahona
Compostela
I. Saona
Isla Mona (U.S.A.)
Guayama
Frederiksted
St. Croix
Basseterre
ST. KITTS & NEVIS
St. John's
ANTIGUA & BARBUDA
Les Cayes
Jacmel
Aquin
Î. à Vache
I. Beata
C. Beata
PUERTO RICO (U.S.A.)
Nevis
Redonda
Antigua
Pointe-à-Gravois
Hispaniola
Antilles
Montserrat (U.K.)
Ste.-Rose
Le Moule
La Désirade
Guadeloupe Passage
Leeward Islands
GUADELOUPE (Fr.)
Pointe-à-Pitre
Marie-Galante (Fr.)
I. de Aves (Venezuela)
Basse-Terre
I. des Saintes (Fr.)
Grand-Bourg
Portsmouth
Dominica Passage
B E A N
S E A
Roseau
DOMINICA
Martinique Passage
Mt. Pelée 1397
Ste.-Marie
Le François
Fort-de-France
Rivière-Pilote
MARTINIQUE (Fr.)
St. Lucia Channel
Castries
Soufrière
ST. LUCIA
St. Vincent Passage
La Soufrière 1234
ST. VINCENT
Speightstown
Kingstown
Bridgetown
THE
BARBADOS
Windward Islands
Hillsborough
GRENADINES
Lesser
Antilles
Aruba (Neth.)
Curaçao
Bonaire
St. George's
GRENADA
Grenadines
Pta. Gallinas
C. San Román
Pen. de Paraguaná
NETH. ANTILLES
Willemstad
I. Blanquilla (Ven.)
Tobago
Pen. de la Guajira
Pta. Espada
Punta Fijo
Is. Las Aves (Ven.)
I. Orchila (Ven.)
Is. Los Hermanos (Ven.)
Scarborough
Ríohacha
Uribia
GUAJIRA
Puerto Cumarebo
Is. Los Roques (Ven.)
Is. Los Testigos (Ven.)
Galera Point
SANTA MARTA
Ciénaga
Golfo de Venezuela
Punta Cardón
Puerto La Vela de Coro
I. de Margarita
La Asunción
Port of Spain
Trinidad
BARRAN-QUILLA
Baranoa
Sierra Nevada de Santa Marta 5800
San Rafael
Altagracia
FALCÓN
Tucacas
Maiquetía
La Guaira
NUEVA ESPARTA
Porlamar
Arima
Río Claro
ATLÁNTICO
Soledad
Sabanalarga
La Concepción
MARACAIBO
Santa Rita
Mene de Mauroa
Puerto Cabello
Maracay
CARACAS
DISTRITO FEDERAL
I. La Tortuga (Ven.)
Cumaná
Carúpano
Caribe
SUCRE
Güiria
G. de Paria
San Fernando
TRINIDAD & TOBAGO
NA
Calamar
Fundación
Valledupar
Agustín Codazzi
Villa del Rosario
Cabimas
Baragua
Carora
San Felipe
YARACUY
VALENCIA
MIRANDA
Río Chico
Puerto La Cruz
C. Codera
Los Teques
Higuerote
Barcelona
Caripito
Serpent's Mouth
Arjona
Carmen
MAGDALENA
Plato
Zambrano
Machiques
Ciudad Ojeda
LARA
BARQUISIMETO
Yaritagua de
Maracaibo
Villa de Cura
San Juan de los Morros
Altagracia de Orituco
Anaco
Caicara
Maturín
DELTA
Since
Sincé
Corozal
CÉSAR
Mene Grande
El Tocuyo
Acarigua
San Carlos
COJEDES
Aragua de Barcelona
Cantaura
MONAGAS
Tucupita
San Marcos
Magangué
Mompós
ZULIA
Betijoque
Trujillo
PORTUGUESA
El Baúl
GUÁRICO
Santa María de Ipire
El Tigre
AMACURO
Planeto
El Banco
Valera
Guanare
Portuguesa
Valle de la Pascua
ANZOÁTEGUI
Soledad
Los Barrancos
Ciudad Guayana
DOBA
libano
Ayapel
Simití
NORTE
Encontrados
San Carlos del Zulia
MÉRIDA
Barinas
Calabozo
Pariaguán
El Pao
Sierra Imataca
Caucasia
DE Ocaña
Cord. de Mérida
Ciudad Bolivia
Libertad
BARINAS
Puerto de Nutrias
San Fernando de Apure
Ciudad Bolívar
El Callao
Upata
BOLÍVAR
SANTANDER
Santa Bárbara
Bruzual
Achaguas
Orinoco
Cúcuta
TÁCHIRA
V E N E Z U E L A
Apure
Caicara
Embalse de Guri
Caroní
Guasipati
Tumeremo

ft m
12 000 4000
9000 3000
6000 2000
4500 1500
3000 1000
1200 400
200
0
m ft

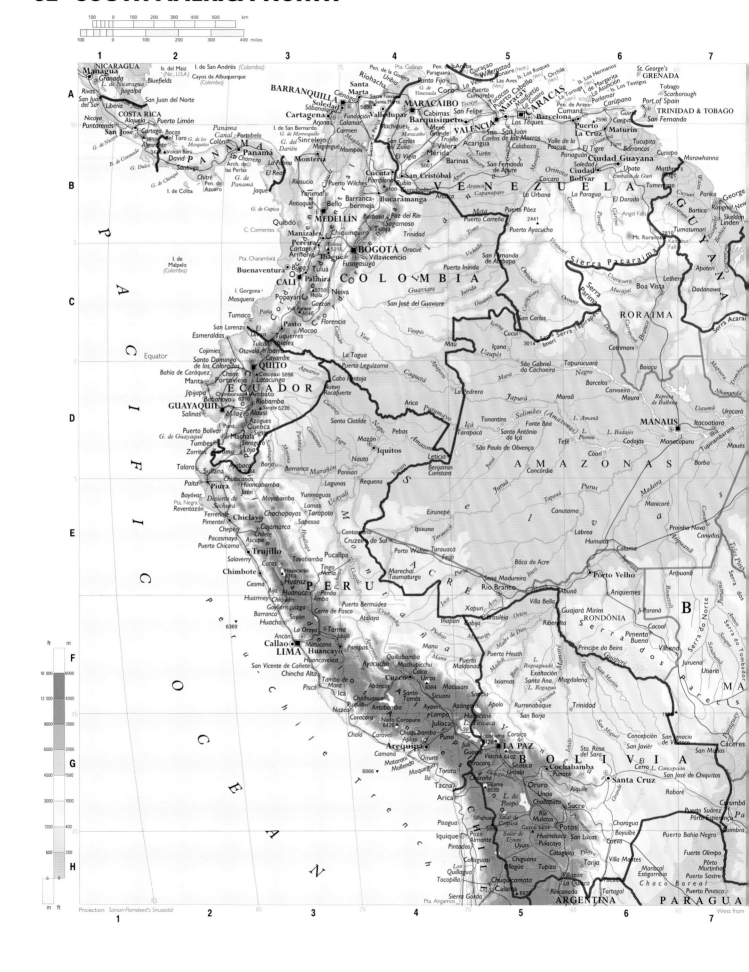

8   9   10   11   12   13

A

A T L A N T I C

B

O C E A N

C

São Paulo
(Braz.)

own
Amsterdam
ieuw Nickerie   Paramaribo
Totness   Nieuw Amsterdam
Kwakoegron   Albina   St-Laurent   Sinnamary
Moengo   Iracoubo   Kourou
Prof Van   Kaw   Cayenne
Blommestein-   St-Georges   Approuague
meer   C. Orange
SURINAM   **FRENCH**   Oiapoque
▲1230   **GUIANA**
Julianatop   Camopi

Equator

Rocas   Fernando de Noronha
(Braz.)

Amapá   I. de Maracá

Meriruma   **AMAPÁ**

Serra Turnucumaque   Serra do
Navio

Araguari

Macapá   I. Caviana
Mazagão   I. Mexiana
Afuá   Chaves   C. Maguarinho
I. Grande   Curuçá   Salinópolis
de Gurupá   Soure
Marajó   **BELÉM**   Bragança
Breves   Vigia   Viseu
Óbidos   Monte   Prainha   Gurupá   Castanhal   Turiaçu   Cururupú
Alegre   Almeirim   Abaetetuba   B. de São Marcos
Faro   Pôrto de Móz   Alcântara   **São Luís**   Barreirinhas
Juruti   Cametá   Pinheiro   Tutóia   Luís Correia
Alenquer   Baião   Rosário   Parnaíba   Camocim
Parintins   Itapecuru-   Granja   Itapipoca
Santarém   Mirim   Viana   **FORTALEZA**
Belterra   Altamira   Santa Inês   Caucaia
Aveiro   Curralinho   Bacabal   Brejo   Piracuruca   Sobral   Cascavel
Brasília Legal   Tucuruí   Coroatá   Piripiri   Maranguape
Itaituba   Represa de   Codó   Campo   Ipu   Quixadá
Tucuruí   Pedreiras   Maior   Oiticica
Acailândia   Caxias   Crateús   Mossoró
MARANHÃO   Senador   Baturité   Aracati
Marabá   **Imperatriz**   Pompeu   Caraúbas   Areia Branca
São João do   Barra   Valença   **CEARÁ**   Russos   Macau
Carajás   Araguaia   do Corda   Colinas   do Piauí   **RIO GRANDE**   Ceará Mirim
Tocantinópolis   Grajaú   Amarante   Iguatu   Caicó   **DO NORTE**   **Natal**
Pôrto Franco   Floriano   Cedro   Sousa   Currais   C. de São Roque
Conceição do   Estreito   Nova Iorque   Oeiras   Picos   Cajàzeiras   Novos   Canguaretama
Araguaia   Carolina   Loreto   Crato   Patos   Alagoa   Mamanguape
Riachão   Uruçuí   **PIAUÍ**   Chapada do Araripe   Juàzeiro   Grande   Cabedelo
Araguaína   São João   Ouricuri   do Norte   **PARAÍBA**   **João Pessoa**
Araguacema   Pedro Afonso   do Piauí   Salgueiro   **Campina**   **Olinda**
Paulistana   Pesqueira   **Grande**   **RECIFE**
Palmas   Santa   Sa. Dois Irmãos   **PERNAMBUCO**   Caruaru   Jaboatão
Filomena   Petrolina   Garanhuns   Victória de Santo Antão
Caracol   Nova Casa   Novo Remanso   Palmares
Conceição do   Represa de   Nova   Paulo Afonso   Palmeira   Rio Largo
Araguaia   **TOCANTINS**   Sobradinho   Juàzeiro   dos   **Maceió**
Pôrto Nacional   Parnaguá   Barra   Senhor-do-   Indios   Arapiraca
Bonfim   **ALAGOAS**
BRAZIL   Xique-Xique   Própria   Penedo
Gurupi   Santa Isabel   Mundo   **SERGIPE**   Capela
do Morro   Novo   Jacobina   **Aracaju**
Peixe   Paraná   **BAHIA**   Queimadas   Capela   São Cristóvão
Campos Belos   Barreiras   Ibotirama   Serrinho   Estância
São Domingos   Santa Maria   Itaberaba   **Feira de**   Santo Amaro
da Vitória   Bom Jesus   **Santana**   Alagoinhas
Posse   da Lapa   Castro   Cachoeira
Carinhanha   Caetité   Alves   Valença   **SALVADOR**
Niquelândia   Brumado   Condeúba   Nazaré   Jequié
DIST.   Formosa   Januária   Monte Azul   Vitória da
FED   Conquista   Itabuna   Ilhéus
Taguatinga   **BRASÍLIA**   São Francisco   Pedra Azul   Canavieiras
Luziânia   Janaúba   Belmonte
Anápolis   Montes   Salinas   Pôrto Seguro
Goiânia   Vianópolis   Claros   Araçuaí   Jequitinhonha   Itamaraju
Pirapora   Teófilo Otoni   Prado   Caravelas
Morrinhos   Ipamen   Diamantina   Nanuque   Conceição da Barra
Rio Verde   Patos de   Corinto   Governador   São Mateus
Jataí   Minas   Araguari   Valadares
Itumbiara   Catalão   Curvelo   Ipatinga   Colatina
Quirinópolis   Ituiutaba   Ibiá   **MINAS GERAIS**   Itabira   Linhares
GOIÁS   Uberlândia   Patrocínio   Sête Lagoas
Prata   Araxá   Caratinga   **Cariacica**
Uberaba   **BELO HORIZONTE**   Ponte Nova   **Vitória**
Campo   Sabará   Nova   **Vila Velha**
Grande   Divinópolis   Lima   Ubá
Ribeirão Prêto   Franca   Conselheiro   Ouro   Cachoeiro de Itapemirim
Andradina   Passos   Prêto   Três Rios
Araçatuba   Guaxupé   São João   Barbacena   **Campos**
Catanduva   Araraquara   Poços de   del Rei   Juiz de Fora
Presidente Epitácio   São Carlos   Caldas   São   Nova Friburgo
Moji-Mirim   Lourenço   Petrópolis
Bauru   Jaú   Volta   **Rio de Janeiro**
Marília   Limeira   Redonda   **Niterói**
Assis   **Piracicaba**   Cabo Frio
Campinas   **RIO DE JANEIRO**

D

E

6059 ▼

F

G

Trindade
(Braz.)

H

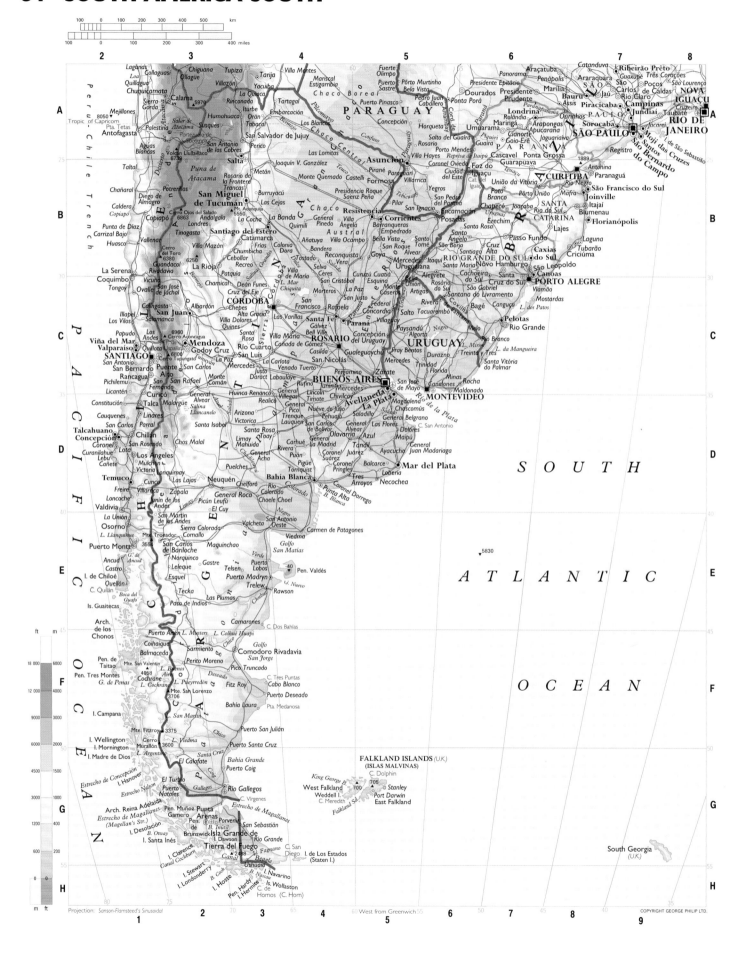

Index to Map Pages

The index contains the names of all principal places and features shown on the maps. Physical features composed of a proper name (Erie) and a description (Lake) are positioned alphabetically by the proper name. The description is positioned after the proper name and is usually abbreviated:

Erie, L., *N. Amer.* **52 D5**

Where a description forms part of a settlement or administrative name however, it is always written in full and put in its true alphabetical position:

Lake Charles, *U.S.A.* . . . **55 K8**

The number in bold type which follows each name in the index refers to the number of the map page where that feature or place will be found. This is usually the largest scale at which the place or feature appears.

The letter and figure which are in bold type immediately after the page number give the grid square on the map page, within which the feature is situated.

Rivers carry the symbol ➔ after their names. A solid square ■ follows the name of a country while an open square □ refers to a first order administrative area.

Al 'Uwaynid, *Si. Arabia* **30** E5
Al 'Uwayqīlah,
 Si. Arabia **30** D4
Al 'Uyūn, *Ḥijāz,*
 Si. Arabia **30** E3
Al 'Uyūn, *Najd,*
 Si. Arabia **30** E4
Al 'Uzayr, *Iraq* **30** D5
Al Wajh, *Si. Arabia* . . . **30** E3
Al Wakrah, *Qatar* **31** E6
Al Wannān, *Si. Arabia* . **30** E5
Al Waqbah, *Si. Arabia* . **30** D5
Al Warī'ah, *Si. Arabia* . **30** E5
Al Wusayl, *Qatar* **31** E6
Ala Dağ, *Turkey* **30** B2
Ala Tau Shankou =
 Dzungarian Gates,
 Asia **24** B3
Alabama □, *U.S.A.* **53** J2
Alabama →, *U.S.A.* **53** K2
Alabaster, *U.S.A.* **53** J2
Alaçam Dağları, *Turkey* **17** E13
Alachua, *U.S.A.* **53** L4
Alagoa Grande, *Brazil* . **63** E11
Alagoas □, *Brazil* **63** E11
Alagoinhas, *Brazil* **63** F11
Alajuela, *Costa Rica* . . **60** D3
Alakurtti, *Russia* **18** A5
Alamarvdasht, *Iran* . . . **31** E7
Alameda, *U.S.A.* **57** J10
Alamo, *U.S.A.* **57** H6
Alamogordo, *U.S.A.* . . . **57** K11
Alamos, *Mexico* **58** B3
Alamosa, *U.S.A.* **57** H11
Åland, *Finland* **7** F19
Ålands hav, *Sweden* . . **7** F18
Alania = North
 Ossetia □, *Russia* . . . **19** F7
Alanya, *Turkey* **19** G5
Alapayevsk, *Russia* . . . **20** D7
Alaşehir, *Turkey* **17** E13
Alaska □, *U.S.A.* **46** B5
Alaska, G. of, *Pac. Oc.* . **46** C5
Alaska Peninsula, *U.S.A.* **46** C4
Alaska Range, *U.S.A.* . . **46** B4
Älät, *Azerbaijan* **19** G8
Alatyr, *Russia* **18** D8
Alausi, *Ecuador* **62** D3
Alava, C., *U.S.A.* **56** B1
Alavus, *Finland* **7** E20
Alawoona, *Australia* . . . **43** E3
'Alayh, *Lebanon* **33** B4
Alba, *Italy* **14** D8
Alba-Iulia, *Romania* . . . **13** E12
Albacete, *Spain* **15** C5
Albacutya, L., *Australia* **43** F3
Albanel, L., *Canada* . . . **48** B5
Albania ■, *Europe* **17** D9
Albany, *Australia* **41** G2
Albany, *Ga., U.S.A.* **53** K3
Albany, *N.Y., U.S.A.* . . . **52** D9
Albany, *Oreg., U.S.A.* . . **56** D2
Albany, *Tex., U.S.A.* . . . **55** J5
Albany →, *Canada* **48** B3
Albardón, *Argentina* . . **64** C3
Albatross B., *Australia* . **42** A3
Albemarle, *U.S.A.* **53** H5
Albemarle Sd., *U.S.A.* . **53** H7
Alberche →, *Spain* **15** C3
Albert, L., *Australia* . . . **43** F2
Albert Edward Ra.,
 Australia **40** C4
Albert L., *Africa* **36** D6
Albert Lea, *U.S.A.* **54** D8
Albert Nile →, *Uganda* **36** D6
Albert Town, *Bahamas* **61** B5
Alberta □, *Canada* **50** C6
Alberton, *Canada* **49** C7
Albertville = Kalemie,
 Dem. Rep. of
 the Congo **36** F5
Albertville, *France* **14** D7
Albertville, *U.S.A.* **53** H2
Albi, *France* **14** E5
Albia, *U.S.A.* **54** E8
Albina, *Surinam* **63** B8
Albion, *Mich., U.S.A.* . . **52** D3
Albion, *Nebr., U.S.A.* . . **54** E6
Alborán, *Medit. S.* **15** E4
Ålborg, *Denmark* **7** H13
Alborz, Reshteh-ye
 Kūhhā-ye, *Iran* . . . **31** C7
Albuquerque, *U.S.A.* . . **57** J10
Albuquerque, Cayos de,
 Caribbean **60** D3
Albury-Wodonga,
 Australia **43** F4
Alcalá de Henares,
 Spain **15** B4
Alcalá la Real, *Spain* . . **15** D4
Álcamo, *Italy* **16** F5
Alcañiz, *Spain* **15** B5
Alcântara, *Brazil* **63** D10
Alcântara, Embalse de,
 Spain **15** C2
Alcantarilla, *Spain* **15** D5
Alcaraz, Sierra de, *Spain* **15** C4
Alcaudete, *Spain* **15** D3
Alcázar de San Juan,
 Spain **15** C4
Alchevsk, *Ukraine* **19** E6
Alcira = Alzira, *Spain* . **15** C5
Alcova, *U.S.A.* **56** E10
Alcoy, *Spain* **15** C5
Aldabra Is., *Seychelles* . **3** E12

Aldama, *Mexico* **59** C5
Aldan, *Russia* **21** D13
Aldan →, *Russia* **21** C13
Aldeburgh, *U.K.* **9** E9
Alderney, *U.K.* **9** H5
Aldershot, *U.K.* **9** F7
Aledo, *U.S.A.* **54** E9
Aleg, *Mauritania* **34** E3
Alegrete, *Brazil* **64** B6
Aleksandriya =
 Oleksandriya, *Ukraine* **13** C14
Aleksandrov Gay,
 Russia **19** D8
Aleksandrovsk-
 Sakhalinskiy, *Russia* . **21** D15
Alençon, *France* **14** B4
Alenquer, *Brazil* **63** D8
Aleppo = Ḥalab, *Syria* . **30** B3
Alès, *France* **14** D6
Alessándria, *Italy* **14** D8
Ålesund, *Norway* **7** E12
Aleutian Is., *Pac. Oc.* . . **46** C2
Aleutian Trench,
 Pac. Oc. **44** C10
Alexander, *U.S.A.* **54** B3
Alexander, Mt.,
 Australia **41** E3
Alexander Arch., *U.S.A.* **46** C6
Alexander City, *U.S.A.* . **53** J3
Alexander I., *Antarctica* **5** C17
Alexandra, *Australia* . . . **43** F4
Alexandra, *N.Z.* **39** L2
Alexandra Falls, *Canada* **50** A5
Alexandria = El
 Iskandarîya, *Egypt* . . **35** B11
Alexandria, *B.C., Canada* **50** C4
Alexandria, *Ont.,
 Canada* **48** C5
Alexandria, *Romania* . . **13** G13
Alexandria, *La., U.S.A.* . **55** K8
Alexandria, *Minn.,
 U.S.A.* **54** C7
Alexandria, *S. Dak.,
 U.S.A.* **54** D6
Alexandria, *Va., U.S.A.* . **52** F7
Alexandria Bay, *U.S.A.* . **52** C8
Alexandrina, L.,
 Australia **43** F2
Alexandroúpolis, *Greece* **17** D11
Alexis →, *Canada* **49** B8
Alexis Creek, *Canada* . . **50** C4
Alford, *U.K.* **8** D8
Alfreton, *U.K.* **8** D6
Alga, *Kazakstan* **19** E10
Ålgård, *Norway* **7** G11
Algarve, *Portugal* **15** D1
Algeciras, *Spain* **15** D3
Algemesí, *Spain* **15** C5
Alger, *Algeria* **34** A6
Algeria ■, *Africa* **34** C6
Alghero, *Italy* **16** D3
Algiers = Alger, *Algeria* **34** A6
Algoa, *U.S.A.* **52** C2
Algoma, *U.S.A.* **54** D7
Algonquin Prov. Park,
 Canada **48** C4
Algorta, *Uruguay* **64** C5
Alhucemas = Al
 Hoceima, *Morocco* . . **34** A5
'Alī al Gharbī, *Iraq* **30** C5
'Alī ash Sharqī, *Iraq* . . **30** C5
'Alī Khēl, *Afghan.* **28** C6
Alī Shāh, *Iran* **30** B5
'Alīābād, Khorāsān, *Iran* **31** C8
'Alīābād, Kordestān, *Iran* **30** C5
'Alīābād, Yazd, *Iran* . . . **31** D7
Aliağa, *Turkey* **17** E12
Aliákmon →, *Greece* . . **17** D11
Alicante, *Spain* **15** C5
Alice →, *Queens.,
 Australia* **42** C3
Alice →, *Queens.,
 Australia* **42** B3
Alice Arm, *Canada* **50** B3
Alice Springs, *Australia* **42** C1
Aliceville, *U.S.A.* **53** J1
Aligarh, *India* **28** F10
Alīgūdarz, *Iran* **31** C6
Alingsås, *Sweden* **7** H15
Alipur, *Pakistan* **28** E7
Alipur Duar, *India* **29** F16
Aliquippa, *U.S.A.* **52** E4
Alitus = Alytus,
 Lithuania **7** J21
Aliwal North, *S. Africa* . **37** L5
Alix, *Canada* **50** C6
Aljustrel, *Portugal* **15** D1
Alkmaar, *Neths.* **11** B4
All American Canal,
 U.S.A. **57** K6
Allagash →, *U.S.A.* . . . **53** B11
Allahabad, *India* **29** G12
Allan, *Canada* **51** C7
Allegheny →, *U.S.A.* . . **52** E5
Alleghany Mts., *U.S.A.* . **52** G6
Allendale, *U.S.A.* **53** J5
Allende, *Mexico* **58** B4
Allentown, *U.S.A.* **52** E9
Alleppey, *India* **28** Q10
Aller →, *Germany* **12** B5
Alliance, *Nebr., U.S.A.* . **54** D3
Alliance, *Ohio, U.S.A.* . **52** E5
Allier →, *France* **14** C5

Alliford Bay, *Canada* . . **50** C2
Alliston, *Canada* **48** D4
Allora, *Australia* **43** D5
Alluitsup Paa,
 Greenland **4** C5
Alma, *Canada* **49** C5
Alma, *Ga., U.S.A.* **53** K4
Alma, *Kans., U.S.A.* . . . **54** F6
Alma, *Mich., U.S.A.* . . . **52** D3
Alma, *Nebr., U.S.A.* . . . **54** E5
Alma Ata = Almaty,
 Kazakstan **20** E8
Almada, *Portugal* **15** C1
Almaden, *Australia* **42** B3
Almadén, *Spain* **15** C3
Almanor, L., *U.S.A.* . . . **56** F3
Almansa, *Spain* **15** C5
Almanzor, Pico, *Spain* . **15** B3
Almanzora →, *Spain* . . **15** D5
Almaty, *Kazakstan* **20** E8
Almazán, *Spain* **15** B4
Almeirim, *Brazil* **63** D8
Almelo, *Neths.* **11** B6
Almendralejo, *Spain* . . **15** C2
Almere-Stad, *Neths.* . . . **11** B5
Almería, *Spain* **15** D4
Almirante, *Panama* **60** E3
Almora, *India* **28** E11
Almnouth, *U.K.* **8** B6
Alnwick, *U.K.* **29** H19
Alon, *Burma* **29** H19
Alor, *Indonesia* **27** F6
Alor Setar, *Malaysia* . . . **26** C2
Aloysius, Mt., *Australia* **41** E4
Alpena, *U.S.A.* **52** C4
Alpha, *Australia* **42** C4
Alphen aan den Rijn,
 Neths. **11** B4
Alpine, *Ariz., U.S.A.* . . . **57** K9
Alpine, *Tex., U.S.A.* . . . **55** K3
Alps, *Europe* **14** C8
Alsace, *France* **14** B7
Alsask, *Canada* **51** C7
Alsasua, *Spain* **15** A4
Alsek →, *U.S.A.* **50** B1
Alsten, *Norway* **6** D15
Alston, *U.K.* **8** C5
Alta, *Norway* **6** B20
Alta Gracia, *Argentina* . **64** C4
Altaelva →, *Norway* . . . **6** B20
Altafjorden, *Norway* . . . **6** A20
Altai = Aerhtai Shan,
 Mongolia **24** B4
Altamaha →, *U.S.A.* . . **53** K5
Altamira, *Brazil* **63** D8
Altamira, *Mexico* **59** C5
Altamura, *Italy* **16** D7
Altanbulag, *Mongolia* . . **24** A5
Altar, *Mexico* **58** A2
Altar, Desierto de,
 Mexico **58** B2
Altata, *Mexico* **58** C3
Altavista, *U.S.A.* **52** G6
Altay, *China* **24** B3
Altea, *Spain* **15** C5
Alto Araguaia, *Brazil* . . **63** G8
Alto Cuchumatanes =
 Cuchumatanes, Sierra
 de los, *Guatemala* . . **60** C1
Alto Molocue, *Mozam.* . **37** H7
Alton, *U.K.* **9** F7
Alton, *U.S.A.* **54** F9
Altoona, *U.S.A.* **52** E6
Altun Kūprī, *Iraq* **30** C5
Altun Shan, *China* **24** C3
Alturas, *U.S.A.* **56** F3
Altus, *U.S.A.* **55** H5
Alucra, *Turkey* **19** F6
Alūksne, *Latvia* **7** H22
Alusi, *Indonesia* **27** F8
Alva, *U.S.A.* **55** G5
Alvarado, *Mexico* **59** D5
Alvarado, *U.S.A.* **55** J6
Alvaro Obregón, Presa,
 Mexico **58** B3
Alvear, *Argentina* **64** B5
Alvesta, *Sweden* **7** H16
Alvin, *U.S.A.* **55** L7
Älvkarleby, *Sweden* . . . **7** F17
Alvord Desert, *U.S.A.* . . **56** E4
Älvsbyn, *Sweden* **6** D19
Alwar, *India* **28** F10
Alxa Zuoqi, *China* **24** C5
Alyangula, *Australia* . . . **42** A2
Alyata = Älät,
 Azerbaijan **19** G8
Alytus, *Lithuania* **7** J21
Alzada, *U.S.A.* **54** C2
Alzira, *Spain* **15** C5
Am-Timan, *Chad* **35** F10
Amadeus, L., *Australia* . **41** D5
Amadjuak L., *Canada* . . **47** B12
Amagasaki, *Japan* **23** G7
Amahai, *Indonesia* **27** E7
Amakusa-Shotō, *Japan* **23** H5
Åmål, *Sweden* **7** G15
Amaliás, *Greece* **17** F9
Amalner, *India* **28** J9
Amambaí, *Brazil* **63** H8
Amambay, Cordillera
 de, *S. Amer.* **64** A5
Amami-Guntō, *Japan* . . **23** L4
Amami-Ō-Shima, *Japan* **23** L4
Amaná, L., *Brazil* **62** D6

Amangeldy, *Kazakstan* **20** D7
Amapá, *Brazil* **63** C8
Amapá □, *Brazil* **63** C8
Amarante, *Brazil* **63** E10
Amaranth, *Canada* **51** C9
Amarillo, *U.S.A.* **55** H4
Amaro, Mte., *Italy* **16** C6
Amasya □, *Turkey* **19** F6
Amata, *Australia* **41** E5
Amatitlán, *Guatemala* . . **60** D1
Amay, *Belgium* **11** D5
Amazon =
 Amazonas →,
 S. Amer. **63** D9
Amazonas □, *Brazil* . . . **62** E6
Amazonas →, *S. Amer.* **63** D9
Ambala, *India* **28** D10
Ambalavao, *Madag.* . . . **37** J9
Ambanja, *Madag.* **37** G9
Ambarchik, *Russia* **21** C17
Ambato, *Ecuador* **62** D3
Ambatolampy, *Madag.* . **37** H9
Ambatondrazaka,
 Madag. **37** H9
Amberg, *Germany* **12** D6
Ambergris Cay, *Belize* . **59** D7
Amberley, *N.Z.* **39** K4
Ambikapur, *India* **29** H13
Ambilobé, *Madag.* **37** G9
Amble, *U.K.* **8** B6
Ambleside, *U.K.* **8** C5
Ambo, *Peru* **62** F3
Amboise, *France* **14** C4
Ambon, *Indonesia* **27** E7
Ambositra, *Madag.* **37** J9
Ambovombe, *Madag.* . . **37** K9
Amboy, *U.S.A.* **57** J6
Amboyna Cay,
 S. China Sea **26** C4
Ambriz, *Angola* **36** F2
Amchitka I., *U.S.A.* **46** C1
Amderma, *Russia* **20** C7
Ameca, *Mexico* **58** C4
Ameca →, *Mexico* **58** C3
Amecameca, *Mexico* . . . **59** D5
Ameland, *Neths.* **11** A5
American Falls, *U.S.A.* . **56** E7
American Falls
 Reservoir, *U.S.A.* . . . **56** E7
American Fork, *U.S.A.* . **56** F8
American Highland,
 Antarctica **5** D6
American Samoa ■,
 Pac. Oc. **39** B13
Americus, *U.S.A.* **53** K3
Amersfoort, *Neths.* **11** B5
Amery Ice Shelf,
 Antarctica **5** C6
Ames, *U.S.A.* **54** E8
Amga, *Russia* **21** C14
Amga →, *Russia* **21** C14
Amgu, *Russia* **21** E14
Amgun →, *Russia* **21** D14
Amherst, *Canada* **49** C7
Amherstburg, *Canada* . . **48** D3
Amiata, Mte., *Italy* **16** C4
Amidon, *U.S.A.* **54** B3
Amiens, *France* **14** B5
Amīrābād, *Iran* **30** C5
Amirante Is., *Seychelles* **3** E12
Amisk L., *Canada* **51** C8
Amistad, Presa de la,
 Mexico **58** B4
Amite, *U.S.A.* **55** K9
Amlia I., *U.S.A.* **46** C2
Amlwch, *U.K.* **8** D3
'Ammān, *Jordan* **33** D4
'Ammān □, *Jordan* **33** D5
Ammanford, *U.K.* **9** F4
Ammassalik = Tasiilaq,
 Greenland **4** C6
Ammon, *U.S.A.* **56** E8
Āmol, *Iran* **31** B7
Amorgós, *Greece* **17** F11
Amory, *U.S.A.* **53** J1
Amos, *Canada* **48** C4
Åmot, *Norway* **7** G13
Amoy = Xiamen, *China* **25** D6
Ampanihy, *Madag.* **37** J8
Ampenan, *Indonesia* . . . **26** F5
Amper →, *Germany* . . . **12** D6
Amqui, *Canada* **49** C6
Amravati, *India* **28** J10
Amreli, *India* **28** J7
Amritsar, *India* **28** D9
Amroha, *India* **28** E11
Amsterdam, *Neths.* **11** B4
Amsterdam, *U.S.A.* **52** D8
Amsterdam, I. =
 Nouvelle-Amsterdam,
 I., *Ind. Oc.* **3** F13
Amstetten, *Austria* **12** D8
Amudarya →,
 Uzbekistan **20** E6
Amundsen Gulf, *Canada* **46** A7
Amundsen Sea,
 Antarctica **5** D15
Amuntai, *Indonesia* . . . **26** E5
Amur →, *Russia* **21** D15
Amurang, *Indonesia* . . . **27** D6
Amuri Pass, *N.Z.* **39** K4
Amursk, *Russia* **21** D14
Amyderya →,
 Uzbekistan **20** E6

An Nabaṭīyah at Taḥta,
 Lebanon **33** B4
An Nabk, *Si. Arabia* . . . **30** D3
An Nabk, *Syria* **33** A5
An Nafūd, *Si. Arabia* . . **30** D4
An Najaf, *Iraq* **30** C5
An Nāşirīyah, *Iraq* **30** D5
An Nhon, *Vietnam* **26** B3
An Nu'ayrīyah,
 Si. Arabia **31** E6
An Nuwayb'ī, W. →,
 Si. Arabia **33** F3
Anabar →, *Russia* . . . **21** B12
'Anabtā, *West Bank* . . . **33** C4
Anaconda, *U.S.A.* **56** C7
Anacortes, *U.S.A.* **56** B2
Anadarko, *U.S.A.* **55** H5
Anadolu, *Turkey* **19** G5
Anadyr, *Russia* **21** C18
Anadyr →, *Russia* **21** C18
Anadyrskiy Zaliv, *Russia* **21** C19
'Ānah, *Iraq* **30** C4
Anaheim, *U.S.A.* **57** K5
Anahim Lake, *Canada* . . **50** C3
Anáhuac, *Mexico* **58** B4
Anakapalle, *India* **29** L13
Anakie, *Australia* **42** C4
Anambas, Kepulauan,
 Indonesia **26** D3
Anambas Is. =
 Anambas, Kepulauan,
 Indonesia **26** D3
Anamosa, *U.S.A.* **54** D9
Anamur, *Turkey* **19** G5
Anan, *Japan* **23** H7
Anantnag, *India* **28** C9
Ananyiv, *Ukraine* **13** E15
Anápolis, *Brazil* **63** G9
Anapu →, *Brazil* **63** D8
Anār, *Iran* **31** D7
Anārak, *Iran* **31** C7
Anatolia = Anadolu,
 Turkey **19** G5
Añatuya, *Argentina* . . . **64** B4
Anaunethad L., *Canada* **51** A8
Anchorage, *U.S.A.* **46** B5
Ancohuma, Nevada,
 Bolivia **62** G5
Ancón, *Peru* **62** F3
Ancona, *Italy* **16** C5
Ancud, *Chile* **64** E2
Ancud, G. de, *Chile* . . . **64** E2
Anda, *China* **25** B7
Andalgalá, *Argentina* . . **64** B3
Åndalsnes, *Norway* . . . **7** E12
Andalucía □, *Spain* . . . **15** D3
Andalusia □, *Spain* . . . **15** D3
Andalusia, *U.S.A.* **53** K2
Andaman Is., *Ind. Oc.* . **3** D14
Andaman Is., *Ind. Oc.* . **3** D14
Andaman Sea, *Ind. Oc.* **26** B1
Andamooka Opal Fields,
 Australia **43** E2
Andapa, *Madag.* **37** G9
Andenes, *Norway* **6** B17
Andenne, *Belgium* **11** D5
Anderson, Alaska,
 U.S.A. **46** B5
Anderson, *Calif., U.S.A.* **56** F2
Anderson, *Ind., U.S.A.* . **52** E3
Anderson, *Mo., U.S.A.* . **55** G7
Anderson, *S.C., U.S.A.* . **53** H4
Anderson →, *Canada* . **46** B7
Andes, Cord. de los,
 S. Amer. **62** H5
Andfjorden, *Norway* . . . **6** B17
Andhra Pradesh □, *India* **28** L11
Andijon, *Uzbekistan* . . . **20** E8
Andikíthira, *Greece* . . . **17** G10
Andīmeshk, *Iran* **31** C6
Andizhan = Andijon,
 Uzbekistan **20** E8
Andoany, *Madag.* **37** G9
Andoom, *Australia* **42** A3
Andorra ■, *Europe* **14** E4
Andorra La Vella,
 Andorra **14** E4
Andover, *U.K.* **9** F6
Andøya, *Norway* **6** B16
Andradina, *Brazil* **63** H8
Andreanof Is., *U.S.A.* . . **46** C2
Andrews, *S.C., U.S.A.* . **53** J6
Andrews, *Tex., U.S.A.* . **55** J3
Ándria, *Italy* **16** D7
Andropov = Rybinsk,
 Russia **18** C6
Ándros, *Greece* **17** F11
Andros I., *Bahamas* . . . **60** B4
Andros Town, *Bahamas* **60** B4
Andselv, *Norway* **6** B18
Andújar, *Spain* **15** C3
Andulo, *Angola* **36** G3
Anegada I., *Virgin Is.* . . **61** C7
Anegada Passage,
 W. Indies **61** C7
Aneto, Pico de, *Spain* . **15** A6
Ang Thong, *Thailand* . . **26** B2
Angamos, Punta, *Chile* . **62** H4
Angara →, *Russia* **21** D11
Angarsk, *Russia* **21** D11
Angas Hills, *Australia* . . **40** D4
Angaston, *Australia* . . . **43** E2
Angaur I., *Pac. Oc.* **27** C8
Ånge, *Sweden* **7** E16

Ángel, Salto = Angel
 Falls, *Venezuela* **62** B6
Ángel de la Guarda, I.,
 Mexico **58** B2
Angel Falls, *Venezuela* . **62** B6
Angeles, *Phil.* **27** A6
Ängelholm, *Sweden* . . . **7** H15
Angels Camp, *U.S.A.* . . **57** G3
Ångermanälven →,
 Sweden **6** E17
Ångermanland, *Sweden* **6** E18
Angers, *France* **14** C3
Ängesån →, *Sweden* . . **6** C20
Angikuni L., *Canada* . . . **51** A9
Anglesey, Isle of □, *U.K.* **8** D3
Angleton, *U.S.A.* **55** L7
Angmagssalik =
 Tasiilaq, *Greenland* . . **4** C6
Ango, *Dem. Rep. of*
 the Congo **36** D5
Angoche, *Mozam.* **37** H7
Angol, *Chile* **64** D2
Angola ■, *Africa* **37** G3
Angoulême, *France* **14** D4
Angoumois, *France* **14** D3
Angra dos Reis, *Brazil* . **64** B7
Angren, *Uzbekistan* . . . **20** E8
Anguilla ■, *W. Indies* . . **61** C7
Angurugu, *Australia* . . . **42** A2
Anholt, *Denmark* **7** H14
Anhui □, *China* **25** C6
Anhwei = Anhui □,
 China **25** C6
Animas, *U.S.A.* **57** H9
Anjalankoski, *Finland* . . **7** F22
Anjou, *France* **14** C3
Ankaboa, Tanjona,
 Madag. **37** J8
Ankang, *China* **25** C5
Ankara, *Turkey* **19** G5
Ankaratra, *Madag.* **37** H9
Ankeny, *U.S.A.* **54** E8
Ann, C., *U.S.A.* **52** D10
Ann Arbor, *U.S.A.* **52** D4
Annaba, *Algeria* **34** A7
Annan, *U.K.* **10** D5
Annapolis, *U.S.A.* **52** F7
Annapolis Royal,
 Canada **49** D6
Annean, L., *Australia* . . **41** E2
Annecy, *France* **14** D7
Anning, *China* **24** D5
Anniston, *U.S.A.* **53** J3
Annobón, *Atl. Oc.* **32** G4
Annotto Bay, *Jamaica* . **60** C4
Anqing, *China* **25** C6
Ansbach, *Germany* **12** D6
Anshan, *China* **25** B7
Anshun, *China* **24** D5
Ansley, *U.S.A.* **54** E5
Anson, *U.S.A.* **55** J5
Anson B., *Australia* **40** B5
Ansongo, *Mali* **34** E6
Ansudu, *Indonesia* **27** E9
Antabamba, *Peru* **62** F4
Antakya, *Turkey* **19** G6
Antalaha, *Madag.* **37** G10
Antalya, *Turkey* **19** G5
Antalya Körfezi, *Turkey* **19** G5
Antananarivo, *Madag.* . **37** H9
Antarctic Pen.,
 Antarctica **5** C18
Antarctica **5** E3
Antequera, *Spain* **15** D3
Antero, Mt., *U.S.A.* **57** G10
Anthony, *Kans., U.S.A.* . **55** G5
Anthony, N. Mex.,
 U.S.A. **57** K10
Anti Atlas, *Morocco* . . . **34** C4
Anti-Lebanon = Ash
 Sharqi, Al Jabal,
 Lebanon **33** B5
Antibes, *France* **14** E7
Anticosti, Î. d', *Canada* **49** C7
Antigo, *U.S.A.* **54** C10
Antigonish, *Canada* . . . **49** C7
Antigua, *W. Indies* **61** C7
Antigua & Barbuda ■,
 W. Indies **61** C7
Antigua Guatemala,
 Guatemala **60** D1
Antilla, *Cuba* **60** B4
Antilles = West Indies,
 Cent. Amer. **61** D7
Antioquia, *Colombia* . . . **62** B3
Antipodes Is., *Pac. Oc.* **44** M9
Antlers, *U.S.A.* **55** H7
Antofagasta, *Chile* **64** A2
Anton, *U.S.A.* **55** J3
Antonina, *Brazil* **64** B7
Antrim, *U.K.* **10** D3
Antrim Plateau,
 Australia **40** C4
Antsirabe, *Madag.* **37** H9
Antsiranana, *Madag.* . . **37** G9
Antsohihy, *Madag.* **37** G9
Antwerp = Antwerpen,
 Belgium **11** C4
Antwerpen, *Belgium* . . . **11** C4
Antwerpen □, *Belgium* **11** C4
Anupgarh, *India* **28** E8
Anuradhapura,
 Sri Lanka **28** Q12
Anveh, *Iran* **31** E7
Anvers = Antwerpen,
 Belgium **11** C4

Anvers I., Antarctica .. 5 C17
Anxi, China 24 B4
Anxious B., Australia .. 43 E1
Anyang, China 25 C6
Anyer-Kidul, Indonesia 27 G11
Anzhero-Sudzhensk, Russia 20 D9
Ánzio, Italy 16 D5
Aoga-Shima, Japan ... 23 H9
Aomen = Macau □, China 25 D6
Aomori, Japan 22 D10
Aomori □, Japan 22 D10
Aoraki Mount Cook, N.Z. 39 K3
Aosta, Italy 14 D7
Aoukâr, Mauritania ... 34 E4
Aozou, Chad 35 D8
Apache, U.S.A. 55 H5
Apache Junction, U.S.A. 57 K8
Apalachee B., U.S.A. .. 53 L4
Apalachicola, U.S.A. .. 53 L3
Apalachicola →, U.S.A. 53 L3
Apaporis →, Colombia 62 D5
Aparri, Phil. 27 A6
Apatity, Russia 18 A5
Apatzingán, Mexico .. 58 D4
Apeldoorn, Neths. 11 B5
Apennines = Appennini, Italy 16 B4
Apia, Samoa 39 A13
Apiacás, Serra dos, Brazil 62 E7
Apizaco, Mexico 59 D5
Aplao, Peru 62 G4
Apo, Mt., Phil. 27 C7
Apollo Bay, Australia .. 43 F3
Apolo, Bolivia 62 F5
Aporé →, Brazil 63 G8
Apostle Is., U.S.A. ... 54 B9
Apostolos Andreas, C., Cyprus 30 C2
Apoteri, Guyana 62 C7
Appalachian Mts., U.S.A. 52 G6
Appennini, Italy 16 B4
Appleby-in-Westmorland, U.K. .. 8 C5
Appleton, U.S.A. 52 C1
Approuague →, Fr. Guiana 63 C8
Aprília, Italy 16 D5
Apucarana, Brazil ... 64 A6
Apure →, Venezuela . 62 B5
Apurimac →, Peru .. 62 F4
Âqâ Jarī, Iran 31 D6
Aqaba = Al 'Aqabah, Jordan 33 F4
'Aqaba, Khalīj al = Aqaba, G. of, Red Sea 30 D2
'Aqdā, Iran 31 C7
Aqmola = Astana, Kazakhstan 20 D8
'Aqrah, Iraq 30 B4
Aqtaū, Kazakhstan ... 20 E6
Aqtöbe, Kazakhstan .. 19 D10
Aquidauana, Brazil ... 63 H7
Aquiles Serdán, Mexico 58 B3
Aquin, Haiti 61 C5
Aquitain, Bassin, France 14 D3
Aqviligjuaq = Pelly Bay, Canada 47 B11
Ar Rachidiya, Morocco 34 B5
Ar Rafid, Syria 33 C4
Ar Raḥḥāliyah, Iraq .. 30 C4
Ar Ramādī, Iraq 30 C4
Ar Ramthā, Jordan .. 33 C5
Ar Raqqah, Syria ... 30 C3
Ar Rass, Si. Arabia .. 30 E4
Ar Rifā'ī, Iraq 30 D5
Ar Riyāḍ, Si. Arabia . 30 E5
Ar Ru'ays, Qatar 31 E6
Ar Rukhaymīyah, Iraq . 30 D5
Ar Ruqayyidah, Si. Arabia 31 E6
Ar Ruṣāfah, Syria ... 30 C3
Ar Ruṭbah, Iraq 30 C4
Ara, India 29 G14
Arab, U.S.A. 53 H2
'Arab, Bahr el →, Sudan 35 G11
Arab, Shatt al →, Asia 31 D6
'Arabābād, Iran 31 C8
Arabian Desert = Es Sahrâ' Esh Sharqîya, Egypt 35 C12
Arabian Gulf = Gulf, The, Asia 31 E6
Arabian Sea, Ind. Oc. . 3 C13
Arabian Sea, Ind. Oc. . 3 C13
Aracaju, Brazil 63 F11
Aracati, Brazil 63 D11
Araçatuba, Brazil ... 63 H8
Aracena, Spain 15 D2
Araçuaí, Brazil 63 G10
'Arad, Israel 33 D4
Arad, Romania 13 E11
Arādān, Iran 31 C7
Arafura Sea, E. Indies . 38 B6
Aragón □, Spain ... 15 B5
Aragón →, Spain .. 15 A5
Araguacema, Brazil .. 63 E9
Araguaia →, Brazil . 63 E9
Araguaína, Brazil ... 63 E9
Araguari, Brazil 63 G9

Araguari →, Brazil ... 63 C9
Arak, Algeria 34 C6
Arāk, Iran 31 C6
Arakan Coast, Burma . 29 K19
Arakan Yoma, Burma . 29 K19
Araks = Aras, Rūd-e →, Asia 30 B5
Aral, Kazakhstan 20 E7
Aral Sea, Asia 20 E7
Aral Tengizi = Aral Sea, Asia 20 E7
Aralsk = Aral, Kazakhstan 20 E7
Aralskoye More = Aral Sea, Asia 20 E7
Aramac, Australia ... 42 C4
Aran I., Ireland 10 D2
Aran Is., Ireland 10 E2
Aranda de Duero, Spain 15 B4
Arandán, Iran 30 C5
Aranjuez, Spain 15 B4
Aransas Pass, U.S.A. . 55 M6
Aranyaprathet, Thailand 26 B2
Arapahoe, U.S.A. ... 54 E5
Arapgir, Turkey 30 B3
Arapiraca, Brazil ... 63 E11
Arapongas, Brazil ... 64 A6
Ar'ar, Si. Arabia 30 D4
Araraquara, Brazil ... 63 H9
Ararat, Australia 43 F3
Ararat, Mt. = Ağrı Dağı, Turkey 19 G7
Araripe, Chapada do, Brazil 63 E11
Aras, Rūd-e →, Asia . 30 B5
Arauca, Colombia ... 62 B4
Arauca →, Venezuela 62 B5
Araxá, Brazil 63 G9
Araya, Pen. de, Venezuela 62 A6
Arba Minch, Ethiopia . 32 F2
Árbatax, Italy 16 E3
Arbīl, Iraq 30 B5
Arborfield, Canada .. 51 C8
Arborg, Canada 51 C9
Arbroath, U.K. 10 C5
Arbuckle, U.S.A. ... 56 G2
Arcachon, France ... 14 D3
Arcadia, Fla., U.S.A. . 53 M5
Arcadia, La., U.S.A. . 55 J8
Arcata, U.S.A. 56 F1
Archangel = Arkhangelsk, Russia . 18 B7
Archer →, Australia . 42 A3
Archer B., Australia .. 42 A3
Arches National Park, U.S.A. 57 G9
Arckaringa Cr. →, Australia 43 D2
Arco, U.S.A. 56 E7
Arcos de la Frontera, Spain 15 D3
Arcot, India 28 N11
Arctic Bay, Canada .. 47 A11
Arctic Ocean, Arctic . 4 B18
Arctic Red River = Tsiigehtchic, Canada 46 B6
Arda →, Bulgaria .. 17 D12
Ardabīl, Iran 31 B6
Ardakān = Sepīdān, Iran 31 D7
Ardakān, Iran 31 C7
Ardenne, Belgium .. 12 D3
Ardennes = Ardenne, Belgium 12 D3
Ardestān, Iran 31 C7
Ardlethan, Australia . 43 E4
Ardmore, U.S.A. 55 H6
Ardrossan, Australia . 43 E2
Arecibo, Puerto Rico . 61 C6
Areia Branca, Brazil . 63 E11
Arena, Pt., U.S.A. ... 56 G2
Arenal, Honduras ... 60 C2
Arendal, Norway ... 7 G13
Arequipa, Peru 62 G4
Arévalo, Spain 15 B3
Arezzo, Italy 16 C4
Arga, Turkey 30 B3
Arganda, Spain 15 B4
Argenta, Canada ... 50 C5
Argentan, France ... 14 B3
Argentário, Mte., Italy 16 C4
Argentia, Canada ... 49 C9
Argentina ■, S. Amer. . 64 D3
Argentina Is., Antarctica 5 C17
Argentino, L., Argentina 64 G2
Argeş →, Romania . 13 F14
Arghandab →, Afghan. 28 D4
Argolikós Kólpos, Greece 17 F10
Árgos, Greece 17 F10
Argostólion, Greece . 17 E9
Arguello, Pt., U.S.A. . 57 J3
Argun →, Russia .. 21 D13
Argyle, L., Australia . 40 C4
Århus, Denmark ... 7 H14
Ariadnoye, Russia .. 22 B7
Ariana, Tunisia 35 A7
Arica, Chile 62 G4
Arica, Colombia 62 D4
Arida, Japan 23 G7
Arinos →, Brazil ... 62 F7
Ario de Rosales, Mexico 58 D4
Aripuanã, Brazil 62 E6

Aripuanã →, Brazil . 62 E6
Ariquemes, Brazil ... 62 E6
Aristazabal I., Canada . 50 C3
Arizona, Argentina .. 64 D3
Arizona □, U.S.A. .. 57 J8
Arizpe, Mexico 58 A2
Arjeplog, Sweden .. 6 D18
Arjona, Colombia ... 62 A3
Arjuna, Indonesia ... 27 G15
Arka, Russia 21 C15
Arkadelphia, U.S.A. . 55 H8
Arkalyk = Arqalyk, Kazakhstan 20 D7
Arkansas □, U.S.A. . 55 H8
Arkansas →, U.S.A. 55 J9
Arkansas City, U.S.A. . 55 G6
Arkaroola, Australia . 43 E2
Arkhángelsk, Russia . 18 B7
Arklow, Ireland 10 E3
Arktichevskiy, Mys, Russia 21 A10
Arlanzón →, Spain . 15 A3
Arlberg Pass, Austria . 12 E6
Arles, France 14 E6
Arlington, Oreg., U.S.A. 56 D3
Arlington, S. Dak., U.S.A. 54 C6
Arlington, Tex., U.S.A. . 55 J6
Arlington, Va., U.S.A. . 52 F7
Arlington, Wash., U.S.A. 56 B2
Arlington Heights, U.S.A. 52 D2
Arlit, Niger 34 E7
Arlon, Belgium 11 E5
Arltunga, Australia .. 42 C1
Armagh, U.K. 10 D3
Armavir, Russia 19 E7
Armenia, Colombia .. 62 C3
Armenia ■, Asia ... 19 F7
Armidale, Australia .. 43 E5
Armour, U.S.A. 54 D5
Armstrong, B.C., Canada 50 C5
Armstrong, Ont., Canada 48 B2
Arnaíjörður, Iceland . 6 D2
Arnaud →, Canada . 47 B12
Arnauti, C., Cyprus .. 30 C2
Arnett, U.S.A. 55 G5
Arnhem, Neths. 11 C5
Arnhem, C., Australia . 42 A2
Arnhem B., Australia . 42 A2
Arnhem Land, Australia 42 A1
Arno →, Italy 16 C4
Arno Bay, Australia .. 43 E2
Arnold, U.K. 8 D6
Arnot, Canada 51 B9
Arnøy, Norway 6 A19
Arnprior, Canada ... 48 C4
Arnsberg, Germany . 12 C5
Arqalyk, Kazakhstan . 20 D7
Arrah = Ara, India .. 29 G14
Arran, France 14 A5
Arras, France 14 A5
Arrée, Mts. d', France 14 B2
Arriaga, Chiapas, Mexico 59 D6
Arriaga, San Luis Potosi, Mexico 58 C4
Arrilalah, Australia .. 42 C3
Arrino, Australia 41 E2
Arrowtown, N.Z. ... 39 L2
Arroyo Grande, U.S.A. 57 J3
Ars, Iran 30 B5
Arsenault L., Canada . 51 B7
Arsenev, Russia 22 B6
Árta, Greece 17 E9
Arteaga, Mexico ... 58 D4
Artemovsk, Russia .. 21 D10
Artemovsk, Ukraine . 19 E6
Artesia, U.S.A. 55 J2
Arthur →, Australia . 42 G3
Arthur Cr. →, Australia 42 C2
Arthur Pt., Australia . 42 C5
Arthur River, Australia 41 F2
Arthur's Pass, N.Z. .. 39 K3
Arthur's Town, Bahamas 61 B4
Artigas, Uruguay ... 64 C5
Artillery L., Canada .. 51 A7
Artois, France 14 A5
Artsyz, Ukraine 13 E15
Artvin, Turkey 19 F7
Aru, Kepulauan, Indonesia 27 F8
Aru Is. = Aru, Kepulauan, Indonesia 27 F8
Arua, Uganda 36 D6
Aruanã, Brazil 63 F8
Aruba ■, W. Indies . 62 A5
Arun →, U.K. 9 G7
Arunachal Pradesh □, India 29 F19
Arusha, Tanzania ... 36 E7
Aruwimi →, Dem. Rep. of the Congo 36 D4
Arvada, Colo., U.S.A. . 54 F2
Arvada, Wyo., U.S.A. . 56 D10
Arvi, C., Australia ... 41 F3
Arvidsjaur, Sweden . 6 D18
Arvika, Sweden 7 G15
Arxan, China 25 B6
Arys, Kazakhstan ... 20 E7
Arzamas, Russia ... 18 C7

Aş Şadr, U.A.E. 31 E7
Aş Şafā, Syria 33 B6
As Saffānīyah, Si. Arabia 31 E6
As Safīrah, Syria ... 30 B3
Aş Şahm, Oman 31 E8
Aş Şājir, Si. Arabia .. 30 E5
As Salamīyah, Syria . 30 C3
As Salmān, Iraq 30 D5
As Salṭ, Jordan 33 C4
As Sal'w'a, Qatar ... 31 E6
As Samāwah, Iraq .. 30 D5
As Sanamayn, Syria . 33 B5
As Sohar = Şuḥār, Oman 31 E8
As Sulaymānīyah, Iraq 30 C5
As Sulaymī, Si. Arabia 30 E4
As Sulayyil, Si. Arabia 32 C4
As Summān, Si. Arabia 30 E5
As Suwaydā', Syria .. 33 C5
As Suwaydā' □, Syria 33 C5
As Suwayq, Oman .. 31 F8
As Şuwayrah, Iraq .. 30 C5
Asad, Buḥayrat al, Syria 30 C3
Asahi-Gawa →, Japan 23 G6
Asahigawa, Japan .. 22 C11
Asamankese, Ghana . 34 G5
Asansol, India 29 H15
Asbestos, Canada .. 49 C5
Asbury Park, U.S.A. . 52 E8
Ascensión, Mexico .. 58 A3
Ascensión, B. de la, Mexico 59 D7
Ascension I., Atl. Oc. . 2 E9
Aschaffenburg, Germany 12 D5
Aschersleben, Germany 12 C6
Áscoli Piceno, Italy .. 16 C5
Ascope, Peru 62 E3
Aseb, Eritrea 32 E3
Asela, Ethiopia 32 F2
Asenovgrad, Bulgaria 17 C11
Aserradero, Mexico . 58 C3
Ash Fork, U.S.A. ... 57 J7
Ash Grove, U.S.A. .. 55 G8
Ash Shabakah, Iraq . 30 D4
Ash Shamāl □, Lebanon 33 A5
Ash Shāmīyah, Iraq . 30 D5
Ash Shāriqah, U.A.E. 31 E7
Ash Sharmah, Si. Arabia 30 D2
Ash Sharqāt, Iraq ... 30 C4
Ash Sharqi, Al Jabal, Lebanon 33 B5
Ash Shaṭrah, Iraq ... 30 D5
Ash Shawbak, Jordan . 30 D2
Ash Shawmari, J., Jordan 33 E5
Ash Shināfiyah, Iraq . 30 D5
Ash Shu'bah, Si. Arabia 30 D5
Ash Shumlūl, Si. Arabia 30 E5
Ash Shūr'ah, Iraq ... 30 C4
Ash Shurayf, Si. Arabia 30 E3
Ash Shuwayfāt, Lebanon 33 B4
Asha, Russia 18 D10
Ashburn, U.S.A. 53 K4
Ashburton, N.Z. 39 K3
Ashburton →, Australia 40 D1
Ashcroft, Canada ... 50 C4
Ashdod, Israel 33 D3
Ashdown, U.S.A. ... 55 J7
Asheboro, U.S.A. ... 53 H6
Ashern, Canada 51 C9
Asherton, U.S.A. ... 55 L5
Asheville, U.S.A. ... 53 H4
Asheweig →, Canada 48 B2
Ashford, Australia .. 43 D5
Ashford, U.K. 9 F8
Ashgabat, Turkmenistan 20 F6
Ashibetsu, Japan ... 22 C11
Ashikaga, Japan ... 23 F9
Ashington, U.K. 8 B6
Ashizuri-Zaki, Japan . 23 H6
Ashkhabad = Ashgabat, Turkmenistan 20 F6
Ashkhāneh, Iran 31 B8
Ashland, Kans., U.S.A. 55 G5
Ashland, Ky., U.S.A. . 52 F4
Ashland, Mont., U.S.A. 56 D10
Ashland, Ohio, U.S.A. . 52 E4
Ashland, Oreg., U.S.A. 56 E2
Ashland, Va., U.S.A. . 52 G7
Ashland, Wis., U.S.A. . 54 B9
Ashley, U.S.A. 54 B5
Ashmore Reef, Australia 40 B3
Ashmyany, Belarus . 7 J21
Ashqelon, Israel ... 33 D3
Ashtabula, U.S.A. ... 52 E5
Ashton, U.S.A. 56 D8
Ashuanipi, L., Canada 49 B6
Asia, Kepulauan, Indonesia 27 D8
Āsīā Bak, Iran 31 C6
Asifabad, India 28 K11
Asinara, G. dell', Italy 16 D3
Asinara, Italy 16 D3
Asino, Russia 20 D9
Asipovichy, Belarus . 13 B15
'Asīr □, Si. Arabia .. 32 D3
'Asir, Ras, Somali Rep. 32 E5
Askersund, Sweden . 7 G16
Askim, Norway 7 G14

Askja, Iceland 6 D5
Askøy, Norway 7 F11
Asmara = Asmera, Eritrea 32 D2
Asmera, Eritrea 32 D2
Åsnen, Sweden 7 H16
Aspen, U.S.A. 57 G10
Aspermont, U.S.A. .. 55 J4
Aspiring, Mt., N.Z. .. 39 L2
Asquith, Canada ... 51 C7
Assam □, India 29 G18
Asse, Belgium 11 D4
Assen, Neths. 11 A6
Assiniboia, Canada .. 51 D7
Assiniboine →, Canada 51 D9
Assiniboine, Mt., Canada 50 C5
Assis, Brazil 63 H8
Assisi, Italy 16 C5
Astana, Kazakhstan . 20 D8
Åstanh, Iran 31 B6
Astara, Azerbaijan .. 19 G8
Asti, Italy 14 D8
Astipálaia, Greece .. 17 F12
Astorga, Spain 15 A2
Astoria, U.S.A. 56 C2
Astrakhan, Russia .. 19 E8
Asturias □, Spain ... 15 A3
Asunción, Paraguay . 64 B5
Asunción Nochixtlán, Mexico 59 D5
Aswân, Egypt 35 D12
Aswân High Dam = Sadd el Aali, Egypt . 35 D12
Asyût, Egypt 35 C12
At Ṭafilah, Jordan .. 33 E4
Aṭ Tā'if, Si. Arabia .. 32 C3
Aṭ Tubayq, Si. Arabia 30 D3
Atacama, Desierto de, Chile 64 A3
Atacama, Salar de, Chile 64 A3
Atalaya, Peru 62 F4
Atami, Japan 23 G9
Atapupu, Indonesia . 27 F6
Atâr, Mauritania ... 34 D3
Atascadero, U.S.A. .. 57 J3
Atasu, Kazakhstan .. 20 E8
Atatürk Baraji, Turkey 19 G6
'Atbara, Sudan 35 E12
'Atbara, Nahr →, Sudan 35 E12
Atbasar, Kazakhstan . 20 D7
Atchafalaya B., U.S.A. 55 L9
Atchison, U.S.A. ... 54 F7
Ateshan, Iran 31 C7
Ath, Belgium 11 D3
Athabasca, Canada . 50 C6
Athabasca →, Canada 51 B6
Athabasca, L., Canada 51 B7
Athens = Athínai, Greece 17 F10
Athens, Ala., U.S.A. . 53 H2
Athens, Ga., U.S.A. . 53 J4
Athens, Ohio, U.S.A. . 52 F4
Athens, Tenn., U.S.A. 53 H3
Athens, Tex., U.S.A. . 55 J7
Atherton, Australia .. 42 B4
Athínai, Greece 17 F10
Athlone, Ireland ... 10 E3
Atholville, Canada .. 49 C6
Áthos, Greece 17 D11
Athy, Ireland 10 E3
Ati, Chad 35 F9
Atik, L., Canada 51 B9
Atikameg →, Canada 48 B3
Atikokan, Canada .. 48 C1
Atikonak L., Canada . 49 B7
Atka, Russia 21 C16
Atka I., U.S.A. 46 C2
Atkinson, U.S.A. ... 54 D5
Atlanta, Ga., U.S.A. . 53 J3
Atlanta, Tex., U.S.A. . 55 J7
Atlantic, U.S.A. 54 E7
Atlantic City, U.S.A. . 52 F8
Atlantic Ocean 2 E9
Atlas Mts. = Haut Atlas, Morocco 34 B4
Atlin, Canada 50 B2
Atlin, L., Canada ... 50 B2
Atlin Prov. Park, Canada 50 B2
Atmore, U.S.A. 53 K2
Atoka, U.S.A. 55 H6
Atrak = Atrek →, Turkmenistan 31 B8
Atrek →, Turkmenistan 31 B8
Atsuta, Japan 22 C10
Attalla, U.S.A. 53 H2
Attapu, Laos 26 B3
Attawapiskat, Canada 48 B3
Attawapiskat →, Canada 48 B3
Attawapiskat L., Canada 48 B2
Attica, U.S.A. 52 E3
Attikamagen L., Canada 49 B6
Attleboro, U.S.A. ... 52 E10
Attock, Pakistan ... 28 C8
Attopeu = Attapu, Laos 26 B3
Attu I., U.S.A. 46 C1
Attur, India 28 P11
Atuel →, Argentina . 64 D3
Atvidaberg, Sweden . 7 G17
Atwater, U.S.A. 57 H3
Atwood, U.S.A. 54 F4

Atyraū, Kazakhstan . 19 E9
Au Sable →, U.S.A. . 52 C4
Aubagne, France ... 14 E6
Aube →, France ... 14 B5
Auburn, Ala., U.S.A. . 53 J3
Auburn, Calif., U.S.A. 56 G3
Auburn, Ind., U.S.A. . 52 E3
Auburn, Maine, U.S.A. 53 C10
Auburn, N.Y., U.S.A. . 52 D7
Auburn, Nebr., U.S.A. 54 E7
Auburn Ra., Australia 43 D5
Auburndale, U.S.A. . 53 L5
Aubusson, France .. 14 D5
Auch, France 14 E4
Auckland, N.Z. 39 G5
Auckland Is., Pac. Oc. 44 N8
Aude →, France ... 14 E5
Auden, Canada 48 B2
Audubon, U.S.A. ... 54 E7
Augathella, Australia . 43 D4
Augsburg, Germany . 12 D6
Augusta, Australia .. 41 F2
Augusta, Italy 16 F6
Augusta, Ark., U.S.A. 55 H9
Augusta, Ga., U.S.A. 53 J5
Augusta, Kans., U.S.A. 55 G6
Augusta, Maine, U.S.A. 47 D13
Augusta, Mont., U.S.A. 56 C7
Augustów, Poland .. 13 B12
Augustus, Mt., Australia 41 D2
Augustus I., Australia 40 C3
Auld, L., Australia .. 40 D3
Ault, U.S.A. 54 E2
Aunis, France 14 C3
Auponhia, Indonesia 27 E7
Aurangabad, Bihar, India 29 G14
Aurangabad, Maharashtra, India . 28 K9
Aurich, Germany ... 12 B4
Aurillac, France 14 D5
Aurora, Colo., U.S.A. 54 F2
Aurora, Ill., U.S.A. .. 52 E1
Aurora, Mo., U.S.A. . 55 G8
Aurora, Nebr., U.S.A. 54 E6
Aurukun, Australia .. 42 A3
Auschwitz = Oświęcim, Poland 13 C10
Austin, Minn., U.S.A. 54 D8
Austin, Nev., U.S.A. . 56 G5
Austin, Tex., U.S.A. . 55 K6
Austin, L., Australia . 41 E2
Austin I., Canada ... 51 A10
Austra, Norway 6 D14
Austral Is. = Tubuai Is., Pac. Oc. 45 K13
Austral Seamount Chain, Pac. Oc. ... 45 K13
Australia ■, Oceania . 38 D6
Australian Alps, Australia 38 E7
Australian Capital Territory □, Australia 43 F4
Australind, Australia . 41 F2
Austria ■, Europe .. 12 E8
Austvågøy, Norway . 6 B16
Autlán, Mexico 58 D4
Autun, France 14 C6
Auvergne, France .. 14 D5
Auvergne, Mts. d', France 14 D5
Auxerre, France 14 C5
Ava, U.S.A. 55 G8
Avallon, France 14 C5
Avalon Pen., Canada 49 C9
Avanos, Turkey 30 B2
Aveiro, Brazil 63 D7
Aveiro, Portugal ... 15 B1
Āvej, Iran 31 C6
Avellaneda, Argentina 64 C5
Avellino, Italy 16 D6
Aversa, Italy 16 D6
Avery, U.S.A. 56 C6
Aves, Is. de, Venezuela 62 A5
Avesta, Sweden 7 F17
Avezzano, Italy 16 C5
Aviemore, U.K. 10 C5
Avignon, France ... 14 E6
Ávila, Spain 15 B3
Avilés, Spain 15 A3
Avoca →, Australia . 43 F3
Avola, Canada 50 C5
Avola, Italy 16 F6
Avon →, Australia . 41 F2
Avon →, Bristol, U.K. 9 F5
Avon →, Dorset, U.K. 9 G6
Avon →, Warks., U.K. 9 E5
Avon Park, U.S.A. .. 53 M5
Avonlea, Canada ... 51 D8
Avonmore, Canada . 51 D8
Avranches, France .. 14 B3
A'waj →, Syria 33 B5
Awaji-Shima, Japan . 23 G7
'Awālī, Bahrain 31 E6
Awash, Ethiopia ... 32 F3
Awatere →, N.Z. ... 39 J5
Awbārī, Libya 35 C8
Awjilah, Libya 35 C10
Axe →, U.K. 9 F5
Axel Heiberg I., Canada 4 B3
Axim, Ghana 34 H5
Axiós →, Greece ... 17 D10
Axminster, U.K. 9 G4
Ayabaca, Peru 62 D3
Ayabe, Japan 23 G7

Ayacucho, *Argentina* . . 64 D5
Ayacucho, *Peru* 62 F4
Ayaguz, *Kazakstan* . . 20 E9
Ayamonte, *Spain* 15 D2
Ayan, *Russia* 21 D14
Ayaviri, *Peru* 62 F4
Aydın, *Turkey* 17 F12
Aydin □, *Turkey* 19 G4
Ayers Rock, *Australia* . 41 E5
Áyios Evstrátios, *Greece* 17 E11
Aykino, *Russia* 18 B8
Aylesbury, *U.K.* 9 F7
Aylmer, L., *Canada* . . . 46 B8
'Ayn, Wādī al, *Oman* . . 31 F7
Ayn Dār, *Si. Arabia* . . 31 E7
Ayn Zālah, *Iraq* 30 B4
Ayon, Ostrov, *Russia* . 21 C17
'Ayoûn el 'Atroûs,
  Mauritania 34 E4
Ayr, *Australia* 42 B4
Ayr, *U.K.* 10 D4
Ayre, Pt. of, *U.K.* 8 C3
Ayton, *Australia* 42 B4
Aytos, *Bulgaria* 17 C12
Ayu, Kepulauan,
  Indonesia 27 D8
Ayutla, *Guatemala* . . . 60 D1
Ayutla, *Mexico* 59 D5
Ayvacık, *Turkey* 17 E12
Ayvalık, *Turkey* 17 E12
Az Zabadānī, *Syria* . . . 33 B5
Az Zāhiriyah, *West Bank* 33 D3
Az Zahrān, *Si. Arabia* . 31 E6
Az Zarqā, *Jordan* 33 C5
Az Zarqā', *U.A.E.* 31 E7
Az Zibār, *Iraq* 30 B5
Az Zāwiyah, *Libya* . . . 35 B8
Az Zilfī, *Si. Arabia* . . . 30 E5
Az Zubayr, *Iraq* 30 D5
Azamgarh, *India* 29 F13
Azangaro, *Peru* 62 F4
Āzar Shahr, *Iran* 30 B5
Azarān, *Iran* 30 B5
Azärbayjan ■,
  Azerbaijan 19 F8
Āzarbāyjān-e Gharbī □,
  Iran 30 B5
Āzarbāyjān-e Sharqī □,
  Iran 30 B5
Azare, *Nigeria* 34 F8
Azbine = Aïr, *Niger* . . 34 E7
Azerbaijan ■, *Asia* . . 19 F8
Azerbaijchan =
  Azerbaijan ■, *Asia* . . 19 F8
Azogues, *Ecuador* . . . 62 D3
Azores, Atl. Oc. 34 A1
Azov, *Russia* 19 E6
Azov, Sea of, *Europe* . 19 E6
Azovskoye More =
  Azov, Sea of, *Europe* 19 E6
Azraq ash Shīshān,
  Jordan 33 D5
Aztec, *U.S.A.* 57 H10
Azúa de Compostela,
  Dom. Rep. 61 C5
Azuaga, *Spain* 15 C3
Azuero, Pen. de,
  Panama 60 E3
Azul, *Argentina* 64 D5

Ba Don, *Vietnam* . . . 26 A3
Baa, *Indonesia* 27 F6
Baarle-Nassau, *Belgium* 11 C4
Bab el Mandeb, *Red Sea* 32 E3
Bābā, Koh-i-, *Afghan.* . 28 B5
Baba Burnu, *Turkey* . . 17 E12
Bābā Kalū, *Iran* 31 D6
Babadag, *Romania* . . 13 F15
Babadayhan,
  Turkmenistan 20 F7
Babaeski, *Turkey* 17 D12
Babahoyo, *Ecuador* . . 62 D3
Babar, *Indonesia* 27 F7
Babb, *U.S.A.* 56 B7
Babelthuap, *Pac. Oc.* . 27 C8
Babinda, *Australia* . . . 42 B4
Babine, *Canada* 50 B3
Babine →, *Canada* . . 50 B3
Babine L., *Canada* . . . 50 B3
Babo, *Indonesia* 27 E8
Bābol, *Iran* 31 B7
Bābol Sar, *Iran* 31 B7
Babruysk, *Belarus* . . . 13 B15
Babuyan Chan., *Phil.* . 27 A6
Babylon, *Iraq* 30 C5
Bac Lieu, *Vietnam* . . . 26 C3
Bacabal, *Brazil* 63 D10
Bacalar, *Mexico* 59 D7
Bacan, Kepulauan,
  Indonesia 27 E7
Bacarra, *Phil.* 27 A6
Bacău, *Romania* 13 E14
Bacerac, *Mexico* 58 A3
Bachelina, *Russia* . . . 20 D7
Back →, *Canada* 46 B9
Bacolod, *Phil.* 27 B6
Bād, *Iran* 31 C7
Bad →, *U.S.A.* 54 C4
Bad Axe, *U.S.A.* 52 D4
Bad Ischl, *Austria* . . . 12 E7
Bad Kissingen, *Germany* 12 C6
Bad Lands, *U.S.A.* . . . 54 D3
Badagara, *India* 28 P9

Badajós, L., *Brazil* 62 D6
Badajoz, *Spain* 15 C2
Badalona, *Spain* 15 B7
Badampahar, *India* . . 29 H15
Badanah, *Si. Arabia* . . 30 D4
Badarinath, *India* . . . 28 D11
Badas, Kepulauan,
  Indonesia 26 D3
Baddo →, *Pakistan* . . 28 F4
Bade, *Indonesia* 27 F9
Baden, *Austria* 12 D9
Baden-Baden, *Germany* 12 D5
Baden-Württemberg □,
  Germany 12 D5
Badgastein, *Austria* . . 12 E7
Badger, *Canada* 49 C8
Bādghīsāt □, *Afghan.* . 28 B3
Badin, *Pakistan* 28 G6
Badlands National Park,
  U.S.A. 54 D3
Badrah, *Iraq* 30 C5
Badulla, *Sri Lanka* . . . 28 R12
Baena, *Spain* 15 D3
Baeza, *Spain* 15 D4
Baffin B., *Canada* 4 B4
Baffin I., *Canada* 47 B12
Bafing →, *Mali* 34 F3
Bafliyūn, *Syria* 30 B3
Bafoulabé, *Mali* 34 F3
Bāfq, *Iran* 31 D7
Bafra, *Turkey* 19 F6
Bāft, *Iran* 31 D8
Bafwasende, *Dem. Rep.
  of the Congo* 36 D5
Bagamoyo, *Tanzania* . 36 F7
Baganga, *Phil.* 27 C7
Bagansiapiapi,
  Indonesia 26 D2
Bagdarin, *Russia* . . . 21 D12
Bagé, *Brazil* 64 C6
Baggs, *U.S.A.* 56 F10
Baghdād, *Iraq* 30 C5
Bagheria, *Italy* 16 E5
Baghlān, *Afghan.* . . . 28 A6
Bagley, *U.S.A.* 54 B7
Bago = Pegu, *Burma* . 29 L20
Bagrationovsk, *Russia* . 7 J19
Baguio, *Phil.* 27 A6
Bahama, Canal Viejo de,
  W. Indies 60 B4
Bahamas ■, *N. Amer.* . 61 B5
Baharampur, *India* . . 29 G16
Bahawalpur, *Pakistan* . 28 E7
Bahia = Salvador, *Brazil* 63 F11
Bahia □, *Brazil* 63 F10
Bahía, Is. de la,
  Honduras 60 C2
Bahía Blanca, *Argentina* 64 D4
Bahía de Caráquez,
  Ecuador 62 D2
Bahía Honda, *Cuba* . . 60 B3
Bahía Laura, *Argentina* 64 F3
Bahía Negra, *Paraguay* 62 H7
Bahir Dar, *Ethiopia* . . 32 E2
Bahmanzād, *Iran* . . . 31 D6
Bahr el Ghazâl □, *Sudan* 35 G11
Bahraich, *India* 29 F12
Bahrain ■, *Asia* 31 E6
Bāhū Kalāt, *Iran* 31 E9
Bai Bung, Mui = Ca
  Mau, Mui, *Vietnam* . . 26 C2
Baia Mare, *Romania* . 13 E12
Baião, *Brazil* 63 D9
Baïbokoum, *Chad* . . . 35 G9
Baidoa, *Somali Rep.* . . 32 G3
Baie Comeau, *Canada* 49 C6
Baie-St-Paul, *Canada* . 49 C5
Baie Trinité, *Canada* . . 49 C6
Baie Verte, *Canada* . . 49 C8
Ba'ījī, *Iraq* 30 C4
Baikal, L. = Baykal, Oz.,
  Russia 21 D11
Baile Atha Cliath =
  Dublin, *Ireland* 10 E3
Băileşti, *Romania* . . . 13 F12
Bainbridge, *U.S.A.* . . . 53 K3
Baing, *Indonesia* 27 F6
Bā'ir, *Jordan* 33 E5
Bairnsdale, *Australia* . 43 F4
Baitadi, *Nepal* 29 E12
Baiyin, *China* 24 C5
Baja, *Hungary* 13 E10
Baja, Pta., *Mexico* . . . 58 B1
Baja California, *Mexico* 58 A1
Baja California □,
  Mexico 58 B2
Baja California Sur □,
  Mexico 58 B2
Bājgīrān, *Iran* 31 B8
Bajimba, Mt., *Australia* 43 D5
Bajo Nuevo, *Caribbean* 60 D3
Bajoga, *Nigeria* 35 F8
Bajool, *Australia* 42 C5
Bakala, *C.A.R.* 32
Bakel, *Senegal* 34 F3
Baker, Calif., *U.S.A.* . . 57 J5
Baker, Mont., *U.S.A.* . . 54 B2
Baker, L., *Canada* . . . 46 B10
Baker I., *Pac. Oc.* . . . 44 G10
Baker I., *U.S.A.* 50 B2
Baker L., *Australia* . . . 41 E4
Baker Lake, *Canada* . . 46 B10
Baker Mt., *U.S.A.* 56 B3
Bakers Creek, *Australia* 42 C4

Baker's Dozen Is.,
  Canada 48 A4
Bakersfield, *U.S.A.* . . . 57 J4
Bākhtarān, *Iran* 30 C5
Bākhtarān □, *Iran* . . . 30 C5
Bakı, *Azerbaijan* 19 F8
Bakkafjörður, *Iceland* . 6 C6
Bakony, *Hungary* . . . 13 E9
Bakony Forest =
  Bakony, *Hungary* . . 13 E9
Bakouma, *C.A.R.* 36 C4
Baku = Bakı, *Azerbaijan* 19 F8
Bakutis Coast,
  Antarctica 5 D15
Baky = Bakı, *Azerbaijan* 19 F8
Bala, *Canada* 48 B5
Bala, L., *U.K.* 8 E4
Balabac I., *Phil.* 26 C5
Balabac Str., *E. Indies* . 26 C5
Balabalangan,
  Kepulauan, *Indonesia* 26 E5
Balad, *Iraq* 30 C5
Balad Rūz, *Iraq* 30 C5
Bālādeh, *Fārs, Iran* . . . 31 D6
Bālādeh, *Māzandaran,
  Iran* 31 B6
Balaghat, *India* 28 J12
Balaghat Ra., *India* . . 28 K10
Balaguer, *Spain* 15 B6
Balaklava, *Ukraine* . . . 19 F5
Balakovo, *Russia* 18 D8
Balancán, *Mexico* . . . 59 D6
Balashov, *Russia* 19 D7
Balasore = Baleshwar,
  India 29 J15
Balaton, *Hungary* . . . 13 E9
Balbina, Reprêsa de,
  Brazil 62 D7
Balboa, *Panama* 60 E4
Balcarce, *Argentina* . . 64 D5
Balcarres, *Canada* . . . 51 C8
Balchik, *Bulgaria* . . . 17 C13
Balclutha, *N.Z.* 39 M2
Balcones Escarpment,
  U.S.A. 55 L5
Bald Hd., *Australia* . . 41 G2
Bald I., *Australia* 41 F2
Bald Knob, *U.S.A.* . . . 55 H9
Baldock L., *Canada* . . 51 B9
Baldwin, *U.S.A.* 52 D3
Baldy Mt., *U.S.A.* 56 B9
Baldy Peak, *U.S.A.* . . . 57 K9
Baleares, Is., *Spain* . . . 15 C7
Balearic Is. = Baleares,
  Is., *Spain* 15 C7
Baleine = Whale →,
  Canada 49 A6
Baler, *Phil.* 27 A6
Baleshwar, *India* 29 J15
Balfate, *Honduras* . . . 60 C2
Bali □, *Indonesia* 26 F5
Bali, Selat, *Indonesia* . 27 H16
Balikeşir, *Turkey* 17 E12
Balikpapan, *Indonesia* 26 E5
Balimbing, *Phil.* 27 C5
Balipara, *India* 29 F18
Balkan Mts. = Stara
  Planina, *Bulgaria* . . 17 C10
Balkhash = Balqash,
  Kazakstan 20 E8
Balkhash, Ozero =
  Balqash Köl,
  Kazakstan 20 E8
Balla, *Bangla.* 29 G17
Balladonia, *Australia* . 41 F3
Ballarat, *Australia* . . . 43 F3
Ballard, L., *Australia* . . 41 E3
Ballater, *U.K.* 10 C5
Ballenas, Canal de,
  Mexico 58 B2
Balleny Is., *Antarctica* . 5 C11
Ballina, *Australia* 43 D5
Ballina, *Ireland* 10 D2
Ballinasloe, *Ireland* . . 10 E2
Ballinger, *U.S.A.* 55 K5
Ballymena, *U.K.* 10 D3
Balmaceda, *Chile* . . . 64 F2
Balmertown, *Canada* . 51 C10
Balmoral, *Australia* . . 43 F3
Balmorhea, *U.S.A.* . . . 55 K3
Balonne →, *Australia* . 43 D4
Balqash, *Kazakstan* . . 20 E8
Balqash Köl, *Kazakstan* 20 E8
Balrampur, *India* 29 F13
Balranald, *Australia* . . 43 E3
Balsas, *Mexico* 59 D5
Balsas →, *Brazil* 63 E9
Balsas →, *Mexico* . . . 58 D4
Balta, *Ukraine* 13 D15
Bălţi, *Moldova* 13 E14
Baltic Sea, *Europe* . . 7 H18
Baltimore, *U.S.A.* 52 F7
Baltiysk, *Russia* 7 J18
Baluchistan □, *Pakistan* 28 F4
Balvi, *Latvia* 7 H22
Balya, *Turkey* 17 E12
Bam, *Iran* 31 D8
Bama, *Nigeria* 35 F8
Bamaga, *Australia* . . 42 A3
Bamaji L., *Canada* . . . 48 B1
Bamako, *Mali* 34 F4
Bambari, *C.A.R.* 36 C4
Bambaroo, *Australia* . 42 B4
Bamberg, *Germany* . . 12 D6

Bamberg, *U.S.A.* 53 J5
Bamfield, *Canada* . . . 50 D3
Bāmiān □, *Afghan.* . . 28 B5
Bampūr, *Iran* 31 E9
Ban Don = Surat Thani,
  Thailand 26 C1
Ban Kantang, *Thailand* 26 C1
Ban Mê Thuột = Buon
  Ma Thuot, *Vietnam* . 26 B3
Banaba, *Kiribati* 44 H8
Banalia, *Dem. Rep. of
  the Congo* 36 D5
Bananal, I. do, *Brazil* . 63 F8
Banaras = Varanasi,
  India 29 G13
Bânâs, Ras, *Egypt* . . . 35 D13
Banbān, *Si. Arabia* . . . 30 E5
Banbury, *U.K.* 9 E6
Bancroft, *Canada* . . . 48 C4
Band Bonī, *Iran* 31 E8
Band Qīr, *Iran* 31 D6
Banda, *India* 28 G12
Banda, Kepulauan,
  Indonesia 27 E7
Banda Aceh, *Indonesia* 26 C1
Banda Banda, Mt.,
  Australia 43 E5
Banda Elat, *Indonesia* . 27 F8
Banda Is. = Banda,
  Kepulauan, *Indonesia* 27 E7
Banda Sea, *Indonesia* . 27 F7
Bandai-San, *Japan* . . 22 F10
Bandān, *Iran* 31 D9
Bandanaira, *Indonesia* 27 E7
Bandar =
  Machilipatnam, *India* 29 L12
Bandar 'Abbās, *Iran* . . 31 E8
Bandar-e Anzalī, *Iran* . 31 B6
Bandar-e Chārak, *Iran* . 31 E7
Bandar-e Deylam, *Iran* 31 D6
Bandar-e Khomeyni,
  Iran 31 D6
Bandar-e Lengeh, *Iran* 31 E7
Bandar-e Maqām, *Iran* 31 E7
Bandar-e Ma'shur, *Iran* 31 D6
Bandar-e Nakhīlū, *Iran* 31 E7
Bandar-e Rīg, *Iran* . . . 31 D6
Bandar-e Torkeman,
  Iran 31 B7
Bandar Maharani =
  Muar, *Malaysia* 26 D2
Bandar Penggaram =
  Batu Pahat, *Malaysia* 26 D2
Bandar Seri Begawan,
  Brunei 26 C4
Bandar Sri Aman,
  Malaysia 26 D4
Bandera, *Argentina* . . 64 B4
Banderas, B. de, *Mexico* 58 C3
Bandırma, *Turkey* . . . 17 D13
Bandon, *Ireland* 10 F2
Bandundu, *Dem. Rep. of
  the Congo* 36 E3
Bandung, *Indonesia* . . 27 G12
Băneh, *Iran* 30 C5
Banes, *Cuba* 61 B4
Banff, *Canada* 50 C5
Banff, *U.K.* 10 C5
Banff Nat. Park, *Canada* 50 C5
Bang Saphan, *Thailand* 26 B1
Bangalore, *India* 28 N10
Bangassou, *C.A.R.* . . . 36 D4
Banggai, *Indonesia* . . 27 E6
Banggai, Kepulauan,
  Indonesia 27 E6
Banggai Arch. =
  Banggai, Kepulauan,
  Indonesia 27 E6
Banggi, *Malaysia* . . . 26 C5
Banghāzī, *Libya* 35 B10
Bangka, Sulawesi,
  Indonesia 27 D7
Bangka, Sumatera,
  Indonesia 26 E3
Bangka, Selat, *Indonesia* 26 E3
Bangkalan, *Indonesia* . 27 G15
Bangkinang, *Indonesia* 26 D2
Bangko, *Indonesia* . . 26 E2
Bangkok, *Thailand* . . 26 B2
Bangladesh ■, *Asia* . . 29 H17
Bangong Co, *India* . . 28 B11
Bangor, Down, *U.K.* . . 10 D4
Bangor, Gwynedd, *U.K.* 8 D3
Bangor, *U.S.A.* 47 D13
Bangued, *Phil.* 27 A6
Bangui, *C.A.R.* 36 D3
Bangweulu, L., *Zambia* 36 G6
Bani, *Dom. Rep.* 61 C5
Banī Sa'd, *Iraq* 30 C5
Bāniyās, *Syria* 30 C3
Banja, Bos.-H. 16 E4
Banjarmasin, *Indonesia* 26 E4
Banjul, *Gambia* 34 F2
Bankipore, *India* 29 G14
Banks I., *B.C., Canada* . 50 C3
Banks I., *N.W.T., Canada* 46 A7
Banks Pen., *N.Z.* 39 K4
Banks Str., *Australia* . . 42 G4
Bankura, *India* 29 H15
Banning, *U.S.A.* 57 K5
Banningville =
  Bandundu, *Dem. Rep.
  of the Congo* 36 E3

Bannu, *Pakistan* 28 C7
Banská Bystrica,
  Slovak Rep. 13 D10
Banswara, *India* 28 H9
Bantaeng, *Indonesia* . 27 F5
Bantry, *Ireland* 10 F2
Bantul, *Indonesia* . . . 27 G14
Banyak, Kepulauan,
  Indonesia 26 D1
Banyo, *Cameroon* . . . 36 C2
Banyumas, *Indonesia* . 27 G13
Banyuwangi, *Indonesia* 27 H16
Banzare Coast,
  Antarctica 5 C9
Banzyville = Mobayi,
  *Dem. Rep. of
  the Congo* 36 D4
Baoding, *China* 25 C6
Baoji, *China* 24 C5
Baoshan, *China* 24 D4
Baotou, *China* 25 B6
Bapatla, *India* 29 M12
Bāqerābād, *Iran* 31 C6
Ba'qūbah, *Iraq* 30 C5
Bar, *Montenegro, Yug.* . 17 C8
Bar, *Ukraine* 13 D14
Bar Harbor, *U.S.A.* . . . 53 C11
Bar-le-Duc, *France* . . 14 B6
Barabai, *Indonesia* . . 26 E5
Baraboo, *U.S.A.* 54 D10
Baracoa, *Cuba* 61 B5
Baradā →, *Syria* 33 B5
Baradine, *Australia* . . 43 E4
Baraga, *U.S.A.* 54 B10
Barahona, *Dom. Rep.* . 61 C5
Barail Range, *India* . . 29 G18
Barakaldo, *Spain* . . . 15 A4
Barakhola, *India* 29 G18
Barakpur, *India* 29 H16
Baralaba, *Australia* . . 42 C4
Baralzon L., *Canada* . . 51 B9
Baramula, *India* 28 B9
Baran, *India* 28 G10
Baranavichy, *Belarus* . . 13 B14
Baranof, *U.S.A.* 50 B2
Baranof I., *U.S.A.* 46 C6
Barapasi, *Indonesia* . . 27 E9
Barat Daya, Kepulauan,
  Indonesia 27 F7
Barataria B., *U.S.A.* . . 55 L10
Barbacena, *Brazil* . . . 63 H10
Barbados ■, *W. Indies* . 61 D8
Barberton, *U.S.A.* 52 E5
Barbosa, *Colombia* . . 62 B4
Barbourville, *U.S.A.* . . 53 G4
Barbuda, *W. Indies* . . 61 C7
Barcaldine, *Australia* . 42 C4
Barcellona Pozzo di
  Gotto, *Italy* 16 E6
Barcelona, *Spain* . . . 15 B7
Barcelona, *Venezuela* . 62 A6
Barcelos, *Brazil* 62 D6
Barco →, *Australia* . . 42 D3
Bardaï, *Chad* 35 D9
Barddhaman, *India* . . 29 H15
Bardejov, *Slovak Rep.* . 13 D11
Bardera, *Somali Rep.* . 32 G3
Bardīyah, *Libya* 35 B10
Bardsey I., *U.K.* 8 E3
Bardstown, *U.S.A.* . . . 52 G3
Bareilly, *India* 28 E11
Barents Sea, *Arctic* . . 4 B9
Barfleur, Pte. de, *France* 14 B3
Bargara, *Australia* . . . 42 C5
Barguzin, *Russia* . . . 21 D11
Barham, *Australia* . . . 43 F3
Barhi, *India* 29 G14
Bari, *Italy* 16 D7
Bari Doab, *Pakistan* . . 28 D8
Barīdī, Ra's, *Si. Arabia* . 30 E3
Barinas, *Venezuela* . . 62 B4
Baring, C., *Canada* . . 46 B8
Barisal, *Bangla.* 29 H17
Barisan, Bukit, *Indonesia* 26 E2
Barito →, *Indonesia* . . 26 E4
Barkakana, *India* . . . 29 H14
Barkley, L., *U.S.A.* . . . 53 G2
Barkley Sound, *Canada* 50 D3
Barkly Roadhouse,
  Australia 42 B2
Barkly Tableland,
  Australia 42 B2
Barkol Kazak Zizhixian,
  China 24 B4
Bârlad, *Romania* 13 E14
Bârlad →, *Romania* . . 13 F14
Barlee, L., *Australia* . . 41 E2
Barlee, Mt., *Australia* . 41 D4
Barletta, *Italy* 16 D7
Barlow L., *Canada* . . . 51 A8
Barmedman, *Australia* . 43 E4
Barmer, *India* 28 G7
Barmera, *Australia* . . 43 E3
Barmouth, *U.K.* 8 E3
Barnard Castle, *U.K.* . . 8 C6
Barnaul, *Russia* 20 D9
Barnesville, *U.S.A.* . . . 53 J3
Barnet, *U.K.* 9 F7
Barneveld, *Neths.* . . . 11 B5
Barnhart, *U.S.A.* 55 K4
Barnsley, *U.K.* 8 D6
Barnstaple, *U.K.* 9 F3
Barnstable Bay =
  Bideford Bay, *U.K.* . . 9 F3

Barnwell, *U.S.A.* 53 J5
Baro, *Nigeria* 34 G7
Baroda = Vadodara,
  India 28 H8
Baron Ra., *Australia* . . 40 D4
Barotseland, *Zambia* . 37 H4
Barpeta, *India* 29 F17
Barques, Pt. Aux, *U.S.A.* 52 C4
Barquísimeto, *Venezuela* 62 A5
Barr Smith Range,
  Australia 41 E3
Barra, *Brazil* 63 F10
Barra, *U.K.* 10 C3
Barra de Navidad,
  Mexico 58 D4
Barra do Corda, *Brazil* 63 E9
Barra Falsa, Pta. da,
  Mozam. 37 J7
Barraba, *Australia* . . . 43 E5
Barrackpur = Barakpur,
  India 29 H16
Barradale Roadhouse,
  Australia 40 D1
Barraigh = Barra, *U.K.* 10 C3
Barranca, *Lima, Peru* . 62 F3
Barranca, *Loreto, Peru* 62 D3
Barrancabermeja,
  Colombia 62 B4
Barrancas, *Venezuela* . 62 B6
Barrancos, *Portugal* . . 15 C2
Barranqueras, *Argentina* 64 B5
Barranquilla, *Colombia* 62 A4
Barraute, *Canada* . . . 48 C4
Barre, *U.S.A.* 52 C9
Barreiras, *Brazil* 63 F10
Barreirinhas, *Brazil* . . 63 D10
Barreiro, *Portugal* . . . 15 C1
Barretos, *Brazil* 63 H9
Barrhead, *Canada* . . . 50 C6
Barrie, *Canada* 48 D4
Barrier Ra., *Australia* . 43 E3
Barrière, *Canada* . . . 50 C4
Barrington L., *Canada* . 51 B8
Barrington Tops,
  Australia 43 E5
Barringun, *Australia* . . 43 D4
Barro do Garças, *Brazil* 63 G8
Barron, *U.S.A.* 54 C9
Barrow, *U.S.A.* 46 A4
Barrow Creek, *Australia* 42 C1
Barrow I., *Australia* . . 40 D2
Barrow-in-Furness, *U.K.* 8 C4
Barrow Pt., *Australia* . . 42 A3
Barrow Ra., *Australia* . 41 E4
Barrow Str., *Canada* . . 4 B3
Barry, *U.K.* 9 F4
Barry's Bay, *Canada* . . 48 C4
Barsham, *Syria* 30 C4
Barsi, *India* 28 K9
Barsoi, *India* 29 G15
Barstow, *U.S.A.* 57 J5
Bartica, *Guyana* 62 B7
Bartlesville, *U.S.A.* . . . 55 G7
Bartlett, L., *Canada* . . 50 A5
Barton upon Humber,
  U.K. 8 D7
Bartow, *U.S.A.* 53 M5
Barú, Volcan, *Panama* . 60 E3
Barysaw, *Belarus* . . . 13 A15
Barzān, *Iraq* 30 B5
Bāsa'idū, *Iran* 31 E7
Basankusa, Dem. Rep.
  of the Congo 36 D3
Basarabeasca, *Moldova* 13 E15
Basel, *Switz.* 14 C7
Bashākerd, Kūhhā-ye,
  Iran 31 E8
Bashaw, *Canada* 50 C6
Bāshī, *Iran* 31 D6
Bashkir Republic =
  Bashkortostan □,
  Russia 18 D10
Bashkortostan □, *Russia* 18 D10
Basilan □, *Phil.* 27 C6
Basilan Str., *Phil.* 27 C6
Basildon, *U.K.* 9 F8
Basim = Washim, *India* 28 J10
Basin, *U.S.A.* 56 D9
Basingstoke, *U.K.* . . . 9 F6
Baskatong, Rés., *Canada* 48 C4
Basle = Basel, *Switz.* . 14 C7
Basque Provinces =
  País Vasco □, *Spain* . 15 A4
Basra = Al Başrah, *Iraq* 30 D5
Bass Str., *Australia* . . 42 F4
Bassano, *Canada* . . . 50 C6
Bassano del Grappa,
  Italy 16 B4
Bassas da India, *Ind. Oc.* 37 J7
Basse-Terre,
  Guadeloupe 61 C7
Basseterre,
  St. Kitts & Nevis . . . 61 C7
Bassein, *Burma* 29 L19
Basset, *U.S.A.* 54 D5
Bastak, *Iran* 31 E7
Baştām, *Iran* 31 B7
Basti, *India* 29 F13
Bastia, *France* 14 E8
Bastogne, *Belgium* . . 11 D5
Bastrop, *La., U.S.A.* . . 55 J9
Bastrop, *Tex., U.S.A.* . 55 K6
Bat Yam, *Israel* 33 C3
Bata, *Eq. Guin.* 36 D1

Bataan □, *Phil.* 27 B6
Batabanó, *Cuba* 60 B3
Batabanó, G. de, *Cuba* 60 B3
Batac, *Phil.* 27 A6
Batagai, *Russia* 21 C14
Batamay, *Russia* 21 C13
Batang, *Indonesia* ... 27 G13
Batangafo, *C.A.R.* 32
Batangas, *Phil.* 27 B6
Batanta, *Indonesia* ... 27 E8
Batavia, *U.S.A.* 52 D6
Batchelor, *Australia* .. 40 B5
Batdambang, *Cambodia* 26 B2
Bateman's B., *Australia* 43 F5
Batemans Bay, *Australia* 43 F5
Bates Ra., *Australia* .. 41 E3
Batesburg-Leesville,
  U.S.A. 53 J5
Batesville, *Ark., U.S.A.* 55 H9
Batesville, *Miss., U.S.A.* 55 H10
Batesville, *Tex., U.S.A.* 55 L5
Bath, *U.K.* 9 F5
Bath, *Maine, U.S.A.* ... 53 D11
Bath, *N.Y., U.S.A.* 52 D7
Bath & North East
  Somerset □, *U.K.* .. 9 F5
Bathurst = Banjul,
  Gambia 34 F2
Bathurst, *Australia* 43 E4
Bathurst, *Canada* 49 C6
Bathurst, C., *Canada* . 46 A7
Bathurst B., *Australia* . 42 A3
Bathurst Harb., *Australia* 42 G4
Bathurst I., *Australia* .. 40 B5
Bathurst I., *Canada* ... 4 B2
Bathurst Inlet, *Canada* . 46 B9
Batlow, *Australia* 43 F4
Batman, *Turkey* 19 G7
Baţn al Ghūl, *Jordan* .. 33 F4
Batna, *Algeria* 34 A7
Baton Rouge, *U.S.A.* .. 55 K9
Batopilas, *Mexico* 58 B3
Batouri, *Cameroon* ... 36 D2
Båtsfjord, *Norway* 6 A23
Battambang =
  Batdambang,
  Cambodia 26 B2
Batticaloa, *Sri Lanka* .. 28 R12
Battipáglia, *Italy* 16 D6
Battle, *U.K.* 9 G8
Battle →, *Canada* 51 C7
Battle Creek, *U.S.A.* .. 52 D3
Battle Harbour, *Canada* 49 B8
Battle Lake, *U.S.A.* 54 B7
Battle Mountain, *U.S.A.* 56 F5
Battleford, *Canada* 51 C7
Batu, *Ethiopia* 32 F2
Batu, Kepulauan,
  Indonesia 26 E1
Batu Is. = Batu,
  Kepulauan, *Indonesia* 26 E1
Batu Pahat, *Malaysia* . 26 D2
Batuata, *Indonesia* ... 27 F6
Baturaja, *Indonesia* ... 26 E2
Baturité, *Brazil* 63 D11
Bau, *Malaysia* 26 D4
Baubau, *Indonesia* 27 F6
Bauchi, *Nigeria* 34 F7
Baudette, *U.S.A.* 54 A7
Bauer, C., *Australia* ... 43 E1
Bauhinia, *Australia* ... 42 C4
Baukau, *Indonesia* 27 F7
Bauld, C., *Canada* 47 C14
Bauru, *Brazil* 63 H9
Bauska, *Latvia* 7 H21
Bautzen, *Germany* 12 C8
Bavānāt, *Iran* 31 D7
Bavaria = Bayern □,
  Germany 12 D6
Bavispe →, *Mexico* ... 58 B3
Bawdwin, *Burma* 29 H20
Bawean, *Indonesia* ... 26 F4
Bawku, *Ghana* 34 F5
Bawlake, *Burma* 29 K20
Baxley, *U.S.A.* 53 K4
Baxter, *U.S.A.* 54 B7
Baxter Springs, *U.S.A.* 55 G7
Bay City, *Mich., U.S.A.* 52 D4
Bay City, *Tex., U.S.A.* . 55 L7
Bay Minette, *U.S.A.* ... 53 K2
Bay Roberts, *Canada* .. 49 C9
Bay St. Louis, *U.S.A.* . 55 K10
Bay Springs, *U.S.A.* ... 55 K10
Bay View, *N.Z.* 39 H6
Bayamo, *Cuba* 60 B4
Bayamón, *Puerto Rico* . 61 C6
Bayan Har Shan, *China* 24 C4
Bayan Hot = Alxa
  Zuoqi, *China* 24 C5
Bayanaūyl, *Kazakstan* . 20 D8
Bayanhongor, *Mongolia* 24 B5
Bayard, *N. Mex., U.S.A.* 57 K9
Bayard, *Nebr., U.S.A.* . 54 E3
Baybay, *Phil.* 27 B6
Bayern □, *Germany* ... 12 D6
Bayeux, *France* 14 C3
Bayfield, *U.S.A.* 54 B9
Bayındır, *Turkey* 17 E12
Baykal, Oz., *Russia* ... 21 D11
Baykan, *Turkey* 30 B4
Baykonur = Bayqongyr,
  Kazakstan 20 E7
Baymak, *Russia* 18 D10
Bayombong, *Phil.* 27 A6

Bayonne, *France* 14 E3
Bayovar, *Peru* 62 E2
Bayqongyr, *Kazakstan* 20 E7
Bayram-Ali =
  Bayramaly,
  Turkmenistan 20 F7
Bayramaly,
  Turkmenistan 20 F7
Bayramiç, *Turkey* 17 E12
Bayreuth, *Germany* ... 12 D6
Bayrūt, *Lebanon* 33 B4
Bayt Lahm, *West Bank* 33 D4
Baytown, *U.S.A.* 55 L7
Baza, *Spain* 15 D4
Bazaruto, I. do, *Mozam.* 37 J7
Bazmān, Kūh-e, *Iran* .. 31 D9
Beach, *U.S.A.* 54 B3
Beachport, *Australia* .. 43 F3
Beachy Hd., *U.K.* 9 G8
Beacon, *Australia* 41 F2
Beacon, *U.S.A.* 52 E9
Beaconsfield, *Australia* 42 G4
Beagle, Canal, *S. Amer.* 64 H3
Beagle Bay, *Australia* . 40 C3
Beals Cr. →, *U.S.A.* ... 55 J4
Bear L., *Canada* 51 B9
Bear L., *U.S.A.* 56 F8
Beardmore, *Canada* ... 48 C2
Beardmore Glacier,
  Antarctica 5 E11
Beardstown, *U.S.A.* ... 54 F9
Béarn, *France* 14 E3
Bearpaw Mts., *U.S.A.* . 56 B9
Bearskin Lake, *Canada* 48 B1
Beata, C., *Dom. Rep.* . 61 C5
Beata, I., *Dom. Rep.* .. 61 C5
Beatrice, *U.S.A.* 54 E6
Beatrice, C., *Australia* . 42 A2
Beatton →, *Canada* ... 50 B4
Beatton River, *Canada* . 50 B4
Beatty, *U.S.A.* 57 H5
Beauce, Plaine de la,
  France 14 B4
Beauceville, *Canada* .. 49 C5
Beaudesert, *Australia* . 43 D5
Beaufort, *Malaysia* ... 26 C5
Beaufort, *N.C., U.S.A.* . 53 H7
Beaufort, *S.C., U.S.A.* . 53 J5
Beaufort Sea, *Arctic* .. 4 B1
Beaufort West, *S. Africa* 37 L4
Beaulieu →, *Canada* .. 50 A6
Beaumaris, *U.K.* 8 D3
Beaumont, *Belgium* ... 11 D4
Beaumont, *U.S.A.* 55 K7
Beaune, *France* 14 C6
Beaupré, *Canada* 49 C5
Beauraing, *Belgium* ... 11 D4
Beauséjour, *Canada* .. 51 C9
Beauvais, *France* 14 B5
Beauval, *Canada* 51 B7
Beaver, *Okla., U.S.A.* . 55 G4
Beaver, *Utah, U.S.A.* .. 57 G7
Beaver →, *B.C.,
  Canada* 50 B4
Beaver →, *Ont.,
  Canada* 48 A2
Beaver →, *Sask.,
  Canada* 51 B7
Beaver →, *U.S.A.* 55 G5
Beaver City, *U.S.A.* ... 54 E5
Beaver Creek, *Canada* 46 B5
Beaver Dam, *U.S.A.* .. 54 D10
Beaver Falls, *U.S.A.* .. 52 E5
Beaver Hill L., *Canada* . 51 C10
Beaver I., *U.S.A.* 52 C3
Beaverhill L., *Canada* . 50 C6
Beaverlodge, *Canada* . 50 B5
Beaverstone →,
  Canada 48 B2
Beaverton, *U.S.A.* 56 D2
Beawar, *India* 28 F9
Beccles, *U.K.* 9 E9
Bečej, *Serbia, Yug.* ... 17 B9
Béchar, *Algeria* 34 B5
Beddouza, Ras, *Morocco* 34 B4
Bedford, *U.K.* 9 E7
Bedford, *Ind., U.S.A.* . 52 F2
Bedford, *Iowa, U.S.A.* . 54 E7
Bedford, *Va., U.S.A.* .. 52 G6
Bedford, C., *Australia* . 42 B4
Bedfordshire □, *U.K.* . 9 E7
Bedourie, *Australia* ... 42 C2
Bedum, *Neths.* 11 A6
Beenleigh, *Australia* .. 43 D5
Be'er Menuha, *Israel* . 30 D2
Be'er Sheva, *Israel* ... 33 D3
Beersheba = Be'er
  Sheva, *Israel* 33 D3
Beeston, *U.K.* 8 E6
Beeville, *U.S.A.* 55 L6
Befale, *Dem. Rep. of
  the Congo* 36 D4
Bega, *Australia* 43 F4
Behbahān, *Iran* 31 D6
Behbehān, *Iran* 31 D6
Behm Canal, *U.S.A.* .. 50 B2
Behshahr, *Iran* 31 B7
Bei Jiang →, *China* ... 25 D6
Bei'an, *China* 25 B7
Beihai, *China* 25 D5
Beijing, *China* 25 C6
Beilen, *Neths.* 11 B6
Beilpajah, *Australia* ... 43 E3

Beinn na Faoghla =
  Benbecula, *U.K.* ... 10 C3
Beira, *Mozam.* 37 H6
Beirut = Bayrūt,
  Lebanon 33 B4
Beiseker, *Canada* 50 C6
Beitbridge, *Zimbabwe* . 37 J6
Beja, *Portugal* 15 C2
Béja, *Tunisia* 35 A7
Bejaia, *Algeria* 34 A7
Béjar, *Spain* 15 B3
Bejestān, *Iran* 31 C8
Békéscsaba, *Hungary* . 13 E11
Bela, *India* 29 G13
Bela, *Pakistan* 28 F5
Bela Crkva, *Serbia, Yug.* 17 B9
Bela Vista, *Brazil* 63 H7
Bela Vista, *Mozam.* ... 37 K6
Belarus ■, *Europe* ... 13 B14
Belau = Palau ■,
  Pac. Oc. 38 A6
Belawan, *Indonesia* ... 26 D1
Belaya →, *Russia* 18 C9
Belaya Tserkov = Bila
  Tserkva, *Ukraine* .. 13 D16
Belcher Is., *Canada* ... 48 A3
Belebey, *Russia* 18 D9
Belém, *Brazil* 63 D9
Belen, *U.S.A.* 57 J10
Belet Uen, *Somali Rep.* 32 G4
Belev, *Russia* 18 D6
Belfast, *U.K.* 10 D4
Belfast, *U.S.A.* 53 C11
Belfield, *U.S.A.* 54 B3
Belfort, *France* 14 C7
Belfry, *U.S.A.* 56 D9
Belgaum, *India* 28 M9
Belgium ■, *Europe* ... 11 D4
Belgorod, *Russia* 19 D6
Belgorod-
  Dnestrovskiy =
  Bilhorod-Dnistrovskyy,
  Ukraine 19 E5
Belgrade = Beograd,
  Serbia, Yug. 17 B9
Belgrade, *U.S.A.* 56 D8
Belhaven, *U.S.A.* 53 H7
Beli Drim →, *Europe* . 17 C9
Belinyu, *Indonesia* ... 26 E3
Beliton Is. = Belitung,
  Indonesia 26 E3
Belitung, *Indonesia* ... 26 E3
Belize ■, *Cent. Amer.* . 59 D7
Belize City, *Belize* 59 D7
Belkovskiy, Ostrov,
  Russia 21 B14
Bell →, *Canada* 48 C4
Bell I., *Canada* 49 B8
Bell-Irving →, *Canada* 50 B3
Bell Peninsula, *Canada* 47 B11
Bell Ville, *Argentina* .. 64 C4
Bella Bella, *Canada* ... 50 C3
Bella Coola, *Canada* .. 50 C3
Bella Unión, *Uruguay* . 64 C5
Bella Vista, *Argentina* . 64 B5
Bellaire, *U.S.A.* 52 E5
Bellary, *India* 28 M10
Bellata, *Australia* 43 D4
Belle-Chasse, *U.S.A.* . 55 L10
Belle Fourche, *U.S.A.* 54 C3
Belle Fourche →,
  U.S.A. 54 C3
Belle Glade, *U.S.A.* ... 53 M5
Belle-Île, *France* 14 C2
Belle Isle, *Canada* 49 B8
Belle Isle, Str. of,
  Canada 49 B8
Belle Plaine, *U.S.A.* ... 54 E8
Bellefontaine, *U.S.A.* . 52 E4
Bellefonte, *U.S.A.* 52 E7
Belleoram, *Canada* ... 49 C8
Belleville, *Canada* 48 D4
Belleville, *Ill., U.S.A.* . 54 F10
Belleville, *Kans., U.S.A.* 54 F6
Bellevue, *Canada* 50 D6
Bellevue, *Idaho, U.S.A.* 56 E6
Bellevue, *Nebr., U.S.A.* 54 E7
Bellin = Kangirsuk,
  Canada 47 B13
Bellingen, *Australia* ... 43 E5
Bellingham, *U.S.A.* ... 46 D7
Bellingshausen Sea,
  Antarctica 5 C17
Bellinzona, *Switz.* 14 C8
Bello, *Colombia* 62 B3
Bellows Falls, *U.S.A.* . 52 D9
Belluno, *Italy* 16 A5
Belmonte, *Brazil* 63 G11
Belmopan, *Belize* 59 D7
Belo Horizonte, *Brazil* . 63 G10
Belo-Tsiribihina, *Madag.* 37 H8
Belogorsk, *Russia* 21 D13
Beloit, *Kans., U.S.A.* .. 54 F5
Beloit, *Wis., U.S.A.* ... 54 D10
Belokorovichi, *Ukraine* 13 C15
Belomorsk, *Russia* 18 B5
Belonia, *India* 29 H17
Beloretsk, *Russia* 18 D10
Belovo, *Russia* 20 D9
Beloye, Ozero, *Russia* 18 B6
Beloye More, *Russia* .. 18 A6
Belozersk, *Russia* 18 B6
Belpre, *U.S.A.* 52 F5

Belt, *U.S.A.* 56 C8
Beltana, *Australia* 43 E2
Belterra, *Brazil* 63 D8
Belton, *U.S.A.* 55 K6
Belton L., *U.S.A.* 55 K6
Beltsy = Bălţi, *Moldova* 13 E14
Belukha, *Russia* 20 E9
Beluran, *Malaysia* 26 C5
Belvidere, *U.S.A.* 54 D10
Belyando →, *Australia* 42 C4
Belyy, Ostrov, *Russia* . 20 B8
Belyy Yar, *Russia* 20 D9
Belzoni, *U.S.A.* 55 J9
Bemberéke, *Benin* 34 F6
Bemidji, *U.S.A.* 54 B7
Ben, *Iran* 31 C6
Ben Lomond, *N.S.W.,
  Australia* 43 E5
Ben Lomond, *Tas.,
  Australia* 42 G4
Ben Nevis, *U.K.* 10 C4
Bena, *Nigeria* 34 F7
Benalla, *Australia* 43 F4
Benares = Varanasi,
  India 29 G13
Benavente, *Spain* 15 A3
Benavides, *U.S.A.* 55 M5
Benbecula, *U.K.* 10 C3
Benbonyathe, *Australia* 43 E2
Bend, *U.S.A.* 56 D3
Bendemeer, *Australia* . 43 E5
Bender Beila,
  Somali Rep. 32 F5
Bendery = Tighina,
  Moldova 13 E15
Bendigo, *Australia* 43 F3
Benē Beraq, *Israel* ... 33 C3
Benevento, *Italy* 16 D6
Bengal, Bay of, *Ind. Oc.* 29 M17
Bengbu, *China* 25 C6
Benghazi = Banghāzī,
  Libya 35 B10
Bengkalis, *Indonesia* . 26 D2
Bengkulu, *Indonesia* .. 26 E2
Bengkulu □, *Indonesia* 26 E2
Bengough, *Canada* ... 51 D7
Benguela, *Angola* 37 G2
Beni, *Dem. Rep. of
  the Congo* 36 D5
Beni →, *Bolivia* 62 F5
Beni Mellal, *Morocco* . 34 B4
Beni Suef, *Egypt* 35 C12
Beniah L., *Canada* 50 A6
Benidorm, *Spain* 15 C5
Benin ■, *Africa* 34 G6
Benin, Bight of, *W. Afr.* 34 H6
Benin City, *Nigeria* ... 34 G7
Benjamin Constant,
  Brazil 62 D4
Benjamin Hill, *Mexico* . 58 A2
Benkelman, *U.S.A.* ... 54 E4
Bennett, *Canada* 50 B2
Bennett, L., *Australia* . 40 D5
Bennetta, Ostrov, *Russia* 21 B15
Bennettsville, *U.S.A.* . 53 H6
Bennington, *U.S.A.* ... 52 D9
Benoni, *S. Africa* 37 K5
Benque Viejo, *Belize* .. 59 D7
Benson, *Ariz., U.S.A.* . 57 L8
Benson, *Minn., U.S.A.* 54 C7
Bent, *Iran* 31 E8
Benteng, *Indonesia* ... 27 F6
Bentinck I., *Australia* .. 42 B2
Benton, *Ark., U.S.A.* .. 55 H8
Benton, *Ill., U.S.A.* ... 54 G10
Benton Harbor, *U.S.A.* 52 D2
Bentonville, *U.S.A.* ... 55 G7
Benue →, *Nigeria* 34 G7
Benxi, *China* 25 B7
Beo, *Indonesia* 27 D7
Beograd, *Serbia, Yug.* 17 B9
Beppu, *Japan* 23 H5
Beqaa Valley = Al Biqâ,
  Lebanon 33 A5
Berat, *Albania* 17 D8
Berati = Berat, *Albania* 17 D8
Berau, Teluk, *Indonesia* 27 E8
Berber, *Sudan* 35 E12
Berbera, *Somali Rep.* . 32 E4
Berbérati, *C.A.R.* 36 D3
Berbice →, *Guyana* ... 62 B7
Berdichev = Berdychiv,
  Ukraine 13 D15
Berdsk, *Russia* 20 D9
Berdyansk, *Ukraine* .. 19 E6
Berdychiv, *Ukraine* ... 13 D15
Berea, *U.S.A.* 52 G3
Berebere, *Indonesia* .. 27 D7
Bereda, *Somali Rep.* .. 32 E5
Berehove, *Ukraine* ... 13 D12
Berekum, *Ghana* 34 G5
Berens →, *Canada* ... 51 C9
Berens I., *Canada* 51 C9
Berens River, *Canada* . 51 C9
Beresford, *U.S.A.* 54 D6
Berestechko, *Ukraine* . 13 C13
Bereza = Byaroza,
  Belarus 13 B13
Berezhany, *Ukraine* ... 13 D13
Berezina =
  Byarezina →,
  Belarus 13 B16
Berezniki, *Russia* 18 B7
Berezniki, *Russia* 18 C10
Berezovo, *Russia* 20 C7

Berga, *Spain* 15 A6
Bergama, *Turkey* 17 E12
Bérgamo, *Italy* 14 D8
Bergen, *Neths.* 11 B4
Bergen, *Norway* 7 F11
Bergen op Zoom, *Neths.* 11 C4
Bergerac, *France* 14 D4
Bergisch Gladbach,
  Germany 11 D7
Berhala, Selat,
  Indonesia 26 E2
Berhampore =
  Baharampur, *India* . 29 G16
Berhampur =
  Brahmapur, *India* .. 29 K14
Bering Sea, *Pac. Oc.* . 46 C1
Bering Strait, *Pac. Oc.* 46 B3
Beringovskiy, *Russia* . 21 C18
Berja, *Spain* 15 D4
Berkeley, *U.S.A.* 56 H2
Berkner I., *Antarctica* . 5 D18
Berkshire Downs, *U.K.* 9 F6
Berlin, *Germany* 12 B7
Berlin, *Md., U.S.A.* ... 52 F8
Berlin, *N.H., U.S.A.* .. 52 C10
Berlin, *Wis., U.S.A.* ... 52 D1
Bermejo →, *Formosa,
  Argentina* 64 B5
Bermejo →, *San Juan,
  Argentina* 64 C3
Bermen, L., *Canada* .. 49 B6
Bermuda ■, *Atl. Oc.* . 2 C6
Bern, *Switz.* 14 C7
Bernalillo, *U.S.A.* 57 J10
Bernburg, *Germany* .. 12 C6
Berne = Bern, *Switz.* . 14 C7
Bernier I., *Australia* ... 41 D1
Bernina, Piz, *Switz.* ... 14 C8
Beroun, *Czech Rep.* .. 12 D8
Berri, *Australia* 43 E3
Berriane, *Algeria* 34 B6
Berrigan, *Australia* ... 43 F4
Berry, *Australia* 43 E5
Berry, *France* 14 C5
Berry Is., *Bahamas* ... 60 A4
Berryville, *U.S.A.* 55 G8
Bershad, *Ukraine* 13 D15
Berthold, *U.S.A.* 54 A4
Berthoud, *U.S.A.* 54 E2
Bertoua, *Cameroon* .. 36 D2
Berwick, *U.S.A.* 52 E7
Berwick-upon-Tweed,
  U.K. 8 B6
Berwyn Mts., *U.K.* ... 8 E4
Besalampy, *Madag.* ... 37 H8
Besançon, *France* 14 C7
Besar, *Indonesia* 26 E5
Besnard L., *Canada* ... 51 B7
Besni, *Turkey* 30 B3
Besor, N. →, *Egypt* .. 33 D3
Bessarabiya, *Moldova* 13 E15
Bessarabka =
  Basarabeasca,
  Moldova 13 E15
Bessemer, *Ala., U.S.A.* 53 J2
Bessemer, *Mich., U.S.A.* 54 B9
Beswick, *Australia* 40 B5
Bet She'an, *Israel* 33 C4
Bet Shemesh, *Israel* .. 33 D4
Betanzos, *Spain* 15 A1
Bétaré Oya, *Cameroon* 36 C2
Bethany, *U.S.A.* 54 E7
Bethel, *U.S.A.* 46 B3
Bethlehem = Bayt
  Lahm, *West Bank* .. 33 D4
Bethlehem, *S. Africa* . 37 K5
Bethlehem, *U.S.A.* ... 52 E8
Béthune, *France* 14 A5
Betoota, *Australia* 42 D3
Betroka, *Madag.* 37 J9
Betsiamites, *Canada* .. 49 C6
Betsiamites →, *Canada* 49 C6
Bettendorf, *U.S.A.* ... 54 E9
Bettiah, *India* 29 F14
Betul, *India* 28 J10
Betung, *Malaysia* 26 D4
Betws-y-Coed, *U.K.* .. 8 D4
Beulah, *Mich., U.S.A.* 52 C2
Beulah, *N. Dak., U.S.A.* 54 B4
Beveren, *Belgium* 11 C4
Beverley, *Australia* ... 41 F2
Beverley, *U.K.* 8 D7
Beverly Hills, *U.S.A.* .. 53 L4
Beverly Hills, *U.S.A.* .. 57 J4
Bexhill, *U.K.* 9 G8
Beyānlū, *Iran* 30 C5
Beyneu, *Kazakstan* ... 19 E10
Beypazarı, *Turkey* 19 F5
Beyşehir Gölü, *Turkey* 19 G5
Béziers, *France* 14 E5
Bezwada = Vijayawada,
  India 29 L12
Bhachau, *India* 28 H7
Bhadrakh, *India* 29 J15
Bhadravati, *India* 28 N9
Bhagalpur, *India* 29 G15
Bhakra Dam, *India* ... 28 D10
Bhamo, *Burma* 29 G20
Bhandara, *India* 28 J11
Bhanrer Ra., *India* 28 H11
Bharat = India ■, *Asia* 28 K11
Bharatpur, *India* 28 F10
Bhatpara, *India* 29 H16
Bhaunagar =
  Bhavnagar, *India* .. 28 J8
Bhavnagar, *India* 28 J8

Bhavnagar, *India* 28 J8
Bhilsa = Vidisha, *India* 28 H10
Bhilwara, *India* 28 G9
Bhima →, *India* 28 L10
Bhind, *India* 28 F11
Bhiwandi, *India* 28 K8
Bhiwani, *India* 28 E10
Bhola, *Bangla.* 29 H17
Bhopal, *India* 28 H10
Bhubaneshwar, *India* . 29 J14
Bhuj, *India* 28 H6
Bhusaval, *India* 28 J9
Bhutan ■, *Asia* 29 F17
Biafra, B. of = Bonny,
  Bight of, *Africa* 36 D1
Biak, *Indonesia* 27 E9
Biała Podlaska, *Poland* 13 B12
Białogard, *Poland* 12 A8
Białystok, *Poland* 13 B12
Biärjmand, *Iran* 31 B7
Biaro, *Indonesia* 27 D7
Biarritz, *France* 14 E3
Bibai, *Japan* 22 C10
Bibby I., *Canada* 51 A10
Biberach, *Germany* ... 12 D5
Bic, *Canada* 49 C6
Bicester, *U.K.* 9 F6
Bicheno, *Australia* 42 G4
Bickerton I., *Australia* . 42 A2
Bida, *Nigeria* 34 G7
Bidar, *India* 28 L10
Biddeford, *U.S.A.* 53 D10
Bideford, *U.K.* 9 F3
Bideford Bay, *U.K.* ... 9 F3
Bié, Planalto de, *Angola* 37 G3
Bieber, *U.S.A.* 56 F3
Biel, *Switz.* 14 C7
Bielefeld, *Germany* ... 12 B5
Biella, *Italy* 14 D8
Bielsk Podlaski, *Poland* 13 B12
Bielsko-Biała, *Poland* . 13 D10
Bien Hoa, *Vietnam* ... 26 B3
Bienne = Biel, *Switz.* . 14 C7
Bienville, L., *Canada* .. 48 A5
Big →, *Canada* 49 B8
Big B., *Canada* 49 A7
Big Belt Mts., *U.S.A.* . 56 C8
Big Bend National Park,
  U.S.A. 55 L3
Big Black →, *U.S.A.* . 55 K9
Big Blue →, *U.S.A.* .. 54 F6
Big Cypress National
  Preserve, *U.S.A.* .. 53 M5
Big Cypress Swamp,
  U.S.A. 53 M5
Big Falls, *U.S.A.* 54 A8
Big Fork →, *U.S.A.* .. 54 A8
Big Horn Mts. =
  Bighorn Mts., *U.S.A.* 56 D10
Big I., *Canada* 50 A5
Big Lake, *U.S.A.* 55 K4
Big Muddy Cr. →,
  U.S.A. 54 A2
Big Pine, *U.S.A.* 57 H4
Big Piney, *U.S.A.* 56 E8
Big Rapids, *U.S.A.* ... 52 D3
Big River, *Canada* 51 C7
Big Sable Pt., *U.S.A.* . 52 C2
Big Salmon →, *Canada* 50 A2
Big Sand L., *Canada* . 51 B9
Big Sandy, *U.S.A.* 56 B8
Big Sandy →, *U.S.A.* 52 F4
Big Sandy Cr. →,
  U.S.A. 54 F3
Big Sioux →, *U.S.A.* . 54 D6
Big Spring, *U.S.A.* ... 55 J4
Big Stone City, *U.S.A.* 54 C6
Big Stone Gap, *U.S.A.* 53 G4
Big Stone L., *U.S.A.* .. 54 C6
Big Timber, *U.S.A.* ... 56 D9
Big Trout L., *Canada* .. 48 B2
Big Trout Lake, *Canada* 48 B2
Biğa, *Turkey* 17 D12
Bigadiç, *Turkey* 17 E13
Biggar, *Canada* 51 C7
Bigge I., *Australia* 40 B4
Biggenden, *Australia* . 43 D5
Biggleswade, *U.K.* 9 E7
Bighorn, *U.S.A.* 56 C10
Bighorn →, *U.S.A.* .. 56 C10
Bighorn L., *U.S.A.* 56 D9
Bighorn Mts., *U.S.A.* . 56 D10
Bigstone L., *Canada* .. 51 C9
Bihać, *Bos.-H.* 12 F8
Bihar, *India* 29 G14
Bihar □, *India* 29 G15
Bihor, Munţii, *Romania* 13 E12
Bijagós, Arquipélago
  dos, *Guinea-Biss.* .. 34 F2
Bijapur, *Karnataka, India* 28 L9
Bijapur, *Mad. P., India* 29 K12
Bijār, *Iran* 30 C5
Bijeljina, *Bos.-H.* 17 B8
Bijnor, *India* 28 E11
Bikaner, *India* 28 E8
Bikfayyā, *Lebanon* ... 33 B4
Bikin, *Russia* 21 E14
Bikin →, *Russia* 22 A7
Bikini Atoll, *Marshall Is.* 38 F8
Bila Tserkva, *Ukraine* . 13 D16
Bilara, *India* 28 F8
Bilaspur, *India* 29 H13
Bilauk Taungdan,
  Thailand 26 B1
Bilbao, *Spain* 15 A4

Bilbo = Bilbao, *Spain* . 15 A4
Bildudalur, *Iceland* . . . 6 D2
Bílé Karpaty, *Europe* . . 13 D9
Bilecik, *Turkey* 19 F5
Bilhorod-Dnistrovskyy,
  Ukraine 19 E5
Bilibino, *Russia* 21 C17
Billabalong Roadhouse,
  Australia 41 E2
Billiluna, *Australia* 40 C4
Billings, *U.S.A.* 56 D9
Billiton Is. = Belitung,
  Indonesia 26 E3
Bilma, *Niger* 35 E8
Biloela, *Australia* 42 C5
Biloxi, *U.S.A.* 55 K10
Bilpa Morea Claypan,
  Australia 42 D3
Biltine, *Chad* 35 F10
Bima, *Indonesia* 27 F5
Bimini Is., *Bahamas* . . 60 A4
Bina-Etawah, *India* . . 28 G11
Bināb, *Iran* 31 B6
Binalbagan, *Phil.* 27 B6
Binalong, *Australia* . . . 43 E4
Bīnālūd, Kūh-e, *Iran* . . 31 B8
Binatang = Bintangor,
  Malaysia 26 D4
Binche, *Belgium* 11 D4
Bindura, *Zimbabwe* . . 37 H6
Bingara, *Australia* 43 D5
Bingham, *U.S.A.* 53 C11
Binghamton, *U.S.A.* . . 52 D8
Bingöl, *Turkey* 30 B4
Binh Dinh = An Nhon,
  Vietnam 26 B3
Binh Son, *Vietnam* . . . 26 A3
Binjai, *Indonesia* 26 D3
Binnaway, *Australia* . . . 43 E4
Binongko, *Indonesia* . . 27 F6
Binscarth, *Canada* 51 C8
Bintan, *Indonesia* 26 D2
Bintangor, *Malaysia* . . 26 D4
Bintulu, *Malaysia* 26 D4
Bintuni, *Indonesia* . . . 27 E8
Binzert = Bizerte,
  Tunisia 35 A7
Bioko, *Eq. Guin.* 36 D1
Bir, *India* 28 K9
Bîr Abu Muḩammad,
  Egypt 33 F3
Bi'r ad Dabbāghāt,
  Jordan 33 E4
Bi'r al Butayyihāt,
  Jordan 33 F4
Bi'r al Mārī, *Jordan* . . . 33 E4
Bi'r al Qattār, *Jordan* . . 33 F4
Bîr Atrun, *Sudan* . . . 35 E11
Bîr Beïda, *Egypt* 33 E3
Bîr el 'Abd, *Egypt* . . . 33 D2
Bîr el Biarât, *Egypt* . . . 33 F3
Bîr el Duweidar, *Egypt* 33 E1
Bîr el Garârât, *Egypt* . . 33 D2
Bîr el Heisi, *Egypt* . . . 33 F3
Bîr el Jafir, *Egypt* 33 E1
Bîr el Mâlḩi, *Egypt* . . . 33 E2
Bîr el Thamâda, *Egypt* . 33 E2
Bîr Gebeil Ḩiṣn, *Egypt* . 33 E2
Bi'r Ghadīr, *Syria* 33 A6
Bîr Ḩasana, *Egypt* 33 E2
Bîr Kaseiba, *Egypt* . . . 33 E2
Bîr Lahfân, *Egypt* 33 E2
Bîr Madkûr, *Egypt* . . . 33 E1
Bîr Mogreïn, *Mauritania* 34 C3
Bi'r Muṭribah, *Kuwait* . 30 D5
Bîr Qaṭia, *Egypt* 33 E1
Bîr Shalatein, *Egypt* . 35 D13
Birch →, *Canada* 50 B6
Birch Hills, *Canada* . . . 51 C7
Birch I., *Canada* 51 C9
Birch L., *N.W.T., Canada* 50 A5
Birch L., *Ont., Canada* . 48 B1
Birch Mts., *Canada* . . . 50 B6
Birch River, *Canada* . . . 51 C8
Birchip, *Australia* 43 F3
Bird, *Canada* 51 B10
Bird I. = Las Aves, Is.,
  W. Indies 61 C7
Birdsville, *Australia* . . . 42 D2
Birdum Cr., *Australia* . . 40 C5
Birecik, *Turkey* 30 B3
Birein, *Israel* 33 E3
Bireuen, *Indonesia* . . . 26 C1
Birjand, *Iran* 31 C8
Birkenhead, *U.K.* 8 D4
Bîrlad = Bârlad,
  Romania 13 E14
Birmingham, *U.K.* 9 E6
Birmingham, *U.S.A.* . . 53 J2
Birmitrapur, *India* . . . 29 H14
Birni Nkonni, *Niger* . . 34 F7
Birnin Kebbi, *Nigeria* . 34 F6
Birobidzhan, *Russia* . . 21 E14
Birr, *Ireland* 10 E3
Birrie →, *Australia* . . . 43 D4
Birsk, *Russia* 18 C10
Birtle, *Canada* 51 C8
Birur, *India* 28 N9
Biržai, *Lithuania* 7 H21
Bisa, *Indonesia* 27 E7
Bisbee, *U.S.A.* 57 L9
Biscay, B. of, *Atl. Oc.* . 14 D1
Biscayne B., *U.S.A.* . . . 53 N5
Biscoe Bay, *Antarctica* . 5 D13
Biscoe Is., *Antarctica* . 5 C17

Biscostasing, *Canada* . . 48 C3
Bishek, *Kyrgyzstan* . . . 20 E8
Bishop, *Calif., U.S.A.* . . 57 H4
Bishop, *Tex., U.S.A.* . . 55 M6
Bishop Auckland, *U.K.* . 8 C6
Bishop's Falls, *Canada* . 49 C8
Bishop's Stortford, *U.K.* . 9 F8
Biskra, *Algeria* 34 B7
Bismarck, *U.S.A.* 54 B4
Bismarck Arch.,
  Papua N. G. 38 B7
Bison, *U.S.A.* 54 C3
Bīsotūn, *Iran* 30 C5
Bissagos = Bijagós,
  Arquipélago dos,
  Guinea-Biss. 34 F2
Bissau, *Guinea-Biss.* . . 34 F2
Bistcho L., *Canada* . . . 50 B5
Bistriṭa, *Romania* . . . 13 E13
Bistriṭa →, *Romania* . 13 E14
Bitlis, *Turkey* 30 B4
Bitola, *Macedonia* . . . 17 D9
Bitolj = Bitola,
  Macedonia 17 D9
Bitter Creek, *U.S.A.* . . 56 F9
Bitterfontein, *S. Africa* . 37 L3
Bitterroot →, *U.S.A.* . . 56 C6
Bitterroot Range, *U.S.A.* 56 D6
Biu, *Nigeria* 35 F8
Biwa-Ko, *Japan* 23 G8
Biwabik, *U.S.A.* 54 B8
Bixby, *U.S.A.* 55 H7
Biysk, *Russia* 20 D9
Bizen, *Japan* 23 G7
Bizerte, *Tunisia* 35 A7
Bjargtangar, *Iceland* . . 6 D1
Bjelovar, *Croatia* 16 B7
Bjørnevatn, *Norway* . . 6 B23
Bjørnøya, *Arctic* 4 B8
Black →, *Ariz., U.S.A.* . 57 K8
Black →, *Ark., U.S.A.* . 55 H9
Black →, *Wis., U.S.A.* . 54 D9
Black Bay Pen., *Canada* 48 C2
Black Birch L., *Canada* . 51 B7
Black Diamond, *Canada* 50 C6
Black Duck →, *Canada* 48 A2
Black Forest =
  Schwarzwald,
  Germany 12 D5
Black Forest, *U.S.A.* . . 54 F2
Black Hills, *U.S.A.* . . . 54 D3
Black I., *Canada* 51 C9
Black L., *Canada* 51 B7
Black L., *U.S.A.* 52 C3
Black Lake, *Canada* . . . 51 B7
Black Mesa, *U.S.A.* . . . 55 G3
Black Mt. = Mynydd Du,
  U.K. 9 F4
Black Mts., *U.K.* 9 F4
Black Range, *U.S.A.* . 57 K10
Black River, *Jamaica* . . 60 C4
Black River Falls, *U.S.A.* 54 C9
Black Sea, *Eurasia* . . . 19 F6
Black Tickle, *Canada* . . 49 B8
Black Volta →, *Africa* . 34 G5
Black Warrior →,
  U.S.A. 53 J2
Blackall, *Australia* 42 C4
Blackball, *N.Z.* 39 K3
Blackbull, *Australia* . . . 42 B3
Blackburn, *U.K.* 8 D5
Blackburn with
  Darwen □, *U.K.* . . . 8 D5
Blackfoot, *U.S.A.* 56 E7
Blackfoot →, *U.S.A.* . . 56 C7
Blackfoot River
  Reservoir, *U.S.A.* . . . 56 E8
Blackie, *Canada* 50 C6
Blackpool, *U.K.* 8 D4
Blackpool □, *U.K.* 8 D4
Blacks Harbour, *Canada* 49 C6
Blacksburg, *U.S.A.* . . . 52 G5
Blackstone, *U.S.A.* . . . 52 G7
Blackstone Ra., *Australia* 41 E4
Blackwater, *Australia* . . 42 C4
Blackwater →, *Ireland* 10 E3
Blackwell, *U.S.A.* 55 G6
Blaenau Ffestiniog, *U.K.* 8 E4
Blaenau Gwent □, *U.K.* 9 F4
Blagodarnoye =
  Blagodarnyy, *Russia* 19 E7
Blagodarnyy, *Russia* . . 19 E7
Blagoevgrad, *Bulgaria* . 17 C10
Blagoveshchensk,
  Russia 21 D13
Blaine, *Minn., U.S.A.* . . 54 C8
Blaine, *Wash., U.S.A.* . 56 B2
Blaine Lake, *Canada* . . 51 C7
Blair, *U.S.A.* 54 E6
Blair Athol, *Australia* . . 42 C4
Blake Pt., *U.S.A.* . . . 54 A10
Blakely, *U.S.A.* 53 K3
Blanc, Mont, *Alps* 14 D7
Blanc-Sablon, *Canada* . 49 B8
Blanca, B., *Argentina* . 64 D4
Blanca Peak, *U.S.A.* . . 57 H11
Blanche, C., *Australia* . 43 E1
Blanche, L., *S. Austral.,*
  Australia 43 D2
Blanche, L., *W. Austral.,*
  Australia 40 D3
Blanco, *U.S.A.* 55 K5
Blanco, C., *Costa Rica* . 60 E2
Blanco, C., *U.S.A.* 56 E1
Blanda →, *Iceland* . . . 6 D3

Blandford Forum, *U.K.* . 9 G5
Blanding, *U.S.A.* 57 H9
Blanes, *Spain* 15 B7
Blankenberge, *Belgium* 11 C3
Blanquilla, I., *Venezuela* 61 D7
Blantyre, *Malawi* 37 H6
Blaydon, *U.K.* 8 C6
Blayney, *Australia* 43 E4
Blaze, Pt., *Australia* . . . 40 B5
Blekinge, *Sweden* 7 H16
Blenheim, *N.Z.* 39 J4
Bletchley, *U.K.* 9 F7
Blida, *Algeria* 34 A6
Bligh Sound, *N.Z.* 39 L1
Blind River, *Canada* . . 48 C3
Bliss, *U.S.A.* 56 E6
Blitar, *Indonesia* 27 H15
Block I., *U.S.A.* 52 E10
Blodgett Iceberg
  Tongue, *Antarctica* . . 5 C9
Bloemfontein, *S. Africa* 37 K5
Bloemhof, *S. Africa* . . 37 K5
Blois, *France* 14 C4
Blönduós, *Iceland* 6 D3
Bloodvein →, *Canada* . 51 C9
Bloomer, *U.S.A.* 54 C9
Bloomfield, *Iowa, U.S.A.* 54 E8
Bloomfield, *N. Mex.,*
  U.S.A. 57 H10
Bloomfield, *Nebr.,*
  U.S.A. 54 D6
Bloomington, *Ill., U.S.A.* 54 E10
Bloomington, *Ind.,*
  U.S.A. 52 F2
Bloomington, *Minn.,*
  U.S.A. 54 C8
Bloomsburg, *U.S.A.* . . 52 E7
Blora, *Indonesia* 27 G14
Blountstown, *U.S.A.* . . 53 K3
Blue Earth, *U.S.A.* . . . 54 D8
Blue Mesa Reservoir,
  U.S.A. 57 G10
Blue Mts., *U.S.A.* 56 D4
Blue Mud B., *Australia* . 42 A2
Blue Nile = Nîl el
  Azraq →, *Sudan* . . . 35 E12
Blue Rapids, *U.S.A.* . . 54 F6
Blue Ridge Mts., *U.S.A.* 53 G5
Blue River, *Canada* . . . 50 C5
Bluefield, *U.S.A.* 52 G5
Bluefields, *Nic.* 60 D3
Bluff, *Australia* 42 C4
Bluff, *N.Z.* 39 M2
Bluff, *U.S.A.* 57 H9
Bluff Knoll, *Australia* . . 41 F2
Bluff Pt., *Australia* . . . 41 E1
Bluffton, *U.S.A.* 52 E3
Blumenau, *Brazil* 64 B7
Blunt, *U.S.A.* 54 C5
Bly, *U.S.A.* 56 E3
Blyth, *U.K.* 8 B6
Blythe, *U.S.A.* 57 K6
Blytheville, *U.S.A.* . . . 55 H10
Bo, *S. Leone* 34 G3
Bo Hai, *China* 25 C6
Boa Vista, *Brazil* 62 C6
Boaco, *Nic.* 60 D2
Bobadah, *Australia* . . . 43 E4
Bobbili, *India* 29 K13
Bobcaygeon, *Canada* . . 48 D4
Bobo-Dioulasso,
  Burkina Faso 34 F5
Bóbr →, *Poland* 12 B8
Bobraomby, Tanjon' i,
  Madag. 37 G9
Bobruysk = Babruysk,
  Belarus 13 B15
Boby, Pic, *Madag.* . . . 37 J9
Bôca do Acre, *Brazil* . . 62 E5
Boca Raton, *U.S.A.* . . . 53 M5
Bocaranga, *C.A.R.* 32
Bocas del Toro, *Panama* 60 E3
Bochnia, *Poland* 13 D11
Bochum, *Germany* . . . 12 C4
Bocoyna, *Mexico* 58 B3
Boddam, *Russia* 21 D12
Boddington, *Australia* . 41 F2
Boden, *Sweden* 6 D19
Bodensee, *Europe* 14 C8
Bodhan, *India* 28 K10
Bodmin, *U.K.* 9 G3
Bodmin Moor, *U.K.* . . . 9 G3
Bodø, *Norway* 6 C16
Bodrog →, *Hungary* . . 13 D11
Bodrum, *Turkey* 17 F12
Boende, Dem. Rep. of
  the Congo 36 E4
Boerne, *U.S.A.* 55 L5
Bogalusa, *U.S.A.* 55 K10
Bogan →, *Australia* . . . 43 D4
Bogan Gate, *Australia* . 43 E4
Bogantungan, *Australia* 42 C4
Bogata, *U.S.A.* 55 J7
Boggabilla, *Australia* . . 43 D5
Boggabri, *Australia* . . . 43 E5
Boglan = Solhan,
  Turkey 30 B4
Bognor Regis, *U.K.* . . . 9 G7
Bogo, *Phil.* 27 B6
Bogong, Mt., *Australia* . 43 F4
Bogor, *Indonesia* . . . 27 G12
Bogotá, *Colombia* 62 C4
Bogotol, *Russia* 20 D9
Bogra, *Bangla.* 29 G16

Boguchany, *Russia* . . . 21 D10
Bohemian Forest =
  Böhmerwald,
  Germany 12 D7
Böhmerwald, *Germany* 12 D7
Bohol □, *Phil.* 27 C6
Bohol Sea, *Phil.* 27 C6
Bohuslän, *Sweden* . . . 7 G14
Boiaçu, *Brazil* 62 D6
Boileau, C., *Australia* . . 40 C3
Boise, *U.S.A.* 56 E5
Boise City, *U.S.A.* 55 G3
Boissevain, *Canada* . . . 51 D8
Bojador C., *W. Sahara* . 34 C3
Bojana →, *Albania* . . . 17 D8
Bojnūrd, *Iran* 31 B8
Bojonegoro, *Indonesia* 27 G14
Bokhara →, *Australia* . 43 D4
Boknafjorden, *Norway* . 7 G11
Bokoro, *Chad* 35 F9
Bokpyin, *Burma* 26 B1
Bolan Pass, *Pakistan* . . 28 E5
Bolaños →, *Mexico* . . . 58 C4
Bolbec, *France* 14 B4
Boldājī, *Iran* 31 D6
Bole, *China* 24 B3
Bolekhiv, *Ukraine* . . . 13 D12
Bolesławiec, *Poland* . . 12 C8
Bolgrad = Bolhrad,
  Ukraine 13 F15
Bolhrad, *Ukraine* 13 F15
Bolivar, *Mo., U.S.A.* . . 55 G8
Bolivar, *Tenn., U.S.A.* . 55 H10
Bolivia ■, *S. Amer.* . . . 62 G6
Bollnäs, *Sweden* 7 F17
Bollon, *Australia* 43 D4
Bolmen, *Sweden* 7 H15
Bolobo, Dem. Rep. of
  the Congo 36 E3
Bologna, *Italy* 16 B4
Bologoye, *Russia* 18 C5
Bolonchenticul, *Mexico* 59 D7
Bolsena, L. di, *Italy* . . . 16 C4
Bolshevik, Ostrov,
  Russia 21 B11
Bolshoi Kavkas =
  Caucasus Mountains,
  Eurasia 19 F7
Bolshoy Anyuy →,
  Russia 21 C17
Bolshoy Begichev,
  Ostrov, *Russia* 21 B12
Bolshoy Lyakhovskiy,
  Ostrov, *Russia* 21 B15
Bolshoy Tyuters, Ostrov,
  Russia 7 G22
Bolsward, *Neths.* 11 A5
Bolt Head, *U.K.* 9 G4
Bolton, *U.K.* 8 D5
Bolu, *Turkey* 19 F5
Bolungavík, *Iceland* . . 6 C2
Bolvadin, *Turkey* 19 G5
Bolzano, *Italy* 16 A4
Bom Jesus da Lapa,
  Brazil 63 F10
Boma, Dem. Rep. of
  the Congo 36 F2
Bombala, *Australia* . . . 43 F4
Bombay = Mumbai,
  India 28 K8
Bomboma, Dem. Rep. of
  the Congo 36 D3
Bømlo, *Norway* 7 G11
Bomu →, *C.A.R.* 36 D4
Bonaire, *Neth. Ant.* . . 62 A5
Bonang, *Australia* 43 F4
Bonanza, *Nic.* 60 D3
Bonaparte Arch.,
  Australia 40 B3
Bonaventure, *Canada* . 49 C6
Bonavista, *Canada* . . . 49 C9
Bonavista, C., *Canada* . 49 C9
Bonavista B., *Canada* . 49 C9
Bondo, Dem. Rep. of
  the Congo 36 D4
Bondoukou, *Ivory C.* . . 34 G5
Bondowoso, *Indonesia* 27 G15
Bone, Teluk, *Indonesia* 27 E6
Bonerate, *Indonesia* . . 27 F6
Bonerate, Kepulauan,
  Indonesia 27 F6
Bong Son = Hoai Nhon,
  Vietnam 26 B3
Bongor, *Chad* 35 F9
Bonham, *U.S.A.* 55 J6
Bonifacio, *France* 14 F8
Bonifacio, Bouches de,
  Medit. S. 16 D3
Bonin Is. = Ogasawara
  Gunto, *Pac. Oc.* 44 E6
Bonn, *Germany* 12 C4
Bonners Ferry, *U.S.A.* . 56 B5
Bonney, L., *Australia* . . 43 F3
Bonnie Rock, *Australia* 41 F2
Bonny, Bight of, *Africa* 36 D1
Bonnyville, *Canada* . . . 51 C6
Bonoi, *Indonesia* 27 E9
Bontang, *Indonesia* . . 26 D5
Bonthe, S. *Leone* 34 G3
Bontoc, *Phil.* 27 A6
Bonython Ra., *Australia* 40 D4
Bookabie, *Australia* . . . 41 F5
Booker, *U.S.A.* 55 G4
Booligal, *Australia* 43 E3

Boonah, *Australia* 43 D5
Boone, *Iowa, U.S.A.* . . 54 D8
Boone, *N.C., U.S.A.* . . 53 G5
Booneville, *Ark., U.S.A.* 55 H8
Booneville, *Miss., U.S.A.* 53 H1
Boonville, *Ind., U.S.A.* . 52 F2
Boonville, *Mo., U.S.A.* . 54 F8
Boonville, *N.Y., U.S.A.* . 52 D8
Boorindal, *Australia* . . . 43 E4
Boorowa, *Australia* . . . 43 E4
Boothia, Gulf of, *Canada* 47 A11
Boothia Pen., *Canada* . 46 A10
Bootle, *U.K.* 8 D4
Booué, *Gabon* 36 E2
Boquete, *Panama* 60 E3
Boquilla, Presa de la,
  Mexico 58 B3
Boquillas del Carmen,
  Mexico 58 B4
Bor, *Serbia, Yug.* 17 B10
Bôr, *Sudan* 35 G12
Bor Mashash, *Israel* . . 33 D3
Bora, *China* 62 D7
Borah Peak, *U.S.A.* . . . 56 D7
Borås, *Sweden* 7 H15
Borāzjān, *Iran* 31 D6
Borba, *Brazil* 62 D7
Bord Khūn-e Now, *Iran* 31 D6
Borda, C., *Australia* . . . 43 F2
Bordeaux, *France* 14 D3
Borden, *Australia* 41 F2
Borden, *Canada* 49 C7
Borden I., *Canada* 4 B2
Borden Pen., *Canada* . 47 A11
Bordertown, *Australia* . 43 F3
Borðeyri, *Iceland* 6 D3
Bordj Fly Ste. Marie,
  Algeria 34 C5
Bordj-in-Eker, *Algeria* . 34 D7
Bordj Omar Driss,
  Algeria 34 C7
Borgå = Porvoo,
  Finland 7 F21
Borgarfjörður, *Iceland* . 6 D7
Borgarnes, *Iceland* . . . 6 D3
Børgefjellet, *Norway* . . 6 D15
Borger, *Neths.* 11 B6
Borger, *U.S.A.* 55 H4
Borgholm, *Sweden* . . . 7 H17
Borhoyn Tal, *Mongolia* 25 B6
Borisoglebsk, *Russia* . . 19 D7
Borisov = Barysaw,
  Belarus 13 A15
Borja, *Peru* 62 D3
Borkou, *Chad* 35 E9
Borkum, *Germany* . . . 12 B4
Borlänge, *Sweden* 7 F16
Borley, C., *Antarctica* . 5 C5
Borneo, E. *Indies* 26 D5
Bornholm, *Denmark* . . 7 J16
Borogontsy, *Russia* . . 21 C14
Borongan, *Phil.* 27 B7
Borovichi, *Russia* 18 C5
Borroloola, *Australia* . . 42 B2
Borşa, *Romania* 13 E13
Borth, *U.K.* 9 E3
Borūjerd, *Iran* 31 C6
Boryslav, *Ukraine* . . . 13 D12
Borzya, *Russia* 21 D12
Bosa, *Italy* 16 D3
Bosanska Gradiška,
  Bos.-H. 16 B7
Bosaso, *Somali Rep* . . 32 F4
Boscastle, *U.K.* 9 G3
Boshrūyeh, *Iran* 31 C8
Bosna →, *Bos.-H.* 17 B8
Bosna i Hercegovina =
  Bosnia-
  Herzegovina ■,
  Europe 16 B7
Bosnia-Herzegovina ■,
  Europe 16 B7
Bosnik, *Indonesia* 27 E9
Bosobolo, Dem. Rep. of
  the Congo 36 D3
Bosporus = İstanbul
  Boğazı, *Turkey* 17 D13
Bosque Farms, *U.S.A.* . 57 J10
Bossangoa, *C.A.R.* . . . 36 C3
Bossier City, *U.S.A.* . . 55 J8
Bosso, *Niger* 35 F8
Bostān, *Iran* 31 D6
Bosten Hu, *China* 24 B3
Boston, *U.K.* 8 E7
Boston, *U.S.A.* 52 D10
Boston Bar, *Canada* . . 50 D4
Boston Mts., *U.S.A.* . . 55 H8
Boswell, *Canada* 50 D5
Botany B., *Australia* . . . 43 E5
Bothaville, *S. Africa* . . 38 E5
Bothnia, G. of, *Europe* . 6 E19
Bothwell, *Australia* . . . 42 G4
Botletle →, *Botswana* . 37 J4
Botoşani, *Romania* . . . 13 E14
Botou, *Burkina Faso* . . 34 F6
Botswana ■, *Africa* . . 37 J4
Bottineau, *U.S.A.* 54 A4
Bottrop, *Germany* . . . 11 C6
Botucatu, *Brazil* 63 H9
Botwood, *Canada* 49 C8
Bou Djébéha, *Mali* . . . 34 E5
Bouafle, *Ivory C.* 34 G4
Bouar, *C.A.R.* 36 C3
Bouârfa, *Morocco* 34 B5
Bouca, *C.A.R.* 32
Boucaut B., *Australia* . 42 A1

Bougainville, C.,
  Australia 40 B4
Bougainville I.,
  Papua N. G. 38 B8
Bougainville Reef,
  Australia 42 B4
Bougie = Bejaia, *Algeria* 34 A7
Bougouni, *Mali* 34 F4
Bouillon, *Belgium* 11 E5
Boulder, *Colo., U.S.A.* . 54 E2
Boulder, *Mont., U.S.A.* . 56 C7
Boulder City, *U.S.A.* . . 57 J6
Boulder Dam = Hoover
  Dam, *U.S.A.* 57 J6
Boulia, *Australia* 42 C2
Boulogne-sur-Mer,
  France 14 A4
Boultoum, *Niger* 35 F8
Bouna, *Ivory C.* 34 G5
Boundiali, *Ivory C.* . . . 34 G4
Bountiful, *U.S.A.* 56 F8
Bounty Is., *Pac. Oc.* . . 44 M9
Bourbonnais, *France* . . 14 C5
Bourdel L., *Canada* . . . 48 A5
Bourem, *Mali* 34 E5
Bourg-en-Bresse, *France* 14 C6
Bourg-St-Maurice,
  France 14 D7
Bourges, *France* 14 C5
Bourgogne, *France* . . . 14 C6
Bourke, *Australia* 43 E4
Bourne, *U.K.* 8 E7
Bournemouth, *U.K.* . . . 9 G6
Bournemouth □, *U.K.* . 9 G6
Bouvet I. = Bouvetøya,
  Antarctica 3 G10
Bouvetøya, *Antarctica* . 3 G10
Bovill, *U.S.A.* 56 C5
Bow →, *Canada* 50 C6
Bow Island, *Canada* . . 50 D6
Bowbells, *U.S.A.* 54 A3
Bowdle, *U.S.A.* 54 C5
Bowelling, *Australia* . . 41 F2
Bowen, *Australia* 42 C4
Bowen Mts., *Australia* . 43 F4
Bowie, *Ariz., U.S.A.* . . 57 K9
Bowie, *Tex., U.S.A.* . . 55 J6
Bowkān, *Iran* 30 B5
Bowland, Forest of, *U.K.* 8 D5
Bowling Green, *Ky.,*
  U.S.A. 52 G2
Bowling Green, *Ohio,*
  U.S.A. 52 E4
Bowling Green, C.,
  Australia 42 B4
Bowman, *U.S.A.* 54 B3
Bowman I., *Antarctica* . 5 C8
Bowral, *Australia* 43 E5
Bowraville, *Australia* . . 43 E5
Bowron →, *Canada* . . . 50 C4
Bowron Lake Prov. Park,
  Canada 50 C4
Bowser L., *Canada* . . . 50 B3
Bowsman, *Canada* . . . 51 C8
Box Cr. →, *Australia* . . 43 E3
Boxmeer, *Neths.* 11 C5
Boxtel, *Neths.* 11 C5
Boyce, *U.S.A.* 55 K8
Boyd L., *Canada* 48 B4
Boyle, *Canada* 50 C6
Boyne →, *Ireland* 10 C5
Boyne City, *U.S.A.* . . . 52 C3
Boynton Beach, *U.S.A.* 53 M6
Boyolali, *Indonesia* . . 27 G14
Boysen Reservoir,
  U.S.A. 56 E9
Boyuibe, *Bolivia* 62 G6
Boyup Brook, *Australia* 41 F2
Boz Dağları, *Turkey* . . 17 E13
Bozburun, *Turkey* 17 F13
Bozcaada, *Turkey* . . . 17 E12
Bozdoğan, *Turkey* . . . 17 F13
Bozeman, *U.S.A.* 56 D8
Bozen = Bolzano, *Italy* . 16 A4
Bozoum, *C.A.R.* 36 C3
Bra, *Italy* 14 D7
Brabant □, *Belgium* . . 11 D4
Brabant L., *Canada* . . . 51 B8
Brač, *Croatia* 16 C7
Bracciano, L. di, *Italy* . 16 C5
Bracebridge, *Canada* . 48 C4
Brach, *Libya* 35 C8
Bräcke, *Sweden* 7 E16
Brackettville, *U.S.A.* . . 55 L4
Bracknell, *U.K.* 9 F7
Bracknell Forest □, *U.K.* 9 F7
Brad, *Romania* 13 E12
Bradenton, *U.S.A.* . . . 53 M4
Bradford, *U.K.* 8 D6
Bradford, *U.S.A.* 52 E6
Bradley, *U.S.A.* 55 J8
Brady, *U.S.A.* 55 K5
Braga, *Portugal* 15 B1
Bragança, *Brazil* 63 D9
Bragança, *Portugal* . . . 15 B2
Brahmanbaria, *Bangla.* 29 H17
Brahmani →, *India* . . . 29 J15
Brahmapur, *India* . . . 29 K14
Brahmaputra →, *India* 29 H16
Braich-y-pwll, *U.K.* . . . 8 E3
Braidwood, *Australia* . . 43 F4
Brăila, *Romania* 13 F14
Brainerd, *U.S.A.* 54 B7
Braintree, *U.K.* 9 F8
Brampton, *Canada* . . . 48 D4

Brampton, U.K. 8 C5
Branco →, Brazil 62 D6
Brandenburg = Neubrandenburg, Germany 12 B7
Brandenburg, Germany 12 B7
Brandenburg □, Germany 12 B6
Brandon, Canada 51 D9
Braniewo, Poland 13 A10
Bransfield Str., Antarctica 5 C18
Branson, U.S.A. 55 G8
Brantford, Canada 48 D3
Bras d'Or L., Canada .. 49 C7
Brasiléia, Brazil 62 F5
Brasília, Brazil 63 G9
Brasília Legal, Brazil .. 63 D7
Braslaw, Belarus 7 J22
Brașov, Romania 13 F13
Brasschaat, Belgium .. 11 C4
Brassey, Banjaran, Malaysia 26 D5
Brassey Ra., Australia . 41 E3
Brasstown Bald, U.S.A. 53 H4
Brastad, Sweden 7 G14
Bratislava, Slovak Rep. 13 D9
Bratsk, Russia 21 D11
Brattleboro, U.S.A. ... 52 D9
Braunau, Austria 12 D7
Braunschweig, Germany 12 B6
Braunton, U.K. 9 F3
Bravo del Norte, Rio → = Grande, Rio →, U.S.A. 55 N6
Brawley, U.S.A. 57 K6
Bray, Ireland 10 E3
Bray, Mt., Australia ... 42 A1
Bray, Pays de, France . 14 B4
Brazeau →, Canada .. 50 C5
Brazil, U.S.A. 52 F2
Brazil ■, S. Amer. 63 F9
Brazos →, U.S.A. 55 L7
Brazzaville, Congo 36 E3
Brčko, Bos.-H. 17 B8
Breaden, L., Australia . 41 E4
Breaksea Sd., N.Z. ... 39 L1
Bream B., N.Z. 39 F5
Bream Hd., N.Z. 39 F5
Brebes, Indonesia 27 G13
Brecht, Belgium 11 C4
Breckenridge, Colo., U.S.A. 56 G10
Breckenridge, Minn., U.S.A. 54 B6
Breckenridge, Tex., U.S.A. 55 J5
Breckland, U.K. 9 E8
Brecon, U.K. 9 F4
Brecon Beacons, U.K. . 9 F4
Breda, Neths. 11 C4
Bredasdorp, S. Africa . 37 L4
Bree, Belgium 11 C5
Bregenz, Austria 12 E5
Breiðafjörður, Iceland . 6 D2
Brejo, Brazil 63 D10
Bremen, Germany 12 B5
Bremer Bay, Australia . 41 F2
Bremer I., Australia ... 42 A2
Bremerhaven, Germany 12 B5
Bremerton, U.S.A. 56 C2
Brenham, U.S.A. 55 K6
Brennerpass, Austria .. 12 E6
Brent, U.S.A. 53 J2
Brentwood, U.K. 9 F8
Bréscia, Italy 14 D9
Breskens, Neths. 11 C3
Breslau = Wrocław, Poland 13 C9
Bressanone, Italy 16 A4
Brest, Belarus 13 B12
Brest, France 14 B1
Brest-Litovsk = Brest, Belarus 13 B12
Bretagne, France 14 B2
Breton, Canada 50 C6
Breton Sd., U.S.A. ... 55 L10
Brett, C., N.Z. 39 F5
Brevard, U.S.A. 53 H4
Breves, Brazil 63 D8
Brewarrina, Australia . 43 E4
Brewer, U.S.A. 53 C11
Brewster, U.S.A. 56 B4
Brewster, Kap = Kangikajik, Greenland 4 B6
Brewton, U.S.A. 53 K2
Brezhnev = Naberezhnyye Chelny, Russia 18 C9
Bria, C.A.R. 32
Briançon, France 14 D7
Bribie I., Australia ... 43 D5
Bribri, Costa Rica 60 E3
Bridgend, U.K. 9 F4
Bridgend □, U.K. 9 F4
Bridgeport, Calif., U.S.A. 57 G4
Bridgeport, Conn., U.S.A. 52 E9
Bridgeport, Nebr., U.S.A. 54 E3
Bridgeport, Tex., U.S.A. 55 J6
Bridger, U.S.A. 56 D9
Bridgeton, U.S.A. 52 F8
Bridgetown, Australia . 41 F2
Bridgetown, Barbados . 61 D8

Bridgetown, Canada .. 49 D6
Bridgewater, Canada .. 49 D7
Bridgewater, C., Australia 43 F3
Bridgewater-Gagebrook, Australia 42 G4
Bridgnorth, U.K. 9 E5
Bridgwater, U.K. 9 F5
Bridgwater B., U.K. ... 9 F4
Bridlington, U.K. 8 C7
Bridlington B., U.K. ... 8 C7
Bridport, Australia ... 42 G4
Bridport, U.K. 9 G5
Brig, Switz. 14 C7
Brigg, U.K. 8 D7
Brigham City, U.S.A. .. 56 F7
Bright, Australia 43 F4
Brighton, Australia ... 43 F2
Brighton, U.K. 9 G7
Brighton, U.S.A. 54 F2
Brindisi, Italy 17 D7
Brinkley, U.S.A. 55 H9
Brion, I., Canada 49 C7
Brisbane, Australia ... 43 D5
Brisbane →, Australia 43 D5
Bristol, U.K. 9 F5
Bristol, Conn., U.S.A. . 52 E9
Bristol, Tenn., U.S.A. . 53 G4
Bristol, City of □, U.K. . 9 F5
Bristol B., U.S.A. 46 C4
Bristol Channel, U.K. . 9 F3
Bristol I., Antarctica .. 5 B1
Bristol L., U.S.A. 57 J5
Bristow, U.S.A. 55 H6
Britain = Great Britain, Europe 10 D5
Britain = Great Britain, Europe 10 D5
British Columbia □, Canada 50 C3
British Indian Ocean Terr. = Chagos Arch., Ind. Oc. 3 E13
British Indian Ocean Terr. = Chagos Arch., Ind. Oc. 3 E13
British Isles, Europe .. 10 D5
British Isles, Europe .. 10 D5
Britt, Canada 48 C3
Brittany = Bretagne, France 14 B2
Britton, U.S.A. 54 C6
Brive-la-Gaillarde, France 14 D4
Brixen = Bressanone, Italy 16 A4
Brixham, U.K. 9 G4
Brno, Czech Rep. 13 D9
Broad →, U.S.A. 53 J5
Broad Arrow, Australia 41 F3
Broad Sd., Australia .. 42 C4
Broadback →, Canada 48 B4
Broadford, Australia .. 43 F4
Broadhurst Ra., Australia 40 D3
Broads, The, U.K. 8 E9
Broadus, U.S.A. 54 C2
Brochet, Canada 51 B8
Brochet, L., Canada .. 51 B8
Brocken, Germany ... 12 C6
Brockport, U.S.A. 52 D7
Brockton, U.S.A. 52 D10
Brockville, Canada ... 48 D4
Brockway, U.S.A. 54 B2
Brodeur Pen., Canada . 47 A11
Brodnica, Poland 13 B10
Brody, Ukraine 13 C13
Brogan, U.S.A. 56 D5
Broken Arrow, U.S.A. . 55 G7
Broken Bow, Nebr., U.S.A. 54 E5
Broken Bow, Okla., U.S.A. 55 H7
Broken Bow Lake, U.S.A. 55 H7
Broken Hill = Kabwe, Zambia 37 G5
Broken Hill, Australia . 43 E3
Bromley □, U.K. 9 F8
Bromsgrove, U.K. ... 9 E5
Brønderslev, Denmark . 7 H13
Brønnøysund, Norway . 6 D15
Brookhaven, U.S.A. ... 55 K9
Brookings, Oreg., U.S.A. 56 E1
Brookings, S. Dak., U.S.A. 54 C6
Brooklyn Park, U.S.A. . 54 C8
Brooks, Canada 50 C6
Brooks Range, U.S.A. . 46 B5
Brooksville, U.S.A. ... 53 L4
Brookton, Australia .. 41 F2
Brookville, U.S.A. 52 E6
Broome, Australia 40 C3
Brothers, U.S.A. 56 E3
Brough, U.K. 8 C5
Broughton Island = Qikiqtarjuaq, Canada 47 B13
Brown, L., Australia .. 41 F2
Brown, Pt., Australia .. 43 E1
Brown Willy, U.K. 9 G3
Brownfield, U.S.A. ... 55 J3
Browning, U.S.A. 56 B7
Brownsville, Oreg., U.S.A. 56 D2

Brownsville, Tenn., U.S.A. 55 H10
Brownsville, Tex., U.S.A. 55 N6
Brownwood, U.S.A. .. 55 K5
Browse I., Australia .. 40 B3
Bruay-la-Buissière, France 14 A5
Bruce, Mt., Australia .. 40 D2
Bruce Rock, Australia . 41 F2
Bruck an der Leitha, Austria 13 D9
Bruck an der Mur, Austria 12 E8
Brue →, U.K. 9 F5
Bruges = Brugge, Belgium 11 C3
Brugge, Belgium 11 C3
Brûlé, Canada 50 C5
Brumado, Brazil 63 F10
Brumunddal, Norway . 7 F14
Bruneau, U.S.A. 56 E6
Bruneau →, U.S.A. .. 56 E6
Brunei = Bandar Seri Begawan, Brunei .. 26 C4
Brunei ■, Asia 26 D4
Brunner, L., N.Z. 39 K3
Brunssum, Neths. ... 11 D5
Brunswick = Braunschweig, Germany 12 B6
Brunswick, Ga., U.S.A. 53 K5
Brunswick, Maine, U.S.A. 53 D11
Brunswick, Md., U.S.A. 52 F7
Brunswick, Mo., U.S.A. 54 F8
Brunswick, Pen. de, Chile 64 G2
Brunswick B., Australia 40 C3
Brunswick Junction, Australia 41 F2
Bruny I., Australia ... 42 G4
Brus Laguna, Honduras 60 C3
Brush, U.S.A. 54 E3
Brussel, Belgium 11 D4
Brussels = Brussel, Belgium 11 D4
Bruthen, Australia ... 43 F4
Bruxelles = Brussel, Belgium 11 D4
Bryan, Ohio, U.S.A. .. 52 E3
Bryan, Tex., U.S.A. ... 55 K6
Bryan, Mt., Australia . 43 E2
Bryansk, Russia 18 D4
Bryce Canyon National Park, U.S.A. 57 H7
Bryne, Norway 7 G11
Bryson City, U.S.A. ... 53 H4
Bsharri, Lebanon 33 A5
Bū Baqarah, U.A.E. .. 31 E8
Bu Craa, W. Sahara .. 34 C3
Bū Ḥasā, U.A.E. 31 F7
Buapinang, Indonesia . 27 E6
Būbiyān, Kuwait 31 D6
Bucaramanga, Colombia 62 B4
Bucasia, Australia 42 C4
Buccaneer Arch., Australia 40 C3
Buchach, Ukraine 13 D13
Buchan, Canada 51 C8
Buchanan, Canada ... 51 C8
Buchanan, Liberia ... 34 G3
Buchanan, L., Queens., Australia 42 C4
Buchanan, L., W. Austral., Australia 41 E3
Buchanan, L., U.S.A. . 55 K5
Buchanan Cr. →, Australia 42 B2
Buchans, Canada 49 C8
Bucharest = Bucureşti, Romania 13 F14
Buckeye, U.S.A. 57 K7
Buckhannon, U.S.A. .. 52 F5
Buckie, U.K. 10 C5
Buckingham, Canada . 48 C4
Buckingham, U.K. ... 9 F7
Buckingham B., Australia 42 A2
Buckinghamshire □, U.K. 9 F7
Buckle Hd., Australia . 40 B4
Buckleboo, Australia . 43 E2
Buckley, U.K. 8 D4
Buckley →, Australia 42 C2
Bucklin, U.S.A. 55 G5
Buctouche, Canada .. 49 C7
Bucureşti, Romania .. 13 F14
Bucyrus, U.S.A. 52 E4
Budalin, Burma 29 H19
Budapest, Hungary .. 13 E10
Budd Coast, Antarctica 5 C8
Bude, U.K. 9 G3
Budennovsk, Russia .. 19 F7
Budgewoi, Australia .. 43 E5
Budjala, Dem. Rep. of the Congo 36 D3
Buena Vista, Colo., U.S.A. 57 G10
Buena Vista, Va., U.S.A. 52 G6
Buena Vista Lake Bed, U.S.A. 57 J4
Buenaventura, Colombia 62 C3
Buenaventura, Mexico 58 B3
Buenos Aires, Argentina 64 C5
Buenos Aires, Costa Rica 60 E3

Buenos Aires, L., Chile 64 F2
Buffalo, Mo., U.S.A. .. 55 G8
Buffalo, N.Y., U.S.A. .. 52 D6
Buffalo, Okla., U.S.A. . 55 G5
Buffalo, S. Dak., U.S.A. 54 C3
Buffalo, Wyo., U.S.A. . 56 D10
Buffalo →, Canada .. 50 A5
Buffalo Head Hills, Canada 50 B5
Buffalo L., Alta., Canada 50 C6
Buffalo L., N.W.T., Canada 50 A5
Buffalo Narrows, Canada 51 B7
Buford, U.S.A. 53 H4
Bug = Buh →, Ukraine 19 E5
Bug →, Poland 13 B11
Buga, Colombia 62 C3
Bugel, Tanjung, Indonesia 27 G14
Bugsuk, Phil. 26 C5
Bugulma, Russia 18 D9
Bugun Shara, Mongolia 24 B5
Buguruslan, Russia ... 18 D9
Buh →, Ukraine 19 E5
Buhl, U.S.A. 56 E6
Builth Wells, U.K. 9 E4
Buir Nur, Mongolia ... 25 B6
Bujumbura, Burundi .. 36 E5
Bukachacha, Russia .. 21 D12
Bukavu, Dem. Rep. of the Congo 36 E5
Bukhara = Bukhoro, Uzbekistan 20 F7
Bukhoro, Uzbekistan . 20 F7
Bukittinggi, Indonesia . 26 E2
Bukoba, Tanzania 36 E6
Bül, Kuh-e, Iran 31 D7
Bula, Indonesia 27 E8
Bulan, Phil. 27 B6
Bulandshahr, India ... 28 E10
Bulawayo, Zimbabwe . 37 J5
Buldan, Turkey 17 E13
Buldar = Valsad, India 28 J8
Bulgan, Mongolia 24 B5
Bulgaria ■, Europe .. 17 C11
Bulgar, Russia 18 D8
Buli, Teluk, Indonesia . 27 D7
Buliluyan, C., Phil. ... 26 C5
Bulkley →, Canada .. 50 B3
Bull Shoals L., U.S.A. . 55 G8
Bullhead City, U.S.A. . 57 J6
Büllingen, Belgium ... 11 D6
Bullock Creek, Australia 42 B3
Bulloo →, Australia . 43 D3
Bulloo L., Australia ... 43 D3
Bulls, N.Z. 39 J5
Bulsar = Valsad, India 28 J8
Bulukumba, Indonesia 27 F6
Bulun, Russia 21 B13
Bumba, Dem. Rep. of the Congo 36 D4
Bumhpa Bum, Burma . 29 F20
Bunbury, Australia ... 41 F2
Buncrana, Ireland ... 10 D3
Bundaberg, Australia . 43 C5
Bundey →, Australia 42 C2
Bundi, India 28 G9
Bundoran, Ireland ... 10 D2
Bungatakada, Japan .. 23 H5
Bungay, U.K. 9 E9
Bungil Cr. →, Australia 43 D4
Bungo-Suidō, Japan .. 23 H6
Bunia, Dem. Rep. of the Congo 36 D6
Bunji, Pakistan 28 B9
Bunkie, U.S.A. 55 K8
Bunnell, U.S.A. 53 L5
Buntok, Indonesia ... 26 E4
Bunyu, Indonesia 26 D5
Buol, Indonesia 27 D6
Buon Ma Thuot, Vietnam 26 B3
Buorkhaya, Mys, Russia 21 B14
Buqayq, Si. Arabia ... 31 E6
Bur Acaba, Somali Rep. 32 G3
Bur Safaga, Egypt ... 30 E2
Bûr Sa'îd, Egypt 35 B12
Bûr Sûdân, Sudan ... 35 E13
Burakin, Australia ... 41 F2
Burao, Somali Rep. .. 32 F4
Buraq, Syria 33 B5
Buraydah, Si. Arabia . 30 E4
Burbank, U.S.A. 57 J4
Burdekin →, Australia 42 B4
Burdur, Turkey 19 G5
Burdwan = Barddhaman, India . 29 H15
Bure, Ethiopia 32 E2
Bure →, U.K. 8 E9
Bureya →, Russia ... 21 E13
Burgas, Bulgaria 17 C12
Burgeo, Canada 49 C8
Burges, Mt., Australia . 41 F3
Burgos, Spain 15 A4
Burgsvik, Sweden ... 7 H18
Burgundy = Bourgogne, France 14 C6
Burhaniye, Turkey ... 17 E12
Burhanpur, India 28 J10
Burias I., Phil. 27 B6
Burica, Pta., Costa Rica 60 E3
Burin, Canada 49 C8
Buriram, Thailand ... 26 A2
Burj Sāfiṭā, Syria 30 C3
Burkburnett, U.S.A. .. 55 H5

Burke →, Australia .. 42 C2
Burke Chan., Canada . 50 C3
Burketown, Australia . 42 B2
Burkina Faso ■, Africa 34 F5
Burk's Falls, Canada .. 48 C4
Burley, U.S.A. 56 E7
Burlington, Canada ... 48 D4
Burlington, Colo., U.S.A. 54 F3
Burlington, Iowa, U.S.A. 54 E9
Burlington, Kans., U.S.A. 54 F7
Burlington, N.C., U.S.A. 53 G6
Burlington, Vt., U.S.A. 52 C9
Burlington, Wash., U.S.A. 56 B2
Burlington, Wis., U.S.A. 52 D1
Burlyu-Tyube, Kazakstan 20 E8
Burma ■, Asia 29 J20
Burnaby I., Canada ... 50 C2
Burnet, U.S.A. 55 K5
Burney, U.S.A. 56 F3
Burnham-on-Sea, U.K. 9 F5
Burnie, Australia 42 G4
Burnley, U.K. 8 D5
Burns, U.S.A. 56 E4
Burns Lake, Canada .. 50 C3
Burnside →, Canada 46 B9
Burnside, L., Australia 41 E3
Burnsville, U.S.A. 54 C8
Burnt L., Canada 49 B7
Burntwood →, Canada 51 B9
Burntwood L., Canada 51 B8
Burqan, Kuwait 30 D5
Burra, Australia 43 E2
Burren Junction, Australia 43 E4
Burriijuck Res., Australia 43 F4
Burro, Serranías del, Mexico 58 B4
Burruyacú, Argentina . 64 B4
Burry Port, U.K. 9 F3
Bursa, Turkey 17 D13
Burstall, Canada 51 C7
Burton, U.S.A. 53 J5
Burton, L., Canada ... 48 B4
Burton upon Trent, U.K. 8 E6
Buru, Indonesia 27 E7
Burûn, Râs, Egypt ... 33 D2
Burundi ■, Africa 36 E5
Burutu, Nigeria 34 G7
Burwell, U.S.A. 54 E5
Bury, U.K. 8 D5
Bury St. Edmunds, U.K. 9 E8
Buryatia □, Russia ... 21 D11
Buşayrah, Syria 30 C4
Büshehr, Iran 31 D6
Büshehr □, Iran 31 D6
Bushell, Canada 51 B7
Bushire = Büshehr, Iran 31 D6
Businga, Dem. Rep. of the Congo 36 D4
Busra ash Shām, Syria 33 C5
Busselton, Australia .. 41 F2
Bussum, Neths. 11 B5
Busto Arsizio, Italy ... 14 D8
Busu-Djanoa, Dem. Rep. of the Congo 36 D4
Busuanga I., Phil. ... 27 B5
Buta, Dem. Rep. of the Congo 36 D4
Butare, Rwanda 36 E5
Butaritari, Kiribati ... 44 G9
Bute Inlet, Canada ... 50 C4
Butembo, Dem. Rep. of the Congo 36 D5
Butha Qi, China 25 B7
Butler, Mo., U.S.A. ... 54 F7
Butler, Pa., U.S.A. ... 52 E6
Buton, Indonesia 27 E6
Butte, Mont., U.S.A. .. 56 C7
Butte, Nebr., U.S.A. .. 54 D5
Butterworth = Gcuwa, S. Africa 37 L5
Butterworth, Malaysia 26 C2
Buttfield, Mt., Australia 41 D4
Button B., Canada ... 51 B10
Butty Hd., Australia .. 41 F3
Butuan, Phil. 27 C7
Butung = Buton, Indonesia 27 E6
Buturlinovka, Russia .. 19 D7
Buxtehude, Germany . 12 B5
Buxton, U.K. 8 D6
Buy, Russia 18 C7
Büyük Menderes →, Turkey 17 F12
Büyükçekmece, Turkey 17 D13
Buzău, Romania 13 F14
Buzău →, Romania .. 13 F14
Buzen, Japan 23 H5
Buzi →, Mozam. 37 H6
Buzuluk, Russia 18 D9
Byarezina →, Belarus 13 B16
Byaroza, Belarus 13 B13
Bydgoszcz, Poland ... 13 B9
Byelarus = Belarus ■, Europe 13 B14
Byelorussia = Belarus ■, Europe 13 B14
Byers, U.S.A. 54 F2
Byford, Australia 41 F2
Bykhaw, Belarus 13 B16
Bykhov = Bykhaw, Belarus 13 B16

Bylas, U.S.A. 57 K8
Bylot, Canada 51 B10
Bylot I., Canada 47 A12
Byrd, C., Antarctica .. 5 C17
Byrock, Australia 43 E4
Byron, C., Australia .. 38 D8
Byron Bay, Australia .. 43 D5
Byrranga, Gory, Russia 21 B11
Byrranga Mts. = Byrranga, Gory, Russia 21 B11
Byske, Sweden 6 D19
Byske älv →, Sweden 6 D19
Bytom, Poland 13 C10
Bytów, Poland 13 A9

Ca Mau, Vietnam 26 C3
Ca Mau, Mui, Vietnam 26 C2
Caála, Angola 37 G3
Caamano Sd., Canada 50 C3
Cabanatuan, Phil. ... 27 A6
Cabano, Canada 49 C6
Cabedelo, Brazil 63 E12
Cabimas, Venezuela .. 62 A4
Cabinda, Angola 36 F2
Cabinda □, Angola ... 36 F2
Cabinet Mts., U.S.A. .. 56 C6
Cabo Blanco, Argentina 64 F3
Cabo Frio, Brazil 63 H10
Cabo Pantoja, Peru .. 62 D3
Cabonga, Réservoir, Canada 48 C4
Cabool, U.S.A. 55 G8
Caboolture, Australia . 43 D5
Cabora Bassa Dam = Cahora Bassa, Represa de, Mozam. 37 H6
Caborca, Mexico 58 A2
Cabot Str., Canada ... 49 C8
Cabra, Spain 15 D3
Cabrera, Spain 15 C7
Cabri, Canada 51 C7
Cabriel →, Spain ... 15 C5
Čačak, Serbia, Yug. .. 17 C9
Cáceres, Brazil 62 G7
Cáceres, Spain 15 C2
Cache Bay, Canada .. 48 C4
Cache Creek, Canada . 50 C4
Cachimbo, Serra do, Brazil 63 E7
Cachoeira, Brazil 63 F11
Cachoeira de Itapemirim, Brazil .. 63 H10
Cachoeira do Sul, Brazil 64 C6
Cacoal, Brazil 62 F6
Cacólo, Angola 36 G3
Caconda, Angola 37 G3
Caddo, U.S.A. 55 H6
Cader Idris, U.K. 9 E4
Cadereyta, Mexico ... 58 B5
Cadibarrawirracanna, L., Australia 43 D2
Cadillac, U.S.A. 52 C3
Cadiz, Phil. 27 B6
Cádiz, Spain 15 D2
Cádiz, G. de, Spain .. 15 D2
Cadiz L., U.S.A. 57 J6
Cadney Park, Australia 43 D1
Cadomin, Canada ... 50 C5
Cadotte Lake, Canada 50 B5
Cadoux, Australia ... 41 F2
Caen, France 14 B3
Caernarfon, U.K. 8 D3
Caernarfon B., U.K. .. 8 D3
Caernarvon = Caernarfon, U.K. .. 8 D3
Caerphilly, U.K. 9 F4
Caerphilly □, U.K. ... 9 F4
Caesarea, Israel 33 C3
Caetité, Brazil 63 F10
Cagayan de Oro, Phil. . 27 C6
Cagayan Is., Phil. ... 27 C5
Cágliari, Italy 16 E3
Cágliari, G. di, Italy .. 16 E3
Caguán →, Colombia 62 D4
Caguas, Puerto Rico . 61 C6
Cahora Bassa, Represa de, Mozam. 37 H6
Cahors, France 14 D4
Cahul, Moldova 13 F15
Caibarién, Cuba 60 B4
Caicara, Venezuela .. 62 B5
Caicó, Brazil 63 E11
Caicos Is., W. Indies . 61 B5
Caicos Passage, W. Indies 61 B5
Caird Coast, Antarctica 5 D1
Cairns, Australia 42 B4
Cairns L., Canada ... 51 C10
Cairo = El Qâhira, Egypt 35 B12
Cairo, Ga., U.S.A. ... 53 K3
Cairo, Ill., U.S.A. 55 G10
Cajamarca, Peru 62 E3
Cajàzeiras, Brazil 63 E11
Calabar, Nigeria 34 H7
Calabozo, Venezuela . 62 B5
Calábria □, Italy 16 E7
Calafate, Argentina .. 64 G2
Calahorra, Spain 15 A5
Calais, France 14 A4
Calais, U.S.A. 53 C12
Calama, Brazil 62 E6
Calama, Chile 62 H5
Calamar, Colombia ... 62 A4

Calamian Group, Phil. . . 27 B5
Calamocha, Spain 15 B5
Calang, Indonesia 26 D1
Calapan, Phil. 27 B6
Călăraşi, Romania . . . 13 F14
Calatayud, Spain 15 B5
Calauag, Phil. 27 B6
Calavite, C., Phil. 27 B6
Calbayog, Phil. 27 B6
Calca, Peru 62 F4
Calcasieu L., U.S.A. . . 55 L8
Calcutta = Kolkata, India 29 H16
Caldas da Rainha,
  Portugal 15 C1
Calder →, U.K. 8 D6
Caldera, Chile 64 B2
Caldwell, Idaho, U.S.A. 56 E5
Caldwell, Kans., U.S.A. 55 G6
Caldwell, Tex., U.S.A. . 55 K6
Caledon →, S. Africa . . 37 L5
Caledon B., Australia . . 42 A2
Calen, Australia 42 C4
Calexico, U.S.A. 57 K6
Calf of Man, U.K. 8 C3
Calgary, Canada 50 C6
Calhoun, U.S.A. 53 H3
Cali, Colombia 62 C3
Calicut, India 28 P9
Caliente, U.S.A. 57 H6
California, U.S.A. 54 F8
California □, U.S.A. . . . 57 H4
California, Baja, Mexico 58 A1
California, Baja, T.N. =
  Baja California □,
  Mexico 58 B2
California, Baja, T.S. =
  Baja California Sur □,
  Mexico 58 B2
California, G. de, Mexico 58 B2
Calingasta, Argentina . 64 C3
Calipatria, U.S.A. 57 K6
Calistoga, U.S.A. 56 G2
Callabonna, L., Australia 43 D3
Callao, Peru 62 F3
Calles, Mexico 59 C5
Calling Lake, Canada . . 50 B6
Calliope, Australia . . . 42 C5
Calne, U.K. 9 F6
Caloundra, Australia . . 43 D5
Calstock, Canada 48 C3
Caltagirone, Italy 16 F6
Caltanissetta, Italy . . . 16 F6
Calulo, Angola 36 G2
Calvert →, Australia . . 42 B2
Calvert I., Canada 50 C3
Calvert Ra., Australia . . 40 D3
Calvi, France 14 E8
Calvià, Spain 15 C7
Calvillo, Mexico 58 C4
Calvinia, S. Africa 37 L3
Cam →, U.K. 9 E8
Cam Ranh, Vietnam . . . 26 B3
Camabatela, Angola . . 36 F3
Camacho, Mexico 58 C4
Camacupa, Angola . . . 37 G3
Camagüey, Cuba 60 B4
Camaná, Peru 62 G4
Camargo, Mexico 59 B5
Camarón, C., Honduras 60 C2
Camarones, Argentina . 64 E3
Camas, U.S.A. 56 D2
Camas Valley, U.S.A. . . 56 E2
Câmballin, Australia . . 40 C3
Cambay = Khambhat,
  India 28 H8
Cambay, G. of =
  Khambhat, G. of, India 28 J8
Cambodia ■, Asia . . . 26 B3
Camborne, U.K. 9 G2
Cambrai, France 14 A5
Cambria, U.S.A. 57 J3
Cambrian Mts., U.K. . . 9 E4
Cambridge, Canada . . 48 D3
Cambridge, Jamaica . . 60 C4
Cambridge, N.Z. 39 G5
Cambridge, U.K. 9 E8
Cambridge, Mass.,
  U.S.A. 52 D10
Cambridge, Minn.,
  U.S.A. 54 C8
Cambridge, Nebr.,
  U.S.A. 54 E4
Cambridge, Ohio, U.S.A. 52 E5
Cambridge Bay =
  Ikaluktutiak, Canada . 46 B9
Cambridge G., Australia 40 B4
Cambridgeshire □, U.K. 9 E7
Cambundi-Catembo,
  Angola 36 G3
Camden, Ala., U.S.A. . . 53 K2
Camden, Ark., U.S.A. . . 55 J8
Camden, Maine, U.S.A. 53 C11
Camden, N.J., U.S.A. . . 52 F8
Camden, S.C., U.S.A. . . 53 H5
Camden Sd., Australia . 40 C3
Camdenton, U.S.A. . . . 55 F8
Cameron, Ariz., U.S.A. . 57 J8
Cameron, La., U.S.A. . . 55 L8
Cameron, Mo., U.S.A. . 54 F7
Cameron, Tex., U.S.A. . 55 K6
Cameron Hills, Canada 50 B5
Cameroon ■, Africa . . 36 C2
Cameroun, Mt.,
  Cameroon 36 D1

Cametá, Brazil 63 D9
Camiguin I., Phil. 27 C6
Camilla, U.S.A. 53 K3
Caminha, Portugal . . . 15 B1
Camino, U.S.A. 56 G3
Camira Creek, Australia 43 D5
Camocim, Brazil 63 D10
Camooweal, Australia . 42 B2
Camopi, Fr. Guiana . . . 63 C8
Camp Hill, U.S.A. 52 E7
Camp Verde, U.S.A. . . . 57 J8
Camp Wood, U.S.A. . . . 55 L5
Campana, I., Chile . . . 64 F1
Campana, Italy 16 D6
Campbell I., Pac. Oc. . . 44 N8
Campbell L., Canada . . 51 A7
Campbell River, Canada 50 C3
Campbell Town,
  Australia 42 G4
Campbellsville, U.S.A. . 52 G3
Campbellton, Canada . . 49 C6
Campbelltown, Australia 43 E5
Campbeltown, U.K. . . . 10 D4
Campeche, Mexico . . . 59 D6
Campeche □, Mexico . . 59 D6
Campeche, Golfo de,
  Mexico 59 D6
Camperdown, Australia 43 F3
Camperville, Canada . . 51 C8
Câmpina, Romania . . . 13 F13
Campina Grande, Brazil 63 E12
Campinas, Brazil 63 H9
Campo Grande, Brazil . 63 H8
Campo Maior, Brazil . . 63 D10
Campos, Brazil 63 H10
Campos Belos, Brazil . 63 F9
Câmpulung, Romania . 13 F13
Camrose, Canada 50 C6
Camsell Portage,
  Canada 51 B7
Çan, Turkey 17 D12
Can Tho, Vietnam 26 B3
Canada ■, N. Amer. . . 46 C10
Cañada de Gómez,
  Argentina 64 C4
Canadian, U.S.A. 55 H4
Canadian →, U.S.A. . . 55 H7
Çanakkale, Turkey . . . 17 D12
Çanakkale Boğazı,
  Turkey 17 D12
Canal Flats, Canada . . 50 C5
Canandaigua, U.S.A. . . 52 D7
Cananea, Mexico 58 A2
Canarias, Is., Atl. Oc. . . 34 C2
Canarreos, Arch. de los,
  Cuba 60 B3
Canary Is. = Canarias,
  Is., Atl. Oc. 34 C2
Canatlán, Mexico 58 C4
Canaveral, C., U.S.A. . . 53 L5
Canavieiras, Brazil . . . 63 G11
Canberra, Australia . . . 43 F4
Canby, Calif., U.S.A. . . 56 F3
Canby, Minn., U.S.A. . . 54 C6
Canby, Oreg., U.S.A. . . 56 D2
Cancún, Mexico 59 C7
Candelo, Australia . . . 43 F4
Candia = Iráklion,
  Greece 17 G11
Candle L., Canada 51 C7
Candlemas I., Antarctica 5 B1
Cando, U.S.A. 54 A5
Canea = Khaniá, Greece 17 G11
Canelones, Uruguay . . 64 C5
Cañete, Chile 64 D2
Cañete, Peru 62 F3
Cangas de Narcea,
  Spain 15 A2
Canguaretama, Brazil . 63 E11
Canguçu, Brazil 64 C6
Caniapiscau →,
  Canada 49 A6
Caniapiscau Rés. de,
  Canada 49 B6
Canicattì, Italy 16 F5
Canim Lake, Canada . . 50 C4
Cañitas, Mexico 58 C4
Çankırı, Turkey 19 F5
Canmore, Canada 50 C5
Cann River, Australia . . 43 F4
Cannanore, India 28 P9
Cannes, France 14 E7
Cannock, U.K. 9 E5
Cannon Ball →, U.S.A. 54 B4
Cannondale Mt.,
  Australia 42 D4
Cannonvale, Australia . 42 C4
Canoas, Brazil 64 B6
Canoe L., Canada 51 B7
Canon City, U.S.A. . . . 54 F2
Canora, Canada 51 C8
Canowindra, Australia . 43 E4
Canso, Canada 49 C7
Cantabria □, Spain . . . 15 A4
Cantabrian Mts. =
  Cantábrica, Cordillera,
  Spain 15 A3
Cantábrica, Cordillera,
  Spain 15 A3
Cantal, Plomb du,
  France 14 D5
Canterbury, Australia . . 42 D3
Canterbury, U.K. 9 F9
Canterbury Bight, N.Z. . 39 L3

Canterbury Plains, N.Z. 39 K3
Canton = Guangzhou,
  China 25 D6
Canton, Ga., U.S.A. . . . 53 H3
Canton, Ill., U.S.A. . . . 54 E9
Canton, Miss., U.S.A. . 55 J9
Canton, Mo., U.S.A. . . . 54 E9
Canton, N.Y., U.S.A. . . 52 C8
Canton, Ohio, U.S.A. . . 52 E5
Canton, S. Dak., U.S.A. 54 D6
Canton L., U.S.A. 55 G5
Canudos, Brazil 62 E7
Canumã →, Brazil . . . 62 D7
Canutama, Brazil 62 E6
Canutillo, U.S.A. 57 L10
Canvey, U.K. 9 F8
Canyon, U.S.A. 55 H4
Canyonlands National
  Park, U.S.A. 57 G9
Canyonville, U.S.A. . . . 56 E2
Cap-aux-Meules,
  Canada 49 C7
Cap-Chat, Canada . . . 49 C6
Cap-de-la-Madeleine,
  Canada 48 C5
Cap-Haïtien, Haiti 61 C5
Capanaparo →,
  Venezuela 62 B5
Cape →, Australia . . . 42 C4
Cape Barren I., Australia 42 G4
Cape Breton Highlands
  Nat. Park, Canada . . 49 C7
Cape Breton I., Canada 49 C7
Cape Charles, U.S.A. . . 52 G8
Cape Coast, Ghana . . . 34 G5
Cape Coral, U.S.A. . . . 53 M5
Cape Dorset, Canada . 47 B12
Cape Fear →, U.S.A. . . 53 H6
Cape Girardeau, U.S.A. 55 G10
Cape May, U.S.A. 52 F8
Cape May Point, U.S.A. 52 F8
Cape Province, S. Africa 37 L3
Cape Tormentine,
  Canada 49 C7
Cape Town, S. Africa . . 37 L3
Cape Verde Is. ■,
  Atl. Oc. 2 D8
Cape York Peninsula,
  Australia 42 A3
Capela, Brazil 63 F11
Capella, Australia 42 C4
Capim →, Brazil 63 D9
Capitan, U.S.A. 57 K11
Capitol Reef National
  Park, U.S.A. 57 G8
Capraia, Italy 14 E8
Capreol, Canada 48 C3
Capri, Italy 16 D6
Capricorn Group,
  Australia 42 C5
Capricorn Ra., Australia 40 D2
Caprivi Strip, Namibia . 37 H4
Captain's Flat, Australia 43 F4
Caquetá →, Colombia . 62 D5
Caracal, Romania 13 F13
Caracas, Venezuela . . . 62 A5
Caracol, Brazil 63 E10
Carajás, Brazil 63 E8
Carajás, Serra dos,
  Brazil 63 E8
Caransebeş, Romania . 13 F12
Caraquet, Canada 49 C6
Caras, Peru 62 E3
Caratasca, L., Honduras 60 C3
Caratinga, Brazil 63 G10
Caraúbas, Brazil 63 E11
Caravaca = Caravaca de
  la Cruz, Spain 15 C5
Caravaca de la Cruz,
  Spain 15 C5
Caravelas, Brazil 63 G11
Caraveli, Peru 62 G4
Carballo, Spain 15 A1
Carberry, Canada 51 D9
Carbó, Mexico 58 B2
Carbonara, C., Italy . . . 16 E3
Carbondale, Colo.,
  U.S.A. 56 G10
Carbondale, Ill., U.S.A. 55 G10
Carbondale, Pa., U.S.A. 52 E8
Carbonear, Canada . . . 49 C9
Carbónia, Italy 16 E3
Carcajou, Canada 50 B5
Carcasse, C., Haiti . . . 61 C5
Carcross, Canada 50 A2
Cardamon Hills, India . 28 Q10
Cárdenas, Cuba 60 B3
Cárdenas,
  San Luis Potosí,
  Mexico 59 C5
Cárdenas, Tabasco,
  Mexico 59 D6
Cardiff, U.K. 9 F4
Cardiff □, U.K. 9 F4
Cardigan, U.K. 9 E3
Cardigan B., U.K. 9 E3
Cardston, Canada 50 D6
Cardwell, Australia . . . 42 B4
Careen L., Canada . . . 51 B7
Carei, Romania 13 E12
Careme = Ciremai,
  Indonesia 27 G13
Carey, U.S.A. 56 E7
Carey, L., Australia . . . 41 E3

Carey L., Canada 51 A8
Carhué, Argentina 64 D4
Caria, Turkey 17 F13
Cariacica, Brazil 63 H10
Caribbean Sea,
  W. Indies 61 D5
Cariboo Mts., Canada . 50 C4
Caribou, U.S.A. 53 B12
Caribou →, Man.,
  Canada 51 B10
Caribou →, N.W.T.,
  Canada 50 A3
Caribou I., Canada . . . 48 C2
Caribou Is., Canada . . 50 A6
Caribou L., Man.,
  Canada 51 B9
Caribou L., Ont., Canada 48 B2
Caribou Mts., Canada . 50 B5
Carichic, Mexico 58 B3
Carinda, Australia 43 E4
Carinhanha, Brazil . . . 63 F10
Carinhanha →, Brazil . 63 F10
Carinthia = Kärnten □,
  Austria 12 E8
Caripito, Venezuela . . . 62 A6
Carleton, Mt., Canada . 49 C6
Carleton Place, Canada 48 C4
Carlin, U.S.A. 56 F5
Carlinville, U.S.A. 54 F10
Carlisle, U.K. 8 C5
Carlisle, U.S.A. 52 E7
Carlow, Ireland 10 E3
Carlsbad, Calif., U.S.A. 57 K5
Carlsbad, N. Mex.,
  U.S.A. 55 J2
Carlsbad Caverns
  National Park, U.S.A. 55 J2
Carlyle, Canada 51 D8
Carman, Canada 51 D9
Carmacks, Canada . . . 46 B6
Carman, Canada 51 D9
Carmarthen, U.K. 9 F3
Carmarthen B., U.K. . . 9 F3
Carmarthenshire □, U.K. 9 F3
Carmaux, France 14 D5
Carmel, U.S.A. 52 E9
Carmelo, Uruguay 64 C4
Carmen, Colombia . . . 62 B3
Carmen →, Mexico . . . 58 A3
Carmen, Paraguay . . . 58 B2
Carmen de Patagones,
  Argentina 64 E4
Carmi, Canada 50 D5
Carmi, U.S.A. 52 F1
Carmila, Australia 42 C4
Carmona, Costa Rica . . 60 E2
Carmona, Spain 15 D3
Carnac, France 14 C2
Carnamah, Australia . . 41 E2
Carnarvon, Australia . . 41 D1
Carnarvon, S. Africa . . 37 L4
Carnarvon Ra., Queens.,
  Australia 42 D4
Carnarvon Ra.,
  W. Austral., Australia 41 E3
Carndonagh, Ireland . . 10 D3
Carnduff, Canada 51 D8
Carnegie, U.S.A. 52 E5
Carnegie, L., Australia . 41 E3
Carnic Alps = Karnische
  Alpen, Europe 12 E7
Carniche Alpi =
  Karnische Alpen,
  Europe 12 E7
Carnot, C.A.R. 36 D3
Carnot, C., Australia . . 43 E2
Carnot B., Australia . . . 40 C3
Caro, U.S.A. 52 D4
Carol City, U.S.A. 53 N5
Carolina, Brazil 63 E9
Carolina, Puerto Rico . . 61 C6
Caroline I., Kiribati . . . 45 H12
Caroline Is., Micronesia 44 G7
Caroni →, Venezuela . . 62 B6
Caronie = Nébrodi,
  Monti, Italy 16 F6
Caroona, Australia . . . 43 E5
Carpathians, Europe . . 13 D11
Carpaţii Meridionali,
  Romania 13 F13
Carpentaria, G. of,
  Australia 42 A2
Carpentras, France . . . 14 D6
Carpi, Italy 16 B4
Carpinteria, U.S.A. . . . 57 J4
Carr Boyd Ra., Australia 40 C4
Carrabelle, U.S.A. 53 L3
Carranza, Presa V.,
  Mexico 58 B4
Carrara, Italy 16 B4
Carrauntoohill, Ireland . 10 E2
Carrick-on-Suir, Ireland 10 E3
Carrieton, Australia . . . 43 E2
Carrington, U.S.A. 54 B5
Carrizal Bajo, Chile . . . 64 B2
Carrizo Cr. →, U.S.A. . 55 G3
Carrizo Springs, U.S.A. 55 L5
Carrizozo, U.S.A. 57 K11
Carroll, U.S.A. 54 D7
Carrollton, Ga., U.S.A. . 53 J3
Carrollton, Ill., U.S.A. . . 54 F9
Carrollton, Ky., U.S.A. . 52 F3
Carrollton, Mo., U.S.A. . 54 F8
Carron →, Canada . . . 51 C8
Carrot →, Canada . . . 51 C8
Carrot River, Canada . . 51 C8
Carruthers, Canada . . . 51 C7
Carson, U.S.A. 54 B4
Carson City, U.S.A. . . . 56 G4
Carson Sink, U.S.A. . . . 56 G4

Causapscal, Canada . . 49 C6
Cauvery →, India 28 P11
Caux, Pays de, France . 14 B4
Cavalier, U.S.A. 54 A6
Cavan, Ireland 10 D3
Cave Creek, U.S.A. . . . 57 K7
Cavendish Ra., Australia 41 E4
Cavendish, Australia . . 43 F3
Caviana, I., Brazil 63 C8
Cavite, Phil. 27 B6
Cawndilla L., Australia . 43 E3
Cawnpore = Kanpur,
  India 28 F12
Caxias, Brazil 63 D10
Caxias do Sul, Brazil . . 64 B6
Cay Sal Bank, Bahamas 60 B4
Cayambe, Ecuador . . . 62 C3
Cayenne, Fr. Guiana . . 63 B8
Cayman Brac,
  Cayman Is. 60 C4
Cayman Is. ■, W. Indies 60 C3
Cayo Romano, Cuba . . 60 B4
Cayuga L., U.S.A. 52 D7
Cazombo, Angola 37 G4
Ceanannus Mor, Ireland 10 E3
Ceará = Fortaleza, Brazil 63 D11
Ceará □, Brazil 63 E11
Ceará Mirim, Brazil . . . 63 E11
Cebaco, I. de, Panama . 60 E3
Cebollar, Argentina . . . 64 B3
Cebu, Phil. 27 B6
Cecil Plains, Australia . 43 D5
Cedar →, U.S.A. 54 E9
Cedar City, U.S.A. 57 H7
Cedar Creek Reservoir,
  U.S.A. 55 J6
Cedar Falls, U.S.A. . . . 54 D8
Cedar Key, U.S.A. 53 L4
Cedar L., Canada 51 C9
Cedar Rapids, U.S.A. . . 54 E9
Cedartown, U.S.A. . . . 53 H3
Cedarvale, Canada . . . 50 B3
Cedral, Mexico 58 C4
Cedro, Brazil 63 E11
Cedros, I. de, Mexico . . 58 B1
Ceduna, Australia 43 E1
Cefalù, Italy 16 E6
Cegléd, Hungary 13 E10
Celaya, Mexico 58 C4
Celebes = Sulawesi,
  Indonesia 27 E6
Celebes = Sulawesi □,
  Indonesia 27 E6
Celebes Sea, Indonesia 27 D6
Celina, U.S.A. 52 E3
Celje, Slovenia 12 E8
Celle, Germany 12 B6
Celtic Sea, Atl. Oc. . . . 10 F2
Cenderwasih, Teluk,
  Indonesia 27 E9
Center, N. Dak., U.S.A. 54 B4
Center, Tex., U.S.A. . . . 55 K7
Centerville, Iowa, U.S.A. 54 E8
Centerville, Tenn.,
  U.S.A. 53 H2
Centerville, Tex., U.S.A. 55 K7
Central, Cordillera,
  Colombia 62 C4
Central, Cordillera,
  Costa Rica 60 E3
Central, Cordillera,
  Dom. Rep. 61 C5
Central African Rep. ■,
  Africa 36 C4
Central Butte, Canada . 51 C7
Central City, Colo.,
  U.S.A. 56 G11
Central City, Ky., U.S.A. 52 G2
Central City, Nebr.,
  U.S.A. 54 E6
Central Makran Range,
  Pakistan 28 F4
Central Patricia, Canada 48 B1
Central Point, U.S.A. . . 56 E2
Centralia, Ill., U.S.A. . . 54 F10
Centralia, Mo., U.S.A. . 54 F8
Centralia, Wash., U.S.A. 56 C2
Cephalonia = Kefallinía,
  Greece 17 E9
Cepu, Indonesia 27 G14
Ceram = Seram,
  Indonesia 27 E7
Ceram Sea = Seram
  Sea, Indonesia 27 E7
Ceredigion □, U.K. . . . 9 E3
Ceres, Argentina 64 B4
Cerignola, Italy 16 D6
Cerigo = Kithira, Greece 17 F10
Çerkezköy, Turkey . . . 17 D12
Cerralvo, I., Mexico . . . 58 C3
Cerritos, Mexico 58 C4
Cerventes, Australia . . 41 F2
Cervera, Spain 15 B6
Cesena, Italy 16 B5
Cēsis, Latvia 7 H21
České Budějovice,
  Czech Rep. 12 D8
Českomoravská
  Vrchovina, Czech Rep. 12 D8
Çeşme, Turkey 17 E12
Cessnock, Australia . . 43 E5
Cetinje,
  Montenegro, Yug. . . 17 C8
Cetraro, Italy 16 E6
Ceuta, N. Afr. 15 E3

Cévennes, France 14 D5
Ceyhan, Turkey 30 B2
Ceylon = Sri Lanka ■,
Asia 28 R12
Chachapoyas, Peru 62 E3
Chachran, Pakistan . . . 28 E7
Chaco ■, U.S.A. 57 H9
Chaco Austral, S. Amer. 64 B4
Chaco Boreal, S. Amer. . 62 H6
Chaco Central, S. Amer. 62 H6
Chacon, C., U.S.A. 50 C2
Chad ■, Africa 35 E9
Chad, L. = Tchad, L.,
Chad 35 F8
Chadan, Russia 21 D10
Chadileuvú →,
Argentina 64 D3
Chadron, U.S.A. 54 D3
Chadyr-Lunga = Ciadâr-
Lunga, Moldova . . 13 E15
Chagai Hills = Chäh
Gay, Afghan. 28 E3
Chagda, Russia 21 D14
Chagos Arch., Ind. Oc. . 3 E13
Chagos Arch., Ind. Oc. . 3 E13
Chäh Äkhvor, Iran . . . 31 C8
Chäh Bahar, Iran 31 E9
Chäh-e Kavir, Iran . . . 31 C8
Chäh Gay, Afghan. . . . 28 E3
Chahar Burjak, Afghan. 28 D3
Chahär Mahäll va
Bakhtiari □, Iran . . 31 C6
Chaibasa, India 29 H14
Chakhänsür, Afghan. . . 28 D3
Chakonipau, L., Canada 49 A6
Chakradharpur, India . . 29 H14
Chakwal, Pakistan . . . 28 C8
Chala, Peru 62 G4
Chalchihuites, Mexico . 58 C4
Chalcis = Khalkís,
Greece 17 E10
Chaleur B., Canada . . . 49 C6
Chalhuanca, Peru 62 F4
Chalisgaon, India 28 J9
Chalk River, Canada . . 48 C4
Chalky Inlet, N.Z. 39 M1
Challapata, Bolivia . . . 62 G5
Challis, U.S.A. 56 D6
Chalmette, U.S.A. 55 L10
Chalon-sur-Saône,
France 14 C6
Châlons-en-Champagne,
France 14 B6
Chalyaphum, Thailand . 26 A2
Chama, U.S.A. 57 H10
Chaman, Pakistan 28 D5
Chamba, India 28 C10
Chambal →, India . . . 28 F11
Chamberlain, U.S.A. . . 54 D5
Chamberlain →,
Australia 40 C4
Chamberlain L., U.S.A. 53 B11
Chambers, U.S.A. 57 J9
Chambersburg, U.S.A. . 52 F7
Chambéry, France 14 D6
Chambeshi →, Zambia 36 G6
Chambord, Canada . . . 49 C5
Chamchamal, Iraq . . . 30 C5
Chamela, Mexico 58 D3
Chamical, Argentina . . 64 C3
Chamonix-Mont Blanc,
France 14 D7
Chamouchouane →,
Canada 48 C5
Champagne, Canada . . 50 A1
Champagne, France . . . 14 B6
Champaign, U.S.A. . . . 52 E1
Champdoré, L., Canada 49 A6
Champlain, U.S.A. . . . 52 C9
Champlain, L., U.S.A. . 52 C9
Champotón, Mexico . . 59 D6
Chañaral, Chile 64 B2
Chanärän, Iran 31 B8
Chandeleur Is., U.S.A. . 55 L10
Chandeleur Sd., U.S.A. 55 L10
Chandigarh, India . . . 28 D10
Chandler, Australia . . . 43 D1
Chandler, Canada 49 C7
Chandler, Ariz., U.S.A. . 57 K8
Chandler, Okla., U.S.A. 55 H6
Chandpur, Bangla. . . . 29 H17
Chandrapur, India . . . 28 K11
Chänf, Iran 31 E9
Chang, Ko, Thailand . . 26 B2
Ch'ang Chiang = Chang
Jiang →, China . . . 25 C7
Chang Jiang →, China 25 C7
Changanacheri, India . 28 Q10
Changane →, Mozam. 37 J6
Changchiak'ou =
Zhangjiakou, China . 25 B6
Ch'angchou =
Changzhou, China . . 25 C6
Changchun, China . . . 25 B7
Changde, China 25 D6
Changhai = Shanghai,
China 25 C7
Changhua, Taiwan . . . 25 D7
Changsha, China 25 D6
Changzhi, China 25 C6
Changzhou, China . . . 25 C6
Channapatna, India . . 28 N10
Channel Is., U.K. 9 H5
Channel Is., U.S.A. . . . 57 K4

Channel Islands
National Park, U.S.A. 57 J3
Channel-Port aux
Basques, Canada . . . 49 C8
Channel Tunnel, Europe 9 F9
Channing, U.S.A. 55 H3
Chantada, Spain 15 A2
Chanthaburi, Thailand . 26 B2
Chantrey Inlet, Canada 46 B10
Chanute, U.S.A. 55 G7
Chao Phraya →,
Thailand 26 B2
Chaozhou, China 25 D6
Chapais, Canada 48 C5
Chapala, L. de, Mexico 58 C4
Chapayev, Kazakstan . 19 D9
Chapayevsk, Russia . . 18 D8
Chapecó, Brazil 64 B6
Chapel Hill, U.S.A. . . . 53 H6
Chapleau, Canada . . . 48 C3
Chaplin, Canada 51 C7
Chaplin L., Canada . . . 51 C7
Chappell, U.S.A. 54 E3
Chapra = Chhapra,
India 29 G14
Chara, Russia 21 D12
Charagua, Bolivia . . . 62 G6
Charambirá, Punta,
Colombia 62 C3
Charaña, Bolivia 62 G5
Charcas, Mexico 58 C4
Chard, U.K. 9 G5
Chardzhou = Chärjew,
Turkmenistan 20 F7
Charente →, France . . 14 D3
Chari →, Chad 35 F8
Chärikär, Afghan. 28 B6
Chariton →, U.S.A. . . 54 F8
Chärjew, Turkmenistan 20 F7
Charleroi, Belgium . . . 11 D4
Charles, C., U.S.A. . . . 52 G8
Charles City, U.S.A. . . 54 D8
Charles L., Canada . . . 51 B6
Charles Town, U.S.A. . 52 F7
Charleston, Ill., U.S.A. 52 F1
Charleston, Miss.,
U.S.A. 55 H9
Charleston, Mo., U.S.A. 55 G10
Charleston, S.C., U.S.A. 53 J6
Charleston, W. Va.,
U.S.A. 52 F5
Charlestown, U.S.A. . . 52 F3
Charleville, Australia . 43 D4
Charleville-Mézières,
France 14 B6
Charlevoix, U.S.A. . . . 52 C3
Charlotte, Mich., U.S.A. 52 D3
Charlotte, N.C., U.S.A. . 53 H5
Charlotte Amalie,
Virgin Is. 61 C7
Charlotte Harbor, U.S.A. 53 M4
Charlotte L., Canada . . 50 C3
Charlottesville, U.S.A. . 52 F6
Charlottetown, Nfld.,
Canada 49 B8
Charlottetown, P.E.I.,
Canada 49 C7
Charlton, Australia . . . 43 F3
Charlton, U.S.A. 54 E8
Charlton I., Canada . . . 48 B4
Charny, Canada 49 C5
Charolles, France 14 C6
Charters Towers,
Australia 42 C4
Chartres, France 14 B4
Chascomús, Argentina 64 D5
Chât, Iran 31 B7
Châteaubriant, France . 14 C3
Châteauguay, L.,
Canada 49 A5
Châteaulin, France . . . 14 B1
Châteauroux, France . . 14 C4
Châtellerault, France . . 14 C4
Chatham = Miramichi,
Canada 49 C6
Chatham, Canada 48 D3
Chatham, U.K. 9 F8
Chatham Is., Pac. Oc. . 44 M10
Chatrapur, India 29 K14
Chattahoochee, U.S.A. 53 K3
Chattahoochee →,
U.S.A. 53 K3
Chattanooga, U.S.A. . . 53 H3
Chatteris, U.K. 9 E8
Chaukan Pass, Burma . 29 F20
Chaumont, France . . . 14 B6
Chauvin, Canada 51 C6
Chaves, Brazil 63 D9
Chaves, Portugal 15 B2
Chaykovskiy, Russia . . 18 C9
Cheb, Czech Rep. 12 C7
Cheboksary, Russia . . 18 C8
Cheboygan, U.S.A. . . . 52 C3
Chech, Erg, Africa . . . 34 D5
Chechenia □, Russia . 19 F8
Checheno-Ingush
Republic =
Chechenia □, Russia 19 F8
Chechnya =
Chechenia □, Russia 19 F8
Checotah, U.S.A. 55 H7
Chedabucto B., Canada 49 C7
Cheduba I., Burma . . . 29 K18
Cheepie, Australia . . . 43 D4
Chegdomyn, Russia . . 21 D14

Chegga, Mauritania . . . 34 C4
Chegutu, Zimbabwe . . 37 H6
Chehalis, U.S.A. 56 C2
Cheju do, S. Korea . . . 25 C7
Chekiang = Zhejiang □,
China 25 D7
Chelan, U.S.A. 56 C4
Chelan, L., U.S.A. 56 B3
Cheleken, Turkmenistan 19 G9
Cheleken Yarymadasy,
Turkmenistan 31 B7
Chelforó, Argentina . . 64 D3
Chelkar = Shalqar,
Kazakstan 20 E6
Chelkar Tengiz,
Solonchak, Kazakstan 20 E7
Chełm, Poland 13 C12
Chełmno, Poland 13 B10
Chelmsford, U.K. 9 F8
Cheltenham, U.K. 9 F5
Chelyabinsk, Russia . . 20 D7
Chemba, Mozam. 37 H6
Chembar, Russia 18 D7
Chemnitz, Germany . . 12 C7
Chemult, U.S.A. 56 E3
Chen, Gora, Russia . . 21 C15
Chenab →, Pakistan . 28 D7
Chenchou =
Zhengzhou, China . . 25 C6
Chengde, China 25 B6
Chengdu, China 24 C5
Chengjiang, China . . . 24 D5
Ch'engtu = Chengdu,
China 24 C5
Chenkán, Mexico 59 D6
Chennai, India 28 N12
Cheo Reo, Vietnam . . 26 B3
Cheom Ksan, Cambodia 26 B2
Chepén, Peru 62 E3
Chepes, Argentina . . . 64 C3
Chepo, Panama 60 E4
Chepstow, U.K. 9 F5
Chequamegon B.,
U.S.A. 54 B9
Cher →, France 14 C4
Cheraw, U.S.A. 53 H6
Cherbourg, France . . . 14 B3
Cherdyn, Russia 18 B10
Cheremkhovo, Russia . 21 D11
Cherepanovo, Russia . 20 D9
Cherepovets, Russia . . 18 C6
Chergui, Chott ech,
Algeria 34 B6
Cherikov = Cherykaw,
Belarus 13 B16
Cherkasy, Ukraine . . . 19 E5
Cherkessk, Russia . . . 19 F7
Cherlak, Russia 20 D8
Chernaya, Russia 21 B9
Chernigov = Chernihiv,
Ukraine 18 D5
Chernihiv, Ukraine . . . 18 D5
Chernivtsi, Ukraine . . 13 D13
Chernobyl = Chornobyl,
Ukraine 13 C16
Chernogorsk, Russia . 21 D10
Chernovtsy =
Chernivtsi, Ukraine . 13 D13
Chernyakhovsk, Russia 7 J19
Chernysheyskiy, Russia 21 C12
Cherokee, Iowa, U.S.A. 54 D7
Cherokee, Okla., U.S.A. 55 G5
Cherokee Village, U.S.A. 55 G9
Cherokees, Grand Lake
O' The, U.S.A. 55 G7
Cherrapunji, India . . . 29 G17
Cherskiy, Russia 21 C17
Cherskogo Khrebet,
Russia 21 C15
Cherven, Belarus 13 B15
Chervonohrad, Ukraine 13 C13
Cherwell →, U.K. 9 F6
Cherykaw, Belarus . . . 13 B16
Chesapeake, U.S.A. . . 52 G7
Chesapeake B., U.S.A. . 52 G7
Cheshire □, U.K. 8 D5
Cheshskaya Guba,
Russia 18 A8
Cheshunt, U.K. 9 F7
Chesil Beach, U.K. . . . 9 G5
Chester, U.K. 8 D5
Chester, Calif., U.S.A. . 56 F3
Chester, Ill., U.S.A. . . 55 G10
Chester, Mont., U.S.A. . 56 B8
Chester, Pa., U.S.A. . . 52 F8
Chester, S.C., U.S.A. . . 53 H5
Chester-le-Street, U.K. . 8 C6
Chesterfield, U.K. 8 D6
Chesterfield, Is., N. Cal. 38 C8
Chesterfield Inlet,
Canada 46 B10
Chesterton Ra.,
Australia 43 D4
Chesuncook L., U.S.A. 53 C11
Chéticamp, Canada . . 49 C7
Chetumal, Mexico . . . 59 D7
Chetumal, B. de, Mexico 59 D7
Chetwynd, Canada . . . 50 B4
Cheviot, The, U.K. . . . 8 B5
Cheviot Hills, U.K. . . . 8 B5
Cheviot Ra., Australia . 43 D3
Chew Bahir, Ethiopia . 32 G2
Chewelah, U.S.A. 56 B5
Cheyenne, Okla., U.S.A. 55 H5
Cheyenne, Wyo., U.S.A. 54 E2

Cheyenne →, U.S.A. . 54 C4
Cheyenne Wells, U.S.A. 54 F3
Cheyne B., Australia . . 41 F2
Chhapra, India 29 G14
Chhatarpur, India 28 G11
Chhindwara, India . . . 28 H11
Chi →, Thailand 26 A3
Chiai, Taiwan 25 D7
Chiamboni, Somali Rep. 36 E8
Chiamussu = Jiamusi,
China 25 B8
Chiapa →, Mexico . . . 59 D6
Chiapa de Corzo,
Mexico 59 D6
Chiapas □, Mexico . . . 59 D6
Chiautla, Mexico 59 D5
Chiávari, Italy 14 D8
Chiavenna, Italy 14 C8
Chiba, Japan 23 G10
Chiba □, Japan 23 G10
Chibemba, Angola . . . 37 H2
Chibia, Angola 37 H2
Chibougamau, Canada 48 C5
Chibougamau, L.,
Canada 48 C5
Chic-Chocs, Mts.,
Canada 49 C6
Chicacole = Srikakulam,
India 29 K13
Chicago, U.S.A. 52 E2
Chicago Heights, U.S.A. 52 E2
Chichagof I., U.S.A. . . 46 C6
Chichén-Itzá, Mexico . 59 C7
Chichester, U.K. 9 G7
Chichester Ra., Australia 40 D2
Chichibu, Japan 23 F9
Ch'ich'ihaerh = Qiqihar,
China 21 E13
Chickasha, U.S.A. 55 H6
Chiclana de la Frontera,
Spain 15 D2
Chiclayo, Peru 62 E3
Chico, U.S.A. 56 G3
Chico →, Chubut,
Argentina 64 E3
Chico →, Santa Cruz,
Argentina 64 G3
Chicontepec, Mexico . 59 C5
Chicopee, U.S.A. 52 D9
Chicoutimi, Canada . . 49 C5
Chidambaram, India . . 28 P11
Chidley, C., Canada . . 47 B13
Chiemsee, Germany . . 12 E7
Chiese →, Italy 14 D9
Chieti, Italy 16 C6
Chignecto B., Canada . 49 C7
Chiguana, Bolivia 62 H5
Chigwell, U.K. 9 F8
Chihli, G. of = Bo Hai,
China 25 C6
Chihuahua, Mexico . . 58 B3
Chihuahua □, Mexico . 58 B3
Chiili, Kazakstan 20 E7
Chik Bollapur, India . . 28 N10
Chilac, Mexico 59 D5
Chilapa, Mexico 59 D5
Chilas, Pakistan 28 B9
Chilaw, Sri Lanka 28 R11
Chilcotin →, Canada . 50 C4
Childers, Australia . . . 43 D5
Childress, U.S.A. 55 H4
Chile ■, S. Amer. 64 D2
Chile Rise, Pac. Oc. . . 45 L18
Chilete, Peru 62 E3
Chililabombwe, Zambia 37 G5
Chilin = Jilin, China . . 25 B7
Chilka L., India 29 K14
Chilko →, Canada . . . 50 C4
Chilko L., Canada 50 C4
Chillagoe, Australia . . 42 B3
Chillán, Chile 64 D2
Chillicothe, Ill., U.S.A. 54 E10
Chillicothe, Mo., U.S.A. 54 F8
Chillicothe, Ohio, U.S.A. 52 F4
Chilliwack, Canada . . . 50 D4
Chiloé, I. de, Chile . . . 64 E2
Chilpancingo, Mexico . 59 D5
Chiltern Hills, U.K. . . . 9 F7
Chilton, U.S.A. 52 C1
Chilung, Taiwan 25 D7
Chilwa, L., Malawi . . . 37 H7
Chimaltitán, Mexico . . 58 C4
Chimán, Panama 60 E4
Chimay, Belgium 11 D4
Chimayo, U.S.A. 57 H11
Chimbay, Uzbekistan . 20 E6
Chimborazo, Ecuador . 62 D3
Chimbote, Peru 62 E3
Chimkent = Shymkent,
Kazakstan 20 E7
Chimoio, Mozam. 37 H6
Chin □, Burma 29 J18
Chinan = Jinan, China 25 C6
Chinandega, Nic. 60 D2
Chinati Peak, U.S.A. . . 55 L2
Chincha Alta, Peru . . . 62 F3
Chinchaga →, Canada 50 B5
Chinchilla, Australia . . 43 D5
Chinchorro, Banco,
Mexico 59 D7
Chinchou = Jinzhou,
China 25 B7

Chincoteague, U.S.A. . 52 G8
Chinde, Mozam. 37 H7
Chindwin →, Burma . . 29 J19
Chingola, Zambia 37 G5
Ch'ingtao = Qingdao,
China 25 C7
Chinguetti, Mauritania 34 D3
Chinhoyi, Zimbabwe . . 37 H6
Chiniot, Pakistan 28 D8
Chínipas, Mexico 58 B3
Chinle, U.S.A. 57 H9
Chinnampo = Namp'o,
N. Korea 25 C7
Chino, Japan 23 G9
Chino Valley, U.S.A. . . 57 J7
Chinon, France 14 C4
Chinook, U.S.A. 56 B9
Chióggia, Italy 16 B5
Chíos = Khíos, Greece 17 E12
Chipata, Zambia 37 G6
Chipley, U.S.A. 53 K3
Chipman, Canada 49 C6
Chippenham, U.K. . . . 9 F5
Chippewa →, U.S.A. . . 54 C8
Chippewa Falls, U.S.A. 54 C9
Chipping Norton, U.K. . 9 F6
Chiputneticook Lakes,
U.S.A. 53 C11
Chiquián, Peru 62 F3
Chiquimula, Guatemala 60 D2
Chiquinquira, Colombia 62 B4
Chirala, India 28 M12
Chirchiq, Uzbekistan . 20 E7
Chiredzi, Zimbabwe . . 37 J6
Chirfa, Niger 35 D8
Chiricahua Peak, U.S.A. 57 L9
Chiriquí, G. de, Panama 60 E3
Chiriquí, L. de, Panama 60 E3
Chirmiri, India 29 H13
Chirripó Grande, Cerro,
Costa Rica 60 E3
Chisapani Garhi, Nepal 29 F14
Chisasibi, Canada 48 B4
Chisholm, Canada . . . 50 C6
Chisholm, U.S.A. 54 B8
Chişinău, Moldova . . . 13 E15
Chisos Mts., U.S.A. . . 55 L3
Chistopol, Russia 18 C9
Chita, Russia 21 D12
Chitose, Japan 22 C10
Chitral, Pakistan 28 B7
Chitré, Panama 60 E3
Chittagong, Bangla. . . 29 H17
Chittagong □, Bangla. 29 G17
Chittaurgarh, India . . . 28 G9
Chittoor, India 28 N11
Chitungwiza, Zimbabwe 37 H6
Chiusi, Italy 16 C4
Chivasso, Italy 14 D7
Chivilcoy, Argentina . . 64 C5
Chkalov = Orenburg,
Russia 18 D10
Choctawhatchee →,
U.S.A. 53 K3
Choele Choel, Argentina 64 D3
Choiseul, Solomon Is. . 38 B8
Choix, Mexico 58 B3
Chojnice, Poland 13 B9
Chōkai-San, Japan . . . 22 E10
Choke Canyon L., U.S.A. 55 L5
Chokurdakh, Russia . . 21 B15
Cholet, France 14 C3
Choluteca, Honduras . 60 D2
Choluteca →,
Honduras 60 D2
Choma, Zambia 37 H5
Chomutov, Czech Rep. 12 C7
Chon Buri, Thailand . . 26 B2
Chone, Ecuador 62 D3
Chŏngjin, N. Korea . . . 25 B7
Chongqing, China . . . 24 D5
Chongqing □, China . . 24 D5
Chŏnju, S. Korea 25 C7
Chonos, Arch. de los,
Chile 64 F2
Chop, Ukraine 13 D12
Chorley, U.K. 8 D5
Chornobyl, Ukraine . . 13 C16
Chorregon, Australia . . 42 C3
Chortkiv, Ukraine 13 D13
Chorzów, Poland 13 C10
Chos-Malal, Argentina 64 D2
Choszczno, Poland . . . 12 B8
Choteau, U.S.A. 56 C7
Chotila, India 28 H7
Chowchilla, U.S.A. . . . 57 H3
Choybalsan, Mongolia . 25 B6
Christchurch, N.Z. . . . 39 K4
Christchurch, U.K. . . . 9 G6
Christiansted, Virgin Is. 61 C7
Christie B., Canada . . . 51 A6
Christina →, Canada . 51 B6
Christmas Cr. →,
Australia 40 C4
Christmas I. = Kiritimati,
Kiribati 45 G12
Christmas I., Ind. Oc. . 44 J2
Christopher L., Australia 40 D4
Chu = Shu, Kazakstan 20 E8
Ch'uanchou =
Quanzhou, China . . 25 D6
Chubbuck, U.S.A. 56 E7
Chūbu □, Japan 23 F8
Chubut →, Argentina . 64 E3

Chuchi L., Canada . . . 50 B4
Chudskoye, Ozero,
Russia 7 G22
Chūgoku □, Japan . . . 23 G6
Chūgoku-Sanchi, Japan 23 G6
Chugwater, U.S.A. . . . 54 E2
Chukchi Sea, Russia . . 21 C19
Chukotskoye Nagorye,
Russia 21 C18
Chula Vista, U.S.A. . . . 57 K5
Chulucanas, Peru 62 E2
Chulym →, Russia . . . 20 D9
Chumbicha, Argentina 64 B3
Chumikan, Russia . . . 21 D14
Chumphon, Thailand . 26 B1
Chuna →, Russia 21 D10
Ch'unch'ŏn, S. Korea . 25 C7
Chungking =
Chongqing, China . . 24 D5
Chunya, Tanzania 36 F6
Chuquibamba, Peru . . 62 G4
Chuquicamata, Chile . 62 H5
Chur, Switz. 14 C8
Churachandpur, India . 29 G18
Churchill, Canada 51 B10
Churchill →, Man.,
Canada 51 B10
Churchill →, Nfld.,
Canada 49 B7
Churchill, C., Canada . 51 B10
Churchill Falls, Canada 49 B7
Churchill L., Canada . . 51 B7
Churchill Pk., Canada . 50 B3
Churu, India 28 E9
Churún Merú = Angel
Falls, Venezuela . . . 62 B6
Chushal, India 28 C11
Chuska Mts., U.S.A. . . 57 H9
Chusovoy, Russia 18 C10
Chute-aux-Outardes,
Canada 49 C6
Chuvash Republic =
Chuvashia □, Russia 18 C8
Chuvashia □, Russia . 18 C8
Chuwärtah, Iraq 30 C5
Ciadâr-Lunga, Moldova 13 E15
Ciamis, Indonesia . . . 27 G13
Cianjur, Indonesia . . . 27 G12
Cianorte, Brazil 64 A6
Cicero, U.S.A. 52 E2
Ciechanów, Poland . . . 13 B11
Ciego de Avila, Cuba . 60 B4
Ciénaga, Colombia . . . 62 A4
Cienfuegos, Cuba 60 B3
Cieszyn, Poland 13 D10
Cieza, Spain 15 C5
Cihuatlán, Mexico . . . 58 D4
Cijara, Embalse de,
Spain 15 C3
Cijulang, Indonesia . . 27 G13
Cilacap, Indonesia . . . 27 G13
Cill Chainnigh =
Kilkenny, Ireland . . . 10 E3
Cilo Daği, Turkey 19 G7
Cimarron, Kans., U.S.A. 55 G4
Cimarron, N. Mex.,
U.S.A. 55 G2
Cimarron →, U.S.A. . . 55 G6
Cimişlia, Moldova . . . 13 E15
Cimone, Mte., Italy . . . 16 B4
Cinca →, Spain 15 B6
Cincar, Bos.-H. 16 C7
Cincinnati, U.S.A. 52 F3
Çine, Turkey 17 F13
Ciney, Belgium 11 D5
Cinto, Mte., France . . . 14 E8
Circle, Alaska, U.S.A. . 46 B5
Circle, Mont., U.S.A. . . 54 B2
Circleville, U.S.A. 52 F4
Cirebon, Indonesia . . . 27 G13
Ciremai, Indonesia . . . 27 G13
Cirencester, U.K. 9 F6
Cisco, U.S.A. 55 J5
Citlaltépetl, Mexico . . 59 D5
Città di Castello, Italy . 16 C5
Ciudad Altamirano,
Mexico 58 D4
Ciudad Bolívar,
Venezuela 62 B6
Ciudad Camargo,
Mexico 58 B3
Ciudad de Valles,
Mexico 59 C5
Ciudad del Carmen,
Mexico 59 D6
Ciudad del Este,
Paraguay 64 B6
Ciudad Delicias =
Delicias, Mexico . . . 58 B3
Ciudad Guayana,
Venezuela 62 B6
Ciudad Guerrero,
Mexico 58 B3
Ciudad Guzmán, Mexico 58 D4
Ciudad Juárez, Mexico 58 A3
Ciudad Madero, Mexico 59 C5
Ciudad Mante, Mexico 59 C5
Ciudad Obregón,
Mexico 58 B3
Ciudad Real, Spain . . 15 C4
Ciudad Rodrigo, Spain 15 B2
Ciudad Trujillo = Santo
Domingo, Dom. Rep. 61 C6
Ciudad Victoria, Mexico 59 C5
Civitanova Marche, Italy 16 C5

Civitavécchia, *Italy* 16 C4
Cizre, *Turkey* 19 G7
Clacton-on-Sea, *U.K.* .. 9 F9
Claire, L., *Canada* 50 B6
Clanton, *U.S.A.* 53 J2
Clare, *Australia* 43 E2
Clare, *U.S.A.* 52 D3
Claremont, *U.S.A.* 52 D9
Claremont Pt., *Australia* 42 A3
Claremore, *U.S.A.* 55 G7
Clarence →, *Australia* 43 D5
Clarence →, *N.Z.* 39 K4
Clarence, I., *Chile* 64 G2
Clarence I., *Antarctica* . 5 C18
Clarence Str., *Australia* 40 B5
Clarence Town,
 Bahamas 61 B5
Clarendon, *U.S.A.* 55 H4
Clarenville, *Canada* 49 C9
Claresholm, *Canada* 50 D6
Clarie Coast, *Antarctica* 5 C9
Clarinda, *U.S.A.* 54 E7
Clarion, *U.S.A.* 54 D8
Clark, *U.S.A.* 54 C6
Clark Fork, *U.S.A.* 56 B5
Clark Fork →, *U.S.A.* .. 56 B5
Clarkdale, *U.S.A.* 57 J7
Clarke City, *Canada* ... 49 B6
Clarke I., *Australia* 42 G4
Clarke Ra., *Australia* ... 42 C4
Clark's Fork →, *U.S.A.* 56 D9
Clark's Harbour, *Canada* 49 D6
Clarks Hill L., *U.S.A.* .. 53 J4
Clarksburg, *U.S.A.* 52 F5
Clarksdale, *U.S.A.* 55 H9
Clarksville, *Ark., U.S.A.* 55 H8
Clarksville, *Tenn., U.S.A.* 53 G2
Clarksville, *Tex., U.S.A.* 55 J7
Claude, *U.S.A.* 55 H4
Claveria, *Phil.* 27 A6
Clay Center, *U.S.A.* ... 54 F6
Claypool, *U.S.A.* 57 K8
Clayton, *N. Mex., U.S.A.* 55 G3
Clayton, *N.Y., U.S.A.* .. 52 C7
Clear, C., *Ireland* 10 F2
Clear Hills, *Canada* 50 B5
Clear L., *U.S.A.* 56 G2
Clear Lake, *Iowa, U.S.A.* 54 D8
Clear Lake, *S. Dak.,*
 U.S.A. 54 C6
Clear Lake Reservoir,
 U.S.A. 56 F3
Clearfield, *Pa., U.S.A.* . 52 E6
Clearfield, *Utah, U.S.A.* 56 F8
Clearlake, *U.S.A.* 56 G2
Clearwater, *Canada* 50 C4
Clearwater, *U.S.A.* 53 M4
Clearwater →, *Alta.,*
 Canada 50 C6
Clearwater →, *Alta.,*
 Canada 51 B6
Clearwater L., *Canada* . 51 C9
Clearwater Mts., *U.S.A.* 56 C6
Clearwater Prov. Park,
 Canada 51 C8
Clearwater River Prov.
 Park, *Canada* 51 B7
Cleburne, *U.S.A.* 55 J6
Clee Hills, *U.K.* 9 E5
Cleethorpes, *U.K.* 8 D7
Cleeve Cloud, *U.K.* 9 F6
Clemson, *U.S.A.* 53 H4
Clerke Reef, *Australia* . 40 C2
Clermont, *Australia* 42 C4
Clermont, *U.S.A.* 53 L5
Clermont-Ferrand,
 France 14 D5
Clervaux, *Lux.* 11 D6
Cleve, *Australia* 43 E2
Clevedon, *U.K.* 9 F5
Cleveland, *Miss., U.S.A.* 55 J9
Cleveland, *Ohio, U.S.A.* 52 E5
Cleveland, *Okla., U.S.A.* 55 G6
Cleveland, *Tenn., U.S.A.* 53 H3
Cleveland, *Tex., U.S.A.* 55 K7
Cleveland, C., *Australia* 42 B4
Cleveland, Mt., *U.S.A.* . 56 B7
Clewiston, *U.S.A.* 53 M5
Clifden, *Ireland* 39 M1
Cliffy Hd., *Australia* ... 41 G2
Clifton, *Australia* 43 D5
Clifton, *Ariz., U.S.A.* .. 57 K9
Clifton, *Colo., U.S.A.* .. 57 G9
Clifton, *Tex., U.S.A.* ... 55 K6
Clifton Beach, *Australia* 42 B4
Climax, *Canada* 51 D7
Clinch →, *U.S.A.* 53 H3
Clingmans Dome,
 U.S.A. 53 H4
Clint, *U.S.A.* 57 L10
Clinton, *B.C., Canada* .. 50 C4
Clinton, *Ont., Canada* .. 48 D3
Clinton, *N.Z.* 39 M2
Clinton, *Ark., U.S.A.* ... 55 H8
Clinton, *Ill., U.S.A.* 54 E10
Clinton, *Ind., U.S.A.* ... 52 F2
Clinton, *Iowa, U.S.A.* .. 54 E9
Clinton, *Miss., U.S.A.* .. 55 J9
Clinton, *Mo., U.S.A.* ... 54 F8
Clinton, *N.C., U.S.A.* ... 53 H6
Clinton, *Okla., U.S.A.* .. 55 H5
Clinton, *S.C., U.S.A.* ... 53 H5
Clinton, *Tenn., U.S.A.* .. 53 G3
Clinton C., *Australia* ... 42 C5

Clinton Colden L.,
 Canada 46 B9
Clintonville, *U.S.A.* 54 C10
Clipperton, I., *Pac. Oc.* . 45 F17
Clitheroe, *U.K.* 8 D5
Cloates, Pt., *Australia* .. 40 D1
Cloncurry, *Australia* ... 42 C3
Cloncurry →, *Australia* . 42 B3
Clones, *Ireland* 10 D3
Clonmel, *Ireland* 10 E3
Cloquet, *U.S.A.* 54 B8
Cloud Bay, *Canada* ... 48 C2
Cloud Peak, *U.S.A.* 56 D10
Cloudcroft, *U.S.A.* 57 K11
Cloverdale, *U.S.A.* 56 G2
Clovis, *Calif., U.S.A.* ... 57 H4
Clovis, *N. Mex., U.S.A.* 55 H3
Cluj-Napoca, *Romania* . 13 E12
Clunes, *Australia* 43 F3
Clutha →, *N.Z.* 39 M2
Clwyd □, *U.K.* 8 D4
Clwyd →, *U.K.* 8 D4
Clyde, *Canada* 50 C6
Clyde, *N.Z.* 39 L2
Clyde →, *U.K.* 10 D4
Clyde, Firth of, *U.K.* ... 10 D4
Clyde River, *Canada* ... 47 A13
Coachella, *U.S.A.* 57 K5
Coachella Canal, *U.S.A.* 57 K6
Coahoma, *U.S.A.* 55 J4
Coahuayana →,
 Mexico 58 D4
Coahuila □, *Mexico* ... 58 B4
Coal →, *Canada* 50 B3
Coalcomán, *Mexico* ... 58 D4
Coaldale, *Canada* 50 D6
Coalgate, *U.S.A.* 55 H6
Coalinga, *U.S.A.* 57 H3
Coalville, *U.K.* 8 E6
Coalville, *U.S.A.* 56 F8
Coari, *Brazil* 62 D6
Coast Mts., *Canada* ... 50 C3
Coast Ranges, *U.S.A.* .. 56 F2
Coatepec, *Mexico* 59 D5
Coatepeque, *Guatemala* 60 D1
Coatesville, *U.S.A.* 52 F8
Coaticook, *Canada* 49 C5
Coats I., *Canada* 47 B11
Coats Land, *Antarctica* . 5 D1
Coatzacoalcos, *Mexico* . 59 D6
Cobalt, *Canada* 48 C4
Cobán, *Guatemala* 60 C1
Cobar, *Australia* 43 E4
Cobargo, *Australia* 43 F4
Cóbh, *Ireland* 10 F2
Cobija, *Bolivia* 62 F5
Cobleskill, *U.S.A.* 52 D8
Cobourg, *Canada* 48 D4
Cobourg Pen., *Australia* 40 B5
Cobram, *Australia* 43 F4
Coburg, *Germany* 12 C6
Cocanada = Kakinada,
 India 29 L13
Cochabamba, *Bolivia* .. 62 G5
Cochin, *India* 28 Q10
Cochin China = Nam-
 Phan, *Vietnam* 26 B3
Cochran, *U.S.A.* 53 J4
Cochrane, *Alta., Canada* 50 C6
Cochrane, *Ont., Canada* 48 C3
Cochrane, *Chile* 64 F2
Cochrane →, *Canada* . 51 B8
Cochrane, L., *Chile* 64 F2
Cockburn, *Australia* ... 43 E3
Cockburn, Canal, *Chile* 64 G2
Cockburn I., *Canada* ... 48 C3
Cockburn Ra., *Australia* 40 C4
Cockermouth, *U.K.* 8 C4
Cocklebiddy, *Australia* . 41 F4
Coco →, *Cent. Amer.* . 60 D3
Coco, I. del, *Pac. Oc.* .. 45 G19
Cocoa, *U.S.A.* 53 L5
Cocobeach, *Gabon* 36 D1
Cocos Is., *Ind. Oc.* 44 J1
Cod, C., *U.S.A.* 52 D10
Codajás, *Brazil* 62 D6
Codó, *Brazil* 63 D10
Cody, *U.S.A.* 56 D9
Coen, *Australia* 42 A3
Cœur d'Alene, *U.S.A.* .. 56 C5
Cœur d'Alene L., *U.S.A.* 56 C5
Coevorden, *Neths.* 11 B6
Coffeyville, *U.S.A.* 55 G7
Coffin B., *Australia* 43 E2
Coffin Bay, *Australia* ... 43 E2
Coffin Bay Peninsula,
 Australia 43 E2
Coffs Harbour, *Australia* 43 E5
Cognac, *France* 14 D3
Cohuna, *Australia* 43 F3
Coiba, I., *Panama* 60 E3
Coig →, *Argentina* 64 G3
Coihaique, *Chile* 64 F2
Coimbatore, *India* 28 P10
Coimbra, *Brazil* 62 G7
Coimbra, *Portugal* 15 B1
Coín, *Spain* 15 D3
Coipasa, Salar de,
 Bolivia 62 G5
Cojimies, *Ecuador* 62 C3
Cojutepeque, *El Salv.* .. 60 D2
Colac, *Australia* 43 F3
Colatina, *Brazil* 63 G10
Colbeck, C., *Antarctica* . 5 D13
Colby, *U.S.A.* 54 F4

Colchester, *U.K.* 9 F8
Cold L., *Canada* 51 C7
Coldstream, *Canada* ... 50 C5
Coldwater, *Kans., U.S.A.* 55 G5
Coldwater, *Mich., U.S.A.* 52 E3
Coleambally, *Australia* . 43 E4
Colebrook, *U.S.A.* 52 C10
Coleman, *U.S.A.* 55 K5
Coleman →, *Australia* . 42 B3
Coleraine, *Australia* 43 F3
Coleraine, *U.K.* 10 A5
Coleridge, L., *N.Z.* 39 K3
Colesberg, *S. Africa* ... 37 L5
Colfax, *La., U.S.A.* 55 K8
Colfax, *Wash., U.S.A.* .. 56 C5
Colhué Huapi, L.,
 Argentina 64 F3
Colima, *Mexico* 58 D4
Colima □, *Mexico* 58 D4
Colima, Nevado de,
 Mexico 58 D4
Colinas, *Brazil* 63 E10
Coll, *U.K.* 10 C3
Collaguasi, *Chile* 62 H5
Collarenebri, *Australia* . 43 D4
College Park, *U.S.A.* ... 53 J3
College Station, *U.S.A.* . 55 K6
Collie, *Australia* 41 F2
Collier B., *Australia* 40 C3
Collier Ra., *Australia* ... 41 D2
Collina, Passo di, *Italy* . 16 B4
Collingwood, *Canada* .. 48 D3
Collingwood, *N.Z.* 39 J4
Collins, *Canada* 48 B2
Collinsville, *Australia* ... 42 C4
Colo →, *Australia* 43 E5
Cologne = Köln,
 Germany 12 C4
Colomb-Béchar =
 Béchar, *Algeria* 34 B5
Colombia ■, *S. Amer.* . 62 C4
Colombo, *Sri Lanka* ... 28 R11
Colón, *Cuba* 60 B3
Colón, *Panama* 60 E4
Colonia Dora, *Argentina* 64 B4
Colonial Beach, *U.S.A.* . 52 F7
Colonsay, *Canada* 51 C7
Colonsay, *U.K.* 10 C3
Colorado □, *U.S.A.* ... 57 G10
Colorado →, *Argentina* 64 D4
Colorado →, *N. Amer.* 57 L6
Colorado →, *U.S.A.* .. 55 L7
Colorado City, *U.S.A.* .. 55 J4
Colorado Plateau, *U.S.A.* 57 H8
Colorado River
 Aqueduct, *U.S.A.* ... 57 J6
Colorado Springs,
 U.S.A. 54 F2
Colotlán, *Mexico* 58 C4
Colstrip, *U.S.A.* 56 D10
Columbia, *Ky., U.S.A.* .. 52 G3
Columbia, *La., U.S.A.* .. 55 J8
Columbia, *Miss., U.S.A.* 55 K10
Columbia, *Mo., U.S.A.* . 54 F8
Columbia, *Pa., U.S.A.* .. 52 E7
Columbia, *S.C., U.S.A.* . 53 J5
Columbia, *Tenn., U.S.A.* 53 H2
Columbia →, *N. Amer.* 56 C1
Columbia, C., *Canada* . 4 A4
Columbia, District of □,
 U.S.A. 52 F7
Columbia, Mt., *Canada* 50 C5
Columbia Basin, *U.S.A.* 56 C4
Columbia Falls, *U.S.A.* . 56 B6
Columbia Mts., *Canada* 50 C5
Columbia Plateau,
 U.S.A. 56 D5
Columbretes, Is., *Spain* 15 C6
Columbus, *Ga., U.S.A.* . 53 J3
Columbus, *Ind., U.S.A.* 52 F3
Columbus, *Kans., U.S.A.* 55 G7
Columbus, *Miss., U.S.A.* 53 J1
Columbus, *Mont.,*
 U.S.A. 56 D9
Columbus, *N. Mex.,*
 U.S.A. 57 L10
Columbus, *Nebr., U.S.A.* 54 E6
Columbus, *Ohio, U.S.A.* 52 F4
Columbus, *Tex., U.S.A.* 55 L6
Colusa, *U.S.A.* 56 G2
Colville, *U.S.A.* 56 B5
Colville →, *U.S.A.* 46 A4
Colville, C., *N.Z.* 39 G5
Colwyn Bay, *U.K.* 8 D4
Comácchio, *Italy* 16 B5
Comalcalco, *Mexico* ... 59 D6
Comallo, *Argentina* ... 64 E2
Comanche, *U.S.A.* 55 K5
Comayagua, *Honduras* 60 D2
Combahee →, *U.S.A.* . 53 J5
Comblain-au-Pont,
 Belgium 11 D5
Comet, *Australia* 42 C4
Comilla, *Bangla.* 29 H17
Comino, C., *Italy* 16 D3
Comitán, *Mexico* 59 D6
Commerce, *Ga., U.S.A.* 53 H4
Commerce, *Tex., U.S.A.* 55 J7
Committee B., *Canada* . 47 B11
Commonwealth B.,
 Antarctica 5 C10
Commoron Cr. →,
 Australia 43 D5

Communism Pk. =
 Kommunizma, Pik,
 Tajikistan 20 F8
Como, *Italy* 14 D8
Como, Lago di, *Italy* ... 14 D8
Comodoro Rivadavia,
 Argentina 64 F3
Comoro Is. =
 Comoros ■, *Ind. Oc.* . 3 E12
Comoros ■, *Ind. Oc.* .. 3 E12
Comox, *Canada* 50 D4
Compiègne, *France* ... 14 B5
Compostela, *Mexico* ... 58 C4
Comrat, *Moldova* 13 E15
Con Son, *Vietnam* 26 C3
Conakry, *Guinea* 34 G3
Conara, *Australia* 42 G4
Concarneau, *France* ... 14 C2
Conceição da Barra,
 Brazil 63 G11
Conceição do Araguaia,
 Brazil 63 E9
Concepción, *Argentina* 64 B3
Concepción, *Bolivia* ... 62 G6
Concepción, *Chile* 64 D2
Concepción, *Mexico* ... 59 D6
Concepción, *Paraguay* . 64 A5
Concepción →, *Mexico* 58 A2
Concepción, Est. de,
 Chile 64 G2
Concepción, L., *Bolivia* 62 G6
Concepción, Punta,
 Mexico 58 B2
Concepción del Oro,
 Mexico 58 C4
Concepción del
 Uruguay, *Argentina* . 64 C5
Conception, Pt., *U.S.A.* 57 J3
Conception B., *Canada* 49 C9
Conception I., *Bahamas* 61 B4
Conchas Dam, *U.S.A.* . 55 H2
Concho, *U.S.A.* 57 J9
Concho →, *U.S.A.* 55 K5
Conchos →,
 Chihuahua, Mexico .. 58 B4
Conchos →,
 Tamaulipas, Mexico . 59 B5
Concord, *Calif., U.S.A.* . 56 H2
Concord, *N.C., U.S.A.* . 53 H5
Concord, *N.H., U.S.A.* . 52 D10
Concordia, *Argentina* .. 64 C5
Concórdia, *Brazil* 62 D5
Concordia, *Mexico* 58 C3
Concordia, *U.S.A.* 54 F6
Concrete, *U.S.A.* 56 B3
Condamine, *Australia* .. 43 D5
Conde, *U.S.A.* 54 C5
Condeúba, *Brazil* 63 F10
Condobolin, *Australia* .. 43 E4
Condon, *U.S.A.* 56 D3
Conegliano, *Italy* 16 B5
Conejos, *Mexico* 58 B4
Confuso →, *Paraguay* . 64 B5
Congleton, *U.K.* 8 D5
Congo (Kinshasa) =
 Congo, Dem. Rep. of
 the ■, *Africa* 36 E4
Congo ■, *Africa* 36 E3
Congo →, *Africa* 36 F2
Congo, Dem. Rep. of
 the ■, *Africa* 36 E4
Congo Basin, *Africa* ... 36 E4
Congress, *U.S.A.* 57 J7
Coniston, *Canada* 48 C3
Conjeeveram =
 Kanchipuram, *India* . 28 N11
Conklin, *Canada* 51 B6
Conn, L., *Ireland* 10 D2
Connacht □, *Ireland* .. 10 E2
Conneaut, *U.S.A.* 52 E5
Connecticut □, *U.S.A.* . 52 E9
Connecticut →, *U.S.A.* 52 E9
Connell, *U.S.A.* 56 C4
Connellsville, *U.S.A.* ... 52 E6
Connemara, *Ireland* ... 10 E2
Connersville, *U.S.A.* ... 52 F3
Connors Ra., *Australia* . 42 C4
Conquest, *Canada* 51 C7
Conrad, *U.S.A.* 56 B8
Conran, C., *Australia* ... 43 F4
Conroe, *U.S.A.* 55 K7
Conselheiro Lafaiete,
 Brazil 63 H10
Consett, *U.K.* 8 C6
Consort, *Canada* 51 C6
Constance = Konstanz,
 Germany 12 E5
Constance, L. =
 Bodensee, *Europe* .. 14 C8
Constanța, *Romania* ... 13 F15
Constantine, *Algeria* ... 34 A7
Constitución, *Chile* 64 D2
Consul, *Canada* 51 D7
Contact, *U.S.A.* 56 F6
Contai, *India* 29 J15
Contamana, *Peru* 62 E4
Contas →, *Brazil* 63 F11
Contwoyto L., *Canada* . 46 B8
Conway = Conwy, *U.K.* 8 D4
Conway →,
 U.K. 8 D4
Conway, *Ark., U.S.A.* .. 55 H8
Conway, *N.H., U.S.A.* .. 52 D10
Conway, *S.C., U.S.A.* .. 53 J6

Conway, L., *Australia* .. 43 D2
Conwy, *U.K.* 8 D4
Conwy □, *U.K.* 8 D4
Conwy →, *U.K.* 8 D4
Coober Pedy, *Australia* 43 D1
Cooinda, *Australia* 40 B5
Cook, *Australia* 41 F5
Cook, *U.S.A.* 54 B8
Cook, B., *Chile* 64 H3
Cook, C., *Canada* 50 C3
Cook, Mt. = Aoraki
 Mount Cook, *N.Z.* ... 39 K3
Cook Inlet, *U.S.A.* 46 C4
Cook Is., *Pac. Oc.* 45 J12
Cook Strait, *N.Z.* 39 J5
Cookeville, *U.S.A.* 53 G3
Cookhouse, *S. Africa* .. 37 L5
Cookstown, *U.K.* 10 B5
Cooktown, *Australia* ... 42 B4
Coolabah, *Australia* ... 43 E4
Cooladdi, *Australia* 43 D4
Coolah, *Australia* 43 E4
Coolamon, *Australia* ... 43 E4
Coolgardie, *Australia* .. 41 F3
Coolidge, *U.S.A.* 57 K8
Coolidge Dam, *U.S.A.* . 57 K8
Cooma, *Australia* 43 F4
Coon Rapids, *U.S.A.* .. 54 C8
Coonabarabran,
 Australia 43 E4
Coonalpyn, *Australia* .. 43 F2
Coonamble, *Australia* .. 43 E4
Coonana, *Australia* 41 F3
Coondapoor, *India* 28 N9
Cooninie, L., *Australia* . 43 D2
Cooper, *U.S.A.* 55 J7
Cooper Cr. →,
 Australia 43 D2
Cooperstown, *N. Dak.,*
 U.S.A. 54 B5
Cooperstown, *N.Y.,*
 U.S.A. 52 D8
Coorabie, *Australia* 41 F5
Coorow, *Australia* 41 E2
Cooroy, *Australia* 43 D5
Coos Bay, *U.S.A.* 56 E1
Coosa →, *U.S.A.* 53 J2
Cootamundra, *Australia* 43 E4
Copainalá, *Mexico* 59 D6
Copán, *Honduras* 60 D2
Cope, *U.S.A.* 54 F3
Copenhagen =
 København, *Denmark* 7 J15
Copiapó, *Chile* 64 B2
Copiapó →, *Chile* 64 B2
Copp L., *Canada* 50 A6
Copper Harbor, *U.S.A.* . 52 B2
Copperas Cove, *U.S.A.* 55 K6
Coppermine =
 Kugluktuk, *Canada* .. 46 B8
Coppermine →,
 Canada 46 B8
Coquet →, *U.K.* 8 B6
Coquilhatville =
 Mbandaka, *Dem. Rep.*
 of the Congo 36 D3
Coquille, *U.S.A.* 56 E1
Coquimbo, *Chile* 64 C2
Corabia, *Romania* 13 G13
Coracora, *Peru* 62 G4
Coraki, *Australia* 43 D5
Coral Gables, *U.S.A.* ... 53 N5
Coral Harbour = Salliq,
 Canada 47 B11
Coral Sea, *Pac. Oc.* ... 38 C8
Coral Sea Islands
 Terr. □, *Australia* ... 38 C8
Coral Springs, *U.S.A.* .. 53 M5
Corato, *Italy* 16 D7
Corbin, *U.S.A.* 52 G3
Corby, *U.K.* 9 E7
Corcaigh = Cork, *Ireland* 10 F2
Corcoran, *U.S.A.* 57 H4
Corcubión, *Spain* 15 A1
Cordele, *U.S.A.* 53 K4
Cordell, *U.S.A.* 55 H5
Córdoba, *Argentina* ... 64 C4
Córdoba, *Mexico* 59 D5
Córdoba, *Spain* 15 D3
Córdoba, Sierra de,
 Argentina 64 C4
Cordova, *U.S.A.* 46 B5
Corella, →, *Australia* .. 42 B3
Corfield, *Australia* 42 C3
Corfu = Kérkira, *Greece* 17 E8
Coria, *Spain* 15 C2
Corigliano Cálabro, *Italy* 16 E7
Coringa Is., *Australia* .. 42 B4
Corinth = Kórinthos,
 Greece 17 F10
Corinth, *U.S.A.* 53 H1
Corinth, G. of =
 Korinthiakós Kólpos,
 Greece 17 E10
Corinto, *Brazil* 63 G10
Corinto, *Nic.* 60 D2
Cork, *Ireland* 10 F2
Çorlu, *Turkey* 17 D12
Cormack L., *Canada* .. 50 A4
Cormorant, *Canada* ... 51 C8
Cormorant L., *Canada* . 51 C8
Corn Is. = Maíz, Is. del,
 Nic. 60 D3

Corner Brook, *Canada* . 49 C8
Corneşti, *Moldova* 13 E15
Corning, *Ark., U.S.A.* .. 55 G9
Corning, *Calif., U.S.A.* . 56 G2
Corning, *Iowa, U.S.A.* . 54 E7
Corning, *N.Y., U.S.A.* .. 52 D7
Cornwall, *Canada* 48 C5
Cornwall □, *U.K.* 9 G3
Corny Pt., *Australia* 43 E2
Coro, *Venezuela* 62 A5
Coroatá, *Brazil* 63 D10
Corocoro, *Bolivia* 62 G5
Coroico, *Bolivia* 62 G5
Coromandel, *N.Z.* 39 G5
Coromandel Coast, *India* 28 N12
Corona, *Calif., U.S.A.* .. 57 K5
Corona, *N. Mex., U.S.A.* 57 J11
Coronach, *Canada* 51 D7
Coronado, B. de,
 Costa Rica 60 E3
Coronation, *Canada* ... 50 C6
Coronation Gulf, *Canada* 46 B8
Coronation I., *Antarctica* 5 C18
Coronation Is., *Australia* 40 B3
Coronel, *Chile* 64 D2
Coronel Dorrego,
 Argentina 64 D4
Coronel Oviedo,
 Paraguay 64 B5
Coronel Pringles,
 Argentina 64 D4
Coronel Suárez,
 Argentina 64 D4
Coropuna, Nevado, *Peru* 62 G4
Corowa, *Australia* 43 F4
Corozal, *Belize* 59 D7
Corpus Christi, *U.S.A.* . 55 M6
Corpus Christi, L.,
 U.S.A. 55 L6
Corrib, L., *Ireland* 10 E2
Corrientes, *Argentina* .. 64 B5
Corrientes →, *Peru* ... 62 D4
Corrientes, C., *Colombia* 62 B3
Corrientes, C., *Cuba* .. 60 B3
Corrientes, C., *Mexico* 58 C3
Corrigan, *U.S.A.* 55 K7
Corrigin, *Australia* 41 F2
Corry, *U.S.A.* 52 E6
Corryong, *Australia* 43 F4
Corse, *France* 14 F8
Corse, C., *France* 14 E8
Corsica = Corse, *France* 14 F8
Corsicana, *U.S.A.* 55 J6
Corte, *France* 14 E8
Cortez, *U.S.A.* 57 H9
Cortland, *U.S.A.* 52 D7
Çorum, *Turkey* 19 F5
Corumbá, *Brazil* 62 G7
Corunna = A Coruña,
 Spain 15 A1
Corvallis, *U.S.A.* 56 D2
Corvette, L. de la,
 Canada 48 B5
Corydon, *U.S.A.* 54 E8
Cosalá, *Mexico* 58 C3
Cosamaloapan, *Mexico* 59 D5
Cosenza, *Italy* 16 E7
Coshocton, *U.S.A.* 52 E5
Cosmo Newberry,
 Australia 41 E3
Costa Blanca, *Spain* ... 15 C5
Costa Brava, *Spain* 15 B7
Costa del Sol, *Spain* ... 15 D3
Costa Dorada, *Spain* .. 15 B6
Costa Rica ■,
 Cent. Amer. 60 E3
Cotabato, *Phil.* 27 C6
Cotagaita, *Bolivia* 62 H5
Côte d'Azur, *France* ... 14 E7
Côte-d'Ivoire = Ivory
 Coast ■, *Africa* 34 G4
Coteau des Prairies,
 U.S.A. 54 C6
Coteau du Missouri,
 U.S.A. 54 B4
Cotentin, *France* 14 B3
Cotonou, *Benin* 34 G6
Cotopaxi, *Ecuador* 62 D3
Cotswold Hills, *U.K.* ... 9 F5
Cottage Grove, *U.S.A.* . 56 E2
Cottbus, *Germany* 12 C8
Cottonwood, *U.S.A.* ... 57 J7
Cotulla, *U.S.A.* 55 L5
Coudersport, *U.S.A.* ... 52 E6
Couedic, C. du, *Australia* 43 F2
Coulee City, *U.S.A.* ... 56 C4
Coulman I., *Antarctica* . 5 D11
Coulonge →, *Canada* . 48 C4
Council, *U.S.A.* 56 D5
Council Bluffs, *U.S.A.* .. 54 E7
Council Grove, *U.S.A.* . 54 F6
Courantyne →,
 S. Amer. 62 B7
Courcelles, *Belgium* ... 11 D4
Courtenay, *Canada* ... 50 D4
Courtrai = Kortrijk,
 Belgium 11 D3
Coushatta, *U.S.A.* 55 J8
Coutts Crossing,
 Australia 43 D5
Couvin, *Belgium* 11 D4
Coventry, *U.K.* 9 E6
Covilhã, *Portugal* 15 B2
Covington, *Ga., U.S.A.* 53 J4
Covington, *Ky., U.S.A.* . 52 F3

Covington, *Okla., U.S.A.* **55** G6
Covington, *Tenn., U.S.A.* **55** H10
Covington, *Va., U.S.A.* **52** G5
Cowal, L., *Australia* **43** E4
Cowan, L., *Australia* **41** F3
Cowan, L., *Canada* **51** C7
Cowangie, *Australia* **43** F3
Cowansville, *Canada* **48** C5
Coward Springs, *Australia* **43** D2
Cowcowing Lakes, *Australia* **41** F2
Cowell, *Australia* **43** E2
Cowes, *U.K.* **9** G6
Cowra, *Australia* **43** E4
Coxim, *Brazil* **63** G8
Cox's Bazar, *Bangla.* **29** J17
Coyuca de Benítez, *Mexico* **59** D4
Coyuca de Catalan, *Mexico* **58** D4
Cozad, *U.S.A.* **54** E5
Cozumel, *Mexico* **59** C7
Cozumel, Isla, *Mexico* **59** C7
Cracow = Kraków, *Poland* **13** C10
Cracow, *Australia* **43** D5
Cradock, *Australia* **43** E2
Cradock, *S. Africa* **37** L5
Craig, *U.S.A.* **56** F10
Craigavon, *U.K.* **10** D3
Craik, *Canada* **51** C7
Crailsheim, *Germany* **12** D6
Craiova, *Romania* **13** F12
Cramsie, *Australia* **42** C3
Cranberry Portage, *Canada* **51** C8
Cranbrook, *Australia* **41** F2
Cranbrook, *Canada* **50** D5
Crandon, *U.S.A.* **54** C10
Crane, *Oreg., U.S.A.* **56** E4
Crane, *Tex., U.S.A.* **55** K3
Crater L., *U.S.A.* **56** E2
Crater Lake National Park, *U.S.A.* **56** E2
Crateús, *Brazil* **63** E10
Crato, *Brazil* **63** E11
Craven, L., *Canada* **48** B4
Crawford, *U.S.A.* **54** D3
Crawfordsville, *U.S.A.* **52** E2
Crawley, *U.K.* **9** F7
Crazy Mts., *U.S.A.* **56** C8
Crean L., *Canada* **51** C7
Cree →, *Canada* **51** B7
Cree L., *Canada* **51** B7
Creede, *U.S.A.* **57** H10
Creel, *Mexico* **58** B3
Creighton, *Canada* **51** C8
Creighton, *U.S.A.* **54** D6
Crema, *Italy* **14** D8
Cremona, *Italy* **14** D9
Cres, *Croatia* **12** F8
Crescent City, *U.S.A.* **56** F1
Creston, *Canada* **50** D5
Creston, *U.S.A.* **54** E7
Crestview, *U.S.A.* **53** K2
Crete = Kríti, *Greece* **17** G11
Crete, *U.S.A.* **54** E6
Créteil, *France* **14** B5
Creus, C. de, *Spain* **15** A7
Creuse →, *France* **14** C4
Crewe, *U.K.* **8** D5
Crewkerne, *U.K.* **9** G5
Criciúma, *Brazil* **64** B7
Crimea □, *Ukraine* **19** E5
Crimean Pen. = Krymskyy Pivostriv, *Ukraine* **19** F5
Crişul Alb →, *Romania* **13** E11
Crişul Negru →, *Romania* **13** E11
Crna →, *Macedonia* **17** D9
Crna Gora = Montenegro □, *Yugoslavia* **17** C8
Crna Gora, *Macedonia* **17** C9
Crna Reka = Crna →, *Macedonia* **17** D9
Croatia ■, *Europe* **12** F9
Crocker, Banjaran, *Malaysia* **26** C5
Crockett, *U.S.A.* **55** K7
Crocodile Is., *Australia* **42** A1
Croix, L. La, *Canada* **48** C1
Croker, C., *Australia* **40** B5
Croker I., *Australia* **40** B5
Cromer, *U.K.* **8** E9
Cromwell, *N.Z.* **39** L2
Crook, *U.K.* **8** C6
Crooked →, *Canada* **50** C4
Crooked →, *U.S.A.* **56** D3
Crooked I., *Bahamas* **61** B5
Crooked Island Passage, *Bahamas* **61** B5
Crookston, *Minn., U.S.A.* **54** B6
Crookston, *Nebr., U.S.A.* **54** D4
Crookwell, *Australia* **43** E4
Crosby, *U.K.* **8** D4
Crosby, *U.S.A.* **54** A3
Crosbyton, *U.S.A.* **55** J4
Cross City, *U.S.A.* **53** L4
Cross Fell, *U.K.* **8** C5
Cross L., *Canada* **51** C9
Cross Lake, *Canada* **51** C9
Cross Sound, *U.S.A.* **46** C6

Crossett, *U.S.A.* **55** J9
Crossville, *U.S.A.* **53** G3
Crotone, *Italy* **16** E7
Crow →, *Canada* **50** B4
Crow Agency, *U.S.A.* **56** D10
Crowell, *U.S.A.* **55** J5
Crowley, *U.S.A.* **55** K9
Crown Point, *U.S.A.* **52** E2
Crownpoint, *U.S.A.* **57** J9
Crows Nest, *Australia* **43** D5
Crowsnest Pass, *Canada* **50** D6
Croydon, *Australia* **42** B3
Croydon □, *U.K.* **9** F7
Crozet, Is., *Ind. Oc.* **3** G12
Cruz, C., *Cuba* **60** C4
Cruz Alta, *Brazil* **64** B6
Cruz del Eje, *Argentina* **64** C4
Cruzeiro, *Brazil* **64** A8
Cruzeiro do Sul, *Brazil* **62** E4
Cry L., *Canada* **50** B3
Crystal Brook, *Australia* **43** E2
Crystal City, *U.S.A.* **55** L5
Crystal Falls, *U.S.A.* **52** B1
Crystal River, *U.S.A.* **53** L4
Crystal Springs, *U.S.A.* **55** K9
Csongrád, *Hungary* **13** E11
Cuamba, *Mozam.* **37** G7
Cuando →, *Angola* **37** H4
Cuangar, *Angola* **37** H3
Cuango = Kwango →, *Africa* **36** E3
Cuanza →, *Angola* **36** F2
Cuarto →, *Argentina* **64** C3
Cuatrociénegas, *Mexico* **58** B4
Cuauhtémoc, *Mexico* **58** B3
Cuba, *U.S.A.* **57** J10
Cuba ■, *W. Indies* **60** B4
Cubango →, *Africa* **37** H4
Cuchumatanes, Sierra de los, *Guatemala* **60** C1
Cuckfield, *U.K.* **9** F7
Cucuí, *Brazil* **62** C5
Cucurpe, *Mexico* **58** A2
Cúcuta, *Colombia* **62** B4
Cuddalore, *India* **28** P11
Cuddapah, *India* **28** M11
Cuddapan, L., *Australia* **42** D3
Cue, *Australia* **41** E2
Cuenca, *Ecuador* **62** D3
Cuenca, *Spain* **15** B4
Cuenca, Serranía de, *Spain* **15** C5
Cuernavaca, *Mexico* **59** D5
Cuero, *U.S.A.* **55** L6
Cuevas del Almanzora, *Spain* **15** D5
Cuevo, *Bolivia* **62** H6
Cuiabá, *Brazil* **63** G7
Cuiabá →, *Brazil* **63** G7
Cuijk, *Neths.* **11** C5
Cuilco, *Guatemala* **60** C1
Cuillin Hills, *U.K.* **10** C3
Cuito →, *Angola* **37** H4
Cuitzeo, L. de, *Mexico* **58** D4
Culbertson, *U.S.A.* **54** A2
Culcairn, *Australia* **43** F4
Culgoa →, *Australia* **43** D4
Culiacán, *Mexico* **58** C3
Culiacán →, *Mexico* **58** C3
Culion, *Phil.* **27** B6
Cullarin Ra., *Australia* **43** E4
Cullen Pt., *Australia* **42** A3
Cullera, *Spain* **15** C5
Cullman, *U.S.A.* **53** H2
Culloden, *U.S.A.* **52** F7
Culpeper, *U.S.A.* **52** F7
Culuene →, *Brazil* **63** F8
Culver, Pt., *Australia* **41** F3
Culverden, *N.Z.* **39** K4
Cumaná, *Venezuela* **62** A6
Cumberland, *Canada* **50** D4
Cumberland, *U.S.A.* **52** F6
Cumberland →, *U.S.A.* **53** G2
Cumberland, L., *U.S.A.* **53** G3
Cumberland I., *U.S.A.* **53** K5
Cumberland Is., *Australia* **42** C4
Cumberland L., *Canada* **51** C8
Cumberland Pen., *Canada* **47** B13
Cumberland Plateau, *U.S.A.* **53** H3
Cumberland Sd., *Canada* **47** B13
Cumborah, *Australia* **43** D4
Cumbria □, *U.K.* **8** C5
Cumbrian Mts., *U.K.* **8** C5
Cumbum, *India* **28** M11
Cuminá →, *Brazil* **63** D7
Cummins, *Australia* **43** E2
Cumnock, *Australia* **43** E4
Cumpas, *Mexico* **58** B3
Cunco, *Chile* **64** D2
Cunderdin, *Australia* **41** F2
Cunene →, *Angola* **37** H2
Cúneo, *Italy* **14** D7
Çüngüş, *Turkey* **30** B3
Cunnamulla, *Australia* **43** D4
Cupar, *Canada* **51** C8
Cupar, *U.K.* **10** C5
Cupica, G. de, *Colombia* **62** B3
Curaçao, *Neth. Ant.* **62** A5
Curanilahue, *Chile* **64** D2
Curaray →, *Peru* **62** D4
Curiapo, *Venezuela* **62** B6
Curicó, *Chile* **64** C2
Curitiba, *Brazil* **64** B7
Curitibanos, *Brazil* **64** B6
Currabubula, *Australia* **43** E5
Currais Novos, *Brazil* **63** E11
Curralinho, *Brazil* **63** D9
Currane, L., *Ireland* **10** E1
Currant, *U.S.A.* **56** G6
Current →, *U.S.A.* **55** G9
Currie, *Australia* **42** F3

Currie, *U.S.A.* **56** F6
Curtea de Argeş, *Romania* **13** F13
Curtis, *U.S.A.* **54** E4
Curtis Group, *Australia* **42** F4
Curtis I., *Australia* **42** C5
Curuápanema →, *Brazil* **63** D7
Curuçá, *Brazil* **63** D9
Curup, *Indonesia* **26** E2
Cururupu, *Brazil* **63** D10
Curuzú Cuatiá, *Argentina* **64** B5
Curvelo, *Brazil* **63** G10
Cushing, *U.S.A.* **55** H6
Cushing, Mt., *Canada* **50** B3
Cusihuiriáchic, *Mexico* **58** B3
Custer, *U.S.A.* **54** D3
Cut Bank, *U.S.A.* **56** B7
Cuthbert, *U.S.A.* **53** K3
Cuttaburra →, *Australia* **43** D3
Cuttack, *India* **29** J14
Cuvier, C., *Australia* **41** D1
Cuvier I., *N.Z.* **39** G5
Cuxhaven, *Germany* **12** B5
Cuyahoga Falls, *U.S.A.* **52** E5
Cuyo, *Phil.* **27** B6
Cuyuni →, *Guyana* **62** B7
Cuzco, *Bolivia* **62** H5
Cuzco, *Peru* **62** F4
Cwmbran, *U.K.* **9** F4
Cyclades = Kikládhes, *Greece* **17** F11
Cygnet, *Australia* **42** G4
Cynthiana, *U.S.A.* **52** F3
Cypress Hills, *Canada* **51** D7
Cypress Hills Prov. Park, *Canada* **51** D7
Cyprus ■, *Asia* **30** C2
Cyrenaica, *Libya* **35** C10
Czar, *Canada* **51** C6
Czech Rep. ■, *Europe* **12** D8
Częstochowa, *Poland* **13** C10

Da Hinggan Ling, *China* **25** B7
Da Lat, *Vietnam* **26** B3
Da Nang, *Vietnam* **26** A3
Da Qaidam, *China* **24** C4
Daba Shan, *China* **25** C5
Dabbagh, Jabal, *Si. Arabia* **30** E2
Dabo = Pasirkuning, *Indonesia* **26** E2
Dabola, *Guinea* **34** F2
Dacca = Dhaka, *Bangla.* **29** H17
Dacca = Dhaka □, *Bangla.* **29** G17
Dachau, *Germany* **12** D6
Dadanawa, *Guyana* **62** C7
Dade City, *U.S.A.* **53** L4
Dadra & Nagar Haveli □, *India* **28** J8
Dadu, *Pakistan* **28** F5
Daet, *Phil.* **27** B6
Dagana, *Senegal* **34** E2
Dagestan □, *Russia* **19** F8
Daghestan Republic = Dagestan □, *Russia* **19** F8
Dağlıq Qarabağ = Nagorno-Karabakh, *Azerbaijan* **19** F8
Dagö = Hiiumaa, *Estonia* **7** G20
Dagupan, *Phil.* **27** A6
Daguragu, *Australia* **40** C5
Dahlak Kebir, *Eritrea* **32** D3
Dahlonega, *U.S.A.* **53** H4
Dahod, *India* **28** H9
Dahomey = Benin ■, *Africa* **34** G6
Dahūk, *Iraq* **30** B3
Dai-Sen, *Japan* **23** G6
Daintree, *Australia* **42** B4
Daió-Misaki, *Japan* **23** G8
Daisetsu-Zan, *Japan* **22** C11
Dajarra, *Australia* **42** C2
Dakar, *Senegal* **34** F2
Dakhla, *W. Sahara* **34** D2
Dakhla, El Wâhât el-, *Egypt* **35** C11
Dakota City, *U.S.A.* **54** D6
Đakovica, *Kosovo, Yug.* **17** C9
Đakovo, *Croatia* **17** C8
Dālakī, *Iran* **31** D6
Dalaman, *Turkey* **17** F13
Dalandzadgad, *Mongolia* **24** B5
Dalap-Uliga-Darrit, *Marshall Is.* **44** G9
Dalarna, *Sweden* **7** F16
Dālbandīn, *Pakistan* **28** E4
Dalbeg, *Australia* **42** C4
Dalby, *Australia* **43** D5
Dale City, *U.S.A.* **52** F7
Dale Hollow L., *U.S.A.* **53** G3
Dalgán, *Iran* **31** E8
Dalhart, *U.S.A.* **55** G3
Dalhousie, *Canada* **49** C6
Dali, *China* **24** D5
Dalian, *China* **25** C7
Daliang Shan, *China* **24** D5
Dāliyat el Karmel, *Israel* **33** C4
Dallas, *Oreg., U.S.A.* **56** D2

Currie, *U.S.A.* **56** F6
Dallas, *Tex., U.S.A.* **55** J6
Dalmã, *U.A.E.* **31** E7
Dalmacija, *Croatia* **16** C7
Dalmas, L., *Canada* **49** B5
Dalmatia = Dalmacija, *Croatia* **16** C7
Dalnegorsk, *Russia* **21** E14
Dalnerechensk, *Russia* **21** E14
Daloa, *Ivory C.* **34** G4
Dalrymple, L., *Australia* **42** C4
Dalsland, *Sweden* **7** G14
Dalton, *Ga., U.S.A.* **53** H3
Dalton, *Nebr., U.S.A.* **54** E3
Dalton Iceberg Tongue, *Antarctica* **5** C9
Dalton-in-Furness, *U.K.* **8** C4
Dalvík, *Iceland* **6** D4
Dalwallinu, *Australia* **41** F2
Daly →, *Australia* **40** B5
Daly L., *Canada* **51** B7
Daly River, *Australia* **40** B5
Daly Waters, *Australia* **42** B1
Daman, *India* **28** J8
Dāmaneh, *Iran* **31** C6
Damanhûr, *Egypt* **35** B12
Damar, *Indonesia* **27** F7
Damaraland, *Namibia* **37** H2
Damascus = Dimashq, *Syria* **33** B5
Damāvand, *Iran* **31** C7
Damāvand, Qolleh-ye, *Iran* **31** C7
Damba, *Angola* **36** F3
Dâmboviţa →, *Romania* **13** F14
Dame Marie, *Haiti* **61** C5
Damghan, *Iran* **31** B7
Damiel, *Spain* **15** C4
Damietta = Dumyât, *Egypt* **35** B12
Damīr Qābū, *Syria* **30** B4
Dammam = Ad Dammām, *Si. Arabia* **31** E6
Damoh, *India* **28** H11
Dampier, *Australia* **40** D2
Dampier, Selat, *Indonesia* **27** E8
Dampier Arch., *Australia* **40** D2
Dana, *Indonesia* **27** F6
Dana, L., *Canada* **48** B4
Danakil Desert, *Ethiopia* **32** E3
Danané, *Ivory C.* **34** G4
Danau Poso, *Indonesia* **27** E6
Danbury, *U.S.A.* **52** E9
Danby L., *U.S.A.* **57** J6
Dandeldhura, *Nepal* **29** E12
Dandeli, *India* **28** M9
Dandenong, *Australia* **43** F4
Dandong, *China* **25** B7
Danger Is. = Pukapuka, *Cook Is.* **45** J11
Dangla Shan = Tanggula Shan, *China* **24** C4
Dangriga, *Belize* **59** D7
Daniel, *U.S.A.* **56** E8
Daniel's Harbour, *Canada* **49** B8
Danilov, *Russia* **18** C7
Dank, *Oman* **31** F8
Dankhar Gompa, *India* **28** C11
Danli, *Honduras* **60** D2
Dannemora, *U.S.A.* **52** C9
Dannevirke, *N.Z.* **39** J6
Dansville, *U.S.A.* **52** D7
Dante, *Somali Rep.* **32** E5
Danube = Dunărea →, *Europe* **13** F15
Danville, *Ill., U.S.A.* **52** E2
Danville, *Ky., U.S.A.* **52** G3
Danville, *Va., U.S.A.* **53** G6
Danzig = Gdańsk, *Poland* **13** A10
Dapaong, *Togo* **34** F6
Dar el Beida = Casablanca, *Morocco* **34** B4
Dar es Salaam, *Tanzania* **36** F7
Dar Mazār, *Iran* **31** D8
Dar'ā, *Syria* **33** C5
Dar'ā □, *Syria* **33** C5
Dārāb, *Iran* **31** D7
Daraj, *Libya* **35** B8
Dārān, *Iran* **31** C6
Dārayyā, *Syria* **33** B5
Darband, *Pakistan* **28** B8
Darband, Kūh-e, *Iran* **31** D8
Darbhanga, *India* **29** F14
D'Arcy, *Canada* **50** C4
Dardanelle, *U.S.A.* **55** H8
Dardanelles = Çanakkale Boğazı, *Turkey* **17** D12
Dārestān, *Iran* **31** D8
Dârfûr, *Sudan* **35** F10
Dargai, *Pakistan* **28** B7
Dargan Ata, *Uzbekistan* **20** E7
Dargaville, *N.Z.* **39** F4
Darhan, *Mongolia* **24** B5
Darica, *Turkey* **17** D13
Darién, G. del, *Colombia* **62** B3
Darjeeling = Darjiling, *India* **29** F16
Darjiling, *India* **29** F16
Darkan, *Australia* **41** F2
Darkhazineh, *Iran* **31** D6

Darling →, *Australia* **43** E3
Darling Downs, *Australia* **43** D5
Darling Ra., *Australia* **41** F2
Darlington, *U.K.* **8** C6
Darlington, *U.S.A.* **53** H6
Darlington □, *U.K.* **8** C6
Darlington Point, *Australia* **43** E4
Darłot, L., *Australia* **41** E3
Darłowo, *Poland* **12** A9
Darmstadt, *Germany* **12** D5
Darnah, *Libya* **35** B10
Darnley, C., *Antarctica* **5** C6
Darnley B., *Canada* **46** B7
Darr →, *Australia* **42** C3
Darrington, *U.S.A.* **56** B3
Dart, C., *Antarctica* **5** D14
Dartford, *U.K.* **9** F8
Dartmoor, *U.K.* **9** G4
Dartmouth, *Canada* **49** D7
Dartmouth, *U.K.* **9** G4
Dartmouth, L., *Australia* **43** D4
Darvaza, *Turkmenistan* **20** E6
Darvel, Teluk = Lahad Datu, Teluk, *Malaysia* **27** D5
Darwen, *U.K.* **8** D5
Darwha, *India* **28** J10
Darwin, *Australia* **40** B5
Daryoi Amu = Amudarya →, *Uzbekistan* **20** E6
Dās, *U.A.E.* **31** E7
Dashen, Ras, *Ethiopia* **32** E2
Dashhowuz = Turkmenistan **20** E6
Dashköpri, *Turkmenistan* **31** B9
Dasht, *Iran* **31** B8
Dasht →, *Pakistan* **28** G2
Datça, *Turkey* **17** F12
Datia, *India* **28** G11
Datong, *China* **25** B6
Datu, Tanjung, *Indonesia* **26** D3
Datu Piang, *Phil.* **27** C6
Datuk, Tanjong = Datu, Tanjung, *Indonesia* **26** D3
Daugava →, *Latvia* **7** H21
Daugavpils, *Latvia* **7** J22
Daulpur, *India* **28** F10
Dauphin, *Canada* **51** C8
Dauphin L., *Canada* **51** C9
Dauphiné, *France* **14** D6
Davangere, *India* **28** M9
Davao, *Phil.* **27** C7
Davao G., *Phil.* **27** C7
Dāvar Panāh, *Iran* **31** E9
Dāvar Panāh, *Iran* **31** E9
Davenport, *Iowa, U.S.A.* **54** E9
Davenport, *Wash., U.S.A.* **56** C4
Davenport Ra., *Australia* **42** C1
Daventry, *U.K.* **9** E6
David, *Panama* **60** E3
David City, *U.S.A.* **54** E6
David Gorodok = Davyd Haradok, *Belarus* **13** B14
Davidson, *Canada* **51** C7
Davis, *U.S.A.* **56** G3
Davis Dam, *U.S.A.* **57** J6
Davis Inlet, *Canada* **49** A7
Davis Mts., *U.S.A.* **55** K2
Davis Sea, *Antarctica* **5** C7
Davis Str., *N. Amer.* **47** B14
Davos, *Switz.* **14** C8
Davy L., *Canada* **51** B7
Davyd Haradok, *Belarus* **13** B14
Dawei, *Burma* **26** B1
Dawes Ra., *Australia* **42** C5
Dawlish, *U.K.* **9** G4
Dawson, *Canada* **46** B6
Dawson, *U.S.A.* **53** K3
Dawson, I., *Chile* **64** G2
Dawson Creek, *Canada* **50** B4
Dawson Inlet, *Canada* **51** A10
Dawson Ra., *Australia* **42** C4
Dax, *France* **14** E3
Daxian, *China* **24** C5
Daxue Shan, *China* **24** C5
Daylesford, *Australia* **43** F3
Dayr az Zawr, *Syria* **30** C4
Daysland, *Canada* **50** C6
Dayton, *Ohio, U.S.A.* **52** F3
Dayton, *Tenn., U.S.A.* **53** H3
Dayton, *Wash., U.S.A.* **56** C4
Dayton, *Wyo., U.S.A.* **56** D10
Daytona Beach, *U.S.A.* **53** L5
Dayville, *U.S.A.* **56** D4
De Aar, *S. Africa* **37** L4
De Funiak Springs, *U.S.A.* **53** K2
De Grey →, *Australia* **40** D2
De Haan, *Belgium* **11** C3
De Kalb, *U.S.A.* **54** E10
De Land, *U.S.A.* **53** L5
De Leon, *U.S.A.* **55** J5
De Panne, *Belgium* **11** C2
De Pere, *U.S.A.* **52** C1
De Queen, *U.S.A.* **55** H7
De Quincy, *U.S.A.* **55** K8
De Ridder, *U.S.A.* **55** K8
De Smet, *U.S.A.* **54** C6
De Soto, *U.S.A.* **54** F9

De Tour Village, *U.S.A.* **52** C4
De Witt, *U.S.A.* **55** H9
Dead Sea, *Asia* **33** D4
Deadwood, *U.S.A.* **54** C3
Deadwood L., *Canada* **50** B3
Deal, *U.K.* **9** F9
Deal I., *Australia* **42** F4
Dean →, *Canada* **50** C3
Dean, Forest of, *U.K.* **9** F5
Dean Chan., *Canada* **50** C3
Deán Funes, *Argentina* **64** C4
Dease →, *Canada* **50** B3
Dease L., *Canada* **50** B2
Dease Lake, *Canada* **50** B2
Death Valley, *U.S.A.* **57** H5
Death Valley Junction, *U.S.A.* **57** H5
Death Valley National Park, *U.S.A.* **57** H5
Debar, *Macedonia* **17** D9
Debden, *Canada* **51** C7
Dębica, *Poland* **13** C11
Debolt, *Canada* **50** B5
Deborah East, L., *Australia* **41** F2
Deborah West, L., *Australia* **41** F2
Debre Markos, *Ethiopia* **32** E2
Debre Tabor, *Ethiopia* **32** E2
Debre Zeyit, *Ethiopia* **32** F2
Debrecen, *Hungary* **13** E11
Decatur, *Ala., U.S.A.* **53** H2
Decatur, *Ga., U.S.A.* **53** J3
Decatur, *Ill., U.S.A.* **54** F10
Decatur, *Ind., U.S.A.* **52** E3
Decatur, *Tex., U.S.A.* **55** J6
Deccan, *India* **28** L11
Deception Bay, *Australia* **43** D5
Deception L., *Canada* **51** B8
Děčín, *Czech Rep.* **12** C8
Decorah, *U.S.A.* **54** D9
Dedéagach = Alexandroúpolis, *Greece* **17** D11
Dee →, *Aberds., U.K.* **10** C5
Dee →, *Wales, U.K.* **8** D4
Deep B., *Canada* **50** A5
Deepwater, *Australia* **43** D5
Deer →, *Canada* **51** B10
Deer L., *Canada* **51** C10
Deer Lake, *Nfld., Canada* **49** C8
Deer Lake, *Ont., Canada* **51** C10
Deer Lodge, *U.S.A.* **56** C7
Deer Park, *U.S.A.* **56** C5
Deer River, *U.S.A.* **54** B8
Deeragun, *Australia* **42** B4
Defiance, *U.S.A.* **52** E3
Dégelis, *Canada* **49** C6
Deggendorf, *Germany* **12** D7
Deh Bid, *Iran* **31** D7
Deh-e Shīr, *Iran* **31** D7
Dehaj, *Iran* **31** D7
Dehak, *Iran* **31** E9
Dehdez, *Iran* **31** D6
Dehestān, *Iran* **31** D7
Dehgolān, *Iran* **30** C5
Dehibat, *Tunisia* **35** B8
Dehlorān, *Iran* **30** C5
Dehnow-e Kühestān, *Iran* **31** E8
Dehra Dun, *India* **28** D11
Deinze, *Belgium* **11** D3
Dej, *Romania* **13** E12
Dekese, *Dem. Rep. of the Congo* **36** E4
Del Norte, *U.S.A.* **57** H10
Del Rio, *U.S.A.* **55** L4
Delambre I., *Australia* **40** D2
Delano, *U.S.A.* **57** J4
Delano Peak, *U.S.A.* **57** G7
Delaronde L., *Canada* **51** C7
Delavan, *U.S.A.* **54** D10
Delaware, *U.S.A.* **52** E4
Delaware □, *U.S.A.* **52** F8
Delaware →, *U.S.A.* **52** F8
Delay →, *Canada* **49** A5
Delegate, *Australia* **43** F4
Delft, *Neths.* **11** B4
Delfzijl, *Neths.* **11** A6
Delgado, C., *Mozam.* **36** G8
Delgo, *Sudan* **35** D12
Delhi, *India* **28** E10
Delhi, *U.S.A.* **55** J9
Delia, *Canada* **50** C6
Delice, *Turkey* **19** G5
Delicias, *Mexico* **58** B3
Delījān, *Iran* **31** C6
Déline, *Canada* **46** B7
Delisle, *Canada* **51** C7
Dell City, *U.S.A.* **57** L11
Dell Rapids, *U.S.A.* **54** D6
Delmenhorst, *Germany* **12** B5
Delonga, Ostrova, *Russia* **21** B15
Deloraine, *Australia* **42** G4
Deloraine, *Canada* **51** D8
Delphi, *U.S.A.* **52** E2
Delphos, *U.S.A.* **52** E3
Delray Beach, *U.S.A.* **53** M5
Delta, *Colo., U.S.A.* **57** G9
Delta, *Utah, U.S.A.* **56** G7
Delta Junction, *U.S.A.* **46** B5
Deltona, *U.S.A.* **53** L5
Delungra, *Australia* **43** D5
Delvinë, *Albania* **17** E9

Demak, *Indonesia* 27 G14
Demanda, Sierra de la,
  Spain 15 A4
Demavand =
  Damāvand, *Iran* 31 C7
Dembidolo, *Ethiopia* .. 32 F1
Demer ➤, *Belgium* .. 11 D4
Deming, *U.S.A.* 57 K10
Demini ➤, *Brazil* 62 D6
Demirci, *Turkey* 17 E13
Demirköy, *Turkey* ... 17 D12
Demopolis, *U.S.A.* 53 J2
Dempo, *Indonesia* 26 E2
Den Burg, *Neths.* 11 A4
Den Haag = 's-
  Gravenhage, *Neths.* .. 11 B4
Den Helder, *Neths.* 11 B4
Den Oever, *Neths.* 11 B5
Denau, *Uzbekistan* 20 F7
Denbigh, *U.K.* 8 D4
Denbighshire □, *U.K.* .. 8 D4
Dendang, *Indonesia* ... 26 E3
Dendermonde, *Belgium* 11 C4
Denham, *Australia* 41 E1
Denham B., *Australia* . 42 C4
Denham Sd., *Australia* 41 E1
Denholm, *Canada* 51 C7
Denia, *Spain* 15 C6
Denial B., *Australia* .. 43 E1
Deniliquin, *Australia* . 43 F3
Denison, *Iowa, U.S.A.* 54 E7
Denison, *Tex., U.S.A.* 55 J6
Denison Plains,
  Australia 40 C4
Denizli, *Turkey* 19 G4
Denman Glacier,
  Antarctica 5 C7
Denmark, *Australia* ... 41 F2
Denmark ■, *Europe* ... 7 J13
Denmark Str., *Atl. Oc.* . 4 C6
Denpasar, *Indonesia* .. 26 F5
Denton, *Mont., U.S.A.* 56 C9
Denton, *Tex., U.S.A.* . 55 J6
D'Entrecasteaux, Pt.,
  Australia 41 F2
D'Entrecasteaux Is.,
  Papua N. G. 38 B8
Denver, *U.S.A.* 54 F2
Denver City, *U.S.A.* ... 55 J3
Deoghar, *India* 29 G15
Deolali, *India* 28 K8
Deoria, *India* 29 F13
Deosai Mts., *Pakistan* . 28 B9
Depuch I., *Australia* ... 40 D2
Deputatskiy, *Russia* .. 21 C14
Dera Ghazi Khan,
  Pakistan 28 D7
Dera Ismail Khan,
  Pakistan 28 D7
Derbent, *Russia* 19 F8
Derby, *Australia* 40 C3
Derby, *U.K.* 8 E6
Derby, *U.S.A.* 55 G6
Derby City □, *U.K.* ... 8 E6
Derbyshire □, *U.K.* ... 8 D6
Derg, L., *Ireland* 10 E2
Dergaon, *India* 29 F19
Dermott, *U.S.A.* 55 J9
Derry = Londonderry,
  U.K. 10 D3
Derwent ➤, *Cumb.,*
  U.K. 8 C4
Derwent ➤, *Derby,*
  U.K. 8 E6
Derwent ➤, *N. Yorks.,*
  U.K. 8 D7
Derwent Water, *U.K.* .. 8 C4
Des Moines, *Iowa,*
  U.S.A. 54 E8
Des Moines, *N. Mex.,*
  U.S.A. 55 G3
Des Moines ➤, *U.S.A.* 54 E9
Desaguadero ➤,
  Bolivia 62 G5
Deschaillons, *Canada* . 49 C5
Deschambault L.,
  Canada 51 C8
Deschutes ➤, *U.S.A.* . 56 D3
Dese, *Ethiopia* 32 E2
Deseado ➤, *Argentina* 64 F3
Desert Center, *U.S.A.* . 57 K6
Desna ➤, *Ukraine* .. 13 C16
Desolación, I., *Chile* .. 64 G2
Despeñaperros, Paso,
  Spain 15 C4
Dessau, *Germany* 12 C7
Dessye = Dese, *Ethiopia* 32 E2
D'Estrees B., *Australia* . 43 F2
Detmold, *Germany* ... 12 C5
Detour, Pt., *U.S.A.* ... 52 C2
Detroit, *U.S.A.* 52 D4
Detroit Lakes, *U.S.A.* . 54 B7
Deurne, *Neths.* 11 C5
Deutsche Bucht,
  Germany 12 A5
Deva, *Romania* 13 F12
Devakottai, *India* 28 Q11
Deventer, *Neths.* 11 B6
Devils Lake, *U.S.A.* ... 54 A5
Devils Paw, *Canada* .. 50 B2
Devils Tower Junction,
  U.S.A. 54 C2
Devine, *U.S.A.* 55 L5
Devizes, *U.K.* 9 F6
Devon, *Canada* 50 C6

Devon □, *U.K.* 9 G4
Devon I., *Canada* 4 B3
Devonport, *Australia* . 42 G4
Devonport, *N.Z.* 39 G5
Dewas, *India* 28 H10
Dexter, *Maine, U.S.A.* . 53 C11
Dexter, *Mo., U.S.A.* .. 55 G10
Dexter, *N. Mex., U.S.A.* 55 J2
Dey-Dey, L., *Australia* . 41 E5
Deyhūk, *Iran* 31 C8
Deyyer, *Iran* 31 E6
Dezadeash L., *Canada* . 50 A1
Dezfūl, *Iran* 31 C6
Dezhneva, Mys, *Russia* 21 C19
Dhahiriya = Az̧
  Z̧āhiriyah, *West Bank* 33 D3
Dhahran = Az̧ Z̧ahrān,
  Si. Arabia 31 E6
Dhaka, *Bangla.* 29 H17
Dhaka □, *Bangla.* 29 G17
Dhamtari, *India* 29 J12
Dhanbad, *India* 29 H15
Dhangarhi, *Nepal* 29 E12
Dhankuta, *Nepal* 29 F15
Dhar, *India* 28 H9
Dharmapuri, *India* 28 N11
Dharwad, *India* 28 M9
Dhaulagiri, *Nepal* 29 E13
Dhenkanal, *India* 29 J14
Dhībān, *Jordan* 33 D4
Dhikti Óros, *Greece* .. 17 G11
Dhírfis = Dhírfis Óros,
  Greece 17 E10
Dhírfis Óros, *Greece* .. 17 E10
Dhodhekánisos, *Greece* 17 F12
Dhrol, *India* 28 H7
Dhuburi, *India* 29 F16
Dhule, *India* 28 J9
Diafarabé, *Mali* 34 F5
Diamantina, *Brazil* ... 63 G10
Diamantina ➤,
  Australia 43 D2
Diamantino, *Brazil* ... 63 F7
Diamond Harbour, *India* 29 H16
Diamond Is., *Australia* 42 B5
Diamond Mts., *U.S.A.* . 56 G6
Diba-Lubue,
  Dem. Rep. of
  the Congo 36 E3
Dibaya-Lubue,
  Dem. Rep. of
  the Congo 36 E3
Dibrugarh, *India* 29 F19
Dickens, *U.S.A.* 55 J4
Dickinson, *U.S.A.* 54 B3
Dickson = Dikson,
  Russia 20 B9
Dickson, *U.S.A.* 53 G2
Didiéni, *Mali* 34 F4
Didsbury, *Canada* 50 C6
Diefenbaker, L., *Canada* 51 C7
Diego de Almagro, *Chile* 64 B2
Diego Garcia, *Ind. Oc.* . 3 E13
Diekirch, *Lux.* 11 E6
Dieppe, *France* 14 B4
Dierks, *U.S.A.* 55 H8
Diest, *Belgium* 11 D5
Differdange, *Lux.* 11 E5
Digby, *Canada* 49 D6
Dighinala, *Bangla.* ... 29 H18
Dighton, *U.S.A.* 54 F4
Digne-les-Bains, *France* 14 D7
Digos, *Phil.* 27 C7
Digranes, *Iceland* 6 C6
Digul ➤, *Indonesia* .. 27 F9
Dihang ➤, *India* ... 29 F19
Dijlah, Nahr ➤, *Asia* . 30 D5
Dijon, *France* 14 C6
Dikhil, *Djibouti* 32 E3
Dikkil = Dikhil, *Djibouti* 32 E3
Diksmuide, *Belgium* .. 11 C2
Dikson, *Russia* 20 B9
Dila, *Ethiopia* 32 F2
Dili, *Indonesia* 27 F7
Dilley, *U.S.A.* 55 L5
Dillingham, *U.S.A.* ... 46 C4
Dillon, *Canada* 51 B7
Dillon, *Mont., U.S.A.* . 56 D7
Dillon, *S.C., U.S.A.* .. 53 H6
Dillon ➤, *Canada* ... 51 B7
Dilolo, *Dem. Rep. of*
  the Congo 36 G4
Dimas, *Mexico* 58 C3
Dimashq, *Syria* 33 B5
Dimashq □, *Syria* 33 B5
Dimboola, *Australia* .. 43 F3
Dîmbovita =
  Dâmbovita ➤,
  Romania 13 F14
Dimbulah, *Australia* .. 42 B4
Dimitrovgrad, *Bulgaria* 17 C11
Dimitrovgrad, *Russia* . 18 D8
Dimitrovo = Pernik,
  Bulgaria 17 C10
Dimmitt, *U.S.A.* 55 H3
Dimona, *Israel* 33 D4
Dinagat, *Phil.* 27 B7
Dinajpur, *Bangla.* 29 G16
Dinan, *France* 14 B2
Dīnān Āb, *Iran* 31 C8
Dinant, *Belgium* 11 D4
Dinar, *Turkey* 19 G4
Dīnār, Kūh-e, *Iran* ... 31 D6
Dinara Planina, *Croatia* 16 C7
Dinard, *France* 14 B2
Dinaric Alps = Dinara
  Planina, *Croatia* 16 C7

Dindigul, *India* 28 P11
Dingle, *Ireland* 10 E1
Dingo, *Australia* 42 C4
Dingwall, *U.K.* 10 C4
Dinh, Mui, *Vietnam* .. 26 B3
Dinhata, *Bangla.* 51 D10
Dinorwic, *Canada* 51 D10
Dinosaur National
  Monument, *U.S.A.* .. 56 F9
Dinosaur Prov. Park,
  Canada 50 C6
Dinuba, *U.S.A.* 57 H4
Dipolog, *Phil.* 27 C6
Dir, *Pakistan* 28 B7
Diriamba, *Nic.* 60 D2
Dirk Hartog I., *Australia* 41 E1
Dirranbandi, *Australia* 43 D4
Disa, *India* 28 G8
Disappointment, C.,
  U.S.A. 56 C2
Disappointment, L.,
  Australia 40 D3
Disaster B., *Australia* . 43 F4
Discovery B., *Australia* 43 F3
Disko = Qeqertarsuaq,
  Greenland 4 C5
Disko Bugt, *Greenland* 4 C5
Disteghil Sar, *Pakistan* . 28 A9
Distrito Federal □, *Brazil* 63 G9
Distrito Federal □,
  Mexico 59 D5
Diu, *India* 28 J7
Divándarreh, *Iran* 30 C5
Divide, *U.S.A.* 56 D7
Dividing Ra., *Australia* . 41 E2
Divinópolis, *Brazil* ... 63 H10
Divnoye, *Russia* 19 E7
Divo, *Ivory C.* 34 G4
Dixon, *U.S.A.* 54 E10
Dixon Entrance, *U.S.A.* 46 C6
Diyālā ➤, *Iraq* 30 C5
Diyarbakir, *Turkey* ... 19 G7
Djakarta = Jakarta,
  Indonesia 27 G12
Djambala, *Congo* 36 E2
Djanet, *Algeria* 34 D7
Djawa = Jawa,
  Indonesia 27 G14
Djelfa, *Algeria* 34 B6
Djerba, I. de, *Tunisia* . 35 B8
Djerid, Chott, *Tunisia* . 34 B7
Djibouti, *Djibouti* 32 E3
Djibouti ■, *Africa* 32 E3
Djolu, *Dem. Rep. of*
  the Congo 36 D4
Djoum, *Cameroon* ... 36 D2
Djourab, Erg du, *Chad* . 35 E9
Djúpivogur, *Iceland* .. 6 D6
Dmitriya Lapteva, Proliv,
  Russia 21 B15
Dnepr ➤ =
  Dnipro ➤, *Ukraine* . 19 E5
Dneprodzerzhinsk =
  Dniprodzerzhynsk,
  Ukraine 19 E5
Dnepropetrovsk =
  Dnipropetrovsk,
  Ukraine 19 E6
Dnestr ➤ =
  Dnister ➤, *Europe* . 13 E16
Dnestrovski = Belgorod,
  Russia 19 D6
Dnieper = Dnipro ➤,
  Ukraine 19 E5
Dniester = Dnister ➤,
  Europe 13 E16
Dnipro ➤, *Ukraine* .. 19 E5
Dniprodzerzhynsk,
  Ukraine 19 E5
Dnipropetrovsk, *Ukraine* 19 E6
Dnister ➤, *Europe* .. 13 E16
Dnistrovskyy Lyman,
  Ukraine 13 E16
Dno, *Russia* 18 C4
Dnyapro = Dnipro ➤,
  Ukraine 19 E5
Doaktown, *Canada* ... 49 C6
Doba, *Chad* 35 G9
Dobbyn, *Australia* 42 B3
Dobele, *Latvia* 7 H20
Doberai, Jazirah,
  Indonesia 27 E8
Dobo, *Indonesia* 27 F8
Doboj, *Bos.-H.* 17 B8
Dobreta-Turnu Severin,
  Romania 13 F12
Dobrich, *Bulgaria* 17 C12
Dobruja, *Europe* 13 F15
Dobrush, *Belarus* 13 B16
Docker River, *Australia* 41 D4
Doctor Arroyo, *Mexico* 58 C4
Doda, L., *Canada* 48 C4
Dodecanese =
  Dhodhekánisos,
  Greece 17 F12
Double Mountain
  Fork ➤, *U.S.A.* 55 J4
Dodge City, *U.S.A.* ... 55 G5
Dodge L., *Canada* 51 B7
Dodgeville, *U.S.A.* 54 D9
Dodson, *U.S.A.* 56 B9
Doesburg, *Neths.* 11 B6
Doetinchem, *Neths.* .. 11 C6
Dog Creek, *Canada* ... 50 C4

Dog L., *Man., Canada* . 51 C9
Dog L., *Ont., Canada* . 48 C2
Doğubayazit, *Turkey* .. 30 B5
Doha = Ad Dawḩah,
  Qatar 31 E6
Dohazari, *Bangla.* 29 H18
Doi, *Indonesia* 27 D7
Dois Irmãos, Sa., *Brazil* 63 E10
Dokkum, *Neths.* 11 A5
Dolak, Pulau, *Indonesia* 27 F9
Dolbeau, *Canada* 49 C5
Dole, *France* 14 C6
Dolgellau, *U.K.* 8 E4
Dolgelley = Dolgellau,
  U.K. 8 E4
Dollard, *Neths.* 11 A7
Dolo, *Ethiopia* 32 G3
Dolomites = Dolomiti,
  Italy 16 A4
Dolomiti, *Italy* 16 A4
Dolores, *Argentina* ... 64 D5
Dolores, *U.S.A.* 57 H9
Dolores ➤, *U.S.A.* ... 57 G9
Dolphin, C., *Falk. Is.* . 64 G5
Dolphin and Union Str.,
  Canada 46 B8
Dombarovskiy, *Russia* . 20 D6
Dombås, *Norway* 7 E13
Domel I. = Letsôk-aw
  Kyun, *Burma* 26 B1
Dominica ■, *W. Indies* 61 C7
Dominica Passage,
  W. Indies 61 C7
Dominican Rep. ■,
  W. Indies 61 C5
Domodóssola, *Italy* ... 14 C8
Domville, Mt., *Australia* 43 D5
Don ➤, *Russia* 19 E6
Don ➤, *Aberds., U.K.* 10 C5
Don ➤, *S. Yorks., U.K.* 8 D7
Don, C., *Australia* 40 B5
Don Benito, *Spain* 15 C3
Donald, *Australia* 43 F3
Donaldsonville, *U.S.A.* 55 K9
Donalsonville, *U.S.A.* . 53 K3
Donau = Dunărea ➤,
  Europe 13 F15
Donau ➤, *Austria* ... 11 D3
Donauwörth, *Germany* 12 D6
Doncaster, *U.K.* 8 D6
Dondo, Teluk, *Indonesia* 27 D6
Dondra Head, *Sri Lanka* 28 S12
Donegal, *Ireland* 10 D2
Donets ➤, *Russia* ... 19 E7
Donetsk, *Ukraine* 19 E6
Dong Hoi, *Vietnam* ... 26 A3
Dongara, *Australia* ... 41 E1
Dongbei, *China* 25 B7
Dongchuan, *China* ... 24 D5
Donggala, *Indonesia* . 27 E5
Dongola, *Sudan* 35 E12
Dongting Hu, *China* .. 25 D6
Donington, C., *Australia* 43 E2
Doniphan, *U.S.A.* 55 G9
Dønna, *Norway* 6 C15
Donna, *U.S.A.* 55 M5
Donnaconna, *Canada* . 49 C5
Donnelly's Crossing,
  N.Z. 39 F4
Donnybrook, *Australia* . 41 F2
Donostia = Donostia-
  San Sebastián, *Spain* 15 A5
Donostia-San Sebastián,
  Spain 15 A5
Dora, L., *Australia* ... 40 D3
Dora Báltea ➤, *Italy* . 14 D8
Doran L., *Canada* 51 A7
Dorchester, *U.K.* 9 G5
Dorchester, C., *Canada* 47 B12
Dordogne ➤, *France* . 14 D3
Dordrecht, *Neths.* 11 C4
Doré L., *Canada* 51 C7
Doré Lake, *Canada* ... 51 C7
Dori, *Burkina Faso* ... 34 F5
Dornbirn, *Austria* 12 E5
Dornoch, *U.K.* 10 C4
Dorohoi, *Romania* 13 E14
Döröö Nuur, *Mongolia* 24 E4
Dorr, *Iran* 31 C6
Dorre I., *Australia* 41 E1
Dorrigo, *Australia* 43 E5
Dorris, *U.S.A.* 56 F3
Dorset □, *U.K.* 9 G5
Dortmund, *Germany* . 12 C4
Dörüneh, *Iran* 31 C8
Dos Bahías, C.,
  Argentina 64 E3
Dos Hermanas, *Spain* . 15 D3
Dosso, *Niger* 34 F6
Dothan, *U.S.A.* 53 K3
Douai, *France* 14 A5
Douala, *Cameroon* ... 36 D1
Douarnenez, *France* .. 14 B1
Double Island Pt.,
  Australia 43 D5
Doubs ➤, *France* 14 C6
Doubtful Sd., *N.Z.* ... 39 L1
Doubtless B., *N.Z.* 39 F4
Douglas, *U.K.* 8 C3
Douglas, *Ariz., U.S.A.* 57 L9
Douglas, *Ga., U.S.A.* . 53 K4
Douglas, *Wyo., U.S.A.* 54 D2
Douglas Chan., *Canada* 50 C3
Douglasville, *U.S.A.* .. 53 J3

Dourada, Serra, *Brazil* . 63 F9
Dourados, *Brazil* 63 H8
Douro ➤, *Europe* 15 B1
Dove ➤, *U.K.* 8 E6
Dove Creek, *U.S.A.* ... 57 H9
Dover, *Australia* 42 G4
Dover, *U.K.* 9 F9
Dover, *Del., U.S.A.* ... 52 F8
Dover, *N.H., U.S.A.* .. 52 D10
Dover, *Ohio, U.S.A.* .. 52 E5
Dover, Pt., *Australia* .. 41 F4
Dover, Str. of, *Europe* . 9 G9
Dover-Foxcroft, *U.S.A.* 53 C11
Dovey = Dyfi ➤, *U.K.* 9 E3
Dovrefjell, *Norway* ... 7 E13
Dow Rūd, *Iran* 31 C6
Dowagiac, *U.S.A.* 52 E2
Dowerin, *Australia* ... 41 F2
Dowghā'i, *Iran* 31 B8
Dowlatābād, *Iran* 31 D8
Downey, *U.S.A.* 56 E7
Downham Market, *U.K.* 9 E8
Downieville, *U.S.A.* ... 56 G3
Downton, Mt., *Canada* . 50 C4
Dowsārī, *Iran* 31 D8
Dozois, Rés., *Canada* . 48 C4
Drachten, *Neths.* 11 A6
Drăgăşani, *Romania* .. 13 F13
Dragichyn, *Belarus* ... 13 B13
Dragoman, Prokhod,
  Bulgaria 17 C10
Draguignan, *France* .. 14 E7
Drain, *U.S.A.* 56 E2
Drake, *U.S.A.* 54 B4
Drake Passage,
  S. Ocean 5 B17
Drakensberg, *S. Africa* 37 L5
Dráma, *Greece* 17 D11
Drammen, *Norway* ... 7 G14
Drangajökull, *Iceland* . 6 C2
Drau = Drava ➤,
  Croatia 17 B8
Drava ➤, *Croatia* ... 17 B8
Drayton Valley, *Canada* 50 C6
Drenthe □, *Neths.* ... 11 B6
Dresden, *Germany* ... 12 C7
Dreux, *France* 14 B4
Driffield, *U.K.* 8 C7
Driggs, *U.S.A.* 56 E8
Drin ➤, *Albania* 17 C8
Drina ➤, *Bos.-H.* ... 17 B8
Drini = Drin ➤,
  Albania 17 C8
Drøbak, *Norway* 7 G14
Drochia, *Moldova* 13 D14
Drogheda, *Ireland* ... 10 E3
Drogichin = Dragichyn,
  Belarus 13 B13
Drogobych =
  Drohobych, *Ukraine* . 13 D12
Drohobych, *Ukraine* .. 13 D12
Droichead Atha =
  Drogheda, *Ireland* .. 10 E3
Droitwich, *U.K.* 9 E5
Dromedary, C., *Australia* 43 F5
Dronfield, *U.K.* 8 D6
Dronten, *Neths.* 11 B5
Drumheller, *Canada* .. 50 C6
Drummond, *U.S.A.* ... 56 C7
Drummond I., *U.S.A.* . 52 C4
Drummond Pt.,
  Australia 43 E2
Drummond Ra.,
  Australia 42 C4
Drummondville, *Canada* 48 C5
Drumright, *U.S.A.* 55 H6
Druskininkai, *Lithuania* 7 J20
Drut ➤, *Belarus* 13 B16
Druzhina, *Russia* 21 C15
Dry Tortugas, *U.S.A.* . 60 B3
Dryden, *Canada* 51 D10
Drygalski I., *Antarctica* . 5 C7
Drysdale ➤, *Australia* 40 B4
Drysdale I., *Australia* . 42 A2
Du Bois, *U.S.A.* 52 E6
Du Gué ➤, *Canada* .. 48 A5
Du Quoin, *U.S.A.* 54 G10
Duaringa, *Australia* ... 42 C4
Dubā, *Si. Arabia* 30 E2
Dubai = Dubayy, *U.A.E.* 31 E7
Dubāsari, *Moldova* ... 13 E15
Dubāsari Vdkhr.,
  Moldova 13 E15
Dubawnt ➤, *Canada* . 51 A8
Dubawnt, L., *Canada* . 51 A8
Dubayy, *U.A.E.* 31 E7
Dubbo, *Australia* 43 E4
Dublin, *Ireland* 10 E3
Dublin, *Ga., U.S.A.* .. 53 J4
Dublin, *Tex., U.S.A.* .. 55 J5
Dubno, *Ukraine* 13 C13
Dubois, *U.S.A.* 56 D7
Dubossary = Dubăsari,
  Moldova 13 E15
Dubossary Vdkhr. =
  Dubăsari Vdkhr.,
  Moldova 13 E15
Dubovka, *Russia* 19 E7
Dubréka, *Guinea* 34 G3
Dubrovitsa =
  Dubrovytsya, *Ukraine* 13 C14
Dubrovnik, *Croatia* ... 17 C8
Dubrovytsya, *Ukraine* . 13 C14
Dubuque, *U.S.A.* 54 D9

Duchess, *Australia* ... 42 C2
Ducie I., *Pac. Oc.* 45 K15
Duck ➤, *U.S.A.* 53 G2
Duck Cr. ➤, *Australia* 40 D2
Duck Lake, *Canada* ... 51 C7
Duck Mountain Prov.
  Park, *Canada* 51 C8
Dudhi, *India* 29 G13
Dudinka, *Russia* 21 C9
Dudley, *U.K.* 9 E5
Duero = Douro ➤,
  Europe 15 B1
Dūghī Kalā, *Afghan.* .. 28 C3
Dugi Otok, *Croatia* ... 12 G8
Duifken Pt., *Australia* . 42 A3
Duisburg, *Germany* ... 12 C4
Dükdamin, *Iran* 31 C8
Dukelský Průsmyk,
  Slovak Rep. 13 D11
Dukhān, *Qatar* 31 E6
Duki, *Pakistan* 28 D6
Duku, *Nigeria* 35 F8
Dulce, *U.S.A.* 57 H10
Dulce ➤, *Argentina* .. 64 C4
Dulce, G., *Costa Rica* . 60 E3
Dulf, *Iraq* 30 C5
Dulit, Banjaran,
  Malaysia 26 D4
Dulq Maghār, *Syria* .. 30 B3
Duluth, *U.S.A.* 54 B8
Dum Duma, *India* 29 F19
Dūmā, *Syria* 33 B5
Dumaguete, *Phil.* 27 C6
Dumai, *Indonesia* 26 D2
Dumaran, *Phil.* 27 B5
Dumas, *Ark., U.S.A.* .. 55 J9
Dumas, *Tex., U.S.A.* .. 55 H4
Dumayr, *Syria* 33 B5
Dumbleyung, *Australia* 41 F2
Dumfries, *U.K.* 10 D5
Dumfries ➤, *Canada* . 48 C4
Dumoine, L., *Canada* . 48 C4
Dumyât, *Egypt* 35 B12
Dún Dealgan =
  Dundalk, *Ireland* ... 10 E3
Dun Laoghaire, *Ireland* 10 E3
Duna = Dunărea ➤,
  Europe 13 F15
Dunaj = Dunărea ➤,
  Europe 13 F15
Dunakeszi, *Hungary* .. 13 E10
Dunărea ➤, *Europe* .. 13 F15
Dunaújváros, *Hungary* 13 E10
Dunav = Dunărea ➤,
  Europe 13 F15
Dunay, *Russia* 22 C6
Dunback, *N.Z.* 39 L3
Dunbar, *U.K.* 10 C5
Duncan, *Canada* 50 D4
Duncan, *Ariz., U.S.A.* 57 K9
Duncan, *Okla., U.S.A.* 55 H6
Duncan, L., *Canada* .. 48 B4
Duncan L., *Canada* ... 50 A6
Duncan Town, *Bahamas* 60 B4
Dundalk, *Ireland* 10 E3
Dundalk, *U.S.A.* 52 F7
Dundas, L., *Australia* . 41 F3
Dundas I., *Canada* 50 C2
Dundas Str., *Australia* . 40 B5
Dundee, *U.K.* 10 C5
Dunedin, *N.Z.* 39 L3
Dunedin, *U.S.A.* 53 L4
Dunedoo, *Australia* ... 43 E4
Dunfermline, *U.K.* 10 C5
Dungarvan, *Ireland* ... 10 E3
Dungeness, *U.K.* 9 G8
Dungog, *Australia* 43 E5
Dungu, *Dem. Rep. of*
  the Congo 36 D5
Dunhuang, *China* 24 B4
Dunk I., *Australia* 42 B4
Dunkeld, *Australia* ... 43 E4
Dunkerque, *France* ... 14 A5
Dunkery Beacon, *U.K.* . 9 F4
Dunkirk = Dunkerque,
  France 14 A5
Dunkirk, *U.S.A.* 52 D6
Dúnleary = Dun
  Laoghaire, *Ireland* .. 10 E3
Dunmara, *Australia* ... 42 B1
Dunmore, *U.S.A.* 52 E8
Dunmore Town,
  Bahamas 60 A4
Dunn, *U.S.A.* 53 H6
Dunnellon, *U.S.A.* 53 L4
Dunning, *U.S.A.* 54 E4
Dunolly, *Australia* 43 F3
Dunphy, *U.S.A.* 56 F5
Dunseith, *U.S.A.* 54 A4
Dunsmuir, *U.S.A.* 56 F2
Dunstable, *U.K.* 9 F7
Dunstan Mts., *N.Z.* ... 39 L2
Dunster, *Canada* 50 C5
Dunvegan L., *Canada* . 51 A7
Dupree, *U.S.A.* 54 C4
Dupuyer, *U.S.A.* 56 B7
Durack ➤, *Australia* . 40 C4
Durack Ra., *Australia* . 40 C4
Durance ➤, *France* .. 14 E6
Durango, *Mexico* 58 C4
Durango, *U.S.A.* 57 H10
Durango □, *Mexico* ... 58 C4
Durant, *Miss., U.S.A.* . 55 J10
Durant, *Okla., U.S.A.* . 55 J6

Durazno, Uruguay 64 C5
Durazzo = Durrës,
 Albania 17 D8
Durban, S. Africa 37 K6
Durbuy, Belgium 11 D5
Düren, Germany 12 C4
Durg, India 29 J12
Durgapur, India 29 H15
Durham, Canada 48 D3
Durham, U.K. 8 C6
Durham, U.S.A. 53 H6
Durham □, U.K. 8 C6
Durmā, Si. Arabia .. 30 E5
Durmitor,
 Montenegro, Yug. .. 17 C8
Durrës, Albania 17 D8
Durrësi = Durrës,
 Albania 17 D8
Dursunbey, Turkey .. 17 E13
Durūz, Jabal ad, Jordan 33 C5
D'Urville, Tanjung,
 Indonesia 27 E9
D'Urville I., N.Z. 39 J4
Dushak, Turkmenistan . 20 F7
Dushanbe, Tajikistan .. 20 F7
Dusky Sd., N.Z. 39 L1
Dussejour, C., Australia 40 B4
Düsseldorf, Germany .. 12 C4
Dutch Harbor, U.S.A. .. 46 C3
Dutton →, Australia .. 42 C3
Duwayhin, Khawr,
 U.A.E. 31 E6
Duyun, China 24 D5
Duzdab = Zāhedān, Iran 31 D9
Dvina, Severnaya →,
 Russia 18 B7
Dvinsk = Daugavpils,
 Latvia 7 J22
Dvinskaya Guba, Russia 18 B6
Dwarka, India 28 H6
Dwellingup, Australia . 41 F2
Dwight, U.S.A. 52 E1
Dyatlovo = Dzyatlava,
 Belarus 13 B13
Dyer, C., Canada 47 B3
Dyer Plateau, Antarctica 5 D17
Dyersburg, U.S.A. .. 55 G10
Dyfi →, U.K. 9 E3
Dymer, Ukraine 13 C16
Dysart, Australia 42 C4
Dzamin Üüd = Borhoyn
 Tal, Mongolia 25 B6
Dzerzhinsk, Russia ... 18 C7
Dzhalinda, Russia ... 21 D13
Dzhambul = Zhambyl,
 Kazakhstan 20 E8
Dzhankoy, Ukraine .. 19 E5
Dzhezkazgan =
 Zhezqazghan,
 Kazakhstan 20 E7
Dzhizak = Jizzakh,
 Uzbekistan 20 E7
Dzhugdzur, Khrebet,
 Russia 21 D14
Dzhungarskiye Vorota =
 Dzungarian Gates,
 Asia 24 B3
Działdowo, Poland ... 13 B11
Dzibilchaltun, Mexico . 59 C7
Dzierżoniów, Poland . 13 C9
Dzilam de Bravo,
 Mexico 59 C7
Dzungaria = Junggar
 Pendi, China 24 B3
Dzungarian Gates, Asia 24 B3
Dzuumod, Mongolia .. 24 B5
Dzyarzhynsk, Belarus . 13 B14
Dzyatlava, Belarus 13 B13

Eabamet L., Canada .. 48 B2
Eads, U.S.A. 54 F3
Eagar, U.S.A. 57 J9
Eagle, Alaska, U.S.A. .. 46 B5
Eagle, Colo., U.S.A. .. 56 G10
Eagle →, Canada 49 B8
Eagle Butte, U.S.A. .. 54 C4
Eagle Grove, U.S.A. .. 54 D8
Eagle L., Canada 51 D10
Eagle L., Calif., U.S.A. 56 F3
Eagle L., Maine, U.S.A. 53 B11
Eagle Lake, Maine,
 U.S.A. 53 B11
Eagle Lake, Tex., U.S.A. 55 L6
Eagle Nest, U.S.A. .. 57 H11
Eagle Pass, U.S.A. .. 55 L4
Eagle Pt., Australia .. 40 C3
Eagle River, Mich.,
 U.S.A. 52 B1
Eagle River, Wis., U.S.A. 54 C10
Eaglehawk, Australia . 43 F3
Ealing □, U.K. 9 F7
Ear Falls, Canada ... 51 C10
Earle, U.S.A. 55 H9
Earlimart, U.S.A. 57 J4
Earnslaw, Mt., N.Z. .. 39 L2
Earth, U.S.A. 55 H3
Easley, U.S.A. 53 H4
East Anglia, U.K. 8 E9
East Angus, Canada .. 49 C5
East Bengal, Bangla. .. 29 H17
East Beskids =
 Vychodné Beskydy,
 Europe 13 D11
East C., N.Z. 39 G7

East Chicago, U.S.A. .. 52 E2
East China Sea, Asia .. 25 D7
East Coulee, Canada .. 50 C6
East Dereham, U.K. .. 9 E8
East Falkland, Falk. Is. 64 G5
East Grand Forks, U.S.A. 54 B6
East Grinstead, U.K. .. 9 F8
East Helena, U.S.A. .. 56 C8
East Kilbride, U.K. ... 10 D4
East Lansing, U.S.A. .. 52 D3
East Liverpool, U.S.A. 52 E5
East London, S. Africa . 37 L5
East Main = Eastmain,
 Canada 48 B4
East Orange, U.S.A. .. 52 E8
East Pacific Ridge,
 Pac. Oc. 45 J17
East Pine, Canada ... 50 B4
East Point, Canada ... 53 J3
East Pt., Canada 49 C7
East Retford = Retford,
 U.K. 8 D7
East Riding of
 Yorkshire □, U.K. .. 8 D7
East St. Louis, U.S.A. . 54 F9
East Schelde =
 Oosterschelde →,
 Neths. 11 C4
East Siberian Sea,
 Russia 21 B17
East Stroudsburg,
 U.S.A. 52 E8
East Sussex □, U.K. .. 9 G8
East Tawas, U.S.A. .. 52 C4
East Timor = Timor
 Timur □, Indonesia . 27 F7
East Toorale, Australia 43 E4
Eastbourne, N.Z. 39 J5
Eastbourne, U.K. 9 G8
Eastend, Canada 51 D7
Easter I. = Pascua, I. de,
 Pac. Oc. 45 K17
Eastern Cr. →,
 Australia 42 C3
Eastern Ghats, India .. 28 N11
Eastern Group = Lau
 Group, Fiji 39 C9
Eastern Group, Australia 41 F3
Easterville, Canada .. 51 C9
Eastland, U.S.A. 55 J5
Eastleigh, U.K. 9 G6
Eastmain, Canada ... 48 B4
Eastmain →, Canada . 48 B4
Eastman, U.S.A. 53 J4
Easton, Md., U.S.A. .. 52 F7
Easton, Pa., U.S.A. .. 52 E8
Eastport, U.S.A. 53 C12
Eaton, U.S.A. 54 E2
Eatonia, Canada 51 C7
Eatonton, U.S.A. 53 J4
Eau Claire, U.S.A. .. 54 C9
Eau Claire, L. à l',
 Canada 48 A5
Ebbw Vale, U.K. 9 F4
Ebeltoft, Denmark ... 7 H14
Eberswalde-Finow,
 Germany 12 B7
Ebetsu, Japan 22 C10
Ebolowa, Cameroon .. 36 D2
Ebro →, Spain 15 B6
Eceabat, Turkey 17 D12
Ech Cheliff, Algeria .. 34 A6
Echigo-Sammyaku,
 Japan 23 F9
Echizen-Misaki, Japan . 23 G7
Echo Bay, N.W.T.,
 Canada 46 B8
Echo Bay, Ont., Canada 48 C3
Echoing →, Canada .. 48 B3
Echternach, Lux. 11 E6
Echuca, Australia 43 F3
Ecija, Spain 15 D3
Eclipse Is., Australia .. 40 B4
Eclipse Sd., Canada .. 47 A11
Ecuador ■, S. Amer. .. 62 D3
Ed Damazin, Sudan .. 35 F12
Ed Debba, Sudan 35 E12
Ed Dueim, Sudan 35 F12
Edam, Canada 51 C7
Edam, Neths. 11 B5
Eddystone Pt., Australia 42 G4
Ede, Neths. 11 B5
Edehon L., Canada ... 51 A9
Eden, Australia 43 F4
Eden, N.C., U.S.A. .. 53 G6
Eden, Tex., U.S.A. .. 55 K5
Eden →, U.K. 8 C4
Edenhope, Australia .. 43 F3
Edenton, U.S.A. 53 G7
Eder →, Germany ... 12 C5
Edgar, U.S.A. 54 E6
Edge Hill, U.K. 9 E6
Edgefield, U.S.A. 53 J5
Edgeley, U.S.A. 54 B5
Edgemont, U.S.A. ... 54 D3
Edgeøya, Svalbard ... 4 B9
Édhessa, Greece 17 D10
Edievale, N.Z. 39 L2
Edina, U.S.A. 54 E8
Edinburg, U.S.A. 55 M5
Edinburgh, U.K. 10 D5
Edineț, Moldova 13 D14
Edirne, Turkey 17 D12
Edithburgh, Australia . 43 F2
Edmond, U.S.A. 55 H6

Edmonds, U.S.A. 56 C2
Edmonton, Australia .. 42 B4
Edmonton, Canada .. 50 C6
Edmund L., Canada .. 48 B1
Edmundston, Canada . 49 C6
Edna, U.S.A. 55 L6
Edremit, Turkey 17 E12
Edremit Körfezi, Turkey 17 E12
Edson, Canada 50 C5
Edward →, Australia . 43 F3
Edward, L., Africa ... 36 E5
Edward River, Australia 42 A3
Edward VII Land,
 Antarctica 5 E13
Edwards Plateau, U.S.A. 55 K4
Edzo, Canada 50 A5
Eeklo, Belgium 11 C3
Effingham, U.S.A. ... 52 F1
Égadi, Ísole, Italy ... 16 F5
Egan Range, U.S.A. .. 56 G6
Eganville, Canada ... 48 C4
Eger = Cheb,
 Czech Rep. 12 C7
Eger, Hungary 13 E11
Egersund, Norway ... 7 G12
Egg L., Canada 51 B7
Éghezée, Belgium ... 11 D4
Egmont, Canada 50 D4
Egmont, C., N.Z. 39 H4
Egmont, Mt. = Taranaki,
 Mt., N.Z. 39 H5
Eğridir, Turkey 19 G5
Eğridir Gölü, Turkey .. 19 G5
Egvekinot, Russia ... 21 C19
Egypt ■, Africa 35 C12
Ehime □, Japan 23 H6
Eibar, Spain 15 A4
Eidsvold, Australia ... 43 D5
Eidsvoll, Norway 7 F14
Eifel, Germany 12 C4
Eigg, U.K. 10 E3
Eighty Mile Beach,
 Australia 40 C3
Eil, Somali Rep. 32 F4
Eildon, Australia 43 F4
Eildon, L., Australia .. 43 F4
Einasleigh, Australia .. 42 B3
Einasleigh →, Australia 42 B3
Eindhoven, Neths. ... 11 C5
Eire = Ireland ■, Europe 10 E2
Eiriksjökull, Iceland .. 6 D3
Eirunepé, Brazil 62 E5
Eisenach, Germany .. 12 C6
Eisenerz, Austria 12 E8
Eivissa, Spain 15 C6
Ejutla, Mexico 59 D5
Ekalaka, U.S.A. 54 C2
Eketahuna, N.Z. 39 J5
Ekibastuz, Kazakstan . 20 D8
Eksjö, Sweden 7 H16
Ekwan →, Canada .. 48 B3
Ekwan Pt., Canada .. 48 B3
El Aaiún, W. Sahara .. 34 C3
El 'Agrūd, Egypt 33 E3
El Alamein, Egypt ... 35 B11
El 'Aqaba, W. →,
 Egypt 33 E2
El Arīḥā, West Bank .. 33 D4
El 'Arîsh, Egypt 33 D2
El 'Arîsh, W. →, Egypt 33 D2
El Asnam = Ech Cheliff,
 Algeria 34 A6
El Bayadh, Algeria ... 34 B6
El Bluff, Nic. 60 D3
El Brûk, W. →, Egypt . 33 E2
El Cajon, U.S.A. 57 K5
El Campo, U.S.A. ... 55 L6
El Centro, U.S.A. ... 57 K6
El Cerro, Bolivia 62 G6
El Cuy, Argentina ... 64 D3
El Cuyo, Mexico 59 C7
El Dátil, Mexico 58 B2
El Dere, Somali Rep. . 32 G4
El Desemboque, Mexico 58 A2
El Diviso, Colombia .. 62 C3
El Djouf, Mauritania .. 34 D4
El Dorado, Ark., U.S.A. 55 J8
El Dorado, Kans., U.S.A. 55 G6
El Dorado, Venezuela . 62 B6
El Escorial, Spain 15 B3
El Faiyûm, Egypt 35 C12
El Fâsher, Sudan 35 F11
El Ferrol = Ferrol, Spain 15 A1
El Fuerte, Mexico 58 B3
El Gal, Somali Rep. .. 32 E5
El Geneina = Al
 Junaynah, Sudan .. 35 F10
El Gîza, Egypt 35 C12
El Goléa, Algeria 34 B6
El Iskandarîya, Egypt . 35 B11
El Istiwa'iya, Sudan .. 35 G11
El Jadida, Morocco .. 34 B4
El Jardal, Honduras .. 60 D2
El Kabrît, G., Egypt .. 33 F2
El Khârga, Egypt 35 C12
El Khartûm, Sudan .. 35 E12
El Kuntilla, Egypt 33 F3
El Maestrazgo, Spain . 15 B5
El Mahalla el Kubra,
 Egypt 35 B12
El Mansûra, Egypt ... 35 B12
El Minyâ, Egypt 35 C12
El Obeid, Sudan 35 F12
El Odaiya, Sudan ... 35 F11

El Oro, Mexico 59 D4
El Oued, Algeria 34 B7
El Palmito, Presa,
 Mexico 58 B3
El Paso, U.S.A. 57 L10
El Porvenir, Mexico .. 58 A3
El Progreso, Honduras 60 C2
El Pueblito, Mexico .. 58 B3
El Puerto de Santa
 María, Spain 15 D2
El Qâhira, Egypt 35 B12
El Qantara, Egypt ... 33 E1
El Quseima, Egypt ... 33 E3
El Real, Panama 62 B3
El Reno, U.S.A. 55 H6
El Rosarito, Mexico .. 58 B2
El Saheira, W. →,
 Egypt 33 E2
El Salto, Mexico 58 C3
El Salvador ■,
 Cent. Amer. 60 D2
El Sauce, Nic. 60 D2
El Sueco, Mexico ... 58 B3
El Suweis, Egypt 35 C12
El Tamarâni, W. →,
 Egypt 33 E3
El Thamad, Egypt ... 33 F3
El Tigre, Venezuela .. 62 B6
El Tîh, Gebal, Egypt .. 33 F2
El Tîna, Khalîg, Egypt . 33 D1
El Tûr, Egypt 30 D2
El Turbio, Argentina .. 64 G2
El Uqsur, Egypt 35 C12
El Venado, Mexico .. 58 C4
El Vergel, Mexico ... 58 B3
El Vigía, Venezuela .. 62 B4
El Wabeira, Egypt ... 33 F2
El Wak, Kenya 36 D8
El Wuz, Sudan 35 E12
Elat, Israel 33 F3
Elâzığ, Turkey 19 G6
Elba, Italy 16 C4
Elba, U.S.A. 53 K2
Elban, Albania 17 D9
Elbasani = Elbasan,
 Albania 17 D9
Elbe →, Europe 12 B5
Elbert, Mt., U.S.A. .. 57 G10
Elberton, U.S.A. 53 H4
Elbeuf, France 14 B4
Elbidtan, Turkey 30 B3
Elbing = Elbląg, Poland 13 A10
Elbląg, Poland 13 A10
Elbow, Canada 51 C7
Elbrus, Asia 19 F7
Elburz Mts. = Alborz,
 Reshteh-ye Kühhä-ye,
 Iran 31 C7
Elche, Spain 15 C5
Elcho I., Australia ... 42 A2
Elda, Spain 15 C5
Elde →, Germany ... 12 B6
Eldon, U.S.A. 54 F8
Eldora, U.S.A. 54 D8
Eldorado, Ill., U.S.A. . 52 G1
Eldorado, Tex., U.S.A. 55 K4
Eldorado Springs,
 U.S.A. 55 G8
Eldoret, Kenya 36 D7
Eleanora, Pk., Australia 41 F3
Elektrostal, Russia ... 18 C6
Elephant Butte
 Reservoir, U.S.A. .. 57 K10
Elephant I., Antarctica 5 C18
Eleuthera, Bahamas .. 60 B4
Elgin, U.K. 10 D5
Elgin, Ill., U.S.A. 52 D1
Elgin, N. Dak., U.S.A. 54 B4
Elgin, Oreg., U.S.A. .. 56 D5
Elgin, Tex., U.S.A. .. 55 K6
Elgon, Mt., Africa ... 36 D6
Eliase, Indonesia 27 F8
Elisabethville =
 Lubumbashi,
 Dem. Rep. of
 the Congo 37 G5
Elista, Russia 19 E7
Elizabeth, Australia .. 43 E2
Elizabeth, U.S.A. 52 E8
Elizabeth City, U.S.A. 53 G7
Elizabethton, U.S.A. . 53 G4
Elizabethtown, U.S.A. 52 G3
Elk →, Canada 50 D5
Elk →, U.S.A. 53 H2
Elk City, U.S.A. 55 H5
Elk Island Nat. Park,
 Canada 50 C6
Elk Lake, Canada ... 48 C3
Elk Point, Canada ... 51 C6
Elk River, Idaho, U.S.A. 56 C5
Elk River, Minn., U.S.A. 54 C8
Elkedra →, Australia . 42 C2
Elkhart, Ind., U.S.A. . 52 E3
Elkhart, Kans., U.S.A. 55 G4
Elkhorn, Canada 51 D8
Elkhorn →, U.S.A. .. 54 E6
Elkhovo, Bulgaria ... 17 C12
Elkin, U.S.A. 53 G5
Elkins, U.S.A. 52 F6
Elko, Canada 50 D5
Elko, U.S.A. 56 F6

Ell, L., Australia 41 E4
Ellef Ringnes I., Canada 4 B2
Ellendale, U.S.A. 54 B5
Ellensburg, U.S.A. .. 56 C3
Ellenville, U.S.A. 52 E8
Ellery, Mt., Australia . 43 F4
Ellesmere, L., N.Z. .. 39 M4
Ellesmere I., Canada . 4 B4
Ellesmere Port, U.K. .. 8 D5
Ellice Is. = Tuvalu ■,
 Pac. Oc. 38 B10
Elliot, Australia 42 B1
Elliot Lake, Canada .. 48 C3
Ellis, U.S.A. 54 F5
Elliston, Australia ... 43 E1
Ellisville, U.S.A. 55 K10
Ellore = Eluru, India . 29 L12
Ellsworth, Kans., U.S.A. 54 F5
Ellsworth, Maine, U.S.A. 53 C11
Ellsworth Land,
 Antarctica 5 D16
Ellsworth Mts.,
 Antarctica 5 D16
Elma, Canada 51 D9
Elma, U.S.A. 56 C2
Elmali, Turkey 19 G4
Elmhurst, U.S.A. 52 E2
Elmira, U.S.A. 52 D7
Elmore, Australia ... 43 F3
Elmshorn, Germany .. 12 B5
Eloy, U.S.A. 57 K8
Elrose, Canada 51 C7
Elsinore = Helsingør,
 Denmark 7 H15
Eltham, N.Z. 39 H5
Eluru, India 29 L12
Elvas, Portugal 15 C2
Elverum, Norway ... 7 F14
Elvire →, Australia .. 40 C4
Elvire, Mt., Australia . 41 E2
Elwell, L., U.S.A. ... 56 B8
Elwood, Ind., U.S.A. . 52 E3
Elwood, Nebr., U.S.A. 54 E5
Elx = Elche, Spain ... 15 C5
Ely, U.K. 9 E8
Ely, Minn., U.S.A. ... 54 B9
Ely, Nev., U.S.A. 56 G6
Elyria, U.S.A. 52 E4
Emāmrūd, Iran 31 B7
Emba, Kazakstan ... 20 E6
Emba →, Kazakstan . 19 E9
Embarcación, Argentina 64 A4
Embarras Portage,
 Canada 51 B6
Embetsu, Japan 22 B10
Embi = Emba,
 Kazakstan 20 E6
Embi = Emba →,
 Kazakstan 19 E9
Embrun, France 14 D7
Emden, Germany ... 12 B4
Emerald, Australia .. 42 C4
Emerson, Canada ... 51 D9
Emet, Turkey 17 E13
Emi Koussi, Chad ... 35 E9
Emine, Nos, Bulgaria . 17 C12
Emmeloord, Neths. .. 11 B5
Emmen, Neths. 11 B6
Emmet, Australia ... 42 C3
Emmetsburg, U.S.A. . 54 D7
Emmett, U.S.A. 56 E5
Emmonak, U.S.A. ... 46 B3
Emo, Canada 51 D10
Empalme, Mexico ... 58 B2
Empangeni, S. Africa . 37 K6
Empedrado, Argentina 64 B5
Emperor Seamount
 Chain, Pac. Oc. .. 44 D9
Emporia, Kans., U.S.A. 54 F6
Emporia, Va., U.S.A. . 53 G7
Emporium, U.S.A. ... 52 E6
Empress, Canada ... 51 C7
Empty Quarter = Rub'
 al Khālī, Si. Arabia . 32 D4
Ems →, Germany ... 12 B4
Emu, Australia 42 C5
Emu Park, Australia .. 42 C5
'En 'Avrona, Israel .. 33 F4
En Nahud, Sudan ... 35 F11
Ena, Japan 23 G8
Enaratoli, Indonesia .. 27 E9
Enard B., U.K. 10 C3
Encarnación, Paraguay 64 B5
Encarnación de Diaz,
 Mexico 58 C4
Encino, U.S.A. 57 J11
Encounter B., Australia 43 F2
Endako, Canada 50 C3
Ende, Indonesia 27 F6
Endeavour Str.,
 Australia 42 A3
Enderbury I., Kiribati . 38 H10
Enderby, Canada ... 50 C5
Enderby I., Australia . 40 D2
Enderby Land,
 Antarctica 5 C5
Enderlin, U.S.A. 54 B6
Endicott, U.S.A. 52 D7
Endyalgout I., Australia 40 B5
Eneabba, Australia .. 41 E2
Enewetak Atoll,
 Marshall Is. 44 F8
Enez, Turkey 17 D12
Enfield, Canada 49 D7

Engadin, Switz. 14 C9
Engaño, C., Dom. Rep. 61 C6
Engaño, C., Phil. 27 A6
Engaru, Japan 22 B11
Engels, Russia 19 D8
Engemann L., Canada . 51 B7
Enggano, Indonesia .. 26 F2
England, U.S.A. 55 H9
England □, U.K. 8 D7
Englee, Canada 49 B8
Englehart, Canada .. 48 C4
Englewood, U.S.A. .. 54 F2
English →, Canada . 51 C10
English Bazar = Ingraj
 Bazar, India 29 G16
English Channel, Europe 9 G6
English River, Canada . 48 C1
Enid, U.S.A. 55 G6
Enkhuizen, Neths. ... 11 B5
Enna, Italy 16 F6
Ennadai, Canada ... 51 A8
Ennadai L., Canada .. 51 A8
Ennedi, Chad 35 E10
Enngonia, Australia .. 43 D4
Ennis, Ireland 10 E2
Ennis, Mont., U.S.A. . 56 D8
Ennis, Tex., U.S.A. .. 55 J6
Enniskillen, U.K. 10 D3
Enns →, Austria 12 D8
Enontekiö, Finland ... 6 B20
Enschede, Neths. ... 11 B6
Ensenada, Mexico .. 58 A1
Ensenada de los
 Muertos, Mexico .. 58 C2
Entebbe, Uganda ... 36 D6
Enterprise, Canada .. 50 A5
Enterprise, Ala., U.S.A. 53 K3
Enterprise, Oreg., U.S.A. 56 D5
Entre Ríos, Bolivia .. 64 A4
Entroncamento,
 Portugal 15 C1
Enugu, Nigeria 34 G7
Eólie, Ís., Italy 16 E6
Epe, Neths. 11 B5
Épernay, France 14 B5
Ephesus, Turkey 17 F12
Ephraim, U.S.A. 56 G8
Ephrata, U.S.A. 56 C4
Épinal, France 14 B7
Epsom, U.K. 9 F7
Equatorial Guinea ■,
 Africa 36 D1
Er Rahad, Sudan ... 35 F12
Er Rif, Morocco 34 A5
Erāwadī Myit =
 Irrawaddy →, Burma 29 M19
Erbil = Arbil, Iraq ... 30 B5
Erçek, Turkey 30 B4
Erçiyaş Dağı, Turkey . 19 G6
Érd, Hungary 13 E10
Erdek, Turkey 17 D12
Erebus, Mt., Antarctica 5 D11
Erechim, Brazil 64 B6
Ereğli, Konya, Turkey . 19 G5
Ereğli, Zonguldak,
 Turkey 19 F5
Eresma →, Spain ... 15 B3
Erewadi Myitwanya =
 Irrawaddy, Mouths of
 the, Burma 29 M19
Erfurt, Germany 12 C6
Erg Iguidi, Africa ... 34 C4
Ergani, Turkey 30 B3
Ergeni Vozvyshennost,
 Russia 19 E7
Érgli, Latvia 7 H21
Érice, Italy 16 E5
Erie, U.S.A. 52 D5
Erie, L., N. Amer. ... 52 D5
Erigavo, Somali Rep. . 32 E4
Eriksdale, Canada ... 51 C9
Erimanthos, Greece .. 17 F9
Erimo-misaki, Japan . 22 D11
Eritrea ■, Africa 32 D2
Erlangen, Germany .. 12 D6
Erldunda, Australia .. 42 D1
Ermelo, Neths. 11 B5
Ermenek, Turkey ... 30 B2
Ermoúpolis = Síros,
 Greece 17 F11
Ernakulam = Cochin,
 India 28 Q10
Ernest Giles Ra.,
 Australia 41 E3
Erode, India 28 P10
Eromanga, Australia . 43 D3
Erramala Hills, India . 28 M11
Erskine, U.S.A. 54 B7
Ertis = Irtysh →,
 Russia 20 C7
Erwin, U.S.A. 53 G4
Erzgebirge, Germany . 12 C7
Erzin, Russia 21 D10
Erzincan, Turkey ... 19 G6
Erzurum, Turkey 19 G7
Es Sahrâ' Esh Sharqîya,
 Egypt 35 C12
Es Sînâ', Egypt 33 F3
Esan-Misaki, Japan .. 22 D10
Esashi, Hokkaidō, Japan 22 B11
Esashi, Hokkaidō, Japan 22 D10
Esbjerg, Denmark ... 7 J13
Escalante, U.S.A. ... 57 H8

Escalante →, U.S.A. . 57 H8
Escalón, Mexico 58 B4
Escambia →, U.S.A. . 53 K2
Escanaba, U.S.A. 52 C2
Esch-sur-Alzette, Lux. . 14 B6
Escondido, U.S.A. 57 K5
Escuinapa, Mexico 58 C3
Escuintla, Guatemala . 60 D1
Esenguly, Turkmenistan 20 F6
Eşfahān, Iran 31 C6
Eşfahān □, Iran 31 C6
Esfarāyen, Iran 31 B8
Esfideh, Iran 31 C8
Esh Sham = Dimashq,
  Syria 33 B5
Esher, U.K. 9 F7
Esil = Ishim →, Russia 20 D8
Esk →, U.K. 8 C7
Eskån, Iran 31 E9
Esker, Canada 49 B6
Eskifjörður, Iceland 6 D7
Eskimo Pt., Canada .. 46 B10
Eskilstuna, Sweden ... 7 G17
Eskişehir, Turkey 19 G5
Esla →, Spain 15 B2
Eslāmābād-e Gharb,
  Iran 30 C5
Eslāmshahr, Iran 31 C6
Eşme, Turkey 17 E13
Esmeraldas, Ecuador . 62 C3
Esnagi L., Canada ... 48 C3
Espanola, Canada 48 C3
Espanola, U.S.A. 57 H10
Esparta, Costa Rica .. 60 E3
Esperance, Australia .. 41 F3
Esperance B., Australia 41 F3
Espichel, C., Portugal . 15 C1
Espinazo, Sierra del =
  Espinhaço, Serra do,
  Brazil 63 G10
Espinhaço, Serra do,
  Brazil 63 G10
Espírito Santo □, Brazil 63 H10
Espíritu Santo, Vanuatu 38 C9
Espíritu Santo, B. del,
  Mexico 59 D7
Espíritu Santo, I.,
  Mexico 58 C2
Espita, Mexico 59 C7
Espoo, Finland 7 F21
Esquel, Argentina 64 E2
Esquimalt, Canada ... 50 D4
Esquina, Argentina ... 64 C5
Essaouira, Morocco .. 34 B4
Essen, Belgium 11 C4
Essen, Germany 12 C4
Essendon, Mt., Australia 41 E3
Essequibo →, Guyana 62 B7
Essex □, U.K. 9 F8
Esslingen, Germany .. 12 D5
Estados, I. de Los,
  Argentina 64 G4
Eştahbānāt, Iran 31 D7
Estância, Brazil 63 F11
Estancia, U.S.A. 57 J10
Estârm, Iran 31 D8
Esteli, Nic. 60 D2
Esterhazy, Canada ... 51 C8
Estevan, Canada 51 D8
Estevan Group, Canada 50 C3
Estherville, U.S.A. ... 54 D7
Eston, Canada 51 C7
Estonia ■, Europe ... 7 G21
Estreito, Brazil 63 E9
Estrela, Serra da,
  Portugal 15 B2
Estremoz, Portugal ... 15 C2
Estrondo, Serra do,
  Brazil 63 E9
Esztergom, Hungary .. 13 E10
Étampes, France 14 B5
Etawah, India 28 F11
Etawney L., Canada .. 51 B9
Ethelbert, Canada 51 C8
Ethiopia ■, Africa ... 32 F3
Etna, Italy 16 F6
Etosha Pan, Namibia . 37 H3
Etowah, U.S.A. 53 H3
Ettelbruck, Lux. 11 E6
Etzatlán, Mexico 58 C4
Etznà, Mexico 59 D6
Euboea = Évvoia,
  Greece 17 E11
Eucla, Australia 41 F4
Euclid, U.S.A. 52 E5
Eucumbene, L.,
  Australia 43 F4
Eudora, U.S.A. 55 J9
Eufaula, Ala., U.S.A. . 53 K3
Eufaula, Okla., U.S.A. 55 H7
Eufaula L., U.S.A. ... 55 H7
Eugene, U.S.A. 56 E2
Eugowra, Australia ... 43 E4
Eulo, Australia 43 D4
Eunice, La., U.S.A. .. 55 K8
Eunice, N. Mex., U.S.A. 55 J3
Eupen, Belgium 11 D6
Euphrates = Furāt, Nahr
  al →, Asia 30 D5
Eureka, Canada 4 B3
Eureka, Calif., U.S.A. . 56 F1
Eureka, Kans., U.S.A. . 55 G6
Eureka, Mont., U.S.A. . 56 B6
Eureka, Nev., U.S.A. . 56 G5
Eureka, S. Dak., U.S.A. 54 C5

Eureka, Mt., Australia . 41 E3
Euroa, Australia 43 F4
Europa, Île, Ind. Oc. . 37 J8
Europa, Picos de, Spain 15 A3
Europa, Pta. de, Gib. . 15 D3
Europoort, Neths. 11 C4
Eustis, U.S.A. 53 L5
Euston, Australia 43 E3
Eutsuk L., Canada ... 50 C3
Evans, Canada 54 E2
Evans, L., Canada ... 48 B4
Evans Head, Australia . 43 D5
Evansburg, Canada .. 50 C5
Evanston, Ill., U.S.A. . 52 D2
Evanston, Wyo., U.S.A. 56 F8
Evansville, U.S.A. ... 52 G2
Evaz, Iran 31 E7
Eveleth, U.S.A. 54 B8
Evensk, Russia 21 C16
Everard, L., Australia . 43 E2
Everard Ranges,
  Australia 41 E5
Everest, Mt., Nepal .. 29 E15
Everett, U.S.A. 56 C2
Everglades, The, U.S.A. 53 N5
Everglades City, U.S.A. 53 N5
Everglades National
  Park, U.S.A. 53 N5
Evergreen, Ala., U.S.A. 53 K2
Evergreen, Mont.,
  U.S.A. 56 B6
Evesham, U.K. 9 E6
Evje, Norway 7 G12
Évora, Portugal 15 C2
Evowghli, Iran 30 B5
Évreux, France 14 B4
Évros →, Bulgaria .. 17 D12
Évry, France 14 B5
Évvoia, Greece 17 E11
Ewing, U.S.A. 54 D5
Ewo, Congo 36 E2
Exaltación, Bolivia ... 62 F5
Excelsior Springs,
  U.S.A. 54 F7
Exe →, U.K. 9 G4
Exeter, U.K. 9 G4
Exeter, U.S.A. 57 H4
Exmoor, U.K. 9 F4
Exmouth, Australia .. 40 D1
Exmouth, U.K. 9 G4
Exmouth G., Australia . 40 D1
Expedition Ra., Australia 42 C4
Extremadura □, Spain . 15 C2
Exuma Sound, Bahamas 60 B4
Eyasi, L., Tanzania ... 36 E6
Eyjafjörður, Iceland ... 6 C4
Eyre (North), L.,
  Australia 43 D2
Eyre (South), L.,
  Australia 43 D2
Eyre, L., Australia ... 38 D6
Eyre Mts., N.Z. 39 L2
Eyre Pen., Australia .. 43 E2
Eysturoy, Færoe Is. .. 6 E9
Eyvānkī, Iran 31 C6
Ezine, Turkey 17 E12

F.Y.R.O.M. =
  Macedonia ■, Europe 17 D9
Fabala, Guinea 34 G4
Fabens, U.S.A. 57 L10
Fabriano, Italy 16 C5
Fachi, Niger 35 E8
Fada, Chad 35 E10
Fada-n-Gourma,
  Burkina Faso 34 F6
Faddeyevskiy, Ostrov,
  Russia 21 B15
Fadghāmī, Syria 30 C4
Faenza, Italy 16 B4
Færoe Is. = Føroyar,
  Atl. Oc. 6 F9
Făgăraş, Romania ... 13 F13
Fagersta, Sweden ... 7 F16
Fagnano, L., Argentina 64 G3
Fahliān, Iran 31 D6
Fahraj, Kermān, Iran . 31 D8
Fahraj, Yazd, Iran ... 31 D7
Fair Haven, U.S.A. .. 52 D9
Fair Isle, U.K. 10 B6
Fairbanks, U.S.A. ... 46 B5
Fairbury, U.S.A. 54 E6
Fairfield, Ala., U.S.A. . 53 J2
Fairfield, Calif., U.S.A. 56 G2
Fairfield, Idaho, U.S.A. 56 E6
Fairfield, Ill., U.S.A. . 52 F1
Fairfield, Iowa, U.S.A. 54 E9
Fairfield, Tex., U.S.A. . 55 K7
Fairford, Canada 51 C9
Fairhope, U.S.A. 53 K2
Fairlie, N.Z. 39 L3
Fairmont, Minn., U.S.A. 54 D7
Fairmont, W. Va., U.S.A. 52 F5
Fairplay, U.S.A. 57 G11
Fairport, U.S.A. 52 D7
Fairview, Canada 50 B5
Fairview, Mont., U.S.A. 54 B2
Fairview, Okla., U.S.A. 55 G5
Fairweather, Mt., U.S.A. 50 B1
Faisalabad, Pakistan . 28 D8
Faith, U.S.A. 54 C3
Faizabad, India 29 F13
Fajardo, Puerto Rico . 61 C6
Fajr, W. →, Si. Arabia 30 D3

Fakenham, U.K. 8 E8
Fakfak, Indonesia 27 E8
Falaise, France 14 B3
Falam, Burma 29 H18
Falcón, Presa, Mexico . 59 B5
Falcon Lake, Canada . 51 D9
Falcon Reservoir, U.S.A. 55 M5
Falconara Marittima,
  Italy 16 C5
Falcone, C. del, Italy . 16 D3
Faleshty = Fălești,
  Moldova 13 E14
Fălești, Moldova 13 E14
Falfurrias, U.S.A. 55 M5
Falher, Canada 50 B5
Falkenberg, Sweden .. 7 H15
Falkland Is. □, Atl. Oc. 64 G5
Falkland Sd., Falk. Is. . 64 G5
Falköping, Sweden ... 7 G15
Fall River, U.S.A. ... 52 E10
Fallon, U.S.A. 56 G4
Falls City, U.S.A. 54 E7
Falmouth, Jamaica .. 60 C4
Falmouth, U.K. 9 G2
Falsa, Pta., Mexico .. 58 B1
Falso, C., Honduras .. 60 C3
Falster, Denmark 7 J14
Fălticeni, Romania ... 13 E14
Falun, Sweden 7 F16
Famagusta, Cyprus .. 30 C2
Famalé, Niger 34 F6
Family L., Canada ... 51 C9
Fannūj, Iran 31 E9
Fanø, Denmark 7 J13
Fano, Italy 16 C5
Fao = Al Fāw, Iraq .. 31 D6
Faradje, Dem. Rep. of
  the Congo 36 D5
Farafangana, Madag. . 37 J9
Farāh, Afghan. 28 C3
Farāh □, Afghan. ... 28 C3
Farah, Guinea 34 F3
Farasān, Jazā'ir,
  Si. Arabia 32 D3
Farasan Is. = Farasān,
  Jazā'ir, Si. Arabia .. 32 D3
Fareham, U.K. 9 G6
Farewell, C., N.Z. ... 39 J4
Farewell C. = Nunap
  Isua, Greenland ... 4 D5
Farghona, Uzbekistan . 20 E8
Fargo, U.S.A. 54 B6
Fār'iah, W. al →,
  West Bank 33 C4
Faribault, U.S.A. 54 C8
Faridabad, India 28 E10
Farīmān, Iran 31 C8
Farina, Australia 43 E2
Farmerville, U.S.A. .. 55 J8
Farmington, Canada . 50 B4
Farmington, Maine,
  U.S.A. 53 C10
Farmington, Mo., U.S.A. 55 G9
Farmington, N. Mex.,
  U.S.A. 57 H9
Farmington, Utah,
  U.S.A. 56 F8
Farmville, U.S.A. ... 52 G6
Farne Is., U.K. 8 B6
Farnham, Mt., Canada . 50 C5
Faro, Brazil 63 D7
Faro, Canada 46 B6
Faro, Portugal 15 D2
Fårö, Sweden 7 H18
Farquhar, C., Australia 41 D1
Farrars Cr. →,
  Australia 42 D3
Farrāshband, Iran ... 31 D7
Farrokhī, Iran 31 C8
Fārs □, Iran 31 D7
Fársala, Greece 17 E10
Farson, U.S.A. 56 E9
Farsund, Norway ... 7 G12
Fartak, Râs, Si. Arabia 30 D2
Fartak, Ra's, Yemen . 32 D5
Fārūj, Iran 31 B8
Farvel, Kap = Nunap
  Isua, Greenland ... 4 D5
Farwell, U.S.A. 55 H3
Fasā, Iran 31 D7
Fasano, Italy 16 D7
Fastiv, Ukraine 13 C15
Fastov = Fastiv, Ukraine 13 C15
Fatagar, Tanjung,
  Indonesia 27 E8
Fatehgarh, India 28 F11
Fatehpur, Raj., India . 28 F9
Fatehpur, Ut. P., India . 29 G12
Fatima, Canada 49 C7
Faulkton, U.S.A. 54 C5
Faure I., Australia ... 41 E1
Fauske, Norway 6 C16
Favara, Italy 16 F5
Favignana, Italy 16 F5
Fawcett, Pt., Australia 40 B5
Fawn →, Canada ... 48 A2
Faxaflói, Iceland 6 D2
Faya-Largeau, Chad .. 35 E9
Fayd, Si. Arabia 30 E4
Fayette, Ala., U.S.A. . 53 J2
Fayette, Mo., U.S.A. . 54 F8
Fayetteville, Ark., U.S.A. 55 G7
Fayetteville, N.C., U.S.A. 53 H6

Fayetteville, Tenn.,
  U.S.A. 53 H2
Fazilka, India 28 D9
Fdérik, Mauritania .. 34 D3
Fear, C., U.S.A. 53 J7
Feather →, U.S.A. .. 56 G3
Featherston, N.Z. ... 39 J5
Fécamp, France 14 B4
Fedala = Mohammedia,
  Morocco 34 B4
Fédéral, Argentina .. 64 C5
Fedeshkūh, Iran 31 D7
Fehmarn, Germany .. 12 A6
Fehmarn Belt =
  Fehmarn Bælt, Europe 7 J14
Feijó, Brazil 62 E4
Feilding, N.Z. 39 J5
Feira de Santana, Brazil 63 F11
Feldkirch, Austria ... 12 E5
Felipe Carrillo Puerto,
  Mexico 59 D7
Felixstowe, U.K. 9 F9
Femer Bælt = Fehmarn
  Bælt, Europe 7 J14
Femunden, Norway .. 7 E14
Fenoarivo Atsinanana,
  Madag. 37 H9
Fens, The, U.K. 8 E7
Fenton, U.S.A. 52 D4
Fenyang, China 25 C6
Feodosiya, Ukraine .. 19 E6
Ferdows, Iran 31 C8
Ferfer, Somali Rep. .. 32 F4
Fergana = Farghona,
  Uzbekistan 20 E8
Fergus Falls, U.S.A. . 54 B6
Ferland, Canada 48 B2
Fermo, Italy 16 C5
Fermont, Canada ... 49 B6
Fernandina Beach,
  U.S.A. 53 K5
Fernando de Noronha,
  Brazil 63 D12
Fernando Póo = Bioko,
  Eq. Guin. 36 D1
Ferndale, U.S.A. 56 B2
Fernie, Canada 50 D5
Fernlees, Australia .. 42 C4
Fernley, U.S.A. 56 G4
Ferozepore = Firozpur,
  India 28 D9
Ferrara, Italy 16 B4
Ferreñafe, Peru 62 E3
Ferret, C., France ... 14 D3
Ferriday, U.S.A. 55 K9
Ferrol, Spain 15 A1
Ferron, U.S.A. 57 G8
Ferryland, Canada .. 49 C9
Fertile, U.S.A. 54 B6
Fès, Morocco 34 B5
Fessenden, U.S.A. .. 54 B5
Festus, U.S.A. 54 F9
Feteşti, Romania ... 13 F14
Fethiye, Turkey 19 G4
Fetlar, U.K. 10 A6
Feuilles →, Canada . 47 C12
Fez = Fès, Morocco . 34 B5
Fezzan, Libya 35 C8
Fianarantsoa, Madag. 37 J9
Field →, Australia .. 42 C2
Field I., Australia ... 40 B5
Fier, Albania 17 D8
Fieri = Fier, Albania . 17 D8
Fifth Cataract, Sudan . 35 E12
Figeac, France 14 D5
Figueira da Foz,
  Portugal 15 B1
Figueres, Spain 15 A7
Figuig, Morocco 34 B5
Fiji ■, Pac. Oc. 39 C8
Filey, U.K. 8 C7
Filey B., U.K. 8 C7
Filiatrá, Greece 17 F9
Filingué, Niger 34 F6
Filipstad, Sweden ... 7 G16
Fillmore, U.S.A. 57 G7
Finger L., Canada ... 48 B1
Fingoè, Mozam. 37 G6
Finisterre, C. = Fisterra,
  C., Spain 15 A1
Finke, Australia 42 D1
Finland ■, Europe .. 6 E12
Finland, G. of, Europe . 7 G21
Finlay →, Canada .. 50 B3
Finley, Australia 43 F4
Finley, U.S.A. 54 B6
Finnigan, Mt., Australia 42 B4
Finniss, C., Australia . 43 E1
Finnmark, Norway .. 6 B20
Finnsnes, Norway ... 6 B18
Finspång, Sweden ... 7 G16
Fiora →, Italy 16 C4
Fiq, Syria 33 C4
Firat = Furāt, Nahr
  al →, Asia 30 D5
Firebag →, Canada . 51 B6
Firedrake L., Canada . 51 A8
Firenze, Italy 16 C4
Firk →, Iraq 30 D5
Firozabad, India 28 F11
Firozpur, India 28 D9

Firūzābād, Iran 31 D7
Firūzkūh, Iran 31 C7
Firvale, Canada 50 C3
Fish →, Namibia ... 37 K3
Fisher, Australia 41 F5
Fisher B., Canada ... 51 C9
Fishguard, U.K. 9 E3
Fishing L., Canada .. 51 C9
Fitchburg, U.S.A. ... 52 D10
Fitz Roy, Argentina .. 64 F3
Fitzgerald, Canada .. 50 B6
Fitzgerald, U.S.A. ... 53 K4
Fitzmaurice →,
  Australia 40 B5
Fitzroy →, Queens.,
  Australia 42 C5
Fitzroy →, W. Austral.,
  Australia 40 C3
Fitzroy, Mte., Argentina 64 F2
Fitzroy Crossing,
  Australia 40 C4
Fiume = Rijeka, Croatia 12 F8
Fizi, Dem. Rep. of
  the Congo 36 E5
Flagstaff, U.S.A. 57 J8
Flagstaff L., U.S.A. .. 53 C10
Flaherty I., Canada .. 48 A4
Flåm, Norway 7 F12
Flambeau →, U.S.A. 54 C9
Flamborough Hd., U.K. 8 C7
Flaming Gorge
  Reservoir, U.S.A. .. 56 F9
Flamingo, Teluk,
  Indonesia 27 F9
Flanders = Flandre,
  Europe 10 F8
Flandre, Europe 10 F8
Flandre Occidentale =
  West-Vlaanderen □,
  Belgium 11 D2
Flandre Orientale =
  Oost-Vlaanderen □,
  Belgium 11 C3
Flandreau, U.S.A. ... 54 C6
Flåsjön, Sweden 6 D16
Flat →, Canada 50 A3
Flathead L., U.S.A. .. 56 C7
Flattery, C., Australia . 42 A4
Flattery, C., U.S.A. .. 56 B1
Flatwoods, U.S.A. .. 52 F4
Flekkefjord, Norway . 7 G12
Flensburg, Germany . 12 A5
Flers, France 14 B3
Flesko, Tanjung,
  Indonesia 27 D6
Fleurieu Pen., Australia 43 F2
Flevoland □, Neths. . 11 B5
Flin Flon, Canada ... 51 C8
Flinders →, Australia 42 B3
Flinders B., Australia . 41 F2
Flinders Group,
  Australia 42 A3
Flinders I., S. Austral.,
  Australia 43 E1
Flinders I., Tas.,
  Australia 42 G4
Flinders Ranges,
  Australia 43 E2
Flinders Reefs, Australia 42 B4
Flint, U.K. 8 D4
Flint, U.S.A. 52 D4
Flint →, U.S.A. 53 K3
Flint I., Kiribati 45 J12
Flintshire □, U.K. ... 8 D4
Flodden, U.K. 8 B5
Floodwood, U.S.A. .. 54 B8
Flora, U.S.A. 52 F1
Florala, U.S.A. 53 K2
Florence = Firenze, Italy 16 C4
Florence, Ala., U.S.A. 53 H2
Florence, Ariz., U.S.A. 57 K8
Florence, Colo., U.S.A. 55 F2
Florence, Oreg., U.S.A. 56 E1
Florence, S.C., U.S.A. 53 H6
Florence, L., Australia 43 D2
Florencia, Colombia . 62 C3
Florennes, Belgium .. 11 D4
Florenville, Belgium .. 11 E5
Flores, Guatemala ... 60 C2
Flores, Indonesia 27 F6
Flores I., Canada ... 50 D3
Flores Sea, Indonesia 27 F6
Floreşti, Moldova ... 13 E15
Floresville, U.S.A. .. 55 L5
Floriano, Brazil 63 E10
Florianópolis, Brazil . 64 B7
Florida, Cuba 60 B4
Florida, Uruguay 64 C5
Florida □, U.S.A. ... 53 L5
Florida B., U.S.A. ... 60 B3
Florida Keys, U.S.A. . 53 N5
Flórina, Greece 17 D9
Florø, Norway 7 F11
Floydada, U.S.A. ... 55 J4
Fluk, Indonesia 27 E7
Flushing = Vlissingen,
  Neths. 11 C3
Fly →, Papua N. G. . 38 B7
Flying Fish, C.,
  Antarctica 5 D15
Foam Lake, Canada . 51 C8

Foça, Turkey 17 E12
Focşani, Romania ... 13 F14
Fóggia, Italy 16 D6
Fogo, Canada 49 C9
Fogo I., Canada 49 C9
Föhr, Germany 12 A5
Foix, France 14 E4
Folda, Nord-Trøndelag,
  Norway 6 D14
Folda, Nordland,
  Norway 6 C16
Foley, U.S.A. 53 K2
Foleyet, Canada 48 C3
Folgefonni, Norway . 7 F12
Foligno, Italy 16 C5
Folkestone, U.K. 9 F9
Folkston, U.S.A. 53 K5
Fond-du-Lac, Canada 51 B7
Fond du Lac, U.S.A. . 54 D10
Fond-du-Lac →,
  Canada 51 B7
Fondi, Italy 16 D5
Fongafale, Tuvalu ... 44 H9
Fonsagrada = A
  Fonsagrada, Spain . 15 A2
Fonseca, G. de,
  Cent. Amer. 60 D2
Fontainebleau, France 14 B5
Fontas →, Canada . 50 B4
Fonte Boa, Brazil ... 62 D5
Fontenay-le-Comte,
  France 14 C3
Fontenelle Reservoir,
  U.S.A. 56 E8
Fontur, Iceland 6 C6
Foochow = Fuzhou,
  China 25 D6
Forbes, Australia 43 E4
Førde, Norway 7 F11
Ford's Bridge, Australia 43 D4
Fordyce, U.S.A. 55 J8
Forel, Mt., Greenland . 4 C6
Foremost, Canada .. 50 D6
Forest, U.S.A. 55 J10
Forest City, Iowa, U.S.A. 54 D8
Forest City, N.C., U.S.A. 53 H5
Forest Grove, U.S.A. . 56 D2
Forestburg, Canada .. 50 C6
Forestier Pen., Australia 42 G4
Forestville, Canada .. 49 C6
Forfar, U.K. 10 C5
Forks, U.S.A. 56 C1
Forlì, Italy 16 B5
Forman, U.S.A. 54 B6
Formby Pt., U.K. ... 8 D4
Formentera, Spain .. 15 C6
Formentor, C. de, Spain 15 C7
Former Yugoslav
  Republic of
  Macedonia =
  Macedonia ■, Europe 17 D9
Fórmia, Italy 16 D5
Formosa = Taiwan ■,
  Asia 25 D7
Formosa, Argentina .. 64 B5
Formosa, Brazil 63 G9
Formosa, Serra, Brazil 63 F8
Føroyar, Atl. Oc. 6 F9
Forrest, Australia ... 41 F4
Forrest, Mt., Australia 41 D4
Forrest City, U.S.A. . 55 H9
Forsayth, Australia .. 42 B3
Forssa, Finland 7 F20
Forst, Germany 12 C8
Forsyth, U.S.A. 56 C10
Fort Albany, Canada . 48 B3
Fort Assiniboine,
  Canada 50 C6
Fort Benton, U.S.A. . 56 C8
Fort Bragg, U.S.A. .. 56 G2
Fort Bridger, U.S.A. . 56 F8
Fort Chipewyan, Canada 51 B6
Fort Collins, U.S.A. . 54 E2
Fort-Coulonge, Canada 48 C4
Fort Davis, U.S.A. .. 55 K3
Fort-de-France,
  Martinique 61 D7
Fort Defiance, U.S.A. 57 J9
Fort Dodge, U.S.A. . 54 D7
Fort Fairfield, U.S.A. 53 B12
Fort Frances, Canada 51 D10
Fort Garland, U.S.A. . 57 H11
Fort George = Chisasibi,
  Canada 48 B4
Fort Good-Hope,
  Canada 46 B7
Fort Hancock, U.S.A. 57 L11
Fort Hertz = Putao,
  Burma 29 F20
Fort Hope, Canada .. 48 B2
Fort Jameson =
  Chipata, Zambia .. 37 G6
Fort Kent, U.S.A. ... 53 B11
Fort Klamath, U.S.A. 56 E3
Fort-Lamy = Ndjamena,
  Chad 35 F8
Fort Laramie, U.S.A. . 54 D2
Fort Lauderdale, U.S.A. 53 M5
Fort Liard, Canada .. 50 A4
Fort Liberté, Haiti ... 61 C5
Fort Lupton, U.S.A. . 54 E2
Fort Mackay, Canada . 50 B6
Fort Macleod, Canada 50 D6
Fort McMurray, Canada 50 B6
Fort McPherson, Canada 46 B6

Fort Madison, *U.S.A.* ... 54 E9
Fort Meade, *U.S.A.* ... 53 M5
Fort Morgan, *U.S.A.* ... 54 E3
Fort Myers, *U.S.A.* ... 53 M5
Fort Nelson, *Canada* ... 50 B4
Fort Nelson →, *Canada* 50 B4
Fort Norman = Tulita,
  Canada 46 B7
Fort Payne, *U.S.A.* ... 53 H3
Fort Peck, *U.S.A.* ... 56 B10
Fort Peck Dam, *U.S.A.* . 56 C10
Fort Peck L., *U.S.A.* ... 56 C10
Fort Pierce, *U.S.A.* ... 53 M5
Fort Pierre, *U.S.A.* ... 54 C4
Fort Providence, *Canada* 50 A5
Fort Qu'Appelle, *Canada* 51 C8
Fort Resolution, *Canada* 50 A6
Fort Rosebery = Mansa,
  Zambia 36 G5
Fort Rupert =
  Waskaganish, *Canada* 48 B4
Fort St. James, *Canada* . 50 C4
Fort St. John, *Canada* .. 50 B4
Fort Sandeman = Zhob,
  Pakistan 28 D6
Fort Saskatchewan,
  Canada 50 C6
Fort Scott, *U.S.A.* 55 G7
Fort Severn, *Canada* .. 48 A2
Fort Shevchenko,
  Kazakstan 19 F9
Fort Simpson, *Canada* . 50 A4
Fort Smith, *Canada* ... 50 B6
Fort Smith, *U.S.A.* 55 H7
Fort Stockton, *U.S.A.* .. 55 K3
Fort Sumner, *U.S.A.* ... 55 H2
Fort Thompson, *U.S.A.* . 54 C5
Fort Trinquet = Bir
  Mogreïn, *Mauritania* 34 C3
Fort Valley, *U.S.A.* 53 J4
Fort Vermilion, *Canada* 50 B5
Fort Walton Beach,
  U.S.A. 53 K2
Fort Wayne, *U.S.A.* ... 52 E3
Fort William, *U.K.* 10 C4
Fort Worth, *U.S.A.* 55 J6
Fort Yates, *U.S.A.* 54 B4
Fort Yukon, *U.S.A.* 46 B5
Fortaleza, *Brazil* 63 D11
Forteau, *Canada* 49 B8
Fortescue →, *Australia* 40 D2
Fortuna, *Calif., U.S.A.* . 56 F1
Fortuna, *N. Dak., U.S.A.* 54 A3
Fortune, *Canada* 49 C8
Fortune B., *Canada* ... 49 C8
Forûr, *Iran* 31 E7
Fosna, *Norway* 6 E14
Fosnavåg, *Norway* ... 7 E11
Fossano, *Italy* 14 D7
Fossil, *U.S.A.* 56 D3
Foster, *Australia* 43 F4
Foster →, *Canada* ... 51 B7
Fosters Ra., *Australia* . 42 C1
Fostoria, *U.S.A.* 52 E4
Fougères, *France* 14 B3
Foul Pt., *Sri Lanka* ... 28 Q12
Foula, *U.K.* 10 A5
Foulness I., *U.K.* 9 F8
Fouman, *Cameroon* .. 36 C2
Fountain, *U.S.A.* 54 F2
Foúrnoi, *Greece* 17 F12
Fourth Cataract, *Sudan* 35 E12
Fouta Djalon, *Guinea* . 34 F3
Foux, Cap-à-, *Haiti* ... 61 C5
Foveaux Str., *N.Z.* ... 39 M2
Fowey, *U.K.* 9 G3
Fowler, *U.S.A.* 54 F3
Fowlers B., *Australia* . 41 F5
Fowman, *Iran* 31 B6
Fox →, *Canada* 51 B10
Fox Creek, *Canada* ... 50 C5
Fox Lake, *Canada* 50 B6
Fox Valley, *Canada* ... 51 C7
Foxe Basin, *Canada* .. 47 B11
Foxe Chan., *Canada* .. 47 B11
Foxe Pen., *Canada* ... 47 B12
Foxton, *N.Z.* 39 J5
Foz do Iguaçu, *Brazil* . 64 B6
Franca, *Brazil* 63 H9
Francavilla Fontana,
  Italy 17 D7
France ■, *Europe* ... 14 C5
Frances, *Australia* ... 43 F3
Frances →, *Canada* .. 50 A3
Frances L., *Canada* ... 50 A3
Franceville, *Gabon* ... 36 E2
Franche-Comté, *France* 14 C6
Francis Case, L., *U.S.A.* 54 D5
Francisco I. Madero,
  Coahuila, Mexico .. 58 B4
Francisco I. Madero,
  Durango, Mexico .. 58 C4
Francistown, *Botswana* 37 C4
François, *Canada* 49 C8
François L., *Canada* .. 50 C3
Franeker, *Neths.* 11 A5
Frankfort, *Ind., U.S.A.* 52 E2
Frankfort, *Kans., U.S.A.* 54 F6
Frankfort, *Ky., U.S.A.* . 52 F3
Frankfurt, *Brandenburg,
  Germany* 12 B8
Frankfurt, *Hessen,
  Germany* 12 C5

Fränkische Alb,
  Germany 12 D6
Frankland →, *Australia* 41 G2
Franklin, *Ky., U.S.A.* .. 53 G2
Franklin, *La., U.S.A.* .. 55 L9
Franklin, *N.H., U.S.A.* . 52 D10
Franklin, *Nebr., U.S.A.* . 54 E5
Franklin, *Pa., U.S.A.* .. 52 E6
Franklin, *Va., U.S.A.* .. 53 G7
Franklin, *W. Va., U.S.A.* 52 F6
Franklin B., *Canada* .. 46 B7
Franklin D. Roosevelt L.,
  U.S.A. 56 B4
Franklin I., *Antarctica* .. 5 D11
Franklin L., *U.S.A.* ... 56 F6
Franklin Mts., *Canada* . 46 B7
Franklin Str., *Canada* . 46 A10
Franklinton, *U.S.A.* ... 55 K9
Franks Pk., *U.S.A.* ... 56 E9
Frankston, *Australia* ... 43 F4
Frantsa Iosifa, Zemlya,
  Russia 20 A6
Franz, *Canada* 48 C3
Franz Josef Land =
  Frantsa Iosifa, Zemlya,
  Russia 20 A6
Fraser →, *B.C., Canada* 50 D4
Fraser →, *Nfld.,
  Canada* 49 A7
Fraser, Mt., *Australia* . 41 E2
Fraser I., *Australia* ... 43 D5
Fraser Lake, *Canada* .. 50 C4
Fraserburgh, *U.K.* 10 C5
Fraserdale, *Canada* .. 48 C3
Fray Bentos, *Uruguay* . 64 C5
Fredericia, *Denmark* ... 7 J13
Frederick, *Md., U.S.A.* . 52 F7
Frederick, *Okla., U.S.A.* 55 H5
Frederick, *S. Dak.,
  U.S.A.* 54 C5
Fredericksburg, *Tex.,
  U.S.A.* 55 K5
Fredericksburg, *Va.,
  U.S.A.* 52 F7
Fredericktown, *U.S.A.* . 55 G9
Frederico I. Madero,
  Presa, *Mexico* 58 B3
Fredericton, *Canada* .. 49 C6
Fredericton Junction,
  Canada 49 C6
Frederikshåb = Paamiut,
  Greenland 4 C5
Frederikshavn, *Denmark* 7 H14
Frederiksted, *Virgin Is.* 61 C7
Fredonia, *Ariz., U.S.A.* 57 H7
Fredonia, *Kans., U.S.A.* 55 G7
Fredonia, *N.Y., U.S.A.* . 52 D6
Fredrikstad, *Norway* . 7 G14
Free State □, *S. Africa* 37 K5
Freels, C., *Canada* ... 49 C9
Freeman, *U.S.A.* 54 D6
Freeport, *Bahamas* .. 60 A4
Freeport, *Ill., U.S.A.* . 54 D10
Freeport, *N.Y., U.S.A.* . 52 E9
Freeport, *Tex., U.S.A.* . 55 L7
Freetown, *S. Leone* .. 34 G3
Frégate, L., *Canada* .. 48 B5
Fregenal de la Sierra,
  Spain 15 C2
Freibourg = Fribourg,
  Switz. 14 C7
Freiburg, *Germany* ... 12 E4
Freire, *Chile* 64 D2
Freising, *Germany* ... 12 D6
Freistadt, *Austria* ... 12 D8
Fréjus, *France* 14 E7
Fremantle, *Australia* . 41 F2
Fremont, *Calif., U.S.A.* 57 H2
Fremont, *Mich., U.S.A.* 52 D3
Fremont, *Nebr., U.S.A.* 54 E6
Fremont, *Ohio, U.S.A.* 52 E4
Fremont →, *U.S.A.* . 57 G8
French Guiana ■,
  S. Amer. 63 C8
French Polynesia ■,
  Pac. Oc. 45 K13
Frenchman Cr. →,
  N. Amer. 56 B10
Frenchman Cr. →,
  U.S.A. 54 E4
Fresco →, *Brazil* 63 E8
Freshfield, C., *Antarctica* 5 C10
Fresnillo, *Mexico* 58 C4
Fresno, *U.S.A.* 57 H4
Fresno Reservoir, *U.S.A.* 56 B9
Frew →, *Australia* ... 42 C2
Freycinet Pen., *Australia* 42 G4
Fria, C., *Namibia* 37 H2
Frías, *Argentina* 64 B3
Fribourg, *Switz.* 14 C7
Friedrichshafen,
  Germany 12 E5
Friendly Is. = Tonga ■,
  Pac. Oc. 39 D11
Friesland □, *Neths.* .. 11 A5
Frio →, *U.S.A.* 55 L5
Friona, *U.S.A.* 55 H3
Fritch, *U.S.A.* 55 H4
Frobisher B., *Canada* . 47 B13
Frobisher Bay = Iqaluit,
  Canada 47 B13
Frobisher L., *Canada* . 51 B7
Frohavet, *Norway* ... 6 E13
Frome, *U.K.* 9 F5
Frome →, *U.K.* 9 G5

Frome, L., *Australia* ... 43 E2
Front Royal, *U.S.A.* ... 52 F6
Frontera, *Mexico* 59 D6
Fronteras, *Mexico* 58 A3
Frosinone, *Italy* 16 D5
Frostburg, *U.S.A.* 52 F6
Frostisen, *Norway* ... 6 B17
Frøya, *Norway* 6 E13
Frunze = Bishkek,
  Kyrgyzstan 20 E8
Frutal, *Brazil* 63 H9
Frýdek-Místek,
  Czech Rep. 13 D10
Fuchou = Fuzhou, *China* 25 D6
Fuchū, *Japan* 23 G6
Fuengirola, *Spain* ... 15 D3
Fuentes de Oñoro,
  Spain 15 B2
Fuerte →, *Mexico* ... 58 B3
Fuerte Olimpo,
  Paraguay 62 H7
Fuerteventura,
  Canary Is. 34 C3
Fuhai, *China* 24 B3
Fuḥaymī, *Iraq* 30 C4
Fuji, *Japan* 23 G9
Fuji-San, *Japan* 23 G9
Fuji-Yoshida, *Japan* .. 23 G9
Fujian □, *China* 25 D6
Fujinomiya, *Japan* ... 23 G9
Fujisawa, *Japan* 23 G9
Fujiyama, Mt. = Fuji-
  San, *Japan* 23 G9
Fukien = Fujian □,
  China 25 D6
Fukuchiyama, *Japan* . 23 G7
Fukue-Shima, *Japan* . 23 H4
Fukui, *Japan* 23 F8
Fukui □, *Japan* 23 G8
Fukuoka, *Japan* 23 H5
Fukuoka □, *Japan* ... 23 H5
Fukushima, *Japan* ... 22 F10
Fukushima □, *Japan* . 22 F10
Fukuyama, *Japan* ... 23 G6
Fulda, *Germany* 12 C5
Fulda →, *Germany* .. 12 C5
Fullerton, *U.S.A.* 54 E6
Fulton, *Mo., U.S.A.* .. 54 F9
Fulton, *N.Y., U.S.A.* . 52 D7
Funabashi, *Japan* ... 23 G10
Funafuti, *Tuvalu* 38 B10
Funchal, *Madeira* ... 34 B2
Fundación, *Colombia* . 62 A4
Fundão, *Portugal* ... 15 B2
Fundy, B. of, *Canada* . 49 D6
Funtua, *Nigeria* 34 F7
Furano, *Japan* 22 C11
Furāt, Nahr al →, *Asia* 30 D5
Fürg, *Iran* 31 D7
Furneaux Group,
  Australia 42 G4
Furqlus, *Syria* 33 A6
Fürstenwalde, *Germany* 12 B8
Fürth, *Germany* 12 D6
Furukawa, *Japan* ... 22 E10
Fury and Hecla Str.,
  Canada 47 B11
Fusagasuga, *Colombia* 62 C4
Fushun, *China* 25 B7
Futuna, *Wall. & F. Is.* . 39 B8
Fuxin, *China* 25 B7
Fuzhou, *China* 25 D6
Fylde, *U.K.* 8 D5
Fyn, *Denmark* 7 J14

Gabela, *Angola* 36 G2
Gabès, *Tunisia* 35 B8
Gabès, G. de, *Tunisia* . 35 B8
Gabon ■, *Africa* 36 E2
Gaborone, *Botswana* . 37 J5
Gābrīk, *Iran* 31 E8
Gabrovo, *Bulgaria* .. 17 C11
Gāch Sār, *Iran* 31 B6
Gachsārān, *Iran* 31 D6
Gadag, *India* 28 M9
Gadarwara, *India* ... 28 H11
Gadhada, *India* 28 J7
Gadsden, *U.S.A.* 53 H3
Gadwal, *India* 28 L10
Gaffney, *U.S.A.* 53 H5
Gafsa, *Tunisia* 34 B7
Gagnoa, *Ivory C.* ... 34 G4
Gagnon, *Canada* ... 49 B6
Gagnon, L., *Canada* . 51 A6
Gail, *U.S.A.* 55 J4
Gaillimh = Galway,
  Ireland 10 E2
Gainesville, *Fla., U.S.A.* 53 L4
Gainesville, *Ga., U.S.A.* 53 H4
Gainesville, *Mo., U.S.A.* 55 G8
Gainesville, *Tex., U.S.A.* 55 J6
Gainsborough, *U.K.* .. 8 D7
Gairdner, L., *Australia* . 43 E2
Galápagos, *Pac. Oc.* . 45 H18
Galashiels, *U.K.* 10 D5
Galați, *Romania* 13 F15
Galatina, *Italy* 17 D8
Galax, *U.S.A.* 53 G5
Galcaio, *Somali Rep.* . 32 F4
Galdhøpiggen, *Norway* 7 F12
Galeana, *Chihuahua,
  Mexico* 58 A3
Galeana, *Nuevo León,
  Mexico* 58 A3

Galela, *Indonesia* 27 D7
Galena, *U.S.A.* 46 B4
Galera Point,
  Trin. & Tob. 61 D7
Galesburg, *U.S.A.* ... 54 E9
Galich, *Russia* 18 C7
Galicia □, *Spain* 15 A2
Galilee = Hagalil, *Israel* 33 C4
Galilee, L., *Australia* .. 42 C4
Galilee, Sea of = Yam
  Kinneret, *Israel* ... 33 C4
Galiuro Mts., *U.S.A.* .. 57 K8
Galiwinku, *Australia* .. 42 A2
Gallatin, *U.S.A.* 53 G2
Galle, *Sri Lanka* 28 R12
Gállego →, *Spain* ... 15 B5
Gallegos →, *Argentina* 64 G3
Gallipoli = Gelibolu,
  Turkey 17 D12
Gallípoli, *Italy* 17 D8
Gallipolis, *U.S.A.* 52 F4
Gällivare, *Sweden* ... 6 C19
Galloway, Mull of, *U.K.* 10 D4
Gallup, *U.S.A.* 57 J9
Galoya, *Sri Lanka* ... 28 Q12
Galva, *U.S.A.* 54 E9
Galveston, *U.S.A.* ... 55 L7
Galveston B., *U.S.A.* . 55 L7
Gálvez, *Argentina* ... 64 C4
Galway, *Ireland* 10 E2
Galway B., *Ireland* .. 10 E2
Gamagori, *Japan* ... 23 G8
Gambia ■, *W. Afr.* .. 34 F2
Gambia →, *W. Afr.* . 34 F2
Gambier, C., *Australia* 40 B5
Gambier Is., *Australia* 43 F2
Gambo, *Canada* 49 C9
Gamboma, *Congo* .. 36 E3
Gamlakarleby =
  Kokkola, *Finland* .. 6 E20
Gammon →, *Canada* . 51 C9
Gan Jiang →, *China* . 25 D6
Ganado, *U.S.A.* 57 J9
Gananoque, *Canada* . 48 D4
Ganāveh, *Iran* 31 D6
Gäncä, *Azerbaijan* .. 19 F8
Gand = Gent, *Belgium* 11 C3
Ganda, *Angola* 37 G2
Gandak →, *Dem. Rep. of
  the Congo* 36 F4
Gandak →, *India* ... 29 G14
Gandava, *Pakistan* .. 28 E5
Gander, *Canada* 49 C9
Gander L., *Canada* .. 49 C9
Gandhi Sagar, *India* . 28 G9
Gandía, *Spain* 15 C5
Ganedidalem = Gani,
  Indonesia 27 E7
Ganga →, *India* 29 H17
Ganganagar, *India* .. 28 E8
Gangaw, *Burma* ... 29 H19
Gangdisê Shan, *China* 29 D12
Ganges = Ganga →,
  India 29 H17
Ganges, *Canada* 50 D4
Gangtok, *India* 29 F16
Gani, *Indonesia* 27 E7
Gannett Peak, *U.S.A.* . 56 E9
Gansu □, *China* 24 C5
Ganta, *Liberia* 34 G4
Gantheaume, C.,
  Australia 43 F2
Gantheaume B.,
  Australia 41 E1
Gantsevichi =
  Hantsavichy, *Belarus* 13 B14
Ganyem = Genyem,
  Indonesia 27 E10
Ganzhou, *China* 25 D6
Gao, *Mali* 34 E5
Gaoua, *Burkina Faso* . 34 F4
Gaoual, *Guinea* 34 F3
Gaoxiong = Kaohsiung,
  Taiwan 25 D7
Gap, *France* 14 D7
Gapuwiyak, *Australia* . 42 A2
Gar, *China* 24 C2
Garabogazköl Aylagy,
  Turkmenistan 19 F9
Garachiné, *Panama* .. 60 E4
Garah, *Australia* 43 D4
Garanhuns, *Brazil* ... 63 E11
Garberville, *U.S.A.* .. 56 F2
Garda, L. di, *Italy* ... 16 B4
Garde L., *Canada* ... 51 A7
Garden City, *Ga., U.S.A.* 53 J5
Garden City, *Kans.,
  U.S.A.* 55 G4
Garden City, *Tex.,
  U.S.A.* 55 K4
Gardez, *Afghan.* 28 C6
Gardiner, *Maine, U.S.A.* 53 C11
Gardiner, *Mont., U.S.A.* 56 D8
Gardiner Canal, *Canada* 50 C3
Gardnerville, *U.S.A.* . 56 G4
Gardo, *Somali Rep.* .. 32 F4
Garfield, *U.S.A.* 56 C5
Garforth, *U.K.* 8 D6
Gargano, Mte., *Italy* . 16 D6
Garibaldi Prov. Park,
  Canada 50 D4
Garigliano →, *Italy* .. 16 D5
Garissa, *Kenya* 36 E7
Garland, *Tex., U.S.A.* . 55 J6

Garland, *Utah, U.S.A.* . 56 F7
Garm, *Tajikistan* 20 F8
Garmāb, *Iran* 31 C8
Garmisch-Partenkirchen,
  Germany 12 E6
Garmsār, *Iran* 31 C7
Garner, *U.S.A.* 54 D8
Garnett, *U.S.A.* 54 F7
Garoe, *Somali Rep.* .. 32 F4
Garonne →, *France* . 14 D3
Garoua, *Cameroon* .. 35 G8
Garrison, *Mont., U.S.A.* 56 C7
Garrison, *N. Dak., U.S.A.* 54 B4
Garrison Res. =
  Sakakawea, L., *U.S.A.* 54 B4
Garry →, *U.K.* 10 C4
Garry, L., *Canada* ... 46 B9
Garson L., *Canada* .. 51 B6
Garut, *Indonesia* 27 G12
Garvie Mts., *N.Z.* ... 39 L2
Garwa = Garoua,
  Cameroon 35 G8
Gary, *U.S.A.* 52 E2
Garzê, *China* 24 C5
Garzón, *Colombia* ... 62 C3
Gas-San, *Japan* 22 E10
Gasan Kuli = Esenguly,
  Turkmenistan 20 F6
Gascogne, *France* .. 14 E4
Gascogne, G. de,
  Europe 14 D2
Gascony = Gascogne,
  France 14 E4
Gascoyne →, *Australia* 41 D1
Gascoyne Junction,
  Australia 41 E2
Gashaka, *Nigeria* ... 35 G8
Gashua, *Nigeria* 35 F8
Gaspé, *Canada* 49 C7
Gaspé, C. de, *Canada* 49 C7
Gaspé, Pén. de, *Canada* 49 C6
Gaspésie, Parc de
  Conservation de la,
  Canada 49 C6
Gasteiz = Vitoria-
  Gasteiz, *Spain* 15 A4
Gastonia, *U.S.A.* 53 H5
Gastre, *Argentina* ... 64 E3
Gata, C. de, *Spain* .. 15 D4
Gata, Sierra de, *Spain* 15 B2
Gataga →, *Canada* . 50 B3
Gateshead, *U.K.* 8 C6
Gatesville, *U.S.A.* ... 55 K6
Gatineau, *Canada* ... 48 C4
Gatineau →, *Canada* 48 C4
Gatineau, Parc Nat. de
  la, *Canada* 48 C4
Gatton, *Australia* ... 43 D5
Gatun, L., *Panama* .. 60 E4
Gau, *Fiji* 39 D8
Gauer L., *Canada* ... 51 B9
Gauhati, *India* 29 F17
Gauja →, *Latvia* ... 7 H21
Gaula →, *Norway* .. 6 E14
Gausta, *Norway* 7 G13
Gāv Koshī, *Iran* 31 D8
Gāvāter, *Iran* 31 E9
Gāvbandī, *Iran* 31 E7
Gávdhos, *Greece* ... 17 G11
Gāvkhūnī, Baţlāq-e, *Iran* 31 C7
Gävle, *Sweden* 7 F17
Gawachab, *Namibia* . 37 D2
Gawilgarh Hills, *India* . 28 J10
Gawler, *Australia* ... 43 E2
Gaxun Nur, *China* ... 24 B5
Gay, *Russia* 18 D10
Gaya, *India* 29 G14
Gaya, *Niger* 34 F6
Gaylord, *U.S.A.* 52 C3
Gayndah, *Australia* .. 43 D5
Gaysin = Haysyn,
  Ukraine 13 D15
Gayvoron = Hayvoron,
  Ukraine 13 D15
Gaza, *Gaza Strip* 33 D3
Gaza Strip □, *Asia* .. 33 D3
Gazanjyk, *Turkmenistan* 31 B7
Gāzbor, *Iran* 31 D8
Gaziantep, *Turkey* ... 19 G6
Gcuwa, *S. Africa* ... 37 L5
Gdańsk, *Poland* 13 A10
Gdańska, Zatoka, *Poland* 13 A10
Gdov, *Russia* 7 G22
Gdynia, *Poland* 13 A10
Gebe, *Indonesia* 27 D7
Gebze, *Turkey* 17 D13
Gedaref, *Sudan* 35 F13
Gediz →, *Turkey* ... 17 E12
Gedser, *Denmark* ... 7 J14
Geegully Cr. →,
  Australia 40 C3
Geel, *Belgium* 11 C4
Geelong, *Australia* .. 43 F3
Geelvink B. =
  Cenderwasih, Teluk,
  Indonesia 27 E9
Geelvink Chan.,
  Australia 41 E1
Geesthacht, *Germany* . 12 B6
Geidam, *Nigeria* 35 F8
Geikie →, *Canada* .. 51 B8
Gejiu, *China* 24 D5
Gel, Meydān-e, *Iran* . 31 D7
Gela, *Italy* 16 F6
Gelderland □, *Neths.* . 11 B6
Geldrop, *Neths.* 11 C5
Geleen, *Neths.* 11 D5

Gelibolu, *Turkey* 17 D12
Gelsenkirchen, *Germany* 12 C4
Gembloux, *Belgium* .. 11 D4
Gemena, *Dem. Rep. of
  the Congo* 36 D3
Gemerek, *Turkey* 30 B3
Gemlik, *Turkey* 17 D13
Genale →, *Ethiopia* . 32 F2
General Acha, *Argentina* 64 D4
General Alvear,
  *Buenos Aires,
  Argentina* 64 D5
General Alvear,
  Mendoza, Argentina . 64 D3
General Belgrano,
  Argentina 64 D5
General Cepeda, *Mexico* 58 B4
General Juan
  Madariaga, *Argentina* 64 D5
General La Madrid,
  Argentina 64 D4
General MacArthur, *Phil.* 27 B7
General Pico, *Argentina* 64 D4
General Pinedo,
  Argentina 64 B4
General Roca, *Argentina* 64 D3
General Santos, *Phil.* . 27 C7
General Treviño, *Mexico* 59 B5
General Trías, *Mexico* . 58 B3
General Villegas,
  Argentina 64 D4
Genesee, *U.S.A.* 56 C5
Genesee →, *U.S.A.* . 52 D7
Geneseo, *Ill., U.S.A.* . 54 E9
Geneseo, *N.Y., U.S.A.* 52 D7
Geneva = Genève,
  Switz. 14 C7
Geneva, *Ala., U.S.A.* . 53 K3
Geneva, *N.Y., U.S.A.* . 52 D7
Geneva, *Nebr., U.S.A.* 54 E6
Geneva, *Ohio, U.S.A.* 52 E5
Geneva, L. = Léman, L.,
  Europe 14 C7
Geneva, L., *U.S.A.* .. 52 D1
Genève, *Switz.* 14 C7
Genil →, *Spain* 15 D3
Genk, *Belgium* 11 D5
Gennargentu, Mti. del,
  Italy 16 D3
Genoa = Génova, *Italy* 14 D8
Genoa, *Australia* 43 F4
Genoa, *U.S.A.* 54 E6
Génova, *Italy* 14 D8
Génova, G. di, *Italy* . 16 C3
Genriyetty, Ostrov,
  Russia 21 B16
Gent, *Belgium* 11 C3
Genteng, *Indonesia* . 27 G12
Genyem, *Indonesia* . 27 E10
Geographe B., *Australia* 41 F2
Geographe Chan.,
  Australia 41 D1
Georga, Zemlya, *Russia* 20 A5
George, *S. Africa* ... 37 L4
George →, *Canada* . 49 A6
George, L., *N.S.W.,
  Australia* 43 F4
George, L., *S. Austral.,
  Australia* 43 F3
George, L., *W. Austral.,
  Australia* 40 D3
George, L., *Fla., U.S.A.* 53 L5
George, L., *N.Y., U.S.A.* 52 D9
George Gill Ra.,
  Australia 40 D5
George River =
  Kangiqsualujjuaq,
  Canada 47 C13
George Sound, *N.Z.* . 39 L1
George Town, *Australia* 42 G4
George Town, *Bahamas* 60 B4
George Town, *Malaysia* 26 C2
George V Land,
  Antarctica 5 C10
George VI Sound,
  Antarctica 5 D17
George West, *U.S.A.* . 55 L5
Georgetown, *Australia* 42 B3
Georgetown, *Ont.,
  Canada* 48 D4
Georgetown, *P.E.I.,
  Canada* 49 C7
Georgetown, *Cayman Is.* 60 C3
Georgetown, *Gambia* . 34 F3
Georgetown, *Guyana* . 62 B7
Georgetown, *Colo.,
  U.S.A.* 56 G11
Georgetown, *Ky., U.S.A.* 52 F3
Georgetown, *Ohio,
  U.S.A.* 52 F4
Georgetown, *S.C.,
  U.S.A.* 53 J6
Georgetown, *Tex.,
  U.S.A.* 55 K6
Georgia ■, *Asia* 19 F7
Georgia □, *U.S.A.* .. 53 J4
Georgia, Str. of, *Canada* 50 D4
Georgian B., *Canada* . 48 C3
Georgina →, *Australia* 42 C2
Georgina-Dezh = Liski,
  Russia 19 D6
Georgiyevsk, *Russia* . 19 F7
Gera, *Germany* 12 C7
Geraardsbergen,
  Belgium 11 D3

Geral de Goiás, Serra,
  Brazil 63 F9
Geraldine, U.S.A. 56 C8
Geraldton, Australia .. 41 E1
Geraldton, Canada ... 48 C2
Gereshk, Afghan. 28 D4
Gering, U.S.A. 54 E3
Gerlach, U.S.A. 56 F4
Germansen Landing,
  Canada 50 B4
Germantown, Pa., U.S.A. 55 M10
Germany ■, Europe .. 12 C6
Germī, Iran 31 B6
Germiston, S. Africa .. 37 K5
Gernika-Lumo, Spain . 15 A4
Gero, Japan 23 G8
Gerona = Girona, Spain 15 B7
Gerrard, Canada 50 C5
Geser, Indonesia 27 E8
Getafe, Spain 15 B4
Gettysburg, Pa., U.S.A. 52 F7
Gettysburg, S. Dak.,
  U.S.A. 54 C5
Getxo, Spain 15 A4
Getz Ice Shelf,
  Antarctica 5 D14
Geyser, U.S.A. 56 C8
Ghaghara →, India .. 29 G14
Ghana ■, W. Afr. ... 34 G5
Ghanzi, Botswana ... 37 J4
Ghardaïa, Algeria ... 34 B6
Gharyān, Libya 35 B8
Ghat, Libya 35 D8
Ghaţţī, Si. Arabia ... 30 D3
Ghawdex = Gozo, Malta 16 F6
Ghazal, Bahr el →,
  Chad 35 F9
Ghazâl, Bahr el →,
  Sudan 35 G12
Ghaziabad, India 28 E10
Ghazipur, India 29 G13
Ghazni, Afghan. 28 C6
Ghazni □, Afghan. ... 28 C6
Ghent = Gent, Belgium 11 C3
Gheorghe Gheorghiu-
  Dej = Oneşti,
  Romania 13 E14
Ghinah, Wādī al →,
  Si. Arabia 30 D3
Ghizao, Afghan. 28 C4
Ghowr □, Afghan. ... 28 C4
Ghudaf, W. al →, Iraq 30 C4
Ghudāmis, Libya 35 B7
Ghugus, India 28 K11
Ghūriān, Afghan. ... 28 B2
Gia Lai = Plei Ku,
  Vietnam 26 B3
Giarabub = Al Jaghbūb,
  Libya 35 C10
Giarre, Italy 16 F6
Gibara, Cuba 60 B4
Gibb River, Australia . 40 C4
Gibbon, U.S.A. 54 E5
Gibeon, Namibia 37 K3
Gibraltar ■, Europe .. 15 D3
Gibraltar, Str. of,
  Medit. S. 15 E3
Gibson Desert, Australia 40 D4
Gibsons, Canada 50 D4
Giddings, U.S.A. 55 K6
Giessen, Germany ... 12 C5
Gīfān, Iran 31 B8
Gift Lake, Canada ... 50 B5
Gifu, Japan 23 G8
Gifu □, Japan 23 G8
Giganta, Sa. de la,
  Mexico 58 B2
Gíglio, Italy 16 C4
Gijón, Spain 15 A3
Gil I., Canada 50 C3
Gila →, U.S.A. 57 K6
Gila Bend, U.S.A. ... 57 K7
Gila Bend Mts., U.S.A. 57 K7
Gīlān □, Iran 31 B6
Gilbert →, Australia . 42 B3
Gilbert Is., Kiribati .. 38 A10
Gilbert River, Australia 42 B3
Gilford I., Canada ... 50 C3
Gilgandra, Australia . 43 E4
Gilgit, India 28 B9
Gilgunnia, Australia . 43 E4
Gillam, Canada 51 B10
Gillen, L., Australia .. 41 E3
Gilles, L., Australia .. 43 E2
Gillette, U.S.A. 54 C2
Gilliat, Australia 42 C3
Gillingham, U.K. 9 F8
Gilmer, U.S.A. 55 J7
Gilmore, L., Australia . 41 F3
Gilroy, U.S.A. 57 H3
Gimli, Canada 51 C9
Gin Gin, Australia ... 43 D5
Gingin, Australia 41 F2
Ginir, Ethiopia 32 F3
Gióna, Óros, Greece . 17 E10
Gippsland, Australia . 43 F4
Girāfi, W. →, Egypt . 33 F3
Girard, U.S.A. 52 G7
Giresun, Turkey 19 F6
Girga, Egypt 35 C12
Giridih, India 29 G15
Girne = Kyrenia, Cyprus 30 D12
Girona, Spain 15 B7
Gironde →, France . 14 D3
Giru, Australia 42 B4

Girvan, U.K. 10 D4
Gisborne, N.Z. 39 H7
Gisenyi, Rwanda 36 E5
Gislaved, Sweden ... 7 H15
Gitega, Burundi 36 E5
Giuba →, Somali Rep. 32 G3
Giurgiu, Romania ... 13 G13
Giza = El Gîza, Egypt 35 C12
Gizhiga, Russia 21 C17
Gizhiginskaya Guba,
  Russia 21 C16
Gizycko, Poland 13 A11
Gjirokastër, Albania . 17 D9
Gjirokastra =
  Gjirokastër, Albania . 17 D9
Gjoa Haven, Canada . 46 B10
Gjøvik, Norway 7 F14
Glace Bay, Canada .. 49 C8
Glacier Bay National
  Park and Preserve,
  U.S.A. 50 B1
Glacier National Park,
  Canada 50 C5
Glacier National Park,
  U.S.A. 56 B7
Glacier Peak, U.S.A. . 56 B3
Gladewater, U.S.A. .. 55 J7
Gladstone, Queens.,
  Australia 42 C5
Gladstone, S. Austral.,
  Australia 43 E2
Gladstone, Canada .. 51 C9
Gladstone, U.S.A. ... 52 C2
Gladwin, U.S.A. 52 D3
Glåma = Glomma →,
  Norway 7 G14
Gláma, Iceland 6 D2
Glasco, U.S.A. 54 F6
Glasgow, U.K. 10 D4
Glasgow, Ky., U.S.A. . 52 G3
Glasgow, Mont., U.S.A. 56 B10
Glaslyn, Canada 51 C7
Glastonbury, U.K. ... 9 F5
Glazov, Russia 18 C9
Gleichen, Canada ... 50 C6
Gleiwitz = Gliwice,
  Poland 13 C10
Glen Canyon, U.S.A. . 57 H8
Glen Canyon Dam,
  U.S.A. 57 H8
Glen Canyon National
  Recreation Area,
  U.S.A. 57 H8
Glen Innes, Australia . 43 D5
Glen Ullin, U.S.A. ... 54 B4
Glencoe, U.S.A. 54 C7
Glendale, Ariz., U.S.A. 57 K7
Glendale, Calif., U.S.A. 57 J4
Glendive, U.S.A. 54 B2
Glendo, U.S.A. 54 D2
Glenelg →, Australia . 43 F3
Glenmorgan, Australia 43 D4
Glennallen, U.S.A. ... 46 B5
Glenns Ferry, U.S.A. . 56 E6
Glenore, Australia ... 42 B3
Glenreagh, Australia . 43 E5
Glenrock, U.S.A. 56 E11
Glenrothes, U.K. 10 C5
Glens Falls, U.S.A. .. 52 D9
Glenville, U.S.A. 52 F5
Glenwood, Canada .. 49 C9
Glenwood, Ark., U.S.A. 55 H8
Glenwood, Iowa, U.S.A. 54 E7
Glenwood, Minn.,
  U.S.A. 54 C7
Glenwood Springs,
  U.S.A. 56 G10
Glettinganes, Iceland . 6 D7
Gliwice, Poland 13 C10
Globe, U.S.A. 57 K8
Głogów, Poland 12 C9
Glomma →, Norway . 7 G14
Glorieuses, Is., Ind. Oc. 37 G9
Glossop, U.K. 8 D6
Gloucester, Australia . 43 E5
Gloucester, U.K. 9 F5
Gloucester I., Australia 42 C4
Gloucester Point, U.S.A. 52 G7
Gloucestershire □, U.K. 9 F5
Glovertown, Canada . 49 C9
Głusk, Belarus 13 B15
Gmünd, Austria 12 D8
Gmunden, Austria ... 12 E7
Gniezno, Poland 13 B9
Gno-no-ura, Japan .. 23 H4
Goa, India 28 M8
Goa □, India 28 M8
Goalen Hd., Australia . 43 F5
Goalpara, India 29 F17
Goba, Ethiopia 32 F2
Gobabis, Namibia ... 37 J3
Gobi, Asia 25 B5
Gobō, Japan 23 H7
Godavari →, India ... 29 L13
Godavari Pt., India .. 29 L13
Godbout, Canada ... 49 C6
Goderich, Canada ... 48 D3
Godfrey Ra., Australia 41 D2
Godhavn =
  Qeqertarsuaq,
  Greenland 4 C5
Godhra, India 28 H8
Godoy Cruz, Argentina 64 C3
Gods →, Canada ... 48 A1

Gods L., Canada 48 B1
Gods River, Canada . 51 C10
Godthåb = Nuuk,
  Greenland 47 B14
Godwin Austen = K2,
  Pakistan 28 B10
Goeie Hoop, Kaap die =
  Good Hope, C. of,
  S. Africa 37 L3
Goéland, L. au, Canada 48 C4
Goeree, Neths. 11 C3
Goes, Neths. 11 C3
Gogama, Canada 48 C3
Gogebic, L., U.S.A. .. 54 B10
Gogra = Ghaghara →,
  India 29 G14
Gogrial, Sudan 35 G11
Goiânia, Brazil 63 G9
Goiás, Brazil 63 G8
Goiás □, Brazil 63 F9
Goio-Erê, Brazil 64 A6
Gojō, Japan 23 G7
Gojra, Pakistan 28 D8
Gökçeada, Turkey ... 17 D11
Gökova Körfezi, Turkey 17 F12
Goktelk, Burma 29 H20
Gol Gol, Australia ... 43 E3
Golan Heights =
  Hagolan, Syria 33 C4
Goläshkerd, Iran ... 31 E8
Golchikha, Russia ... 4 B12
Golconda, U.S.A. ... 56 F5
Gold Beach, U.S.A. .. 56 E1
Gold Coast, W. Afr. .. 34 H5
Gold Hill, U.S.A. 56 E2
Gold River, Canada .. 50 D3
Golden, Canada 50 C5
Golden, B., N.Z. 39 J4
Golden Gate, U.S.A. . 56 H2
Golden Hinde, Canada 50 D3
Goldendale, U.S.A. .. 56 D3
Goldfield, U.S.A. 57 H5
Goldsand L., Canada . 51 B8
Goldsboro, U.S.A. ... 53 H7
Goldsmith, U.S.A. ... 55 K3
Goldsworthy, Australia 40 D2
Goldthwaite, U.S.A. . 55 K5
Goleniów, Poland ... 12 B8
Golestānak, Iran ... 31 D7
Golfito, Costa Rica .. 60 E3
Golfo Aranci, Italy ... 16 C3
Goliad, U.S.A. 55 L6
Golpäyegän, Iran ... 31 C6
Golspie, U.K. 10 C5
Goma, Dem. Rep. of
  the Congo 36 E5
Gombe, Nigeria 35 F8
Gomel = Homyel,
  Belarus 13 B16
Gomera, Canary Is. .. 34 C2
Gómez Palacio, Mexico 58 B4
Gomishān, Iran 31 B7
Gomogomo, Indonesia 27 F8
Gomoh, India 29 H15
Gompa = Ganta, Liberia 34 G4
Gonābād, Iran 31 C8
Gonaïves, Haiti 61 C5
Gonâve, G. de la, Haiti 61 C5
Gonâve, I. de la, Haiti . 61 C5
Gonbad-e Kāvūs, Iran . 31 B7
Gonda, India 29 F12
Gonder, Ethiopia ... 32 E2
Gondia, India 28 J12
Gönen, Turkey 17 D12
Gonghe, China 24 C5
Gongolgon, Australia . 43 E4
Gonzales, Calif., U.S.A. 57 H3
Gonzales, Tex., U.S.A. 55 L6
Good Hope, C. of,
  S. Africa 37 L3
Gooding, U.S.A. 56 E6
Goodland, U.S.A. ... 54 F4
Goodlow, Canada ... 50 B4
Goodooga, Australia . 43 D4
Goole, U.K. 8 D7
Goolgowi, Australia . 43 E4
Goolwa, Australia ... 43 F2
Goomalling, Australia 41 F2
Goombalie, Australia 43 D4
Goomeri, Australia .. 43 D5
Goondiwindi, Australia 43 D5
Goongarrie, L., Australia 41 F3
Goonyella, Australia . 42 C4
Goose →, Canada ... 49 B7
Goose Creek, U.S.A. . 53 J5
Goose L., U.S.A. 56 F3
Grain Coast, W. Afr. . 34 H3
Grajaú, Brazil 63 E9
Grajaú →, Brazil ... 63 D10
Grampian Highlands =
  Grampian Mts., U.K. 10 C4
Grampian Mts., U.K. . 10 C4
Grampians, The,
  Australia 43 F3
Gran Canaria, Canary Is. 34 C2
Gran Chaco, S. Amer. 64 B4
Gran Paradiso, Italy . 14 D7
Gran Sasso d'Itália, Italy 16 C5
Granada, Nic. 60 D2
Granada, Spain 15 D4
Granada, U.S.A. 55 F3
Granby, Canada 48 C5
Granby, U.S.A. 56 F11
Grand →, Mo., U.S.A. 54 F8
Grand →, S. Dak.,
  U.S.A. 54 C4
Grand →, Canada .. 48 D4

Gorízia, Italy 16 B5
Gorki = Nizhniy
  Novgorod, Russia ... 18 C7
Gorkiy = Nizhniy
  Novgorod, Russia ... 18 C7
Gorkovskoye Vdkhr.,
  Russia 18 C7
Görlitz, Germany 12 C8
Gorlovka = Horlivka,
  Ukraine 19 E6
Gorna Dzhumayo =
  Blagoevgrad, Bulgaria 17 C10
Gorna Oryakhovitsa,
  Bulgaria 17 C11
Gorno-Altay □, Russia 20 D9
Gorno-Altaysk, Russia 20 D9
Gornyatski, Russia ... 18 A11
Gornyy, Russia 22 B6
Gorodenka =
  Horodenka, Ukraine . 13 D13
Gorodok = Horodok,
  Ukraine 13 D12
Gorokhov = Horokhiv,
  Ukraine 13 C13
Gorong, Kepulauan,
  Indonesia 27 E8
Gorontalo, Indonesia . 27 D6
Gorzów Wielkopolski,
  Poland 12 B8
Gosford, Australia ... 43 E5
Goshen, U.S.A. 52 E3
Goshogawara, Japan . 22 D10
Goslar, Germany 12 C6
Gospič, Croatia 12 F8
Gosport, U.K. 9 G6
Gosse →, Australia . 42 B1
Göta älv →, Sweden . 7 H14
Göta kanal, Sweden . 7 G16
Götaland, Sweden ... 7 G15
Göteborg, Sweden .. 7 H14
Gotha, Germany 12 C6
Gothenburg =
  Göteborg, Sweden .. 7 H14
Gothenburg, U.S.A. . 54 E4
Gotland, Sweden ... 7 H18
Gotō-Rettō, Japan ... 23 H4
Gotska Sandön, Sweden 7 G18
Götsu, Japan 23 G6
Gott Pk., Canada ... 50 C4
Göttingen, Germany . 12 C5
Gottwaldov = Zlín,
  Czech Rep. 13 D9
Gouda, Neths. 11 B4
Gough I., Atl. Oc. ... 2 G9
Gouin, Rés., Canada . 48 C5
Goulburn, Australia . 43 E4
Goulimine, Morocco . 34 C3
Gouverneur, U.S.A. . 52 C8
Governador Valadares,
  Brazil 63 G10
Governor's Harbour,
  Bahamas 60 A4
Gowan Ra., Australia . 42 D4
Gowanda, U.S.A. ... 52 D6
Gower, U.K. 9 F3
Goya, Argentina 64 B5
Goyder Lagoon,
  Australia 43 D2
Goyllarisquisga, Peru . 62 F3
Goz Beïda, Chad 35 F10
Gozo, Malta 16 F6
Graaff-Reinet, S. Africa 37 L4
Gračac, Croatia 12 F8
Gracias a Dios, C.,
  Honduras 60 D3
Grado, Spain 15 A2
Grady, U.S.A. 55 H3
Grafham Water, U.K. . 9 E7
Grafton, Australia ... 43 D5
Grafton, N. Dak., U.S.A. 54 A6
Grafton, W. Va., U.S.A. 52 F5
Graham, Canada 48 C1
Graham, U.S.A. 55 J5
Graham, Mt., U.S.A. . 57 K9
Graham Bell, Ostrov =
  Russia 20 A7
Graham I., B.C., Canada 50 C2
Graham I., N.W.T.,
  Canada 46 C6
Graham Land,
  Antarctica 5 C17
Grahamstown, S. Africa 37 L5
Grajaú, Brazil 63 E9

Grand Bahama,
  Bahamas 60 A4
Grand Bank, Canada . 49 C8
Grand Bassam, Ivory C. 34 G5
Grand-Bourg,
  Guadeloupe 61 C7
Grand Canyon, U.S.A. 57 H7
Grand Canyon National
  Park, U.S.A. 57 H7
Grand Cayman,
  Cayman Is. 60 C3
Grand Centre, Canada 51 C6
Grand Coulee, U.S.A. 56 C4
Grand Coulee Dam,
  U.S.A. 56 C4
Grand Erg du Bilma,
  Niger 35 E8
Grand Erg Occidental,
  Algeria 34 B6
Grand Erg Oriental,
  Algeria 34 B7
Grand Falls, Canada . 49 C6
Grand Falls-Windsor,
  Canada 49 C8
Grand Forks, Canada . 50 D5
Grand Forks, U.S.A. . 54 B6
Grand Haven, U.S.A. . 52 D2
Grand I., U.S.A. 54 B2
Grand Island, U.S.A. . 54 E5
Grand Isle, U.S.A. ... 55 L9
Grand Junction, U.S.A. 57 G9
Grand L., N.B., Canada 49 C6
Grand L., Nfld., Canada 49 C8
Grand L., Nfld., Canada 49 B8
Grand L., U.S.A. 55 L8
Grand Lake, U.S.A. .. 56 F11
Grand Manan I., Canada 49 D6
Grand Marais, Canada 52 B9
Grand Marais, U.S.A. 52 B3
Grand-Mère, Canada . 48 C5
Grand Portage, U.S.A. 54 B10
Grand Prairie, U.S.A. . 55 J6
Grand Rapids, Canada 51 C9
Grand Rapids, Mich.,
  U.S.A. 52 D2
Grand Rapids, Minn.,
  U.S.A. 54 B8
Grand St-Bernard, Col
  du, Europe 14 D7
Grand Teton, U.S.A. . 56 E8
Grand Teton National
  Park, U.S.A. 56 E8
Grand Union Canal, U.K. 9 E7
Grand View, Canada . 51 C8
Grande →, Bolivia .. 62 G6
Grande →, Bahia,
  Brazil 63 F10
Grande →,
  Minas Gerais, Brazil . 63 H8
Grande, B., Argentina . 64 G3
Grande, Rio →, U.S.A. 55 N6
Grande Baleine, R. de
  la →, Canada 48 A4
Grande Cache, Canada 50 C5
Grande-Entrée, Canada 49 C7
Grande Prairie, Canada 50 B5
Grande-Rivière, Canada 49 C7
Grande-Vallée, Canada 49 C6
Grandfalls, U.S.A. ... 55 K3
Grandview, U.S.A. ... 56 C4
Granger, U.S.A. 56 F9
Grangeville, U.S.A. .. 56 D5
Granisle, Canada ... 50 C3
Granite City, U.S.A. . 54 F9
Granite Falls, U.S.A. . 54 C7
Granite L., Canada .. 49 C8
Granite Pk., U.S.A. .. 56 D9
Granity, N.Z. 39 J3
Granja, Brazil 63 D10
Granollers, Spain ... 15 B7
Grant, U.S.A. 54 E4
Grant, Mt., U.S.A. ... 56 G4
Grant City, U.S.A. ... 54 E7
Grant I., Australia ... 40 B5
Grant Range, U.S.A. . 57 G6
Grantham, U.K. 8 E7
Grants, U.S.A. 57 J10
Grants Pass, U.S.A. . 56 E2
Grantsville, U.S.A. .. 56 F7
Granville, France 14 B3
Granville, N. Dak.,
  U.S.A. 54 A4
Granville, N.Y., U.S.A. 52 D9
Granville L., Canada . 51 B8
Grass →, Canada ... 51 B9
Grass Range, U.S.A. . 56 C9
Grass River Prov. Park,
  Canada 51 C8
Grass Valley, Calif.,
  U.S.A. 56 G3
Grass Valley, Oreg.,
  U.S.A. 56 D3
Grassano, Italy
Grasse, France 14 E7
Grasslands Nat. Park,
  Canada 51 D7
Grassy, Australia ... 42 G3
Graulhet, France ... 14 E4
Gravelbourg, Canada 51 D7
's-Gravenhage, Neths. 11 B4
Gravenhurst, Canada 48 D4
Gravesend, Australia . 43 D5
Gravesend, U.K. 9 F8
Gravois, Pointe-à-, Haiti 61 C5
Grayling, U.S.A. 52 C3
Grays Harbor, U.S.A. 56 C1

Grays L., U.S.A. 56 E8
Graz, Austria 12 E8
Greasy L., Canada .. 50 A4
Great Abaco I.,
  Bahamas 60 A4
Great Artesian Basin,
  Australia 42 C3
Great Australian Bight,
  Australia 41 F5
Great Bahama Bank,
  Bahamas 60 B4
Great Barrier I., N.Z. . 39 G5
Great Barrier Reef,
  Australia 42 B4
Great Basin, U.S.A. . 56 G5
Great Basin Nat. Park,
  U.S.A. 56 G6
Great Bear →, Canada 46 B7
Great Bear L., Canada 46 B7
Great Belt = Store Bælt,
  Denmark 7 J14
Great Bend, U.S.A. .. 54 F5
Great Britain, Europe . 10 D5
Great Britain, Europe . 10 D5
Great Codroy, Canada 49 C8
Great Dividing Ra.,
  Australia 42 C4
Great Driffield =
  Driffield, U.K. 8 C7
Great Exuma I.,
  Bahamas 60 B4
Great Falls, U.S.A. .. 56 C8
Great Guana Cay,
  Bahamas 60 B4
Great Inagua I.,
  Bahamas 61 B5
Great Indian Desert =
  Thar Desert, India .. 28 F8
Great Karoo, S. Africa . 37 L4
Great Lake, Australia . 42 G4
Great Malvern, U.K. . 9 E5
Great Miami →, U.S.A. 52 F3
Great Ormes Head, U.K. 8 D4
Great Ouse →, U.K. . 8 E8
Great Palm I., Australia 42 B4
Great Ruaha →,
  Tanzania 36 F7
Great Saint Bernard
  Pass = Grand St-
  Bernard, Col du,
  Europe 14 D7
Great Salt L., U.S.A. . 56 F7
Great Salt Lake Desert,
  U.S.A. 56 F7
Great Salt Plains L.,
  U.S.A. 55 G5
Great Sandy Desert,
  Australia 40 D3
Great Sangi = Sangihe,
  Pulau, Indonesia .. 27 D7
Great Slave L., Canada 50 A5
Great Smoky Mts. Nat.
  Park, U.S.A. 53 H4
Great Snow Mt., Canada 50 B4
Great Stour =
  Stour →, U.K. 9 F9
Great Victoria Desert,
  Australia 41 E4
Great Wall, China ... 25 C5
Great Whernside, U.K. 8 C6
Great Yarmouth, U.K. 9 E9
Greater Antilles,
  W. Indies 61 C5
Greater London □, U.K. 9 F7
Greater Manchester □,
  U.K. 8 D5
Greater Sunda Is.,
  Indonesia 26 F4
Gredos, Sierra de, Spain 15 B3
Greece ■, Europe ... 17 E9
Greeley, Colo., U.S.A. 54 E2
Greeley, Nebr., U.S.A. 54 E5
Greem-Bell, Ostrov,
  Russia 20 A7
Green, U.S.A. 56 E2
Green →, Ky., U.S.A. 52 G2
Green →, Utah, U.S.A. 57 G9
Green B., U.S.A. 52 C2
Green Bay, U.S.A. ... 52 C2
Green C., Australia .. 43 F5
Green Cove Springs,
  U.S.A. 53 L5
Green Lake, Canada . 51 C7
Green River, Utah,
  U.S.A. 57 G8
Green River, Wyo.,
  U.S.A. 56 F9
Green Valley, U.S.A. . 57 L8
Greenbush, U.S.A. .. 54 A6
Greencastle, U.S.A. . 52 F2
Greenfield, Ind., U.S.A. 52 F3
Greenfield, Iowa, U.S.A. 54 E7
Greenfield, Mass.,
  U.S.A. 52 D9
Greenfield, Mo., U.S.A. 55 G8
Greenland ■, N. Amer. 4 C5
Greenland Sea, Arctic . 4 B7
Greenock, U.K. 10 D4
Greenough, Australia . 41 E1
Greenough →,
  Australia 41 E1
Greensboro, Ga., U.S.A. 53 J4
Greensboro, N.C.,
  U.S.A. 53 G6
Greensburg, Ind., U.S.A. 52 F3

Hatteras, C.

Greensburg, Kans., U.S.A. 55 G5
Greensburg, Pa., U.S.A. 52 E6
Greenvale, Australia 42 B4
Greenville, Ala., U.S.A. 53 K2
Greenville, Calif., U.S.A. 56 F3
Greenville, Maine, U.S.A. 53 C11
Greenville, Mich., U.S.A. 52 D3
Greenville, Miss., U.S.A. 55 J9
Greenville, Mo., U.S.A. 55 G9
Greenville, N.C., U.S.A. 53 H7
Greenville, Ohio, U.S.A. 52 E3
Greenville, Pa., U.S.A. 52 E5
Greenville, S.C., U.S.A. 53 H4
Greenville, Tenn., U.S.A. 53 G4
Greenville, Tex., U.S.A. 55 J6
Greenwater Lake Prov. Park, Canada 51 C8
Greenwich □, U.K. 9 F8
Greenwood, Canada 50 D5
Greenwood, Ark., U.S.A. 55 H7
Greenwood, Ind., U.S.A. 52 F2
Greenwood, Miss., U.S.A. 55 J9
Greenwood, S.C., U.S.A. 53 H4
Greenwood, Mt., Australia 40 B5
Gregory, U.S.A. 54 D5
Gregory →, Australia 42 B2
Gregory, L., S. Austral., Australia 43 D2
Gregory, L., W. Austral., Australia 41 E2
Gregory Downs, Australia 42 B2
Gregory L., Australia 40 D4
Gregory Ra., Queens., Australia 42 B3
Gregory Ra., W. Austral., Australia 40 D3
Greifswald, Germany 12 A7
Greiz, Germany 12 C7
Gremikha, Russia 18 A6
Grenå, Denmark 7 H14
Grenada, U.S.A. 55 J10
Grenada ■, W. Indies 62 A6
Grenadines, W. Indies 61 D7
Grenen, Denmark 7 H14
Grenfell, Australia 43 E4
Grenfell, Canada 51 C8
Grenoble, France 14 D6
Grenville, C., Australia 42 A3
Grenville Chan., Canada 50 C3
Gresham, U.S.A. 56 D2
Gresik, Indonesia 27 G15
Grevenmacher, Lux. 11 E6
Grey →, Canada 49 C8
Grey →, N.Z. 39 K3
Grey, C., Australia 42 A2
Grey Ra., Australia 43 D3
Greybull, U.S.A. 56 D9
Greymouth, N.Z. 39 K3
Greytown, N.Z. 39 J5
Gribbell I., Canada 50 C3
Gridley, U.S.A. 56 G3
Griffin, U.S.A. 53 J3
Griffith, Australia 43 E4
Grimari, C.A.R. 32
Grimaylov = Hrymayliv, Ukraine 13 D14
Grimsby, U.K. 8 D7
Grímsey, Iceland 6 C5
Grimshaw, Canada 50 B5
Grimstad, Norway 7 G13
Grinnell, U.S.A. 54 E8
Gris-Nez, C., France 14 A4
Groais I., Canada 49 B8
Grodno = Hrodna, Belarus 13 B12
Grodzyanka = Hrodzyanka, Belarus 13 B15
Groesbeck, U.S.A. 55 K6
Grójec, Poland 13 C11
Grong, Norway 6 D15
Groningen, Neths. 11 A6
Groningen □, Neths. 11 A6
Groom, U.S.A. 55 H4
Groote Eylandt, Australia 42 A2
Grootfontein, Namibia 37 H3
Gros C., Canada 50 A6
Gros Morne Nat. Park, Canada 49 C8
Grosser Arber, Germany 12 D7
Grosseto, Italy 16 C4
Grossglockner, Austria 12 E7
Groswater B., Canada 49 B8
Groton, U.S.A. 54 C5
Grouard Mission, Canada 50 B5
Groundhog →, Canada 48 C3
Grouw, Neths. 11 A5
Grove Hill, U.S.A. 53 K2
Groves, U.S.A. 55 L8
Groveton, U.S.A. 52 C10
Groznyy, Russia 19 F8
Grudziądz, Poland 13 B10
Grundy Center, U.S.A. 54 D8
Gruver, U.S.A. 55 G4
Gryazi, Russia 18 D6
Gryazovets, Russia 18 C7
Gua, India 29 H14
Guacanayabo, G. de, Cuba 60 B4
Guadalajara, Mexico 58 C4
Guadalajara, Spain 15 B4
Guadalcanal, Solomon Is. 38 B9
Guadalete →, Spain 15 D2
Guadalquivir →, Spain 15 D2
Guadalupe = Guadeloupe ■, W. Indies 61 C7
Guadalupe, U.S.A. 57 J3
Guadalupe →, U.S.A. 55 L6
Guadalupe, Sierra de, Spain 15 C3
Guadalupe Bravos, Mexico 58 A3
Guadalupe Mts. Nat. Park, U.S.A. 55 K2
Guadalupe Peak, U.S.A. 55 K2
Guadalupe y Calvo, Mexico 58 B3
Guadarrama, Sierra de, Spain 15 B4
Guadeloupe ■, W. Indies 61 C7
Guadeloupe Passage, W. Indies 61 C7
Guadiana →, Portugal 15 D2
Guadix, Spain 15 D4
Guafo, Boca del, Chile 64 E2
Guainía →, Colombia 62 C5
Guaíra, Brazil 64 A6
Guaitecas, Is., Chile 64 E2
Guajará-Mirim, Brazil 62 F5
Guajira, Pen. de la, Colombia 62 A4
Gualán, Guatemala 60 C2
Gualeguaychú, Argentina 64 C5
Guam ■, Pac. Oc. 44 F6
Guamúchil, Mexico 58 B3
Guanabacoa, Cuba 60 B3
Guanacaste, Cordillera del, Costa Rica 60 D2
Guanaceví, Mexico 58 B3
Guanahani = San Salvador I., Bahamas 61 B5
Guanajay, Cuba 60 B3
Guanajuato, Mexico 58 C4
Guanajuato □, Mexico 58 C4
Guandacol, Argentina 64 B3
Guane, Cuba 60 B3
Guangdong □, China 25 D6
Guangxi Zhuangzu Zizhiqu □, China 25 D5
Guangzhou, China 25 D6
Guanipa →, Venezuela 62 B6
Guantánamo, Cuba 61 B4
Guápiles, Costa Rica 60 D3
Guaporé →, Brazil 62 F5
Guaqui, Bolivia 62 G5
Guarapuava, Brazil 64 B6
Guarda, Portugal 15 B2
Guardafui, C. = Asir, Ras, Somali Rep. 32 E5
Guárico □, Venezuela 62 B5
Guasave, Mexico 58 B3
Guasdualito, Venezuela 62 B4
Guatemala, Guatemala 60 D1
Guatemala ■, Cent. Amer. 60 C1
Guaviare →, Colombia 62 C5
Guaxupé, Brazil 63 H9
Guayama, Puerto Rico 61 C6
Guayaquil, Ecuador 62 D3
Guayaquil, G. de, Ecuador 62 D2
Guaymas, Mexico 58 B2
Gubkin, Russia 19 D6
Gudbrandsdalen, Norway 7 F14
Guddu Barrage, Pakistan 28 E6
Gudur, India 28 M11
Guecho = Getxo, Spain 15 A4
Guelph, Canada 48 D3
Guéret, France 14 C4
Guernica = Gernika-Lumo, Spain 15 A4
Guernsey, U.K. 9 H5
Guernsey, U.S.A. 54 D2
Guerrero □, Mexico 59 D5
Gügher, Iran 31 D8
Guhakolak, Tanjung, Indonesia 27 G11
Guidónia-Montecélio, Italy 16 C5
Guijá, Mozam. 37 J6
Guildford, U.K. 9 F7
Guilin, China 25 D6
Guillaume-Delisle L., Canada 48 A4
Guimarães, Portugal 15 B1
Guimaras □, Phil. 27 B6
Guinea ■, W. Afr. 34 F3
Guinea, Gulf of, Atl. Oc. 3 D10
Guinea, Gulf of, Atl. Oc. 3 D10
Guinea-Bissau ■, Africa 34 F3
Güines, Cuba 60 B3
Guingamp, France 14 B2
Güiria, Venezuela 62 A6
Guiuan, Phil. 27 B7
Guiyang, China 24 D5
Guizhou □, China 24 D5
Gujarat □, India 28 H7
Gujranwala, Pakistan 28 C9
Gujrat, Pakistan 28 C9
Gulargambone, Australia 43 E4
Gulbarga, India 28 L10
Gulbene, Latvia 7 H22
Gulf, The, Asia 31 E6
Gulfport, U.S.A. 55 K10
Gulgong, Australia 43 E4
Gull Lake, Canada 51 C7
Güllük, Turkey 17 F12
Gulshad, Kazakstan 20 E8
Gulu, Uganda 36 D6
Gumel, Nigeria 34 F7
Gumlu, Australia 42 B4
Gumma □, Japan 23 F9
Gumzai, Indonesia 27 F8
Guna, India 28 G10
Gunisao →, Canada 51 C9
Gunisao L., Canada 51 C9
Gunnbjørn Fjeld, Greenland 4 C6
Gunnedah, Australia 43 E5
Gunnewin, Australia 43 D4
Gunningbar Cr. →, Australia 43 E4
Gunnison, Colo., U.S.A. 57 G10
Gunnison, Utah, U.S.A. 56 G8
Gunnison →, U.S.A. 57 G9
Gunpowder, Australia 42 B2
Guntakal, India 28 M10
Guntersville, U.S.A. 53 H2
Guntur, India 29 L12
Gunungapi, Indonesia 27 F7
Gunungsitoli, Indonesia 26 D1
Gunza, Angola 36 G2
Gupis, Pakistan 28 A8
Gurdaspur, India 28 C9
Gurdon, U.S.A. 55 J8
Gurgueia →, Brazil 63 E10
Guri, Embalse de, Venezuela 62 B6
Gurkha, Nepal 29 E14
Gurley, Australia 43 D4
Gürün, Turkey 19 G6
Gurupá, Brazil 63 D8
Gurupá, I. Grande de, Brazil 63 D8
Gurupi, Brazil 63 F9
Gurupi →, Brazil 63 D9
Guryev = Atyraū, Kazakstan 19 E9
Gusau, Nigeria 34 F7
Gusev, Russia 7 J20
Gushgy, Turkmenistan 20 F7
Gusinoozersk, Russia 21 D11
Gustavus, U.S.A. 50 B1
Gustine, U.S.A. 57 H3
Güstrow, Germany 12 B7
Gütersloh, Germany 12 C5
Gutha, Australia 41 E2
Guthalungra, Australia 42 B4
Guthrie, Okla., U.S.A. 55 H6
Guthrie, Tex., U.S.A. 55 J4
Guttenberg, U.S.A. 54 D9
Guyana ■, S. Amer. 62 C7
Guyane française = French Guiana ■, S. Amer. 63 C8
Guyenne, France 14 D4
Guymon, U.S.A. 55 G4
Guyra, Australia 43 E5
Guzmán, L. de, Mexico 58 A3
Gvardeysk, Russia 7 J19
Gwa, Burma 29 L19
Gwabegar, Australia 43 E4
Gwādar, Pakistan 28 G3
Gwalior, India 28 F11
Gwanda, Zimbabwe 37 J5
Gweru, Zimbabwe 37 H5
Gwinn, U.S.A. 52 B2
Gwydir →, Australia 43 D4
Gwynedd □, U.K. 8 E3
Gyandzha = Gäncä, Azerbaijan 19 F8
Gyaring Hu, China 24 C4
Gydanskiy Poluostrov, Russia 20 C8
Gympie, Australia 43 D5
Gyöngyös, Hungary 13 E10
Győr, Hungary 13 E9
Gypsum Pt., Canada 50 A6
Gypsumville, Canada 51 C9
Gyula, Hungary 13 E11
Gyumri, Armenia 19 F7
Gyzylarbat, Turkmenistan 20 F6
Gyzyletrek, Turkmenistan 31 B7

Ha 'Arava →, Israel 33 E4
Haaksbergen, Neths. 11 B6
Haapsalu, Estonia 7 G20
Haarlem, Neths. 11 B4
Haast →, N.Z. 39 K2
Haast Bluff, Australia 40 D5
Hab Nadi Chauki, Pakistan 28 G5
Habay, Canada 50 B5
Ḩabbānīyah, Iraq 30 C4
Haboro, Japan 22 B10
Ḩabshān, U.A.E. 31 F7
Hachijō-Jima, Japan 23 H9
Hachinohe, Japan 22 D10
Hachiōji, Japan 23 G9
Hadarba, Ras, Sudan 35 D13
Hadarom □, Israel 33 E4
Hadd, Ra's al, Oman 32 C6
Hadejia, Nigeria 34 F7
Ḩadera, Israel 33 C3
Ḩadera, N. →, Israel 33 C3
Haderslev, Denmark 7 J13
Hadhramaut = Ḩaḑramawt, Yemen 32 D4
Hadibu, Yemen 32 E5
Ḩaḑramawt, Yemen 32 D4
Ḩadrānīyah, Iraq 30 C4
Hadrian's Wall, U.K. 8 B5
Haeju, N. Korea 25 C7
Haerhpin = Harbin, China 25 B7
Hafar al Bāţin, Si. Arabia 30 D5
Ḩafirat al 'Aydā, Si. Arabia 30 E3
Ḩafit, Oman 31 F7
Ḩafit, Jabal, Oman 31 E7
Hafizabad, Pakistan 28 C8
Haflong, India 29 G18
Hafnarfjörður, Iceland 6 D3
Haft Gel, Iran 31 D6
Hafun, Ras, Somali Rep. 32 E5
Hagalil, Israel 33 C4
Hagen, Germany 12 C4
Hagerman, U.S.A. 55 J2
Hagerstown, U.S.A. 52 F7
Hagfors, Sweden 7 F15
Hagi, Japan 23 G5
Hagolan, Syria 33 C4
Hagondange, France 14 B7
Hague, C. de la, France 14 B3
Hague, The = 's-Gravenhage, Neths. 11 B4
Haguenau, France 14 B7
Haifa = Ḩefa, Israel 33 C4
Haikou, China 25 D6
Ḩā'il, Si. Arabia 30 E4
Hailar, China 25 B6
Hailey, U.S.A. 56 E6
Haileybury, Canada 48 C4
Hailuoto, Finland 6 D21
Hainan □, China 25 E5
Hainaut □, Belgium 11 D4
Haines, Alaska, U.S.A. 50 B1
Haines, Oreg., U.S.A. 56 D5
Haines City, U.S.A. 53 L5
Haines Junction, Canada 50 A1
Haiphong, Vietnam 24 D5
Haiti ■, W. Indies 61 C5
Haiya, Sudan 35 E13
Hajdúböszörmény, Hungary 13 E11
Ḩājjī Muḩsin, Iraq 30 C5
Ḩājjīābād, Iran 31 D7
Ḩājjīābād-e Zarrīn, Iran 31 C7
Hajnówka, Poland 13 B12
Hakkâri, Turkey 30 B4
Hakken-Zan, Japan 23 G7
Hakodate, Japan 22 D10
Haku-San, Japan 23 F8
Hakui, Japan 23 F8
Hala, Pakistan 28 G6
Ḩalab, Syria 30 B3
Ḩalabjah, Iraq 30 C5
Halaib, Sudan 35 D13
Hälat 'Ammār, Si. Arabia 30 D3
Halbā, Lebanon 33 A5
Halberstadt, Germany 12 C6
Halcombe, N.Z. 39 J5
Halcon, Phil. 27 B6
Halden, Norway 7 G14
Haldia, India 29 H16
Haldwani, India 28 E11
Hale →, Australia 42 C2
Halesowen, U.K. 9 E5
Haleyville, U.S.A. 53 H2
Halfmoon Bay, N.Z. 39 M2
Halfway →, Canada 50 B4
Haliburton, Canada 48 C4
Halifax, Australia 42 B4
Halifax, Canada 49 D7
Halifax, U.K. 8 D6
Halifax B., Australia 42 B4
Halīl →, Iran 31 E8
Hall Beach = Sanirajak, Canada 47 B11
Hall Pen., Canada 47 B13
Hall Pt., Australia 40 C3
Halland, Sweden 7 H15
Halle, Belgium 11 D4
Halle, Germany 12 C6
Hällefors, Sweden 7 G16
Hallett, Australia 43 E2
Hallettsville, U.S.A. 55 L6
Hallingdalselvi →, Norway 7 F13
Hallock, U.S.A. 54 A6
Halls Creek, Australia 40 C4
Hallsberg, Sweden 7 G16
Halmahera, Indonesia 27 D7
Halmstad, Sweden 7 H15
Hälsingborg = Helsingborg, Sweden 7 H15
Hälsingland, Sweden 7 F16
Halstead, U.K. 9 F8
Halti, Finland 6 B19
Halton □, U.K. 8 D5
Haltwhistle, U.K. 8 C5
Ḩalul, Qatar 31 E7
Ḩalvān, Iran 31 C8
Hamada, Japan 23 G6
Hamadān, Iran 31 C6
Hamadān □, Iran 31 C6
Ḩamāh, Syria 30 C3
Hamamatsu, Japan 23 G8
Hamar, Norway 7 F14
Hamâta, Gebel, Egypt 30 E2
Hambantota, Sri Lanka 28 R12
Hamber Prov. Park, Canada 50 C5
Hamburg, Germany 12 B5
Hamburg, Ark., U.S.A. 55 J9
Hamburg, N.Y., U.S.A. 52 D6
Ḩamḑ, W. al →, Si. Arabia 30 E3
Häme, Finland 7 F20
Hämeenlinna, Finland 7 F21
Hamelin Pool, Australia 41 E1
Hameln, Germany 12 B5
Hamerkaz □, Israel 33 C3
Hamersley Ra., Australia 40 D2
Hami, China 24 B4
Hamilton, Australia 43 F3
Hamilton, Canada 48 D4
Hamilton, N.Z. 39 G5
Hamilton, U.K. 10 D4
Hamilton, Ala., U.S.A. 53 H1
Hamilton, Mont., U.S.A. 56 C6
Hamilton, N.Y., U.S.A. 52 D8
Hamilton, Ohio, U.S.A. 52 F3
Hamilton, Tex., U.S.A. 55 K5
Hamilton →, Australia 42 C2
Hamilton Inlet, Canada 49 B8
Hamina, Finland 7 F22
Hamlet, U.S.A. 53 H6
Hamley Bridge, Australia 43 E2
Hamlin = Hameln, Germany 12 B5
Hamlin, U.S.A. 55 J4
Hamm, Germany 12 C4
Ḩammār, Hawr al, Iraq 30 D5
Hammerfest, Norway 6 A20
Hammond, Ind., U.S.A. 52 E2
Hammond, La., U.S.A. 55 K9
Hammonton, U.S.A. 52 F8
Hampden, N.Z. 39 L3
Hampshire □, U.K. 9 F6
Hampshire Downs, U.K. 9 F6
Hampton, Canada 49 C6
Hampton, Ark., U.S.A. 55 J8
Hampton, Iowa, U.S.A. 54 D8
Hampton, S.C., U.S.A. 53 J5
Hampton, Va., U.S.A. 52 G7
Hampton Tableland, Australia 41 F4
Han Pijesak, Bos.-H. 17 B8
Hanak, Si. Arabia 30 E3
Hanamaki, Japan 22 E10
Hanau, Germany 12 C5
Hancock, U.S.A. 54 B10
Handa, Japan 23 G8
Handan, China 25 C6
Hanegev, Israel 33 E4
Hanford, U.S.A. 57 H4
Hangayn Nuruu, Mongolia 24 B4
Hangchou = Hangzhou, China 25 C7
Hangzhou, China 25 C7
Hangzhou Wan, China 25 C7
Ḩanīdh, Si. Arabia 31 E6
Ḩanīsh, Yemen 32 E3
Hankinson, U.S.A. 54 B6
Hanko, Finland 7 G20
Hanksville, U.S.A. 57 G8
Hanle, India 28 C11
Hanmer Springs, N.Z. 39 K4
Hann →, Australia 40 C4
Hann, Mt., Australia 40 C4
Hanna, Canada 50 C6
Hanna, U.S.A. 56 F10
Hannah B., Canada 48 B4
Hannibal, U.S.A. 54 F9
Hannover, Germany 12 B5
Hanoi, Vietnam 24 D5
Hanover = Hannover, Germany 12 B5
Hanover, Canada 48 D3
Hanover, N.H., U.S.A. 52 D9
Hanover, Pa., U.S.A. 52 F7
Hanover, I., Chile 64 G2
Hansi, India 28 E9
Hanson, L., Australia 43 E2
Hantsavichy, Belarus 13 B14
Hanzhong, China 24 C5
Haora, India 29 H16
Haparanda, Sweden 6 D21
Happy, U.S.A. 55 H4
Happy Camp, U.S.A. 56 F2
Happy Valley-Goose Bay, Canada 49 B7
Hapur, India 28 E10
Ḩaql, Si. Arabia 33 F3
Har, Indonesia 27 F8
Har Hu, China 24 C4
Har Us Nuur, Mongolia 24 B4
Har Yehuda, Israel 33 D3
Ḩaraḑ, Si. Arabia 32 C4
Haranomachi, Japan 22 F10
Harare, Zimbabwe 37 H6
Harbin, China 25 B7
Harbor Beach, U.S.A. 52 D4
Harbour Breton, Canada 49 C8
Harbour Deep, Canada 49 B8
Hardangerfjorden, Norway 7 F12
Hardangervidda, Norway 7 F12
Hardenberg, Neths. 11 B6
Harderwijk, Neths. 11 B5
Hardey →, Australia 40 D2
Hardin, U.S.A. 56 D10
Harding Ra., Australia 40 C3
Hardisty, Canada 50 C6
Hardoi, India 28 F12
Hardwar = Haridwar, India 28 E11
Hardy, Pen., Chile 64 H3
Hare B., Canada 49 B8
Hareid, Norway 7 E12
Harer, Ethiopia 32 F3
Hargeisa, Somali Rep. 32 F3
Hari →, Indonesia 26 E2
Haridwar, India 28 E11
Harim, Jabal al, Oman 31 E8
Haringhata →, Bangla. 29 J16
Harīrūd →, Asia 28 A2
Härjedalen, Sweden 7 E15
Harlan, Iowa, U.S.A. 54 E7
Harlan, Ky., U.S.A. 53 G4
Harlech, U.K. 8 E3
Harlem, U.S.A. 56 B9
Harlingen, Neths. 11 A5
Harlingen, U.S.A. 55 M6
Harlow, U.K. 9 F8
Harlowton, U.S.A. 56 C9
Harney Basin, U.S.A. 56 E4
Harney L., U.S.A. 56 E4
Harney Peak, U.S.A. 54 D3
Härnösand, Sweden 7 E17
Harp L., Canada 49 A7
Harper, Liberia 34 H4
Harricana →, Canada 48 B4
Harriman, U.S.A. 53 H3
Harrington Harbour, Canada 49 B8
Harris, U.K. 10 C3
Harris L., Australia 43 E2
Harrisburg, Ill., U.S.A. 55 G10
Harrisburg, Nebr., U.S.A. 54 E3
Harrisburg, Pa., U.S.A. 52 E7
Harrison, Ark., U.S.A. 55 G8
Harrison, Nebr., U.S.A. 54 D3
Harrison, C., Canada 49 B8
Harrison L., Canada 50 D4
Harrisonburg, U.S.A. 52 F6
Harrisonville, U.S.A. 54 F7
Harrisville, U.S.A. 52 C4
Harrodsburg, U.S.A. 52 G3
Harrogate, U.K. 8 C6
Harrow □, U.K. 9 F7
Harry S. Truman Reservoir, U.S.A. 54 F7
Harsīn, Iran 30 C5
Harstad, Norway 6 B17
Hart, U.S.A. 52 D2
Hart, L., Australia 43 E2
Hartford, Conn., U.S.A. 52 E9
Hartford, Ky., U.S.A. 52 G2
Hartford, S. Dak., U.S.A. 54 D6
Hartford, Wis., U.S.A. 54 D10
Hartford City, U.S.A. 52 E3
Hartland, Canada 49 C6
Hartland Pt., U.K. 9 F3
Hartlepool, U.K. 8 C6
Hartlepool □, U.K. 8 C6
Hartley Bay, Canada 50 C3
Hartney, Canada 51 D8
Hartselle, U.S.A. 53 H2
Hartshorne, U.S.A. 55 H7
Hartsville, U.S.A. 53 H5
Hartwell, U.S.A. 53 H4
Harvand, Iran 31 D7
Harvey, Australia 41 F2
Harvey, Ill., U.S.A. 52 E2
Harvey, N. Dak., U.S.A. 54 B5
Harwich, U.K. 9 F9
Haryana □, India 28 E10
Haryn →, Belarus 13 B14
Harz, Germany 12 C6
Hasa □, Si. Arabia 31 E6
Ḩasanābād, Iran 31 C7
Hashimoto, Japan 23 G7
Hashtjerd, Iran 31 C6
Haskell, U.S.A. 55 J5
Haslemere, U.K. 9 F7
Hasselt, Belgium 11 D5
Hassi Messaoud, Algeria 34 B7
Hässleholm, Sweden 7 H15
Hastings, N.Z. 39 H6
Hastings, U.K. 9 G8
Hastings, Mich., U.S.A. 52 D3
Hastings, Minn., U.S.A. 54 C8
Hastings, Nebr., U.S.A. 54 E5
Hastings Ra., Australia 43 E5
Hat Yai, Thailand 26 C2
Hatay = Antalya, Turkey 19 G5
Hatch, U.S.A. 57 K10
Hatchet L., Canada 51 B8
Hateruma-Shima, Japan 23 M1
Hatfield P.O., Australia 43 E3
Hatgal, Mongolia 24 A5
Hathras, India 28 F11
Hatia, Bangla. 29 H17
Hato Mayor, Dom. Rep. 61 C6
Hattah, Australia 43 E3
Hatteras, C., U.S.A. 53 H8

Hattiesburg, *U.S.A.* 55 K10
Hatvan, *Hungary* 13 E10
Hau Bon = Cheo Reo,
Vietnam 26 B3
Haugesund, *Norway* . . 7 G11
Haukipudas, *Finland* . . 6 D21
Haultain →, *Canada* . . 51 B7
Hauraki G., *N.Z.* 39 G5
Haut Atlas, *Morocco* . . 34 B4
Hautes Fagnes = Hohe
Venn, *Belgium* 11 D6
Havana = La Habana,
Cuba 60 B3
Havana, *U.S.A.* 54 E9
Havant, *U.K.* 9 G7
Havasu, L., *U.S.A.* . . . 57 J6
Havel →, *Germany* . . . 12 B7
Havelock, *Canada* 48 D4
Havelock, *N.Z.* 39 J4
Havelock, *U.S.A.* 53 H7
Haverfordwest, *U.K.* . . 9 F3
Haverhill, *U.S.A.* 52 D10
Havířov, *Czech.* 13 D10
Havlíčkův Brod,
Czech Rep. 12 D8
Havre, *U.S.A.* 56 B9
Havre-Aubert, *Canada* . 49 C7
Havre-St.-Pierre, *Canada* 49 B7
Haw →, *U.S.A.* 53 H6
Hawaiian Is., *Pac. Oc.* . 45 E12
Hawaiian Ridge,
Pac. Oc. 45 E11
Hawarden, *U.S.A.* 54 D6
Hawea, L., *N.Z.* 39 L2
Hawera, *N.Z.* 39 H5
Hawick, *U.K.* 10 D5
Hawk Junction, *Canada* 48 C3
Hawke B., *N.Z.* 39 H6
Hawker, *Australia* 43 E2
Hawkesbury, *Canada* . . 48 C5
Hawkesbury I., *Canada* 50 C3
Hawkesbury Pt.,
Australia 42 A1
Hawkinsville, *U.S.A.* . . 53 J4
Hawley, *U.S.A.* 54 B6
Hawrān, W. →, *Iraq* . . 30 C4
Hawsh Mūssá, *Lebanon* 33 B4
Hawthorne, *U.S.A.* . . . 56 G4
Hay, *Australia* 43 E3
Hay →, *Australia* 42 C2
Hay →, *Canada* 50 A5
Hay, C., *Australia* 40 B4
Hay L., *Canada* 50 B5
Hay-on-Wye, *U.K.* . . . 9 E4
Hay River, *Canada* . . . 50 A5
Hay Springs, *U.S.A.* . . 54 D3
Haya = Tehoru,
Indonesia 27 E7
Hayachine-San, *Japan* . 22 E10
Hayden, *Australia* 56 F10
Hayden, *Australia* 41 F2
Hayes, *U.S.A.* 54 C4
Hayes →, *Canada* 48 A1
Hayes Creek, *Australia* . 40 B5
Hayle, *U.K.* 9 G2
Hayling I., *U.K.* 9 G7
Hayrabolu, *Turkey* . . . 17 D12
Hays, *Canada* 50 C6
Hays, *U.S.A.* 54 F5
Haysyn, *Ukraine* 13 D15
Hayvoron, *Ukraine* . . . 13 D15
Hayward, *Calif., U.S.A.* 57 G2
Hayward, *Wis., U.S.A.* . 54 B9
Haywards Heath, *U.K.* . 9 G7
Hazafon □, *Israel* 33 C4
Hazārān, Küh-e, *Iran* . . 31 D8
Hazard, *U.S.A.* 52 G4
Hazaribag, *India* 29 H14
Hazelton, *Canada* 50 B3
Hazelton, *U.S.A.* 54 B4
Hazen, *U.S.A.* 54 B4
Hazlehurst, *Ga., U.S.A.* 53 K4
Hazlehurst, *Miss., U.S.A.* 55 K9
Hazleton, *U.S.A.* 52 E9
Hazlett, L., *Australia* . . 40 D4
Hazro, *Turkey* 30 B4
Head of Bight, *Australia* 41 F5
Healdsburg, *U.S.A.* . . . 56 G2
Healdton, *U.S.A.* 55 H6
Healesville, *Australia* . . 43 F4
Heard I., *Ind. Oc.* 3 G13
Hearne, *U.S.A.* 55 K6
Hearst, *Canada* 48 C3
Heart →, *U.S.A.* 54 B4
Heart's Content, *Canada* 49 C9
Heath Pt., *Canada* 49 C7
Heavener, *U.S.A.* 55 H7
Hebbronville, *U.S.A.* . . 55 M5
Hebei □, *China* 25 C6
Hebel, *Australia* 43 D4
Heber City, *U.S.A.* . . . 56 F8
Heber Springs, *U.S.A.* . 55 H9
Hebert, *Canada* 51 C7
Hebgen L., *U.S.A.* . . . 56 D8
Hebron = Al Khalīl,
West Bank 33 D4
Hebron, *Canada* 47 C13
Hebron, *N. Dak., U.S.A.* 54 B3
Hebron, *Nebr., U.S.A.* . 54 E6
Hecate Str., *Canada* . . 50 C2
Hechi, *China* 24 D5
Hechuan, *China* 24 C5
Hecla, *U.S.A.* 54 C5
Hecla I., *Canada* 51 C9

Hede, *Sweden* 7 E15
Hedemora, *Sweden* . . . 7 F16
Heerde, *Neths.* 11 B6
Heerenveen, *Neths.* . . . 11 B5
Heerhugowaard, *Neths.* 11 B4
Heerlen, *Neths.* 14 A6
Hefa, *Israel* 33 C4
Hefa □, *Israel* 33 C4
Hefei, *China* 25 C6
Hegang, *China* 25 B8
Heidelberg, *Germany* . . 12 D5
Heilbronn, *Germany* . . 12 D5
Heilongjiang □, *China* . 25 B7
Heilunkiang =
Heilongjiang □, *China* 25 B7
Heimaey, *Iceland* 6 E3
Heinola, *Finland* 7 F22
Hejaz = Ḥijāz □,
Si. Arabia 30 E3
Hekimhan, *Turkey* . . . 30 B3
Hekla, *Iceland* 6 E4
Hekou, *China* 24 D5
Helen Atoll, *Pac. Oc.* . 27 D8
Helena, *Ark., U.S.A.* . . 55 H9
Helena, *Mont., U.S.A.* . 56 C7
Helensville, *N.Z.* 39 G5
Helenvale, *Australia* . . 42 B4
Helgeland, *Norway* . . . 6 C15
Helgoland, *Germany* . . 12 A4
Heligoland = Helgoland,
Germany 12 A4
Heligoland B. =
Deutsche Bucht,
Germany 12 A5
Hella, *Iceland* 6 E3
Hellespont = Çanakkale
Boğazı, *Turkey* 17 D12
Hellevoetsluis, *Neths.* . 11 C4
Hellín, *Spain* 15 C5
Helmand □, *Afghan.* . . 28 D4
Helmand →, *Afghan.* . . 28 D2
Helmond, *Neths.* 11 C5
Helmsdale, *U.K.* 10 C5
Helper, *U.S.A.* 56 G8
Helsingborg, *Sweden* . . 7 H15
Helsingfors = Helsinki,
Finland 7 F21
Helsingør, *Denmark* . . 7 H15
Helsinki, *Finland* 7 F21
Helston, *U.K.* 9 G2
Helvellyn, *U.K.* 8 C4
Helwân, *Egypt* 35 C12
Hemel Hempstead, *U.K.* 9 F7
Hemet, *U.S.A.* 57 K5
Hemingford, *U.S.A.* . . 54 D3
Hempstead, *U.S.A.* . . . 55 K6
Hemse, *Sweden* 7 H18
Henan □, *China* 25 C6
Henares →, *Spain* . . . 15 B4
Henashi-Misaki, *Japan* . 22 D10
Henderson, *Ky., U.S.A.* 52 G2
Henderson, *N.C., U.S.A.* 53 H6
Henderson, *Nev., U.S.A.* 57 H6
Henderson, *Tenn.,*
U.S.A. 53 H1
Henderson, *Tex., U.S.A.* 55 J7
Hendersonville, *N.C.,*
U.S.A. 53 H4
Hendersonville, *Tenn.,*
U.S.A. 53 G2
Hendījān, *Iran* 31 D6
Hendorābī, *Iran* 31 E7
Hengelo, *Neths.* 11 B6
Hengyang, *China* 25 D6
Henlopen, C., *U.S.A.* . . 52 F8
Hennessey, *U.S.A.* . . . 55 G6
Henrietta, *U.S.A.* 55 J5
Henrietta, Ostrov =
Genriyetty, Ostrov,
Russia 21 B16
Henrietta Maria, C.,
Canada 48 A3
Henry, *U.S.A.* 54 E10
Henryetta, *U.S.A.* 55 H7
Hentiyn Nuruu,
Mongolia 25 B5
Henty, *Australia* 43 F4
Henzada, *Burma* 29 L19
Heppner, *U.S.A.* 56 D4
Héraðsflói, *Iceland* . . . 6 D6
Héraðsvötn →, *Iceland* 6 D4
Herald Cays, *Australia* . 42 B4
Herāt, *Afghan.* 28 B3
Herāt □, *Afghan.* 28 B3
Herbert →, *Australia* . . 42 B4
Herberton, *Australia* . . 42 B4
Herceg-Novi,
Montenegro, Yug. . . 17 C8
Herchmer, *Canada* . . . 51 B10
Herðubreið, *Iceland* . . 6 D5
Hereford, *U.K.* 9 E5
Hereford, *U.S.A.* 55 H3
Herefordshire □, *U.K.* . 9 E5
Herentals, *Belgium* . . . 11 C4
Herford, *Germany* . . . 12 B5
Herington, *U.S.A.* 54 F6
Herkimer, *U.S.A.* 52 D8
Herm, *U.K.* 9 H5
Hermann, *U.S.A.* 54 F9
Hermannsburg,
Australia 40 D5
Hermidale, *Australia* . . 43 E4
Hermiston, *U.S.A.* . . . 56 D4
Hermite, I., *Chile* 64 H3

Hermon, Mt. = Shaykh,
J. ash, *Lebanon* 33 B4
Hermosillo, *Mexico* . . . 58 B2
Hernád →, *Hungary* . . 13 D11
Hernando, *U.S.A.* 55 H10
Herne, *Germany* 11 C7
Herne Bay, *U.K.* 9 F9
Herning, *Denmark* . . . 7 H13
Heroica = Caborca,
Mexico 58 A2
Heroica Nogales =
Nogales, *Mexico* . . . 58 A2
Heron Bay, *Canada* . . . 48 C2
Herreid, *U.S.A.* 54 C4
Herrin, *U.S.A.* 55 G10
Herriot, *Canada* 51 B8
Herstal, *Belgium* 11 D5
Hertford, *U.K.* 9 F7
Hertford, *U.S.A.* 53 G7
Hertfordshire □, *U.K.* . 9 F7
's-Hertogonbosch,
Neths. 11 C5
Hervey B., *Australia* . . 42 C5
Herzliyya, *Israel* 33 C3
Ḥeṣār, *Fārs, Iran* 31 D6
Ḥeṣār, *Markazi, Iran* . . 31 C6
Hesperia, *U.S.A.* 57 J5
Hesse = Hessen □,
Germany 12 C5
Hessen □, *Germany* . . 12 C5
Hettinger, *U.S.A.* 54 C3
Hewitt, *U.S.A.* 55 K6
Hexham, *U.K.* 8 C5
Heysham, *U.K.* 8 C5
Heywood, *Australia* . . . 43 F3
Hialeah, *U.S.A.* 53 N5
Hiawatha, *U.S.A.* 54 F7
Hibbing, *U.S.A.* 54 B8
Hibbs B., *Australia* . . . 42 G4
Hibernia Reef, *Australia* 40 B3
Hickman, *U.S.A.* 55 G10
Hickory, *U.S.A.* 53 H5
Hicks, L., *Canada* 51 A8
Hicks, Pt., *Australia* . . 43 F4
Hida-Gawa →, *Japan* . 23 G8
Hida-Sammyaku, *Japan* 23 F8
Hidaka-Sammyaku,
Japan 22 C11
Hidalgo, *Mexico* 59 C5
Hidalgo □, *Mexico* . . . 59 C5
Hidalgo, Presa M.,
Mexico 58 B3
Hidalgo del Parral,
Mexico 58 B3
Hierro, *Canary Is.* . . . 34 C2
Higashiajima-San,
Japan 22 F10
Higashiōsaka, *Japan* . . 23 G7
Higgins, *U.S.A.* 55 G4
High Atlas = Haut Atlas,
Morocco 34 B4
High Level, *Canada* . . 50 B5
High Point, *U.S.A.* . . . 53 H6
High Prairie, *Canada* . . 50 B5
High River, *Canada* . . . 50 C6
High Tatra = Tatry,
Slovak Rep. 13 D11
High Wycombe, *U.K.* . . 9 F7
Highland Park, *U.S.A.* . 52 D2
Highmore, *U.S.A.* 54 C5
Highrock L., *Man.,*
Canada 51 B8
Highrock L., *Sask.,*
Canada 51 B7
Higüey, *Dom. Rep.* . . . 61 C6
Hiiumaa, *Estonia* 7 G20
Ḥijāz □, *Si. Arabia* . . . 30 E3
Hijo = Tagum, *Phil.* . . 27 C7
Hikari, *Japan* 23 H5
Hiko, *U.S.A.* 57 H6
Hikone, *Japan* 23 G8
Hikurangi, *N.Z.* 39 F5
Hikurangi, Mt., *N.Z.* . . 39 H6
Hildesheim, *Germany* . 12 B5
Hill →, *Australia* 41 F2
Hill City, *Idaho, U.S.A.* 56 E6
Hill City, *Kans., U.S.A.* 54 F5
Hill City, *S. Dak., U.S.A.* 54 D3
Hill Island L., *Canada* . 51 A7
Hillegom, *Neths.* 11 B4
Hillerød, *Denmark* . . . 7 J15
Hillsboro, *Kans., U.S.A.* 54 F6
Hillsboro, *N. Dak.,*
U.S.A. 54 B6
Hillsboro, *N.H., U.S.A.* 52 D10
Hillsboro, *Ohio, U.S.A.* 52 F4
Hillsboro, *Tex., U.S.A.* 55 J6
Hillsborough, *Grenada* . 61 D7
Hillsdale, *U.S.A.* 52 E3
Hillsport, *Canada* 48 C2
Hillston, *Australia* . . . 43 E4
Hilo, *U.S.A.* 45 J17
Hilton Head Island,
U.S.A. 53 J5
Hilversum, *Neths.* 11 B5
Himachal Pradesh □,
India 28 D10
Himalaya, *Asia* 29 E14
Himatnagar, *India* 28 H8
Himeji, *Japan* 23 G7
Himi, *Japan* 23 F8
Ḥimṣ, *Syria* 33 A5
Ḥimṣ □, *Syria* 33 A6
Hinche, *Haiti* 61 C5
Hinchinbrook I.,
Australia 42 B4

Hinckley, *U.K.* 9 E6
Hinckley, *U.S.A.* 54 B8
Hindmarsh, L., *Australia* 43 F3
Hindu Kush, *Asia* 28 B7
Hindubagh, *Pakistan* . . 28 D5
Hindupur, *India* 28 N10
Hines Creek, *Canada* . . 50 B5
Hinesville, *U.S.A.* 53 K5
Hinganghat, *India* 28 J11
Hingham, *U.S.A.* 56 B8
Hingoli, *India* 28 K10
Hinna = Imi, *Ethiopia* . 32 F3
Hinnøya, *Norway* 6 B16
Hinojosa del Duque,
Spain 15 C3
Hinton, *Canada* 50 C5
Hinton, *U.S.A.* 52 G5
Hirado, *Japan* 23 H4
Hirakud Dam, *India* . . 29 J13
Hiratsuka, *Japan* 23 G9
Hiroo, *Japan* 22 C11
Hirosaki, *Japan* 22 D10
Hiroshima, *Japan* 23 G6
Hiroshima □, *Japan* . . . 23 G6
Hisar, *India* 28 E9
Hisb →, *Iraq* 30 D5
Ḥismá, *Si. Arabia* 30 D3
Hispaniola, *W. Indies* . 61 C5
Hit, *Iraq* 30 C4
Hita, *Japan* 23 H5
Hitachi, *Japan* 23 F10
Hitchin, *U.K.* 9 F7
Hitoyoshi, *Japan* 23 H5
Hitra, *Norway* 6 E13
Hixon, *Canada* 50 C4
Ḥiyyon, N. →, *Israel* . 33 E4
Hjalmar L., *Canada* . . . 51 A7
Hjälmaren, *Sweden* . . . 7 G16
Hjørring, *Denmark* . . . 7 H13
Hkakabo Razi, *Burma* . 29 E20
Hlyboka, *Ukraine* 13 D13
Ho Chi Minh City =
Thanh Pho Ho Chi
Minh, *Vietnam* 26 B3
Hoai Nhon, *Vietnam* . . 26 B3
Hoare B., *Canada* 47 B13
Hobart, *Australia* 42 G4
Hobart, *U.S.A.* 55 H5
Hobbs, *U.S.A.* 55 J3
Hobbs Coast, *Antarctica* 5 D14
Hobe Sound, *U.S.A.* . . 53 M5
Hoboken, *Denmark* . . . 7 H13
Hoburgen, *Sweden* . . . 7 H18
Hodaka-Dake, *Japan* . . 23 F8
Hodgeville, *Canada* . . . 51 C7
Hodgson, *Canada* 51 C9
Hódmezővásárhely,
Hungary 13 E11
Hodna, Chott el, *Algeria* 34 A6
Hodonín, *Czech Rep.* . . 13 D9
Hoek van Holland =
Hoek van Holland,
Neths. 11 C4
Hof, *Germany* 12 C6
Höfn, *Iceland* 6 D6
Hofors, *Sweden* 7 F17
Hofsjökull, *Iceland* . . . 6 D4
Hōfu, *Japan* 23 G5
Hogan Group, *Australia* 43 F4
Hogarth, Mt., *Australia* 42 C2
Hoggar = Ahaggar,
Algeria 34 D7
Hogsty Reef, *Bahamas* . 61 B5
Hohe Venn, *Belgium* . . 11 D6
Hohenwald, *U.S.A.* . . . 53 H2
Hoher Rhön = Rhön,
Germany 12 C5
Hohhot, *China* 25 B6
Hoi An, *Vietnam* 26 A3
Hoisington, *U.S.A.* . . . 54 F5
Hōjō, *Japan* 23 H6
Hokianga Harbour, *N.Z.* 39 F4
Hokitika, *N.Z.* 39 K3
Hokkaidō □, *Japan* . . . 22 C11
Holbrook, *Australia* . . . 43 F4
Holbrook, *U.S.A.* 57 J8
Holden, *U.S.A.* 56 G7
Holdenville, *U.S.A.* . . . 55 H6
Holdrege, *U.S.A.* 54 E5
Holguín, *Cuba* 60 B4
Hollandale, *U.S.A.* . . . 55 J9
Hollandia = Jayapura,
Indonesia 27 E10
Hollidaysburg, *U.S.A.* . 52 E6
Hollis, *U.S.A.* 55 H5
Hollister, *Calif., U.S.A.* 57 H3
Hollister, *Idaho, U.S.A.* 56 E6
Holly Hill, *U.S.A.* 53 L5
Holly Springs, *U.S.A.* . 55 H10
Hollywood, *U.S.A.* . . . 53 N5
Holman, *Canada* 46 A8
Hólmavík, *Iceland* . . . 6 D3
Holmen, *U.S.A.* 54 D9
Holmes Reefs, *Australia* 42 B4
Holmsund, *Sweden* . . . 6 E19
Holroyd →, *Australia* . 42 A3
Holstebro, *Denmark* . . 7 H13
Holsworthy, *U.K.* 9 G3
Holton, *Canada* 49 B8
Holton, *U.S.A.* 54 F7
Holtville, *U.S.A.* 57 K6
Holwerd, *Neths.* 11 A5
Holy I., *Angl., U.K.* . . . 8 D3
Holy I., *Northumb., U.K.* 8 B6
Holyhead, *U.K.* 8 D3

Holyoke, *Colo., U.S.A.* . 54 E3
Holyoke, *Mass., U.S.A.* 52 D9
Holyrood, *Canada* 49 C9
Homalin, *Burma* 29 G19
Homand, *Iran* 31 C8
Homathko →, *Canada* . 50 C4
Hombori, *Mali* 34 E5
Home B., *Canada* 47 B13
Home Hill, *Australia* . . 42 B4
Homedale, *U.S.A.* 56 E5
Homer, *Alaska, U.S.A.* . 46 C4
Homer, *La., U.S.A.* . . . 55 J8
Homestead, *Australia* . 42 C4
Homestead, *U.S.A.* . . . 53 N5
Homs = Ḥimṣ, *Syria* . . 33 A5
Homyel, *Belarus* 13 B16
Hon Chong, *Vietnam* . . 26 B2
Honan = Henan □,
China 25 C6
Honbetsu, *Japan* 22 C11
Hondo, *Japan* 23 H5
Hondo, *U.S.A.* 55 L5
Hondo →, *Belize* 59 D7
Honduras ■,
Cent. Amer. 60 D2
Honduras, G. de,
Caribbean 60 C2
Hønefoss, *Norway* . . . 7 F14
Honey L., *U.S.A.* 56 F3
Honfleur, *France* 14 B4
Hong →, *Vietnam* 24 D5
Hong Kong □, *China* . . 25 D6
Hongjiang, *China* 25 D5
Hongshui He →, *China* 25 D5
Honguedo, Détroit d',
Canada 49 C7
Honjo, *Japan* 22 E10
Honningsvåg, *Norway* . 6 A21
Honolulu, *U.S.A.* 45 E12
Honshū, *Japan* 25 C8
Honshū, *Japan* 25 C8
Hood, Mt., *U.S.A.* 56 D3
Hood, Pt., *Australia* . . 41 F2
Hood River, *U.S.A.* . . . 56 D3
Hoodsport, *U.S.A.* . . . 56 C2
Hoogeveen, *Neths.* . . . 11 B6
Hoogezand-Sappemeer,
Neths. 11 A6
Hooghly = Hugli →,
India 29 J16
Hooker, *U.S.A.* 55 G4
Hooker Creek, *Australia* 40 C5
Hoonah, *U.S.A.* 50 B1
Hooper Bay, *U.S.A.* . . . 46 B3
Hoopeston, *U.S.A.* . . . 52 E2
Hoorn, *Neths.* 11 B5
Hoover, *U.S.A.* 53 J2
Hoover Dam, *U.S.A.* . . 57 J6
Hope, *Canada* 50 D4
Hope, *U.S.A.* 55 J8
Hope, L., *S. Austral.,*
Australia 43 D2
Hope, L., *W. Austral.,*
Australia 41 F3
Hope Town, *Bahamas* . 60 A4
Hopedale, *Canada* . . . 49 A7
Hopei = Hebei □, *China* 25 C6
Hopelchén, *Mexico* . . . 59 D7
Hopetoun, *Vic.,*
Australia 43 F3
Hopetoun, *W. Austral.,*
Australia 41 F3
Hopetown, *S. Africa* . . 37 K4
Hopevale, *Australia* . . 42 B4
Hopewell, *U.S.A.* 52 G7
Hopkins, L., *Australia* . 40 D4
Hopkinsville, *U.S.A.* . . 53 G2
Hopland, *U.S.A.* 56 G2
Hoquiam, *U.S.A.* 56 C2
Horden Hills, *Australia* 40 D5
Horlick Mts., *Antarctica* 5 E15
Horlivka, *Ukraine* 19 E6
Hormak, *Iran* 31 D9
Hormoz, *Iran* 31 E7
Hormoz, Jaz.-ye, *Iran* . 31 E8
Hormozgān □, *Iran* . . . 31 E8
Hormuz, Küh-e, *Iran* . . 31 E7
Hormuz, Str. of,
The Gulf 31 E8
Horn, *Austria* 12 D8
Horn, *Iceland* 6 C2
Horn →, *Canada* 50 A5
Horn, Cape = Hornos,
C. de, *Chile* 64 H3
Horn I., *Australia* 42 A3
Horn Mts., *Canada* . . . 50 A5
Hornavan, *Sweden* . . . 6 C17
Hornbeck, *U.S.A.* 55 K8
Hornbrook, *U.S.A.* . . . 56 F2
Horncastle, *U.K.* 8 D7
Hornell, *U.S.A.* 52 D7
Hornell L., *Canada* . . . 50 A5
Hornepayne, *Canada* . . 48 C3
Hornos, C. de, *Chile* . . 64 H3
Hornsea, *U.K.* 8 D7
Horobetsu, *Japan* 22 C10
Horodenka, *Ukraine* . . 13 D13
Horodok, *Khmelnytskyy,*
Ukraine 13 D14

Horodok, *Lviv, Ukraine* 13 D12
Horokhiv, *Ukraine* . . . 13 C13
Horqin Youyi Qianqi,
China 25 B7
Horqueta, *Paraguay* . . 64 A5
Horse Creek, *U.S.A.* . . 54 E3
Horse Is., *Canada* 49 B8
Horsefly L., *Canada* . . 50 C4
Horsens, *Denmark* . . . 7 J13
Horsham, *Australia* . . . 43 F3
Horsham, *U.K.* 9 F7
Horten, *Norway* 7 G14
Horton, *U.S.A.* 54 F7
Horton →, *Canada* . . . 46 B7
Horwood L., *Canada* . . 48 C3
Hose, Gunung-Gunung,
Malaysia 26 D4
Ḥoseynābād, *Khuzestān,*
Iran 31 C6
Ḥoseynābād, *Kordestān,*
Iran 30 C5
Hoshangabad, *India* . . 28 H10
Hoshiarpur, *India* 28 D9
Hospet, *India* 28 M10
Hoste, I., *Chile* 64 H3
Hot Creek Range, *U.S.A.* 56 G6
Hot Springs, *Ark., U.S.A.* 55 H8
Hot Springs, *S. Dak.,*
U.S.A. 54 D3
Hotagen, *Sweden* 6 E16
Hotan, *China* 24 C2
Hotazel, *S. Africa* 37 K4
Hotchkiss, *U.S.A.* 57 G10
Hotham, C., *Australia* . 40 B5
Hoting, *Sweden* 6 D17
Hotte, Massif de la, *Haiti* 61 C5
Houffalize, *Belgium* . . 11 D5
Houghton, *U.S.A.* 54 B10
Houghton L., *U.S.A.* . . 52 C3
Houhora Heads, *N.Z.* . 39 F4
Houlton, *U.S.A.* 53 B12
Houma, *U.S.A.* 55 L9
Houston, *Canada* 50 C3
Houston, *Mo., U.S.A.* . 55 G9
Houston, *Tex., U.S.A.* . 55 L7
Houtman Abrolhos,
Australia 41 E1
Hovd, *Mongolia* 24 B4
Hove, *U.K.* 9 G7
Hoveyzeh, *Iran* 31 D6
Hövsgöl Nuur, *Mongolia* 24 A5
Howard, *Australia* 43 D5
Howard, *U.S.A.* 54 C6
Howe, *U.S.A.* 56 E7
Howe, C., *Australia* . . . 43 F5
Howell, *U.S.A.* 52 D4
Howick Group, *Australia* 42 A4
Howitt, L., *Australia* . . 43 D2
Howland I., *Pac. Oc.* . . 44 G10
Howrah = Haora, *India* 29 H16
Höxter, *Germany* 12 C5
Hoy, *U.K.* 10 B5
Høyanger, *Norway* . . . 7 F12
Hoyerswerda, *Germany* 12 C8
Hoylake, *U.K.* 8 D4
Hpa-an = Pa-an, *Burma* 29 L20
Hpungan Pass, *Burma* . 29 F20
Hradec Králové,
Czech Rep. 12 C8
Hrodna, *Belarus* 13 B12
Hrodzyanka, *Belarus* . . 13 B15
Hron →, *Slovak Rep.* . 13 E10
Hrvatska = Croatia ■,
Europe 12 F9
Hrymayliv, *Ukraine* . . . 13 D14
Hsenwi, *Burma* 29 H20
Hsiamen = Xiamen,
China 25 D6
Hsian = Xi'an, *China* . 25 C5
Hsinchu, *Taiwan* 25 D7
Hsinhailien =
Lianyungang, *China* . 25 C6
Hsüchou = Xuzhou,
China 25 C6
Hua Hin, *Thailand* . . . 26 B1
Huachinera, *Mexico* . . 58 A3
Huacho, *Peru* 62 F3
Huai He →, *China* . . . 25 C6
Huainan, *China* 25 C6
Huaiyin, *China* 25 C6
Huajuapan de Leon,
Mexico 59 D5
Hualapai Peak, *U.S.A.* . 57 J7
Huallaga →, *Peru* 62 E3
Huambo, *Angola* 37 G3
Huancabamba, *Peru* . . 62 E3
Huancane, *Peru* 62 G5
Huancavelica, *Peru* . . . 62 F3
Huancayo, *Peru* 62 F3
Huanchaca, *Bolivia* . . . 62 H5
Huang Hai = Yellow
Sea, *China* 25 C7
Huang He →, *China* . . 25 C6
Huangshan, *China* . . . 25 D6
Huangshi, *China* 25 C6
Huánuco, *Peru* 62 E3
Huaraz, *Peru* 62 E3
Huarmey, *Peru* 62 F3
Huascarán, *Peru* 62 E3
Huasco, *Chile* 64 B2
Huatabampo, *Mexico* . 58 B3
Huautla de Jiménez,
Mexico 59 D5
Huay Namota, *Mexico* . 58 C4

Hubbard, U.S.A. 55 K6
Hubbart Pt., Canada ... 51 B10
Hubei □, China 25 C6
Hucknall, U.K. 8 D6
Huddersfield, U.K. 8 D6
Hudiksvall, Sweden ... 7 F17
Hudson, Canada 48 B1
Hudson, N.Y., U.S.A. .. 52 D9
Hudson, Wis., U.S.A. .. 54 C8
Hudson, Wyo., U.S.A. .. 56 E9
Hudson →, U.S.A. 52 E8
Hudson Bay, N.W.T.,
   Canada 47 C11
Hudson Bay, Sask.,
   Canada 51 C8
Hudson Falls, U.S.A. .. 52 D9
Hudson Mts., Antarctica 5 D16
Hudson Str., Canada .. 47 B13
Hudson's Hope, Canada 50 B4
Hue, Vietnam 26 A3
Huehuetenango,
   Guatemala 60 C1
Huejúcar, Mexico 58 C4
Huelva, Spain 15 D2
Huesca, Spain 15 A5
Huetamo, Mexico 58 D4
Hugh →, Australia ... 42 D1
Hughenden, Australia . 42 C3
Hughes, Australia 41 F4
Hugli →, India 29 J16
Hugo, Colo., U.S.A. .. 54 F3
Hugo, Okla., U.S.A. ... 55 H7
Hugoton, U.S.A. 55 G4
Huichapán, Mexico ... 59 C5
Huila, Nevado del,
   Colombia 62 C3
Huinca Renancó,
   Argentina 64 C4
Huisache, Mexico 58 C4
Huixtla, Mexico 59 D6
Huize, China 24 D5
Hukawng Valley, Burma 29 F20
Ḥulayfa', Si. Arabia .. 30 E4
Huld = Ulaanjirem,
   Mongolia 24 B5
Hull = Kingston upon
   Hull, U.K. 8 D7
Hull, Canada 48 C4
Hull →, U.K. 8 D7
Hulst, Neths. 11 C4
Hulun Nur, China 25 B6
Humahuaca, Argentina 64 A3
Humaitá, Brazil 62 E6
Humber →, U.K. 8 D7
Humboldt, Canada ... 51 C7
Humboldt, Iowa, U.S.A. 54 D7
Humboldt, Tenn., U.S.A. 55 H10
Humboldt →, U.S.A. . 56 F4
Humboldt Gletscher,
   Greenland 4 B4
Hume, L., Australia ... 43 F4
Humenné, Slovak Rep. 13 D11
Humphreys Peak, U.S.A. 57 J8
Hün, Libya 35 C9
Húnaflói, Iceland 6 D3
Hunan □, China 25 D6
Hundred Mile House,
   Canada 50 C4
Hunedoara, Romania . 13 F12
Hungary ■, Europe .. 13 E10
Hungerford, Australia . 43 D3
Hüngnam, N. Korea .. 25 C7
Hunsrück, Germany .. 12 D4
Hunstanton, U.K. 8 E8
Hunter I., Australia .. 42 G3
Hunter I., Canada 50 C3
Hunter Ra., Australia . 43 E5
Hunterville, N.Z. 39 H5
Huntingburg, U.S.A. .. 52 F2
Huntingdon, Canada . 48 C5
Huntingdon, U.K. 9 E7
Huntingdon, U.S.A. .. 52 E7
Huntington, Ind., U.S.A. 52 E3
Huntington, Oreg.,
   U.S.A. 56 D5
Huntington, Utah,
   U.S.A. 56 G8
Huntington, W. Va.,
   U.S.A. 52 F4
Huntington Beach,
   U.S.A. 57 K5
Huntly, N.Z. 39 G5
Huntly, U.K. 10 C5
Huntsville, Canada ... 48 C4
Huntsville, Ala., U.S.A. 53 H2
Huntsville, Tex., U.S.A. 55 K7
Huonville, Australia .. 42 G4
Hupeh = Hubei □,
   China 25 C6
Hür, Iran 31 D8
Hurghada, Egypt 35 C12
Hurley, N. Mex., U.S.A. 57 K9
Hurley, Wis., U.S.A. .. 54 B9
Huron, Calif., U.S.A. .. 57 H3
Huron, Ohio, U.S.A. .. 52 E4
Huron, S. Dak., U.S.A. 54 C5
Huron, L., U.S.A. 52 C4
Hurricane, U.S.A. 57 H7
Hurunui →, N.Z. 39 K4
Húsavík, Iceland 6 C5
Huşi, Romania 13 E15
Huskvarna, Sweden .. 7 H16
Hustadvika, Norway .. 6 E12
Hutchinson, Kans.,
   U.S.A. 55 F6
Hutchinson, Minn.,
   U.S.A. 54 C7

Hutte Sauvage, L. de la,
   Canada 49 A7
Hutton, Mt., Australia . 43 D4
Huy, Belgium 11 D5
Huzhou, China 25 C7
Hvammstangi, Iceland . 6 D3
Hvar, Croatia 16 C7
Hvítá →, Iceland 6 D3
Hwang Ho = Huang
   He →, China 25 C6
Hwange, Zimbabwe .. 37 H5
Hyannis, Mass., U.S.A. 52 E10
Hyannis, Nebr., U.S.A. 54 E4
Hyargas Nuur, Mongolia 24 B4
Hydaburg, U.S.A. 50 B2
Hyden, Australia 41 F2
Hyder, U.S.A. 50 B2
Hyderabad, India 28 L11
Hyderabad, Pakistan . 28 G6
Hyères, France 14 E7
Hyères, Îs. d', France . 14 E7
Hyland →, Canada .. 50 B3
Hyndman Peak, U.S.A. 56 E6
Hyōgo □, Japan 23 G7
Hyrum, U.S.A. 56 F8
Hysham, U.S.A. 56 C10
Hythe, U.K. 9 F9
Hyūga, Japan 23 H5
Hyvinge = Hyvinkää,
   Finland 7 F21
Hyvinkää, Finland 7 F21

I-n-Gall, Niger 34 E7
Iaco →, Brazil 62 E5
Ialomiţa →, Romania 13 F14
Iaşi, Romania 13 E14
Iba, Phil. 27 A6
Ibadan, Nigeria 34 G6
Ibagué, Colombia 62 C3
Ibar →, Serbia, Yug. . 17 C9
Ibaraki □, Japan 23 F10
Ibarra, Ecuador 62 C3
Iberville, Canada 48 C5
Iberville, Lac d', Canada 48 A5
Ibiá, Brazil 63 G9
Ibioapaba, Sa. da, Brazil 63 D10
Ibiza = Eivissa, Spain . 15 C6
Ibonma, Indonesia ... 27 E8
Ibotirama, Brazil 63 F10
Ibrāhīm →, Lebanon . 33 A4
'Ibri, Oman 31 F8
Ibu, Indonesia 27 D7
Ibusuki, Japan 23 J5
Ica, Peru 62 F3
Iça →, Brazil 62 D5
Içana, Brazil 62 C5
Içana →, Brazil 62 C5
İçel = Mersin, Turkey . 19 G5
Iceland ■, Europe ... 6 D4
Ich'ang = Yichang,
   China 25 C6
Ichchapuram, India .. 29 K14
Ichihara, Japan 23 G10
Ichilo →, Bolivia 62 G6
Ichinohe, Japan 22 D10
Ichinomiya, Japan ... 23 G8
Ichinoseki, Japan ... 22 E10
Ida Grove, U.S.A. 54 D7
Idabel, U.S.A. 55 J7
Idaho □, U.S.A. 56 D7
Idaho City, U.S.A. ... 56 E6
Idaho Falls, U.S.A. ... 56 E7
Idar-Oberstein, Germany 12 D4
Idfû, Egypt 35 D12
Ídhi Óros, Greece ... 17 G11
Ídhra, Greece 17 F10
Idi, Indonesia 26 C1
Idiofa, Dem. Rep. of
   the Congo 36 E3
Idlib, Syria 30 C3
Ieper, Belgium 11 D2
Ierápetra, Greece ... 17 G11
Iesi, Italy 16 C5
Ifakara, Tanzania ... 36 F7
'Ifāl, W. al →,
   Si. Arabia 30 D2
Ife, Nigeria 34 G6
Iférouâne, Niger 34 E7
Iffley, Australia 42 B3
Ifni, Morocco 34 C3
Iforas, Adrar des, Mali 34 E6
Ifould, L., Australia .. 41 F5
Igarapava, Brazil 63 H9
Igarka, Russia 20 C9
Iggesund, Sweden ... 7 F17
Iglésias, Italy 16 E3
Igloolik, Canada 47 B11
Igluligaarjuk, Canada . 47 B10
Iglulik = Igloolik,
   Canada 47 B11
Ignace, Canada 48 C1
İğneada Burnu, Turkey 17 D13
Igoumenítsa, Greece . 17 E9
Iguaçu →, Brazil 64 B6
Iguaçu, Cat. del, Brazil 64 B6
Iguaçu Falls = Iguaçu,
   Cat. del, Brazil 64 B6
Iguala, Mexico 59 D5
Igualada, Spain 15 B6
Iguassu = Iguaçu →,
   Brazil 64 B6
Iguatu, Brazil 63 E11
Iharana, Madag. ... 37 G10

Iheya-Shima, Japan .. 23 L3
Ihosy, Madag. 37 J9
Ii, Finland 6 D21
Ii-Shima, Japan 23 L3
Iida, Japan 23 G8
Iijoki →, Finland 6 D21
Iisalmi, Finland 6 E22
Iiyama, Japan 23 F9
Iizuka, Japan 23 H5
Ijebu-Ode, Nigeria .. 34 G6
IJmuiden, Neths. 11 B4
IJssel →, Neths. 11 B5
IJsselmeer, Neths. ... 11 B5
Ikaluktutiak, Canada . 46 B9
Ikare, Nigeria 34 G7
Ikaría, Greece 17 F12
Ikeda, Japan 23 G6
Ikela, Dem. Rep. of
   the Congo 36 E4
Iki, Japan 23 H4
Ikopa →, Madag. ... 37 H9
Ilagan, Phil. 27 A6
Ílâm, Iran 30 C5
Ilam □, Iran 30 C5
Ilanskiy, Russia 21 D10
Iława, Poland 13 B10
Ile-à-la-Crosse, Canada 51 B7
Ile-à-la-Crosse, Lac,
   Canada 51 B7
Île-de-France □, France 14 B5
Ilebo, Dem. Rep. of
   the Congo 36 E4
Ilek, Russia 20 D6
Ilek →, Russia 18 D9
Ilesha, Nigeria 34 G6
Ilford, Canada 51 B9
Ilfracombe, Australia . 42 C3
Ilfracombe, U.K. 9 F3
Ilhéus, Brazil 63 F11
Ili →, Kazakhstan ... 20 E8
Iliamna L., U.S.A. ... 46 C4
Iligan, Phil. 27 C6
Ilkeston, U.K. 8 E6
Ilkley, U.K. 8 D6
Illampu = Ancohuma,
   Nevada, Bolivia ... 62 G5
Illana B., Phil. 27 C6
Illapel, Chile 64 C2
Iller →, Germany ... 12 D6
Illimani, Nevado, Bolivia 62 G5
Illinois □, U.S.A. 54 E10
Illium = Troy, Turkey . 17 E12
Illizi, Algeria 34 C7
Illoqqortoormiit,
   Greenland 4 B6
Ilmajoki, Finland 7 E20
Ilmen, Ozero, Russia . 18 C5
Ilo, Peru 62 G4
Iloilo, Phil. 27 B6
Ilorin, Nigeria 34 G6
Ilwaki, Indonesia ... 27 F7
Imabari, Japan 23 G6
Imandra, Ozero, Russia 18 A5
Imari, Japan 23 H4
Imatra, Finland 18 B4
Imbil, Australia 43 D5
imeni 26 Bakinskikh
   Komissarov =
   Neftçala, Azerbaijan . 19 G8
imeni 26 Bakinskikh
   Komissarov,
   Turkmenistan 31 B7
Imeri, Serra, Brazil .. 62 C5
Imi, Ethiopia 32 F3
Imlay, U.S.A. 56 F4
Immingham, U.K. ... 8 D7
Immokalee, U.S.A. .. 53 M5
Ímola, Italy 16 B4
Imperatriz, Brazil ... 63 E9
Impéria, Italy 14 E8
Imperial, Canada ... 51 C7
Imperial, Calif., U.S.A. 57 N11
Imperial, Nebr., U.S.A. 54 E4
Imperial Dam, U.S.A. . 57 K6
Imperieuse Reef,
   Australia 40 C2
Impfondo, Congo ... 36 D3
Imphal, India 29 G18
İmroz = Gökçeada,
   Turkey 17 D11
Imuris, Mexico 58 A2
Imuruan B., Phil. ... 27 B5
In Salah, Algeria 34 C6
Ina, Japan 23 G8
Inangahua Junction,
   N.Z. 39 J3
Inanwatan, Indonesia 27 E8
Iñapari, Peru 62 F5
Inari, Finland 6 B22
Inarijärvi, Finland ... 6 B22
Inawashiro-Ko, Japan 22 F10
Inca, Spain 15 C7
Ince Burun, Turkey .. 19 F5
İncesu, Turkey 30 B2
Inch'ŏn, S. Korea ... 25 C7
İncirliova, Turkey ... 17 F12
Incline Village, U.S.A. 56 G4
Incomáti →, Mozam. 37 K6
Indalsälven →,
   Sweden 7 E17
Indaw, Burma 29 G20
Independence, Calif.,
   U.S.A. 57 H4
Independence, Iowa,
   U.S.A. 54 D9

Independence, Kans.,
   U.S.A. 55 G7
Independence, Ky.,
   U.S.A. 52 F3
Independence, Mo.,
   U.S.A. 54 F7
Independence Fjord,
   Greenland 4 A6
Independence Mts.,
   U.S.A. 56 F5
India ■, Asia 28 K11
Indian →, U.S.A. ... 53 M5
Indian Cabins, Canada 50 B5
Indian Harbour, Canada 49 B8
Indian Head, Canada . 51 C8
Indian Ocean 3 E13
Indian Springs, U.S.A. 57 G6
Indiana, U.S.A. 52 E6
Indiana □, U.S.A. ... 52 F3
Indianapolis, U.S.A. . 52 F2
Indianola, Iowa, U.S.A. 54 E8
Indianola, Miss., U.S.A. 55 J9
Indiga, Russia 18 A8
Indigirka →, Russia . 21 B15
Indio, U.S.A. 57 K5
Indonesia ■, Asia ... 26 F5
Indore, India 28 H9
Indramayu, Indonesia 27 G13
Indravati →, India .. 29 K12
Indre □, France 14 C4
Indre →, France 14 C4
Indulkana, Australia . 43 D1
Indus →, Pakistan .. 28 G5
Inebolu, Turkey 19 F5
Infiernillo, Presa del,
   Mexico 58 D4
Ingersoll, Canada ... 48 D3
Ingham, Australia ... 42 B4
Ingleborough, U.K. .. 8 C5
Inglewood, Queens.,
   Australia 43 D5
Inglewood, Vic.,
   Australia 43 F3
Inglewood, N.Z. 39 H5
Inglewood, U.S.A. ... 57 K4
Ingólfshöfði, Iceland . 6 E5
Ingomar, U.S.A. 56 C10
Ingonish, Canada ... 49 C7
Ingraj Bazar, India .. 29 G16
Ingrid Christensen
   Coast, Antarctica .. 5 C6
Ingulec = Inhulec,
   Ukraine 19 E5
Ingushetia □, Russia . 19 F8
Inhambane, Mozam. . 37 J7
Inharrime, Mozam. .. 37 J7
Inhulec, Ukraine 19 E5
Ining = Yining, China 20 E9
Inirida →, Colombia . 62 C5
Injune, Australia 43 D4
Inklin →, Canada ... 50 B2
Inle L., Burma 29 J20
Inn →, Austria 12 D7
Innamincka, Australia 43 D3
Inner Hebrides, U.K. . 10 C3
Inner Mongolia = Nei
   Monggol Zizhiqu □,
   China 25 B6
Innetalling I., Canada . 48 A4
Innisfail, Australia ... 42 B4
Innisfail, Canada 50 C6
In'noshima, Japan ... 23 G6
Innsbruck, Austria ... 12 E6
Inongo, Dem. Rep. of
   the Congo 36 E3
Inoucdjouac = Inukjuak,
   Canada 47 C12
Inowrocław, Poland . 13 B10
Inscription, C., Australia 41 E1
Insein, Burma 29 L20
Inta, Russia 18 A11
Interlaken, Switz. ... 14 C7
International Falls,
   U.S.A. 54 A8
Inukjuak, Canada ... 47 C12
Inútil, B., Chile 64 G2
Inuvik, Canada 46 B6
Invercargill, N.Z. 39 M2
Inverell, Australia ... 43 D5
Invergordon, U.K. ... 10 C4
Inverloch, Australia .. 43 F4
Invermere, Canada .. 50 C5
Inverness, Canada ... 49 C7
Inverness, U.K. 10 C4
Inverness, U.S.A. ... 53 L4
Inverurie, U.K. 10 C5
Investigator Group,
   Australia 43 E1
Investigator Str.,
   Australia 43 F2
Inya, Russia 20 D9
Inyo Mts., U.S.A. ... 57 H5
Inyokern, U.S.A. 57 J5
Inza, Russia 18 D8
Iō-Jima, Japan 23 J5
Ioánnina, Greece ... 17 E9
Iola, U.S.A. 55 G7
Ione, U.S.A. 56 G3
Ionia, U.S.A. 52 D3
Ionian Sea, Medit. S. . 17 E7
Ionian Is. = Iónioi Nísoi,
   Greece 17 E9
Iónioi Nísoi, Greece .. 17 E9
Íos, Greece 17 F11
Iowa □, U.S.A. 54 D8

Iowa →, U.S.A. 54 E9
Iowa City, U.S.A. 54 E9
Iowa Falls, U.S.A. ... 54 D8
Iowa Park, U.S.A. ... 55 J5
Ipameri, Brazil 63 G9
Ipatinga, Brazil 63 G10
Ipiales, Colombia ... 62 C3
Ipin = Yibin, China .. 24 D5
Ipixuna, Brazil 62 E4
Ipoh, Malaysia 26 D2
Ippy, C.A.R. 36 C4
Ipsala, Turkey 17 D12
Ipswich, Australia ... 43 D5
Ipswich, U.K. 9 E9
Ipswich, U.S.A. 54 C5
Ipu, Brazil 63 D10
Iqaluit, Canada 47 B13
Iquique, Chile 62 H4
Iquitos, Peru 62 D4
Irabu-Jima, Japan .. 23 M2
Iracoubo, Fr. Guiana . 63 B8
Irafshān, Iran 31 E9
Iráklion, Greece 17 G11
Iran ■, Asia 31 C7
Iran, Gunung-Gunung,
   Malaysia 26 D4
Iran Ra. = Iran, Gunung-
   Gunung, Malaysia .. 26 D4
Īränshahr, Iran 31 E9
Irapuato, Mexico 58 C4
Iraq ■, Asia 30 C5
Irbid, Jordan 33 C4
Irbid □, Jordan 33 C5
Ireland ■, Europe ... 10 E2
Irian Jaya □, Indonesia 27 E9
Iringa, Tanzania 36 F7
Iriomote-Jima, Japan . 23 M1
Iriona, Honduras 60 C2
Iriri →, Brazil 63 D8
Irish Republic ■, Europe 10 E3
Irish Republic ■, Europe 10 E3
Irish Sea, U.K. 8 D3
Irkutsk, Russia 21 D11
Irma, Canada 51 C6
Irō-Zaki, Japan 23 G9
Iron Baron, Australia . 43 E2
Iron Gate = Portile de
   Fier, Europe 13 F12
Iron Knob, Australia .. 43 E2
Iron Mountain, U.S.A. 52 C1
Iron River, U.S.A. ... 54 B10
Ironton, Mo., U.S.A. . 55 G9
Ironton, Ohio, U.S.A. . 52 F4
Ironwood, U.S.A. ... 54 B9
Iroquois Falls, Canada 48 C3
Irpin, Ukraine 13 C16
Irrara Cr. →, Australia 43 D4
Irrawaddy □, Burma . 29 L19
Irrawaddy →, Burma 29 M19
Irrawaddy, Mouths of
   the, Burma 29 M19
Irricana, Canada 50 C6
Irtysh →, Russia ... 20 C7
Irún, Spain 15 A5
Irunea = Pamplona,
   Spain 15 A5
Irvine, Canada 51 D6
Irvine, U.K. 10 D4
Irvine, U.S.A. 52 G4
Irving, U.S.A. 55 J6
Irwin →, Australia .. 41 E1
Irymple, Australia ... 43 E3
Isaac →, Australia .. 42 C4
Isabel, U.S.A. 54 C4
Isabela, Phil. 27 C6
Isabela, I., Mexico ... 58 C3
Isabela, Cord., Nic. .. 60 D2
Isabella Ra., Australia 40 D3
Ísafjarðardjúp, Iceland 6 C2
Ísafjörður, Iceland ... 6 C2
Isahaya, Japan 23 H5
Isana = Içana →, Brazil 62 C5
Isar →, Germany ... 12 D7
Ischia, Italy 16 D5
Isdell →, Australia .. 40 C3
Ise, Japan 23 G8
Ise-Wan, Japan 23 G8
Isère □, France 14 D6
Isère →, France 14 D6
Isérnia, Italy 16 D6
Isfahan = Eşfahān, Iran 31 C6
Ishigaki-Shima, Japan 23 M2
Ishikari-Gawa →,
   Japan 22 C10
Ishikari-Sammyaku,
   Japan 22 C11
Ishikari-Wan, Japan . 22 C10
Ishikawa □, Japan .. 23 F8
Ishim, Russia 20 D7
Ishim →, Russia ... 20 D8
Ishinomaki, Japan ... 22 E10
Ishioka, Japan 23 F10
Ishkuman, Pakistan . 28 A8
Ishpeming, U.S.A. .. 52 B2
Isil Kul, Russia 20 D8
Isiro, Dem. Rep. of
   the Congo 36 D5
Isisford, Australia ... 42 C3
İskenderun, Turkey .. 19 G6
İskenderun Körfezi,
   Turkey 19 G6
İskŭr →, Bulgaria ... 17 C11
Iskut →, Canada ... 50 B2
Islamabad, Pakistan . 28 C8
Island L., Canada ... 51 C10
Island Lagoon, Australia 43 E2

Island Pond, U.S.A. .. 52 C10
Islands, B. of, Canada . 49 C8
Islands, B. of, N.Z. ... 39 F5
Islay, U.K. 10 D3
Isle →, France 14 D3
Isle aux Morts, Canada 49 C8
Isle of Wight □, U.K. . 9 G6
Isle Royale, U.S.A. .. 54 B10
Isle Royale National
   Park, U.S.A. 54 B10
Ismail = Izmayil,
   Ukraine 13 F15
Ismâ'ilîya, Egypt 35 B12
Isparta, Turkey 19 G5
İspica, Italy 16 F6
Israel ■, Asia 33 D3
Issoire, France 14 D5
Issyk-Kul, Ozero = Ysyk-
   Köl, Ozero, Kyrgyzstan 20 E8
İstanbul, Turkey 17 D13
İstanbul Boğazı, Turkey 17 D13
Istiaia, Greece 17 E10
Istokpoga, L., U.S.A. . 53 M5
Istra, Croatia 12 F7
Istres, France 14 E6
Istria = Istra, Croatia . 12 F7
Itaberaba, Brazil 63 F10
Itabira, Brazil 63 G10
Itabuna, Brazil 63 F11
Itacaunas →, Brazil . 63 E9
Itacoatiara, Brazil ... 62 D7
Itaipú, Reprêsa de,
   Brazil 64 B6
Itaituba, Brazil 63 D7
Itajaí, Brazil 64 B7
Italy ■, Europe 16 C5
Itamaraju, Brazil 63 G11
Itapecuru-Mirim, Brazil 63 D10
Itaperuna, Brazil 63 H10
Itapicuru →, Bahia,
   Brazil 63 F11
Itapicuru →,
   Maranhão, Brazil .. 63 D10
Itapipoca, Brazil 63 D11
Itaqui, Brazil 64 B5
Itchen →, U.K. 9 G6
Ithaca = Itháki, Greece 17 E9
Ithaca, U.S.A. 52 D7
Itháki, Greece 17 E9
Itiquira →, Brazil ... 63 G7
Ito, Japan 23 G9
Itu Ōshima →, S. China Sea 26 B4
Itoigawa, Japan 23 F8
Itonamas →, Bolivia 62 F6
Ituiutaba, Brazil 63 G9
Itumbiara, Brazil 63 G9
Ituna, Canada 51 C8
Iturbe, Argentina ... 64 A3
Iturup, Ostrov, Russia 21 E15
Ituxi →, Brazil 62 E6
Itzehoe, Germany ... 12 B5
Ivalo, Finland 6 B22
Ivalojoki →, Finland . 6 B22
Ivanava, Belarus ... 13 B13
Ivanhoe, Australia .. 43 E3
Ivanhoe, U.S.A. 54 C6
Ivano-Frankivsk, Ukraine 13 D13
Ivano-Frankovsk =
   Ivano-Frankivsk,
   Ukraine 13 D13
Ivanovo = Ivanava,
   Belarus 13 B13
Ivanovo, Russia 18 C7
Ivatsevichy, Belarus . 13 B13
Ivdel, Russia 18 B11
Ivory Coast, W. Afr. .. 34 H4
Ivory Coast ■, Africa . 34 G4
Ivrea, Italy 14 D7
Ivujivik, Canada 47 B12
Ivybridge, U.K. 9 G4
Iwaizumi, Japan 22 E10
Iwaki, Japan 23 F10
Iwakuni, Japan 23 G6
Iwamizawa, Japan .. 22 C10
Iwanai, Japan 22 C10
Iwata, Japan 23 G8
Iwate □, Japan 22 E10
Iwate-San, Japan ... 22 E10
Iwo, Nigeria 34 G6
Ixiamas, Bolivia 62 F5
Ixtepec, Mexico 59 D5
Ixtlán del Río, Mexico 58 C4
Iyo, Japan 23 H6
Izabal, L. de, Guatemala 60 C2
Izamal, Mexico 59 C7
Izena-Shima, Japan .. 23 L3
Izhevsk, Russia 18 C9
Izhma →, Russia ... 18 A9
Izmayil, Ukraine 13 F15
İzmir, Turkey 17 E12
İzmit = Kocaeli, Turkey 19 F4
İznik Gölü, Turkey ... 17 D13
Izra, Syria 33 C5
Izu-Shotō, Japan ... 23 G10
Izúcar de Matamoros,
   Mexico 59 D5
Izumi-Sano, Japan .. 23 G7
Izumo, Japan 23 G6
Izyaslav, Ukraine ... 13 C14

Jabalpur, India 28 H11
Jabbūl, Syria 30 B3
Jabiru, Australia 40 B5
Jablah, Syria 30 C3

Jablonec nad Nisou,
Czech Rep. 12 C8
Jaboatão, Brazil 63 E11
Jaca, Spain 15 A5
Jacareí, Brazil 64 A7
Jackman, U.S.A. 53 C10
Jacksboro, U.S.A. 55 J5
Jackson, Ala., U.S.A. . 53 K2
Jackson, Calif., U.S.A. 56 G3
Jackson, Ky., U.S.A. .. 52 G4
Jackson, Mich., U.S.A. 52 D3
Jackson, Minn., U.S.A. 54 D7
Jackson, Miss., U.S.A. 55 J9
Jackson, Mo., U.S.A. . 55 G10
Jackson, Ohio, U.S.A. . 52 F4
Jackson, Tenn., U.S.A. 53 H1
Jackson, Wyo., U.S.A. . 56 E8
Jackson B., N.Z. 39 K2
Jackson L., U.S.A. 56 E8
Jacksons, N.Z. 39 K3
Jackson's Arm, Canada 49 C8
Jacksonville, Ala.,
U.S.A. 53 J3
Jacksonville, Ark.,
U.S.A. 55 H8
Jacksonville, Fla., U.S.A. 53 K5
Jacksonville, Ill., U.S.A. 54 F9
Jacksonville, N.C.,
U.S.A. 53 H7
Jacksonville, Tex.,
U.S.A. 55 K7
Jacksonville Beach,
U.S.A. 53 K5
Jacmel, Haiti 61 C5
Jacob Lake, U.S.A. ... 57 H7
Jacobabad, Pakistan .. 28 E6
Jacobina, Brazil 63 F10
Jacques Cartier, Dét. de,
Canada 49 C7
Jacques-Cartier, Mt.,
Canada 49 C6
Jacques Cartier, Parc
Prov., Canada 49 C5
Jacundá →, Brazil ... 63 D8
Jadotville = Likasi,
Dem. Rep. of
the Congo 36 G5
Jaén, Peru 62 E3
Jaén, Spain 15 D4
Jaffa = Tel Aviv-Yafo,
Israel 33 C3
Jaffa, C., Australia ... 43 F2
Jaffna, Sri Lanka 28 Q12
Jagadhri, India 28 D10
Jagdalpur, India 29 K13
Jaghin →, Iran 31 E8
Jagodina, Serbia, Yug. 17 C9
Jagraon, India 28 D9
Jagtial, India 28 K11
Jaguariaíva, Brazil .. 64 A7
Jaguaribe →, Brazil . 63 D11
Jagüey Grande, Cuba . 60 B3
Jahrom, Iran 31 D7
Jailolo, Indonesia ... 27 D7
Jailolo, Selat, Indonesia 27 D7
Jaipur, India 28 F9
Jājarm, Iran 31 B8
Jakarta, Indonesia ... 27 G12
Jakobstad = Pietarsaari,
Finland 6 E20
Jal, U.S.A. 55 J3
Jalālābād, Afghan. ... 28 B7
Jalapa, Guatemala ... 60 D2
Jalapa Enriquez, Mexico 59 D5
Jalasjärvi, Finland ... 7 E20
Jalgaon, India 28 J9
Jalībah, Iraq 30 D5
Jalisco □, Mexico ... 58 D4
Jalna, India 28 K9
Jalón →, Spain 15 B5
Jalpa, Mexico 58 C4
Jalpaiguri, India 29 F16
Jaluit I., Marshall Is. . 44 G8
Jalūlā, Iraq 30 C5
Jamaica ■, W. Indies . 60 C4
Jamalpur, Bangla. ... 29 G16
Jamalpur, India 29 G15
Jamanxim →, Brazil . 62 D7
Jambi, Indonesia 26 E2
Jambi □, Indonesia .. 26 E2
James →, S. Dak.,
U.S.A. 54 D6
James →, Va., U.S.A. 52 G7
James B., Canada ... 48 B3
James Ranges, Australia 40 D5
James Ross I.,
Antarctica 5 C18
Jamestown, Australia 43 E2
Jamestown, N. Dak.,
U.S.A. 54 B5
Jamestown, N.Y., U.S.A. 52 D6
Jamīlābād, Iran 31 C6
Jamiltepec, Mexico .. 59 D5
Jamkhandi, India 28 L9
Jammu, India 28 C9
Jammu & Kashmir □,
India 28 B10
Jamnagar, India 28 H7
Jämsä, Finland 7 F21
Jamshedpur, India ... 29 H15
Jämtland, Sweden ... 6 E15
Jan L., Canada 51 C8
Jan Mayen, Arctic ... 4 B7
Janakkala, Finland ... 7 F21
Janaúba, Brazil 63 G10

Jand, Pakistan 28 C8
Jandaq, Iran 31 C7
Jandowae, Australia .. 43 D5
Janesville, U.S.A. ... 54 D10
Janin, West Bank 33 C4
Janos, Mexico 58 A3
Januária, Brazil 63 G10
Jaora, India 28 H9
Japan ■, Asia 23 G8
Japan, Sea of, Asia .. 22 E7
Japan Trench, Pac. Oc. 44 D6
Japen = Yapen,
Indonesia 27 E9
Japurá →, Brazil 62 D5
Jaqué, Panama 60 E4
Jarábulus, Syria 30 B3
Jarama →, Spain ... 15 B4
Jarash, Jordan 33 C4
Jardines de la Reina,
Arch. de los, Cuba . 60 B4
Jargalant = Hovd,
Mongolia 24 B4
Jari →, Brazil 63 D8
Jarīr, W. al →,
Si. Arabia 30 E4
Jarosław, Poland 13 C12
Jarrahdale, Australia . 41 F2
Jarrahi →, Iran 31 D6
Järvenpää, Finland .. 7 F21
Jarvis I., Pac. Oc. ... 45 H12
Jarwa, India 29 F13
Jāsimīyah, Iraq 30 C5
Jāsk, Iran 31 E8
Jasło, Poland 13 D11
Jasper, Canada 50 C5
Jasper, Ala., U.S.A. .. 53 J2
Jasper, Fla., U.S.A. .. 53 K4
Jasper, Ind., U.S.A. .. 52 F2
Jasper, Tex., U.S.A. .. 55 K8
Jasper Nat. Park,
Canada 50 C5
Jászberény, Hungary . 13 E10
Jataí, Brazil 63 G8
Jatibarang, Indonesia . 27 G13
Jatinegara, Indonesia . 27 G12
Játiva = Xàtiva, Spain . 15 C5
Jaú, Brazil 63 H9
Jauja, Peru 62 F3
Jaunpur, India 29 G13
Java = Jawa, Indonesia 27 G14
Java Barat □, Indonesia 27 G12
Java Sea, Indonesia .. 26 E3
Java Tengah □,
Indonesia 27 G14
Java Timur □, Indonesia 27 G15
Java Trench, Ind. Oc. . 26 F3
Javhlant = Uliastay,
Mongolia 24 B4
Jawa, Indonesia 27 G14
Jaya, Puncak, Indonesia 27 E9
Jayanti, India 29 F16
Jayapura, Indonesia .. 27 E10
Jayawijaya,
Pegunungan,
Indonesia 27 E9
Jaynagar, India 29 F15
Jayrūd, Syria 30 C3
Jayton, U.S.A. 55 J4
Jāz Mūrīān, Hāmūn-e,
Iran 31 E8
Jazīreh-ye Shīf, Iran . 31 D6
Jazminal, Mexico ... 58 C4
Jazzīn, Lebanon 33 B4
Jean, U.S.A. 57 J6
Jean Marie River,
Canada 50 A4
Jean Rabel, Haiti ... 61 C5
Jeanerette, U.S.A. ... 55 L9
Jeanette =
Zhannetty, Ostrov,
Russia 21 B16
Jebāl Bārez, Küh-e, Iran 31 D8
Jebel, Bahr el →,
Sudan 35 G12
Jedburgh, U.K. 10 D5
Jedda = Jiddah,
Si. Arabia 32 C2
Jeddore L., Canada .. 49 C8
Jędrzejów, Poland ... 13 C11
Jefferson, Iowa, U.S.A. 54 D7
Jefferson, Tex., U.S.A. 55 J7
Jefferson, Mt., Nev.,
U.S.A. 56 G5
Jefferson, Mt., Oreg.,
U.S.A. 56 D3
Jefferson City, Mo.,
U.S.A. 54 F8
Jefferson City, Tenn.,
U.S.A. 53 G4
Jeffersontown, U.S.A. 52 F3
Jeffersonville, U.S.A. . 52 F3
Jeffrey City, U.S.A. .. 56 E10
Jega, Nigeria 34 F6
Jēkabpils, Latvia 7 H21
Jekyll I., U.S.A. 53 K5
Jelenia Góra, Poland . 12 C8
Jelgava, Latvia 7 H20
Jellicoe, Canada 48 C2
Jemaja, Indonesia ... 27 D3
Jember, Indonesia ... 27 H15
Jembongan, Malaysia . 26 C5
Jena, Germany 12 C6
Jena, U.S.A. 55 K8
Jenkins, U.S.A. 52 G4
Jennings, U.S.A. 55 K8
Jepara, Indonesia ... 27 G14
Jeparit, Australia ... 43 F3

Jequié, Brazil 63 F10
Jequitinhonha, Brazil . 63 G10
Jequitinhonha →,
Brazil 63 G11
Jérémie, Haiti 61 C5
Jerez, Punta, Mexico . 59 C5
Jerez de García Salinas,
Mexico 58 C4
Jerez de la Frontera,
Spain 15 D2
Jerez de los Caballeros,
Spain 15 C2
Jericho = El Arīḥā,
West Bank 33 D4
Jericho, Australia 42 C4
Jerilderie, Australia .. 43 F4
Jerome, U.S.A. 56 E6
Jerramungup, Australia 41 F2
Jersey, U.K. 9 H5
Jersey City, U.S.A. .. 52 E8
Jersey Shore, U.S.A. . 52 E7
Jerseyville, U.S.A. ... 54 F9
Jerusalem, Israel ... 33 D4
Jervis B., Australia ... 43 F5
Jervis Inlet, Canada . 50 C4
Jesi = Iesi, Italy 16 C5
Jesselton = Kota
Kinabalu, Malaysia . 26 C5
Jessore, Bangla. 29 H16
Jesup, U.S.A. 53 K5
Jesús Carranza, Mexico 59 D5
Jetmore, U.S.A. 55 F5
Jevnaker, Norway ... 7 F14
Jeyḥūnābād, Iran 31 C6
Jeypore, India 29 K13
Jhal Jhao, Pakistan .. 28 F4
Jhalawar, India 28 G10
Jhang Maghiana,
Pakistan 28 D8
Jhansi, India 28 G11
Jharsuguda, India ... 29 J14
Jhelum, Pakistan 28 C8
Jhelum →, Pakistan . 28 D8
Jhunjhunu, India 28 E9
Ji-Paraná, Brazil 62 F6
Ji'an, China 25 D6
Jiangcheng, China .. 24 D5
Jiangmen, China 25 D6
Jiangsu □, China 25 C7
Jiangxi □, China 25 D6
Jiaxing, China 25 C7
Jiayi = Chiai, Taiwan . 25 D7
Jiayu, China 25 C6
Jibuti = Djibouti ■,
Africa 32 E3
Jicarón, I., Panama .. 60 E3
Jiddah, Si. Arabia ... 32 C2
Jido, India 29 E19
Jiggalong, Australia . 40 D3
Jihlava, Czech Rep. .. 12 D8
Jihlava →, Czech Rep. 13 D9
Jijiga, Ethiopia 32 F3
Jilin, China 25 B7
Jilin □, China 25 B7
Jilong = Chilung,
Taiwan 25 D7
Jima, Ethiopia 32 F2
Jiménez, Mexico 58 B4
Jinan, China 25 C6
Jindabyne, Australia . 43 F4
Jindřichův Hradec,
Czech Rep. 12 D8
Jingdezhen, China .. 25 D6
Jinggu, China 24 D5
Jinhua, China 25 D6
Jining,
Nei Monggol Zizhiqu,
China 25 B6
Jining, Shandong, China 25 C6
Jinja, Uganda 36 D6
Jinnah Barrage,
Pakistan 28 C7
Jinotega, Nic. 60 D2
Jinotepe, Nic. 60 D2
Jinsha Jiang →, China 24 D5
Jinzhou, China 25 B7
Jiparaná →, Brazil .. 62 E6
Jipijapa, Ecuador ... 62 D2
Jiquilpan, Mexico ... 58 D4
Jisr ash Shughūr, Syria 30 C3
Jitarning, Australia .. 41 F2
Jiu →, Romania 13 F12
Jiujiang, China 25 D6
Jixi, China 25 B8
Jīzān, Si. Arabia 32 D3
Jizl, Wādī al, Si. Arabia 30 E3
Jizō-Zaki, Japan 23 G6
Jizzakh, Uzbekistan . 20 E7
Joaçaba, Brazil 64 B6
João Pessoa, Brazil .. 63 E12
Joaquín V. González,
Argentina 64 B4
Jodhpur, India 28 F8
Joensuu, Finland ... 18 B4
Jõetsu, Japan 23 F9
Jõgeva, Estonia 7 G22
Jogjakarta =
Yogyakarta, Indonesia 27 G14
Johannesburg, S. Africa 37 K5
John Day, U.S.A. 56 D4
John Day →, U.S.A. . 56 D3
John D'Or Prairie,
Canada 50 B5
John H. Kerr Reservoir,
U.S.A. 53 G6

John's Ra., Australia .. 42 C1
Johnson, U.S.A. 55 G4
Johnson City, Tenn.,
U.S.A. 53 G4
Johnson City, Tex.,
U.S.A. 55 K5
Johnson's Crossing,
Canada 50 A2
Johnston, L., Australia 41 F3
Johnston Falls =
Mambilima Falls,
Zambia 36 G5
Johnston I., Pac. Oc. . 45 F11
Johnstone Str., Canada 50 C3
Johnstown, N.Y., U.S.A. 52 D8
Johnstown, Pa., U.S.A. 52 E6
Johor Baharu, Malaysia 26 D2
Jōhvi, Estonia 7 G22
Joinville, Brazil 64 B7
Joinville I., Antarctica . 5 C18
Jojutla, Mexico 59 D5
Jokkmokk, Sweden .. 6 C18
Jökulsá á Bru →,
Iceland 6 D6
Jökulsá á Fjöllum →,
Iceland 6 C5
Jolfā,
Āzarbājān-e Sharqī,
Iran 30 B5
Jolfā, Eşfahān, Iran .. 31 C6
Joliet, U.S.A. 52 E1
Joliette, Canada 48 C5
Jolo, Phil. 27 C6
Jombang, Indonesia . 27 G15
Jonava, Lithuania ... 7 J21
Jones Sound, Canada . 4 B3
Jonesboro, Ark., U.S.A. 55 H9
Jonesboro, La., U.S.A. 55 J8
Joniškis, Lithuania .. 7 H20
Jönköping, Sweden .. 7 H16
Jonquière, Canada .. 49 C5
Joplin, U.S.A. 55 G7
Jordan ■, Asia 33 E5
Jordan →, Asia 33 D4
Jordan Valley, U.S.A. . 56 E5
Jorhat, India 29 F19
Jörn, Sweden 6 D19
Jorong, Indonesia ... 26 E4
Jørpeland, Norway .. 7 G11
Jos, Nigeria 34 G7
Joseph, L., Canada .. 49 B6
Joseph Bonaparte G.,
Australia 40 B4
Joshua Tree National
Park, U.S.A. 57 K5
Jostedalsbreen, Norway 7 F12
Jotunheimen, Norway . 7 F13
Jourdanton, U.S.A. .. 55 L5
Jovellanos, Cuba ... 60 B3
Juan Aldama, Mexico . 58 C4
Juan de Fuca Str., B.C.,
Canada 50 D4
Juan de Fuca Str., B.C.,
Canada 50 D4
Juan Fernández, Arch.
de, Pac. Oc. 45 L20
Juankoski, Finland .. 6 E23
Juárez, Argentina ... 64 D5
Juárez, Sierra de,
Mexico 58 A1
Juàzeiro, Brazil 63 E10
Juàzeiro do Norte, Brazil 63 E11
Juba, Sudan 35 H12
Jubayl, Lebanon 33 A4
Jubbah, Si. Arabia .. 30 D4
Jubbulpore = Jabalpur,
India 28 H11
Jubilee L., Australia .. 41 E4
Juby, C., Morocco ... 34 C3
Júcar = Xúquer →,
Spain 15 C5
Júcaro, Cuba 60 B4
Juchitán, Mexico ... 59 D5
Judaea = Har Yehuda,
Israel 33 D3
Judith →, U.S.A. ... 56 C9
Judith Gap, U.S.A. .. 56 C9
Jugoslavia =
Yugoslavia ■, Europe 17 B9
Juigalpa, Nic. 60 D2
Juiz de Fora, Brazil .. 63 H10
Julesburg, U.S.A. ... 54 E3
Juli, Peru 62 G5
Julia Cr. →, Australia 42 C3
Julia Creek, Australia . 42 C3
Juliaca, Peru 62 G4
Julian, U.S.A. 57 K5
Julian, L., Canada ... 48 B4
Julianatop, Surinam . 63 C7
Julianehåb = Qaqortoq,
Greenland 4 C5
Julimes, Mexico 58 B3
Jullundur, India 28 D9
Jumentos Cays,
Bahamas 60 B4
Jumilla, Spain 15 C5
Jumla, Nepal 29 E13
Jumna = Yamuna →,
India 29 G12
Junagadh, India 28 J7
Junction, Tex., U.S.A. 55 K5
Junction, Utah, U.S.A. 57 G7
Junction B., Australia . 42 A1

Junction City, Kans.,
U.S.A. 54 F6
Junction City, Oreg.,
U.S.A. 56 D2
Junction Pt., Australia 42 A1
Jundah, Australia ... 42 C3
Jundiaí, Brazil 64 A7
Juneau, U.S.A. 50 B2
Junee, Australia 43 E4
Jungfrau, Switz. 14 C7
Junggar Pendi, China 24 B3
Junín, Argentina 64 C4
Junín de los Andes,
Argentina 64 D2
Jūniyah, Lebanon ... 33 B4
Juntura, U.S.A. 56 E4
Jur, Nahr el →, Sudan 35 G11
Jura = Jura, Mts. du,
Europe 14 C7
Jura = Schwäbische
Alb, Germany 12 D5
Jura, U.K. 10 D4
Jura, Mts. du, Europe . 14 C7
Jurado, Colombia 62 B3
Jurbarkas, Lithuania . 7 J20
Jurien, Australia 41 F2
Jūrmala, Latvia 7 H20
Juruá →, Brazil 62 D5
Juruena, Brazil 62 F7
Juruena →, Brazil .. 62 E7
Juruti, Brazil 63 D7
Justo Daract, Argentina 64 C3
Jutaí →, Brazil 62 D5
Juticalpa, Honduras . 60 D2
Jutland = Jylland,
Denmark 7 H13
Juventud, I. de la, Cuba 60 B3
Jüy Zar, Iran 30 C5
Jwaneng, Botswana . 37 J4
Jylland, Denmark ... 7 H13
Jyväskylä, Finland .. 7 E21

K2, Pakistan 28 B10
Kaap Plateau, S. Africa 37 K4
Kaapstad = Cape Town,
S. Africa 37 L3
Kabaena, Indonesia . 27 F6
Kabala, S. Leone 34 G3
Kabale, Uganda 36 E6
Kabalo, Dem. Rep. of
the Congo 36 F5
Kabanjahe, Indonesia . 26 D1
Kabardino-Balkar
Republic =
Kabardino-Balkaria □,
Russia 19 F7
Kabardino-Balkaria □,
Russia 19 F7
Kabarega Falls =
Murchison Falls,
Uganda 36 D6
Kabasalan, Phil. 27 C6
Kabetogama, U.S.A. . 54 A8
Kabinakagami L.,
Canada 48 C3
Kabinda, Dem. Rep. of
the Congo 36 F4
Kabompo →, Zambia 37 G4
Kabongo, Dem. Rep. of
the Congo 36 F5
Kabūd Gonbad, Iran . 31 B8
Kābul, Afghan. 28 B6
Kābul □, Afghan. ... 28 B6
Kābul →, Pakistan .. 28 C8
Kaburuang, Indonesia 27 D7
Kabwe, Zambia 37 G5
Kachchh, Gulf of, India 28 H6
Kachchh, Rann of, India 28 H7
Kachin □, Burma ... 29 G20
Kachiry, Kazakstan .. 20 D8
Kaçkar, Turkey 19 F7
Kadan Kyun, Burma . 26 B1
Kadina, Australia ... 43 E2
Kadirli, Turkey 30 B3
Kadiyevka = Stakhanov,
Ukraine 19 E6
Kadoka, U.S.A. 54 D4
Kadoma, Zimbabwe . 37 H5
Kâdugli, Sudan 35 F11
Kaduna, Nigeria 34 F7
Kaédi, Mauritania ... 34 E2
Kaesŏng, N. Korea .. 25 C7
Kāf, Si. Arabia 30 D3
Kafan = Kapan,
Armenia 19 G8
Kafanchan, Nigeria . 34 G7
Kafirévs, Ákra, Greece 17 E11
Kafue, Zambia 37 H5
Kaga Bandoro, C.A.R. 36 C3
Kagan, Uzbekistan .. 20 F7
Kagawa □, Japan ... 23 G7
Kağızman, Turkey ... 30 B4
Kagoshima, Japan .. 23 J5
Kagoshima □, Japan . 23 J5
Kagul = Cahul, Moldova 13 F15
Kahak, Iran 31 B6
Kahama →, Indonesia 31 E4
Kahayan →, Indonesia 26 E4
Kahnūj, Iran 31 E8
Kahoka, U.S.A. 54 E9
Kahramanmaraş, Turkey 19 G6
Kai, Kepulauan,
Indonesia 27 F8
Kai Besar, Indonesia . 27 F8
Kai Is. = Kai,
Kepulauan, Indonesia 27 F8

Kai Kecil, Indonesia . 27 F8
Kaiapoi, N.Z. 39 K4
Kaieteur Falls, Guyana 62 B7
Kaifeng, China 25 C6
Kaikohe, N.Z. 39 F4
Kaikoura, N.Z. 39 K4
Kaikoura Ra., N.Z. ... 39 J4
Kaimana, Indonesia . 27 E8
Kaimanawa Mts., N.Z. 39 H5
Kaingaroa Forest, N.Z. 39 H6
Kainji Res., Nigeria .. 34 F6
Kainuu, Finland 6 D23
Kaipara Harbour, N.Z. 39 G5
Kaironi, Indonesia ... 27 E8
Kairouan, Tunisia ... 35 A8
Kaiserslautern, Germany 12 D4
Kaitaia, N.Z. 39 F4
Kaitangata, N.Z. 39 M2
Kajaani, Finland 6 D22
Kajabbi, Australia ... 42 C3
Kajana = Kajaani,
Finland 6 D22
Kajo Kaji, Sudan 35 H12
Kakabeka Falls, Canada 48 C2
Kakadu Nat. Park,
Australia 40 B5
Kakamega, Kenya ... 36 D6
Kakanui Mts., N.Z. .. 39 L3
Kake, Japan 23 G6
Kake, U.S.A. 50 B2
Kakegawa, Japan ... 23 G9
Kakeroma-Jima, Japan 23 K4
Kakhovka, Ukraine .. 19 E5
Kakhovske Vdskh.,
Ukraine 19 E5
Kakinada, India 29 L13
Kakisa →, Canada .. 50 A5
Kakisa L., Canada .. 50 A5
Kakogawa, Japan ... 23 G7
Kakwa →, Canada .. 50 C5
Kâl Güsheh, Iran ... 31 D8
Kal Safid, Iran 30 C5
Kalaallit Nunaat =
Greenland ■,
N. Amer. 4 C5
Kalabagh, Pakistan . 28 C7
Kalabahi, Indonesia . 27 F6
Kalach, Russia 19 D7
Kaladan →, Burma .. 29 J18
Kaladar, Canada 48 D7
Kalahari, Africa 37 J4
Kalajoki, Finland ... 6 D20
Kālak, Iran 31 E8
Kalakan, Russia 21 D12
K'alak'unlun Shank'ou =
Karakoram Pass,
Pakistan 28 B10
Kalama, U.S.A. 56 D2
Kalámai, Greece ... 17 F10
Kalamata = Kalámai,
Greece 17 F10
Kalamazoo, U.S.A. .. 52 D3
Kalamazoo →, U.S.A. 52 D2
Kalan, Turkey 30 B3
Kalannie, Australia .. 41 F2
Kalāntari, Iran 31 C7
Kalao, Indonesia ... 27 F6
Kalaotoa, Indonesia . 27 F6
Kalat, Pakistan 28 E5
Kalāteh, Iran 31 B7
Kalāteh-ye Ganj, Iran . 31 E8
Kalbarri, Australia .. 41 E1
Kalce, Slovenia 12 C6
Kale, Turkey 17 F13
Kalegauk Kyun, Burma 29 M20
Kalemie, Dem. Rep. of
the Congo 36 F5
Kalewa, Burma 29 H19
Kaleybar, Iran 30 B5
Kalgan = Zhangjiakou,
China 25 B6
Kalgoorlie-Boulder,
Australia 41 F3
Kaliakra, Nos, Bulgaria 17 C13
Kalianda, Indonesia . 27 F3
Kalibo, Phil. 27 B6
Kalima, Dem. Rep. of
the Congo 36 E5
Kalimantan □, Indonesia 26 E4
Kalimantan Barat □,
Indonesia 26 E4
Kalimantan Selatan □,
Indonesia 26 E5
Kalimantan Tengah □,
Indonesia 26 E4
Kalimantan Timur □,
Indonesia 26 D5
Kálimnos, Greece .. 17 F12
Kaliningrad, Russia . 7 J19
Kalinkavichy, Belarus 13 B15
Kalinkovichi =
Kalinkavichy, Belarus 13 B15
Kalispell, U.S.A. 56 B6
Kalisz, Poland 13 C10
Kalix, Sweden 6 D20
Kalix →, Sweden ... 6 D20
Kalkarindji, Australia 40 C5
Kallavesi, Finland ... 6 E22
Kalmar, Sweden 7 H17
Kalmyk Republic =
Kalmykia □, Russia . 19 E8

Kalmykia □, Russia . . . 19 E8
Kalmykovo, Kazakstan . 19 E9
Kalocsa, Hungary 13 E10
Kaluga, Russia 18 D6
Kalundborg, Denmark . 7 J14
Kalush, Ukraine 13 D13
Kalutara, Sri Lanka . . . 28 R12
Kalya, Russia 18 B10
Kama →, Russia 18 C9
Kamaishi, Japan 22 E10
Kamaran, Yemen 32 D3
Kambalda, Australia . . . 41 F3
Kambarka, Russia 18 C9
Kamchatka, Poluostrov, Russia 21 D16
Kamchatka Pen. = Kamchatka, Poluostrov, Russia . . . 21 D16
Kamchiya →, Bulgaria 17 C12
Kamen, Russia 20 D9
Kamen-Rybolov, Russia 22 B6
Kamenjak, Rt., Croatia . 12 F7
Kamenka, Russia 18 A7
Kamenka Bugskaya = Kamyanka-Buzka, Ukraine 13 C13
Kamensk Uralskiy, Russia 20 D7
Kamenskoye, Russia . 21 C17
Kameoka, Japan 23 G7
Kamiah, U.S.A. 56 C5
Kamilukuak, L., Canada 51 A8
Kamin-Kashyrskyy, Ukraine 13 C13
Kamina, Dem. Rep. of the Congo 36 F5
Kaminak L., Canada . . 51 A10
Kaministiquia, Canada . 48 C1
Kaminoyama, Japan . . 22 E10
Kamloops, Canada . . . 50 C4
Kamo, Japan 22 F9
Kampala, Uganda . . . 36 D6
Kampang Chhnang, Cambodia 26 B2
Kampar, Malaysia . . . 26 D2
Kampar →, Indonesia 26 D2
Kampen, Neths. 11 B5
Kampene, Dem. Rep. of the Congo 36 E5
Kampong Saom, Cambodia 26 B2
Kampong Saom, Chaak, Cambodia 26 B2
Kampot, Cambodia . . 26 B2
Kampuchea = Cambodia ■, Asia . 26 B3
Kampungbaru = Tolitoli, Indonesia . . 27 D6
Kamrau, Teluk, Indonesia 27 E8
Kamsack, Canada . . . 51 C8
Kamskoye Vdkhr., Russia 18 C10
Kamuchawie L., Canada 51 B8
Kamui-Misaki, Japan . 22 C10
Kamyanets-Podilskyy, Ukraine 13 D14
Kamyanka-Buzka, Ukraine 13 C13
Kämyärän, Iran 30 C5
Kamyshin, Russia . . . 19 D8
Kanaaupscow, Canada 48 B4
Kanaaupscow →, Canada 47 C12
Kanab, U.S.A. 57 H7
Kanab →, U.S.A. . . . 57 H7
Kanagi, Japan 22 D10
Kanairiktok →, Canada 49 A7
Kananga, Dem. Rep. of the Congo 36 F4
Kanash, Russia 18 C8
Kanastraíon, Ákra = Palioúrion, Ákra, Greece 17 E10
Kanawha →, U.S.A. . . 52 F4
Kanazawa, Japan . . . 23 F8
Kanchanaburi, Thailand 26 B1
Kanchenjunga, Nepal . 29 F16
Kanchipuram, India . . 28 N11
Kandahar = Qandahār, Afghan. 28 D4
Kandalaksha, Russia . 18 A5
Kandalakshskiy Zaliv, Russia 18 A6
Kandangan, Indonesia . 26 E5
Kandanghaur, Indonesia 27 G13
Kandavu, Fiji 39 D8
Kandi, Benin 34 F6
Kandla, India 28 H7
Kandos, Australia . . . 43 E4
Kandy, Sri Lanka . . . 28 R12
Kane, U.S.A. 52 E6
Kane Basin, Greenland 4 B4
Kangān, Fārs, Iran . . 31 E7
Kangān, Hormozgān, Iran 31 E8
Kangaroo I., Australia . 43 F2
Kangaroo Mts., Australia 42 C3
Kangasala, Finland . . 7 F21
Kangāvar, Iran 31 C6
Kangean, Kepulauan, Indonesia 26 F5
Kangean Is. = Kangean, Kepulauan, Indonesia 26 F5

Kangikajik, Greenland . 4 B6
Kangiqsliniq = Rankin Inlet, Canada 46 B10
Kangiqsualujjuaq, Canada 47 C13
Kangiqsujuaq, Canada . 47 B12
Kangiqtugaapik = Clyde River, Canada 47 A13
Kangirsuk, Canada . . . 47 B13
Kangto, India 29 F18
Kaniapiskau = Caniapiscau →, Canada 49 A6
Kaniapiskau, Res. = Caniapiscau Rés. de, Canada 49 B6
Kanin, Poluostrov, Russia 18 A8
Kanin Nos, Mys, Russia 18 A7
Kanin Pen. = Kanin, Poluostrov, Russia . 18 A8
Kaniva, Australia . . . 43 F3
Kankaanpää, Finland . 7 F20
Kankakee, U.S.A. . . . 52 E2
Kankakee →, U.S.A. . 52 E1
Kankan, Guinea 34 F4
Kanker, India 29 J12
Kannapolis, U.S.A. . . 53 H5
Kannauj, India 28 F11
Kannod, India 28 H10
Kano, Nigeria 34 F7
Kan'onji, Japan 23 G6
Kanowit, Malaysia . . 26 D4
Kanoya, Japan 23 J5
Kanpetlet, Burma . . . 29 J18
Kanpur, India 28 F12
Kansas □, U.S.A. . . . 54 F6
Kansas →, U.S.A. . . . 54 F7
Kansas City, Kans., U.S.A. 54 F7
Kansas City, Mo., U.S.A. 54 F7
Kansk, Russia 21 D10
Kansu = Gansu □, China 24 C5
Kantö □, Japan 23 F9
Kantö-Sanchi, Japan . 23 G9
Kanuma, Japan 23 F9
Kanye, Botswana . . . 37 J5
Kaohsiung, Taiwan . . 25 D7
Kaolack, Senegal . . . 34 F2
Kapan, Armenia . . . 19 G8
Kapanga, Dem. Rep. of the Congo 36 F4
Kapchagai = Qapshaghay, Kazakstan 20 E8
Kapela = Velika Kapela, Croatia 12 F8
Kapfenberg, Austria . 12 E8
Kapiri Mposhi, Zambia 37 G5
Kapiskau →, Canada . 48 B3
Kapit, Malaysia 26 D4
Kapiti I., N.Z. 39 J5
Kaplan, U.S.A. 55 K8
Kapoeta, Sudan 35 H12
Kaposvár, Hungary . . 13 E9
Kapsukas = Marijampolė, Lithuania 7 J20
Kapuas →, Indonesia 26 E3
Kapuas Hulu, Pegunungan, Malaysia 26 D4
Kapuas Hulu Ra. = Kapuas Hulu, Pegunungan, Malaysia 26 D4
Kapunda, Australia . . 43 E2
Kapuni, N.Z. 39 H5
Kapuskasing, Canada . 48 C3
Kapuskasing →, Canada 48 C3
Kaputar, Australia . . 43 E5
Kaputir, Kenya 36 D7
Kara, Russia 20 C7
Kara Bogaz Gol, Zaliv = Garabogazköl Aylagy, Turkmenistan . . . 19 F9
Kara Kalpak Republic = Karakalpakstan □, Uzbekistan 20 E6
Kara Kum, Turkmenistan 20 F6
Kara Sea, Russia . . . 20 B7
Karabiğa, Turkey . . . 17 D12
Karabük, Turkey . . . 19 F5
Karaburun, Turkey . . 17 E12
Karabutak = Qarabutaq, Kazakstan 20 E7
Karacabey, Turkey . . 17 D13
Karacasu, Turkey . . . 17 F13
Karachey-Cherkessia □, Russia 19 F7
Karachi, Pakistan . . . 28 G5
Karad, India 28 L9
Karaganda = Qaraghandy, Kazakstan 20 E8
Karagayly, Kazakstan . 20 E8
Karaginskiy, Ostrov, Russia 21 D17
Karagiye, Vpadina, Kazakstan 19 F9

Karagiye Depression = Karagiye, Vpadina, Kazakstan 19 F9
Karaikal, India 28 P11
Karaikkudi, India . . . 28 P11
Karaj, Iran 31 C6
Karakalpakstan □, Uzbekistan 20 E6
Karakelong, Indonesia 27 D7
Karakitang, Indonesia . 27 D7
Karaklis = Vanadzor, Armenia 19 F7
Karakoram Pass, Pakistan 28 B10
Karakoram Ra., Pakistan 28 B10
Karalon, Russia . . . 21 D12
Karama, Jordan 33 D4
Karaman, Turkey . . . 19 G5
Karamay, China 24 B3
Karambu, Indonesia . . 26 E5
Karamea Bight, N.Z. . 39 J3
Karand, Iran 30 C5
Karanganyar, Indonesia 27 G13
Karasburg, Namibia . . 37 K3
Karasino, Russia . . . 20 C9
Karasjok, Norway . . . 6 B21
Karasuk, Russia . . . 20 D8
Karasuyama, Japan . . 23 F10
Karatau = Qarataū, Kazakstan 20 E8
Karatau, Khrebet, Kazakstan 20 E7
Karatsu, Japan 23 H5
Karaul, Russia 20 B9
Karawang, Indonesia . 27 G12
Karawanken, Europe . 12 E8
Karayazı, Turkey . . . 19 G7
Karazhal, Kazakstan . 20 E8
Karbalā', Iraq 30 C5
Karcag, Hungary . . . 13 E11
Kardhitsa, Greece . . . 17 E9
Kärdla, Estonia 7 G20
Kareima, Sudan 35 E12
Karelia □, Russia . . . 18 A5
Karelian Republic = Karelia □, Russia . . 18 A5
Kärevändar, Iran . . . 31 E9
Kargasok, Russia . . . 20 D9
Kargat, Russia 20 D9
Kargil, India 28 B10
Kargopol, Russia . . . 18 B6
Karian, Iran 31 E8
Kariba, L., Zimbabwe . 37 H5
Kariba Dam, Zimbabwe 37 H5
Kariba Gorge, Zambia . 37 H5
Karimata, Kepulauan, Indonesia 26 E3
Karimata, Selat, Indonesia 26 E3
Karimata Is. = Karimata, Kepulauan, Indonesia 26 E3
Karimnagar, India . . . 28 K11
Karimunjawa, Kepulauan, Indonesia 26 F4
Karin, Somali Rep. . . 32 E4
Karīt, Iran 31 C8
Kariya, Japan 23 G8
Karkaralinsk = Qarqaraly, Kazakstan 20 E8
Karkheh →, Iran . . . 30 D5
Karkinitska Zatoka, Ukraine 19 E5
Karkinitskiy Zaliv = Karkinitska Zatoka, Ukraine 19 E5
Karl-Marx-Stadt = Chemnitz, Germany . 12 C7
Karlovac, Croatia . . . 12 F8
Karlovo, Bulgaria . . . 17 C11
Karlovy Vary, Czech Rep. 12 C7
Karlsbad = Karlovy Vary, Czech Rep. . . 12 C7
Karlsborg, Sweden . . 7 G16
Karlshamn, Sweden . . 7 H16
Karlskoga, Sweden . . 7 G16
Karlskrona, Sweden . . 7 H16
Karlsruhe, Germany . . 12 D5
Karlstad, Sweden . . . 7 G15
Karlstad, U.S.A. . . . 54 A6
Karmi'el, Israel 33 C4
Karnak, Egypt 35 C12
Karnal, India 28 E10
Karnali →, Nepal . . . 29 E12
Karnaphuli Res., Bangla. 29 H18
Karnataka □, India . . 28 N10
Karnes City, U.S.A. . . 55 L6
Karnische Alpen, Europe 12 E7
Kärnten □, Austria . . 12 E8
Karonga, Malawi . . . 36 F6
Karoonda, Australia . . 43 F2
Karora, Sudan 35 E13
Kárpathos, Greece . . 17 G12
Karpinsk, Russia . . . 18 C11
Karpogory, Russia . . 18 B7
Karpuz Burnu = Apostolos Andreas, C., Cyprus 30 C2
Karratha, Australia . . 40 D2
Karsakpay, Kazakstan . 20 E7
Karshi = Qarshi, Uzbekistan 20 F7
Kartaly, Russia 20 D7
Karufa, Indonesia . . . 27 E8

Karumba, Australia . . 42 B3
Kārūn →, Iran 31 D6
Karungu, Kenya 36 E6
Karviná, Czech Rep. . . 13 D10
Karwar, India 28 M9
Kasai →, Dem. Rep. of the Congo 36 E3
Kasama, Zambia 36 G6
Kasaragod, India . . . 28 N9
Kasba L., Canada . . . 51 A8
Käseh Garän, Iran . . . 30 C5
Kasempa, Zambia . . . 37 G5
Kasenga, Dem. Rep. of the Congo 36 G5
Kasese, Uganda 36 D6
Kashaf, Iran 31 C9
Kāshān, Iran 31 C6
Kashechewan, Canada . 48 B3
Kashi, China 24 C2
Kashiwazaki, Japan . . 23 F9
Kashk-e Kohneh, Afghan. 28 B3
Kashkü'īyeh, Iran . . . 31 D7
Kāshmar, Iran 31 C8
Kashmir, Asia 28 C10
Kashun Noerh = Gaxun Nur, China 24 B5
Kasimov, Russia . . . 18 D7
Kasiruta, Indonesia . . 27 E7
Kaskaskia →, U.S.A. . 54 G10
Kaskattama →, Canada 51 B10
Kaskinen, Finland . . . 7 E19
Kaslo, Canada 50 D5
Kasmere L., Canada . . 51 B8
Kasongo, Dem. Rep. of the Congo 36 E5
Kasongo Lunda, Dem. Rep. of the Congo 36 F3
Kásos, Greece 17 G12
Kassalâ, Sudan 35 E13
Kassel, Germany . . . 12 C5
Kasson, U.S.A. 54 C8
Kastamonu, Turkey . . 19 F5
Kasterlee, Belgium . . 11 C4
Kastoria, Greece . . . 17 D9
Kasumi, Japan 23 G7
Kasur, Pakistan 28 D9
Katahdin, Mt., U.S.A. . 53 C11
Katanga □, Dem. Rep. of the Congo 36 F4
Katangi, India 28 J11
Katanning, Australia . 41 F2
Kateríni, Greece . . . 17 D10
Katha, Burma 29 G20
Katherîna, Gebel, Egypt 30 D2
Katherine, Australia . . 40 B5
Katherine Gorge, Australia 40 B5
Kathiawar, India . . . 28 H7
Kathikas, India 29 G15
Katima Mulilo, Zambia 37 H4
Katingan = Mendawai →, Indonesia 26 E4
Katiola, Ivory C. . . . 34 G4
Katmandu, Nepal . . . 29 F14
Katoomba, Australia . 43 E5
Katowice, Poland . . . 13 C10
Katrineholm, Sweden . 7 G17
Katsina, Nigeria . . . 34 F7
Katsumoto, Japan . . . 23 H4
Katsuura, Japan . . . 23 G10
Katsuyama, Japan . . . 23 F8
Kattegat, Denmark . . 7 H14
Katwijk, Neths. 11 B4
Kauai, U.S.A. 55 J6
Kaufman, U.S.A. . . . 55 J6
Kauhajoki, Finland . . 7 E20
Kaukauna, U.S.A. . . . 52 C1
Kaunas, Lithuania . . . 7 J20
Kautokeino, Norway . 6 B20
Kavacha, Russia . . . 21 C17
Kavalerovo, Russia . . 22 B7
Kavali, India 28 M12
Kavála, Greece 17 D11
Kavār, Iran 31 D7
Kavīr, Dasht-e, Iran . . 31 C7
Kaw, Fr. Guiana . . . 63 C8
Kawagoe, Japan 23 G9
Kawaguchi, Japan . . . 23 G9
Kawanoe, Japan 23 G6
Kawardha, India . . . 29 J12
Kawasaki, Japan . . . 23 G9
Kawasi, Indonesia . . . 27 E7
Kawerau, N.Z. 39 H6
Kawhia Harbour, N.Z. . 39 H5
Kawio, Kepulauan, Indonesia 27 D7
Kawnro, Burma 29 H21
Kawthoolei = Kawthule □, Burma . 29 L20
Kawthule □, Burma . . 29 L20
Kaya, Burkina Faso . . 34 F4
Kayah □, Burma . . . 29 K20
Kayan →, Indonesia . 26 D5
Kaycee, U.S.A. 56 E10
Kayeli, Indonesia . . . 27 E7
Kayenta, U.S.A. 57 H8
Kayes, Mali 34 F3
Kayin = Kawthule □, Burma 29 L20
Kayoa, Indonesia . . . 27 D7
Kayseri, Turkey 19 G6
Kaysville, U.S.A. . . . 56 F8

Kazachye, Russia . . . 21 B14
Kazakstan ■, Asia . . . 20 E7
Kazan, Russia 18 C8
Kazan →, Canada . . . 51 A9
Kazan-Rettö, Pac. Oc. . 44 E6
Kazanlük, Bulgaria . . 17 C11
Kazatin = Kozyatyn, Ukraine 13 D15
Käzerün, Iran 31 D6
Kazi Magomed = Qazimämmäd, Azerbaijan 31 A6
Kazuno, Japan 22 D10
Kazym →, Russia . . . 20 C7
Kéa, Greece 17 F11
Kearney, U.S.A. 54 E5
Kearny, U.S.A. 57 K8
Keban, Turkey 19 G6
Keban Baraji, Turkey . 19 G6
Kebnekaise, Sweden . . 6 C18
Kebri Dehar, Ethiopia . 32 F3
Kebumen, Indonesia . . 27 G13
Kechika →, Canada . . 50 B3
Kecskemét, Hungary . 13 E10
Kedainiai, Lithuania . . 7 J21
Kedgwick, Canada . . 49 C6
Kediri, Indonesia . . . 27 G15
Keeley L., Canada . . . 51 C7
Keeling Is. = Cocos Is., Ind. Oc. 44 J1
Keelung = Chilung, Taiwan 25 D7
Keene, U.S.A. 52 D9
Keer-Weer, C., Australia 42 A3
Keetmanshoop, Namibia 37 K3
Keewatin, Canada . . . 51 D10
Keewatin →, Canada . 51 B8
Kefallinía, Greece . . . 17 E9
Kefamenanu, Indonesia 27 F6
Kefar Sava, Israel . . . 33 C3
Keffi, Nigeria 34 G7
Keflavik, Iceland . . . 6 D2
Keg River, Canada . . 50 B5
Kegaska, Canada . . . 49 B7
Keighley, U.K. 8 D6
Keila, Estonia 7 G21
Keimoes, S. Africa . . . 37 K4
Keitele, Finland 6 E22
Keith, Australia 43 F3
Keizer, U.S.A. 56 D2
Kejimkujik Nat. Park, Canada 49 D6
Kejser Franz Joseph Fd., Greenland 4 B6
Kekri, India 28 G9
Kelang, Malaysia . . . 26 D2
Kelkit, Turkey 19 F6
Kelkit →, Turkey . . . 19 F6
Kellerberrin, Australia . 41 F2
Kellett, C., Canada . . 4 B1
Kellogg, U.S.A. 56 C5
Kells = Ceanannus Mor, Ireland 10 E3
Kelowna, Canada . . . 50 D5
Kelso, N.Z. 39 L2
Kelso, U.S.A. 56 C2
Keluang, Malaysia . . 26 D2
Kelvington, Canada . . 51 C8
Kem, Russia 18 B5
Kem →, Russia 18 B5
Kema, Indonesia . . . 27 D7
Kemah, Turkey 30 B3
Kemaman, Malaysia . . 26 D2
Kemano, Canada . . . 50 C3
Kemerovo, Russia . . . 20 D9
Kemi, Finland 6 D21
Kemi älv = Kemijoki →, Finland 6 D21
Kemijärvi, Finland . . 6 C22
Kemijoki →, Finland . 6 D21
Kemmerer, U.S.A. . . . 56 F8
Kemp, L., U.S.A. . . . 55 J5
Kemp Land, Antarctica . 5 C5
Kempsey, Australia . . 43 E5
Kempt, L., Canada . . 48 C5
Kempten, Germany . . 12 E6
Kempton, Australia . . 42 G4
Kemptville, Canada . . 48 D4
Kenai, U.S.A. 46 B4
Kendal, Indonesia . . . 27 G14
Kendal, U.K. 8 C5
Kendall, Australia . . . 43 E5
Kendall, U.S.A. 53 N5
Kendall →, Australia . 42 A3
Kendallville, U.S.A. . . 52 E3
Kendari, Indonesia . . 27 E6
Kendawangan, Indonesia 26 E4
Kendrapara, India . . . 29 J15
Kenedy, U.S.A. 55 L6
Kenema, S. Leone . . . 34 G3
Keng Tawng, Burma . 29 J21
Keng Tung, Burma . . 29 J21
Kenitra, Morocco . . . 34 B3
Kenmare, Ireland . . . 10 E2
Kenmare, U.S.A. . . . 54 A3
Kenmare →, Ireland . 10 E1
Kennebec →, U.S.A. . 53 D11
Kennedy Ra., Australia 41 D2
Kennedy Taungdeik, Burma 29 H18
Kennet →, U.K. 9 F7
Kenneth Ra., Australia . 41 D2
Kennett, U.S.A. 55 G9
Kennewick, U.S.A. . . 56 C4
Kenogami →, Canada 48 B3

Kenora, Canada 51 D10
Kenosha, U.S.A. 52 D2
Kensington, Canada . . 49 C7
Kent, U.S.A. 55 K2
Kent □, U.K. 9 F8
Kent Group, Australia . 42 F4
Kent Pen., Canada . . 46 B9
Kentau, Kazakstan . . 20 E7
Kentland, U.S.A. . . . 52 E2
Kenton, U.S.A. 52 E4
Kentucky □, U.S.A. . . 52 G3
Kentucky →, U.S.A. . 52 F3
Kentucky L., U.S.A. . . 53 G2
Kentville, Canada . . . 49 C7
Kentwood, U.S.A. . . . 55 K9
Kenya ■, Africa 36 D7
Kenya, Mt., Kenya . . 36 E7
Keokuk, U.S.A. 54 E9
Kepi, Indonesia 27 F9
Kerala □, India 28 P10
Kerama-Rettö, Japan . 23 L3
Kerang, Australia . . . 43 F3
Keraudren, C., Australia 40 C2
Kerava, Finland 7 F21
Kerch, Ukraine 19 E6
Kerguelen, Ind. Oc. . . 3 G13
Kericho, Kenya 36 E7
Kerinci, Indonesia . . . 26 E2
Kerki, Turkmenistan . . 20 F7
Kérkira, Greece 17 E8
Kerkrade, Neths. . . . 11 D6
Kermadec Is., Pac. Oc. . 38 E11
Kermadec Trench, Pac. Oc. 44 L10
Kermān, Iran 31 D8
Kermān □, Iran 31 D8
Kermān, Biābān-e, Iran 31 D8
Kermānshāh = Bākhtarān, Iran . . . 30 C5
Kermit, U.S.A. 55 K3
Kern →, U.S.A. 57 J4
Kernow = Cornwall □, U.K. 9 G3
Kerrobert, Canada . . 51 C7
Kerrville, U.S.A. . . . 55 K5
Kerulen →, Asia . . . 25 B6
Kerzaz, Algeria 34 C5
Kesagami →, Canada . 48 B4
Kesagami L., Canada . 48 B3
Keşan, Turkey 17 D12
Kesennuma, Japan . . 22 E10
Keshit, Iran 31 D8
Kestenga, Russia . . . 18 A5
Keswick, U.K. 8 C4
Ket →, Russia 20 D9
Ketapang, Indonesia . 26 E4
Ketchikan, U.S.A. . . . 50 B2
Ketchum, U.S.A. . . . 56 E6
Ketef, Khalîg Umm el, Egypt 30 F2
Kętrzyn, Poland 13 A11
Kettering, U.K. 9 E7
Kettering, U.S.A. . . . 52 F3
Kettle →, Canada . . . 51 B11
Kettle Falls, U.S.A. . . 56 B4
Keuruu, Finland 7 E21
Kewanee, U.S.A. . . . 54 E10
Kewaunee, U.S.A. . . . 52 C2
Keweenaw B., U.S.A. . 52 B1
Keweenaw Pen., U.S.A. 52 B2
Keweenaw Pt., U.S.A. . 52 B2
Key Largo, U.S.A. . . . 53 N5
Key West, U.S.A. . . . 60 B3
Keynsham, U.K. 9 F5
Keyser, U.S.A. 52 F6
Kezhma, Russia 21 D11
Khabarovsk, Russia . . 21 E14
Khabr, Iran 31 D8
Khābūr →, Syria . . . 30 C4
Khachmas = Xaçmaz, Azerbaijan 19 F8
Khairpur, Pakistan . . 28 F6
Khakassia □, Russia . . 20 D9
Khalafābād, Iran . . . 31 D6
Khalīlī, Iran 31 E7
Khalkhāl, Iran 31 B6
Khalkis, Greece 17 E10
Khalmer-Sede = Tazovskiy, Russia . . 20 C8
Khalmer Yu, Russia . . 20 C7
Khalturin, Russia . . . 18 C8
Khalūf, Oman 32 C6
Khambhat, India . . . 28 H8
Khambhat, G. of, India 28 J8
Khamir, Iran 31 E7
Khamir, Yemen 32 D3
Khamsa, Egypt 33 E1
Khān Abū Shāmat, Syria 33 B5
Khān Azād, Iraq . . . 30 C5
Khān Mujiddah, Iraq . 30 C4
Khān Shaykhūn, Syria . 30 C3
Khān Yūnis, Gaza Strip 33 D3
Khānbāghī, Iran . . . 31 B7
Khandwa, India 28 J10
Khandyga, Russia . . . 21 C14
Khāneh, Iran 30 B5
Khanewal, Pakistan . . 28 D7
Khaniá, Greece 17 G11
Khanion, Kólpos, Greece 17 G10
Khanka, L., Asia . . . 21 E14
Khankendy = Xankändi, Azerbaijan 19 G8
Khanty-Mansiysk, Russia 20 C7

Khapcheranga, Russia . 21 E12
Kharagpur, India ... 29 H15
Kharan Kalat, Pakistan . 28 E4
Kharānaq, Iran 31 C7
Kharda, India 28 K9
Khârga, El Wâhât-el,
Egypt 35 C12
Khargon, India 28 J9
Khārk, Jazireh-ye, Iran . 31 D6
Kharkov = Kharkiv,
Ukraine 19 E6
Kharkiv, Ukraine 19 E6
Kharovsk, Russia 18 C7
Kharta, Turkey 17 D13
Khartoum = El
Khartûm, Sudan ... 35 E12
Khasan, Russia 22 C5
Khāsh, Iran 28 E2
Khashm el Girba, Sudan 35 F13
Khaskovo, Bulgaria ... 17 D11
Khatanga, Russia 21 B11
Khatanga →, Russia .. 21 B11
Khātūnābād, Iran 31 D7
Khatyrka, Russia 21 C18
Khaybar, Harrat,
Si. Arabia 30 E4
Khayelitsha, S. Africa . 37 L3
Khāzimiyah, Iraq 30 C4
Khed Brahma, India .. 28 G8
Khemisset, Morocco . 34 B4
Khemmarat, Thailand . 26 A2
Khenāmān, Iran 31 D8
Khenchela, Algeria ... 34 A7
Khersān →, Iran 31 D6
Kherson, Ukraine 19 E5
Kheta →, Russia 21 B11
Khilok, Russia 21 D12
Khíos, Greece 17 E12
Khiuma = Hiiumaa,
Estonia 7 G20
Khiva, Uzbekistan ... 20 E7
Khiyāv, Iran 30 B5
Khmelnik, Ukraine ... 13 D14
Khmelnitskiy =
Khmelnytskyy,
Ukraine 13 D14
Khmelnytskyy, Ukraine 13 D14
Khmer Rep. =
Cambodia ■, Asia . 26 B3
Khodoriv, Ukraine ... 13 D13
Khodzent = Khudzhand,
Tajikistan 20 E7
Khojak Pass, Afghan. . 28 D5
Kholm, Russia 18 C5
Kholmsk, Russia 21 E15
Khomeyn, Iran 31 C6
Khomeynī Shahr, Iran . 31 C6
Khon Kaen, Thailand . 26 A2
Khong →, Cambodia . 26 B3
Khonuu, Russia 21 C15
Khoper →, Russia ... 19 D6
Khóra Sfakíon, Greece . 17 G11
Khorāsān □, Iran 31 C8
Khorat = Nakhon
Ratchasima, Thailand 26 B2
Khorramābād,
Khorāsān, Iran ... 31 C8
Khorramābād,
Lorestān,
Iran 31 C6
Khorrāmshahr, Iran .. 31 D6
Khorugh, Tajikistan .. 20 F8
Khosravi, Iran 31 D6
Khosrowābād,
Khuzestān, Iran .. 31 D6
Khosrowābād,
Kordestān, Iran .. 30 C5
Khosûyeh, Iran 31 D7
Khotyn, Ukraine 13 D14
Khouribga, Morocco . 34 B4
Khowst, Afghan. 28 C6
Khoyniki, Belarus ... 13 C15
Khu Khan, Thailand . 26 B2
Khudzhand, Tajikistan . 20 E7
Khuff, Si. Arabia 30 E5
Khūgiāni, Afghan. ... 28 D4
Khulna, Bangla. 29 H16
Khulna □, Bangla. .. 29 H16
Khūnsorkh, Iran 31 E8
Khūr, Iran 31 C8
Khurayş, Si. Arabia .. 31 E6
Khuriyā Muriyā, Jazā 'ir,
Oman 32 D6
Khūrmāl, Iraq 30 C5
Khurr, Wādī al, Iraq .. 30 C4
Khūsf, Iran 31 C8
Khush, Afghan. 28 C3
Khushab, Pakistan .. 28 C8
Khust, Ukraine 13 D12
Khuzdar, Pakistan ... 28 F5
Khūzestān □, Iran ... 31 D6
Khvāf, Iran 31 C9
Khvājeh, Iran 30 B5
Khvānsār, Iran 31 D7
Khvor, Iran 31 C7
Khvorgū, Iran 31 E8
Khvormūj, Iran 31 D6
Khvoy, Iran 30 B5
Khyber Pass, Afghan. . 28 B7
Kiama, Australia 43 E5
Kiamba, Phil. 27 C6
Kiangsi = Jiangxi □,
China 25 D6
Kiangsu = Jiangsu □,
China 25 C7

Kibombo, Dem. Rep. of
the Congo 36 E5
Kibre Mengist, Ethiopia 32 F2
Kibwezi, Kenya 36 E7
Kichmengskiy Gorodok,
Russia 18 B8
Kicking Horse Pass,
Canada 50 C5
Kidal, Mali 34 E6
Kidderminster, U.K. ... 9 E5
Kidnappers, C., N.Z. .. 39 H6
Kidsgrove, U.K. 8 D5
Kidston, Australia ... 42 B3
Kiel, Germany 12 A6
Kiel Canal = Nord-
Ostsee-Kanal,
Germany 12 A5
Kielce, Poland 13 C11
Kielder Water, U.K. ... 8 B5
Kieler Bucht, Germany 12 A6
Kiev = Kyyiv, Ukraine . 13 C16
Kiffa, Mauritania 34 E3
Kifri, Iraq 30 C5
Kigali, Rwanda 36 E6
Kigoma-Ujiji, Tanzania 36 E5
Kihnu, Estonia 7 G21
Kii-Sanchi, Japan ... 23 G8
Kii-Suidō, Japan 23 H7
Kikaiga-Shima, Japan . 23 K4
Kikinda, Serbia, Yug. . 17 B9
Kikládhes, Greece ... 17 F11
Kikwit, Dem. Rep. of
the Congo 36 E3
Kilcoy, Australia 43 D5
Kilgore, U.S.A. 55 J7
Kilimanjaro, Tanzania . 36 E7
Kilis, Turkey 30 B3
Kiliya, Ukraine 13 F15
Kilkenny, Ireland ... 10 E3
Kilkís, Greece 17 D10
Killarney, Australia .. 43 D5
Killarney, Canada ... 51 D9
Killarney, Ireland ... 10 E2
Killdeer, U.S.A. 54 B3
Killeen, U.S.A. 55 K6
Killíni, Greece 17 F10
Kilmarnock, U.K. 10 D4
Kilmore, Australia ... 43 F3
Kilosa, Tanzania 36 F7
Kilrush, Ireland 10 E2
Kilwa Kivinje, Tanzania 36 F7
Kim, U.S.A. 55 G3
Kimaam, Indonesia .. 27 F9
Kimba, Australia 43 E2
Kimball, Nebr., U.S.A. 54 E3
Kimball, S. Dak., U.S.A. 54 D5
Kimberley, Australia . 40 C4
Kimberley, Canada .. 50 D5
Kimberley, S. Africa . 37 K4
Kimberly, U.S.A. 56 E6
Kimmirut, Canada ... 47 B13
Kimpese, Dem. Rep. of
the Congo 36 F2
Kimry, Russia 18 C6
Kinabalu, Gunong,
Malaysia 26 C5
Kinaskan L., Canada . 50 B2
Kinbasket L., Canada . 50 C5
Kincardine, Canada .. 48 D3
Kincolith, Canada ... 50 B3
Kinder Scout, U.K. ... 8 D6
Kindersley, Canada .. 51 C7
Kindia, Guinea 34 F3
Kindu, Dem. Rep. of
the Congo 36 E5
Kineshma, Russia ... 18 C7
King, L., Australia ... 41 F2
King, Mt., Australia .. 42 D4
King City, U.S.A. 57 H3
King Cr. →, Australia . 42 C2
King Edward →,
Australia 40 B4
King Frederick VI
Land = Kong Frederik
VI Kyst, Greenland . 4 C5
King George B., Falk. Is. 64 G4
King George I.,
Antarctica 5 C18
King George Is., Canada 47 C11
King I. = Kadan Kyun,
Burma 26 B1
King I., Australia 42 F3
King I., Canada 50 C3
King Leopold Ranges,
Australia 40 C4
King Sd., Australia ... 40 C3
King William I., Canada 46 B10
Kingaok = Bathurst
Inlet, Canada 46 B9
Kingaroy, Australia .. 43 D5
Kingoonya, Australia . 43 E2
Kingfisher, U.S.A. ... 55 H6
Kingirbān, Iraq 30 C5
Kingisepp = Kuressaare,
Estonia 7 G20
Kingman, Ariz., U.S.A. 57 J6
Kingman, Kans., U.S.A. 55 G5
Kings →, U.S.A. 57 H4
Kings Canyon National
Park, U.S.A. 57 H4
King's Lynn, U.K. 8 E8
Kings Mountain, U.S.A. 53 H5
King's Peak, U.S.A. .. 56 F8
Kingsbridge, U.K. ... 9 G4

Kingsburg, U.S.A. 57 H4
Kingscote, Australia .. 43 F2
Kingsford, U.S.A. ... 52 C1
Kingsland, U.S.A. ... 53 K5
Kingsport, U.S.A. ... 53 G4
Kingston, Canada ... 48 D4
Kingston, Jamaica ... 60 C4
Kingston, N.Z. 39 L2
Kingston, N.Y., U.S.A. 52 E9
Kingston, Pa., U.S.A. . 52 E8
Kingston South East,
Australia 43 F2
Kingston upon Hull,
U.K. 8 D7
Kingston upon Hull □,
U.K. 8 D7
Kingston-upon-
Thames □, U.K. ... 9 F7
Kingstown, St. Vincent 61 D7
Kingstree, U.S.A. ... 53 J6
Kingsville, Canada .. 48 D3
Kingsville, U.S.A. ... 55 M6
Kingwood, U.S.A. ... 55 K7
Kınık, Turkey 17 E12
Kinistino, Canada ... 51 C7
Kinkala, Congo 36 E2
Kinki □, Japan 23 H8
Kinleith, N.Z. 39 H5
Kinna, Sweden 7 H15
Kinngait = Cape Dorset,
Canada 47 B12
Kino, Mexico 58 B2
Kinoje →, Canada .. 48 B3
Kinomoto, Japan ... 23 G8
Kinoosao, Canada .. 51 B8
Kinsale, Ireland 10 F2
Kinsha = Chang
Jiang →, China ... 25 C7
Kinshasa, Dem. Rep. of
the Congo 36 E3
Kinsley, U.S.A. 55 G5
Kinston, U.S.A. 53 H7
Kintore Ra., Australia . 40 D4
Kinushseo →, Canada 48 A3
Kinuso, Canada 50 B5
Kiosk, Canada 48 C4
Kiowa, Kans., U.S.A. . 55 G5
Kiowa, Okla., U.S.A. . 55 H7
Kipahigan L., Canada . 51 B8
Kiparissía, Greece ... 17 F9
Kiparissiakós Kólpos,
Greece 17 F9
Kipawa, L., Canada .. 48 C4
Kipling, Canada 51 C8
Kipushi, Dem. Rep. of
the Congo 37 G5
Kirensk, Russia 21 D11
Kirghizia =
Kyrgyzstan ■, Asia . 20 E8
Kirghizstan =
Kyrgyzstan ■, Asia . 20 E8
Kirgiziya Steppe,
Eurasia 19 E10
Kiribati ■, Pac. Oc. .. 38 B10
Kırıkkale, Turkey ... 19 G5
Kirillov, Russia 18 C6
Kirin = Jilin, China .. 25 B7
Kiritimati, Kiribati ... 45 G12
Kirkby, U.K. 8 D5
Kirkby Lonsdale, U.K. . 8 C5
Kirkcaldy, U.K. 10 C5
Kirkcudbright, U.K. .. 10 D4
Kirkee, India 28 K8
Kirkenes, Norway ... 6 B23
Kirkjubæjarklaustur,
Iceland 6 E4
Kirkkonummi, Finland . 7 F21
Kirkland Lake, Canada . 48 C3
Kırklareli, Turkey ... 17 D12
Kirksville, U.S.A. 54 E8
Kirkūk, Iraq 30 C5
Kirkwall, U.K. 10 B5
Kirov, Russia 18 C8
Kirovabad = Gäncä,
Azerbaijan 19 F8
Kirovakan = Vanadzor,
Armenia 19 F7
Kirovograd =
Kirovohrad, Ukraine . 19 E5
Kirovohrad, Ukraine . 19 E5
Kirovsk = Babadayhan,
Turkmenistan 20 F7
Kirovsk, Russia 18 A5
Kirovskiy, Kamchatka,
Russia 21 D16
Kirovskiy, Primorsk,
Russia 22 B6
Kirsanov, Russia ... 18 D7
Kırşehir, Turkey 19 G5
Kirthar Range, Pakistan 28 F5
Kirtland, U.S.A. 57 H9
Kiruna, Sweden 6 C19
Kiryū, Japan 23 F9
Kisalaya, Nic. 60 D3
Kisangani, Dem. Rep. of
the Congo 36 D5
Kisar, Indonesia 27 F7
Kishanganj, India ... 29 F16
Kishangarh, India ... 28 F7
Kishinev = Chişinău,
Moldova 13 E15
Kishiwada, Japan ... 23 G7
Kishtwar, India 28 C9

Kisii, Kenya 36 E6
Kiskőrös, Hungary ... 13 E10
Kiskunfélegyháza,
Hungary 13 E10
Kiskunhalas, Hungary . 13 E10
Kislovodsk, Russia .. 19 F7
Kiso-Gawa →, Japan . 23 G8
Kiso-Sammyaku, Japan 23 G8
Kisofukushima, Japan . 23 G8
Kissidougou, Guinea . 34 G3
Kissimmee, U.S.A. .. 53 L5
Kissimmee →, U.S.A. 53 M5
Kississing L., Canada . 51 B8
Kisumu, Kenya 36 E6
Kit Carson, U.S.A. .. 54 F3
Kita, Mali 34 F4
Kitaibaraki, Japan ... 23 F10
Kitakami, Japan 22 E10
Kitakami-Gawa →,
Japan 22 E10
Kitakami-Sammyaku,
Japan 22 E10
Kitakata, Japan 22 F9
Kitakyūshū, Japan .. 23 H5
Kitale, Kenya 36 D7
Kitami, Japan 22 C11
Kitami-Sammyaku,
Japan 22 B11
Kitchener, Canada .. 48 D3
Kitega = Gitega,
Burundi 36 E5
Kithira, Greece 17 F10
Kithnos, Greece 17 F11
Kitimat, Canada 50 C3
Kitinen →, Finland .. 6 C22
Kitsuki, Japan 23 H5
Kittakittaooloo, L.,
Australia 43 D2
Kittanning, U.S.A. .. 52 E6
Kittery, U.S.A. 53 D10
Kittilä, Finland 6 C21
Kitui, Kenya 36 E7
Kitwanga, Canada .. 50 B3
Kitwe, Zambia 37 G5
Kivarli, India 28 G8
Kivertsi, Ukraine ... 13 C13
Kivu, L., Dem. Rep. of
the Congo 36 E5
Kiyev = Kyyiv, Ukraine 13 C16
Kiyevskoye Vdkhr. =
Kyyivske Vdskh.,
Ukraine 13 C16
Kizel, Russia 18 C10
Kızıl Irmak →, Turkey 19 F6
Kızıltepe, Turkey ... 30 B4
Kizlyar, Russia 19 F8
Kizyl-Arvat =
Gyzylarbat,
Turkmenistan 20 F6
Kjölur, Iceland 6 D4
Kladno, Czech Rep. .. 12 C8
Klagenfurt, Austria .. 12 E8
Klaipeda, Lithuania .. 7 J19
Klaksvík, Færoe Is. .. 6 E9
Klamath →, U.S.A. .. 56 F1
Klamath Falls, U.S.A. . 56 E3
Klamath Mts., U.S.A. . 56 F2
Klamono, Indonesia . 27 E8
Klappan →, Canada . 50 B3
Klarälven →, Sweden 7 G15
Klatovy, Czech Rep. . 12 D7
Klazienaveen, Neths. . 11 B6
Kleena Kleene, Canada 50 C4
Klerksdorp, S. Africa . 37 K5
Kletsk = Klyetsk,
Belarus 13 B14
Kletskiy, Russia 19 E7
Klickitat, U.S.A. 56 D3
Klinaklini →, Canada . 50 C3
Kłodzko, Poland 13 C9
Klouto, Togo 34 G6
Kluane L., Canada .. 46 B6
Kluane Nat. Park,
Canada 50 A1
Kluczbork, Poland ... 13 C10
Klukwan, U.S.A. 50 B1
Klyetsk, Belarus 13 B14
Klyuchevskaya, Gora,
Russia 21 D17
Knaresborough, U.K. . 8 C6
Knee L., Man., Canada 48 A1
Knee L., Sask., Canada 51 B7
Knight Inlet, Canada . 50 C3
Knighton, U.K. 9 E4
Knob, C., Australia .. 41 F2
Knokke-Heist, Belgium 11 C3
Knossós, Greece 17 G11
Knox, U.S.A. 52 E2
Knox Coast, Antarctica 5 C8
Knoxville, Iowa, U.S.A. 54 E8
Knoxville, Tenn., U.S.A. 53 H4
Koartac = Quaqtaq,
Canada 47 B13
Koba, Indonesia 27 F8
Kobarid, Slovenia ... 12 E7
Kobayashi, Japan ... 23 J5
Kobdo = Hovd,
Mongolia 24 B4
Kōbe, Japan 23 G7
København, Denmark . 7 J15
Koblenz, Germany .. 12 C4
Kobryn, Belarus 13 B13
Kocaeli, Turkey 19 F4
Kočani, Macedonia .. 17 D10
Koch Bihar, India ... 29 F16

Kōchi, Japan 23 H6
Kōchi □, Japan 23 H6
Kochiu = Gejiu, China . 24 D5
Kodiak, U.S.A. 46 C4
Kodiak I., U.S.A. 46 C4
Kofiau, Indonesia ... 27 E7
Koforidua, Ghana ... 34 G5
Kōfu, Japan 23 G9
Koga, Japan 23 F9
Kogaluk →, Canada . 49 A7
Køge, Denmark 7 J15
Kohat, Pakistan 28 C7
Kohima, India 29 G19
Kohkīlūyeh va Būyer
Aḥmadi □, Iran ... 31 D6
Kohler Ra., Antarctica . 5 D15
Kohtla-Järve, Estonia . 7 G22
Koillismaa, Finland .. 6 D23
Kojonup, Australia .. 41 F2
Kojūr, Iran 31 B6
Kokand = Qŭqon,
Uzbekistan 20 E8
Kokas, Indonesia ... 27 E8
Kokchetav = Kökshetaū,
Kazakstan 20 D7
Kokemäenjoki →,
Finland 7 F19
Kokkola, Finland ... 6 E20
Koko Kyunzu, Burma . 29 M18
Kokomo, U.S.A. 52 E2
Kökshetaū, Kazakstan . 20 D7
Koksoak →, Canada . 47 C13
Kokstad, S. Africa ... 37 L5
Kokubu, Japan 23 J5
Kola, Indonesia 27 F8
Kola, Russia 18 A5
Kola Pen. = Kolskiy
Poluostrov, Russia . 18 A6
Kolaka, Indonesia ... 27 E6
Kolar, India 28 N11
Kolar Gold Fields, India 28 N11
Kolari, Finland 6 C20
Kolayat, India 28 F8
Kolchugino = Leninsk-
Kuznetskiy, Russia . 20 D9
Kolding, Denmark .. 7 J13
Kolepom = Dolak,
Pulau, Indonesia .. 27 F9
Kolguyev, Ostrov,
Russia 18 A8
Kolhapur, India 28 L9
Kolín, Czech Rep. ... 12 C8
Kolkas rags, Latvia .. 7 H20
Kolkata, India 29 H16
Kollum, Neths. 11 A6
Köln, Germany 12 C4
Koło, Poland 13 B10
Kołobrzeg, Poland .. 12 A8
Kolomna, Russia ... 18 C6
Kolomyya, Ukraine . 13 D13
Kolonodale, Indonesia . 27 E6
Kolosib, India 29 G18
Kolpashevo, Russia . 20 D9
Kolpino, Russia 18 C5
Kolskiy Poluostrov,
Russia 18 A6
Kolskiy Zaliv, Russia . 18 A5
Kolwezi, Dem. Rep. of
the Congo 36 G5
Kolyma →, Russia .. 21 C17
Kolymskoye Nagorye,
Russia 21 C16
Kôm Ombo, Egypt .. 35 D12
Komandorskiye Is. =
Komandorskiye
Ostrova, Russia ... 21 D17
Komandorskiye Ostrova,
Russia 21 D17
Komárno, Slovak Rep. . 13 E10
Komatsu, Japan 23 F8
Komatsujima, Japan . 23 H7
Komi □, Russia 18 B10
Kommunarsk =
Alchevsk, Ukraine . 19 E6
Kommunizma, Pik,
Tajikistan 20 F8
Komodo, Indonesia . 27 F5
Komoran, Pulau,
Indonesia 27 F9
Komoro, Japan 23 F9
Komotini, Greece ... 17 D11
Kompong Cham,
Cambodia 26 B3
Kompong Chhnang =
Kampang Chhnang,
Cambodia 26 B2
Kompong Som =
Kampong Saom,
Cambodia 26 B2
Kompong Som,
Chhung = Kampong
Saom, Chaak,
Canada 47 B13
Kompong Thom,
Cambodia 26 B2
Komrat = Comrat,
Moldova 13 E15
Komsomolets, Ostrov,
Russia 21 A10
Komsomolsk, Russia . 21 D14
Kon Tum, Vietnam .. 26 B3
Konarhā □, Afghan. .. 28 B7
Konch, India 28 G11
Kondinin, Australia .. 41 F2

Kondoa, Tanzania ... 36 E7
Kondopaga, Russia .. 18 B5
Kondratyevo, Russia . 21 D10
Köneürgench,
Turkmenistan 20 E6
Konevo, Russia 18 B6
Kong = Khong →,
Cambodia 26 B3
Kong, Ivory C. 34 G5
Kong, Koh, Cambodia . 26 B2
Kong Christian IX Land,
Greenland 4 C6
Kong Christian X Land,
Greenland 4 B6
Kong Frederik IX Land,
Greenland 4 C5
Kong Frederik VI Kyst,
Greenland 4 C5
Kong Frederik VIII Land,
Greenland 4 B6
Kong Oscar Fjord,
Greenland 4 B6
Konglu, Burma 29 F20
Kongolo, Dem. Rep. of
the Congo 36 F5
Kongsberg, Norway . 7 G13
Kongsvinger, Norway . 7 F15
Königsberg =
Kaliningrad, Russia . 7 J19
Konin, Poland 13 B10
Konjic, Bos.-H. 17 C7
Konosha, Russia ... 18 B7
Kōnosu, Japan 23 F9
Konotop, Ukraine .. 19 D5
Końskie, Poland 13 C11
Konstanz, Germany . 12 E5
Kont, Iran 31 E9
Kontagora, Nigeria .. 34 F7
Konya, Turkey 19 G5
Koocanusa, L., Canada 56 B6
Kookynie, Australia .. 41 E3
Koolyanobbing,
Australia 41 F2
Koonibba, Australia .. 43 E1
Koorawatha, Australia . 43 E4
Koorda, Australia ... 41 F2
Kooskia, U.S.A. 56 C6
Kootenay →, U.S.A. . 50 D5
Kootenay L., Canada . 50 D5
Kootenay Nat. Park,
Canada 50 C5
Kopaonik, Yugoslavia . 17 C9
Kópavogur, Iceland . 6 D3
Koper, Slovenia 12 F7
Kopervik, Norway ... 7 G11
Kopet Dagh, Asia ... 31 B8
Kopi, Australia 43 E2
Köping, Sweden 7 G17
Koppeh Dāgh = Kopet
Dagh, Asia 31 B8
Koprivnica, Croatia .. 16 A7
Kopychyntsi, Ukraine . 13 D13
Korab, Macedonia .. 17 D9
Korça = Korçë, Albania 17 D9
Korce = Korçë, Albania 17 D9
Korçë, Albania 17 D9
Korčula, Croatia 16 C7
Kord Kūy, Iran 31 B7
Kord Sheykh, Iran .. 31 D7
Kordestān □, Iran ... 30 C5
Kordofân, Sudan ... 35 F11
Korea, North ■, Asia . 25 C7
Korea, South ■, Asia . 25 C7
Korea Bay, Korea ... 25 C7
Korea Strait, Asia ... 25 C7
Korets, Ukraine 13 C14
Korhogo, Ivory C. ... 34 G4
Korinthiakós Kólpos,
Greece 17 E10
Kórinthos, Greece .. 17 F10
Kōriyama, Japan ... 22 F10
Korla, China 24 B3
Korneshty = Corneşti,
Moldova 13 E15
Koro, Fiji 39 C8
Koro, Ivory C. 34 G4
Koro Sea, Fiji 39 C9
Korogwe, Tanzania .. 36 F7
Koronadal, Phil. 27 C6
Koror, Palau 27 C8
Körös →, Hungary .. 13 E11
Korosten, Ukraine .. 13 C15
Korostyshev, Ukraine . 13 C15
Korsakov, Russia ... 21 E15
Korshunovo, Russia . 21 D12
Korsør, Denmark ... 7 J14
Kortrijk, Belgium ... 11 D3
Koryakskoye Nagorye,
Russia 21 C18
Kos, Greece 17 F12
Koschagyl, Kazakstan . 19 E9
Kościan, Poland ... 13 B9
Kosciusko, U.S.A. .. 55 J10
Kosciuszko, Mt.,
Australia 43 F4
Kosha, Sudan 35 D12
K'oshih = Kashi, China 24 C2
Koshiki-Rettō, Japan . 23 J4
Košice, Slovak Rep. . 13 D11
Koslan, Russia 18 B8
Kosovo □, Yugoslavia . 17 C9
Kosovska Mitrovica,
Kosovo, Yug. 17 C9
Kossou, L. de, Ivory C. 34 G4
Kôstî, Sudan 35 F12

Kostopil, Ukraine 13 C14
Kostroma, Russia 18 C7
Kostrzyn, Poland 12 B8
Koszalin, Poland 12 A9
Kota, India 28 G9
Kota Baharu, Malaysia 26 C2
Kota Belud, Malaysia . 26 C5
Kota Kinabalu, Malaysia 26 C5
Kota Kubu Baharu,
  Malaysia 26 D2
Kota Tinggi, Malaysia . 26 D2
Kotabaru, Indonesia ... 26 E5
Kotabumi, Indonesia .. 26 E2
Kotamobagu, Indonesia 27 D6
Kotcho L., Canada 50 B4
Kotelnich, Russia 18 C8
Kotelnikovo, Russia ... 19 E7
Kotelnyy, Ostrov, Russia 21 B14
Kotka, Finland 7 F22
Kotlas, Russia 18 B8
Kotor,
  Montenegro, Yug. .. 17 C8
Kotovsk, Ukraine 13 E15
Kotri, Pakistan 28 G6
Kotturu, India 28 M10
Kotuy →, Russia 21 B11
Kotzebue, U.S.A. 46 B3
Koudougou,
  Burkina Faso 34 F5
Kouilou →, Congo .. 36 E2
Koula Moutou, Gabon . 36 E2
Koulen = Kulen,
  Cambodia 26 B2
Koumala, Australia ... 42 C4
Koumra, Chad 35 G9
Kounradskiy, Kazakstan 20 E8
Kountze, U.S.A. 55 K7
Kourou, Fr. Guiana ... 63 B8
Kousseri, Cameroon .. 35 F8
Kouvola, Finland 7 F22
Kovdor, Russia 18 A5
Kovel, Ukraine 13 C13
Kovrov, Russia 18 C7
Kowanyama, Australia 42 B3
Köyceğiz, Turkey 17 F13
Koza, Japan 23 L3
Kozan, Turkey 30 B2
Kozáni, Greece 17 D9
Kozhikode = Calicut,
  India 28 P9
Kozhva, Russia 18 A10
Kozyatyn, Ukraine ... 13 D15
Kra, Isthmus of = Kra,
  Kho Khot, Thailand 26 B1
Kra, Kho Khot, Thailand 26 B1
Kracheh, Cambodia ... 26 B3
Kragan, Indonesia ... 27 G14
Kragerø, Norway ... 7 G13
Kragujevac, Serbia, Yug. 17 B9
Krajina, Bos.-H. 16 B7
Krakatau = Rakata,
  Pulau, Indonesia ... 26 F3
Krakatoa = Rakata,
  Pulau, Indonesia ... 26 F3
Kraków, Poland 13 C10
Kraljevo, Serbia, Yug. . 17 C9
Kramatorsk, Ukraine .. 19 E6
Kramfors, Sweden ... 7 E17
Kranj, Slovenia 12 E8
Krasavino, Russia 18 B8
Kraskino, Russia 21 E14
Kraśnik, Poland 13 C12
Krasnoarmeysk, Russia 19 D5
Krasnodar, Russia 19 E6
Krasnokamsk, Russia . 18 C10
Krasnoperekopsk,
  Ukraine 19 E5
Krasnorechenskiy,
  Russia 22 B7
Krasnoselkup, Russia . 20 C9
Krasnoturinsk, Russia . 18 C11
Krasnouralsk, Russia . 18 C10
Krasnoufimsk, Russia . 18 C10
Krasnousolskiy, Russia 18 D10
Krasnovishersk, Russia 18 B10
Krasnovodsk =
  Türkmenbashi,
  Turkmenistan 19 G9
Krasnoyarsk, Russia .. 21 D10
Krasnyy Kut, Russia .. 19 D8
Krasnyy Luch, Ukraine 19 E6
Krasnyy Yar, Russia .. 19 E8
Kratie = Kracheh,
  Cambodia 26 B3
Krau, Indonesia 27 E10
Krefeld, Germany 12 C4
Kremen, Croatia 12 F8
Kremenchug =
  Kremenchuk, Ukraine 19 E5
Kremenchuk, Ukraine . 19 E5
Kremenchuksk Vdskh.,
  Ukraine 19 E5
Kremenets, Ukraine .. 13 C13
Kremmling, U.S.A. ... 56 F10
Krems, Austria 12 D8
Kretinga, Lithuania ... 9 J19
Kribi, Cameroon 36 D1
Krichev = Krychaw,
  Belarus 13 B16
Krishna →, India ... 29 M12
Krishnanagar, India .. 29 H16
Kristiansand, Norway . 7 G13
Kristianstad, Sweden . 7 H16
Kristiansund, Norway . 6 E12

Kristiinankaupunki,
  Finland 7 E19
Kristinehamn, Sweden 7 G16
Kristinestad =
  Kristiinankaupunki,
  Finland 7 E19
Kríti, Greece 17 G11
Krivoy Rog = Kryvyy
  Rih, Ukraine 19 E5
Krk, Croatia 12 F8
Krong Kaoh Kong,
  Cambodia 26 B2
Kronprins Olav Kyst,
  Antarctica 5 C5
Kronshtadt, Russia ... 18 B4
Kroonstad, S. Africa .. 37 K5
Kropotkin, Russia 19 E7
Krosno, Poland 13 D11
Krotoszyn, Poland ... 13 C9
Krung Thep = Bangkok,
  Thailand 26 B2
Krupki, Belarus 13 A15
Kruševac, Serbia, Yug. 17 C9
Krychaw, Belarus 13 B16
Krymskyy Poluostrov =
  Krymskyy Pivostriv,
  Ukraine 19 F5
Krymskyy Pivostriv,
  Ukraine 19 F5
Kryvyy Rih, Ukraine .. 19 E5
Ksar el Kebir, Morocco 34 B4
Ksar es Souk = Ar
  Rachidiya, Morocco . 34 B5
Kuala Belait, Malaysia . 26 D4
Kuala Lipis, Malaysia .. 26 D2
Kuala Lumpur, Malaysia 26 D2
Kuala Sepetang,
  Malaysia 26 D2
Kuala Terengganu,
  Malaysia 26 C2
Kualajelai, Indonesia .. 26 E4
Kualakapuas, Indonesia 26 E4
Kualakurun, Indonesia . 26 E4
Kualapembuang,
  Indonesia 26 E4
Kualasimpang,
  Indonesia 26 D1
Kuandang, Indonesia . 27 D6
Kuangchou =
  Guangzhou, China .. 25 D6
Kuantan, Malaysia ... 26 D2
Kuba = Quba,
  Azerbaijan 19 F8
Kuban →, Russia ... 19 E6
Kubokawa, Japan 23 H6
Kuching, Malaysia ... 26 D4
Kuchino-eruba-Jima,
  Japan 23 J5
Kuchino-Shima, Japan 23 K4
Kuchinotsu, Japan ... 23 H5
Kucing = Kuching,
  Malaysia 26 D4
Kuda, India 28 H7
Kudat, Malaysia 26 C5
Kudus, Indonesia 27 G14
Kudymkar, Russia ... 18 C9
Kueiyang = Guiyang,
  China 24 D5
Kufra Oasis = Al Kufrah,
  Libya 35 D10
Kufstein, Austria 12 E7
Kugluktuk, Canada ... 46 B8
Kugong I., Canada ... 48 A4
Kūhbonān, Iran 31 D8
Kühestak, Iran 31 E8
Kuhin, Iran 31 B6
Kūhīrī, Iran 31 E9
Kühpāyeh, Eşfahan, Iran 31 C7
Kühpāyeh, Kermān, Iran 31 D8
Kührān, Kūh-e, Iran .. 31 E8
Kuito, Angola 37 G3
Kuiu I., U.S.A. 50 B2
Kuji, Japan 22 D10
Kujū-San, Japan 23 H5
Kukës, Albania 17 C9
Kukësi = Kukës, Albania 17 C9
Kula, Turkey 17 E13
Kulasekarappattinam,
  India 28 Q11
Kuldiga, Latvia 7 H19
Kuldja = Yining, China 20 E9
Kulen, Cambodia 26 B2
Kulgera, Australia ... 42 D1
Kulin, Australia 41 F2
Kulob, Tajikistan 20 F7
Kulsary, Kazakstan ... 19 E9
Kulumbura, Australia . 40 B4
Kulunda, Russia 20 D8
Külvand, Iran 31 D7
Kulwin, Australia 43 F3
Kulyab = Kūlob,
  Tajikistan 20 F7
Kuma →, Russia ... 19 F8
Kumagaya, Japan 23 F9
Kumai, Indonesia 26 E4
Kumamba, Kepulauan,
  Indonesia 27 E9
Kumamoto, Japan ... 23 H5
Kumamoto □, Japan . 23 H5
Kumanovo, Macedonia 17 C9
Kumara, N.Z. 39 K3
Kumarina, Australia .. 41 D2
Kumasi, Ghana 34 G5

Kumayri = Gyumri,
  Armenia 19 F7
Kumba, Cameroon ... 36 D1
Kumbakonam, India .. 28 P11
Kumbarilla, Australia .. 43 D5
Kumbia, Australia 43 D5
Kume-Shima, Japan .. 23 L3
Kumertau, Russia 18 D10
Kumla, Sweden 7 G16
Kumo, Nigeria 35 F8
Kumon Bum, Burma . 29 F20
Kunashir, Ostrov, Russia 21 E15
Kunda, Estonia 7 G22
Kunghit I., Canada ... 50 C2
Kungrad = Qŭnghirot,
  Uzbekistan 20 E6
Kungsbacka, Sweden . 7 H15
Kungur, Russia 18 C10
Kuningan, Indonesia .. 27 G13
Kunlong, Burma 29 H21
Kunlun Shan, Asia ... 24 C3
Kunming, China 24 D5
Kununurra, Australia . 40 C4
Kunya-Urgench =
  Köneürgench,
  Turkmenistan 20 E6
Kuopio, Finland 6 E22
Kupa →, Croatia ... 12 F9
Kupang, Indonesia ... 27 F6
Kupreanof I., U.S.A. .. 50 B2
Kupyansk-Uzlovoi,
  Ukraine 19 E6
Kuqa, China 24 B3
Kür →, Azerbaijan .. 19 G8
Kür Dili, Azerbaijan .. 31 B6
Kura = Kür →,
  Azerbaijan 19 G8
Kuranda, Australia ... 42 B4
Kurashiki, Japan 23 G6
Kurayoshi, Japan 23 G6
Kürdzhali, Bulgaria .. 17 D11
Kure, Japan 23 G6
Kuressaare, Estonia .. 7 G20
Kurgan, Russia 20 D7
Kuria Maria Is. =
  Khurīyā Murīyā, Jazā
  'ir, Oman 32 D6
Kuridala, Australia ... 42 C3
Kurigram, Bangla. ... 29 G16
Kurikka, Finland 7 E20
Kuril Is. = Kurilskiye
  Ostrova, Russia ... 21 E15
Kuril Trench, Pac. Oc. . 44 C7
Kurilsk, Russia 21 E15
Kurilskiye Ostrova,
  Russia 21 E15
Kurino, Japan 23 J5
Kurinskaya Kosa = Kür
  Dili, Azerbaijan 31 B6
Kurnool, India 28 M11
Kuro-Shima, Japan .. 23 J4
Kuro-Shima, Okinawa,
  Japan 23 M2
Kurow, N.Z. 39 L3
Kurri Kurri, Australia .. 43 E5
Kurrimine, Australia .. 42 B4
Kurshskiy Zaliv, Russia 7 J19
Kursk, Russia 18 D6
Kuruçay, Turkey 30 B3
Kuruktag, China 24 B3
Kuruman, S. Africa .. 37 K4
Kurume, Japan 23 H5
Kurunegala, Sri Lanka . 28 R12
Kurya, Russia 18 B10
Kuş Gölü, Turkey ... 17 D12
Kuşadası, Turkey 17 F12
Kusatsu, Japan 23 F9
Kusawa L., Canada .. 50 A1
Kushikino, Japan 23 J5
Kushima, Japan 23 J5
Kushimoto, Japan ... 23 H7
Kushiro, Japan 22 C12
Kushiro-Gawa →,
  Japan 22 C12
Kūshk, Iran 31 D8
Kushka = Gushgy,
  Turkmenistan 20 F7
Kūshkī, Iran 30 C5
Kushtia, Bangla. 29 H16
Kushva, Russia 18 C10
Kuskokwim B., U.S.A. 46 C3
Kussharo-Ko, Japan .. 22 C12
Kustanay = Qostanay,
  Kazakstan 20 D7
Kut, Ko, Thailand ... 26 B2
Kütahya, Turkey 19 G5
Kutaisi, Georgia 19 F7
Kutaraja = Banda Aceh,
  Indonesia 26 C1
Kutch, Gulf of =
  Kachchh, Gulf of,
  India 28 H6
Kutch, Rann of =
  Kachchh, Rann of,
  India 28 H7
Kutno, Poland 13 B10
Kutu, Dem. Rep. of
  the Congo 36 E3
Kutum, Sudan 35 F10
Kuujjuaq, Canada ... 47 C13
Kuujjuarapik, Canada . 48 A4
Kuusamo, Finland ... 6 D23
Kuusankoski, Finland . 7 F22

Kuwait = Al Kuwayt,
  Kuwait 30 D5
Kuwait ■, Asia 30 D5
Kuwana, Japan 23 G8
Kuybyshev = Samara,
  Russia 18 D9
Kuybyshev, Russia ... 20 D8
Kuybyshevskoye Vdkhr.,
  Russia 18 C8
Küyeh, Iran 30 B5
Küysanjaq, Iraq 30 B5
Kuyto, Ozero, Russia . 18 B5
Kuyumba, Russia 21 C10
Kuzey Anadolu Dağları,
  Turkey 19 F6
Kuznetsk, Russia 18 D8
Kuzomen, Russia 18 A6
Kvænangen, Norway . 6 A19
Kvaløy, Norway 6 B18
Kvarner, Croatia 12 F8
Kvarnerič, Croatia ... 12 F8
Kwa-Nobuhle, S. Africa 37 L5
Kwakoegron, Surinam . 63 B7
KwaMashu, S. Africa . 37 K6
Kwando →, Africa .. 37 H4
Kwangju, S. Korea ... 25 C7
Kwangsi-Chuang =
  Guangxi Zhuangzu
  Zizhiqu □, China ... 25 D5
Kwangtung =
  Guangdong □, China 25 D6
Kwataboahegan →,
  Canada 48 B3
Kwatisore, Indonesia . 27 E8
Kweichow = Guizhou □,
  China 24 D5
Kwekwe, Zimbabwe . 37 H5
Kwidzyn, Poland 13 B10
Kwinana New Town,
  Australia 41 F2
Kwoka, Indonesia ... 27 E8
Kyabra Cr. →,
  Australia 43 D3
Kyabram, Australia .. 43 F4
Kyakhta, Russia 21 D11
Kyancutta, Australia .. 43 E2
Kyaukpadaung, Burma 29 J19
Kyaukpyu, Burma ... 29 K18
Kyaukse, Burma 29 J20
Kyle, Canada 51 C7
Kymijoki →, Finland . 7 F22
Kyneton, Australia ... 43 F3
Kynuna, Australia ... 42 C3
Kyō-ga-Saki, Japan .. 23 G7
Kyogle, Australia 43 D5
Kyoga, L., Uganda ... 36 D6
Kyongpyaw, Burma .. 29 L19
Kyōto, Japan 23 G7
Kyōto □, Japan 23 G7
Kyrenia, Cyprus 30 C2
Kyrgyzstan ■, Asia .. 20 E8
Kyrönjoki →, Finland . 6 E19
Kystatyam, Russia ... 21 C13
Kyunhla, Burma 29 H19
Kyuquot Sound, Canada 50 D3
Kyūshū, Japan 23 H5
Kyūshū □, Japan 23 H5
Kyūshū-Sanchi, Japan 23 H5
Kyustendil, Bulgaria .. 17 C10
Kyusyur, Russia 21 B13
Kyyiv, Ukraine 13 C16
Kyyivske Vdskh.,
  Ukraine 13 C16
Kyzyl, Russia 21 D10
Kyzyl Kum, Uzbekistan 20 E7
Kyzyl-Kyya, Kyrgyzstan 20 E8
Kzyl-Orda = Qyzylorda,
  Kazakstan 20 E7

La Alcarria, Spain 15 B4
La Asunción, Venezuela 62 A6
La Baie, Canada 49 C5
La Banda, Argentina .. 64 B4
La Barca, Mexico 58 C4
La Barge, U.S.A. 56 E8
La Belle, U.S.A. 53 M5
La Biche →, Canada . 50 B4
La Biche, L., Canada . 50 C6
La Bomba, Mexico ... 58 A1
La Carlota, Argentina . 64 C4
La Ceiba, Honduras .. 60 C2
La Chaux-de-Fonds,
  Switz. 14 C7
La Chorrera, Panama . 60 E4
La Cocha, Argentina .. 64 B3
La Concepción, Panama 60 E3
La Concordia, Mexico . 59 D6
La Coruña = A Coruña,
  Spain 15 A1
La Crescent, U.S.A. .. 54 D9
La Crete, Canada 50 B5
La Crosse, Kans., U.S.A. 54 F5
La Crosse, Wis., U.S.A. 54 D9
La Cruz, Costa Rica .. 60 D2
La Cruz, Mexico 58 C3
La Désirade,
  Guadeloupe 61 C7
La Escondida, Mexico . 58 C5
La Esperanza, Cuba .. 60 B3
La Esperanza, Honduras 60 D2
La Estrada = A Estrada,
  Spain 15 A1
La Fayette, U.S.A. ... 53 H3
La Fé, Cuba 60 B3

La Follette, U.S.A. ... 53 G3
La Grande, U.S.A. ... 56 D4
La Grande →, Canada 48 B5
La Grande Deux, Rés.,
  Canada 48 B4
La Grande Quatre, Rés.,
  Canada 48 B5
La Grande Trois, Rés.,
  Canada 48 B4
La Grange, Ga., U.S.A. 53 J3
La Grange, Ky., U.S.A. 52 F3
La Grange, Tex., U.S.A. 55 L6
La Guaira, Venezuela . 62 A5
La Habana, Cuba 60 B3
La Independencia,
  Mexico 59 D6
La Isabela, Dom. Rep. . 61 C5
La Junta, U.S.A. 55 F3
La Libertad, Guatemala 60 C1
La Libertad, Mexico .. 58 B2
La Línea de la
  Concepción, Spain .. 15 D3
La Loche, Canada ... 51 B7
La Louvière, Belgium . 11 D4
La Malbaie, Canada .. 49 C5
La Mancha, Spain ... 15 C4
La Martre, L., Canada 50 A5
La Mesa, U.S.A. 57 K5
La Misión, Mexico ... 58 A1
La Moure, U.S.A. ... 54 B5
La Oroya, Peru 62
La Palma, Canary Is. . 34 C2
La Palma, Panama ... 60 E4
La Palma del Condado,
  Spain 15 D2
La Paragua, Venezuela 62 B6
La Paz, Entre Ríos,
  Argentina 64 C5
La Paz, San Luis,
  Argentina 64 C3
La Paz, Bolivia 62 G5
La Paz, Honduras ... 60 D2
La Paz, Mexico 58 C2
La Paz Centro, Nic. .. 60 D2
La Pedrera, Colombia . 62 D5
La Pérade, Canada ... 49 C5
La Perouse Str., Asia .. 22 B11
La Pesca, Mexico 59 C5
La Piedad, Mexico ... 58 C4
La Pine, U.S.A. 56 E3
La Plata, Argentina .. 64 D5
La Pocatière, Canada . 49 C5
La Porte, Ind., U.S.A. . 52 E2
La Porte, Tex., U.S.A. . 55 L7
La Purísima, Mexico .. 58 B2
La Push, U.S.A. 56 C1
La Quiaca, Argentina . 62 H5
La Rioja, Argentina .. 64 B3
La Rioja □, Spain ... 15 A4
La Robla, Spain 15 A3
La Roche-en-Ardenne,
  Belgium 11 D5
La Roche-sur-Yon,
  France 14 C3
La Rochelle, France .. 14 C3
La Roda, Spain 15 C4
La Romana, Dom. Rep. 61 C6
La Ronge, Canada ... 51 B7
La Salle, U.S.A. 54 E10
La Sarre, Canada 48 C4
La Scie, Canada 49 C8
La Serena, Chile 64 B2
La Seu d'Urgell, Spain 15 A6
La Seyne-sur-Mer,
  France 14 E6
La Soufrière, St. Vincent 61 D7
La Spézia, Italy 14 D8
La Tagua, Colombia .. 62 C4
La Tortuga, Venezuela 62 A5
La Tuque, Canada ... 48 C5
La Unión, Chile 64 E2
La Unión, El Salv. ... 60 D2
La Unión, Mexico 58 D4
La Urbana, Venezuela 62 B5
La Vall d'Uixó, Spain . 15 C5
La Vega, Dom. Rep. .. 61 C5
La Vela de Coro,
  Venezuela 62 A5
La Venta, Mexico 59 D6
La Ventura, Mexico .. 58 C4
Labe = Elbe →,
  Europe 12 B5
Labé, Guinea 34 F3
Laberge, L., Canada .. 50 A1
Labinsk, Russia 19 F7
Laboulaye, Argentina . 64 C4
Labrador, Canada ... 49 B7
Labrador City, Canada 49 B6
Labrador Sea, Atl. Oc. . 47 C14
Lábrea, Brazil 62 E6
Labuan, Malaysia ... 26 C5
Labuan, Pulau, Malaysia 26 C5
Labuha, Indonesia ... 27 E7
Labuhan, Indonesia .. 27 G11
Labuhanbajo, Indonesia 27 F6
Labuk, Telok, Malaysia 26 C5
Labytnangi, Russia ... 20 C7
Labyrinth, L., Australia 43 E2
Lac Bouchette, Canada 49 C5
Lac Edouard, Canada . 48 C5
Lac La Biche, Canada . 50 C6
Lac la Martre = Wha Ti,
  Canada 46 B8
Lac La Ronge Prov.
  Park, Canada 51 B7

Lac-Mégantic, Canada . 49 C5
Lac Seul, Res., Canada 48 B1
Lacanau, France 14 D3
Lacantún →, Mexico 59 D6
Laccadive Is. =
  Lakshadweep Is.,
  Ind. Oc. 3 D13
Lacepede B., Australia . 43 F2
Lacepede Is., Australia 40 C3
Lachine, Canada 48 C5
Lachlan →, Australia . 43 E3
Lachute, Canada 48 C5
Lacombe, Canada ... 50 C6
Laconia, U.S.A. 52 D10
Ladakh Ra., India ... 28 C11
Lādiz, Iran 31 D9
Ladoga, L. =
  Ladozhskoye Ozero,
  Russia 18 B5
Ladozhskoye Ozero,
  Russia 18 B5
Lady Elliott I., Australia 42 C5
Ladysmith, Canada .. 50 D4
Ladysmith, S. Africa . 37 K5
Ladysmith, U.S.A. ... 54 C9
Lae, Papua N. G. 38 B7
Læsø, Denmark 7 H14
Lafayette, Colo., U.S.A. 54 F2
Lafayette, Ind., U.S.A. 52 E2
Lafayette, La., U.S.A. . 55 K9
Lafayette, Tenn., U.S.A. 53 G2
Laferte →, Canada .. 50 A5
Lafia, Nigeria 34 G7
Lafleche, Canada 51 D7
Lagarfljót →, Iceland . 6 D6
Lågen →, Oppland,
  Norway 7 F14
Lågen →, Vestfold,
  Norway 7 G14
Laghouat, Algeria 34 B6
Lagonoy G., Phil. 27 B6
Lagos, Nigeria 34 G6
Lagos, Portugal 15 D1
Lagos de Moreno,
  Mexico 58 C4
Lagrange, Australia .. 40 C3
Lagrange B., Australia 40 C3
Laguna, Brazil 64 B7
Laguna, U.S.A. 57 J10
Lagunas, Chile 64 A3
Lagunas, Peru 62 E3
Lahad Datu, Malaysia . 27 C5
Lahad Datu, Teluk,
  Malaysia 27 D5
Lahat, Indonesia 26 E2
Lahewa, Indonesia ... 26 D1
Lāhījān, Iran 31 B6
Lahn →, Germany .. 12 C4
Laholm, Sweden 7 H15
Lahore, Pakistan 28 D9
Lahti, Finland 7 F21
Lahtis = Lahti, Finland 7 F21
Laï, Chad 35 G9
Laila = Laylá, Si. Arabia 32 C4
Lainio älv →, Sweden 6 C20
Lairg, U.K. 10 B4
Laizhou, China 25 C6
Laja →, Mexico 58 C4
Lajes, Brazil 64 B6
Lake Andes, U.S.A. .. 54 D5
Lake Anse, U.S.A. ... 55 K8
Lake Cargelligo,
  Australia 43 E4
Lake Charles, U.S.A. . 55 K8
Lake City, Colo., U.S.A. 57 G10
Lake City, Fla., U.S.A. . 53 K4
Lake City, Mich., U.S.A. 52 C3
Lake City, Minn., U.S.A. 54 C8
Lake City, S.C., U.S.A. 53 J6
Lake Cowichan, Canada 50 D4
Lake District, U.K. ... 8 C4
Lake Grace, Australia . 41 F2
Lake Harbour =
  Kimmirut, Canada .. 47 B13
Lake Havasu City, U.S.A. 57 J6
Lake Jackson, U.S.A. . 55 L7
Lake Junction, U.S.A. . 56 D8
Lake King, Australia .. 41 F2
Lake Lenore, Canada . 51 C8
Lake Louise, Canada . 50 C5
Lake Mead National
  Recreation Area,
  U.S.A. 57 J6
Lake Mills, U.S.A. ... 54 D8
Lake Providence, U.S.A. 55 J9
Lake Superior Prov.
  Park, Canada 48 C3
Lake Village, U.S.A. .. 55 J9
Lake Wales, U.S.A. .. 53 M5
Lake Worth, U.S.A. .. 53 M5
Lakefield, Canada ... 48 D4
Lakeland, Australia .. 42 B3
Lakeland, U.S.A. 53 M5
Lakemba, Fiji 39 D9
Lakeport, U.S.A. 56 G2
Lakes Entrance,
  Australia 43 F4
Lakeside, Ariz., U.S.A. 57 J9
Lakeside, Nebr., U.S.A. 54 D3
Lakeview, U.S.A. 56 E3
Lakeville, U.S.A. 54 C8
Lakewood, Ohio, U.S.A. 52 E5
Lakin, U.S.A. 55 G4
Lakitusaki →, Canada 48 B3

Lakonikós Kólpos, Greece ... 17 F10
Lakor, Indonesia ... 27 F7
Lakota, Ivory C. ... 34 G4
Lakota, U.S.A. ... 54 A5
Laksefjorden, Norway ... 6 A22
Lakselv, Norway ... 6 A21
Lakshadweep Is., Ind. Oc. ... 3 D13
Lala Ghat, India ... 29 G18
L'Albufera, Spain ... 15 C5
Lālī, Iran ... 31 C6
Lalibela, Ethiopia ... 32 E2
Lalín, Spain ... 15 A1
Lamaing, Burma ... 29 M20
Lamar, Colo., U.S.A. ... 54 F3
Lamar, Mo., U.S.A. ... 55 G7
Lamas, Peru ... 62 E3
Lambaréné, Gabon ... 36 E2
Lambasa, Fiji ... 39 C8
Lambert Glacier, Antarctica ... 5 D6
Lambi Kyun, Burma ... 26 B1
Lame Deer, U.S.A. ... 56 D10
Lamego, Portugal ... 15 B2
Lamèque, Canada ... 49 C7
Lameroo, Australia ... 43 F3
Lamesa, U.S.A. ... 55 J4
Lamía, Greece ... 17 E10
Lamon B., Phil. ... 27 B6
Lamont, Canada ... 50 C6
Lamont, U.S.A. ... 56 E10
Lampa, Peru ... 62 G4
Lampasas, U.S.A. ... 55 K5
Lampazos de Naranjo, Mexico ... 58 B4
Lampedusa, Medit. S. ... 16 G5
Lampeter, U.K. ... 9 E3
Lampione, Medit. S. ... 16 G5
Lampman, Canada ... 51 D8
Lampung □, Indonesia ... 26 F2
Lamu, Kenya ... 36 E8
Lamy, U.S.A. ... 57 J11
Lanak La, India ... 28 B11
Lanak'o Shank'ou = Lanak La, India ... 28 B11
Lancang Jiang →, China ... 24 D5
Lancashire □, U.K. ... 8 D5
Lancaster, U.K. ... 8 C5
Lancaster, Calif., U.S.A. ... 57 J4
Lancaster, Ky., U.S.A. ... 52 G3
Lancaster, N.H., U.S.A. ... 52 C10
Lancaster, Ohio, U.S.A. ... 52 F4
Lancaster, Pa., U.S.A. ... 52 E7
Lancaster, S.C., U.S.A. ... 53 H5
Lancaster, Wis., U.S.A. ... 54 D9
Lancaster Sd., Canada ... 47 A11
Lancelin, Australia ... 41 F2
Lanchow = Lanzhou, China ... 24 C5
Lanciano, Italy ... 16 C6
Landeck, Austria ... 12 E6
Lander, U.S.A. ... 56 E9
Lander →, Australia ... 40 D5
Landes, France ... 14 D3
Landi Kotal, Pakistan ... 28 B7
Land's End, U.K. ... 9 G2
Landsborough Cr. →, Australia ... 42 C3
Landshut, Germany ... 12 D7
Landskrona, Sweden ... 7 J15
Lanett, U.S.A. ... 53 J3
La'nga Co, China ... 29 D12
Langar, Iran ... 31 C9
Langara I., Canada ... 50 C2
Langdon, U.S.A. ... 54 A5
Langeland, Denmark ... 7 J14
Langeberg, Canada ... 51 C8
Langenburg, Canada ... 51 C8
Langjökull, Iceland ... 6 D3
Langkawi, Pulau, Malaysia ... 26 C1
Langkon, Malaysia ... 26 C5
Langlade, St- P. & M. ... 49 C8
Langøya, Norway ... 6 B16
Langreo, Spain ... 15 A3
Langres, France ... 14 C6
Langres, Plateau de, France ... 14 C6
Langsa, Indonesia ... 26 D1
Langtry, U.S.A. ... 55 L4
Languedoc, France ... 14 E5
Lanigan, Canada ... 51 C7
Länkäran, Azerbaijan ... 19 G8
Lannion, France ... 14 B2
L'Annonciation, Canada ... 48 C5
Lansdowne, Australia ... 43 E5
Lansdowne House, Canada ... 48 B2
L'Anse, U.S.A. ... 52 B1
L'Anse au Loup, Canada ... 49 B8
L'Anse aux Meadows, Canada ... 49 B8
Lansing, U.S.A. ... 52 D3
Lanusei, Italy ... 16 E3
Lanzarote, Canary Is. ... 34 C3
Lanzhou, China ... 24 C5
Laoag, Phil. ... 27 A6
Laoang, Phil. ... 27 B7
Laon, France ... 14 B5
Laona, U.S.A. ... 52 C1
Laos ■, Asia ... 26 D4
Lapeer, U.S.A. ... 52 D4

Lappeenranta, Finland ... 7 F23
Lappland, Europe ... 6 B21
Lapseki, Turkey ... 17 D12
Laptev Sea, Russia ... 21 B13
Lapua, Finland ... 6 E20
L'Aquila, Italy ... 16 C5
Lār, Āzarbāyjān-e Sharqī, Iran ... 30 B5
Lār, Fārs, Iran ... 31 E7
Laramie, U.S.A. ... 54 E2
Laramie →, U.S.A. ... 56 F11
Laramie Mts., U.S.A. ... 54 E2
Larantuka, Indonesia ... 27 F6
Larat, Indonesia ... 27 F8
Larder Lake, Canada ... 48 C4
Laredo, U.S.A. ... 55 M5
Laredo Sd., Canada ... 50 C3
Largo, U.S.A. ... 53 M4
Largs, U.K. ... 10 F3
Lariang, Indonesia ... 27 E5
Larimore, U.S.A. ... 54 B6
Lārīn, Iran ... 31 C7
Lárisa, Greece ... 17 E10
Larnaca, Cyprus ... 30 C2
Larne, U.K. ... 10 D4
Larned, U.S.A. ... 54 F5
Larose, U.S.A. ... 55 L9
Larrimah, Australia ... 40 C5
Larsen Ice Shelf, Antarctica ... 5 C17
Larvik, Norway ... 7 G14
Las Animas, U.S.A. ... 54 F3
Las Anod, Somali Rep. ... 32 F4
Las Aves, Is., W. Indies ... 61 C7
Las Cejas, Argentina ... 64 B4
Las Cruces, U.S.A. ... 57 K10
Las Flores, Argentina ... 64 D5
Las Lajas, Argentina ... 64 D2
Las Lomitas, Argentina ... 64 A4
Las Palmas, Canary Is. ... 34 C2
Las Plumas, Argentina ... 64 E3
Las Tablas, Panama ... 60 E3
Las Truchas, Mexico ... 58 D4
Las Varillas, Argentina ... 64 C4
Las Vegas, N. Mex., U.S.A. ... 57 J11
Las Vegas, Nev., U.S.A. ... 57 H6
Lash-e Joveyn, Afghan. ... 28 D2
Lashburn, Canada ... 51 C7
Lashio, Burma ... 29 H20
Läsjerd, Iran ... 31 C7
Lassen Pk., U.S.A. ... 56 F3
Lassen Volcanic National Park, U.S.A. ... 56 F3
Last Mountain L., Canada ... 51 C7
Lastoursville, Gabon ... 36 E2
Lastovo, Croatia ... 16 C7
Latacunga, Ecuador ... 62 D3
Latakia = Al Lādhiqīyah, Syria ... 30 C2
Latchford, Canada ... 48 C4
Latham, Australia ... 41 E2
Latina, Italy ... 16 D5
Latium = Lazio □, Italy ... 16 C5
Latouche Treville, C., Australia ... 40 C3
Latrobe, Australia ... 42 G4
Latvia ■, Europe ... 7 H20
Lau Group, Fiji ... 39 C9
Lauchhammer, Germany ... 12 C7
Laughlin, U.S.A. ... 57 J6
Laukaa, Finland ... 7 E21
Launceston, Australia ... 42 G4
Launceston, U.K. ... 9 G3
Laura, Australia ... 42 B3
Laurel, Miss., U.S.A. ... 55 K10
Laurel, Mont., U.S.A. ... 56 D9
Laurens, U.S.A. ... 53 H4
Laurentian Plateau, Canada ... 49 B6
Lauria, Italy ... 16 E6
Laurie L., Canada ... 51 B8
Laurinburg, U.S.A. ... 53 H6
Laurium, U.S.A. ... 52 B1
Lausanne, Switz. ... 14 C7
Laut, Indonesia ... 26 D3
Laut, Pulau, Indonesia ... 26 E5
Laut Kecil, Kepulauan, Indonesia ... 26 E5
Lautoka, Fiji ... 39 C7
Laval, France ... 14 B3
Lāvar Meydān, Iran ... 31 D7
Laverton, Australia ... 41 E3
Lávrion, Greece ... 17 F11
Lawas, Malaysia ... 26 D5
Lawele, Indonesia ... 27 F6
Lawng Pit, Burma ... 29 G20
Lawqah, Si. Arabia ... 30 D4
Lawrence, N.Z. ... 39 L2
Lawrence, Kans., U.S.A. ... 54 F7
Lawrence, Mass., U.S.A. ... 52 D10
Lawrenceburg, Ind., U.S.A. ... 52 F3
Lawrenceburg, Tenn., U.S.A. ... 53 H2
Lawrenceville, U.S.A. ... 53 J4
Lawton, U.S.A. ... 55 H5
Lawu, Indonesia ... 27 G14
Laylá, Si. Arabia ... 32 C4
Laylān, Iraq ... 30 C5
Laytonville, U.S.A. ... 56 G2
Lazio □, Italy ... 16 C5
Lazo, Russia ... 22 C6

Le Creusot, France ... 14 C6
Le François, Martinique ... 61 D7
Le Havre, France ... 14 B4
Le Mans, France ... 14 C4
Le Mars, U.S.A. ... 54 D6
Le Mont-St-Michel, France ... 14 B3
Le Moule, Guadeloupe ... 61 C7
Le Puy-en-Velay, France ... 14 D5
Le Sueur, U.S.A. ... 54 C8
Le Touquet-Paris-Plage, France ... 14 A4
Le Tréport, France ... 14 A4
Le Verdon-sur-Mer, France ... 14 D3
Lea →, U.K. ... 9 F8
Lead, U.S.A. ... 54 C3
Leader, Canada ... 51 C7
Leadville, U.S.A. ... 57 G10
Leaf →, U.S.A. ... 55 K10
Leaf Rapids, Canada ... 51 B9
Leamington, Canada ... 48 D3
Leamington, U.S.A. ... 56 G7
Leamington Spa = Royal Leamington Spa, U.K. ... 9 E6
Learmonth, Australia ... 40 D1
Leask, Canada ... 51 C7
Leatherhead, U.K. ... 9 F7
Leavenworth, Kans., U.S.A. ... 54 F7
Leavenworth, Wash., U.S.A. ... 56 C3
Lebak, Phil. ... 27 C6
Lebanon, Ind., U.S.A. ... 52 E2
Lebanon, Kans., U.S.A. ... 54 F5
Lebanon, Ky., U.S.A. ... 52 G3
Lebanon, Mo., U.S.A. ... 55 G8
Lebanon, N.H., U.S.A. ... 52 D9
Lebanon, Oreg., U.S.A. ... 56 D2
Lebanon, Pa., U.S.A. ... 52 E7
Lebanon, Tenn., U.S.A. ... 53 G2
Lebanon ■, Asia ... 33 B5
Lebel-sur-Quévillon, Canada ... 48 C4
Lębork, Poland ... 13 A9
Lebrija, Spain ... 15 D2
Lebu, Chile ... 64 D2
Lecce, Italy ... 17 D8
Lecco, Italy ... 14 D8
Lech →, Germany ... 12 D6
Łęczyca, Poland ... 13 B10
Leduc, Canada ... 50 C6
Leech L., U.S.A. ... 54 B7
Leeds, U.K. ... 8 D6
Leeds, U.S.A. ... 53 J2
Leek, Neths. ... 11 A6
Leek, U.K. ... 8 D5
Leeman, Australia ... 41 E1
Leer, Germany ... 12 B4
Leesburg, U.S.A. ... 53 L5
Leesville, U.S.A. ... 55 K8
Leeton, Australia ... 43 E4
Leeuwarden, Neths. ... 11 A5
Leeuwin, C., Australia ... 41 F2
Leeward Is., Atl. Oc. ... 61 C7
Lefroy, L., Australia ... 41 F3
Leganés, Spain ... 15 B4
Legazpi, Phil. ... 27 B6
Legendre I., Australia ... 40 D2
Leghorn = Livorno, Italy ... 16 C4
Legionowo, Poland ... 13 B11
Legnago, Italy ... 16 B4
Legnica, Poland ... 12 C9
Leh, India ... 28 B10
Lehigh Acres, U.S.A. ... 53 M5
Leicester, U.K. ... 9 E6
Leicester City □, U.K. ... 9 E6
Leicestershire □, U.K. ... 9 E6
Leichhardt →, Australia ... 42 B2
Leichhardt Ra., Australia ... 42 C4
Leiden, Neths. ... 11 B4
Leie →, Belgium ... 11 C3
Leigh Creek, Australia ... 43 E2
Leine →, Germany ... 12 B5
Leinster, Australia ... 41 E3
Leinster □, Ireland ... 10 E3
Leipzig, Germany ... 12 C7
Leiria, Portugal ... 15 C1
Leirvik, Norway ... 7 G11
Leisler, Mt., Australia ... 40 D4
Leith Hill, U.K. ... 9 F7
Leitrim, Ireland ... 10 D3
Leizhou Bandao, China ... 25 D6
Lek →, Neths. ... 11 C4
Leka, Norway ... 6 D14
Lékva Óros, Greece ... 17 G11
Leland, Mich., U.S.A. ... 52 C3
Leland, Miss., U.S.A. ... 55 J9
Leleque, Argentina ... 64 E2
Lelystad, Neths. ... 11 B5
Léman, L., Europe ... 14 C7
Lemhi Ra., U.S.A. ... 56 D7
Lemmer, Neths. ... 11 B5
Lemmon, U.S.A. ... 54 C3
Lemoore, U.S.A. ... 57 H4
Lemvig, Denmark ... 7 H13
Lena →, Russia ... 21 B13
Lendeh, Iran ... 31 D6

Leningrad = Sankt-Peterburg, Russia ... 18 C5
Leninogorsk, Kazakstan ... 20 D9
Leninsk, Russia ... 19 E8
Leninsk-Kuznetskiy, Russia ... 20 D9
Lenkoran = Länkäran, Azerbaijan ... 19 G8
Lenmalu, Indonesia ... 27 E8
Lennox, U.S.A. ... 54 D6
Lennoxville, Canada ... 52 A5
Lenoir, U.S.A. ... 53 H5
Lenoir City, U.S.A. ... 53 H3
Lenore L., Canada ... 51 C8
Lens, France ... 14 A5
Lensk, Russia ... 21 C12
Lentini, Italy ... 16 F6
Lenya, Burma ... 26 B1
Leoben, Austria ... 12 E8
Leodhas = Lewis, U.K. ... 10 B3
Leola, U.S.A. ... 54 C5
Leominster, U.K. ... 9 E5
Leominster, U.S.A. ... 52 D10
León, Mexico ... 58 C4
León, Nic. ... 60 D2
León, Spain ... 15 A3
Leon, U.S.A. ... 54 E8
Leon →, U.S.A. ... 55 K6
León, Montes de, Spain ... 15 A2
Leonardtown, U.S.A. ... 52 F7
Leongatha, Australia ... 43 F4
Leonora, Australia ... 41 E3
Léopold II, Lac = Mai-Ndombe, L., Dem. Rep. of the Congo ... 36 E3
Leopoldsburg, Belgium ... 11 C5
Léopoldville = Kinshasa, Dem. Rep. of the Congo ... 36 E3
Leoti, U.S.A. ... 54 F4
Leova, Moldova ... 13 E15
Leoville, Canada ... 51 C7
Lepel = Lyepyel, Belarus ... 18 D4
Leppävirta, Finland ... 7 E22
Lerdo, Mexico ... 58 B4
Lérida = Lleida, Spain ... 15 B6
Lerwick, U.K. ... 10 A6
Les Cayes, Haiti ... 61 C5
Les Sables-d'Olonne, France ... 14 C3
Lesbos = Lésvos, Greece ... 17 E12
Leshan, China ... 24 D5
Leshukonskoye, Russia ... 18 B8
Leskov I., Antarctica ... 5 B1
Leskovac, Serbia, Yug. ... 17 C9
Lesopilnoye, Russia ... 22 A7
Lesotho ■, Africa ... 37 K5
Lesozavodsk, Russia ... 21 E14
Lesse →, Belgium ... 11 D4
Lesser Antilles, W. Indies ... 61 D7
Lesser Slave L., Canada ... 50 B5
Lesser Sunda Is., Indonesia ... 27 F6
Lessines, Belgium ... 11 D3
Lestock, Canada ... 51 C8
Lesuer I., Australia ... 40 B4
Lésvos, Greece ... 17 E12
Leszno, Poland ... 13 C9
Letchworth, U.K. ... 9 F7
Lethbridge, Canada ... 50 D6
Lethem, Guyana ... 62 C7
Leti, Kepulauan, Indonesia ... 27 F7
Leti Is. = Leti, Kepulauan, Indonesia ... 27 F7
Leticia, Colombia ... 62 D5
Letong, Indonesia ... 26 D3
Letpadan, Burma ... 29 L19
Letpan, Burma ... 29 K19
Letsôk-aw Kyun, Burma ... 26 B1
Letterkenny, Ireland ... 10 B4
Leuser, G., Indonesia ... 26 D1
Leuven, Belgium ... 11 D4
Leuze-en-Hainaut, Belgium ... 11 D3
Levádhia, Greece ... 17 E10
Levanger, Norway ... 6 E14
Levelland, U.S.A. ... 55 J3
Leveque C., Australia ... 40 C3
Levice, Slovak Rep. ... 13 D10
Levin, N.Z. ... 39 J5
Lévis, Canada ... 49 C5
Levis, L., Canada ... 50 A5
Levittown, U.S.A. ... 52 E9
Lévkas, Greece ... 17 E9
Levkôsia = Nicosia, Cyprus ... 30 C2
Levskigrad = Karlovo, Bulgaria ... 17 C11
Levuka, Fiji ... 39 C8
Lewes, U.K. ... 9 G8
Lewis, U.K. ... 10 B3
Lewis →, U.S.A. ... 56 C2
Lewis Ra., Australia ... 40 D4
Lewis Range, U.S.A. ... 56 C7
Lewisburg, Tenn., U.S.A. ... 53 H2
Lewisburg, W. Va., U.S.A. ... 52 G5
Lewisporte, Canada ... 49 C8
Lewiston, Idaho, U.S.A. ... 56 C5
Lewiston, Maine, U.S.A. ... 53 C11

Lewistown, Mont., U.S.A. ... 56 C9
Lewistown, Pa., U.S.A. ... 52 E7
Lexington, Ill., U.S.A. ... 54 E10
Lexington, Ky., U.S.A. ... 52 F3
Lexington, Mo., U.S.A. ... 54 F8
Lexington, N.C., U.S.A. ... 53 H5
Lexington, Nebr., U.S.A. ... 54 E5
Lexington, Tenn., U.S.A. ... 53 H1
Lexington, Va., U.S.A. ... 52 G6
Lexington Park, U.S.A. ... 52 F7
Leyburn, U.K. ... 8 C6
Leyland, U.K. ... 8 D5
Leyte □, Phil. ... 27 B6
Lezha = Lezhë, Albania ... 17 D8
Lezhë, Albania ... 17 D8
Lhasa, China ... 24 D4
Lhazê, China ... 24 D3
Lhokkruet, Indonesia ... 26 D1
Lhokseumawe, Indonesia ... 26 C1
L'Hospitalet de Llobregat, Spain ... 15 B7
Lianga, Phil. ... 27 C7
Liangpran, Indonesia ... 26 D4
Lianyungang, China ... 25 C6
Liaoning □, China ... 25 B7
Liaoyang, China ... 25 B7
Liaoyuan, China ... 25 B7
Liard →, Canada ... 50 A4
Liard River, Canada ... 50 B3
Libau = Liepāja, Latvia ... 7 H19
Libby, U.S.A. ... 56 B6
Libenge, Dem. Rep. of the Congo ... 36 D3
Liberal, U.S.A. ... 55 G4
Liberec, Czech Rep. ... 12 C8
Liberia, Costa Rica ... 60 D2
Liberia ■, W. Afr. ... 34 G4
Liberty, Mo., U.S.A. ... 54 F7
Liberty, N.Y., U.S.A. ... 52 E8
Liberty, Tex., U.S.A. ... 55 K7
Libobo, Tanjung, Indonesia ... 27 E7
Libourne, France ... 14 D3
Libramont, Belgium ... 11 E5
Libreville, Gabon ... 36 D1
Libya ■, N. Afr. ... 35 C9
Libyan Desert = Lîbîya, Sahrâ', Africa ... 35 C10
Licantén, Chile ... 64 D2
Licata, Italy ... 16 F5
Lichfield, U.K. ... 9 E6
Lichinga, Mozam. ... 37 G7
Licking →, U.S.A. ... 52 F3
Lida, Belarus ... 7 K21
Lidköping, Sweden ... 7 G15
Liebig, Mt., Australia ... 40 D5
Liechtenstein ■, Europe ... 14 C8
Liège, Belgium ... 11 D5
Liège □, Belgium ... 11 D5
Liegnitz = Legnica, Poland ... 12 C9
Lienyünchiangshih = Lianyungang, China ... 25 C6
Lienz, Austria ... 12 E7
Liepāja, Latvia ... 7 H19
Lier, Belgium ... 11 C4
Lièvre →, Canada ... 48 C4
Liffey →, Ireland ... 10 E3
Lifford, Ireland ... 10 B4
Lifudzin, Russia ... 22 B7
Lightning Ridge, Australia ... 43 D4
Liguria □, Italy ... 14 D8
Ligurian Sea, Medit. S. ... 16 C3
Lihou Reefs and Cays, Australia ... 42 B5
Lijiang, China ... 24 D5
Likasi, Dem. Rep. of the Congo ... 36 G5
Lille, France ... 14 A5
Lille Bælt, Denmark ... 7 J13
Lillehammer, Norway ... 7 F14
Lillesand, Norway ... 7 G13
Lillian Pt., Australia ... 41 E4
Lillooet, Canada ... 50 C4
Lillooet →, Canada ... 50 D4
Lilongwe, Malawi ... 37 G6
Liloy, Phil. ... 27 C6
Lim →, Bos.-H. ... 17 C8
Lima, Indonesia ... 27 E7
Lima, Peru ... 62 F3
Lima, Mont., U.S.A. ... 56 D7
Lima, Ohio, U.S.A. ... 52 E3
Lima →, Portugal ... 15 B1
Liman, Indonesia ... 27 G14
Limassol, Cyprus ... 30 C2
Limay →, Argentina ... 64 D3
Limay Mahuida, Argentina ... 64 D3
Limbang, Brunei ... 26 D5
Limbaži, Latvia ... 7 H21
Limbe, Cameroon ... 36 D1
Limburg, Germany ... 12 C5
Limburg □, Belgium ... 11 C5
Limburg □, Neths. ... 11 C5
Limeira, Brazil ... 63 H9
Limerick, Ireland ... 10 E2
Limestone →, Canada ... 51 B10
Limfjorden, Denmark ... 7 H13
Limia = Lima →, Portugal ... 15 B1
Limingen, Norway ... 6 D15

Limmen Bight, Australia ... 42 A2
Limmen Bight →, Australia ... 42 B2
Limnos, Greece ... 17 E11
Limoges, France ... 14 D4
Limón, Costa Rica ... 60 E3
Limon, U.S.A. ... 54 F3
Limousin, France ... 14 D4
Limoux, France ... 14 E5
Limpopo →, Africa ... 37 K6
Limuru, Kenya ... 36 E7
Linares, Chile ... 64 D2
Linares, Mexico ... 59 C5
Linares, Spain ... 15 C4
Lincoln, Argentina ... 64 C4
Lincoln, N.Z. ... 39 K4
Lincoln, U.K. ... 8 D7
Lincoln, Ill., U.S.A. ... 54 E10
Lincoln, Kans., U.S.A. ... 54 F5
Lincoln, Maine, U.S.A. ... 53 C11
Lincoln, N. Mex., U.S.A. ... 57 K11
Lincoln, Nebr., U.S.A. ... 54 E6
Lincoln City, U.S.A. ... 56 D1
Lincoln Hav = Lincoln Sea, Arctic ... 4 A5
Lincoln Sea, Arctic ... 4 A5
Lincolnshire □, U.K. ... 8 D7
Lincolnshire Wolds, U.K. ... 8 D7
Lincolnton, U.S.A. ... 53 H5
Lind, U.S.A. ... 56 C4
Linden, Guyana ... 62 B7
Linden, Ala., U.S.A. ... 53 J2
Linden, Tex., U.S.A. ... 55 J7
Lindesnes, Norway ... 7 H12
Líndhos, Greece ... 17 F13
Lindi, Tanzania ... 36 F7
Lindsay, Canada ... 48 D4
Lindsay, Calif., U.S.A. ... 57 H4
Lindsay, Okla., U.S.A. ... 55 H6
Lindsborg, U.S.A. ... 54 F6
Lingayen, Phil. ... 27 A6
Lingayen G., Phil. ... 27 A6
Lingen, Germany ... 12 B4
Lingga, Indonesia ... 26 E2
Lingga, Kepulauan, Indonesia ... 26 E2
Lingga Arch. = Lingga, Kepulauan, Indonesia ... 26 E2
Lingle, U.S.A. ... 54 D2
Linguère, Senegal ... 34 E2
Linhai, China ... 25 D7
Linhares, Brazil ... 63 G10
Linköping, Sweden ... 7 G16
Linosa, I., Medit. S. ... 16 G5
Lins, Brazil ... 63 H9
Linton, Ind., U.S.A. ... 52 F2
Linton, N. Dak., U.S.A. ... 54 B4
Linxia, China ... 24 C5
Linz, Austria ... 12 D8
Lion, G. du, France ... 14 E6
Lions, G. of = Lion, G. du, France ... 14 E6
Lipa, Phil. ... 27 B6
Lípari, Italy ... 16 E6
Lípari, Is. = Eólie, Ís., Italy ... 16 E6
Lipcani, Moldova ... 13 D14
Lipetsk, Russia ... 18 D6
Lipkany = Lipcani, Moldova ... 13 D14
Lipovcy Manzovka, Russia ... 22 B6
Lipovets, Ukraine ... 13 D15
Lippe →, Germany ... 12 C4
Lipscomb, U.S.A. ... 55 G4
Liptrap C., Australia ... 43 F4
Liria = Lliria, Spain ... 15 C5
Lisala, Dem. Rep. of the Congo ... 36 D4
Lisboa, Portugal ... 15 C1
Lisbon = Lisboa, Portugal ... 15 C1
Lisbon, U.S.A. ... 54 B6
Lisbon Falls, U.S.A. ... 53 D10
Lisburn, U.K. ... 10 D3
Lisichansk = Lysychansk, Ukraine ... 19 E6
Lisieux, France ... 14 B4
Liski, Russia ... 19 D6
Lismore, Australia ... 43 D5
Lista, Norway ... 7 G12
Lister, Mt., Antarctica ... 5 D11
Liston, Australia ... 43 D5
Listowel, Canada ... 48 D3
Listowel, Ireland ... 10 E2
Litani →, Lebanon ... 33 B4
Litchfield, Ill., U.S.A. ... 54 F10
Litchfield, Minn., U.S.A. ... 54 C7
Lithgow, Australia ... 43 E5
Lithinon, Ákra, Greece ... 17 G11
Lithuania ■, Europe ... 7 J20
Litoměřice, Czech Rep. ... 12 C8
Little Abaco I., Bahamas ... 60 A4
Little Barrier I., N.Z. ... 39 G5
Little Belt Mts., U.S.A. ... 56 C8
Little Blue →, U.S.A. ... 54 F6
Little Buffalo →, Canada ... 50 A6
Little Cayman, Cayman Is. ... 60 C3
Little Churchill →, Canada ... 51 B9

Little Colorado →, U.S.A. 57 H8
Little Current, Canada . 48 C3
Little Current →, Canada 48 B3
Little Falls, Minn., U.S.A. 54 C7
Little Falls, N.Y., U.S.A. 52 D8
Little Fork →, U.S.A. . . 54 A8
Little Grand Rapids, Canada 51 C9
Little Humboldt →, U.S.A. 56 F5
Little Inagua I., Bahamas 61 B5
Little Laut Is. = Laut Kecil, Kepulauan, Indonesia 26 E5
Little Mecatina = Petit-Mécatina →, Canada 49 B8
Little Missouri →, U.S.A. 54 B3
Little Ouse →, U.K. . . 9 E9
Little Red →, U.S.A. . 55 H9
Little River, N.Z. 39 K4
Little Rock, U.S.A. . . . 55 H8
Little Sable Pt., U.S.A. . 52 D2
Little Sioux →, U.S.A. 54 E6
Little Smoky →, Canada 50 C5
Little Snake →, U.S.A. 56 F9
Little Wabash →, U.S.A. 52 G1
Little White →, U.S.A. 54 D4
Littlefield, U.S.A. 55 J3
Littlehampton, U.K. ... 9 G7
Littleton, U.S.A. 52 C10
Liukang Tenggaja = Sabalana, Kepulauan, Indonesia 27 F5
Liuwa Plain, Zambia . 37 G4
Liuzhou, China 25 D5
Live Oak, U.S.A. 53 K4
Livermore, Mt., U.S.A. . 55 K2
Livermore Falls, U.S.A. 53 C11
Liverpool, Canada ... 49 D7
Liverpool, U.K. 8 D4
Liverpool Bay, U.K. ... 8 D4
Liverpool Plains, Australia 43 E5
Liverpool Ra., Australia 43 E5
Livingston, Guatemala 60 C2
Livingston, Ala., U.S.A. 53 J1
Livingston, Mont., U.S.A. 56 D8
Livingston, S.C., U.S.A. 53 J5
Livingston, Tenn., U.S.A. 53 G3
Livingston, Tex., U.S.A. 55 K7
Livingston, L., U.S.A. . . 55 K7
Livingstone, Zambia . 37 H5
Livny, Russia 18 D6
Livonia, U.S.A. 52 D4
Livorno, Italy 16 C4
Lizard I., Australia ... 42 A4
Lizard Pt., U.K. 9 H2
Ljubljana, Slovenia .. 12 E8
Ljungan →, Sweden . 7 E17
Ljungby, Sweden 7 H15
Ljusdal, Sweden 7 F17
Ljusnan →, Sweden .. 7 F17
Ljusne, Sweden 7 F17
Llancanelo, Salina, Argentina 64 D3
Llandeilo, U.K. 9 F4
Llandovery, U.K. 9 F4
Llandrindod Wells, U.K. 9 E4
Llandudno, U.K. 8 D4
Llanelli, U.K. 9 F3
Llanes, Spain 15 A4
Llangollen, U.K. 8 E4
Llanidloes, U.K. 9 E4
Llano, U.S.A. 55 K5
Llano →, U.S.A. 55 K5
Llano Estacado, U.S.A. 55 J3
Llanos, S. Amer. 62 C4
Llanquihue, L., Chile . 64 E1
Llanwrtyd Wells, U.K. . 9 E4
Lleida, Spain 15 B6
Llera, Mexico 59 C5
Lleyn Peninsula, U.K. . 8 E3
Lliria, Spain 15 C5
Llobregat →, Spain .. 15 B7
Lloret de Mar, Spain .. 15 B7
Lloyd B., Australia ... 42 A3
Lloyd L., Canada 51 B7
Lloydminster, Canada . 51 C7
Llucmajor, Spain 15 C7
Llullaillaco, Volcán, S. Amer. 64 A3
Loa, U.S.A. 57 G8
Loa →, Chile 64 A2
Loaita I., S. China Sea . 26 B4
Loange →, Dem. Rep. of the Congo 36 E4
Lobatse, Botswana 37 K5
Lobería, Argentina ... 64 D5
Lobito, Angola 37 G2
Lobos, I., Mexico 58 B2
Locarno, Switz. 14 C8
Loch Garman = Wexford, Ireland 10 E3
Loche, L. La, Canada . 51 B7
Lochem, Neths. 11 B6
Loches, France 14 C4
Lochnagar, Australia . 42 C4
Lock, Australia 43 E2

Lock Haven, U.S.A. .. 52 E7
Lockeport, Canada ... 49 D6
Lockhart, Australia ... 43 F4
Lockhart, U.S.A. 55 L6
Lockhart, L., Australia . 41 F2
Lockhart River, Australia 42 A3
Lockney, U.S.A. 55 H4
Lockport, U.S.A. 52 D6
Lod, Israel 33 D3
Lodeinoye Pole, Russia 18 B5
Lodge Bay, Canada .. 49 B8
Lodge Grass, U.S.A. . . 56 D10
Lodgepole Cr. →, U.S.A. 54 E2
Lodhran, Pakistan ... 28 E7
Lodi, Italy 14 D8
Lodi, U.S.A. 56 G3
Lodja, Dem. Rep. of the Congo 36 E4
Lodwar, Kenya 36 D7
Łódź, Poland 13 C10
Loei, Thailand 26 A2
Lofoten, Norway 6 B15
Logan, Iowa, U.S.A. . . 54 E7
Logan, Ohio, U.S.A. . . 52 F4
Logan, Utah, U.S.A. . . 56 F8
Logan, W. Va., U.S.A. . 52 G5
Logan, Mt., Canada . . 46 B5
Logansport, Ind., U.S.A. 52 E2
Logansport, La., U.S.A. 55 K8
Logone →, Chad 35 F9
Logroño, Spain 15 A4
Lohardaga, India 29 H14
Lohja, Finland 7 F21
Lohjan →, China 24 B4
Loi-kaw, Burma 29 K20
Loimaa, Finland 7 F20
Loir →, France 14 C3
Loire →, France 14 C2
Loja, Ecuador 62 D3
Loja, Spain 15 D3
Loji = Kawasi, Indonesia 27 E7
Lokeren, Belgium 11 C3
Lokitaung, Kenya 36 D7
Lokkan tekojärvi, Finland 6 C22
Lokoja, Nigeria 34 G7
Lolland, Denmark 7 J14
Lolo, U.S.A. 56 C6
Lom, Bulgaria 17 C10
Loma, U.S.A. 56 C8
Lomami →, Dem. Rep. of the Congo 36 D4
Lombadina, Australia . 40 C3
Lombárdia □, Italy ... 14 D8
Lombardy = Lombárdia □, Italy ... 14 D8
Lomblen, Indonesia . . . 27 F6
Lombok, Indonesia ... 26 F5
Lomé, Togo 34 G6
Lomela, Dem. Rep. of the Congo 36 E4
Lomela →, Dem. Rep. of the Congo 36 E4
Lommel, Belgium 11 C5
Lomond, Canada 50 C6
Lomond, L., U.K. 10 C4
Lompobatang, Indonesia 27 F5
Lompoc, U.S.A. 57 J3
Łomza, Poland 13 B12
Loncoche, Chile 64 D2
Londa, India 28 M9
London, Canada 48 D3
London, U.K. 9 F7
London, Ky., U.S.A. . . 52 G3
London, Ohio, U.S.A. . 52 F4
London, Greater □, U.K. 9 F7
Londonderry, U.K. ... 10 B5
Londonderry, □., Australia 40 B4
Londonderry, I., Chile . 64 H2
Londres, Argentina ... 64 B3
Londrina, Brazil 64 A6
Lone Pine, U.S.A. 57 H4
Long B., U.S.A. 53 J6
Long Beach, Calif., U.S.A. 57 K4
Long Beach, Wash., U.S.A. 56 C1
Long Branch, U.S.A. .. 52 E9
Long Creek, U.S.A. ... 56 D4
Long Eaton, U.K. 8 E6
Long I., Australia 42 C4
Long I., Bahamas 61 B4
Long I., Canada 48 B4
Long Island Sd., U.S.A. 52 E9
Long L., Canada 48 C2
Long Lake, U.S.A. ... 52 D8
Long Prairie →, U.S.A. 54 C7
Long Range Mts., Canada 49 C8
Long Reef, Australia .. 40 B4
Long Spruce, Canada . 51 B10
Long Str. = Longa, Proliv, Russia 4 C16
Long Xuyen, Vietnam . 26 B3
Longa, Proliv, Russia . . 4 C16
Longbenton, U.K. 8 B6
Longboat Key, U.S.A. . 53 M4
Longford, Australia ... 42 G4
Longford, Ireland 10 E3
Longiram, Indonesia . 26 E5
Longlac, Canada 48 C2

Longmont, U.S.A. 54 E2
Longnawan, Indonesia 26 D4
Longreach, Australia .. 42 C3
Longview, Tex., U.S.A. 55 J7
Longview, Wash., U.S.A. 56 C2
Lonoke, U.S.A. 55 H9
Lons-le-Saunier, France 14 C6
Looe, U.K. 9 G3
Lookout, C., Canada .. 48 A3
Lookout, C., U.S.A. ... 53 H7
Loon →, Alta., Canada 50 B5
Loon →, Man., Canada 51 B8
Loon Lake, Canada .. 51 C7
Loongana, Australia .. 41 F4
Lop Nor = Lop Nur, China 24 B4
Lop Nur, China 24 B4
Lopatina, Gora, Russia 21 D15
Lopez, C., Gabon 36 E1
Lopphavet, Norway .. 6 A19
Lora →, Afghan. 28 D4
Lora, Hämün-i-, Pakistan 28 E4
Lora Cr. →, Australia . 43 D2
Lora del Río, Spain ... 15 D3
Lorain, U.S.A. 52 E4
Loralai, Pakistan 28 D6
Lorca, Spain 15 D5
Lord Howe I., Pac. Oc. . 38 E8
Lord Howe Ridge, Pac. Oc. 44 L8
Lordsburg, U.S.A. 57 K9
Loreto, Brazil 63 E9
Loreto, Mexico 58 B2
Lorient, France 14 C2
Lorne, Australia 43 F3
Lorraine □, France ... 14 B7
Los Alamos, U.S.A. . . 57 J10
Los Andes, Chile 64 C2
Los Angeles, Chile ... 64 D2
Los Angeles, U.S.A. . . 57 K4
Los Angeles, Bahia de, Mexico 58 B2
Los Angeles Aqueduct, U.S.A. 57 J5
Los Banos, U.S.A. 57 H3
Los Blancos, Argentina 64 A4
Los Chiles, Costa Rica . 60 D3
Los Hermanos Is., Venezuela 62 A6
Los Lunas, U.S.A. . . . 57 J10
Los Mochis, Mexico .. 58 B3
Los Palacios, Cuba ... 60 B3
Los Reyes, Mexico ... 58 D4
Los Roques Is., Venezuela 62 A5
Los Teques, Venezuela 62 A5
Los Testigos, Is., Venezuela 62 A6
Los Vilos, Chile 64 C2
Lošinj, Croatia 12 F8
Lostwithiel, U.K. 9 G3
Lot →, France 14 D4
Lota, Chile 64 D2
Loṭfābād, Iran 31 B8
Loubomo, Congo 36 E2
Louga, Senegal 34 E2
Loughborough, U.K. .. 8 E6
Louis Trichardt, S. Africa 37 J5
Louis XIV, Pte., Canada 48 B4
Louisa, U.S.A. 52 F4
Louisbourg, Canada .. 49 C8
Louise I., Canada 50 C2
Louiseville, Canada ... 48 C5
Louisiade Arch., Papua N. G. 38 C8
Louisiana, U.S.A. 54 F9
Louisiana □, U.S.A. .. 55 K9
Louisville, Ky., U.S.A. . 52 F3
Louisville, Miss., U.S.A. 55 J10
Loulé, Portugal 15 D1
Loup City, U.S.A. 54 E5
Loups Marins, Lacs des, Canada 48 A5
Lourdes, France 14 E3
Lourenço-Marques = Maputo, Mozam. .. 37 K6
Louth, Australia 43 E4
Louth, U.K. 8 D7
Louvain = Leuven, Belgium 11 D4
Lovech, Bulgaria 17 C11
Loveland, U.S.A. 54 E2
Lovell, U.S.A. 56 D9
Lovelock, U.S.A. 56 F4
Loviisa, Finland 7 F22
Loving, U.S.A. 55 J2
Lovington, U.S.A. 55 J3
Lovisa = Loviisa, Finland 7 F22
Low, L., Canada 48 B4
Low Pt., Australia 41 F4
Low Tatra = Nizké Tatry, Slovak Rep. . 13 D10
Lowell, U.S.A. 52 D10
Lower Alkali L., U.S.A. . 56 F3
Lower Arrow L., Canada 50 D5
Lower California = Baja California, Mexico .. 58 A1
Lower Hutt, N.Z. 39 J5
Lower Manitou L., Canada 51 D10
Lower Post, Canada ... 50 B3

Lower Red L., U.S.A. .. 54 B7
Lower Saxony = Niedersachsen □, Germany 12 B5
Lower Tunguska = Tunguska, Nizhnyaya →, Russia 21 C9
Lowestoft, U.K. 9 E9
Łowicz, Poland 13 B10
Lowville, U.S.A. 52 D8
Loxton, Australia 43 E3
Loyalty Is. = Loyauté, Is., N. Cal. 38 D9
Loyang = Luoyang, China 25 C6
Loyauté, Is., N. Cal. .. 38 D9
Loyev = Loyew, Belarus 13 C16
Loyew, Belarus 13 C16
Luachimo, Angola ... 36 F4
Lualaba →, Dem. Rep. of the Congo 36 D5
Luanda, Angola 36 F2
Luang, Thale, Thailand 26 C2
Luangwa →, Zambia . 37 G6
Luanshya, Zambia ... 37 G5
Luapula →, Africa ... 36 F5
Luarca, Spain 15 A2
Luau, Angola 36 G4
Lubana, Ozero = Lubānas Ezers, Latvia 7 H22
Lubānas Ezers, Latvia . 7 H22
Lubang Is., Phil. 27 B6
Lubbock, U.S.A. 55 J4
Lübeck, Germany 12 B6
Lubero = Luofu, Dem. Rep. of the Congo 36 E5
Lubilash →, Dem. Rep. of the Congo 36 F4
Lubin, Poland 12 C9
Lublin, Poland 13 C12
Lubnān, Jabal, Lebanon 33 B4
Lubny, Ukraine 20 D4
Lubudi, Dem. Rep. of the Congo 36 F5
Lubuklinggau, Indonesia 26 E2
Lubuksikaping, Indonesia 26 D2
Lubumbashi, Dem. Rep. of the Congo 37 G5
Lubutu, Dem. Rep. of the Congo 36 E5
Lucania, Mt., Canada . 46 B5
Lucca, Italy 16 C4
Lucea, Jamaica 60 C4
Lucedale, U.S.A. 53 K1
Lucena, Phil. 27 B6
Lucena, Spain 15 D3
Lučenec, Slovak Rep. . 13 D10
Lucerne = Luzern, Switz. 14 C8
Lucero, Mexico 58 A3
Lucinda, Australia ... 42 B4
Lucindale, Australia .. 43 F3
Luckenwalde, Germany 12 B7
Lucknow, India 29 F12
Lüda = Dalian, China . 25 C7
Lüderitz, Namibia 37 K3
Ludhiana, India 28 D9
Ludington, U.S.A. ... 52 D2
Ludlow, U.K. 9 E5
Ludlow, U.S.A. 57 J5
Ludvika, Sweden 7 F16
Ludwigsburg, Germany 12 D5
Ludwigshafen, Germany 12 D5
Lufira →, Dem. Rep. of the Congo 36 F5
Lufkin, U.S.A. 55 K7
Luga, Russia 18 C4
Lugano, Switz. 14 C8
Lugansk = Luhansk, Ukraine 19 E6
Lugenda →, Mozam. . 37 G7
Lugh Ganana, Somali Rep. 32 G3
Lugo, Italy 16 B4
Lugo, Spain 15 A2
Lugoj, Romania 13 F11
Lugovoy, Kazakstan .. 20 E8
Luhansk, Ukraine 19 E6
Luimneach = Limerick, Ireland 10 E2
Luís Correia, Brazil .. 63 D10
Luitpold Coast, Antarctica 5 D1
Luiza, Dem. Rep. of the Congo 36 F4
Lukanga Swamp, Zambia 37 G5
Lukenie →, Dem. Rep. of the Congo 36 E3
Łuków, Poland 13 C12
Lule älv →, Sweden . 6 D19
Luleå, Sweden 6 D20
Lüleburgaz, Turkey ... 17 D12
Luling, U.S.A. 55 L6
Lulonga →, Dem. Rep. of the Congo 36 D3
Lulua →, Dem. Rep. of the Congo 36 E4
Luluabourg = Kananga, Dem. Rep. of the Congo 36 F4
Lumajang, Indonesia . . 27 H15

Lumbala N'guimbo, Angola 37 G4
Lumberton, U.S.A. ... 53 H6
Lumsden, Canada ... 51 C8
Lumsden, N.Z. 39 L2
Lumut, Tanjung, Indonesia 26 E3
Lund, Sweden 7 J15
Lundazi, Zambia 37 G6
Lundu, Malaysia 26 D3
Lundy, U.K. 9 F3
Lune →, U.K. 8 C5
Lüneburg, Germany .. 12 B6
Lüneburg Heath = Lüneburger Heide, Germany 12 B6
Lüneburger Heide, Germany 12 B6
Lunenburg, Canada .. 49 D7
Lunéville, France 14 B7
Lunglei, India 29 H18
Luni, India 28 G8
Luni →, India 28 G7
Luninets = Luninyets, Belarus 13 B14
Luning, U.S.A. 56 G4
Luninyets, Belarus ... 13 B14
Luofu, Dem. Rep. of the Congo 36 E5
Luoyang, China 25 C6
Lupanshui, China ... 24 D5
Luray, U.S.A. 52 F6
Lurgan, U.K. 10 D3
Lusaka, Zambia 37 H5
Lusambo, Dem. Rep. of the Congo 36 E4
Luseland, Canada ... 51 C7
Lushnja = Lushnjë, Albania 17 D8
Lushnjë, Albania 17 D8
Lusk, U.S.A. 54 D2
Lūt, Dasht-e, Iran ... 31 D8
Luta = Dalian, China . 25 C7
Lutherstadt Wittenberg, Germany 12 C7
Luton, U.K. 9 F7
Luton □, U.K. 9 F7
Lutselke, Canada 51 A6
Lutsk, Ukraine 13 C13
Lützow Holmbukta, Antarctica 5 C4
Luverne, Ala., U.S.A. . 53 K2
Luverne, Minn., U.S.A. 54 D6
Luvua →, Dem. Rep. of the Congo 36 F5
Luwuk, Indonesia ... 27 E6
Luxembourg, Lux. ... 14 B7
Luxembourg □, Belgium 11 E5
Luxembourg ■, Europe 14 B7
Luxi, China 24 D4
Luxor = El Uqsur, Egypt 35 C12
Luza, Russia 18 B8
Luzern, Switz. 14 C8
Luzhou, China 24 D5
Luziânia, Brazil 63 G9
Luzon, Phil. 27 A6
Lviv, Ukraine 13 D13
Lvov = Lviv, Ukraine . 13 D13
Lyakhavichy, Belarus . 13 B14
Lyakhovskiye, Ostrova, Russia 21 B15
Lyallpur = Faisalabad, Pakistan 28 D8
Lycksele, Sweden 6 D18
Lydda = Lod, Israel .. 33 D3
Lydenburg, S. Africa .. 37 K6
Lydia, Turkey 17 E13
Lyell, N.Z. 39 J4
Lyell I., Canada 50 C2
Lyepyel, Belarus 18 D4
Lyman, U.S.A. 56 F8
Lyme B., U.K. 9 G4
Lyme Regis, U.K. 9 G5
Lymington, U.K. 9 G6
Łyna →, Poland 7 J19
Lynchburg, U.S.A. ... 52 G6
Lynd →, Australia ... 42 B3
Lynd Ra., Australia .. 43 D4
Lynden, U.S.A. 56 B2
Lyndhurst, Australia .. 43 E2
Lyndon →, Australia . 41 D1
Lyndonville, U.S.A. .. 52 D10
Lyngen, Norway 6 B19
Lynher Reef, Australia 40 C3
Lynn, U.S.A. 52 D10
Lynn Lake, Canada .. 51 B8
Lynn, U.K. 9 F4
Lyntupy, Belarus 7 J22
Lynx L., Canada 51 A7
Lyon, France 14 D6
Lyonnais, France 14 D6
Lyons = Lyon, France . 14 D6
Lyons, Ga., U.S.A. ... 53 J4
Lyons, Kans., U.S.A. .. 54 F5
Lyons, →, Australia .. 41 E2
Lys = Leie →, Belgium 11 C3
Lysva, Russia 18 C10
Lytham St. Anne's, U.K. 8 D4
Lyttelton, N.Z. 39 K4
Lytton, Canada 50 C4
Lyubertsy, Russia ... 18 C6
Lyuboml, Ukraine ... 13 C13

Ma'adaba, Jordan 33 E4
Ma'ān, Jordan 33 E4
Ma'ān □, Jordan 33 F5
Maanselkä, Finland .. 6 C23
Ma'anshan, China ... 25 C6
Maarianhamina, Finland 7 F18
Ma'arrat an Nu'mān, Syria 30 C3
Maas →, Neths. 11 C4
Maaseik, Belgium ... 11 C5
Maassin, Phil. 27 B6
Maastricht, Neths. ... 14 A6
Mabel L., Canada ... 50 C5
Mablethorpe, U.K. ... 8 D8
McAlester, U.S.A. 55 H7
McAllen, U.S.A. 55 M5
MacAlpine L., Canada . 46 B9
Macamic, Canada ... 48 C4
Macao = Macau □, China 25 D6
Macapá, Brazil 63 C8
McArthur →, Australia 42 B2
McArthur, Port, Australia 42 B2
Macau, Brazil 63 E11
Macau □, China 25 D6
McBride, Canada 50 C4
McCall, U.S.A. 56 D5
McCamey, U.S.A. 55 K3
McCammon, U.S.A. .. 56 E7
McCauley I., Canada . 50 C2
Macclenny, U.S.A. ... 53 K4
Macclesfield, U.K. ... 8 D5
M'Clintock Chan., Canada 46 A9
McClintock Ra., Australia 40 C4
McCloud, U.S.A. 56 F2
McCluer I., Australia . 40 B5
M'Clure Str., Canada . 4 B2
McClusky, U.S.A. 54 B4
McComb, U.S.A. 55 K9
McConaughy, L., U.S.A. 54 E4
McCook, U.S.A. 54 E4
McCreary, Canada ... 51 C9
McCusker →, Canada 51 B7
McDame, Canada ... 50 B3
McDermitt, U.S.A. ... 56 F5
Macdonald, L., Australia 40 D4
McDonald Is., Ind. Oc. . 3 G13
MacDonnell Ranges, Australia 40 D5
MacDowell L., Canada . 48 B1
Macedonia = Makedhonía □, Greece 17 D10
Macedonia ■, Europe . 17 D9
Maceió, Brazil 63 E11
Macerata, Italy 16 C5
McFarlane →, Canada 51 B7
Macfarlane, L., Australia 43 E2
McGehee, U.S.A. 55 J9
McGill, U.S.A. 56 G6
Macgillycuddy's Reeks, Ireland 10 E2
McGregor, U.S.A. ... 54 D9
McGregor Ra., Australia 43 D3
Mach, Pakistan 28 E5
Māch Kowr, Iran 31 E9
Machado = Jiparaná →, Brazil 62 E6
Machakos, Kenya ... 36 E7
Machala, Ecuador ... 62 D3
Machattie, L., Australia 42 C2
Machias, U.S.A. 53 C12
Machichi →, Canada . 51 B10
Machilipatnam, India . 29 L12
Machiques, Venezuela 62 A4
Machupicchu, Peru .. 62 F4
Machynlleth, U.K. ... 9 E4
McIlwraith Ra., Australia 42 A3
McInnes L., Canada . 51 C10
McIntosh, U.S.A. 54 C4
McIntosh L., Canada . 51 B8
Macintosh Ra., Australia 41 E4
Macintyre →, Australia 43 D5
Mackay, Australia ... 42 C4
Mackay, U.S.A. 56 E7
MacKay →, Canada . 50 B6
Mackay, L., Australia . 40 D4
McKay Ra., Australia . 40 D3
McKeesport, U.S.A. .. 52 E6
Mackenzie, Canada .. 50 B4
McKenzie, U.S.A. 53 G1
Mackenzie →, Australia 42 C4
Mackenzie →, Canada 46 B6
McKenzie →, U.S.A. . 56 D2
Mackenzie Bay, Canada 4 B1
Mackenzie City = Linden, Guyana 62 B7
Mackenzie Mts., Canada 46 B6
Mackinaw City, U.S.A. 52 C3
McKinlay, Australia .. 42 C3
McKinlay →, Australia 42 C3
McKinley, Mt., U.S.A. . 46 B4
McKinley Sea, Arctic . 4 A7
McKinney, U.S.A. ... 55 J6
Macklin, Canada 51 C7
Macksville, Australia . 43 E5
McLaughlin, U.S.A. .. 54 C4
Maclean, Australia ... 43 D5
McLean, U.S.A. 55 H4
McLeansboro, U.S.A. . 54 F10
Maclear, S. Africa ... 37 L5

Macleay →, *Australia* 43 E5
McLennan, *Canada* ... 50 B5
McLeod →, *Canada* ... 50 C5
MacLeod, B., *Canada* . 51 A7
McLeod, L., *Australia* . 41 D1
MacLeod Lake, *Canada* 50 C4
McLoughlin, Mt., *U.S.A.* 56 E2
McMinnville, *Oreg.,*
U.S.A. 56 D2
McMinnville, *Tenn.,*
U.S.A. 53 H3
McMurdo Sd.,
Antarctica 5 D11
McMurray = Fort
McMurray, *Canada* . 50 B6
Macomb, *U.S.A.* 54 E9
Mâcon, *France* 14 C6
Macon, *Ga., U.S.A.* .. 53 J4
Macon, *Miss., U.S.A.* . 53 J1
Macon, *Mo., U.S.A.* .. 54 F8
Macoun L., *Canada* .. 51 B8
McPherson, *U.S.A.* 54 F6
McPherson Ra.,
Australia 43 D5
Macquarie →,
Australia 43 E4
Macquarie Harbour,
Australia 42 G4
Macquarie Is., *Pac. Oc.* 44 N7
MacRobertson Land,
Antarctica 5 D6
Macusani, *Peru* 62 F4
Macuspana, *Mexico* .. 59 D6
Madadeni, *S. Africa* .. 37 K6
Madagascar ■, *Africa* 37 J9
Madā'in Sālih,
Si. Arabia 30 E3
Madama, *Niger* 35 D8
Madame I., *Canada* ... 49 C7
Madang, *Papua N. G.* . 38 B7
Madaripur, *Bangla.* ... 29 H17
Madauk, *Burma* 29 L20
Madawaska →,
Canada 48 C4
Madaya, *Burma* 29 H20
Maddalena, *Italy* 16 D3
Madeira, *Atl. Oc.* 34 B2
Madeira →, *Brazil* ... 62 D7
Madeleine, Îs. de la,
Canada 49 C7
Madera, *Mexico* 58 B3
Madera, *U.S.A.* 57 H3
Madha, *India* 28 L9
Madhya Pradesh □,
India 28 J11
Madidi →, *Bolivia* ... 62 F5
Madikeri, *India* 28 N9
Madill, *U.S.A.* 55 H6
Madimba, *Dem. Rep. of*
the Congo 36 E3
Ma'din, *Syria* 30 C3
Madingou, *Congo* ... 36 E2
Madison, *Fla., U.S.A.* . 53 K4
Madison, *Ind., U.S.A.* . 52 F3
Madison, *Nebr., U.S.A.* 54 E6
Madison, *S. Dak., U.S.A.* 54 D6
Madison, *Wis., U.S.A.* . 54 D10
Madison →, *U.S.A.* ... 56 D8
Madison Heights, *U.S.A.* 52 G6
Madisonville, *Ky., U.S.A.* 52 G2
Madisonville, *Tex.,*
U.S.A. 55 K7
Madiun, *Indonesia* ... 27 G14
Madona, *Latvia* 7 H22
Madrakah, Ra's al,
Oman 32 D6
Madras = Chennai,
India 28 N12
Madras = Tamil
Nadu □, *India* ... 28 P10
Madras, *U.S.A.* 56 D3
Madre, Laguna, *U.S.A.* 55 M6
Madre, Sierra, *Phil.* .. 27 A6
Madre de Dios →,
Bolivia 62 F5
Madre de Dios, I., *Chile* 64 G1
Madre del Sur, Sierra,
Mexico 59 D5
Madre Occidental,
Sierra, *Mexico* ... 58 B3
Madre Oriental, Sierra,
Mexico 58 C5
Madrid, *Spain* 15 B4
Madura, *Australia* ... 41 F4
Madura, *Indonesia* ... 27 G15
Madura, Selat,
Indonesia 27 G15
Madurai, *India* 28 Q11
Madurantakam, *India* . 28 N11
Mae Sot, *Thailand* ... 26 A1
Maebashi, *Japan* 23 F9
Maesteg, *U.K.* 9 F4
Maestra, Sierra, *Cuba* . 60 B4
Maevatanana, *Madag.* . 37 H9
Mafeking, *Canada* ... 51 C8
Mafeteng, *Lesotho* ... 37 K5
Maffra, *Australia* 43 F4
Mafia I., *Tanzania* ... 36 F7
Mafra, *Brazil* 64 B7
Mafra, *Portugal* 15 C1
Magadan, *Russia* ... 21 D16
Magallanes, Estrecho
de, *Chile* 64 G2
Magangué, *Colombia* . 62 B4
Makarovo, *Russia* ... 21 D11

Magdalen Is. =
Madeleine, Îs. de la,
Canada 49 C7
Magdalena, *Argentina* . 64 D5
Magdalena, *Bolivia* ... 62 F6
Magdalena, *Mexico* ... 58 A2
Magdalena, *U.S.A.* ... 57 J10
Magdalena →,
Colombia 62 A4
Magdalena →, *Mexico* 58 A2
Magdalena, B., *Mexico* 58 C2
Magdalena, Llano de la,
Mexico 58 C2
Magdeburg, *Germany* . 12 B6
Magdelaine Cays,
Australia 42 B5
Magee, *U.S.A.* 55 K10
Magelang, *Indonesia* . 27 G14
Magellan's Str. =
Magallanes, Estrecho
de, *Chile* 64 G2
Magenta, L., *Australia* . 41 F2
Magerøya, *Norway* ... 6 A21
Maggiore, Lago, *Italy* . 14 D8
Maghâgha, *Egypt* 35 C12
Maghreb, *N. Afr.* 34 B5
Magistralnyy, *Russia* .. 21 D11
Magnetic Pole (North) =
North Magnetic Pole,
Canada 4 B2
Magnetic Pole (South) =
South Magnetic Pole,
Antarctica 5 C9
Magnitogorsk, *Russia* . 18 D10
Magnolia, *Ark., U.S.A.* . 55 J8
Magnolia, *Miss., U.S.A.* 55 K9
Magog, *Canada* 49 C5
Magosa = Famagusta,
Cyprus 30 C2
Magozal, *Mexico* 59 C5
Magpie, L., *Canada* ... 49 B7
Magrath, *Canada* ... 50 D6
Maguarinho, C., *Brazil* . 63 D9
Magusa = Famagusta,
Cyprus 30 C2
Maguse L., *Canada* ... 51 A9
Maguse Pt., *Canada* . 51 A10
Magwe, *Burma* 29 J19
Mahābād, *Iran* 30 B5
Mahabo, *Madag.* 37 J8
Mahajanga, *Madag.* .. 37 H9
Mahakam →,
Indonesia 26 E5
Mahalapye, *Botswana* . 37 J5
Mahallāt, *Iran* 31 C6
Māhān, *Iran* 31 D8
Mahanadi →, *India* .. 29 J15
Maharashtra □, *India* . 28 J9
Mahasham, W. →,
Egypt 33 E3
Mahattat ash Shīdīyah,
Jordan 33 F4
Mahattat 'Unayzah,
Jordan 33 E4
Mahbubnagar, *India* .. 28 L10
Maḥdah, *Oman* 31 E7
Mahdia, *Tunisia* 35 A8
Mahenge, *Tanzania* .. 36 F7
Maheno, *N.Z.* 39 L3
Mahesana, *India* 28 H8
Mahia Pen., *N.Z.* 39 H6
Mahilyow, *Belarus* ... 13 B16
Mahnomen, *U.S.A.* ... 54 B7
Mahón = Maó, *Spain* . 15 C8
Mahone Bay, *Canada* . 49 D7
Mai-Ndombe, L.,
Dem. Rep. of
the Congo 36 E3
Maïcurú →, *Brazil* ... 63 D8
Maidenhead, *U.K.* ... 9 F7
Maidstone, *Canada* .. 51 C7
Maidstone, *U.K.* 9 F8
Maiduguri, *Nigeria* ... 35 F8
Maijdi, *Bangla.* 29 H17
Maikala Ra., *India* ... 29 J12
Main →, *Germany* ... 12 C5
Main, *France* 14 C3
Maine □, *U.S.A.* 53 C11
Maine □, *U.S.A.* 53 C11
Maingkwan, *Burma* .. 29 F20
Mainit, L., *Phil.* 27 C7
Mainland, *Orkney, U.K.* 10 B5
Mainland, *Shet., U.K.* . 10 A6
Mainoru, *Australia* ... 42 A1
Mainz, *Germany* 12 C5
Maipú, *Argentina* ... 64 D5
Maiquetía, *Venezuela* . 62 A5
Mairabari, *India* 29 F18
Maisí, *Cuba* 61 B5
Maisí, Pta. de, *Cuba* . 61 B5
Maitland, *N.S.W.,*
Australia 43 E5
Maitland, *S. Austral.,*
Australia 43 E2
Maiz, Is. del, *Nic.* ... 60 D3
Maizuru, *Japan* 23 G7
Majalengka, *Indonesia* 27 G13
Majene, *Indonesia* ... 27 E5
Majorca = Mallorca,
Spain 15 C7
Makale, *Indonesia* ... 27 E5
Makarikari =
Makgadikgadi Salt
Pans, *Botswana* ... 37 J5

Makasar = Ujung
Pandang, *Indonesia* . 27 F5
Makasar, Selat,
Indonesia 27 E5
Makasar, Str. of =
Makasar, Selat,
Indonesia 27 E5
Makat, *Kazakstan* ... 19 E9
Makedhonía □, *Greece* 17 D10
Makedonija =
Macedonia ■, *Europe* 17 D9
Makeyevka = Makiyivka,
Ukraine 19 E6
Makgadikgadi Salt Pans,
Botswana 37 J5
Makhachkala, *Russia* .. 19 F8
Makhmūr, *Iraq* 30 C4
Makian, *Indonesia* ... 27 D7
Makinsk, *Kazakstan* .. 20 D8
Makiyivka, *Ukraine* ... 19 E6
Makkah, *Si. Arabia* ... 32 C2
Makkovik, *Canada* ... 49 A8
Makó, *Hungary* 13 E11
Makokou, *Gabon* 36 D2
Makrai, *India* 28 H10
Makran Coast Range,
Pakistan 28 G4
Mākū, *Iran* 30 B5
Makurazaki, *Japan* ... 23 J5
Makurdi, *Nigeria* 34 G7
Makūyeh, *Iran* 31 D7
Mala, Pta., *Panama* .. 60 E3
Malabar Coast, *India* . 28 P9
Malabo = Rey Malabo,
Eq. Guin. 36 D1
Malacca, Str. of,
Indonesia 26 D2
Malad City, *U.S.A.* ... 56 E7
Maladzyechna, *Belarus* 13 A14
Málaga, *Spain* 15 D3
Malagasy Rep. =
Madagascar ■, *Africa* 37 J9
Malaita, *Solomon Is.* . 38 B9
Malakāl, *Sudan* 35 G12
Malakand, *Pakistan* .. 28 B7
Malakula, *Vanuatu* ... 38 C9
Malamala, *Indonesia* . 27 E6
Malanda, *Australia* ... 42 B4
Malang, *Indonesia* ... 27 G15
Malangen, *Norway* ... 6 B18
Malanje, *Angola* 36 F3
Mälaren, *Sweden* ... 7 G17
Malargüe, *Argentina* . 64 D3
Malartic, *Canada* 48 C4
Malaryta, *Belarus* 13 C13
Malatya, *Turkey* 19 G6
Malawi ■, *Africa* 37 G6
Malawi, L. = Nyasa, L.,
Africa 37 G6
Malay Pen., *Asia* 26 D2
Malay Pen., *Asia* 26 D2
Malaya Vishera, *Russia* 18 C5
Malaybalay, *Phil.* 27 C7
Malāyer, *Iran* 31 C6
Malaysia ■, *Asia* 26 D4
Malazgirt, *Turkey* ... 19 G7
Malbon, *Australia* ... 42 C3
Malbooma, *Australia* . 43 E1
Malbork, *Poland* 13 B10
Malcolm, *Australia* ... 41 E3
Malcolm, Pt., *Australia* 41 F3
Maldegem, *Belgium* .. 11 C3
Malden, *U.S.A.* 55 G10
Malden I., *Kiribati* ... 45 H12
Maldives ■, *Ind. Oc.* . 3 D13
Maldonado, *Uruguay* . 64 C6
Maldonado, Punta,
Mexico 59 D5
Malé Karpaty,
Slovak Rep. 13 D9
Maléa, Ákra, *Greece* . 17 F10
Malegaon, *India* 28 J9
Malek Kandī, *Iran* ... 30 B5
Malema, *Mozam.* 37 G7
Maleny, *Australia* ... 43 D5
Malgomaj, *Sweden* ... 6 D17
Malha, *Sudan* 35 E11
Malheur →, *U.S.A.* .. 56 D5
Malheur L., *U.S.A.* ... 56 E4
Mali ■, *Africa* 34 E5
Mali →, *Burma* 29 G20
Mali Kyun, *Burma* ... 26 B1
Maliku, *Indonesia* ... 27 E6
Malili, *Indonesia* 27 E6
Malimba, Mts.,
Dem. Rep. of
the Congo 36 F5
Malin Hd., *Ireland* ... 10 D3
Malindi, *Kenya* 36 E8
Malines = Mechelen,
Belgium 11 C4
Malino, *Indonesia* ... 27 D6
Malita, *Phil.* 27 C7
Maliwun, *Burma* 26 B1
Malkara, *Turkey* 17 D12
Mallacoota Inlet,
Australia 43 F4
Mallaig, *U.K.* 10 C4
Mallawī, *Egypt* 35 C12
Mallicolo = Malakula,
Vanuatu 38 C9
Mallorca, *Spain* 15 C7
Mallow, *Ireland* 10 E2
Malmberget, *Sweden* . 6 C19
Malmédy, *Belgium* ... 11 D6

Malmö, *Sweden* 7 J15
Maloelap, *Phil.* 27 B6
Malone, *U.S.A.* 52 C8
Måløy, *Norway* 7 F11
Malpelo, I. de, *Colombia* 62 C2
Malta ■, *Europe* 16 G6
Malta, *Idaho, U.S.A.* .. 56 E7
Malta, *Mont., U.S.A.* .. 56 B10
Malton, *U.K.* 8 C7
Maluku, *Indonesia* ... 27 E7
Maluku □, *Indonesia* . 27 E7
Maluku Sea = Molucca
Sea, *Indonesia* ... 27 E6
Malvan, *India* 28 L8
Malvern, *U.S.A.* 55 H8
Malvern Hills, *U.K.* ... 9 E5
Malvinas, Is. = Falkland
Is. □, *Atl. Oc.* 64 G5
Malyn, *Ukraine* 13 C15
Malyy Lyakhovskiy,
Ostrov, *Russia* ... 21 B15
Mama, *Russia* 21 D12
Mamanguape, *Brazil* . 63 E11
Mamarr Mitlā, *Egypt* . 33 E1
Mamasa, *Indonesia* .. 27 E5
Mamberamo →,
Indonesia 27 E9
Mambilima Falls,
Zambia 36 G5
Mamburao, *Phil.* 27 B6
Mameigwess L., *Canada* 48 B2
Mammoth, *U.S.A.* ... 57 K8
Mammoth Cave
National Park, *U.S.A.* 52 G3
Mamoré →, *Bolivia* .. 62 F5
Mamou, *Guinea* 34 F3
Mamuju, *Indonesia* .. 27 E5
Man, *Ivory C.* 34 G4
Man, I. of, *U.K.* 8 C3
Man Na, *Burma* 29 H20
Mana →, *Fr. Guiana* . 63 B8
Manaar, G. of =
Mannar, G. of, *Asia* 28 Q11
Manacapuru, *Brazil* .. 62 D6
Manacor, *Spain* 15 C7
Manado, *Indonesia* .. 27 D6
Managua, *Nic.* 60 D2
Managua, L. de, *Nic.* . 60 D2
Manakara, *Madag.* ... 37 J9
Manama = Al
Manāmah, *Bahrain* . 31 E6
Mananjary, *Madag.* .. 37 J9
Manaos = Manaus,
Brazil 62 D7
Manapire →,
Venezuela 62 B5
Manapouri, *N.Z.* 39 L1
Manapouri, L., *N.Z.* .. 39 L1
Manār, Jabal, *Yemen* . 32 E3
Manas, *China* 24 B3
Manas →, *India* 29 F17
Manassa, *U.S.A.* 57 H11
Manaung, *Burma* ... 29 K18
Manaus, *Brazil* 62 D7
Manawan L., *Canada* . 51 B8
Manbij, *Syria* 30 B3
Manchegorsk, *Russia* . 20 C4
Manchester, *U.K.* 8 D5
Manchester, *Ga., U.S.A.* 53 J3
Manchester, *Iowa,*
U.S.A. 54 D9
Manchester, *Ky., U.S.A.* 52 G4
Manchester, *N.H.,*
U.S.A. 52 D10
Manchester, *Tenn.,*
U.S.A. 53 H2
Manchester L., *Canada* 51 A7
Manchuria = Dongbei,
China 25 B7
Mand →, *Iran* 31 D7
Mandal, *Norway* 7 G12
Mandala, Puncak,
Indonesia 27 E10
Mandalay, *Burma* ... 29 J20
Mandale = Mandalay,
Burma 29 J20
Mandalī, *Iraq* 30 C5
Mandan, *U.S.A.* 54 B4
Mandar, Teluk,
Indonesia 27 E5
Mandaue, *Phil.* 27 B6
Mandi, *India* 28 D10
Mandimba, *Mozam.* .. 37 G7
Mandioli, *Indonesia* .. 27 E7
Mandla, *India* 29 H12
Mandorah, *Australia* .. 40 B5
Mandritsara, *Madag.* . 37 H9
Mandsaur, *India* 28 G9
Mandurah, *Australia* . 41 F2
Mandvi, *India* 28 H6
Mandya, *India* 28 N10
Maneh, *Iran* 31 B8
Maneroo Cr. →,
Australia 42 C3
Manfalūt, *Egypt* 35 C12
Manfredónia, *Italy* ... 16 D6
Mangabeiras, Chapada
das, *Brazil* 63 F9
Mangalia, *Romania* .. 13 G15
Mangalore, *India* 28 N9
Mangaung, *S. Africa* . 37 K5
Mangaweka, *N.Z.* ... 39 H5
Manggar, *Indonesia* .. 26 E3
Manggawitu, *Indonesia* 27 E8
Mao, *Chad* 35 F9

Mangkalihat, Tanjung,
Indonesia 27 D5
Mangla Dam, *Pakistan* 28 C8
Mangnai, *China* 24 C4
Mango, *Togo* 34 F6
Mangoche, *Malawi* .. 37 G7
Mangoky →, *Madag.* . 37 J8
Mangole, *Indonesia* .. 27 E6
Mangonui, *N.Z.* 39 F4
Mangueira, L. da, *Brazil* 64 C6
Manguéni, Plateau du,
Niger 35 D8
Mangum, *U.S.A.* 55 H5
Mangyshlak Poluostrov,
Kazakstan 19 E9
Manhattan, *U.S.A.* ... 54 F6
Manica, *Mozam.* 37 H6
Manicoré, *Brazil* 62 E6
Manicouagan →,
Canada 49 C6
Manicouagan, Rés.,
Canada 49 B6
Manifah, *Si. Arabia* .. 31 E6
Manifold, C., *Australia* . 42 C5
Manigotagan, *Canada* . 51 C9
Manigotagan →,
Canada 51 C9
Manihiki, *Cook Is.* ... 45 J11
Manila, *Phil.* 27 B6
Manila, *U.S.A.* 56 F9
Manila B., *Phil.* 27 B6
Manilla, *Australia* 43 E5
Maningrida, *Australia* . 42 A1
Manipur □, *India* 29 G19
Manipur →, *Burma* .. 29 H19
Manisa, *Turkey* 17 E12
Manistee, *U.S.A.* 52 C2
Manistee →, *U.S.A.* . 52 C2
Manistique, *U.S.A.* ... 52 C2
Manito L., *Canada* ... 51 C7
Manitoba □, *Canada* . 51 B9
Manitoba, L., *Canada* . 51 C9
Manitou, *Canada* ... 51 D9
Manitou, *U.S.A.* 52 C2
Manitou Is., *U.S.A.* ... 52 C3
Manitou Springs, *U.S.A.* 54 F2
Manitoulin I., *Canada* . 48 C3
Manitouwadge, *Canada* 48 C2
Manitowoc, *U.S.A.* ... 52 C2
Manizales, *Colombia* . 62 B3
Manjhand, *Pakistan* .. 28 G6
Manjil, *Iran* 31 B6
Manjimup, *Australia* .. 41 F2
Manjra →, *India* 28 K10
Mankato, *Kans., U.S.A.* 54 F5
Mankato, *Minn., U.S.A.* 54 C8
Mankota, *Canada* ... 51 D7
Manmad, *India* 28 J9
Mann Ranges, *Australia* 41 E5
Manna, *Indonesia* ... 26 E2
Mannahill, *Australia* .. 43 E3
Mannar, *Sri Lanka* ... 28 Q11
Mannar, G. of, *Asia* .. 28 Q11
Mannar I., *Sri Lanka* .. 28 Q11
Mannheim, *Germany* . 12 D5
Manning, *Canada* ... 50 B5
Manning, *U.S.A.* 53 J5
Manning Prov. Park,
Canada 50 D4
Mannum, *Australia* .. 43 E2
Manokwari, *Indonesia* . 27 E8
Manono, *Dem. Rep. of*
the Congo 36 F5
Manosque, *France* ... 14 E6
Manouane →, *Canada* 49 C5
Manouane, L., *Canada* 49 B5
Manresa, *Spain* 15 B6
Mansel I., *Canada* ... 47 B11
Mansfield, *Australia* .. 43 F4
Mansfield, *U.K.* 8 D6
Mansfield, *La., U.S.A.* . 55 J8
Mansfield, *Ohio, U.S.A.* 52 E4
Manson Creek, *Canada* 50 B4
Manta, *Ecuador* 62 D2
Mantalingajan, Mt., *Phil.* 26 C5
Manteca, *U.S.A.* 57 H3
Manteo, *U.S.A.* 53 H8
Mantes-la-Jolie, *France* 14 B4
Manthani, *India* 28 K11
Manti, *U.S.A.* 56 G8
Manton, *U.S.A.* 52 C3
Mántova, *Italy* 16 B4
Mänttä, *Finland* 7 E21
Mantua = Mántova,
Italy 16 B4
Manu, *Peru* 62 F4
Manu →, *Peru* 62 F4
Manua Is.,
Amer. Samoa 39 B14
Manuel Alves →, *Brazil* 63 F9
Manui, *Indonesia* 27 E6
Manukau, *N.Z.* 39 G5
Manuripi →, *Bolivia* . 62 F5
Many, *U.S.A.* 55 K8
Manych-Gudilo, Ozero,
Russia 19 E7
Manzai, *Pakistan* 28 C7
Manzanares, *Spain* .. 15 C4
Manzanillo, *Cuba* ... 60 B4
Manzanillo, *Mexico* .. 58 D4
Manzanillo, Pta.,
Panama 60 E4
Manzano Mts., *U.S.A.* . 57 J10
Manzarīyeh, *Iran* 31 C6
Manzhouli, *China* ... 25 B6

Maó, *Spain* 15 C8
Maoke, Pegunungan,
Indonesia 27 E9
Maoming, *China* 25 D6
Mapam Yumco, *China* . 24 C3
Mapastepec, *Mexico* . 59 D6
Mapia, Kepulauan,
Indonesia 27 D8
Mapimí, *Mexico* 58 B4
Mapimí, Bolsón de,
Mexico 58 B4
Maple Creek, *Canada* . 51 D7
Mapleton, *U.S.A.* 56 D2
Mapuera →, *Brazil* .. 62 D7
Maputo, *Mozam.* 37 K6
Maqnā, *Si. Arabia* ... 30 D2
Maquela do Zombo,
Angola 36 F3
Maquinchao, *Argentina* 64 E3
Maquoketa, *U.S.A.* .. 54 D9
Mar Chiquita, L.,
Argentina 64 C4
Mar del Plata, *Argentina* 64 D5
Mar Menor, *Spain* ... 15 D5
Maraã, *Brazil* 62 D5
Marabá, *Brazil* 63 E9
Maracá, I. de, *Brazil* . 63 C8
Maracaibo, *Venezuela* . 62 A4
Maracaibo, L. de,
Venezuela 62 B4
Maracay, *Venezuela* .. 62 A5
Maradi, *Niger* 34 F7
Marägheh, *Iran* 30 B5
Marāh, *Si. Arabia* ... 30 E5
Marajó, I. de, *Brazil* .. 63 D9
Maräkand, *Iran* 30 B5
Maralinga, *Australia* .. 41 F5
Marana, *U.S.A.* 57 K8
Maranboy, *Australia* .. 40 B5
Marand, *Iran* 30 B5
Maranguape, *Brazil* .. 63 D11
Maranhão = São Luís,
Brazil 63 D10
Maranhão □, *Brazil* .. 63 E9
Maranoa →, *Australia* 43 D4
Marañón →, *Peru* ... 62 D4
Marão, *Mozam.* 37 J6
Maraş =
Kahramanmaraş,
Turkey 19 G6
Marathon, *Australia* .. 42 C3
Marathon, *Canada* ... 48 C2
Marathon, *U.S.A.* ... 55 K3
Maratua, *Indonesia* .. 27 D5
Maravatío, *Mexico* .. 58 D4
Marawih, *U.A.E.* 31 E7
Marbella, *Spain* 15 D3
Marble Bar, *Australia* . 40 D2
Marble Falls, *U.S.A.* .. 55 K5
Marburg, *Germany* ... 12 C5
March, *U.K.* 9 E8
Marche, *France* 14 C4
Marche-en-Famenne,
Belgium 11 D5
Marchena, *Spain* 15 D3
Marco, *U.S.A.* 53 N5
Marcus I. =
Minami-
Tori-Shima, *Pac. Oc.* 44 E7
Marcus Necker Ridge,
Pac. Oc. 44 F9
Mardan, *Pakistan* ... 28 B8
Mardin, *Turkey* 19 G7
Mareeba, *Australia* .. 42 B4
Marek = Stanke
Dimitrov, *Bulgaria* . 17 C10
Marengo, *U.S.A.* 54 E8
Marfa, *U.S.A.* 55 K2
Margaret →, *Australia* 40 C4
Margaret Bay, *Canada* . 50 C3
Margaret L., *Canada* .. 50 B5
Margaret River,
Australia 41 F2
Margarita, I. de,
Venezuela 62 A6
Margaritovo, *Russia* .. 22 C7
Margate, *U.K.* 9 F9
Märgow, Dasht-e,
Afghan. 28 D3
Marguerite, *Canada* .. 50 C4
Mari El □, *Russia* ... 18 C8
Mari Republic = Mari
El □, *Russia* 18 C8
Maria I., *N. Terr.,*
Australia 42 A2
Maria I., *Tas., Australia* 42 G4
Maria van Diemen, C.,
N.Z. 39 F4
Marian, *Australia* 42 C4
Marian L., *Canada* ... 50 A5
Mariana Trench,
Pac. Oc. 44 F6
Marianao, *Cuba* 60 B3
Marianna, *Ark., U.S.A.* 55 H9
Marianna, *Fla., U.S.A.* 53 K3
Marias →, *U.S.A.* ... 56 C8
Mariato, Punta, *Panama* 60 E3
Maribor, *Slovenia* ... 12 E8
Maricopa, *Ariz., U.S.A.* 57 K7
Maricopa, *Calif., U.S.A.* 57 J4
Marié →, *Brazil* 62 D5
Marie Byrd Land,
Antarctica 5 D14
Marie-Galante,
Guadeloupe 61 C7

Mariecourt =
Kangiqsujuaq, *Canada* 47 B12
Mariembourg, *Belgium* 11 D4
Mariental, *Namibia* ... 37 J3
Mariestad, *Sweden* ... 7 G15
Marietta, *Ga., U.S.A.* . 53 J3
Marietta, *Ohio, U.S.A.* . 52 F5
Mariinsk, *Russia* 20 D9
Marijampole, *Lithuania* 7 J20
Marília, *Brazil* 63 H9
Marin, *Spain* 15 A1
Marinduque, *Phil.* 27 B6
Marinette, *U.S.A.* 52 C2
Maringá, *Brazil* 64 A6
Marion, *Ala., U.S.A.* .. 53 J2
Marion, *Ill., U.S.A.* .. 55 G10
Marion, *Ind., U.S.A.* .. 52 E3
Marion, *Iowa, U.S.A.* .. 54 D9
Marion, *Kans., U.S.A.* . 54 F6
Marion, *N.C., U.S.A.* .. 53 H5
Marion, *Ohio, U.S.A.* .. 52 E4
Marion, *S.C., U.S.A.* .. 53 H6
Marion, *Va., U.S.A.* .. 53 G5
Marion, *L., U.S.A.* 53 J5
Mariposa, *U.S.A.* 57 H4
Mariscal Estigarribia,
Paraguay 62 H6
Maritime Alps =
Maritimes, Alpes,
Europe 14 D7
Maritimes, Alpes,
Europe 14 D7
Maritsa = Évros →,
Bulgaria 17 D12
Mariupol, *Ukraine* ... 19 E6
Marīvān, *Iran* 30 C5
Marj 'Uyūn, *Lebanon* .. 33 B4
Markazī □, *Iran* 31 C6
Marked Tree, *U.S.A.* .. 55 H9
Market Drayton, *U.K.* .. 8 E5
Market Harborough,
U.K. 9 E7
Market Rasen, *U.K.* 8 D7
Markham, Mt.,
Antarctica 5 E11
Markovo, *Russia* 21 C17
Marks, *Russia* 18 D8
Marksville, *U.S.A.* 55 K8
Marla, *Australia* 43 D1
Marlborough, *Australia* 42 C4
Marlborough, *U.K.* 9 F6
Marlborough Downs,
U.K. 9 F6
Marlin, *U.S.A.* 55 K6
Marlow, *U.S.A.* 55 H6
Marmagao, *India* 28 M8
Marmara, *Turkey* 17 D12
Marmara, Sea of =
Marmara Denizi,
Turkey 17 D13
Marmara Denizi, *Turkey* 17 D13
Marmaris, *Turkey* 17 F13
Marmion, Mt., *Australia* 41 E2
Marmion L., *Canada* .. 48 C1
Marmolada, Mte., *Italy* 16 A4
Marmora, *Canada* 48 D4
Marne →, *France* 14 B5
Maroantsetra, *Madag.* . 37 H9
Marondera, *Zimbabwe* 37 H6
Maroni →, *Fr. Guiana* 63 B8
Maroochydore, *Australia* 43 D5
Maroona, *Australia* 43 F3
Maroua, *Cameroon* .. 35 F8
Marovoay, *Madag.* 37 H9
Marquesas Is. =
Marquises, Is.,
Pac. Oc. 45 H14
Marquette, *U.S.A.* 52 B2
Marquises, Is., *Pac. Oc.* 45 H14
Marra, Djebel, *Sudan* . 35 F10
Marrakech, *Morocco* .. 34 B4
Marrawah, *Australia* .. 42 G3
Marree, *Australia* 43 D2
Marrero, *U.S.A.* 55 L9
Marrowie Cr. →,
Australia 43 E4
Marrupa, *Mozam.* 37 G7
Mars Hill, *U.S.A.* 53 B12
Marsá Matrûh, *Egypt* . 35 B11
Marsabit, *Kenya* 36 D7
Marsala, *Italy* 16 F5
Marsden, *Australia* 43 E4
Marseille, *France* 14 E6
Marseilles = Marseille,
France 14 E6
Marsh I., *U.S.A.* 55 L9
Marshall, *Ark., U.S.A.* . 55 H8
Marshall, *Mich., U.S.A.* 52 D3
Marshall, *Minn., U.S.A.* 54 C7
Marshall, *Mo., U.S.A.* . 54 F8
Marshall, *Tex., U.S.A.* . 55 J7
Marshall →, *Australia* . 42 C2
Marshall Is. ■, *Pac. Oc.* 38 A10
Marshalltown, *U.S.A.* .. 54 D8
Marshfield, *Mo., U.S.A.* 55 G8
Marshfield, *Wis., U.S.A.* 54 C9
Marshûn, *Iran* 31 B6
Märsta, *Sweden* 7 G17
Mart, *U.S.A.* 55 K6
Martaban, *Burma* 29 L20
Martaban, G. of, *Burma* 29 L20
Martapura, *Kalimantan,
Indonesia* 26 E4
Martapura, *Sumatera,
Indonesia* 26 E2

Martelange, *Belgium* .. 11 E5
Martha's Vineyard,
U.S.A. 52 E10
Martigny, *Switz.* 14 C7
Martigues, *France* 14 E6
Martin, *Slovak Rep.* .. 13 D10
Martin, *S. Dak., U.S.A.* 54 D4
Martin, *Tenn., U.S.A.* . 55 G10
Martin, *L., U.S.A.* 53 J3
Martina Franca, *Italy* .. 16 D7
Martinborough, *N.Z.* .. 39 J5
Martinez, *U.S.A.* 53 J4
Martinique ■, *W. Indies* 61 D7
Martinique Passage,
W. Indies 61 C7
Martins Ferry, *U.S.A.* . 52 E5
Martinsburg, *U.S.A.* .. 52 F7
Martinsville, *Ind., U.S.A.* 52 F2
Martinsville, *Va., U.S.A.* 53 G6
Marton, *N.Z.* 39 J5
Martos, *Spain* 15 D4
Marudi, *Malaysia* 26 D4
Ma'ruf, *Afghan.* 28 D5
Marugame, *Japan* 23 G6
Marv Dasht, *Iran* 31 D7
Marvast, *Iran* 31 D7
Marvel Loch, *Australia* 41 F2
Marwar, *India* 28 G8
Mary, *Turkmenistan* .. 20 F7
Maryborough = Port
Laoise, *Ireland* ... 10 E3
Maryborough, *Queens.,
Australia* 43 D5
Maryborough, *Vic.,
Australia* 43 F3
Maryfield, *Canada* ... 51 D8
Maryland □, *U.S.A.* .. 52 F7
Maryport, *U.K.* 8 C4
Mary's Harbour, *Canada* 49 B8
Marystown, *Canada* .. 49 C8
Marysville, *Canada* .. 50 D5
Marysville, *Calif., U.S.A.* 56 G3
Marysville, *Kans., U.S.A.* 54 F6
Marysville, *Ohio, U.S.A.* 52 E4
Maryville, *Mo., U.S.A.* 54 E7
Maryville, *Tenn., U.S.A.* 53 H4
Marzûq, *Libya* 35 C8
Masaka, *Uganda* 36 E6
Masalembo, Kepulauan,
Indonesia 26 F4
Masalima, Kepulauan,
Indonesia 26 F5
Masamba, *Indonesia* .. 27 E6
Masan, *S. Korea* 25 C7
Masandam, Ra's, *Oman* 31 E8
Masasi, *Tanzania* 36 G7
Masaya, *Nic.* 60 D2
Masbate, *Phil.* 27 B6
Mascara, *Algeria* 34 A4
Mascota, *Mexico* 58 C4
Masela, *Indonesia* 27 F7
Maseru, *Lesotho* 37 K5
Mashābih, *Si. Arabia* .. 30 E3
Mashhad, *Iran* 31 B8
Mashīz, *Iran* 31 D8
Mâshkel, Hâmûn-i-,
Pakistan 28 E3
Mashki Chāh, *Pakistan* 28 E3
Mashonaland,
Zimbabwe 37 H6
Masindi, *Uganda* 36 D6
Maşīrah, *Oman* 32 C6
Maşīrah, Khalīj, *Oman* 32 C6
Masjed Soleyman, *Iran* 31 D6
Mask, L., *Ireland* 10 E2
Maskin, *Oman* 31 F8
Masoala, Tanjon' i,
Madag. 37 H10
Masohi = Amahai,
Indonesia 27 E7
Mason, *U.S.A.* 55 K5
Mason City, *U.S.A.* .. 54 D8
Masqat, *Oman* 32 C6
Massa, *Italy* 14 D9
Massachusetts □, *U.S.A.* 52 D10
Massakory, *Chad* 35 F9
Massangena, *Mozam.* . 37 J6
Massango, *Angola* 36 F3
Massawa = Mitsiwa,
Eritrea 32 D2
Massena, *U.S.A.* 52 C8
Massénya, *Chad* 35 F9
Masset, *Canada* 50 C2
Massif Central, *France* . 14 D5
Massillon, *U.S.A.* 52 E5
Massinga, *Mozam.* 37 J7
Masson I., *Antarctica* . 5 C7
Mastanli =
Momchilgrad,
Bulgaria 17 D11
Masterton, *N.Z.* 39 J5
Mastuj, *Pakistan* 28 A8
Mastung, *Pakistan* .. 28 E5
Masty, *Belarus* 13 B13
Masuda, *Japan* 23 G5
Masvingo, *Zimbabwe* . 37 J6
Maşyāf, *Syria* 30 C3
Matabeleland,
Zimbabwe 37 H5
Matachewan, *Canada* . 48 C3
Matadi, *Dem. Rep. of
the Congo* 36 F2
Matagalpa, *Nic.* 60 D2
Matagami, *Canada* ... 48 C4
Matagami, L., *Canada* . 48 C4

Matagorda B., *U.S.A.* . 55 L6
Matagorda I., *U.S.A.* . 55 L6
Matak, *Indonesia* 26 D3
Matamoros, *Campeche,
Mexico* 59 D6
Matamoros, *Coahuila,
Mexico* 58 B4
Matamoros,
Tamaulipas, Mexico . 59 B5
Ma'tan as Sarra, *Libya* 35 D10
Matane, *Canada* 49 C6
Matanzas, *Cuba* 60 B3
Matapan, C. = Taínaron,
Ákra, *Greece* 17 F10
Matapédia, *Canada* ... 49 C6
Matara, *Sri Lanka* 28 S12
Mataram, *Indonesia* .. 26 F5
Matarani, *Peru* 62 G4
Mataranka, *Australia* . 40 B5
Matarma, Râs, *Egypt* . 33 E1
Mataró, *Spain* 15 B7
Mataura, *N.Z.* 39 M2
Matehuala, *Mexico* .. 58 C4
Matera, *Italy* 16 D7
Mathis, *U.S.A.* 55 L6
Mathráki, *Greece* 17 E8
Mathura, *India* 28 F10
Mati, *Phil.* 27 C7
Matías Romero, *Mexico* 59 D5
Matiri Ra., *N.Z.* 39 J4
Matlock, *U.K.* 8 D6
Mato Grosso □, *Brazil* 63 F8
Mato Grosso, Planalto
do, *Brazil* 63 G8
Mato Grosso do Sul □,
Brazil 63 G8
Matochkin Shar, *Russia* 20 B6
Matosinhos, *Portugal* . 15 B1
Maţruh, *Oman* 32 C6
Matsue, *Japan* 23 G6
Matsumae, *Japan* 22 D10
Matsumoto, *Japan* ... 23 F9
Matsusaka, *Japan* 23 G8
Matsuura, *Japan* 23 H4
Matsuyama, *Japan* ... 23 H6
Mattancheri, *India* ... 28 Q10
Mattawa, *Canada* 48 C4
Matterhorn, *Switz.* ... 14 D7
Matthew Town,
Bahamas 61 B5
Matthew's Ridge,
Guyana 62 B6
Mattice, *Canada* 48 C3
Mattô, *Japan* 23 F8
Mattoon, *U.S.A.* 52 F1
Matucana, *Peru* 62 F3
Matún = Khowst,
Afghan. 28 C6
Maturín, *Venezuela* .. 62 B6
Mau Ranipur, *India* .. 28 G11
Maubeuge, *France* ... 14 A6
Maud, Pt., *Australia* .. 40 D1
Maude, *Australia* 43 E3
Maudin Sun, *Burma* .. 29 M19
Maués, *Brazil* 62 D7
Mauganj, *India* 29 G12
Maughold Hd., *U.K.* .. 8 C3
Maulamyaing =
Moulmein, *Burma* .. 29 L20
Maumee, *U.S.A.* 52 E4
Maumee →, *U.S.A.* .. 52 E4
Maumere, *Indonesia* .. 27 F6
Maun, *Botswana* 37 H4
Maungmagan Kyunzu,
Burma 26 B1
Maupin, *U.S.A.* 56 D3
Maurepas, L., *U.S.A.* . 55 K9
Maurice, L., *Australia* . 41 E5
Mauricie, Parc Nat. de
la, *Canada* 48 C5
Mauritania ■, *Africa* .. 34 D3
Mauritius ■, *Ind. Oc.* . 3 F12
Mauston, *U.S.A.* 54 D9
Mawk Mai, *Burma* ... 29 J20
Mawlaik, *Burma* 29 H19
Mawlamyine =
Moulmein, *Burma* .. 29 L20
Mawqaq, *Si. Arabia* .. 30 E4
Mawson Coast,
Antarctica 5 C6
Max, *U.S.A.* 54 B4
Maxcanú, *Mexico* 59 C6
Maxhamish L., *Canada* 50 B4
Maxwelton, *Australia* . 42 C3
May, C., *U.S.A.* 52 F8
May Pen, *Jamaica* ... 60 C4
Maya →, *Russia* 21 D14
Maya Mts., *Belize* 59 D7
Mayaguana, *Bahamas* . 61 B5
Mayagüez, *Puerto Rico* 61 C6
Mayamey, *Iran* 31 B7
Mayanup, *Australia* .. 41 F2
Mayapan, *Mexico* 59 C7
Mayari, *Cuba* 61 B4
Maydān, *Iraq* 30 C5
Maydena, *Australia* ... 42 G4
Mayenne →, *France* . 14 C3
Mayer, *U.S.A.* 57 J7
Mayerthorpe, *Canada* . 50 C5
Mayfield, *U.S.A.* 53 G1
Mayhill, *U.S.A.* 57 K11
Maykop, *Russia* 19 F7

Maynard Hills, *Australia* 41 E2
Mayne →, *Australia* . 42 C3
Mayo, *Canada* 46 B6
Mayon Volcano, *Phil.* . 27 B6
Mayor I., *N.Z.* 39 G6
Mayotte, *Ind. Oc.* 37 G9
Maysville, *U.S.A.* 52 F4
Mayu, *Indonesia* 27 D7
Mayville, *U.S.A.* 54 B6
Mayya, *Russia* 21 C14
Mazabuka, *Zambia* ... 37 H5
Mazagán = El Jadida,
Morocco 34 B4
Mazagão, *Brazil* 63 D8
Mazán, *Peru* 62 D4
Māzandarān □, *Iran* .. 31 B7
Mazapil, *Mexico* 58 C4
Mazara del Vallo, *Italy* 16 F5
Mazarrón, *Spain* 15 D5
Mazaruni →, *Guyana* 62 B7
Mazatán, *Mexico* 58 B2
Mazatenango,
Guatemala 60 D1
Mazatlán, *Mexico* 58 C3
Mažeikiai, *Lithuania* . 7 H20
Māzhān, *Iran* 31 C8
Mazīnān, *Iran* 31 B8
Mazoe →, *Mozam.* .. 37 H6
Mazurian Lakes =
Mazurski, Pojezierze,
Poland 13 B11
Mazurski, Pojezierze,
Poland 13 B11
Mazyr, *Belarus* 13 B15
Mbabane, *Swaziland* . 37 K6
Mbaïki, *C.A.R.* 36 D3
Mbala, *Zambia* 36 F6
Mbale, *Uganda* 36 D6
Mbalmayo, *Cameroon* . 36 D2
Mbandaka, *Dem. Rep. of
the Congo* 36 D3
Mbanza Congo, *Angola* 36 F2
Mbanza Ngungu,
*Dem. Rep. of
the Congo* 36 F2
Mbarara, *Uganda* 36 E6
Mbeya, *Tanzania* 36 F6
Mbini □, *Eq. Guin.* ... 36 D2
Mbour, *Senegal* 34 F2
Mbuji-Mayi, *Dem. Rep.
of the Congo* 36 F4
Mdantsane, *S. Africa* . 37 L5
Mead, L., *U.S.A.* 57 H6
Meade, *U.S.A.* 55 G4
Meadow Lake, *Canada* 51 C7
Meadow Lake Prov.
Park, *Canada* 51 C7
Meadow Valley
Wash →, *U.S.A.* .. 57 H6
Meadville, *U.S.A.* 52 E5
Meaford, *Canada* 48 D3
Mealy Mts., *Canada* .. 49 B8
Meander River, *Canada* 50 B5
Meares, C., *U.S.A.* ... 56 D2
Mearim →, *Brazil* ... 63 D10
Meath □, *Ireland* 10 E3
Meath Park, *Canada* . 51 C7
Meaux, *France* 14 B5
Mebechi-Gawa →,
Japan 22 D10
Mecca = Makkah,
Si. Arabia 32 C2
Mechelen, *Belgium* ... 11 C4
Mecheria, *Algeria* 34 B5
Mecklenburg, *Germany* 12 B6
Mecklenburger Bucht,
Germany 12 A6
Medan, *Indonesia* 26 D1
Medanosa, Pta.,
Argentina 64 F3
Médéa, *Algeria* 34 A6
Medellín, *Colombia* ... 62 B3
Medelpad, *Sweden* ... 7 E17
Medemblik, *Neths.* ... 11 B5
Medford, *Oreg., U.S.A.* 56 E2
Medford, *Wis., U.S.A.* . 54 C9
Medgidia, *Romania* ... 13 F15
Mediaş, *Romania* 13 E13
Medicine Bow, *U.S.A.* . 56 F10
Medicine Bow Pk.,
U.S.A. 56 F10
Medicine Bow Ra.,
U.S.A. 56 F10
Medicine Hat, *Canada* . 51 D6
Medicine Lake, *U.S.A.* . 54 A2
Medicine Lodge, *U.S.A.* 55 G5
Medina = Al Madinah,
Si. Arabia 30 E3
Medina, *N. Dak., U.S.A.* 54 B5
Medina, *N.Y., U.S.A.* . 52 D6
Medina, *Ohio, U.S.A.* . 52 E3
Medina →, *U.S.A.* .. 55 L5
Medina del Campo,
Spain 15 B3
Medina L., *U.S.A.* 55 L5
Medina Sidonia, *Spain* 15 D3
Medinipur, *India* 29 H15
Mediterranean Sea,
Europe 3 C10
Mediterranean Sea,
Europe 3 C10
Médoc, *France* 14 D3
Medveditsa →, *Russia* 19 E7
Medvezhi, Ostrava,
Russia 21 B17
Medvezhyegorsk, *Russia* 18 B5

Medway □, *U.K.* 9 F8
Medway →, *U.K.* 9 F8
Meekatharra, *Australia* 41 E2
Meeker, *U.S.A.* 56 F10
Meelpaeg Res., *Canada* 49 C8
Meerut, *India* 28 E10
Meeteetse, *U.S.A.* 56 D9
Mega, *Ethiopia* 32 G2
Mégara, *Greece* 17 F10
Meghalaya □, *India* .. 29 G17
Mégiscane, L., *Canada* 48 C4
Meharry, Mt., *Australia* 40 D2
Mehlville, *U.S.A.* 54 F9
Mehr Jān, *Iran* 31 C7
Mehrābād, *Iran* 30 B5
Mehrīz, *Iran* 30 C5
Mehrīz, *Iran* 31 D7
Meiktila, *Burma* 29 J19
Meissen, *Germany* ... 12 C7
Meizhou, *China* 25 D6
Mejillones, *Chile* 64 A2
Mekele, *Ethiopia* 32 E2
Mekhtar, *Pakistan* ... 28 D6
Meknès, *Morocco* 34 B4
Mekong →, *Asia* 26 C3
Mekongga, *Indonesia* . 27 E6
Mekvari = Kür →,
Azerbaijan 19 G8
Melagiri Hills, *India* ... 28 N10
Melaka, *Malaysia* 26 D2
Melalap, *Malaysia* 26 C5
Melanesia, *Pac. Oc.* .. 44 H7
Melbourne, *Australia* . 43 F4
Melbourne, *U.S.A.* 53 L5
Melchor Múzquiz,
Mexico 58 B4
Melchor Ocampo,
Mexico 58 C4
Mélèzes →, *Qué.,
Canada* 47 C12
Mélèzes →, *Qué.,
Canada* 48 A5
Melfort, *Canada* 51 C8
Melhus, *Norway* 6 E14
Melilla, *N. Afr.* 15 E4
Melita, *Canada* 51 D8
Melitopol, *Ukraine* ... 19 E6
Melk, *Austria* 12 D8
Mellansel, *Sweden* ... 6 E18
Mellerud, *Sweden* ... 7 G15
Mellette, *U.S.A.* 54 C5
Melo, *Uruguay* 64 C5
Melolo, *Indonesia* 27 F6
Melrose, *Australia* 43 E4
Melrose, *Minn., U.S.A.* 54 C7
Melrose, *N. Mex., U.S.A.* 55 H3
Melstone, *U.S.A.* 56 C10
Melton Mowbray, *U.K.* 8 E7
Melun, *France* 14 B5
Melville, *Canada* 51 C8
Melville, *C., Australia* . 42 A3
Melville, L., *Canada* .. 49 B8
Melville, B., *Australia* . 42 A2
Melville I., *Australia* .. 40 B5
Melville I., *Canada* ... 4 B2
Melville Pen., *Canada* . 47 B11
Memboro, *Indonesia* . 27 F5
Memel = Klaipeda,
Lithuania 7 J19
Memmingen, *Germany* 12 E6
Mempawah, *Indonesia* 26 D3
Memphis, *Tenn., U.S.A.* 55 H10
Memphis, *Tex., U.S.A.* 55 H4
Mena, *U.S.A.* 55 H7
Menai Strait, *U.K.* 8 D3
Ménaka, *Mali* 34 E5
Menan = Chao
Phraya →, *Thailand* 26 B2
Menard, *U.S.A.* 55 K5
Mendawai →,
Indonesia 26 E4
Mende, *France* 14 D5
Mendez, *Mexico* 59 B5
Mendip Hills, *U.K.* 9 F5
Mendocino, *U.S.A.* ... 56 G2
Mendocino, C., *U.S.A.* 56 F1
Mendooran, *Australia* . 43 E4
Mendota, *Calif., U.S.A.* 57 H3
Mendota, *Ill., U.S.A.* . 54 E10
Mendoza, *Argentina* .. 64 C3
Mene Grande,
Venezuela 62 B4
Menemen, *Turkey* ... 17 E12
Menen, *Belgium* 11 D3
Menggala, *Indonesia* . 26 E3
Mengzi, *China* 24 D5
Menihek, *Canada* 49 B6
Menihek L., *Canada* .. 49 B6
Menin = Menen,
Belgium 11 D3
Menindee, *Australia* .. 43 E3
Menindee L., *Australia* 43 E3
Meningie, *Australia* ... 43 F2
Menominee, *U.S.A.* ... 52 C2
Menominee →, *U.S.A.* 52 C2
Menomonie, *U.S.A.* .. 54 C9
Menongue, *Angola* ... 37 G3
Menorca, *Spain* 15 C8
Mentawai, Kepulauan,
Indonesia 26 E1
Mentor, *U.S.A.* 52 E5
Menzelinsk, *Russia* .. 18 C9
Menzies, *Australia* ... 41 E3

Me'ona, *Israel* 33 B4
Meoqui, *Mexico* 58 B3
Meppel, *Neths.* 11 B6
Merabéllou, Kólpos,
Greece 17 G11
Merak, *Indonesia* 27 F12
Meramangye, L.,
Australia 41 E5
Meran = Merano, *Italy* 16 A4
Merano, *Italy* 16 A4
Merauke, *Indonesia* .. 27 F10
Merbein, *Australia* 43 E3
Merca, *Somali Rep.* ... 32 G3
Mercedes,
*Buenos Aires,
Argentina* 64 C5
Mercedes, *Corrientes,
Argentina* 64 B5
Mercedes, *San Luis,
Argentina* 64 C3
Mercedes, *Uruguay* .. 64 C5
Mercedes, *U.S.A.* 55 M6
Mercer, *N.Z.* 39 G5
Mercy C., *Canada* 47 B13
Mere, *U.K.* 9 F5
Meredith, C., *Falk. Is.* . 64 G4
Meredith, L., *U.S.A.* .. 55 H4
Mergui, *Burma* 26 B1
Mergui Arch. = Myeik
Kyunzu, *Burma* ... 26 B1
Mérida, *Mexico* 59 C7
Mérida, *Spain* 15 C2
Mérida, *Venezuela* ... 62 B4
Mérida, Cord. de,
Venezuela 62 B4
Mérida, Cord. de,
Venezuela 62 B4
Meriden, *U.K.* 9 E6
Meriden, *U.S.A.* 52 E9
Meridian, *Idaho, U.S.A.* 56 E5
Meridian, *Miss., U.S.A.* 53 J1
Merimbula, *Australia* . 43 F4
Merinda, *Australia* 42 C4
Meringur, *Australia* ... 43 E3
Merir, *Pac. Oc.* 27 D8
Merirumã, *Brazil* 63 C8
Merkel, *U.S.A.* 55 J5
Mermaid Reef, *Australia* 40 C2
Merredin, *Australia* ... 41 F2
Merrill, *Oreg., U.S.A.* . 56 E3
Merrill, *Wis., U.S.A.* .. 54 C10
Merriman, *U.S.A.* 54 D4
Merritt, *Canada* 50 C4
Merritt Island, *U.S.A.* . 53 L5
Merriwa, *Australia* 43 E5
Merry I., *Canada* 48 A4
Merryville, *U.S.A.* 55 K8
Mersch, *Lux.* 11 E6
Mersea I., *U.K.* 9 F8
Merseburg, *Germany* . 12 C6
Mersey →, *U.K.* 8 D4
Merseyside □, *U.K.* .. 8 D4
Mersin, *Turkey* 19 G5
Mersing, *Malaysia* ... 26 D2
Merthyr Tydfil, *U.K.* .. 9 F4
Merthyr Tydfil □, *U.K.* 9 F4
Mértola, *Portugal* 15 D2
Mertzon, *U.S.A.* 55 K4
Meru, *Kenya* 36 D7
Meru, *Tanzania* 36 E7
Mesa, *U.S.A.* 57 K8
Mesa Verde National
Park, *U.S.A.* 57 H9
Mesgouez, L., *Canada* 48 B5
Meshed = Mashhad,
Iran 31 B8
Mesilinka →, *Canada* 50 B4
Mesilla, *U.S.A.* 57 K10
Mesolóngion, *Greece* . 17 E9
Mesopotamia = Al
Jazirah, *Iraq* 30 C5
Mesquite, *U.S.A.* 57 H6
Messad, *Algeria* 34 B6
Messina, *Italy* 16 E6
Messina, *S. Africa* 37 J6
Messina, Str. di, *Italy* . 16 F6
Messini, *Greece* 17 F10
Messiniakós Kólpos,
Greece 17 F10
Mesta →, *Bulgaria* .. 17 D11
Meta →, *S. Amer.* ... 62 B5
Meta Incógnita
Peninsula, *Canada* . 47 B13
Metabetchouan, *Canada* 49 C5
Metairie, *U.S.A.* 55 L9
Metaline Falls, *U.S.A.* . 56 B5
Metán, *Argentina* 64 B4
Methven, *N.Z.* 39 K3
Metlakatla, *U.S.A.* 46 C6
Metropolis, *U.S.A.* 55 G10
Metu, *Ethiopia* 32 F2
Metz, *France* 14 B7
Meulaboh, *Indonesia* . 26 D1
Meureudu, *Indonesia* . 26 C1
Meuse →, *Europe* ... 14 A6
Mexia, *U.S.A.* 55 K6
Mexiana, I., *Brazil* 63 D9
Mexicali, *Mexico* 57 N10
Mexican Water, *U.S.A.* 57 H9
México, *Mexico* 59 D5
México, *U.S.A.* 54 F9
México □, *Mexico* 59 D5
Mexico ■, *Cent. Amer.* 58 C4

Mexico, G. of,
  Cent. Amer. 59 C7
Meydān-e Naftūn, Iran 31 D6
Meydani, Ra's-e, Iran . 31 E8
Meymaneh, Afghan. ... 28 B4
Mezen, Russia 18 A7
Mezen →, Russia 18 A7
Mézenc, Mt., France ... 14 D6
Mezhdurechenskiy,
  Russia 20 D7
Mezökövesd, Hungary . 13 E11
Mezötúr, Hungary 13 E11
Mezquital, Mexico 58 C4
Mhow, India 28 H9
Miahuatlán, Mexico ... 59 D5
Miami, Fla., U.S.A. ... 53 N5
Miami, Okla., U.S.A. .. 55 G7
Miami, Tex., U.S.A. ... 55 H4
Miami Beach, U.S.A. .. 53 N5
Miandarreh, Iran 31 C7
Miandowāb, Iran 30 B5
Miandrivazo, Madag. .. 37 H9
Miāneh, Iran 30 B5
Mianwali, Pakistan ... 28 C7
Miass, Russia 18 D11
Michalovce, Slovak Rep. 13 D11
Michigan □, U.S.A. ... 52 C3
Michigan, L., U.S.A. .. 52 D2
Michigan City, U.S.A. . 52 E2
Michipicoten I., Canada 48 C2
Michoacan □, Mexico . 58 D4
Michurin, Bulgaria 17 C12
Michurinsk, Russia ... 18 D7
Mico, Pta., Nic. 60 D3
Micronesia, Pac. Oc. .. 44 G7
Micronesia, Federated
  States of ■, Pac. Oc. 38 A8
Midai, Indonesia 26 D3
Midale, Canada 51 D8
Middelburg, Neths. ... 11 C3
Middelburg, S. Africa . 37 L5
Middle Alkali L., U.S.A. 56 F3
Middle I., Australia ... 41 F3
Middle Loup →, U.S.A. 54 E5
Middle Sackville,
  Canada 49 D7
Middleburg, U.S.A. ... 53 K5
Middlebury, U.S.A. ... 52 C9
Middlemount, Australia 42 C4
Middleport, U.S.A. ... 52 F4
Middlesboro, U.S.A. .. 53 G4
Middlesbrough, U.K. .. 8 C6
Middlesbrough □, U.K. 8 C6
Middlesex, Belize 60 C2
Middleton, Australia .. 42 C3
Middleton, Canada 49 D6
Middleton Cr. →,
  Australia 42 C3
Middletown, N.Y.,
  U.S.A. 52 E8
Middletown, Ohio,
  U.S.A. 52 F3
Midhurst, U.K. 9 G7
Midi, Canal du →,
  France 14 E4
Midland, Canada 48 D4
Midland, Mich., U.S.A. 52 D3
Midland, Tex., U.S.A. . 55 K3
Midlothian, U.S.A. ... 55 J6
Midway Is., Pac. Oc. .. 44 E10
Midwest, U.S.A. 56 E10
Midwest City, U.S.A. . 55 H6
Midyat, Turkey 30 B4
Midžor, Bulgaria 17 C10
Mie □, Japan 23 G8
Międzychód, Poland .. 12 B8
Międzyrzec Podlaski,
  Poland 13 C12
Mielec, Poland 13 C11
Miercurea-Ciuc,
  Romania 13 E13
Mieres, Spain 15 A3
Mifraz Ḥefa, Israel ... 33 C4
Miguel Alemán, Presa,
  Mexico 59 D5
Mihara, Japan 23 G6
Mikhaylovgrad =
  Montana, Bulgaria . 17 C10
Mikhaylovka, Russia .. 19 D7
Mikkeli, Finland 7 F22
Mikkwa →, Canada .. 50 B6
Mikonos, Greece 17 F11
Mikun, Russia 18 B9
Milaca, U.S.A. 54 C8
Milagro, Ecuador 62 D3
Milan = Milano, Italy .. 14 D8
Milan, Mo., U.S.A. ... 54 E8
Milan, Tenn., U.S.A. .. 53 H1
Milang, Australia 43 F2
Milano, Italy 14 D8
Milâs, Turkey 17 F12
Milazzo, Italy 16 E6
Milbank, U.S.A. 54 C6
Milbanke Sd., Canada . 50 C3
Milden, Canada 51 C7
Mildenhall, U.K. 9 E8
Mildura, Australia 43 E3
Miles, Australia 43 D5
Miles City, U.S.A. ... 54 B2
Milestone, Canada ... 51 D8
Miletus, Turkey 17 F12
Milford, Del., U.S.A. .. 52 F8
Milford, Utah, U.S.A. . 57 G7
Milford Haven, U.K. .. 9 F2
Milford Sd., N.Z. 39 L1

Milḥ, Bahr al, Iraq 30 C4
Milikapiti, Australia .. 40 B5
Miling, Australia 41 F2
Milk →, U.S.A. 56 B10
Milk River, Canada ... 50 D6
Mill I., Antarctica 5 C8
Millau, France 14 D5
Mille Lacs, L. des,
  Canada 48 C1
Mille Lacs L., U.S.A. . 54 B8
Milledgeville, U.S.A. .. 53 J4
Millen, U.S.A. 53 J5
Miller, U.S.A. 54 C5
Millicent, Australia ... 43 F3
Millington, U.S.A. ... 55 H10
Millinocket, U.S.A. .. 53 C11
Millmerran, Australia . 43 D5
Millom, U.K. 8 C4
Millville, U.S.A. 52 F8
Millwood L., U.S.A. .. 55 J8
Milo, U.S.A. 53 C11
Milos, Greece 17 F11
Milparinka, Australia .. 43 D3
Milton, Canada 49 D7
Milton, N.Z. 39 M2
Milton, Fla., U.S.A. .. 53 K2
Milton, Pa., U.S.A. ... 52 E7
Milton-Freewater, U.S.A. 56 D4
Milton Keynes, U.K. .. 9 E7
Milton Keynes □, U.K. 9 E7
Milwaukee, U.S.A. ... 52 D2
Milwaukee Deep,
  Atl. Oc. 61 C6
Milwaukie, U.S.A. ... 56 D2
Min Jiang →, Fujian,
  China 25 D6
Min Jiang →, Sichuan,
  China 24 D5
Minā Su'ud, Si. Arabia 31 D6
Minā'al Aḥmadī, Kuwait 31 D6
Minago →, Canada .. 51 C9
Minaki, Canada 51 D10
Minami-Tori-Shima,
  Pac. Oc. 44 E7
Minas, Uruguay 64 C5
Minas, Sierra de las,
  Guatemala 60 C2
Minas Basin, Canada . 49 C7
Minas Gerais □, Brazil 63 G9
Minatitlán, Mexico ... 59 D6
Minbu, Burma 29 J19
Mindanao, Phil. 27 C6
Mindanao Sea = Bohol
  Sea, Phil. 27 C6
Mindanao Trench,
  Pac. Oc. 44 E7
Minden, Germany 12 B5
Minden, La., U.S.A. .. 55 J8
Minden, Nev., U.S.A. . 56 G4
Mindiptana, Indonesia . 27 F10
Mindoro, Phil. 27 B6
Mindoro Str., Phil. .. 27 B6
Mine, Japan 23 G5
Minehead, U.K. 9 F4
Mineola, U.S.A. 55 J7
Mineral Wells, U.S.A. . 55 J5
Mingäçevir Su Anbarı,
  Azerbaijan 19 F8
Mingan, Canada 49 B7
Mingechaurskoye
  Vdkhr. = Mingäçevir
  Su Anban, Azerbaijan 19 F8
Mingela, Australia ... 42 B4
Mingenew, Australia .. 41 E2
Mingera Cr. →,
  Australia 42 C2
Mingin, Burma 29 H19
Minho = Miño →,
  Spain 15 A2
Minho, Portugal 15 B1
Minidoka, U.S.A. 56 E7
Minigwal, L., Australia . 41 E3
Minilya →, Australia . 41 D1
Minilya Roadhouse,
  Australia 41 D1
Minipi L., Canada ... 49 B7
Mink L., Canada 50 A5
Minna, Nigeria 34 G7
Minneapolis, Kans.,
  U.S.A. 54 F6
Minneapolis, Minn.,
  U.S.A. 54 C8
Minnedosa, Canada .. 51 C9
Minnesota □, U.S.A. . 54 B8
Minnesota →, U.S.A. . 54 C8
Minnewaukan, U.S.A. . 54 A5
Minnipa, Australia ... 43 E2
Minnitaki L., Canada . 48 C1
Mino, Japan 23 G8
Miño →, Spain 15 A2
Minorca = Menorca,
  Spain 15 C8
Minot, U.S.A. 54 A4
Minsk, Belarus 13 B14
Mińsk Mazowiecki,
  Poland 13 B11
Mintabie, Australia ... 43 D1
Minto, Canada 49 C6
Minto, L., Canada ... 48 A5
Minton, Canada 51 D8
Minturn, U.S.A. 56 G10
Minusinsk, Russia ... 21 D10

Minutang, India 29 E20
Miquelon, Canada ... 48 C4
Miquelon, St- P. & M. . 49 C8
Mladá Boleslav,
  Czech Rep. 12 C8
Mlanje, Pic, Malawi .. 37 H7
Mława, Poland 13 B11
Mljet, Croatia 16 C7
Mo i Rana, Norway .. 6 C16
Moa, Cuba 61 B4
Moa, Indonesia 27 F7
Moa →, Brazil 62 G7
Moala, Fiji 39 D8
Moama, Australia ... 43 F3
Moba, Dem. Rep. of
  the Congo 36 F5
Mobārakābād, Iran ... 31 D7
Mobaye, C.A.R. 36 D4
Mobayi, Dem. Rep. of
  the Congo 36 D4
Moberley Lake, Canada 50 B4
Moberly, U.S.A. 54 F8
Mobile, U.S.A. 53 K1
Mobile B., U.S.A. ... 53 K2
Mobridge, U.S.A. ... 54 C4
Mobutu Sese Seko, L. =
  Albert L., Africa ... 36 D6
Moçambique, Mozam. . 37 H8
Moçâmedes = Namibe,
  Angola 37 H2
Mochudi, Botswana .. 37 J5
Mocimboa da Praia,
  Mozam. 36 G8
Moclips, U.S.A. 56 C1
Mocoa, Colombia ... 62 C3
Mocorito, Mexico ... 58 B3
Moctezuma, Mexico .. 58 B3
Moctezuma →, Mexico 59 C5
Mocuba, Mozam. 37 H7
Mocúzari, Presa, Mexico 58 B3
Modane, France 14 D7
Módena, Italy 16 B4
Modena, U.S.A. 57 H7
Modesto, U.S.A. 57 H3
Módica, Italy 16 F6
Moe, Australia 43 F4
Moengo, Surinam ... 63 B8
Mogadishu =
  Muqdisho,
  Somali Rep. 32 G4
Mogador = Essaouira,
  Morocco 34 B4
Mogami-Gawa →,
  Japan 22 E10
Mogaung, Burma 29 G20
Mogi das Cruzes, Brazil 64 A7
Mogi-Mirim, Brazil ... 63 H9
Mogilev = Mahilyow,
  Belarus 13 B16
Mogilev-Podolskiy =
  Mohyliv-Podilskyy,
  Ukraine 13 D14
Mogocha, Russia 21 D12
Mogok, Burma 29 H20
Mogollon Rim, U.S.A. . 57 J8
Mogumber, Australia . 41 F2
Mohács, Hungary 13 F10
Mohall, U.S.A. 54 A4
Moḥammadābād, Iran . 31 B8
Mohammedia, Morocco 34 B4
Mohave, L., U.S.A. .. 57 J6
Mohyliv-Podilskyy,
  Ukraine 13 D14
Moisaküla, Estonia ... 7 G21
Moisie, Canada 49 B6
Moisie →, Canada .. 49 B6
Mojave, U.S.A. 57 J4
Mojave Desert, U.S.A. . 57 J5
Mojokerto, Indonesia . 27 G15
Mokai, N.Z. 39 H5
Mokau, N.Z. 39 H5
Mokokchung, India .. 29 F19
Mokra Gora, Yugoslavia 17 C9
Mol, Belgium 11 C5
Molchanovo, Russia .. 20 D9
Mold, U.K. 8 D4
Moldavia = Moldova ■,
  Europe 13 E15
Molde, Norway 6 E12
Moldova ■, Europe .. 13 E15
Moldoveanu, Vf.,
  Romania 13 F13
Mole →, U.K. 9 F7
Mole Creek, Australia . 42 G4
Molepolole, Botswana . 37 J5
Molfetta, Italy 16 D7
Moline, U.S.A. 54 E9
Mollendo, Peru 62 G4
Mollerin, L., Australia . 41 F2
Molodechno =
  Maladzyechna,
  Belarus 13 A14
Molokai, U.S.A. 52 H16
Molong, Australia ... 43 E4
Molopo →, Africa ... 37 K4
Molotov = Perm, Russia 18 C10
Molson L., Canada .. 51 C9
Molu, Indonesia 27 F8
Molucca Sea, Indonesia 27 E6
Moluccas = Maluku,
  Indonesia 27 E7
Moma, Mozam. 37 H7
Mombasa, Kenya ... 36 E7
Mombetsu, Japan ... 22 B11
Mizpe Ramon, Israel . 33 E3
Momchilgrad, Bulgaria 17 D11
Mompós, Colombia .. 62 B4
Møn, Denmark 7 J15

Mjölby, Sweden 7 G16
Mjøsa, Norway 7 F14
Miraj, India 28 L9
Miram Shah, Pakistan . 28 C7
Miramichi, Canada ... 49 C6
Miramichi B., Canada . 49 C7
Miranda, Brazil 63 H7
Miranda →, Brazil .. 62 G7
Miranda de Ebro, Spain 15 A4
Miranda do Douro,
  Portugal 15 B2
Mirbāṭ, Oman 32 D5
Miri, Malaysia 26 D4
Miriam Vale, Australia . 42 C5
Mirim, L., S. Amer. ... 64 C6
Mirnyy, Russia 21 C12
Mirond L., Canada .. 51 B8
Mirpur Khas, Pakistan . 28 G6
Mirtağ, Turkey 30 B4
Mirzapur, India 29 G13
Mirzapur-cum-
  Vindhyachal =
  Mirzapur, India 29 G13
Misantla, Mexico ... 59 D5
Misawa, Japan 22 D10
Miscou I., Canada .. 49 C7
Mish'āb, Ra's al,
  Si. Arabia 31 D6
Mishan, China 25 B8
Mishawaka, U.S.A. .. 52 E2
Mishima, Japan 23 G9
Miskah, Si. Arabia .. 30 E4
Miskitos, Cayos, Nic. . 60 D3
Miskolc, Hungary ... 13 D11
Misool, Indonesia ... 27 E8
Misrātah, Libya 35 B9
Missanabie, Canada . 48 C3
Missinaibi →, Canada 48 B3
Missinaibi L., Canada . 48 C3
Mission, Canada 50 D4
Mission, S. Dak., U.S.A. 54 D4
Mission, Tex., U.S.A. . 55 M5
Mission Beach, Australia 42 B4
Mission Viejo, U.S.A. . 57 K5
Missisa L., Canada .. 48 B2
Mississagi →, Canada 48 B4
Mississauga, Canada . 48 C3
Mississippi □, U.S.A. . 55 J10
Mississippi →, U.S.A. 55 L10
Mississippi River Delta,
  U.S.A. 55 L9
Mississippi Sd., U.S.A. 55 K10
Missoula, U.S.A. 56 C7
Missouri □, U.S.A. .. 54 F8
Missouri →, U.S.A. .. 54 F9
Missouri City, U.S.A. . 55 L7
Missouri Valley, U.S.A. 54 E7
Mistassini, Canada .. 49 B5
Mistassini →, Canada 49 C5
Mistassini, L., Canada 48 B5
Mistastin L., Canada . 49 A7
Mistinibi, L., Canada . 49 A7
Misty L., Canada ... 51 B8
Misurata = Misrātah,
  Libya 35 B9
Mitchell, Australia ... 43 D4
Mitchell, Nebr., U.S.A. 54 E3
Mitchell, Oreg., U.S.A. 56 D3
Mitchell, S. Dak., U.S.A. 54 D6
Mitchell →, Australia . 42 B3
Mitchell, Mt., U.S.A. . 53 H4
Mitchell Ranges,
  Australia 42 A2
Mitilíni, Greece 17 E12
Mito, Japan 23 F10
Mitrovica = Kosovska
  Mitrovica,
  Kosovo, Yug. 17 C9
Mitsiwa, Eritrea 32 D2
Mitsukaidō, Japan ... 23 F9
Mittagong, Australia . 43 E5
Mittimatalik = Pond
  Inlet, Canada 47 A12
Mitú, Colombia 62 C4
Mitumba, Mts.,
  Dem. Rep. of
  the Congo 36 F5
Mitwaba, Dem. Rep. of
  the Congo 36 F5
Mixteco →, Mexico .. 59 D5
Miyagi □, Japan 22 E10
Miyāh, W. el →, Syria 30 C3
Miyake-Jima, Japan .. 23 G9
Miyako, Japan 22 E10
Miyako-Jima, Japan .. 23 M2
Miyako-Rettō, Japan . 23 M2
Miyakonojō, Japan .. 23 J5
Miyanoura-Dake, Japan 23 J5
Miyazaki, Japan 23 J5
Miyazu, Japan 23 G7
Miyet, Bahr el = Dead
  Sea, Asia 33 D4
Miyoshi, Japan 23 G6
Mizdah, Libya 35 B8
Mizoram □, India ... 29 H18

Mona, Canal de la,
  W. Indies 61 C6
Mona, Isla, Puerto Rico 61 C6
Mona, Pta., Costa Rica 60 E3
Monaco ■, Europe ... 14 E7
Monahans, U.S.A. ... 55 K3
Monar, Sierra del,
  Spain 15 B5
Monarch Mt., Canada . 50 C3
Monashee Mts., Canada 50 C5
Monastir = Bitola,
  Macedonia 17 D9
Moncayo, Sierra del,
  Spain 15 B5
Monchegorsk, Russia . 18 A5
Mönchengladbach,
  Germany 12 C4
Monchique, Portugal . 15 D1
Monclova, Mexico ... 58 B4
Moncton, Canada ... 49 C7
Mondego →, Portugal 15 B1
Mondeodo, Indonesia 27 E6
Mondovì, Italy 14 D7
Mondrain I., Australia . 41 F3
Monessen, U.S.A. ... 52 E6
Monett, U.S.A. 55 G8
Monforte de Lemos,
  Spain 15 A2
Mong Hsu, Burma .. 29 J21
Mong Kung, Burma .. 29 J20
Mong Nai, Burma ... 29 J20
Mong Pawk, Burma .. 29 H21
Mong Ton, Burma ... 29 J21
Mong Wa, Burma ... 29 J22
Mong Yai, Burma ... 29 H21
Mongalla, Sudan 35 G12
Mongers, L., Australia . 41 E2
Monghyr = Munger,
  India 29 G15
Mongibello = Etna, Italy 16 F6
Mongo, Chad 35 F9
Mongolia ■, Asia ... 21 E10
Mongu, Zambia 37 H4
Monkey Mia, Australia 41 E1
Monkey River, Belize . 59 D7
Monkoto, Dem. Rep. of
  the Congo 36 E4
Monmouth, U.K. 9 F5
Monmouth, Ill., U.S.A. 54 E9
Monmouth, Oreg.,
  U.S.A. 56 D2
Monmouthshire □, U.K. 9 F5
Mono L., U.S.A. 57 H4
Monópoli, Italy 16 D7
Monroe, Ga., U.S.A. .. 53 J4
Monroe, La., U.S.A. .. 55 J8
Monroe, Mich., U.S.A. 52 E4
Monroe, N.C., U.S.A. . 53 H5
Monroe, Utah, U.S.A. . 57 G7
Monroe, Wis., U.S.A. . 54 D10
Monroe City, U.S.A. . 54 F9
Monroeville, U.S.A. .. 53 K2
Monrovia, Liberia ... 34 G3
Mons, Belgium 11 D3
Monse, Indonesia ... 27 E6
Mont-de-Marsan, France 14 E3
Mont-Joli, Canada ... 49 C6
Mont-Laurier, Canada . 48 C4
Mont-Louis, Canada . 49 C6
Mont-St-Michel, Le = Le
  Mont-St-Michel,
  France 14 B3
Mont Tremblant, Parc
  Recr. du, Canada .. 48 C5
Montagu I., Antarctica . 5 B1
Montague, Canada ... 49 C7
Montague, I., Mexico . 58 A2
Montague Ra., Australia 41 E2
Montague Sd., Australia 40 B4
Montalbán, Spain ... 15 B5
Montana, Bulgaria .. 17 C10
Montaña, Peru 62 E4
Montana □, U.S.A. .. 56 C9
Montargis, France ... 14 C5
Montauban, France .. 14 D4
Montauk Pt., U.S.A. . 52 E10
Montbéliard, France . 14 C7
Montceau-les-Mines,
  France 14 C6
Monte Albán, Mexico . 59 D5
Monte Alegre, Brazil . 63 D8
Monte Azul, Brazil ... 63 G10
Monte Bello Is.,
  Australia 40 D2
Monte-Carlo, Monaco . 14 E7
Monte Caseros,
  Argentina 64 C5
Monte Comán,
  Argentina 64 C3
Monte Cristi, Dom. Rep. 61 C5
Monte Quemado,
  Argentina 64 B4
Monte Santu, C. di, Italy 16 D3
Monte Vista, U.S.A. .. 57 H10
Montebello, Canada .. 48 C5
Montecristo, Italy ... 16 C4
Montego Bay, Jamaica 60 C4
Montélimar, France .. 14 D6
Montello, U.S.A. 54 D10
Montemorelos, Mexico 59 B5
Montenegro □,
  Yugoslavia 17 C8
Montepuez, Mozam. . 37 G7
Monterey, U.S.A. ... 57 H3
Montería, Colombia .. 62 B3
Monterrey, Mexico .. 58 B4

Montes Claros, Brazil . 63 G10
Montesano, U.S.A. .. 56 C2
Montesilvano, Italy .. 16 C6
Montevideo, Uruguay . 64 C5
Montevideo, U.S.A. .. 54 C7
Montezuma, U.S.A. .. 54 E8
Montgomery = Sahiwal,
  Pakistan 28 D8
Montgomery, U.K. .. 9 E4
Montgomery, Ala.,
  U.S.A. J2
Montgomery, W. Va.,
  U.S.A. 52 F5
Montgomery City,
  U.S.A. 54 F9
Monticello, Ark., U.S.A. 55 J9
Monticello, Fla., U.S.A. 53 K4
Monticello, Ind., U.S.A. 52 E2
Monticello, Iowa, U.S.A. 54 D9
Monticello, Ky., U.S.A. 53 G3
Monticello, Minn.,
  U.S.A. 54 C8
Monticello, Miss., U.S.A. 55 K9
Monticello, Utah, U.S.A. 57 H9
Montijo, Portugal ... 15 C1
Montilla, Spain 15 D3
Montluçon, France .. 14 C5
Montmagny, Canada . 49 C5
Montmartre, Canada . 51 C8
Montmorillon, France . 14 C4
Monto, Australia 42 C5
Montoro, Spain 15 C3
Montpelier, Idaho,
  U.S.A. 56 E8
Montpelier, Vt., U.S.A. 52 C9
Montpellier, France .. 14 E5
Montréal, Canada ... 48 C5
Montreal →, Canada . 48 C3
Montreal L., Canada . 51 C7
Montreal Lake, Canada 51 C7
Montreux, Switz. ... 14 C7
Montrose, U.K. 10 C5
Montrose, U.S.A. ... 57 G10
Monts, Pte. des, Canada 49 C6
Montserrat ■, W. Indies 61 C7
Monywa, Burma 29 H19
Monza, Italy 14 D8
Monze, Zambia 37 H5
Monze, C., Pakistan .. 28 G5
Monzón, Spain 15 B6
Moonah →, Australia 42 C2
Moonda, L., Australia . 42 D3
Moonie, Australia ... 43 D5
Moonie →, Australia . 43 D4
Moonta, Australia ... 43 E2
Moora, Australia ... 41 F2
Moorcroft, U.S.A. ... 54 C2
Moore →, Australia . 41 F2
Moore, L., Australia .. 41 E2
Moore Park, Australia 42 C5
Moore Reefs, Australia 42 B4
Moorefield, U.S.A. .. 52 F6
Moorhead, U.S.A. ... 54 B6
Moose →, Canada .. 48 B3
Moose Factory, Canada 48 B3
Moose Jaw, Canada . 51 C7
Moose Jaw →, Canada 51 C7
Moose Lake, Canada . 51 C8
Moose Lake, U.S.A. .. 54 B8
Moose Mountain Prov.
  Park, Canada 51 D8
Moosehead L., U.S.A. . 53 C11
Mooselookmeguntic L.,
  U.S.A. 53 C10
Moosomin, Canada .. 51 C8
Moosonee, Canada .. 48 B3
Mopti, Mali 34 F5
Moquegua, Peru 62 G4
Mora, Sweden 7 F16
Mora, Minn., U.S.A. .. 54 C8
Mora, N. Mex., U.S.A. 57 J11
Mora →, U.S.A. 55 H2
Moradabad, India ... 28 E11
Morafenobe, Madag. . 37 H8
Moramanga, Madag. . 37 H9
Moran, Kans., U.S.A. . 55 G7
Moran, Wyo., U.S.A. . 56 E8
Moranbah, Australia . 42 C4
Morant Cays, Jamaica 60 C4
Morant Pt., Jamaica . 60 C4
Moratuwa, Sri Lanka . 28 R11
Morava →,
  Serbia, Yug. 17 B9
Morava →,
  Slovak Rep. 13 D9
Moravian Hts. =
  Českomoravská
  Vrchovina, Czech Rep. 12 D8
Morawa, Australia ... 41 E2
Morawhanna, Guyana 62 B7
Moray Firth, U.K. ... 10 C5
Morden, Canada ... 51 D9
Mordovian Republic =
  Mordvinia □, Russia 18 D7
Mordvinia □, Russia . 18 D7
Moreau →, U.S.A. .. 54 C4
Morecambe, U.K. ... 8 C5
Morecambe B., U.K. . 8 C5
Moree, Australia ... 43 D4
Morehead, U.S.A. ... 52 F4
Morehead City, U.S.A. 53 H7
Morelia, Mexico 58 D4
Morella, Australia ... 42 C3
Morella, Spain 15 B5
Morelos, Mexico 58 B3

Morelos □, *Mexico* ... 59 D5
Morena, Sierra, *Spain* . 15 C3
Moresby I., *Canada* ... 50 C2
Moreton I., *Australia* .. 43 D5
Morgan, *U.S.A.* 56 F8
Morgan City, *U.S.A.* ... 55 L9
Morganfield, *U.S.A.* ... 52 G2
Morganton, *U.S.A.* 53 H5
Morgantown, *U.S.A.* ... 52 F6
Morghak, *Iran* 31 D8
Moriarty, *U.S.A.* 57 J10
Morice L., *Canada* ... 50 C3
Morinville, *Canada* 50 C6
Morioka, *Japan* 22 E10
Moris, *Mexico* 58 B3
Morlaix, *France* 14 B2
Mornington, *Australia* . 43 F4
Mornington, I., *Chile* .. 64 F1
Mornington I., *Australia* 42 B2
Moro G., *Phil.* 27 C6
Morocco ■, *N. Afr.* ... 34 B4
Morogoro, *Tanzania* .. 36 F7
Moroleón, *Mexico* 58 C4
Morombe, *Madag.* 37 J8
Morón, *Cuba* 60 B4
Morón de la Frontera,
  Spain 15 D3
Morona →, *Peru* 62 D3
Morondava, *Madag.* .. 37 J8
Moroni, *U.S.A.* 56 G8
Morotai, *Indonesia* ... 27 D7
Moroto, *Uganda* 36 D6
Morpeth, *U.K.* 8 B6
Morphou, *Cyprus* 30 C2
Morrilton, *U.S.A.* 55 H8
Morrinhos, *Brazil* 63 G9
Morrinsville, *N.Z.* 39 G5
Morris, *Canada* 51 D9
Morris, *Ill., U.S.A.* ... 54 E10
Morris, *Minn., U.S.A.* . 54 C7
Morris, Mt., *Australia* . 41 E5
Morristown, *Ariz.,
  U.S.A.* 57 K7
Morristown, *Tenn.,
  U.S.A.* 53 G4
Morro Bay, *U.S.A.* 57 J3
Morrosquillo, G. de,
  Colombia 60 E4
Morshansk, *Russia* ... 18 D7
Morteros, *Argentina* .. 64 C4
Mortlach, *Canada* 51 C7
Mortlake, *Australia* ... 43 F3
Morton, *Tex., U.S.A.* .. 55 J3
Morton, *Wash., U.S.A.* . 56 C2
Morundah, *Australia* .. 43 E4
Moruya, *Australia* 43 F5
Morvan, *France* 14 C6
Morven, *Australia* 43 D4
Morwell, *Australia* 43 F4
Morzhovets, Ostrov,
  Russia 18 A7
Moscos Is., *Burma* ... 26 B1
Moscow = Moskva,
  Russia 18 C6
Moscow, *U.S.A.* 56 C5
Mosel →, *Europe* 14 A7
Moselle = Mosel →,
  Europe 14 A7
Moses Lake, *U.S.A.* ... 56 C4
Mosgiel, *N.Z.* 39 L3
Moshi, *Tanzania* 36 E7
Mosjøen, *Norway* 6 D15
Moskenesøya, *Norway* 6 C15
Moskenstraumen,
  Norway 6 C15
Moskva, *Russia* 18 C6
Moson-magyaróvár,
  Hungary 13 E9
Mosquera, *Colombia* . 62 C3
Mosquero, *U.S.A.* 55 H3
Mosquitia, *Honduras* . 60 C3
Mosquito Coast =
  Mosquitia, *Honduras* 60 C3
Mosquito L., *Canada* . 51 A8
Mosquitos, G. de los,
  Panama 60 E3
Moss, *Norway* 7 G14
Moss Vale, *Australia* . 43 E5
Mossbank, *Canada* ... 51 D7
Mossburn, *N.Z.* 39 L2
Mosselbaai, *S. Africa* . 37 L4
Mossendjo, *Congo* ... 36 E2
Mossgiel, *Australia* ... 43 E3
Mossman, *Australia* .. 42 B4
Mossoró, *Brazil* 63 E11
Most, *Czech Rep.* 12 C7
Mostaganem, *Algeria* . 34 A6
Mostar, *Bos.-H.* 17 C7
Mostardas, *Brazil* 64 C6
Mostiska = Mostyska,
  Ukraine 13 D12
Mosty = Masty, *Belarus* 13 B13
Mostyska, *Ukraine* ... 13 D12
Mosul = Al Mawşil, *Iraq* 30 B4
Motagua →,
  Guatemala 60 C2
Motala, *Sweden* 7 G16
Motihari, *India* 29 F14
Motozintla de Mendoza,
  Mexico 59 D6
Motril, *Spain* 15 D4
Mott, *U.S.A.* 54 B3
Motueka, *N.Z.* 39 J4
Motueka →, *N.Z.* 39 J4
Motul, *Mexico* 59 C7

Mouchalagane →,
  Canada 49 B6
Moúdhros, *Greece* ... 17 E11
Mouila, *Gabon* 36 E2
Moulamein, *Australia* . 43 F3
Moulins, *France* 14 C5
Moulmein, *Burma* ... 29 L20
Moulouya, O. →,
  Morocco 34 B5
Moultrie, *U.S.A.* 53 K4
Moultrie, L., *U.S.A.* ... 53 J5
Mound City, *Mo., U.S.A.* 54 E7
Mound City, *S. Dak.,
  U.S.A.* 54 C4
Moundou, *Chad* 35 G9
Moundsville, *U.S.A.* .. 52 F5
Mount Airy, *U.S.A.* ... 53 G5
Mount Barker,
  S. Austral., Australia 43 F2
Mount Barker,
  W. Austral., Australia 41 F2
Mount Beauty, *Australia* 43 F4
Mount Burr, *Australia* . 43 F3
Mount Carmel, *U.S.A.* . 52 F2
Mount Coolon, *Australia* 42 C4
Mount Desert I., *U.S.A.* 53 C11
Mount Dora, *U.S.A.* .. 53 L5
Mount Edziza Prov.
  Park, *Canada* 50 B2
Mount Forest, *Canada* . 48 D3
Mount Gambier,
  Australia 43 F3
Mount Garnet, *Australia* 42 B4
Mount Hope, *N.S.W.,
  Australia* 43 E4
Mount Hope, *S. Austral.,
  Australia* 43 E2
Mount Isa, *Australia* .. 42 C2
Mount Larcom,
  Australia 42 C5
Mount Lofty Ra.,
  Australia 43 E2
Mount Magnet,
  Australia 41 E2
Mount Maunganui, *N.Z.* 39 G6
Mount Molloy, *Australia* 42 B4
Mount Morgan,
  Australia 42 C5
Mount Pearl, *Canada* . 49 C9
Mount Perry, *Australia* 43 D5
Mount Pleasant, *Iowa,
  U.S.A.* 54 E9
Mount Pleasant, *Mich.,
  U.S.A.* 52 D3
Mount Pleasant, *S.C.,
  U.S.A.* 53 J6
Mount Pleasant, *Tenn.,
  U.S.A.* 53 H2
Mount Pleasant, *Tex.,
  U.S.A.* 55 J7
Mount Pleasant, *Utah,
  U.S.A.* 56 G8
Mount Rainier Nat. Park,
  U.S.A. 56 C3
Mount Revelstoke Nat.
  Park, *Canada* 50 C5
Mount Robson Prov.
  Park, *Canada* 50 C5
Mount Shasta, *U.S.A.* . 56 F2
Mount Sterling, *Ill.,
  U.S.A.* 54 F9
Mount Sterling, *Ky.,
  U.S.A.* 52 F4
Mount Surprise,
  Australia 42 B3
Mount Vernon, *Ill.,
  U.S.A.* 52 F1
Mount Vernon, *Ind.,
  U.S.A.* 54 F10
Mount Vernon, *Ohio,
  U.S.A.* 52 E4
Mount Vernon, *Wash.,
  U.S.A.* 56 B2
Mountain Ash, *U.K.* .. 9 F4
Mountain City, *Nev.,
  U.S.A.* 56 F6
Mountain City, *Tenn.,
  U.S.A.* 53 G5
Mountain Grove, *U.S.A.* 55 G8
Mountain Home, *Ark.,
  U.S.A.* 55 G8
Mountain Home, *Idaho,
  U.S.A.* 56 E6
Mountain Iron, *U.S.A.* . 54 B8
Mountain View, *U.S.A.* 55 H8
Mountainair, *U.S.A.* ... 57 J10
Moura, *Australia* 42 C4
Moura, *Brazil* 62 D6
Moura, *Portugal* 15 C2
Mourdi, Dépression du,
  Chad 35 E10
Mourilyan, *Australia* .. 42 B4
Mouscron, *Belgium* .. 11 D3
Moussoro, *Chad* 35 F9
Moutong, *Indonesia* .. 27 D6
Movas, *Mexico* 58 B3
Mowandjum, *Australia* 40 C3
Moyale, *Kenya* 36 D7
Moyen Atlas, *Morocco* 34 B4
Moyne, L. le, *Canada* . 49 A6
Moyobamba, *Peru* ... 62 E3
Moyyero →, *Russia* .. 21 C11
Moyynty, *Kazakstan* .. 20 E8

Mozambique =
  Moçambique, *Mozam.* 37 H8
Mozambique ■, *Africa* 37 H7
Mozambique Chan.,
  Africa 3 F11
Mozambique Chan.,
  Africa 3 F11
Mozdok, *Russia* 19 F7
Mozdūrān, *Iran* 31 B9
Mozhnābād, *Iran* 31 C9
Mozyr = Mazyr, *Belarus* 13 B15
Mpanda, *Tanzania* ... 36 F6
Mpika, *Zambia* 37 G6
Mpwapwa, *Tanzania* . 36 F7
M'sila →, *Algeria* 34 A6
Mstislavl = Mstsislaw,
  Belarus 13 A16
Mstsislaw, *Belarus* ... 13 A16
Mtwara Mikindani,
  Tanzania 36 G8
Mu Us Shamo, *China* . 25 C5
Muang Khong, *Laos* .. 26 B3
Muar, *Malaysia* 26 D2
Muarabungo, *Indonesia* 26 E2
Muaraenim, *Indonesia* 26 E2
Muarajuloi, *Indonesia* . 26 E4
Muarakaman, *Indonesia* 26 E5
Muaratebo, *Indonesia* . 26 E2
Muaratembesi,
  Indonesia 26 E2
Muaratewe, *Indonesia* . 26 E4
Mubarraz = Al
  Mubarraz, *Si. Arabia* 31 E6
Mubi, *Nigeria* 35 F8
Mucajaí →, *Brazil* ... 62 C6
Muckadilla, *Australia* . 43 D4
Mucuri, *Brazil* 63 G11
Mudanjiang, *China* ... 25 B7
Mudanya, *Turkey* 17 D13
Muddy Cr. →, *U.S.A.* 57 H8
Mudgee, *Australia* ... 43 E4
Mudjatik →, *Canada* . 51 B7
Mueller Ra., *Australia* . 40 C4
Muerto, Mar, *Mexico* . 59 D6
Mufulira, *Zambia* 37 G5
Mughayrā', *Si. Arabia* . 30 D3
Mugi, *Japan* 23 H7
Muğla, *Turkey* 17 F13
Mugu, *Nepal* 29 E13
Muhammad, Ras, *Egypt* 30 E2
Muhammad Qol, *Sudan* 35 D13
Mühlhausen, *Germany* . 12 C6
Mühlig Hofmann fjell,
  Antarctica 5 D3
Muhos, *Finland* 6 D22
Muhu, *Estonia* 7 G20
Muir, L., *Australia* 41 F2
Mujnak, *Uzbekistan* .. 20 E6
Mukacheve, *Ukraine* . 13 D12
Mukacheve =
  Mukacheve, *Ukraine* . 13 D12
Mukah, *Malaysia* 26 D4
Mukden = Shenyang,
  China 25 B7
Mukhtuya = Lensk,
  Russia 21 C12
Mukinbudin, *Australia* . 41 F2
Mukomuko, *Indonesia* . 26 E2
Muktsar, *India* 28 D9
Mukutawa →, *Canada* 51 C9
Mula, *Spain* 15 C5
Mulchén, *Chile* 64 D2
Mulde →, *Germany* .. 12 C7
Mule Creek Junction,
  U.S.A. 54 D2
Muleba, *Tanzania* 58 B2
Muleshoe, *U.S.A.* 55 H3
Mulgrave, *Canada* ... 49 C7
Mulhacén, *Spain* 15 D4
Mülheim, *Germany* ... 25 C6
Mulhouse, *France* ... 14 C7
Mull, *U.K.* 10 C4
Mullaittivu, *Sri Lanka* . 28 Q12
Mullen, *U.S.A.* 54 D4
Mullens, *U.S.A.* 52 G5
Muller, Pegunungan,
  Indonesia 26 D4
Mullewa, *Australia* ... 41 E2
Mulligan →, *Australia* 42 D2
Mullingar, *Ireland* ... 10 E3
Mullins, *U.S.A.* 53 H6
Mullumbimby, *Australia* 43 D5
Multan, *Pakistan* 28 D7
Mulvane, *U.S.A.* 55 G6
Mumbai, *India* 28 K8
Mun →, *Thailand* ... 26 A2
Muna, *Indonesia* 27 F6
Munamagi, *Estonia* .. 7 H22
München, *Germany* .. 12 D6
Munchen-Gladbach =
  Mönchengladbach,
  Germany 12 C4
Muncho Lake, *Canada* . 50 B3
Muncie, *U.S.A.* 52 E3
Muncoonie, L., *Australia* 42 D2
Mundabbera, *Australia* 43 D5
Munday, *U.S.A.* 55 J5
Münden, *Germany* ... 12 C5
Mundiwindi, *Australia* . 40 D3
Mundo Novo, *Brazil* .. 63 F10
Mundrabilla, *Australia* . 41 F4
Mungallala, *Australia* . 43 D4
Mungallala Cr. →,
  Australia 43 D4
Mungana, *Australia* .. 42 B3

Mungbere, *Dem. Rep. of
  the Congo* 36 D5
Munger, *India* 29 G15
Munich = München,
  Germany 12 D6
Munising, *U.S.A.* 52 B2
Munku-Sardyk, *Russia* 21 D11
Muñoz Gamero, Pen.,
  Chile 64 G2
Munroe L., *Canada* ... 51 B9
Münster, *Germany* ... 12 C4
Munster □, *Ireland* .. 10 E2
Muntadgin, *Australia* . 41 F2
Muntok, *Indonesia* ... 26 E3
Muonio, *Finland* 6 C20
Muonionjoki →,
  Finland 6 C20
Muqdisho, *Somali Rep.* 32 G4
Mur →, *Austria* 13 E9
Murakami, *Japan* 22 E9
Murallón, Cerro, *Chile* . 64 F2
Murang'a, *Kenya* 36 E7
Murashi, *Russia* 18 C8
Murat →, *Turkey* 19 G7
Muratlı, *Turkey* 17 D12
Murayama, *Japan* ... 22 E10
Murban, *U.A.E.* 31 F7
Murchison →,
  Australia 41 E1
Murchison, Mt.,
  Antarctica 5 D11
Murchison Falls,
  Uganda 36 D6
Murchison Ra., *Australia* 42 C1
Murcia, *Spain* 15 D5
Murcia □, *Spain* 15 D5
Murdo, *U.S.A.* 54 D4
Murdoch Pt., *Australia* . 42 A3
Mureş →, *Romania* .. 13 E11
Mureşul = Mureş →,
  Romania 13 E11
Murfreesboro, *N.C.,
  U.S.A.* 53 G7
Murfreesboro, *Tenn.,
  U.S.A.* 53 H2
Murgab = Murghob,
  Tajikistan 20 F8
Murgab →,
  Turkmenistan 31 B9
Murgenella, *Australia* . 40 B5
Murghob, *Tajikistan* .. 20 F8
Murgon, *Australia* ... 43 D5
Muria, *Indonesia* 27 G14
Müritz, *Germany* 12 B7
Murmansk, *Russia* ... 18 A5
Murom, *Russia* 18 C7
Muroran, *Japan* 22 C10
Muroto, *Japan* 23 H7
Muroto-Misaki, *Japan* . 23 H7
Murphy, *U.S.A.* 56 E5
Murray, *Ky., U.S.A.* ... 53 G1
Murray, *Utah, U.S.A.* . 56 F8
Murray →, *Australia* . 43 F2
Murray, L., *U.S.A.* 53 H5
Murray Bridge, *Australia* 43 F2
Murray Harbour,
  Canada 49 C7
Murrumbidgee →,
  Australia 43 E3
Murrumburrah,
  Australia 43 E4
Murrurundi, *Australia* . 43 E5
Murtle L., *Canada* ... 50 C5
Murtoa, *Australia* 43 F3
Mururoa, *Pac. Oc.* ... 45 K14
Murwara, *India* 29 H12
Murwillumbah, *Australia* 43 D5
Mürzzuschlag, *Austria* . 12 E8
Muş, *Turkey* 19 G7
Mûsa, Gebel, *Egypt* .. 30 D2
Musa Khel, *Pakistan* .. 28 D6
Mûsa Qal'eh, *Afghan.* . 28 C4
Musaffargarh, *Pakistan* 28 D7
Musala, *Bulgaria* 17 C10
Musala, *Indonesia* ... 26 D1
Musay'īd, *Qatar* 31 E6
Muscat = Masqaţ,
  Oman 32 C6
Muscat & Oman =
  Oman ■, *Asia* 32 C6
Muscatine, *U.S.A.* ... 54 E9
Musgrave Harbour,
  Canada 49 C9
Musgrave Ranges,
  Australia 41 E5
Mushie, *Dem. Rep. of
  the Congo* 36 E3
Musi →, *Indonesia* .. 26 E2
Muskeg →, *Canada* . 50 A4
Muskegon, *U.S.A.* ... 52 D2
Muskegon →, *U.S.A.* 52 D2
Muskegon Heights,
  U.S.A. 52 D2
Muskogee, *U.S.A.* ... 55 H7
Muskwa →, *Canada* . 50 B4
Muslimiyah, *Syria* ... 30 B3
Musoma, *Tanzania* ... 36 E6
Musquaro, L., *Canada* . 49 B7
Musquodoboit Harbour,
  Canada 49 D7
Musselburgh, *U.K.* ... 10 F5
Musselshell →, *U.S.A.* 56 C10
Mustafakemalpaşa,
  Turkey 17 D13
Mustang, *Nepal* 29 E13

Musters, L., *Argentina* . 64 F3
Muswellbrook, *Australia* 43 E5
Mût, *Egypt* 35 C11
Mut, *Turkey* 30 B2
Muting, *Indonesia* ... 27 F10
Mutoray, *Russia* 21 C11
Mutsu, *Japan* 22 D10
Mutsu-Wan, *Japan* .. 22 D10
Muttaburra, *Australia* . 42 C3
Mutare, *Zimbabwe* .. 37 H6
Muweilih, *Egypt* 33 E3
Muy Muy, *Nic.* 60 D2
Muzaffarabad, *Pakistan* 28 B8
Muzaffarnagar, *India* . 28 E10
Muzaffarpur, *India* ... 29 F14
Muzhi, *Russia* 18 A11
Mvuma, *Zimbabwe* .. 37 H6
Mwanza, *Dem. Rep. of
  the Congo* 36 F5
Mwanza, *Tanzania* ... 36 E6
Mweka, *Dem. Rep. of
  the Congo* 36 E4
Mweru, L., *Zambia* ... 36 F5
Mwinilunga, *Zambia* . 37 G4
My Tho, *Vietnam* 26 B3
Myanaung, *Burma* ... 29 K19
Myanmar = Burma ■,
  Asia 29 J20
Myaungmya, *Burma* .. 29 L19
Mycenæ = Mikínai,
  Greece 17 F10
Myeik Kyunzu, *Burma* . 26 B1
Myers Chuck, *U.S.A.* . 50 B2
Myingyan, *Burma* ... 29 J19
Myitkyina, *Burma* 29 G20
Mykines, *Færoe Is.* .. 6 E9
Mykolayiv, *Ukraine* .. 19 E5
Mymensingh, *Bangla.* . 29 G17
Mynydd Du, *U.K.* 9 F4
Mýrdalsjökull, *Iceland* . 6 E4
Myrtle Beach, *U.S.A.* . 53 J6
Myrtle Creek, *U.S.A.* .. 56 E2
Myrtle Point, *U.S.A.* .. 56 E1
Mysia, *Turkey* 17 E12
Mysore = Karnataka □,
  India 28 N10
Mysore, *India* 28 N10
Myszków, *Poland* 13 C10
Mytishchi, *Russia* 18 C6
Mývatn, *Iceland* 6 D5
Mzuzu, *Malawi* 36 G6

Na Hearadh = Harris,
  U.K. 10 C3
Naab →, *Germany* .. 12 D6
Naantali, *Finland* 7 F19
Nababeep, *S. Africa* .. 37 K3
Nabari, *Japan* 23 G8
Nabawa, *Australia* ... 41 E1
Nabberu, L., *Australia* . 41 E3
Naberezhnyye Chelny,
  Russia 18 C9
Nabeul, *Tunisia* 35 A8
Nabīd, *Iran* 31 D8
Nabire, *Indonesia* ... 27 E9
Nabisipi →, *Canada* . 49 B7
Nablus = Nābulus,
  West Bank 33 C4
Nābulus, *West Bank* . 33 C4
Nacala, *Mozam.* 37 G8
Nacaome, *Honduras* . 60 D2
Naches, *U.S.A.* 56 C3
Nachicapau, L., *Canada* 49 A6
Nachingwea, *Tanzania* 36 G7
Nacimiento L., *U.S.A.* . 57 J3
Naco, *Mexico* 58 A3
Nacogdoches, *U.S.A.* . 55 K7
Nácori Chico, *Mexico* . 58 B3
Nacozari, *Mexico* 58 A3
Nadiad, *India* 28 H8
Nador, *Morocco* 34 B5
Nadūshan, *Iran* 31 C7
Nadvirna, *Ukraine* ... 13 D13
Nadvoitsy, *Russia* ... 18 B5
Nadvornaya =
  Nadvirna, *Ukraine* . 13 D13
Nadym, *Russia* 20 C8
Nadym →, *Russia* ... 20 C8
Nærbø, *Norway* 7 G11
Næstved, *Denmark* .. 7 J14
Naft-e Safīd, *Iran* 31 D6
Naftshahr, *Iran* 30 C5
Nafud Desert = An
  Nafūd, *Si. Arabia* .. 30 D4
Naga, *Phil.* 27 B6
Nagahama, *Japan* ... 23 G8
Nagai, *Japan* 22 E10
Nagaland □, *India* ... 29 G19
Nagano, *Japan* 23 F9
Nagano □, *Japan* ... 23 F9
Nagaoka, *Japan* 23 F9
Nagappattinam, *India* . 28 P11
Nagar Parkar, *Pakistan* 28 G7
Nagasaki, *Japan* 23 H4
Nagasaki □, *Japan* .. 23 H4
Nagato, *Japan* 23 G5
Nagaur, *India* 28 F8
Nagercoil, *India* 28 Q10
Naginēh, *Iran* 31 C8
Nagīr, *Pakistan* 28 A9
Nagornyy, *Russia* 21 D13
Nagorno-Karabakh,
  Azerbaijan 19 F8
Nagoya, *Japan* 23 G8
Nagpur, *India* 28 J11

Nagua, *Dom. Rep.* ... 61 C6
Nagykanizsa, *Hungary* . 13 E9
Nagykőrös, *Hungary* .. 13 E10
Naha, *Japan* 23 L3
Nahanni Butte, *Canada* 50 A4
Nahanni Nat. Park,
  Canada 50 A4
Nahariyya, *Israel* 30 C2
Nahāvand, *Iran* 31 C6
Naicá, *Mexico* 58 B3
Naicam, *Canada* 51 C8
Naikoon Prov. Park,
  Canada 50 C2
Nain, *Canada* 49 A7
Nā'īn, *Iran* 31 C7
Nainpur, *India* 28 H12
Nairn, *U.K.* 10 C5
Nairobi, *Kenya* 36 E7
Naissaar, *Estonia* 7 G21
Najafābād, *Iran* 31 C6
Najd, *Si. Arabia* 32 B3
Najibabad, *India* 28 E11
Najmah, *Si. Arabia* .. 31 E6
Nakadōri-Shima, *Japan* 23 H4
Nakaminato, *Japan* .. 23 F10
Nakamura, *Japan* ... 23 H6
Nakano, *Japan* 23 F9
Nakano-Shima, *Japan* . 23 K4
Nakashibetsu, *Japan* . 22 C12
Nakfa, *Eritrea* 32 D2
Nakhfar al Buşayyah,
  Iraq 30 D5
Nakhichevan =
  Naxçıvan, *Azerbaijan* 19 G8
Nakhichevan Republic =
  Naxçıvan □,
  Azerbaijan 19 G8
Nakhl, *Egypt* 33 F2
Nakhl-e Taqī, *Iran* ... 31 E7
Nakhodka, *Russia* ... 21 E14
Nakhon Phanom,
  Thailand 26 A2
Nakhon Ratchasima,
  Thailand 26 B2
Nakhon Sawan,
  Thailand 26 A2
Nakhon Si Thammarat,
  Thailand 26 C2
Nakina, *Canada* 48 B2
Nakskov, *Denmark* .. 7 J14
Nakuru, *Kenya* 36 E7
Nakusp, *Canada* 50 C5
Nal →, *Pakistan* 28 G4
Nalchik, *Russia* 19 F7
Nalgonda, *India* 28 L11
Nallamalai Hills, *India* . 28 M11
Nam Co, *China* 24 C4
Nam-Phan, *Vietnam* . 26 B3
Nam Tok, *Thailand* ... 26 B1
Namak, Daryācheh-ye,
  Iran 31 C7
Namak, Kavīr-e, *Iran* . 31 C8
Namakzār, Daryācheh-
  ye, *Iran* 31 C9
Namaland, *Namibia* .. 37 K3
Namangan, *Uzbekistan* 20 E8
Namapa, *Mozam.* 37 G7
Namber, *Indonesia* ... 27 E8
Nambour, *Australia* .. 43 D5
Nambucca Heads,
  Australia 43 E5
Namcha Barwa, *China* 24 D4
Namew L., *Canada* ... 51 C8
Namib Desert =
  Namibwoestyn,
  Namibia 37 J3
Namibe, *Angola* 37 H2
Namibia ■, *Africa* ... 37 J3
Namibwoestyn, *Namibia* 37 J3
Namlea, *Indonesia* ... 27 E7
Namoi →, *Australia* . 43 E4
Nampa, *U.S.A.* 56 E5
Nampō-Shotō, *Japan* . 23 J10
Nampula, *Mozam.* ... 37 H7
Namrole, *Indonesia* .. 27 E7
Namse Shankou, *China* 29 E13
Namsen →, *Norway* . 6 D14
Namsos, *Norway* 6 D14
Namtsy, *Russia* 21 C13
Namtu, *Burma* 29 H20
Namu, *Canada* 50 C3
Namur, *Belgium* 11 D4
Namur □, *Belgium* .. 11 D4
Nan-ch'ang =
  Nanchang, *China* .. 25 D6
Nanaimo, *Canada* ... 50 D4
Nanango, *Australia* .. 43 D5
Nanao, *Japan* 23 F8
Nanchang, *China* 25 D6
Nanching = Nanjing,
  China 25 C6
Nanchong, *China* 24 C5
Nancy, *France* 14 B7
Nanda Devi, *India* ... 28 D11
Nandan, *Japan* 23 G7
Nandewar Ra., *Australia* 43 E5
Nandi, *Fiji* 39 C7
Nandyal, *India* 28 M11
Nanga-Eboko,
  Cameroon 36 D2
Nanga Parbat, *Pakistan* 28 B9
Nangapinoh, *Indonesia* 26 E4

Nangarhār □, Afghan. . . 28 B7
Nangatayap, Indonesia 26 E4
Nanjing, China 25 C6
Nanking = Nanjing,
China 25 C6
Nankoku, Japan 23 H6
Nanning, China 24 D5
Nannup, Australia 41 F2
Nanping, China 25 D6
Nansei-Shotō = Ryūkyū-
rettō, Japan 23 M3
Nansen Sd., Canada . . 4 A3
Nanshan I.,
S. China Sea 26 B5
Nantes, France 14 C3
Nanticoke, U.S.A. 52 E7
Nanton, Canada 50 C6
Nantong, China 25 C7
Nantucket I., U.S.A. . . 62 E10
Nantwich, U.K. 8 D5
Nanuque, Brazil 63 G10
Nanusa, Kepulauan,
Indonesia 27 D7
Nanutarra Roadhouse,
Australia 40 D2
Nanyang, China 25 C6
Nanyuki, Kenya 36 D7
Nao, C. de la, Spain . . 15 C6
Naococane, L., Canada 49 B5
Napa, U.S.A. 56 G2
Napanee, Canada 48 D4
Napier, N.Z. 39 H6
Napier Broome B.,
Australia 40 B4
Napier Pen., Australia . 42 A2
Naples = Nápoli, Italy . 16 D6
Naples, U.S.A. 53 M5
Napo →, Peru 62 D4
Napoleon, N. Dak.,
U.S.A. 54 B5
Napoleon, Ohio, U.S.A. 52 E3
Nápoli, Italy 16 D6
Naqb, Ra's an, Jordan . 33 F4
Naqqāsh, Iran 31 C6
Nara, Japan 23 G7
Nara, Mali 34 E4
Nara □, Japan 23 G8
Nara Visa, U.S.A. 55 H3
Naracoorte, Australia . 43 F3
Naradhan, Australia . . 43 E4
Narasapur, India 29 L12
Narathiwat, Thailand . 26 C2
Narayanganj, Bangla. . 29 H17
Narayanpet, India . . . 28 L10
Narbonne, France . . . 14 E5
Nardin, Iran 31 B7
Nardò, Italy 17 D8
Narembeen, Australia . 41 F2
Naretha, Australia . . . 41 F3
Narew →, Poland . . . 13 B11
Narin, Afghan. 28 A6
Narita, Japan 23 G10
Narmada →, India . . . 28 J8
Narmland, Sweden . . . 7 F15
Narodnaya, Russia . . . 18 A10
Narooma, Australia . . 43 F5
Narrabri, Australia . . . 43 E4
Narran →, Australia . . 43 D4
Narrandera, Australia . 43 E4
Narrogin, Australia . . . 41 F2
Narromine, Australia . . 43 E4
Narrow Hills Prov. Park,
Canada 51 C8
Narsimhapur, India . . . 28 H11
Naruto, Japan 23 G7
Narva, Estonia 18 C4
Narva →, Russia 7 G22
Narvik, Norway 6 B17
Naryan-Mar, Russia . . 18 A9
Narym, Russia 20 D9
Naryn, Kyrgyzstan . . . 20 E8
Nasa, Norway 6 C16
Naseby, N.Z. 39 L3
Naser, Buheirat en,
Egypt 35 D12
Nashua, Mont., U.S.A. 56 B10
Nashua, N.H., U.S.A. . 52 D10
Nashville, Ark., U.S.A. 55 J8
Nashville, Ga., U.S.A. . 53 K4
Nashville, Tenn., U.S.A. 53 G2
Nasik, India 28 K8
Nasirabad, India 28 F9
Naskaupi →, Canada . 49 B7
Naşrābād, Iran 31 C6
Naşrīān-e Pā'īn, Iran . 30 C5
Nass →, Canada 50 C3
Nassau, Bahamas . . . 60 A4
Nassau, B., Chile 64 H3
Nasser, L. = Naser,
Buheirat en, Egypt . 35 D12
Nasser City = Kôm
Ombo, Egypt 35 D12
Nässjö, Sweden 7 H16
Nastapoka →, Canada 48 A4
Nastapoka, Is., Canada 48 A4
Natal, Brazil 63 E11
Natal, Indonesia 26 D1
Natal, S. Africa 37 K6
Naţanz, Iran 31 C6
Natashquan, Canada . 49 B7
Natashquan →,
Canada 49 B7
Natchez, U.S.A. 55 K9
Natchitoches, U.S.A. . . 55 K8
Nathalia, Australia . . . 43 F4

Nathdwara, India 28 G8
Natimuk, Australia . . . 43 F3
Nation →, Canada . . . 50 B4
Natitingou, Benin 34 F6
Natividad, I., Mexico . . 58 B1
Natkyizin, Burma 26 B1
Natron, L., Tanzania . . 36 E7
Natuna Besar,
Kepulauan, Indonesia 26 D3
Natuna Is. = Natuna
Besar, Kepulauan,
Indonesia 26 D3
Natuna Selatan,
Kepulauan, Indonesia 26 D3
Naturaliste, C., Tas.,
Australia 42 G4
Naturaliste, C.,
W. Austral., Australia 38 E4
Noujaat = Repulse Bay,
Canada 47 B11
Naumburg, Germany . . 12 C6
Nā'ūr at Tunayb, Jordan 33 D4
Nauru ■, Pac. Oc. . . . 38 B9
Naushahra = Nowshera,
Pakistan 28 C8
Nauta, Peru 62 D4
Nautanwa, India 29 F13
Nautla, Mexico 59 C5
Nava, Mexico 58 B4
Navahrudak, Belarus . 13 B13
Navajo Reservoir, U.S.A. 57 H10
Navalmoral de la Mata,
Spain 15 C3
Navarino, I., Chile . . . 64 H3
Navarra □, Spain 15 A5
Navasota, U.S.A. 55 K6
Navassa, I., W. Indies . 61 C5
Năvodari, Romania . . 13 F15
Navoi = Nawoiy,
Uzbekistan 20 E7
Navojoa, Mexico 58 B3
Navolato, Mexico 58 C3
Návpaktos, Greece . . 17 E9
Návplion, Greece . . . 17 F10
Navsari, India 28 J8
Nawabshah, Pakistan . 28 F6
Nawakot, Nepal 29 F14
Nawalgarh, India 28 F9
Nawoiy, Uzbekistan . . 20 E7
Naxçivan, Azerbaijan . 19 G8
Naxçıvan □, Azerbaijan 19 G8
Náxos, Greece 17 F11
Nay, Mui, Vietnam . . . 26 B3
Nāy Band, Būshehr, Iran 31 E7
Nāy Band, Khorāsān,
Iran 31 C8
Nayakhan, Russia . . . 21 C16
Nayarit □, Mexico . . . 58 C4
Nayoro, Japan 22 B11
Nayyāl, W. →,
Si. Arabia 30 D3
Nazaré, Brazil 63 F11
Nazareth = Nazerat,
Israel 33 C4
Nazas, Mexico 58 B4
Nazas →, Mexico . . . 58 B4
Nazca, Peru 62 F4
Naze, The, U.K. 9 F9
Nazerat, Israel 33 C4
Nāzik, Iran 30 B5
Nazilli, Turkey 17 F13
Nazko, Canada 50 C4
Nazko →, Canada . . . 50 C4
Nazret, Ethiopia 32 F2
Nazwá, Oman 32 C6
Ndalatando, Angola . . 36 F2
Ndélé, C.A.R. 36 C4
Ndjamena, Chad 35 F8
Ndola, Zambia 37 G5
Neagh, Lough, U.K. . . 10 D3
Neah Bay, U.S.A. 56 B1
Neale, L., Australia . . 40 D5
Near Is., U.S.A. 46 C1
Neath, U.K. 9 F4
Neath Port Talbot □,
U.K. 9 F4
Nebine Cr. →,
Australia 43 D4
Nebitdag, Turkmenistan 19 G9
Nebo, Australia 42 C4
Nebraska □, U.S.A. . . 54 E5
Nebraska City, U.S.A. . 54 E7
Nébrodi, Monti, Italy . 16 F6
Necedah, U.S.A. 54 C9
Nechako →, Canada . 50 C4
Neches →, U.S.A. . . . 55 L8
Neckar →, Germany . 12 D5
Necochea, Argentina . 64 D5
Needles, Canada 50 D5
Needles, U.S.A. 57 J6
Needles, The, U.K. . . . 9 G6
Neemuch = Nimach,
India 28 G9
Neenah, U.S.A. 52 C1
Neepawa, Canada . . . 51 C9
Neftçala, Azerbaijan . 19 G8
Neftekumsk, Russia . . 19 F7
Nefyn, U.K. 8 E3
Negapatam =
Nagappattinam, India 28 P11
Negaunee, U.S.A. . . . 52 B2
Negele, Ethiopia 32 F2
Negev Desert =
Hanegev, Israel . . . 33 E4
Negombo, Sri Lanka . . 28 R11

Negotin, Serbia, Yug. . 17 B10
Negra, Pta., Peru . . . 62 E2
Negrais, C. = Maudin
Sun, Burma 29 M19
Negril, Jamaica 60 C4
Negro →, Argentina . . 64 E4
Negro →, Brazil 62 D7
Negro →, Uruguay . . 64 C5
Negros, Phil. 27 C6
Neguac, Canada 49 C6
Nehāvand, Iran 31 C6
Nehbandān, Iran 31 D9
Nei Monggol Zizhiqu □,
China 25 B6
Neijiang, China 24 D5
Neillsville, U.S.A. 54 C9
Neilton, U.S.A. 56 C2
Neiva, Colombia 62 C3
Nejanilini L., Canada . 51 B9
Nejd = Najd, Si. Arabia 32 B3
Nekā, Iran 31 B7
Nekemte, Ethiopia . . . 32 F2
Neksø, Denmark 7 J16
Nelia, Australia 42 C3
Neligh, U.S.A. 54 D5
Nelkan, Russia 21 D14
Nellore, India 28 M11
Nelson, Canada 50 D5
Nelson, N.Z. 39 J4
Nelson, U.K. 8 D5
Nelson, U.S.A. 57 J7
Nelson →, Canada . . 51 C9
Nelson, C., Australia . 43 F3
Nelson, Estrecho, Chile 64 G2
Nelson Bay, Australia . 43 E5
Nelson Forks, Canada . 50 B4
Nelson House, Canada 51 B9
Nelson L., Canada . . . 51 B8
Nelspruit, S. Africa . . . 37 K6
Néma, Mauritania . . . 34 E4
Neman, Russia 7 J20
Neman →, Lithuania . 7 J19
Nemeiben L., Canada . 51 B7
Némiscau, Canada . . . 48 B4
Némiscau, L., Canada . 48 B4
Nemunas →, Lithuania 7 J19
Nemuro, Japan 22 C12
Nemuro-Kaikyō, Japan 22 C12
Nen Jiang →, China . . 25 B7
Nenagh, Ireland 10 E2
Nene →, U.K. 9 E8
Nenjiang, China 25 B7
Neodesha, U.S.A. . . . 55 G7
Neosho, U.S.A. 55 G7
Neosho →, U.S.A. . . . 55 H7
Nepal ■, Asia 29 F14
Nepalganj, Nepal 29 E12
Nephi, U.S.A. 56 G8
Nerang, Australia . . . 43 D5
Nerchinsk, Russia . . . 21 D12
Néret, L., Canada . . . 49 B5
Neretva →, Croatia . . 17 C7
Neringa, Lithuania . . . 7 J19
Neryungri, Russia . . . 21 D13
Ness, L., U.K. 10 C4
Ness City, U.S.A. 54 F5
Nesterov, Poland 13 C12
Nesvizh = Nyasvizh,
Belarus 13 B14
Netanya, Israel 33 C3
Nete →, Belgium . . . 11 C4
Netherdale, Australia . 42 C4
Netherlands ■, Europe 11 C5
Netherlands Antilles ■,
W. Indies 62 A5
Nettilling L., Canada . . 47 B12
Netzahualcoyotl, Presa,
Mexico 59 D6
Neubrandenburg,
Germany 12 B7
Neuchâtel, Switz. . . . 14 C7
Neuchâtel, Lac de,
Switz. 14 C7
Neufchâteau, Belgium . 11 E5
Neumünster, Germany 12 A5
Neunkirchen, Germany 12 D4
Neuquén, Argentina . . 64 D3
Neuruppin, Germany . 12 B7
Neuse →, U.S.A. 53 H7
Neusiedler See, Austria 13 E9
Neustrelitz, Germany . 12 B7
Neva →, Russia 18 C5
Nevada, Iowa, U.S.A. . 54 D8
Nevada, Mo., U.S.A. . . 55 G7
Nevada □, U.S.A. . . . 56 G5
Nevada, Sierra, Spain . 15 D4
Nevada, Sierra, U.S.A. 56 G3
Nevada City, U.S.A. . . 56 G3
Nevel, Russia 18 C4
Nevers, France 14 C5
Nevertire, Australia . . 43 E4
Neville, Canada 51 D7
Nevinnomyssk, Russia 19 F7
Nevis, W. Indies 61 C7
Nevşehir, Turkey 30 B2
Nevyansk, Russia . . . 18 C11
New →, U.S.A. 52 F5
New Aiyansh, Canada . 50 B3
New Albany, Ind.,
U.S.A. 52 F3
New Albany, Miss.,
U.S.A. 55 H10
New Amsterdam,
Guyana 62 B7

New Angledool,
Australia 43 D4
New Baltimore, U.S.A. 52 D4
New Bedford, U.S.A. . . 52 E10
New Bern, U.S.A. 53 H7
New Boston, U.S.A. . . 55 J7
New Braunfels, U.S.A. 55 L5
New Brighton, N.Z. . . 39 K4
New Britain,
Papua N. G. 38 B8
New Britain, U.S.A. . . 52 E9
New Brunswick, U.S.A. 52 E8
New Brunswick □,
Canada 49 C6
New Caledonia ■,
Pac. Oc. 38 D9
New Castle = Castilla-
La Mancha □, Spain 15 C4
New Castle, Ind., U.S.A. 52 F3
New Castle, Pa., U.S.A. 52 E5
New Delhi, India 28 E10
New Denver, Canada . 50 D5
New England, U.S.A. . 54 B3
New England Ra.,
Australia 43 E5
New Forest, U.K. 9 G6
New Glasgow, Canada 49 C7
New Guinea, Oceania . 38 B6
New Hampshire □,
U.S.A. 52 D10
New Hampton, U.S.A. . 54 D8
New Haven, U.S.A. . . . 52 E9
New Hazelton, Canada 50 B3
New Hebrides =
Vanuatu ■, Pac. Oc. 38 C9
New Iberia, U.S.A. . . . 55 K9
New Ireland,
Papua N. G. 38 B8
New Jersey □, U.S.A. . 52 E8
New Lexington, U.S.A. 52 F4
New Liskeard, Canada 48 C4
New London, Conn.,
U.S.A. 52 E9
New London, Wis.,
U.S.A. 54 C10
New Madrid, U.S.A. . . 55 G10
New Martinsville, U.S.A. 52 F5
New Meadows, U.S.A. 56 D5
New Mexico □, U.S.A. 57 J10
New Norcia, Australia . 41 F2
New Norfolk, Australia 42 G4
New Orleans, U.S.A. . . 55 L9
New Philadelphia,
U.S.A. 52 F3
New Plymouth, N.Z. . . 39 H5
New Plymouth, U.S.A. 56 E5
New Port Richey, U.S.A. 53 L4
New Providence,
Bahamas 60 A4
New Quay, U.K. 9 E3
New Radnor, U.K. . . . 9 E4
New Richmond, Canada 49 C6
New Richmond, U.S.A. 54 C8
New Roads, U.S.A. . . . 55 K9
New Rockford, U.S.A. . 54 B5
New Romney, U.K. . . . 9 G8
New Salem, U.S.A. . . . 54 B4
New Siberian I. =
Novaya Sibir, Ostrov,
Russia 21 B16
New Siberian Is. =
Novosibirskiye
Ostrova, Russia . . . 21 B15
New Smyrna Beach,
U.S.A. 53 L5
New South Wales □,
Australia 43 E4
New Town, U.S.A. . . . 54 B3
New Tredegar, U.K. . . 9 F4
New Ulm, U.S.A. 54 C7
New Waterford, Canada 49 C7
New York, U.S.A. 52 E9
New York □, U.S.A. . . 52 D8
New York Mts., U.S.A. 57 J6
New Zealand ■,
Oceania 39 J6
Newark, Del., U.S.A. . 52 F8
Newark, N.J., U.S.A. . 52 E8
Newark, N.Y., U.S.A. . 52 D7
Newark, Ohio, U.S.A. . 52 E4
Newark-on-Trent, U.K. 8 D7
Newberg, U.S.A. 56 D2
Newberry, Mich., U.S.A. 52 B3
Newberry, S.C., U.S.A. 53 H5
Newburgh, U.S.A. . . . 52 E9
Newbury, U.K. 9 F6
Newburyport, U.S.A. . 53 D10
Newcastle, Australia . . 43 E5
Newcastle, N.B., Canada 49 C6
Newcastle, Ont., Canada 48 D4
Newcastle, S. Africa . . 37 K5
Newcastle Emlyn, U.K. 9 E3
Newcastle Ra., Australia 40 C5
Newcastle-under-Lyme,
U.K. 8 D5
Newcastle-upon-Tyne,
U.K. 8 C6
Newcastle Waters,
Australia 42 B1
Newdegate, Australia . 41 F2
Newell, Australia 42 B4
Newell, U.S.A. 54 C3
Newfoundland □,
Canada 49 B8
Newhaven, U.K. 9 G8

Newkirk, U.S.A. 55 G6
Newlyn, U.K. 9 G2
Newman, Australia . . 40 D2
Newmarket, U.K. 9 E8
Newnan, U.S.A. 53 J3
Newport, I. of W., U.K. 9 G6
Newport, Newp., U.K. . 9 F5
Newport, Ark., U.S.A. . 55 H9
Newport, Ky., U.S.A. . 52 F3
Newport, N.H., U.S.A. . 52 D9
Newport, Oreg., U.S.A. 56 D1
Newport, R.I., U.S.A. . 52 E10
Newport, Tenn., U.S.A. 53 H4
Newport, Vt., U.S.A. . . 52 C9
Newport, Wash., U.S.A. 56 B5
Newport □, U.K. 9 F4
Newport Beach, U.S.A. 57 K5
Newport News, U.S.A. 52 G7
Newport Pagnell, U.K. 9 E7
Newquay, U.K. 9 G2
Newry, U.K. 10 D3
Newton, Ill., U.S.A. . . 54 F10
Newton, Iowa, U.S.A. . 54 E8
Newton, Kans., U.S.A. 55 F6
Newton, Mass., U.S.A. 52 D10
Newton, Miss., U.S.A. 53 J10
Newton, N.C., U.S.A. . 53 H5
Newton, N.J., U.S.A. . 52 E8
Newton, Tex., U.S.A. . 55 K8
Newton Abbot, U.K. . . 9 G4
Newton Aycliffe, U.K. . 8 C6
Newtown, U.K. 9 E4
Neya, Russia 18 C7
Neyrīz, Iran 31 D7
Neyshābūr, Iran 31 B8
Nezhin = Nizhyn,
Ukraine 19 D5
Nezperce, U.S.A. 56 C5
Ngabang, Indonesia . . 26 D3
Ngabordamlu, Tanjung,
Indonesia 27 F8
Ngami Depression,
Botswana . . . . — (not listed)
N'Gage, Angola 36 F3
Nganglong Kangri,
China 29 C12
Ngaoundéré, Cameroon 36 C2
Ngapara, N.Z. 39 L3
Ngawi, Indonesia . . . 27 G14
Ngoring Hu, China . . . 24 C4
Nguigmi, Niger 35 F8
Nguiu, Australia 40 B5
Ngukurr, Australia . . . 42 A1
Ngulu Atoll, Pac. Oc. . 27 C9
Nguru, Nigeria 35 F8
Nha Trang, Vietnam . . 26 B3
Nhamundá →, Brazil . 63 D7
Nhill, Australia 43 F3
Nhulunbuy, Australia . 42 A2
Niagara Falls, Canada 48 D4
Niagara Falls, U.S.A. . 52 D6
Niah, Malaysia 26 D4
Niamey, Niger 34 F6
Nias, Indonesia 26 D1
Nibāk, Si. Arabia 31 E7
Nicaragua ■,
Cent. Amer. 60 D2
Nicaragua, L. de, Nic. . 60 D2
Nicastro, Italy 16 E7
Nice, France 14 E7
Niceville, U.S.A. 53 K2
Nichicun, L., Canada . 49 B5
Nichinan, Japan 23 J5
Nicholás, Canal,
W. Indies 60 B3
Nicholasville, U.S.A. . 52 G3
Nicholson, Australia . . 40 C4
Nicholson →, Australia 42 B2
Nicholson L., Canada . 51 A8
Nicholson Ra., Australia 41 E2
Nicobar Is., Ind. Oc. . 3 D14
Nicobar Is., Ind. Oc. . 3 D14
Nicola, Canada 50 C4
Nicolls Town, Bahamas 60 A4
Nicosia, Cyprus 30 C2
Nicoya, Costa Rica . . 60 D2
Nicoya, G. de,
Costa Rica 60 E3
Nicoya, Pen. de,
Costa Rica 60 E2
Nidd →, U.K. 8 D6
Niedersachsen □,
Germany 12 B5
Niemen = Neman →,
Lithuania 7 J19
Nienburg, Germany . . 12 B5
Nieuw Amsterdam,
Surinam 63 B7
Nieuw Nickerie,
Surinam 63 B7
Nieuwpoort, Belgium . 11 C2
Niğde, Turkey 19 G5
Niger ■, W. Afr. 34 E7
Niger →, W. Afr. 34 G7
Nigeria ■, W. Afr. . . . 34 G7
Nightcaps, N.Z. 39 L2
Nii-Jima, Japan 23 G9
Niigata, Japan 22 F9
Niigata □, Japan 23 F9
Niihama, Japan 23 H6
Niihau, U.S.A. . . . . . — (not listed)
Niimi, Japan 23 G6
Nijil, Jordan 33 E4
Nijkerk, Neths. 11 B5
Nijmegen, Neths. . . . 11 C5
Nijverdal, Neths. 11 B6
Nik Pey, Iran 31 B6

Nikiniki, Indonesia . . . 27 F6
Nikkō, Japan 23 F9
Nikolayev = Mykolayiv,
Ukraine 19 E5
Nikolayevsk, Russia . . 19 E8
Nikolayevsk-na-Amur,
Russia 21 D15
Nikolskoye, Russia . . 21 D17
Nikopol, Ukraine 19 E5
Nikshahr, Iran 31 E9
Nikšić,
Montenegro, Yug. . 17 C8
Nîl, Nahr en →, Africa 35 B12
Nîl el Abyad →, Sudan 35 E12
Nîl el Azraq →, Sudan 35 E12
Nila, Indonesia 27 F7
Nile = Nîl, Nahr en →,
Africa 35 B12
Niles, U.S.A. 52 E2
Nimach, India 28 G9
Nîmes, France 14 E6
Nimfaíon, Ákra =
Pinnes, Ákra, Greece 17 D11
Nimmitabel, Australia . 43 F4
Ninawá, Iraq 30 B4
Nindigully, Australia . . 43 D4
Nineveh = Ninawá, Iraq 30 B4
Ningbo, China 25 D7
Ningjing Shan, China . 24 D4
Ningpo = Ningbo,
China 25 D7
Ningsia Hui A.R. =
Ningxia Huizu
Zizhiqu □, China . . 24 C5
Ningxia Huizu
Zizhiqu □, China . . 24 C5
Ninove, Belgium 11 D4
Niobrara, U.S.A. 54 D6
Niobrara →, U.S.A. . . 54 D6
Nioro du Sahel, Mali . 34 E4
Niort, France 14 C3
Nipawin, Canada 51 C8
Nipigon, Canada 48 C2
Nipigon, L., Canada . . 48 C2
Nipishish L., Canada . 49 B7
Nipissing, L., Canada . 48 C4
Nipomo, U.S.A. 57 J3
Niquelândia, Brazil . . 63 F9
Nīr, Iran 30 B5
Nirasaki, Japan 23 G9
Nirmal, India 28 K11
Nirmali, India 29 F15
Niš, Serbia, Yug. 17 C9
Nişāb, Si. Arabia 30 D5
Nişāb, Yemen 32 E4
Nishinomiya, Japan . . 23 G7
Nishino'omote, Japan . 23 J5
Nishiwaki, Japan 23 G7
Niskibi →, Canada . . 48 A2
Nissum Bredning,
Denmark 7 H13
Nistru = Dnister →,
Europe 13 E16
Nisutlin →, Canada . . 50 A2
Nitchequon, Canada . 49 B5
Niterói, Brazil 63 H10
Nitra, Slovak Rep. . . . 13 D10
Nitra →, Slovak Rep. . 13 E10
Niuafo'ou, Tonga 39 B11
Niue, Cook Is. 45 J11
Niut, Indonesia 26 D4
Nivala, Finland 6 E21
Nivelles, Belgium . . . 11 D4
Nivernais, France . . . 14 C5
Nixon, U.S.A. 55 L6
Nizamabad, India . . . 28 K11
Nizamghat, India 29 E19
Nizhne Kolymsk, Russia 21 C17
Nizhnekamsk, Russia . 18 C9
Nizhnevartovsk, Russia 20 C8
Nizhniy Novgorod,
Russia 18 C7
Nizhniy Tagil, Russia . 18 C10
Nizhyn, Ukraine 19 D5
Nizip, Turkey 30 B3
Nizké Tatry, Slovak Rep. 13 D10
Nkhotakota, Malawi . . 37 G6
Nkongsamba,
Cameroon 36 D1
Nmai →, Burma 29 G20
Noakhali = Maijdi,
Bangla. 29 H17
Nobeoka, Japan 23 H5
Noblesville, U.S.A. . . 52 E3
Nocera Inferiore, Italy . 16 D6
Nocona, U.S.A. 55 J6
Noda, Japan 23 G9
Nogales, Mexico 58 A2
Nogales, U.S.A. 57 L8
Nōgata, Japan 23 H5
Noggerup, Australia . . 41 F2
Noginsk, Russia 21 C10
Nogoa →, Australia . . 42 C4
Noire, Mts., France . . 14 B2
Noirmoutier, Î. de,
France 14 C2
Nojima-Zaki, Japan . . 23 G9
Nok Kundi, Pakistan . 28 E3
Nokia, Finland 7 F20
Nokomis, Canada . . . 51 C8
Nokomis L., Canada . 51 B8
Nola, C.A.R. 36 D3
Nombre de Dios,
Panama 60 E4

Nome, *U.S.A.* 46 B3
Nomo-Zaki, *Japan* 23 H4
Nonacho L., *Canada* . . 51 A7
Nonda, *Australia* 42 C3
Nong Khai, *Thailand* . . 26 A2
Nonoava, *Mexico* 58 B3
Nonoava →, *Mexico* . . 58 B3
Noonamah, *Australia* . . 40 B5
Noord Brabant □,
  Neths. 11 C5
Noord Holland □,
  Neths. 11 B4
Noordbeveland, *Neths.* . 11 C3
Noordoostpolder, *Neths.* 11 B5
Noordwijk, *Neths.* 11 B4
Nootka I., *Canada* 50 D3
Nopiming Prov. Park,
  Canada 51 C9
Noralee, *Canada* 50 C3
Noranda = Rouyn-
  Noranda, *Canada* . . 48 C4
Nord-Ostsee-Kanal,
  Germany 12 A5
Nordaustlandet,
  Svalbard 4 B9
Nordegg, *Canada* 50 C5
Norderney, *Germany* . . 12 B4
Norderstedt, *Germany* . 12 B6
Nordfjord, *Norway* . . . 7 F11
Nordfriesische Inseln,
  Germany 12 A5
Nordhausen, *Germany* 12 C6
Norðoyar, *Færoe Is.* . . 6 E9
Nordkapp, *Norway* . . . 6 A21
Nordkapp, *Svalbard* . . 4 A9
Nordkinn-halvøya,
  Norway 6 A22
Nordrhein-Westfalen □,
  Germany 12 C4
Nordvik, *Russia* 21 B12
Norfolk, *Nebr., U.S.A.* . 54 D6
Norfolk, *Va., U.S.A.* . . 52 G7
Norfolk □, *U.K.* 9 E8
Norfork I., *Pac. Oc.* . . 38 D9
Norfork L., *U.S.A.* . . . 55 G8
Norilsk, *Russia* 21 C9
Norma, Mt., *Australia* . 42 C3
Normal, *U.S.A.* 54 E10
Norman, *U.S.A.* 55 H6
Norman →, *Australia* . 42 B3
Norman Wells, *Canada* 46 B7
Normanby →,
  Australia 42 A3
Normandie, *France* . . . 14 B4
Normandin, *Canada* . . 48 C5
Normandy =
  Normandie, *France* . 14 B4
Normanhurst, Mt.,
  Australia 41 E3
Normanton, *Australia* . 42 B3
Normétal, *Canada* . . . 48 C4
Norquay, *Canada* 51 C8
Norquinco, *Argentina* . 64 E2
Norrbotten □, *Sweden* 6 C19
Norris Point, *Canada* . 49 C8
Norristown, *U.S.A.* . . . 52 E8
Norrköping, *Sweden* . . 7 G17
Norrland, *Sweden* . . . 7 E16
Norrtälje, *Sweden* . . . 7 G18
Norseman, *Australia* . . 41 F3
Norsk, *Russia* 21 D14
Norte, Serra do, *Brazil* 62
North, *C., Canada* . . . 49 C7
North Adams, *U.S.A.* . 52 D9
North Arm, *Canada* . . 50 A5
North Augusta, *U.S.A.* 53 J5
North Battleford,
  Canada 51 C7
North Bay, *Canada* . . 48 C4
North Belcher Is.,
  Canada 48 A4
North Bend, *U.S.A.* . . 56 E1
North C., *Canada* . . . 49 C7
North C., *N.Z.* 39 F4
North Canadian →,
  U.S.A. 55 H7
North Cape =
  Nordkapp, *Norway* . 6 A21
North Cape =
  Nordkapp, *Svalbard* 4 A9
North Caribou L.,
  Canada 48 B1
North Carolina □, *U.S.A.* 53 H6
North Cascades
  National Park, *U.S.A.* 56 B3
North Channel, *Canada* 48 C3
North Channel, *U.K.* . . 10 D4
North Charleston, *U.S.A.* 53 J6
North Chicago, *U.S.A.* 52 D2
North Dakota □, *U.S.A.* 54 B5
North Downs, *U.K.* . . 9 F8
North East Frontier
  Agency = Arunachal
  Pradesh □, *India* . . 29 F19
North East
  Lincolnshire □, *U.K.* 8 D7
North Foreland, *U.K.* . 9 F9
North Fork Grand →,
  U.S.A. 54 C3
North Fork Red →,
  U.S.A. 55 H5
North Frisian Is. =
  Nordfriesische Inseln,
  Germany 12 A5
North Hd., *Australia* . . 41 F1

North Henik L., *Canada* 51 A9
North I., *N.Z.* 39 H5
North Knife →, *Canada* 51 B10
North Korea ■, *Asia* . 25 C7
North Lakhimpur, *India* 29 F19
North Las Vegas, *U.S.A.* 57 H6
North Lincolnshire □,
  U.K. 8 D7
North Little Rock, *U.S.A.* 55 H8
North Loup →, *U.S.A.* 54 E5
North Magnetic Pole,
  Canada 4 B2
North Minch, *U.K.* . . . 10 B4
North Moose L., *Canada* 51 C8
North Myrtle Beach,
  U.S.A. 53 J6
North Nahanni →,
  Canada 50 A4
North Ossetia □, *Russia* 19 F7
North Pagai, I. = Pagai
  Utara, Pulau,
  Indonesia 26 E2
North Palisade, *U.S.A.* 57 H4
North Platte, *U.S.A.* . . 54 E4
North Platte →, *U.S.A.* 54 E4
North Pole, *Arctic* . . . 4 A
North Portal, *Canada* . 51 D8
North Powder, *U.S.A.* . 56 D5
North Rhine
  Westphalia =
  Nordrhein-
  Westfalen □,
  Germany 12 C4
North River, *Canada* . . 49 B8
North
  Saskatchewan →,
  Canada 51 C7
North Sea, *Europe* . . . 10 C7
North Seal →, *Canada* 51 B9
North Somerset □, *U.K.* 9 F5
North Sporades =
  Vóriai Sporádhes,
  Greece 17 E10
North Sydney, *Canada* 49 C7
North Taranaki Bight,
  N.Z. 39 H5
North Thompson →,
  Canada 50 C4
North Tonawanda,
  U.S.A. 52 D6
North Truchas Pk.,
  U.S.A. 57 J11
North Twin I., *Canada* 48 B4
North Tyne →, *U.K.* . . 8 B5
North Uist, *U.K.* 10 C3
North Vancouver,
  Canada 50 D4
North Vernon, *U.S.A.* . 52 F3
North Wabasca L.,
  Canada 50 B6
North Walsham, *U.K.* . 8 E9
North West C., *Australia* 40 D1
North West Christmas I.
  Ridge, *Pac. Oc.* . . . 45 G11
North West Frontier □,
  Pakistan 28 C7
North West Highlands,
  U.K. 10 C4
North West River,
  Canada 49 B7
North Wildwood, *U.S.A.* 52 F8
North York Moors, *U.K.* 8 C7
North Yorkshire □, *U.K.* 8 C6
Northallerton, *U.K.* . . . 8 C6
Northam, *Australia* . . . 41 F2
Northampton, *Australia* 41 E1
Northampton, *U.K.* . . . 9 E7
Northampton, *U.S.A.* . 52 D9
Northamptonshire □,
  U.K. 9 E7
Northcliffe, *Australia* . . 41 F2
Northeast Providence
  Chan., *W. Indies* . . 60 A4
Northern Circars, *India* 29 L13
Northern Indian L.,
  Canada 51 B9
Northern Ireland □, *U.K.* 10 D3
Northern Light L.,
  Canada 48 C1
Northern Marianas ■,
  Pac. Oc. 44 F6
Northern Territory □,
  Australia 40 D5
Northfield, *U.S.A.* . . . 54 C8
Northland □, *N.Z.* . . . 39 F4
Northome, *U.S.A.* . . . 54 B7
Northport, *Ala., U.S.A.* 53 J2
Northport, *Wash.,
  U.S.A.* 56 B5
Northumberland □, *U.K.* 8 B6
Northumberland, C.,
  Australia 43 F3
Northumberland Is.,
  Australia 42 C4
Northumberland Str.,
  Canada 49 C7
Northwest Providence
  Channel, *W. Indies* . 60 A4
Northwest Territories □,
  Canada 46 B9
Northwood, *Iowa,
  U.S.A.* 54 D8
Northwood, *N. Dak.,
  U.S.A.* 54 B6
Norton, *U.S.A.* 54 F5

Norton Sd., *U.S.A.* . . . 46 B3
Norwalk, *Conn., U.S.A.* 52 E9
Norwalk, *Iowa, U.S.A.* 54 E8
Norwalk, *Ohio, U.S.A.* 52 E4
Norway, *Maine, U.S.A.* 53 C10
Norway, *Mich., U.S.A.* 52 C2
Norway ■, *Europe* . . . 6 E14
Norway House, *Canada* 51 C9
Norwegian Sea, *Atl. Oc.* 4 C8
Norwich, *U.K.* 9 E9
Norwich, *Conn., U.S.A.* 52 E9
Norwich, *N.Y., U.S.A.* 52 D8
Noshiro, *Japan* 22 D10
Noşratābād, *Iran* 31 D8
Nossob →, *S. Africa* . 37 K4
Nosy Barren, *Madag.* . 37 H8
Nosy Be, *Madag.* . . . 37 G9
Nosy Boraha, *Madag.* . 37 H9
Nosy Varika, *Madag.* . 37 J9
Noteć →, *Poland* . . . 12 B8
Notikewin →, *Canada* 50 B5
Notodden, *Norway* . . . 7 G13
Notre Dame B., *Canada* 49 C8
Notre Dame de
  Koartac = Quaqtaq,
  Canada 47 B13
Notre Dame
  d'Ivujivic = Ivujivik,
  Canada 47 B12
Notre-Dame-du-Nord,
  Canada 48 C4
Nottaway →, *Canada* 48 B4
Nottingham, *U.K.* . . . 8 E6
Nottingham, City of □,
  U.K. 8 E6
Nottingham I., *Canada* 47 B12
Nottinghamshire □, *U.K.* 8 E6
Nottoway →, *U.S.A.* . 52 G7
Nouâdhibou, *Mauritania* 34 D2
Nouâdhibou, Ras,
  Mauritania 34 D2
Nouakchott, *Mauritania* 34 E1
Nouméa, *N. Cal.* 38 D9
Nouveau Comptoir =
  Wemindji, *Canada* . 48 B4
Nouvelle-Amsterdam, I.,
  Ind. Oc. 3 F13
Nouvelle-Calédonie =
  New Caledonia ■,
  Pac. Oc. 38 D9
Nova Casa Nova, *Brazil* 63 E10
Nova Friburgo, *Brazil* . 63 H10
Nova Gaia = Cambundi-
  Catembo, *Angola* . 36 G3
Nova Iguaçu, *Brazil* . . 64 A8
Nova Iorque, *Brazil* . . 63 E10
Nova Lima, *Brazil* . . . 63 G10
Nova Lisboa = Huambo,
  Angola 37 G3
Nova Scotia □, *Canada* 49 C7
Nova Venécia, *Brazil* . 63 G10
Nova Zagora, *Bulgaria* 17 C11
Novara, *Italy* 14 D8
Novaya Ladoga, *Russia* 18 B5
Novaya Lyalya, *Russia* 18 C11
Novaya Sibir, Ostrov,
  Russia 21 B16
Novaya Zemlya, *Russia* 20 B6
Nové Zámky,
  Slovak Rep. 13 D10
Novgorod, *Russia* . . . 18 C5
Novgorod-Severskiy =
  Novhorod-Siverskyy,
  Ukraine 18 D5
Novhorod-Siverskyy,
  Ukraine 18 D5
Novi Ligure, *Italy* . . . 14 D8
Novi Pazar, *Serbia, Yug.* 17 C9
Novi Sad, *Serbia, Yug.* 17 B8
Nôvo Hamburgo, *Brazil* 64 B6
Novo Mesto, *Slovenia* . 16 B6
Novo Remanso, *Brazil* . 63 E10
Novoataysk, *Russia* . . 20 D9
Novocherkassk, *Russia* 19 E7
Novogrudok =
  Navahrudak, *Belarus* 13 B13
Novohrad-Volynskyy,
  Ukraine 13 C14
Novokachalinsk, *Russia* 22 B6
Novokazalinsk =
  Zhangaqazaly,
  Kazakstan 20 E7
Novokuybyshevsk,
  Russia 18 D8
Novokuznetsk, *Russia* . 20 D9
Novomoskovsk, *Russia* 18 D6
Novorossiysk, *Russia* . 19 F6
Novorybornoye, *Russia* 21 B11
Novoselytsya, *Ukraine* . 13 D14
Novoshakhtinsk, *Russia* 19 E6
Novosibirsk, *Russia* . . 20 D9
Novosibirskiye Ostrova,
  Russia 21 B15
Novotroitsk, *Russia* . . 18 D10
Novouzensk, *Russia* . . 19 D8
Novovolynsk, *Ukraine* . 13 C13
Novska, *Croatia* 16 B7
Novvy Urengoy, *Russia* 20 C8
Novyy Bor, *Russia* . . . 18 A9
Novyy Port, *Russia* . . 20 C8
Now Shahr, *Iran* 31 B6
Nowa Sól, *Poland* . . . 12 C8
Nowata, *U.S.A.* 55 G7
Nowbarān, *Iran* 31 C6
Nowghāb, *Iran* 31 C8

Nowgong, *India* 29 F18
Nowra-Bomaderry,
  Australia 43 E5
Nowshera, *Pakistan* . . 28 C8
Nowy Sącz, *Poland* . . 13 D11
Nowy Targ, *Poland* . . 13 D11
Nowy Tomyśl, *Poland* . 12 B9
Noxon, *U.S.A.* 56 C6
Noyabr'sk, *Russia* . . . 20 C8
Noyon, *France* 14 B5
Nsanje, *Malawi* 37 H7
Nu Jiang →, *China* . . 24 D4
Nu Shan, *China* 24 D4
Nubian Desert =
  Nûbîya, Es Sahrâ en,
  Sudan 35 D12
Nûbîya, Es Sahrâ en,
  Sudan 35 D12
Nuboai, *Indonesia* . . . 27 E9
Nueces →, *U.S.A.* . . 55 M6
Nueltin L., *Canada* . . . 51 A9
Nueva Gerona, *Cuba* . 60 B3
Nueva Rosita, *Mexico* . 58 B4
Nueva San Salvador,
  El Salv. 60 D2
Nuéve de Julio,
  Argentina 64 D4
Nuevitas, *Cuba* 60 B4
Nuevo, G., *Argentina* . 64 E4
Nuevo Casas Grandes,
  Mexico 58 A3
Nuevo Guerrero, *Mexico* 59 B5
Nuevo Laredo, *Mexico* 59 B5
Nuevo León □, *Mexico* 58 C5
Nuevo Rocafuerte,
  Ecuador 62 D3
Nugget Pt., *N.Z.* 39 M2
Nuhaka, *N.Z.* 39 H6
Nukey Bluff, *Australia* . 43 E2
Nukhuyb, *Iraq* 30 C4
Nuku'alofa, *Tonga* . . . 39 E12
Nukus, *Uzbekistan* . . . 20 E6
Nullagine, *Australia* . . 40 D3
Nullagine →, *Australia* 40 D3
Nullarbor, *Australia* . . 41 F5
Nullarbor Plain,
  Australia 41 F4
Numalla, L., *Australia* . 43 D3
Numan, *Nigeria* 35 G8
Numata, *Japan* 23 F9
Numazu, *Japan* 23 G9
Numbulwar, *Australia* . 42 A2
Numfoor, *Indonesia* . . 27 E8
Numurkah, *Australia* . . 43 F4
Nunaksaluk I., *Canada* . 49 A7
Nunap Isua, *Greenland* 4 D5
Nunavut □, *Canada* . . 47 B11
Nuneaton, *U.K.* 10 E6
Nungarin, *Australia* . . 41 F2
Nunivak I., *U.S.A.* . . . 46 B3
Nunkun, *India* 28 C10
Núoro, *Italy* 16 D3
Nūrābād, *Iran* 31 E8
Nuremberg = Nürnberg,
  Germany 12 D6
Nuri, *Mexico* 58 B3
Nuriootpa, *Australia* . . 43 E2
Nurmes, *Finland* 6 E23
Nürnberg, *Germany* . . 12 D6
Nurran, L. = Terewah,
  L., *Australia* 43 D4
Nurrari Lakes, *Australia* 41 E5
Nusa Barung, *Indonesia* 27 H15
Nusa Kambangan,
  Indonesia 27 G13
Nusa Tenggara Barat □,
  Indonesia 26 F5
Nusa Tenggara
  Timur □, *Indonesia* . 27 F6
Nusaybin, *Turkey* . . . 19 G7
Nushki, *Pakistan* 28 E5
Nuuk, *Greenland* 47 B14
Nuwakot, *Nepal* 29 E13
Nuweiba', *Egypt* 30 D2
Nuweveldberge,
  S. Africa 37 L4
Nuyts, C., *Australia* . . 41 F5
Nuyts, Pt., *Australia* . . 41 G2
Nuyts Arch., *Australia* . 43 E1
Nyabing, *Australia* . . . 41 F2
Nyagan, *Russia* 20 C7
Nyahururu, *Kenya* . . . 36 D7
Nyainqentanglha Shan,
  China 24 D4
Nyâlâ, *Sudan* 35 F10
Nyandoma, *Russia* . . . 18 B7
Nyasa, L., *Africa* 37 G6
Nyasvizh, *Belarus* . . . 13 B14
Nyazepetrovsk, *Russia* 18 C10
Nyíregyháza, *Hungary* . 13 E11
Nyíri, *Russia* 20 C8
Nyírbogár, *Russia* . . . 20 C8
Nyiregyháza, *Hungary* 13 E11
Nykøbing, *Storstrøm,
  Denmark* 7 J14
Nykøbing, *Vestsjælland,
  Denmark* 7 J14
Nykøbing, *Viborg,
  Denmark* 7 H13
Nyköping, *Sweden* . . . 7 G17
Nylstroom, *S. Africa* . . 37 J5
Nymagee, *Australia* . . 43 E4
Nynäshamn, *Sweden* . 7 G17
Nyngan, *Australia* . . . 43 E4
Nyoman = Neman →,
  Lithuania 7 J19

Nysa, *Poland* 13 C9
Nysa →, *Europe* 12 B8
Nyssa, *U.S.A.* 56 E5
Nyunzu, *Dem. Rep. of
  the Congo* 36 F5
Nyurba, *Russia* 21 C12
Nzega, *Tanzania* 36 E6
Nzérékoré, *Guinea* . . . 34 G4
Nzeto, *Angola* 36 F2

Ō-Shima, *Japan* 23 G9
Oacoma, *U.S.A.* 54 D5
Oahe, L., *U.S.A.* 54 C4
Oahe Dam, *U.S.A.* . . . 54 C4
Oak Harbor, *U.S.A.* . . 56 B2
Oak Hill, *U.S.A.* 52 G5
Oak Ridge, *U.S.A.* . . . 53 G3
Oakan-Dake, *Japan* . . 22 C12
Oakdale, *U.S.A.* 55 K8
Oakes, *U.S.A.* 54 B5
Oakesdale, *U.S.A.* . . . 56 C5
Oakey, *Australia* 43 D5
Oakham, *U.K.* 9 E7
Oakland, *U.S.A.* 57 H2
Oakley, *Idaho, U.S.A.* . 56 E7
Oakley, *Kans., U.S.A.* . 54 F4
Oakover →, *Australia* . 40 D3
Oakridge, *U.S.A.* 56 E2
Oamaru, *N.Z.* 39 L3
Oates Land, *Antarctica* 5 C11
Oatlands, *Australia* . . . 42 G4
Oaxaca, *Mexico* 59 D5
Oaxaca □, *Mexico* . . . 59 D5
Ob →, *Russia* 20 C7
Oba, *Canada* 48 C3
Obama, *Japan* 23 G7
Oban, *U.K.* 10 C4
Obbia, *Somali Rep.* . . 32 F4
Oberhausen, *Germany* 12 C4
Oberlin, *Kans., U.S.A.* . 54 F4
Oberlin, *La., U.S.A.* . . 55 K8
Oberon, *Australia* . . . 43 E4
Obi, Kepulauan,
  Indonesia 27 E7
Obi Is. = Obi,
  Kepulauan, *Indonesia* 27 E7
Óbidos, *Brazil* 63 D7
Obihiro, *Japan* 22 C11
Obilatu, *Indonesia* . . . 27 E7
Obluchye, *Russia* . . . 21 E14
Obo, *C.A.R.* 36 C5
Oboyan, *Russia* 20 D4
Obozerskaya =
  Obozerskiy, *Russia* . 18 B7
Obozerskiy, *Russia* . . 18 B7
Obskaya Guba, *Russia* 20 C8
Obuasi, *Ghana* 34 G5
Ocala, *U.S.A.* 53 L4
Ocampo, *Chihuahua,
  Mexico* 58 B3
Ocampo, *Tamaulipas,
  Mexico* 59 C5
Ocaña, *Spain* 15 C4
Ocanomowoc, *U.S.A.* . 54 D10
Occidental, Cordillera,
  Colombia 62 C3
Ocean City, *Md., U.S.A.* 52 F8
Ocean City, *N.J., U.S.A.* 52 F8
Ocean Falls, *Canada* . 50 C3
Ocean I. = Banaba,
  Kiribati 44 H8
Ocean Park, *U.S.A.* . . 56 C1
Oceanside, *U.S.A.* . . . 57 K5
Ocilla, *U.S.A.* 53 K4
Ocmulgee →, *U.S.A.* . 53 K4
Ocniţa, *Moldova* 13 D14
Oconee →, *U.S.A.* . . 53 K4
Oconto, *U.S.A.* 52 C2
Oconto Falls, *U.S.A.* . . 52 C1
Ocosingo, *Mexico* . . . 59 D6
Ocotal, *Nic.* 60 D2
Ocotlán, *Mexico* 58 C4
Ocotlán de Morelos,
  Mexico 59 D5
Ōda, *Japan* 23 G6
Ódáðahraun, *Iceland* . 6 D5
Odate, *Japan* 22 D10
Odawara, *Japan* 23 G9
Odda, *Norway* 7 F12
Odei →, *Canada* 51 B9
Ödemiş, *Turkey* 17 E13
Odense, *Denmark* . . . 7 J14
Oder →, *Europe* 12 B8
Odesa, *Ukraine* 19 E5
Odessa = Odesa,
  Ukraine 19 E5
Odessa, *Tex., U.S.A.* . 55 K3
Odessa, *Wash., U.S.A.* 56 C4
Odienné, *Ivory C.* . . . 34 G4
Odintsovo, *Russia* . . . 18 C6
Odorheiu Secuiesc,
  Romania 13 E13
Odra = Oder →,
  Europe 12 B8
Odzi, *Zimbabwe* 37 H6
Oeiras, *Brazil* 63 E10
Oelrichs, *U.S.A.* 54 D3
Oelwein, *U.S.A.* 54 D9
Oenpelli, *Australia* . . . 40 B5
Ofanto →, *Italy* 16 D7
Offa, *Nigeria* 34 G6

Offenbach, *Germany* . 12 C5
Offenburg, *Germany* . . 12 D4
Ofotfjorden, *Norway* . . 6 B17
Ōfunato, *Japan* 22 E10
Oga, *Japan* 22 E9
Oga-Hantō, *Japan* . . . 22 E9
Ōgaki, *Japan* 23 G8
Ogallala, *U.S.A.* 54 E4
Ogasawara Gunto,
  Pac. Oc. 44 E6
Ogbomosho, *Nigeria* . 34 G6
Ogden, *U.S.A.* 56 F7
Ogdensburg, *U.S.A.* . . 52 C8
Ogeechee →, *U.S.A.* . 53 K5
Oglio →, *Italy* 16 B4
Ogmore, *Australia* . . . 42 C4
Ogoki, *Canada* 48 B2
Ogoki →, *Canada* . . . 48 B2
Ogoki L., *Canada* . . . 48 B2
Ogoki Res., *Canada* . . 48 B2
Ogooué →, *Gabon* . . 36 E1
Ogowe = Ogooué →,
  Gabon 36 E1
Ogre, *Latvia* 7 H21
Ogurchinskiy, Ostrov,
  Turkmenistan 31 B7
Ohai, *N.Z.* 39 L2
Ohakune, *N.Z.* 39 H5
Ohata, *Japan* 22 D10
Ohau, L., *N.Z.* 39 L2
Ohio □, *U.S.A.* 52 E3
Ohio →, *U.S.A.* 52 G1
Ohře →, *Czech Rep.* . 12 C8
Ohrid, *Macedonia* . . . 17 D9
Ohridsko Jezero,
  Macedonia 17 D9
Oiapoque, *Brazil* 63
Oil City, *U.S.A.* 52 E6
Oise →, *France* 14 B5
Ōita, *Japan* 23 H5
Ōita □, *Japan* 23 H5
Oiticica, *Brazil* 63 E10
Ojacaliente, *Mexico* . . 58 C4
Ojai, *U.S.A.* 57 J4
Ojinaga, *Mexico* 58 B4
Ojiya, *Japan* 23 F9
Ojos del Salado, Cerro,
  Argentina 64 B3
Oka →, *Russia* 18 C7
Okaba, *Indonesia* . . . 27 F9
Okahandja, *Namibia* . . 37 J3
Okanagan L., *Canada* . 50 D5
Okanogan, *U.S.A.* . . . 56 B4
Okanogan →, *U.S.A.* . 56 B4
Okara, *Pakistan* 28 D8
Okavango Swamps,
  Botswana 37 H4
Okaya, *Japan* 23 F9
Okayama, *Japan* 23 G6
Okayama □, *Japan* . . 23 G6
Okazaki, *Japan* 23 G8
Okeechobee, *U.S.A.* . . 53 M5
Okeechobee, L., *U.S.A.* 53 M5
Okefenokee Swamp,
  U.S.A. 53 K4
Okehampton, *U.K.* . . . 9 G4
Okha, *Russia* 21 D15
Okhotsk, *Russia* 21 D15
Okhotsk, Sea of, *Asia* . 21 D15
Okhotskiy Perevoz,
  Russia 21 C14
Okhtyrka, *Ukraine* . . . 19 D5
Oki-Shotō, *Japan* . . . 23 F6
Okinawa □, *Japan* . . . 23 L4
Okinawa-Guntō, *Japan* 23 L4
Okinawa-Jima, *Japan* . 23 L4
Okino-erabu-Shima,
  Japan 23 L4
Oklahoma □, *U.S.A.* . 55 H6
Oklahoma City, *U.S.A.* 55 H6
Okmulgee, *U.S.A.* . . . 55 H7
Oknitsa = Ocniţa,
  Moldova 13 D14
Okolona, *U.S.A.* 55 J10
Okotoks, *Canada* . . . 50 C6
Oksibil, *Indonesia* . . . 27 E10
Oksovskiy, *Russia* . . . 18 B6
Oktabrsk = Oktyabrsk,
  Kazakstan 19 E10
Oktabrsk, *Kazakstan* . 19 E10
Oktyabrskiy =
  Aktsyabrski, *Belarus* 13 B15
Oktyabrskiy, *Russia* . . 18 D9
Oktyabrskoy Revolyutsii,
  Ostrov, *Russia* . . . 21 B10
Okuru, *N.Z.* 39 K2
Okushiri-Tō, *Japan* . . 22 C9
Ola, *U.S.A.* 55 H8
Ólafsfjörður, *Iceland* . 6 C4
Ólafsvík, *Iceland* 6 D2
Olancha, *U.S.A.* 57 H4
Olanchito, *Honduras* . . 60 C2
Öland, *Sweden* 7 H17
Olary, *Australia* 43 E3
Olathe, *U.S.A.* 54 F7
Olavarría, *Argentina* . . 64 D4
Oława, *Poland* 13 C9
Ólbia, *Italy* 16 D3
Old Bahama Chan. =
  Bahama, Canal Viejo
  de, *W. Indies* 60 B4
Old Castile = Castilla y
  Leon □, *Spain* . . . 15 B3
Old Crow, *Canada* . . . 46 B6

Old Perlican, *Canada* . . 49 C9
Old Town, *U.S.A.* 53 C11
Old Wives L., *Canada* . . 51 C7
Oldbury, *U.K.* 9 F5
Oldenburg, *Germany* . . 12 B5
Oldenzaal, *Neths.* 11 B6
Oldham, *U.K.* 8 D5
Oldman →, *Canada* . . . 50 D6
Olds, *Canada* 50 C6
Olean, *U.S.A.* 52 D6
Olekma →, *Russia* 21 C13
Olekminsk, *Russia* . . . 21 C13
Oleksandriya, *Ukraine* . 13 C14
Olenegorsk, *Russia* . . 18 A5
Olenek, *Russia* 21 C12
Olenek →, *Russia* . . . 21 B13
Oléron, Î. d', *France* . . 14 D3
Oleśnica, *Poland* 13 C9
Olevsk, *Ukraine* 13 C14
Olga, *Russia* 21 E14
Olga, L., *Canada* 48 C4
Olga, Mt., *Australia* . . 41 E5
Olhão, *Portugal* 15 D2
Olifants →, *Africa* . . . 37 J6
Ólimbos, Óros, *Greece* 17 D10
Olinda, *Brazil* 63 E12
Olivenza, *Spain* 15 C2
Oliver, *Canada* 50 D5
Oliver L., *Canada* 51 B8
Ollagüe, *Chile* 62 H5
Olney, *Ill., U.S.A.* . . . 52 F1
Olney, *Tex., U.S.A.* . . 55 J5
Olomane →, *Canada* . . 49 B7
Olomouc, *Czech Rep.* . 13 D9
Olonets, *Russia* 18 B5
Olongapo, *Phil.* 27 B6
Olot, *Spain* 15 A7
Olovyannaya, *Russia* . 21 D12
Oloy →, *Russia* 21 C16
Olsztyn, *Poland* 13 B11
Olt →, *Romania* 13 G13
Oltenița, *Romania* . . . 13 F14
Olton, *U.S.A.* 55 H3
Olympia, *Greece* 17 F9
Olympia, *U.S.A.* 56 C2
Olympic Dam, *Australia* 43 E2
Olympic Mts., *U.S.A.* . 56 C2
Olympic Nat. Park,
U.S.A. 56 C2
Olympus, *Cyprus* 30 C2
Olympus, Mt. =
Ólimbos, Óros,
Greece 17 D10
Olympus, Mt. = Uludağ,
Turkey 17 D13
Olympus, Mt., *U.S.A.* . 56 C2
Om →, *Russia* 20 D8
Ōma, *Japan* 22 D10
Ōmachi, *Japan* 23 F8
Omae-Zaki, *Japan* . . . 23 G9
Ōmagari, *Japan* 22 E10
Omagh, *U.K.* 10 D3
Omaha, *U.S.A.* 54 E7
Omak, *U.S.A.* 56 B4
Oman ■, *Asia* 32 C6
Oman, G. of, *Asia* . . . 31 E8
Omaruru, *Namibia* . . . 37 J3
Omate, *Peru* 62 G4
Ombai, Selat, *Indonesia* 27 F6
Omboué, *Gabon* 36 E1
Ombrone →, *Italy* . . . 16 C4
Omdurmân, *Sudan* . . 35 E12
Omeo, *Australia* 43 F4
Ometepe, I. de, *Nic.* . 60 D2
Ometepec, *Mexico* . . . 59 D5
Ominato, *Japan* 22 D10
Omineca →, *Canada* . . 50 B4
Ōmiya, *Japan* 23 G9
Ommen, *Neths.* 11 B6
Omo →, *Ethiopia* . . . 32 F2
Omolon →, *Russia* . . 21 C16
Omono-Gawa →,
Japan 22 E10
Omsk, *Russia* 20 D8
Omsukchan, *Russia* . . 21 C16
Ōmu, *Japan* 22 B11
Omul, Vf., *Romania* . . 13 F13
Ōmura, *Japan* 23 H4
Omuramba →,
Namibia 37 H4
Ōmuta, *Japan* 23 H5
Onaga, *U.S.A.* 54 F6
Onalaska, *U.S.A.* . . . 54 D9
Onancock, *U.S.A.* . . . 52 G8
Onang, *Indonesia* . . . 27 E5
Onaping L., *Canada* . . 48 C3
Onavas, *Mexico* 58 B3
Onawa, *U.S.A.* 54 D6
Onda, *Spain* 15 C5
Ondangua, *Namibia* . . 37 H3
Öndörhaan, *Iceland* . 6 D1
One Tree, *Australia* . . 43 E3
Onega, *Russia* 18 B6
Onega →, *Russia* . . . 18 B6
Onega, G. of =
Onezhskaya Guba,
Russia 18 B6
Onega, L. = Onezhskoye
Ozero, *Russia* . . . 18 B6
Oneida, *U.S.A.* 52 D8
Oneida L., *U.S.A.* . . . 52 D8
O'Neill, *U.S.A.* 54 D5
Onekotan, Ostrov,
Russia 21 E16

Oneonta, *U.S.A.* 52 D8
Oneşti, *Romania* 13 E14
Onezhskaya Guba,
Russia 18 B6
Onezhskoye Ozero,
Russia 18 B6
Ongarue, *N.Z.* 39 H5
Ongerup, *Australia* . . 41 F2
Ongole, *India* 28 M12
Onida, *U.S.A.* 54 C4
Onilahy →, *Madag.* . . 37 J8
Onitsha, *Nigeria* 34 G7
Onoda, *Japan* 23 G5
Onslow, *Australia* . . . 40 D2
Onslow B., *U.S.A.* . . . 53 H7
Ontake-San, *Japan* . . 23 G8
Ontario, *Calif., U.S.A.* 57 J5
Ontario, *Oreg., U.S.A.* 56 D5
Ontario □, *Canada* . . 48 B3
Ontario, L., *N. Amer.* . 48 D4
Ontonagon, *U.S.A.* . . 54 B10
Oodnadatta, *Australia* 43 D2
Ooldea, *Australia* . . . 41 F5
Oombulgurri, *Australia* 40 C4
Oorindi, *Australia* . . . 42 C3
Oost-Vlaanderen □,
Belgium 11 C3
Oostende, *Belgium* . . 11 C2
Oosterhout, *Neths.* . . 11 C4
Oosterschelde →,
Neths. 11 C4
Oosterwolde, *Neths.* . 11 B6
Ootacamund =
Udagamandalam,
India 28 P10
Ootsa L., *Canada* . . . 50 C3
Opala, *Dem. Rep. of
the Congo* 36 E4
Opanake, *Sri Lanka* . 28 R12
Opasatika, *Canada* . . 48 C3
Opasquia Prov. Park,
Canada 48 B1
Opava, *Czech Rep.* . . 13 D9
Opelika, *U.S.A.* 53 J3
Opelousas, *U.S.A.* . . 55 K8
Opémisca, L., *Canada* 48 C5
Opheim, *U.S.A.* 56 B10
Ophthalmia Ra.,
Australia 40 D2
Opinaca →, *Canada* . . 48 B4
Opinaca, Rés., *Canada* 48 B4
Opinnagau →, *Canada* 48 B3
Opiscoteo, L., *Canada* 49 B6
Opole, *Poland* 13 C9
Oporto = Porto,
Portugal 15 B1
Opotiki, *N.Z.* 39 H6
Opp, *U.S.A.* 53 K2
Oppdal, *Norway* 7 E13
Opportunity, *U.S.A.* . . 56 C5
Opua, *N.Z.* 39 F5
Opunake, *N.Z.* 39 H4
Oracle, *U.S.A.* 57 K8
Oradea, *Romania* . . . 13 E11
Öræfajökull, *Iceland* . 6 D5
Orai, *India* 28 G11
Oral = Zhayyq →,
Kazakstan 19 E9
Oral, *Kazakstan* 19 D9
Oran, *Algeria* 34 A5
Orange, *Australia* . . . 43 E4
Orange, *France* 14 D6
Orange, *Tex., U.S.A.* . 55 K8
Orange, *Va., U.S.A.* . . 52 F6
Orange →, *S. Africa* . 37 K3
Orange, C., *Brazil* . . . 63 C8
Orange Free State =
Free State □, *S. Africa* 37 K5
Orange Grove, *U.S.A.* 55 M6
Orange Walk, *Belize* . 59 D7
Orangeburg, *U.S.A.* . . 53 J5
Orangeville, *Canada* . 48 D3
Oranienburg, *Germany* 12 B7
Oranje = Orange →,
S. Africa 37 K3
Oranje Vrystaat = Free
State □, *S. Africa* . 37 K5
Orapa, *Botswana* . . . 37 J5
Oras, *Phil.* 27 B7
Orașul Stalin = Brașov,
Romania 13 F13
Orbetello, *Italy* 16 C4
Orbost, *Australia* . . . 43 F4
Orchard City, *U.S.A.* . 57 G10
Orchila, I., *Venezuela* 62 A5
Ord, *U.S.A.* 54 E5
Ord →, *Australia* . . . 40 C4
Ord, Mt., *Australia* . . 40 C4
Orderville, *U.S.A.* . . . 57 H7
Ordos = Mu Us Shamo,
China 25 C5
Ordu, *Turkey* 19 F6
Ordway, *U.S.A.* 54 F3
Ordzhonikidze =
Vladikavkaz, *Russia* 19 F7
Ore Mts. = Erzgebirge,
Germany 12 C7
Örebro, *Sweden* 7 G16
Oregon, *U.S.A.* 54 D10
Oregon □, *U.S.A.* . . . 56 E3
Oregon City, *U.S.A.* . 56 D2
Orekhovo-Zuyevo,
Russia 18 C6
Orel, *Russia* 18 D6
Orem, *U.S.A.* 56 F8

Ören, *Turkey* 17 F12
Orenburg, *Russia* . . . 18 D10
Orense = Ourense,
Spain 15 A2
Orepuki, *N.Z.* 39 M1
Orestiás, *Greece* . . . 17 D12
Orestes Pereyra, *Mexico* 58 B3
Orford Ness, *U.K.* . . 9 E9
Orgaz, *Spain* 15 C4
Orgeyev = Orhei,
Moldova 13 E15
Orhaneli, *Turkey* . . . 17 E13
Orhangazi, *Turkey* . . 17 D13
Orhei, *Moldova* 13 E15
Orhon Gol →,
Mongolia 24 A5
Oriental, Cordillera,
Colombia 62 B4
Orihuela, *Spain* 15 C5
Orinoco →, *Venezuela* 62 B6
Orion, *Canada* 51 D6
Orissa □, *India* 29 K14
Orissaare, *Estonia* . . 7 G20
Oristano, *Italy* 16 E3
Oristano, G. di, *Italy* . 16 E3
Orizaba, *Mexico* 59 D5
Orkanger, *Norway* . . 6 E13
Orkla →, *Norway* . . . 6 E13
Orkney Is., *U.K.* 10 B5
Orland, *U.S.A.* 56 G2
Orlando, *U.S.A.* 53 L5
Orléanais, *France* . . . 14 C4
Orléans, *France* 14 C4
Orléans, I. d', *Canada* 49 C5
Ormara, *Pakistan* . . . 28 G4
Ormoc, *Phil.* 27 B6
Ormond, *N.Z.* 39 H6
Ormond Beach, *U.S.A.* 53 L5
Ormskirk, *U.K.* 8 D5
Örnsköldsvik, *Sweden* 6 E18
Oro →, *Mexico* 58 B3
Oro Valley, *U.S.A.* . . 57 K8
Orocué, *Colombia* . . . 62 C4
Orofino, *U.S.A.* 56 C5
Orol Dengizi = Aral Sea,
Asia 20 E7
Oromocto, *Canada* . . 49 C6
Orono, *U.S.A.* 53 C11
Oroqen Zizhiqi, *China* 25 A7
Oroquieta, *Phil.* 27 C6
Orosháza, *Hungary* . . 13 E11
Orotukan, *Russia* . . . 21 C16
Oroville, *Calif., U.S.A.* 56 G3
Oroville, *Wash., U.S.A.* 56 B4
Orroroo, *Australia* . . 43 E2
Orsha, *Belarus* 18 D5
Orsk, *Russia* 20 D6
Orşova, *Romania* . . . 13 F12
Ortaca, *Turkey* 17 F13
Ortegal, C., *Spain* . . 15 A2
Orthez, *France* 14 E3
Ortigueira, *Spain* . . . 15 A2
Ortles, *Italy* 14 C9
Ortón →, *Bolivia* . . . 62 F5
Ortonville, *U.S.A.* . . . 54 C6
Orûmîyeh, *Iran* 30 B5
Orûmîyeh, Daryâcheh-
ye, *Iran* 30 B5
Oruro, *Bolivia* 62 G5
Orust, *Sweden* 7 G14
Oruzgân □, *Afghan.* . 28 C5
Orvieto, *Italy* 16 C5
Orwell →, *U.K.* 9 F9
Oryakhovo, *Bulgaria* . 17 C10
Osa, *Russia* 18 C10
Osa, Pen. de, *Costa Rica* 60 E3
Osage, *U.S.A.* 54 D8
Osage →, *U.S.A.* . . . 54 F9
Osage City, *U.S.A.* . . 54 F7
Ōsaka, *Japan* 23 G7
Osawatomie, *U.S.A.* . 54 F7
Osborne, *U.S.A.* 54 F5
Osceola, *Ark., U.S.A.* 55 H10
Osceola, *Iowa, U.S.A.* 54 E8
Oscoda, *U.S.A.* 52 C4
Ösel = Saaremaa,
Estonia 7 G20
Oude Rijn →, *Neths.* . 11 B4
Oudenaarde, *Belgium* 11 D3
Oudtshoorn, *S. Africa* 37 L4
Ouessant, Î. d', *France* 14 B1
Ouesso, *Congo* 36 D3
Ouest, Pte. de l', *Canada* 49 C7
Ouezzane, *Morocco* . . 34 B4
Oujda, *Morocco* 34 B5
Oulainen, *Finland* . . . 6 D21
Oulu, *Finland* 6 D21
Oulujärvi, *Finland* . . . 6 D22
Oulujoki →, *Finland* . 6 D21
Oum Chalouba, *Chad* 35 E10
Oum Hadjer, *Chad* . . 35 F9
Ounasjoki →, *Finland* 6 C21
Ounianga Sérir, *Chad* 35 E10
Our →, *Lux.* 11 E6
Ouray, *U.S.A.* 57 G10
Ourense, *Spain* 15 A2
Ouricuri, *Brazil* 63 E10
Ourinhos, *Brazil* 64 A7
Ouro Prêto, *Brazil* . . 63 H10
Ourthe →, *Belgium* . . 11 D5
Ouse →, *E. Susx., U.K.* 9 G8
Ouse →, *N. Yorks.,
U.K.* 8 D7
Outaouais →, *Canada* 48 C5
Outardes →, *Canada* . 49 C6

Osorno, *Chile* 64 E2
Osoyoos, *Canada* . . . 50 D5
Ospika →, *Canada* . . 50 B4
Osprey Reef, *Australia* 42 A4
Oss, *Neths.* 11 C5
Ossa, Mt., *Australia* . 42 G4
Óssa, Óros, *Greece* . 17 E10
Ossabaw I., *U.S.A.* . . 53 K5
Ossokmanuan L.,
Canada 49 B7
Ossora, *Russia* 21 D17
Ostend = Oostende,
Belgium 11 C2
Oster, *Ukraine* 13 C16
Österdalälven, *Sweden* 7 F16
Østerdalen, *Norway* . 7 F14
Östersund, *Sweden* . 6 E16
Ostfriesische Inseln,
Germany 12 B4
Ostrava, *Czech Rep.* . 13 D10
Ostróda, *Poland* 13 B10
Ostroh, *Ukraine* 13 C14
Ostrołęka, *Poland* . . . 13 B11
Ostrów Mazowiecka,
Poland 13 B11
Ostrów Wielkopolski,
Poland 13 C9
Ostrowiec-
Świętokrzyski, *Poland* 13 C11
Ostuni, *Italy* 17 D7
Ōsumi-Kaikyō, *Japan* 23 J5
Ōsumi-Shotō, *Japan* . 23 J5
Osuna, *Spain* 15 D3
Oswego, *U.S.A.* 52 D7
Oswestry, *U.K.* 8 E4
Oświęcim, *Poland* . . . 13 C10
Otago □, *N.Z.* 39 L2
Otago Harbour, *N.Z.* . 39 L3
Ōtake, *Japan* 23 G6
Otaki, *N.Z.* 39 J5
Otaru, *Japan* 22 C10
Otaru-Wan = Ishikari-
Wan, *Japan* 22 C10
Otavalo, *Ecuador* . . . 62 C3
Otelnuk L., *Canada* . . 49 A6
Otjiwarongo, *Namibia* 37 J3
Otoineppu, *Japan* . . . 22 B11
Otorohanga, *N.Z.* . . . 39 H5
Otoskwin →, *Canada* . 48 B2
Otra →, *Norway* . . . 7 G13
Otranto, *Italy* 17 D8
Otranto, C. d', *Italy* . 17 D8
Otranto, Str. of, *Italy* 17 D8
Ōtsu, *Japan* 23 G7
Ōtsuki, *Japan* 23 G9
Ottawa =
Outaouais →,
Canada 48 C5
Ottawa, *Canada* 48 C4
Ottawa, *Ill., U.S.A.* . . 54 E10
Ottawa, *Kans., U.S.A.* 54 F7
Ottawa Is., *Canada* . . 47 C11
Otter L., *Canada* . . . 51 B8
Ottery St. Mary, *U.K.* 9 G4
Ottumwa, *U.S.A.* . . . 54 E8
Oturkpo, *Nigeria* . . . 34 G7
Otway, B., *Chile* 64 G2
Otway, C., *Australia* . 43 F3
Otwock, *Poland* 13 B11
Ou-Sammyaku, *Japan* 22 E10
Ouachita →, *U.S.A.* . 55 K9
Ouachita, L., *U.S.A.* . 55 H8
Ouachita Mts., *U.S.A.* 55 H7
Ouadda, *C.A.R.* 32
Ouagadougou,
Burkina Faso . . . 34 F5
Ouahran = Oran,
Algeria 34 A5
Ouallene, *Algeria* . . . 34 D6
Ouanda Djallé, *C.A.R.* 32
Ouargla, *Algeria* . . . 34 B7
Ouarzazate, *Morocco* 34 B4
Oubangi →, *Dem. Rep.
of the Congo* . . . 36 E3
Ouddorp, *Neths.* . . . 11 C3
Oude Rijn →, *Neths.* . 11 B4

Outer Hebrides, *U.K.* . 10 C3
Outjo, *Namibia* 37 J3
Outlook, *Canada* . . . 51 C7
Outokumpu, *Finland* . 6 E23
Ouyen, *Australia* . . . 43 F3
Ovalau, *Fiji* 39 C8
Ovalle, *Chile* 64 C2
Ovamboland, *Namibia* 37 H3
Overflakkee, *Neths.* . 11 C4
Overijssel □, *Neths.* . 11 B6
Overland Park, *U.S.A.* 54 F7
Overton, *U.S.A.* 57 H6
Övertorneå, *Sweden* . 6 C20
Oviedo, *Spain* 15 A3
Øvre Årdal, *Norway* . 7 F12
Ovruch, *Ukraine* . . . 13 C15
Owaka, *N.Z.* 39 M2
Owambo =
Ovamboland, *Namibia* 37 H3
Owase, *Japan* 23 G8
Owatonna, *U.S.A.* . . . 54 C8
Owbeh, *Afghan.* 28 B3
Owen Sound, *Canada* 48 D3
Owen Stanley Ra.,
Papua N. G. 38 B7
Owens →, *U.S.A.* . . . 57 H5
Owens L., *U.S.A.* . . . 57 J5
Owensboro, *U.S.A.* . . 52 G2
Owl →, *Canada* 51 B10
Owo, *Nigeria* 34 G7
Owosso, *U.S.A.* 52 D3
Owyhee, *U.S.A.* 56 F5
Owyhee →, *U.S.A.* . . 56 E5
Owyhee, L., *U.S.A.* . . 56 E5
Öxarfjörður, *Iceland* . 6 C5
Oxbow, *Canada* 51 D8
Oxelösund, *Sweden* . 7 G17
Oxford, *N.Z.* 39 K4
Oxford, *U.K.* 9 F6
Oxford, *Miss., U.S.A.* 55 H10
Oxford, *N.C., U.S.A.* . 53 G6
Oxford, *Ohio, U.S.A.* . 52 F3
Oxford L., *Canada* . . 51 C9
Oxfordshire □, *U.K.* . 9 F6
Oxnard, *U.S.A.* 57 J4
Oxus = Amudarya →,
Uzbekistan 20 E6
Oya, *Malaysia* 26 D4
Oyama, *Japan* 23 F9
Oyem, *Gabon* 36 D2
Oyen, *Canada* 51 C6
Oymyakon, *Russia* . . 21 C15
Oyo, *Nigeria* 34 G6
Ōyūbari, *Japan* 22 C11
Ozamiz, *Phil.* 27 C6
Ozark, *Ala., U.S.A.* . . 53 K3
Ozark, *Ark., U.S.A.* . . 55 H8
Ozark, *Mo., U.S.A.* . . 55 G8
Ozark Plateau, *U.S.A.* 55 G9
Ozarks, L. of the, *U.S.A.* 54 F8
Ozona, *U.S.A.* 55 K4
Ozuluama, *Mexico* . . 59 C5

Pa-an, *Burma* 29 L20
Pa Sak →, *Thailand* . 26 B2
Paamiut, *Greenland* . 4 C5
Paarl, *S. Africa* 37 L3
Pab Hills, *Pakistan* . . 28 F5
Pabianice, *Poland* . . 13 C10
Pabna, *Bangla.* . . . 29 G16
Pacaja →, *Brazil* . . . 63 D8
Pacaraima, Sa.,
S. Amer. 62 C6
Pacasmayo, *Peru* . . . 62 E3
Pachitea →, *Peru* . . . 62 E4
Pachpadra, *India* . . . 28 G8
Pachuca, *Mexico* . . . 59 C5
Pacific, *Canada* 50 C3
Pacific-Antarctic Ridge,
Pac. Oc. 45 M16
Pacific Grove, *U.S.A.* . 57 H3
Pacific Ocean, *Pac. Oc.* 45 G14
Pacitan, *Indonesia* . . 27 H14
Padaido, Kepulauan,
Indonesia 27 E9
Padang, *Indonesia* . . 26 E2
Padangpanjang,
Indonesia 26 E2
Padangsidempuan,
Indonesia 26 D1
Paddle Prairie, *Canada* 50 B5
Paddockwood, *Canada* 51 C7
Paderborn, *Germany* . 12 C5
Pádova, *Italy* 16 B4
Padre I., *U.S.A.* 55 M6
Padstow, *U.K.* 9 G3
Padua = Pádova, *Italy* 16 B4
Paducah, *Ky., U.S.A.* . 52 G1
Paducah, *Tex., U.S.A.* 55 H4
Paeroa, *N.Z.* 39 G5
Pag, *Croatia* 12 F8
Pagadian, *Phil.* 27 C6
Pagai Selatan, Pulau,
Indonesia 26 E2
Pagai Utara, Pulau,
Indonesia 26 E2
Pagastikós Kólpos,
Greece 17 E10
Pagatan, *Indonesia* . . 26 E5
Page, *U.S.A.* 57 H8
Pago Pago,
Amer. Samoa . . . 39 B13

Pagosa Springs, *U.S.A.* 57 H10
Pagwa River, *Canada* 48 B2
Pahiatua, *N.Z.* 39 J5
Pahokee, *U.S.A.* 53 M5
Pahrump, *U.S.A.* . . . 57 H6
Paide, *Estonia* 7 G21
Paignton, *U.K.* 9 G4
Päijänne, *Finland* . . . 7 F21
Painan, *Indonesia* . . . 26 E2
Paint Hills = Wemindji,
Canada 48 B4
Paint L., *Canada* 51 B9
Painted Desert, *U.S.A.* 57 J8
Paintsville, *U.S.A.* . . 52 G4
País Vasco □, *Spain* . 15 A4
Paisley, *U.K.* 10 D4
Paisley, *U.S.A.* 56 E3
Paita, *Peru* 62 E2
Pajares, Puerto de,
Spain 15 A3
Pak Phanang, *Thailand* 26 C2
Pakistan ■, *Asia* 28 E7
Pakokku, *Burma* . . . 29 J19
Pakowki L., *Canada* . 51 D6
Paktiā □, *Afghan.* . . . 28 C6
Pakwach, *Uganda* . . 36 D6
Pakxe, *Laos* 26 A3
Pala, *Chad* 35 G9
Palacios, *U.S.A.* 55 L6
Palagruža, *Croatia* . . 16 C7
Palam, *India* 28 K10
Palampur, *India* . . . 28 C10
Palana, *Australia* . . . 42 F4
Palana, *Russia* 21 D16
Palanan, *Phil.* 27 A6
Palanan Pt., *Phil.* . . . 27 A6
Palanga, *Lithuania* . . 7 J19
Palangkaraya, *Indonesia* 26 E4
Palani Hills, *India* . . 28 P10
Palanpur, *India* 28 G8
Palapye, *Botswana* . . 37 J5
Palatka, *Russia* 21 C16
Palatka, *U.S.A.* 53 L5
Palau ■, *Pac. Oc.* . . . 38 A6
Palawan, *Phil.* 26 C5
Palayankottai, *India* . 28 Q10
Paldiski, *Estonia* . . . 7 G21
Paleleh, *Indonesia* . . 27 D6
Palembang, *Indonesia* 26 E2
Palencia, *Spain* 15 A3
Palenque, *Mexico* . . . 59 D6
Palermo, *Italy* 16 E5
Palermo, *U.S.A.* 56 G3
Palestina, *Chile* 64 A3
Palestine, *Asia* 33 D4
Palestine, *U.S.A.* . . . 55 K7
Paletwa, *Burma* 29 J18
Palghat, *India* 28 P10
Palgrave, Mt., *Australia* 40 D2
Pali, *India* 28 G8
Palikir, *Micronesia* . . 44 G7
Palioúrion, Ákra, *Greece* 17 E10
Palisades Reservoir,
U.S.A. 56 E8
Paliseul, *Belgium* . . . 11 E5
Palitana, *India* 28 J7
Palizada, *Mexico* . . . 59 D6
Palk Bay, *India* . . . 28 Q11
Palk Strait, *Asia* . . . 28 Q11
Palkânah, *Iraq* 30 C5
Pallanza = Verbánia,
Italy 14 D8
Pallarenda, *Australia* . 42 B4
Pallinup →, *Australia* 41 F2
Palm Bay, *U.S.A.* . . . 53 L5
Palm Beach, *U.S.A.* . 53 M6
Palm Coast, *U.S.A.* . . 53 L5
Palm Is., *Australia* . . 42 B4
Palm Springs, *U.S.A.* 57 K5
Palma, B. de, *Spain* . 15 C7
Palma de Mallorca,
Spain 15 C7
Palma Soriano, *Cuba* . 60 B4
Palmares, *Brazil* . . . 63 E11
Palmas, *Brazil* 64 B6
Palmas, C., *Liberia* . . 34 H4
Pálmas, G. di, *Italy* . . 16 E3
Palmdale, *U.S.A.* . . . 57 J4
Palmeira dos Índios,
Brazil 63 E11
Palmer, *U.S.A.* 46 B5
Palmer →, *Australia* . 42 B3
Palmer Arch., *Antarctica* 5 C17
Palmer Lake, *U.S.A.* . 54 F2
Palmer Land, *Antarctica* 5 D18
Palmerston, *N.Z.* . . . 39 L3
Palmerston North, *N.Z.* 39 J5
Palmetto, *U.S.A.* . . . 53 M4
Palmi, *Italy* 16 E6
Palmira, *Colombia* . . 62 C3
Palmyra = Tudmur,
Syria 30 C3
Palmyra, *U.S.A.* 54 F9
Palmyra Is., *Pac. Oc.* . 45 G11
Palopo, *Indonesia* . . 27 E6
Palos, C. de, *Spain* . . 15 D5
Palu, *Indonesia* 27 E5
Palu, *Turkey* 19 G7
Pamanukan, *Indonesia* 27 G12
Pamiers, *France* . . . 14 E4
Pamir, *Tajikistan* . . . 20 F8
Pamlico →, *U.S.A.* . . 53 H7
Pamlico Sd., *U.S.A.* . 53 H8
Pampa, *U.S.A.* 55 H4

Pampanua, Indonesia . 27 E6
Pampas, Argentina ... 64 D4
Pampas, Peru 62 F4
Pamplona, Colombia .. 62 B4
Pamplona, Spain 15 A5
Pana, U.S.A. 54 F10
Panaca, U.S.A. 57 H6
Panaitan, Indonesia . 27 G11
Panaji, India 28 M8
Panamá, Panama 60 E4
Panama ■, Cent. Amer. 60 E4
Panamá, G. de, Panama 60 E4
Panama Canal, Panama 60 E4
Panama City, U.S.A. . 53 K3
Panamint Range, U.S.A. 57 H5
Panão, Peru 62 E3
Panay, Phil. 27 B6
Panay, G., Phil. 27 B6
Pančevo, Serbia, Yug. . 17 B9
Pandan, Phil. 27 B6
Pandegelang, Indonesia 27 G12
Pandharpur, India 28 L9
Pando, L. = Hope, L.,
  Australia 43 D2
Pandora, Costa Rica .. 60 E3
Panevežys, Lithuania .. 7 J21
Panfilov, Kazakstan .. 20 E8
Pang-Long, Burma ... 29 H21
Pang-Yang, Burma ... 29 H21
Pangani, Tanzania 36 F7
Pangfou = Bengbu,
  China 25 C6
Pangkah, Tanjung,
  Indonesia 27 G15
Pangkajene, Indonesia . 27 E5
Pangkalanbrandan,
  Indonesia 26 D1
Pangkalanbuun,
  Indonesia 26 E4
Pangkalpinang,
  Indonesia 26 E3
Pangnirtung, Canada . 47 B13
Panguitch, U.S.A. 57 H7
Pangutaran Group, Phil. 27 C6
Panhandle, U.S.A. ... 55 H4
Panjgur, Pakistan ... 28 F4
Panjim = Panaji, India . 28 M8
Panjinad Barrage,
  Pakistan 28 E7
Panna, India 28 G12
Pannawonica, Australia 40 D2
Pannirtuuq =
  Pangnirtung, Canada 47 B13
Panorama, Brazil 63 H8
Pantanal, Brazil 62 H7
Pantar, Indonesia 27 F6
Pante Macassar,
  Indonesia 27 F6
Pantelleria, Italy 16 F4
Pánuco, Mexico 59 C5
Paola, U.S.A. 54 F7
Paonia, U.S.A. 57 G10
Paoting = Baoding,
  China 25 C6
Paot'ou = Baotou,
  China 25 B6
Paoua, C.A.R. 36 C3
Pápa, Hungary 13 E9
Papagayo →, Mexico 59 D5
Papagayo, G. de,
  Costa Rica 60 D2
Papakura, N.Z. 39 G5
Papantla, Mexico 59 C5
Papar, Malaysia 26 C5
Papeete, Tahiti 45 J13
Papigochic →, Mexico 58 B3
Papua, G. of,
  Papua N. G. 38 B7
Papua New Guinea ■,
  Oceania 38 B7
Papudo, Chile 64 C2
Papun, Burma 29 K20
Papunya, Australia ... 40 D5
Pará = Belém, Brazil . 63 D9
Pará □, Brazil 63 D8
Paraburdoo, Australia . 40 D2
Paracatu, Brazil 63 G9
Paracel Is., S. China Sea 26 A4
Parachilna, Australia . 43 E2
Paradip, India 29 J15
Paradise, U.S.A. 56 G3
Paradise →, Canada . 49 B8
Paradise Hill, Canada . 51 C7
Paradise River, Canada 49 B8
Paradise Valley, U.S.A. 56 F5
Parado, Indonesia 27 F5
Paragould, U.S.A. ... 55 G9
Paragua →, Venezuela 62 B6
Paraguaçu →, Brazil . 63 F11
Paraguaná, Pen. de,
  Venezuela 62 A5
Paraguari, Paraguay .. 64 B5
Paraguay ■, S. Amer. . 62 H7
Paraguay →, Paraguay 64 B5
Paraíba = João Pessoa,
  Brazil 63 E12
Paraíba □, Brazil 63 E11
Paraíso, Mexico 59 D6
Parak, Iran 31 E7
Parakou, Benin 34 G6
Paramaribo, Surinam . 63 B7
Paramushir, Ostrov,
  Russia 21 D16

Paran →, Israel 33 E4
Paraná, Argentina ... 64 C4
Paranã, Brazil 63 F9
Paraná □, Brazil 64 A6
Paraná →, Argentina . 64 C5
Paranaguá, Brazil ... 64 B7
Paranaíba, Brazil 63 G8
Paranaíba →, Brazil . 63 H8
Paranapanema →,
  Brazil 63 H8
Parang, Maguindanao,
  Phil. 27 C6
Parang, Sulu, Phil. ... 27 C6
Parângul Mare, Vf.,
  Romania 13 F12
Paraparaumu, N.Z. ... 39 J5
Parbhani, India 28 K10
Parchim, Germany ... 12 B6
Pardes Hanna-Karkur,
  Israel 33 C3
Pardo →, Bahia, Brazil 63 G11
Pardo →,
  Mato Grosso, Brazil 63 H8
Pardubice, Czech Rep. . 12 C8
Pare, Indonesia 27 G15
Parecis, Serra dos,
  Brazil 62 F7
Paren, Russia 21 C17
Parent, Canada 48 C5
Parent, L., Canada .. 48 C4
Parepare, Indonesia .. 27 E5
Párga, Greece 17 E9
Pariaguán, Venezuela . 62 B6
Paricutín, Cerro, Mexico 58 D4
Parigi, Indonesia 27 E6
Parika, Guyana 62 B7
Parima, Serra, Brazil . 62 C6
Parinari, Peru 62 D4
Parintins, Brazil 63 D7
Pariparit Kyun, Burma 29 M18
Paris, France 14 B5
Paris, Idaho, U.S.A. .. 56 E8
Paris, Ky., U.S.A. ... 52 F3
Paris, Tenn., U.S.A. . 53 G1
Paris, Tex., U.S.A. .. 55 J7
Park City, U.S.A. ... 55 G6
Park Falls, U.S.A. ... 54 C9
Park Hills, U.S.A. ... 55 G9
Park Range, U.S.A. .. 56 G10
Park Rapids, U.S.A. . 54 B7
Park River, U.S.A. .. 54 A6
Parkå Bandar, Iran .. 31 E8
Parkano, Finland 7 E20
Parker, U.S.A. 57 J6
Parker Dam, U.S.A. . 57 J6
Parkersburg, U.S.A. . 52 F5
Parkes, Australia ... 43 E4
Parkston, U.S.A. 54 D6
Parksville, Canada ... 50 D4
Parla, Spain 15 B4
Parma, Italy 14 D9
Parma, Idaho, U.S.A. . 56 E5
Parma, Ohio, U.S.A. . 52 E5
Parnaguá, Brazil 63 F10
Parnaíba, Brazil 63 D10
Parnaíba →, Brazil .. 63 D10
Parnassós, Greece ... 17 E10
Pärnu, Estonia 7 G21
Paroo →, Australia .. 43 E3
Páros, Greece 17 F11
Parowan, U.S.A. 57 H7
Parral, Chile 64 D2
Parras, Mexico 58 B4
Parrett →, U.K. 9 F4
Parris I., U.S.A. 53 J5
Parrsboro, Canada ... 49 C7
Parry Is., Canada ... 4
Parry Sound, Canada . 48 C4
Parsnip →, Canada .. 50 B4
Parsons, U.S.A. 55 G7
Parsons Ra., Australia . 42 A2
Partinico, Italy 16 E5
Partridge I., Canada . 48 A2
Paru →, Brazil 63 D8
Parvān □, Afghan. ... 28 B6
Parvatipuram, India . 29 K13
Pasadena, Canada ... 49 C8
Pasadena, Calif., U.S.A. 57 J4
Pasadena, Tex., U.S.A. 55 L7
Pascagoula, U.S.A. .. 55 K10
Pascagoula →, U.S.A. 55 K10
Pașcani, Romania ... 13 E14
Pasco, U.S.A. 56 C4
Pasco, Cerro de, Peru . 62 F3
Pasco, I., Australia ... 40 D2
Pascua, I. de, Pac. Oc. 45 K17
Pasfield L., Canada .. 51 B7
Pashmakli = Smolyan,
  Bulgaria 17 D11
Pasir Mas, Malaysia .. 26 C2
Pasirian, Indonesia .. 27 H15
Pasirkuning, Indonesia 26 E2
Paskūh, Iran 31 E9
Pasley, C., Australia . 41 F3
Pašman, Croatia 12 G8
Pasni, Pakistan 28 G3
Paso de Indios,
  Argentina 64 E3
Paso Robles, U.S.A. . 57 J3
Paspébiac, Canada ... 49 C6
Passau, Germany ... 12 D7
Passero, C., Italy ... 16 F6
Passo Fundo, Brazil .. 64 B6
Passos, Brazil 63 H9

Pastavy, Belarus 7 J22
Pastaza →, Peru 62 D3
Pasto, Colombia 62 C3
Pasuruan, Indonesia . 27 G15
Patagonia, Argentina . 64 F3
Patagonia, U.S.A. ... 57 L8
Patambar, Iran 31 D9
Patan, India 28 H8
Patani, Indonesia 27 D7
Patchewollock, Australia 43 F3
Patchogue, U.S.A. ... 52 E9
Patea, N.Z. 39 H5
Paternò, Italy 16 F6
Pateros, U.S.A. 56 B4
Paterson, U.S.A. 52 E8
Paterson Ra., Australia 40 D3
Pathankot, India 28 C9
Pathfinder Reservoir,
  U.S.A. 56 E10
Pati, Indonesia 27 G14
Patía →, Colombia ... 62 C3
Patiala, India 28 D10
Patkai Bum, India ... 29 F19
Pátmos, Greece 17 F12
Patna, India 29 G14
Pato Branco, Brazil .. 64 B6
Patos, Brazil 63 E11
Patos, L. dos, Brazil .. 64 C6
Patos de Minas, Brazil . 63 G9
Patquía, Argentina .. 64 C3
Pátrai, Greece 17 E9
Pátraikós Kólpos,
  Greece 17 E9
Patras = Pátrai, Greece 17 E9
Patrocínio, Brazil 63 G9
Pattani, Thailand 26 C2
Pattaya, Thailand 26 B2
Patten, U.S.A. 53 C11
Patterson, Calif., U.S.A. 57 H3
Patterson, La., U.S.A. . 55 L9
Patuakhali, Bangla. .. 29 H17
Patuanak, Canada ... 51 B7
Patuca →, Honduras . 60 C3
Patuca, Punta, Honduras 60 C3
Pátzcuaro, Mexico ... 58 D4
Pau, France 14 E3
Pauk, Burma 29 J19
Paul I., Canada 49 A7
Paulatuk, Canada ... 46 B7
Paulis = Isiro,
  Dem. Rep. of
  the Congo 36 D5
Paulistana, Brazil ... 63 E10
Paulo Afonso, Brazil . 63 E11
Pauls Valley, U.S.A. . 55 H6
Päveh, Iran 30 C5
Pavia, Italy 14 D8
Pävilosta, Latvia 7 H19
Pavlodar, Kazakstan . 20 D8
Pavlograd = Pavlohrad,
  Ukraine 19 E6
Pavlohrad, Ukraine .. 19 E6
Pavlovo, Russia 18 C7
Pavlovsk, Russia 19 D7
Pavlovskaya, Russia .. 19 E6
Pawhuska, U.S.A. ... 55 G6
Pawnee, U.S.A. 55 G6
Pawnee City, U.S.A. . 54 E6
Pawtucket, U.S.A. ... 52 E10
Paxoí, Greece 17 E9
Paxton, Ill., U.S.A. .. 52 E1
Paxton, Nebr., U.S.A. 54 E4
Payakumbuh, Indonesia 26 E2
Payette, U.S.A. 56 D5
Payne Bay = Kangirsuk,
  Canada 47 B13
Payne L., Canada ... 47 C12
Paynes Find, Australia 41 E2
Paynesville, U.S.A. .. 54 C7
Paysandú, Uruguay .. 64 C5
Payson, U.S.A. 57 J8
Paz →, Guatemala .. 60 D1
Paz, B. la, Mexico ... 58 C2
Pāzanān, Iran 31 D6
Pazardzhik, Bulgaria . 17 C11
Peace →, Canada ... 50 B6
Peace Point, Canada . 50 B6
Peace River, Canada . 50 B5
Peach Springs, U.S.A. 57 J7
Peachland, Canada ... 50 D5
Peachtree City, U.S.A. 53 J3
Peak, The = Kinder
  Scout, U.K. 8 D6
Peak District, U.K. .. 8 D6
Peak Hill, N.S.W.,
  Australia 43 E4
Peak Hill, W. Austral.,
  Australia 41 E2
Peak Ra., Australia .. 42 C4
Peake Cr. →, Australia 43 D2
Peale, Mt., U.S.A. ... 57 G9
Pearl →, U.S.A. 55 K10
Pearsall, U.S.A. 55 L5
Peary Land, Greenland 4 A6
Pease →, U.S.A. 55 H5
Peawanuck, Canada .. 47 C11
Pebane, Mozam. 37 H7
Pebas, Peru 62 D4
Peć, Kosovo, Yug. ... 17 C9
Pechenga, Russia ... 18 A5
Pechenizhyn, Ukraine 13 D13
Pechora, Russia 18 A10
Pechora →, Russia .. 18 A9
Pechorskaya Guba,
  Russia 18 A9

Pečory, Russia 7 H22
Pecos, U.S.A. 55 K3
Pecos →, U.S.A. 55 L3
Pécs, Hungary 13 E10
Pedder, L., Australia . 42 G4
Pédernales, Dom. Rep. 61 C5
Pedirka, Australia ... 43 D2
Pedra Azul, Brazil ... 63 G10
Pedreiras, Brazil 63 D10
Pedro Afonso, Brazil . 63 E9
Pedro Cays, Jamaica . 60 C4
Pedro Juan Caballero,
  Paraguay 63 H7
Pee Dee →, U.S.A. .. 53 J6
Peebinga, Australia .. 43 E3
Peekskill, U.S.A. 52 E9
Peel, U.K. 8 C3
Peel →, Australia ... 43 E5
Peel →, Canada 46 B6
Peel Sound, Canada . 46 A10
Peera Peera Poolanna
  L., Australia 43 D2
Peerless Lake, Canada 50 B6
Peers, Canada 50 C5
Pegasus Bay, N.Z. ... 39 K4
Pegu, Burma 29 L20
Pegu Yoma, Burma .. 29 K20
Pehuajó, Argentina .. 64 D4
Peine, Germany 12 B6
Peip'ing = Beijing,
  China 25 C6
Peipus, L. = Chudskoye,
  Ozero, Russia 7 G22
Peixe, Brazil 63 F9
Peixe →, Brazil 63 H8
Pekalongan, Indonesia 27 G13
Pekanbaru, Indonesia . 26 D2
Pekin, U.S.A. 54 E10
Peking = Beijing, China 25 C6
Pelabuhan Kelang,
  Malaysia 26 D2
Pelabuhan Ratu, Teluk,
  Indonesia 27 G12
Pelabuhanratu,
  Indonesia 27 G12
Pelagie, Is., Italy 16 G5
Pelaihari, Indonesia .. 26 E4
Peleaga, Vf., Romania 13 F12
Pelée, Mt., Martinique 61 D7
Pelée, Pt., Canada ... 48 D3
Pelee I., Canada 48 D3
Peleng, Indonesia ... 27 E6
Pelican, U.S.A. 50 B1
Pelican L., Canada ... 51 C8
Pelican Narrows,
  Canada 51 B8
Peljesac, Croatia 16 C7
Pelkosenniemi, Finland 6 C22
Pella, U.S.A. 54 E8
Pello, Finland 6 C21
Pelly →, Canada 46 B6
Pelly Bay, Canada ... 47 B11
Peloponnese =
  Pelopónnisos □,
  Greece 17 F10
Pelopónnisos □, Greece 17 F10
Pelorus Sd., N.Z. 39 J4
Pelotas, Brazil 64 C6
Pelvoux, Massif du,
  France 14 D7
Pemalang, Indonesia . 27 G13
Pematangsiantar,
  Indonesia 26 D1
Pemba, Mozam. 37 G8
Pemba I., Tanzania .. 36 F7
Pemberton, Australia . 41 F2
Pemberton, Canada .. 50 C4
Pembina, U.S.A. 54 A6
Pembroke, Canada .. 48 C4
Pembroke, U.K. 9 F3
Pembrokeshire □, U.K. 9 F3
Pen-y-Ghent, U.K. .. 8 C5
Penang = Pinang,
  Malaysia 26 C2
Penápolis, Brazil 63 H8
Peñarroya-Pueblonuevo,
  Spain 15 C3
Penarth, U.K. 9 F4
Peñas, C. de, Spain .. 15 A3
Peñas, G. de, Chile .. 64 F2
Pench'i = Benxi, China 25 B7
Pend Oreille →, U.S.A. 56 B5
Pend Oreille, L., U.S.A. 56 C5
Pendembu, S. Leone . 34 G3
Pender B., Australia . 40 C3
Pendleton, U.S.A. ... 56 D4
Penedo, Brazil 63 F11
Penetanguishene,
  Canada 48 D4
Pengalengan, Indonesia 27 G12
Penguin, Australia ... 42 G4
Peniche, Portugal ... 15 C1
Penida, Indonesia ... 26 F5
Peninsular Malaysia □,
  Malaysia 26 D2
Penitente, Serra do,
  Brazil 63 E9
Penkridge, U.K. 8 E5
Penmarch, Pte. de,
  France 14 C1
Penn Hills, U.S.A. ... 52 E6
Penn Yan, U.S.A. ... 52 D7
Pennant, Canada 51 C7
Penner →, India 28 M12

Pennines, U.K. 8 C5
Pennsylvania □, U.S.A. 52 E7
Penny, Canada 50 C4
Penobscot →, U.S.A. . 53 C11
Penobscot B., U.S.A. . 53 C11
Penola, Australia 43 F3
Penong, Australia ... 41 F5
Penonomé, Panama .. 60 E3
Penrith, Australia ... 43 E5
Penrith, U.K. 8 C5
Penryn, U.K. 9 G2
Pensacola, U.S.A. ... 53 K2
Pensacola Mts.,
  Antarctica 5 E1
Pense, Canada 51 C8
Penshurst, Australia . 43 F3
Penticton, Canada ... 50 D5
Pentland, Australia .. 42 C4
Pentland Firth, U.K. . 10 B5
Penza, Russia 18 D8
Penzance, U.K. 9 G2
Penzhino, Russia 21 C17
Penzhinskaya Guba,
  Russia 21 C17
Peoria, Ariz., U.S.A. . 57 K7
Peoria, Ill., U.S.A. ... 54 E10
Pera Hd., Australia .. 42 A3
Perabumulih, Indonesia 26 E2
Peräpohjola, Finland . 6 C22
Percé, Canada 49 C7
Perche, Collines du,
  France 14 B4
Percival Lakes, Australia 40 D4
Percy Is., Australia .. 42 C5
Perdido, Mte., Spain . 15 A6
Perdu, Mt. = Perdido,
  Mte., Spain 15 A6
Pereira, Colombia ... 62 C3
Perenjori, Australia .. 41 E2
Pereyaslav-
  Khmelnytskyy,
  Ukraine 19 D5
Pérez, I., Mexico 59 C7
Pergamino, Argentina 64 C4
Perham, U.S.A. 54 B7
Perhentian, Kepulauan,
  Malaysia 26 C2
Péribonca →, Canada 49 C5
Péribonca, L., Canada 49 B5
Perico, Argentina ... 64 A3
Pericos, Mexico 58 B3
Périgueux, France ... 14 D4
Perijá, Sierra de,
  Colombia 62 B4
Perito Moreno,
  Argentina 64 F2
Perlas, Arch. de las,
  Panama 60 E4
Perlas, Punta de, Nic. . 60 D3
Perm, Russia 18 C10
Pernambuco = Recife,
  Brazil 63 E12
Pernambuco □, Brazil 63 E11
Pernatty Lagoon,
  Australia 43 E2
Pernik, Bulgaria 17 C10
Peron Is., Australia .. 40 B5
Peron Pen., Australia . 41 E1
Perow, Canada 50 C3
Perpendicular Pt.,
  Australia 43 E5
Perpignan, France ... 14 E5
Perry, Fla., U.S.A. ... 53 K4
Perry, Ga., U.S.A. ... 53 J4
Perry, Iowa, U.S.A. .. 54 E7
Perry, Okla., U.S.A. . 55 G6
Perryton, U.S.A. 55 G4
Perryville, U.S.A. ... 55 G10
Persepolis, Iran 31 D7
Pershotravensk, Ukraine 13 C14
Persia = Iran ■, Asia . 31 C7
Persian Gulf = Gulf,
  The, Asia 31 E6
Perth, Australia 41 F2
Perth, Canada 48 D4
Perth, U.K. 10 C5
Perth Amboy, U.S.A. . 52 E8
Perth-Andover, Canada 49 C6
Peru, Ind., U.S.A. ... 52 E2
Peru ■, S. Amer. 62 D4
Peru-Chile Trench,
  Pac. Oc. 62 G3
Perúgia, Italy 16 C5
Pervomaysk, Ukraine . 19 E5
Pervouralsk, Russia .. 18 C10
Pésaro, Italy 16 C5
Pescara, Italy 16 C6
Peshawar, Pakistan .. 28 B7
Peshkopi, Albania ... 17 D9
Peshtigo, U.S.A. 52 C2
Pesqueira, Brazil 63 E11
Petah Tiqwa, Israel .. 33 C3
Petaluma, U.S.A. ... 56 G2
Pétange, Lux. 11 E5
Petatlán, Mexico 58 D4
Petauke, Zambia 37 G6
Petawawa, Canada .. 48 C4
Petén Itzá, L.,
  Guatemala 60 C2
Peter I.s Øy, Antarctica 5 C16
Peter Pond L., Canada 51 B7
Peterbell, Canada ... 48 C3
Peterborough, Australia 43 E2
Peterborough, Canada . 48 D4

Peterborough, U.K. .. 9 E7
Peterborough □, U.K. . 9 E7
Peterhead, U.K. 10 C6
Peterlee, U.K. 8 C6
Petermann Ranges,
  Australia 40 E5
Petersburg, Alaska,
  U.S.A. 46 C6
Petersburg, Va., U.S.A. 52 G7
Petersburg, W. Va.,
  U.S.A. 52 F6
Petersfield, U.K. 9 F7
Petit Goâve, Haiti ... 61 C5
Petit Jardin, Canada . 49 C8
Petit Lac Manicouagan,
  Canada 49 B6
Petit-Mécatina →,
  Canada 49 B8
Petit-Mécatina, I. du,
  Canada 49 B8
Petitcodiac, Canada .. 49 C6
Petite Baleine →,
  Canada 48 A4
Petite Saguenay,
  Canada 49 C5
Petitot →, Canada ... 50 A4
Petitsikapau L., Canada 49 B6
Petlad, India 28 H8
Peto, Mexico 59 C7
Petone, N.Z. 39 J5
Petoskey, U.S.A. 52 C3
Petra, Jordan 33 E4
Petra, Ostrova, Russia 4 B13
Petra Velikogo, Zaliv,
  Russia 22 C6
Petrich, Bulgaria 17 D10
Petrified Forest National
  Park, U.S.A. 57 J9
Petrikov = Pyetrikaw,
  Belarus 13 B15
Petrograd = Sankt-
  Peterburg, Russia .. 18 C5
Petrolândia, Brazil ... 63 E11
Petrolia, Canada 48 D3
Petrolina, Brazil 63 E10
Petropavl, Kazakstan . 20 D7
Petropavlovsk =
  Petropavl, Kazakstan 20 D7
Petropavlovsk-
  Kamchatskiy, Russia 21 D16
Petrópolis, Brazil 63 H10
Petroşani, Romania .. 13 F12
Petrovaradin,
  Serbia, Yug. 17 B8
Petrovsk, Russia 18 D8
Petrovsk-Zabaykalskiy,
  Russia 21 D11
Petrozavodsk, Russia . 18 B5
Peureulak, Indonesia . 26 D1
Pevek, Russia 21 C18
Pforzheim, Germany . 12 D5
Phagwara, India 28 D9
Phalodi, India 28 F8
Phan Rang, Vietnam . 26 B3
Phan Thiet, Vietnam . 26 B3
Phangan, Ko, Thailand 26 C2
Phangnga, Thailand . 26 C1
Pharr, U.S.A. 55 M5
Phatthalung, Thailand 26 C2
Phelps, L., Canada .. 51 B8
Phenix City, U.S.A. .. 53 J3
Phet Buri, Thailand .. 26 B1
Phetchabun, Thailand 26 A2
Phetchaburi = Phet
  Buri, Thailand 26 B1
Philadelphia, Miss.,
  U.S.A. 55 J10
Philadelphia, Pa., U.S.A. 52 F8
Philip, U.S.A. 54 C4
Philippeville, Belgium 11 D4
Philippi, U.S.A. 52 F5
Philippi L., Australia . 42 C2
Philippines ■, Asia ... 27 B6
Philippopolis = Plovdiv,
  Bulgaria 17 C11
Philipsburg, U.S.A. .. 56 C7
Phillip I., Australia .. 43 F4
Phillips, U.S.A. 54 C9
Phillipsburg, U.S.A. . 54 F5
Philomath, U.S.A. ... 56 D2
Phitsanulok, Thailand 26 A2
Phnom Dangrek,
  Thailand 26 B2
Phnom Penh, Cambodia 26 B2
Phnum Penh = Phnom
  Penh, Cambodia ... 26 B2
Phoenix, U.S.A. 57 K7
Phoenix Is., Kiribati . 44 H10
Phong →, Thailand .. 26 A2
Phosphate Hill, Australia 42 C2
Phra Nakhon Si
  Ayutthaya, Thailand . 26 B2
Phu Quoc, Dao, Vietnam 26 B2
Phuket, Thailand 26 C1
Piacenza, Italy 14 D8
Pian Cr. →, Australia . 43 E4
Pianosa, Italy 16 C4
Piapot, Canada 51 D7
Piatra Neamţ, Romania 13 E14
Piauí □, Brazil 63 E10
Piauí →, Brazil 63 E10
Piave →, Italy 16 B5
Pibor Post, Sudan ... 35 G12
Picardie, France 14 B5

Picardy

Picardy = Picardie, France 14 B5
Picayune, U.S.A. 55 K10
Pichilemu, Chile 64 C2
Pickerel L., Canada 48 C1
Pickering, U.K. 8 C7
Pickering, Vale of, U.K. 8 C7
Pickle Lake, Canada 48 B1
Pickwick L., U.S.A. 53 H1
Pico Truncado, Argentina 64 F3
Picos, Brazil 63 E10
Picton, Australia 43 E5
Picton, Canada 48 D4
Picton, N.Z. 39 J5
Pictou, Canada 49 C7
Picture Butte, Canada 50 D6
Picún Leufú, Argentina 64 D3
Pidurutalagala, Sri Lanka 28 R12
Piedmont = Piemonte □, Italy 14 D7
Piedmont, U.S.A. 53 J3
Piedras Negras, Mexico 58 B4
Pieksämäki, Finland 7 E22
Piemonte □, Italy 14 D7
Pierceland, Canada 51 C7
Pierre, U.S.A. 54 C4
Piet Retief, S. Africa 37 K6
Pietarsaari, Finland 6 E20
Pietermaritzburg, S. Africa 37 K6
Pietersburg, S. Africa 37 J5
Pietrosul, Vf., Maramureş, Romania 13 E13
Pietrosul, Vf., Suceava, Romania 13 E13
Piggott, U.S.A. 55 G9
Pigüe, Argentina 64 D4
Pihlajavesi, Finland 7 F23
Pijijiapan, Mexico 59 D6
Pikangikum Berens, Canada 51 C10
Pikes Peak, U.S.A. 54 F2
Pikeville, U.S.A. 52 G4
Pikwitonei, Canada 51 B9
Piła, Poland 13 B9
Pilar, Paraguay 64 B5
Pilaya →, Bolivia 62 H6
Pilbara, Australia 40 D2
Pilcomayo →, Paraguay 64 B5
Pilibhit, India 28 E11
Pilica →, Poland 13 C11
Pilliga, Australia 43 E4
Pílos, Greece 17 F9
Pilot Mound, Canada 51 D9
Pilot Point, U.S.A. 55 J6
Pilot Rock, U.S.A. 56 D4
Pilsen = Plzeň, Czech Rep. 12 D7
Pima, U.S.A. 57 K9
Pimba, Australia 43 E2
Pimenta Bueno, Brazil 62 F6
Pimentel, Peru 62 E3
Pinang, Malaysia 26 C2
Pinar del Río, Cuba 60 B3
Pınarhisar, Turkey 17 D12
Pinatubo, Mt., Phil. 27 A6
Pincher Creek, Canada 50 D6
Pinchi L., Canada 50 C4
Pinckneyville, U.S.A. 54 F10
Pińczów, Poland 13 C11
Pindar, Australia 41 E2
Pindos Óros, Greece 17 E9
Pindus Mts. = Pindos Óros, Greece 17 E9
Pine →, B.C., Canada 50 B4
Pine →, Sask., Canada 51 B7
Pine, C., Canada 49 C9
Pine Bluff, U.S.A. 55 H9
Pine Bluffs, U.S.A. 54 E2
Pine City, U.S.A. 54 C8
Pine Creek, Australia 40 B5
Pine Falls, Canada 51 C9
Pine Pass, Canada 50 B4
Pine Point, Canada 50 A6
Pine Ridge, U.S.A. 54 D3
Pine River, Canada 51 C8
Pine River, U.S.A. 54 B7
Pinedale, U.S.A. 56 E9
Pinega →, Russia 18 B8
Pinehill, Australia 42 C4
Pinehouse L., Canada 51 B7
Pineimuta →, Canada 48 B1
Pinerolo, Italy 14 D7
Pinetop, U.S.A. 57 J9
Pineville, U.S.A. 55 K8
Ping →, Thailand 26 A2
Pingaring, Australia 41 F2
Pingdingshan, China 25 C6
Pingdong, Taiwan 25 D7
Pingelly, Australia 41 F2
Pingliang, China 24 C5
Pingrup, Australia 41 F2
P'ingtung, Taiwan 25 D7
Pingxiang, China 24 D5
Pinheiro, Brazil 63 D9
Pinhel, Portugal 15 B2
Pini, Indonesia 26 D1
Piniós →, Greece 17 E10
Pinjarra, Australia 41 F2
Pink Mountain, Canada 50 B4
Pinnaroo, Australia 43 F3
Pínnes, Ákra, Greece 17 D11
Pinos, Mexico 58 C4
Pinos Pt., U.S.A. 57 H3
Pinotepa Nacional, Mexico 59 D5
Pinrang, Indonesia 27 E5
Pinsk, Belarus 13 B14
Pintados, Chile 62 H5
Pinyug, Russia 18 B8
Pioche, U.S.A. 57 H6
Piombino, Italy 16 C4
Pioner, Ostrov, Russia 21 B10
Piorini, L., Brazil 62 D6
Piotrków Trybunalski, Poland 13 C10
Pīp, Iran 31 E9
Pipestone, U.S.A. 54 D6
Pipestone →, Canada 48 B2
Pipestone Cr. →, Canada 51 D8
Pipmuacan, Rés., Canada 49 C5
Pippingarra, Australia 40 D2
Piqua, U.S.A. 52 E3
Piquiri →, Brazil 64 A6
Pīr Sohrāb, Iran 31 E9
Piracicaba, Brazil 63 H9
Piracuruca, Brazil 63 D10
Piræus = Piraiévs, Greece 17 F10
Piraiévs, Greece 17 F10
Pirané, Argentina 64 B5
Pirapora, Brazil 63 G10
Pírgos, Greece 17 F9
Pirimapun, Indonesia 27 F9
Pirin Planina, Bulgaria 17 D10
Pirineos = Pyrénées, Europe 14 E4
Piripiri, Brazil 63 D10
Pirmasens, Germany 12 D4
Pirot, Serbia, Yug. 17 C10
Piru, Indonesia 27 E7
Pisa, Italy 16 C4
Pisagua, Chile 62 G4
Pisco, Peru 62 F3
Písek, Czech Rep. 12 D8
Pishan, China 24 C2
Pīshīn, Iran 31 E9
Pising, Indonesia 27 F6
Pistóia, Italy 16 C4
Pistol B., Canada 51 A10
Pisuerga →, Spain 15 B3
Pit →, U.S.A. 56 F2
Pitarpunga, L., Australia 43 E3
Pitcairn I., Pac. Oc. 45 K14
Pite älv →, Sweden 6 D19
Piteå, Sweden 6 D19
Piteşti, Romania 13 F13
Pithapuram, India 29 L13
Pithara, Australia 41 F2
Pitt I., Canada 50 C3
Pittsburg, Kans., U.S.A. 55 G7
Pittsburg, Tex., U.S.A. 55 J7
Pittsburgh, U.S.A. 52 E6
Pittsfield, Ill., U.S.A. 54 F9
Pittsfield, Maine, U.S.A. 53 C11
Pittsfield, Mass., U.S.A. 52 D9
Pittsworth, Australia 43 D5
Pituri →, Australia 42 C2
Piura, Peru 62 E2
Placentia, Canada 49 C9
Placentia B., Canada 49 C9
Placerville, U.S.A. 56 G3
Placetas, Cuba 60 B4
Plainfield, U.S.A. 52 E8
Plains, Mont., U.S.A. 56 C6
Plains, Tex., U.S.A. 55 J3
Plainview, Nebr., U.S.A. 54 D6
Plainview, Tex., U.S.A. 55 H4
Plainwell, U.S.A. 52 D3
Pláka, Ákra, Greece 17 G12
Plana Cays, Bahamas 61 B5
Plano, U.S.A. 55 J6
Plant City, U.S.A. 53 M4
Plaquemine, U.S.A. 55 K9
Plasencia, Spain 15 B2
Plaster Rock, Canada 49 C6
Plastun, Russia 22 B8
Plata, Río de la, S. Amer. 64 C5
Plátani →, Italy 16 F5
Platte, U.S.A. 54 D5
Platte →, Mo., U.S.A. 54 F7
Platte →, Nebr., U.S.A. 54 E7
Platteville, U.S.A. 54 D9
Plattsburgh, U.S.A. 52 C9
Plattsmouth, U.S.A. 54 E7
Plauen, Germany 12 C7
Plavinas, Latvia 7 H21
Playgreen L., Canada 51 C9
Pleasant Bay, Canada 49 C7
Pleasanton, U.S.A. 55 L5
Pleasantville, U.S.A. 52 F8
Plei Ku, Vietnam 26 B3
Plenty →, Australia 42 C2
Plenty, B. of, N.Z. 39 G6
Plentywood, U.S.A. 54 A2
Plesetsk, Russia 18 B7
Plessisville, Canada 49 C5
Plétipi, L., Canada 49 B5
Pleven, Bulgaria 17 C11
Plevlja, Montenegro, Yug. 17 C8
Płock, Poland 13 B10
Plöckenstein, Germany 12 D7
Ploieşti, Romania 13 F14
Plonge, Lac la, Canada 51 B7
Plovdiv, Bulgaria 17 C11
Plummer, U.S.A. 56 C5
Plumtree, Zimbabwe 37 J5
Plungė, Lithuania 7 J19
Plymouth, U.K. 9 G3
Plymouth, Ind., U.S.A. 52 E2
Plymouth, N.C., U.S.A. 53 H7
Plymouth, Wis., U.S.A. 52 D2
Plynlimon = Pumlumon Fawr, U.K. 9 E4
Plzeň, Czech Rep. 12 D7
Po →, Italy 16 B5
Po Hai = Bo Hai, China 25 C6
Pobeda, Russia 21 C15
Pobedy, Pik, Kyrgyzstan 20 E8
Pocahontas, Ark., U.S.A. 55 G9
Pocahontas, Iowa, U.S.A. 54 D7
Pocatello, U.S.A. 56 E7
Pochutla, Mexico 59 D5
Pocito Casas, Mexico 58 B2
Pocomoke City, U.S.A. 52 F8
Poços de Caldas, Brazil 63 H9
Podgorica, Montenegro, Yug. 17 C8
Podilska Vysochyna, Ukraine 13 D14
Podolsk, Russia 18 C6
Podporozhye, Russia 18 B5
Pogranitšnyi, Russia 22 B5
Poh, Indonesia 27 E6
Pohjanmaa, Finland 6 E20
Pohnpei, Micronesia 44 G7
Poinsett, C., Antarctica 5 C8
Point Baker, U.S.A. 50 B2
Point Edward, Canada 48 D3
Point Hope, U.S.A. 46 B3
Point L., Canada 46 B8
Point Pedro, Sri Lanka 28 Q12
Point Pleasant, U.S.A. 52 F4
Pointe-à-Pitre, Guadeloupe 61 C7
Pointe-Noire, Congo 36 E2
Poisonbush Ra., Australia 40 D3
Poissonnier Pt., Australia 40 C2
Poitiers, France 14 C4
Poitou, France 14 C3
Pojoaque, U.S.A. 57 J11
Pokaran, India 28 F7
Pokataroo, Australia 43 D4
Poko, Dem. Rep. of the Congo 36 D5
Pokrovsk = Engels, Russia 19 D8
Pokrovsk, Russia 21 C13
Pola = Pula, Croatia 12 F7
Polacca, U.S.A. 57 J8
Polan, Iran 31 E9
Poland ■, Europe 13 C10
Polar Bear Prov. Park, Canada 48 A2
Polatsk, Belarus 18 C4
Polessk, Russia 7 J19
Polesye = Pripet Marshes, Europe 13 B15
Polevskoy, Russia 18 C11
Police, Poland 12 B8
Polillo Is., Phil. 27 B6
Políyiros, Greece 17 D10
Pollachi, India 28 P10
Polnovat, Russia 20 C7
Polonne, Ukraine 13 C14
Polonnoye = Polonne, Ukraine 13 C14
Polson, U.S.A. 56 C6
Poltava, Ukraine 19 E5
Põltsamaa, Estonia 7 G21
Polunochnoye, Russia 20 C7
Põlva, Estonia 7 G22
Polyarny, Russia 18 A5
Polynesia, Pac. Oc. 45 J11
Polynésie française = French Polynesia ■, Pac. Oc. 45 K13
Pomaro, Mexico 58 D4
Pombal, Portugal 15 C1
Pomeroy, Ohio, U.S.A. 52 F4
Pomeroy, Wash., U.S.A. 56 C5
Pomézia, Italy 16 D5
Pomona, Australia 43 D5
Pomona, U.S.A. 57 J5
Pomorskie, Pojezierze, Poland 13 B9
Pompano Beach, U.S.A. 53 M5
Pompeys Pillar, U.S.A. 56 D10
Ponape = Pohnpei, Micronesia 44 G7
Ponask L., Canada 48 B1
Ponca, U.S.A. 54 D6
Ponca City, U.S.A. 55 G6
Ponce, Puerto Rico 61 C6
Ponchatoula, U.S.A. 55 K9
Poncheville, L., Canada 48 B4
Pond Inlet, Canada 47 A12
Pondicherry, India 28 P11
Ponds, I. of, Canada 49 B8
Ponferrada, Spain 15 A2
Ponnani, India 28 P9
Ponoka, Canada 50 C6
Ponorogo, Indonesia 27 G14
Ponoy, Russia 18 A7
Ponoy →, Russia 18 A7
Ponta Grossa, Brazil 64 B6
Ponta Pora, Brazil 63 H7
Pontarlier, France 14 C7
Pontchartrain L., U.S.A. 55 K10
Ponte Nova, Brazil 63 H10
Ponteix, Canada 51 D7
Pontevedra, Spain 15 A1
Pontiac, Ill., U.S.A. 54 E10
Pontiac, Mich., U.S.A. 52 D4
Pontianak, Indonesia 26 E3
Pontine Is. = Ponziane, Ísole, Italy 16 D5
Pontine Mts. = Kuzey Anadolu Dağları, Turkey 19 F6
Pontivy, France 14 B2
Pontoise, France 14 B5
Ponton →, Canada 50 B5
Pontypool, U.K. 9 F4
Ponziane, Ísole, Italy 16 D5
Poochera, Australia 43 E1
Poole, U.K. 9 G6
Poole □, U.K. 9 G6
Poona = Pune, India 28 K8
Pooncarie, Australia 43 E3
Poopelloe L., Australia 43 E3
Poopó, L. de, Bolivia 62 G5
Popayán, Colombia 62 C3
Poperinge, Belgium 11 D2
Popilta L., Australia 43 E3
Popio L., Australia 43 E3
Poplar, U.S.A. 54 A2
Poplar →, Canada 51 C9
Poplar Bluff, U.S.A. 55 G9
Poplarville, U.S.A. 55 K10
Popocatépetl, Volcán, Mexico 59 D5
Popokabaka, Dem. Rep. of the Congo 36 F3
Poprad, Slovak Rep. 13 D11
Porbandar, India 28 J6
Porcher I., Canada 50 C2
Porcupine →, Canada 51 B8
Porcupine →, U.S.A. 46 B5
Pordenone, Italy 16 B5
Pori, Finland 7 F19
Porlamar, Venezuela 62 A6
Poronaysk, Russia 21 E15
Poroshiri-Dake, Japan 22 C11
Porpoise B., Antarctica 5 C9
Porsangen, Norway 6 A21
Porsgrunn, Norway 7 G13
Port Alberni, Canada 50 D4
Port Alice, Canada 50 C3
Port Allegany, U.S.A. 52 E6
Port Allen, U.S.A. 55 K9
Port Alma, Australia 42 C5
Port Angeles, U.S.A. 56 B2
Port Antonio, Jamaica 60 C4
Port Aransas, U.S.A. 55 M6
Port Arthur, Australia 42 G4
Port Arthur, U.S.A. 55 L8
Port au Choix, Canada 49 B8
Port au Port B., Canada 49 C8
Port-au-Prince, Haiti 61 C5
Port Augusta, Australia 43 E2
Port Austin, U.S.A. 52 C4
Port Blandford, Canada 49 C9
Port Bradshaw, Australia 42 A2
Port Broughton, Australia 43 E2
Port Campbell, Australia 43 F3
Port-Cartier, Canada 49 B6
Port Chalmers, N.Z. 39 L3
Port Charlotte, U.S.A. 53 M4
Port Chester, U.S.A. 52 E9
Port Clements, Canada 50 C2
Port Clinton, U.S.A. 52 E4
Port Colborne, Canada 48 D4
Port Coquitlam, Canada 50 D4
Port Curtis, Australia 42 C5
Port Darwin, Australia 40 B5
Port Darwin, Falk. Is. 64 G5
Port Davey, Australia 42 G4
Port-de-Paix, Haiti 61 C5
Port Dickson, Malaysia 26 D2
Port Douglas, Australia 42 B4
Port Edward, Canada 50 C2
Port Elgin, Canada 48 D3
Port Elizabeth, S. Africa 37 L5
Port Erin, U.K. 8 C3
Port Essington, Australia 40 B5
Port Etienne = Nouâdhibou, Mauritania 34 D2
Port Fairy, Australia 43 F3
Port-Gentil, Gabon 36 E1
Port Germein, Australia 43 E2
Port Gibson, U.S.A. 55 K9
Port Harcourt, Nigeria 34 H7
Port Hardy, Canada 50 C3
Port Harrison = Inukjuak, Canada 47 C12
Port Hawkesbury, Canada 49 C7
Port Hedland, Australia 40 D2
Port Henry, U.S.A. 52 C9
Port Hood, Canada 49 C7
Port Hope, Canada 48 D4
Port Hope Simpson, Canada 49 B8
Port Huron, U.S.A. 52 D4
Port Jefferson, U.S.A. 52 E9
Port Kelang = Pelabuhan Kelang, Malaysia 26 D2
Port Kenny, Australia 43 E1
Port Lairge = Waterford, Ireland 10 E3
Port Laoise, Ireland 10 E3
Port Lavaca, U.S.A. 55 L6
Port Lincoln, Australia 43 E2
Port Loko, S. Leone 34 G3
Port Lyautey = Kenitra, Morocco 34 B4
Port MacDonnell, Australia 43 F3
Port McNeill, Canada 50 C3
Port Macquarie, Australia 43 E5
Port Maria, Jamaica 60 C4
Port Mellon, Canada 50 D4
Port-Menier, Canada 49 C7
Port Morant, Jamaica 60 C4
Port Moresby, Papua N. G. 38 B7
Port Musgrave, Australia 42 A3
Port Neches, U.S.A. 55 L8
Port Nolloth, S. Africa 37 K3
Port Nouveau-Québec = Kangiqsualujjuaq, Canada 47 C13
Port of Spain, Trin. & Tob. 62 A6
Port Orange, U.S.A. 53 L5
Port Orford, U.S.A. 56 E1
Port Pegasus, N.Z. 39 M1
Port Perry, Canada 48 D4
Port Phillip B., Australia 43 F3
Port Pirie, Australia 43 E2
Port Radium = Echo Bay, Canada 46 B8
Port Renfrew, Canada 50 D4
Port Roper, Australia 42 A2
Port Safaga = Bûr Safâga, Egypt 30 E2
Port Said = Bûr Sa'îd, Egypt 35 B12
Port St. Joe, U.S.A. 53 L3
Port St. Johns = Umzimvubu, S. Africa 37 L5
Port St. Lucie, U.S.A. 53 M5
Port Shepstone, S. Africa 37 L6
Port Simpson, Canada 50 C2
Port Stanley = Stanley, Falk. Is. 64 G5
Port Stanley, Canada 48 D3
Port Sudan = Bûr Sûdân, Sudan 35 E13
Port Sulphur, U.S.A. 55 L10
Port Talbot, U.K. 9 F4
Port Townsend, U.S.A. 56 B2
Port-Vendres, France 14 E5
Port Vila, Vanuatu 38 C9
Port Vladimir, Russia 18 A5
Port Wakefield, Australia 43 E2
Port Washington, U.S.A. 52 D2
Port Weld = Kuala Sepetang, Malaysia 26 D2
Porta Orientalis, Romania 13 F12
Portadown, U.K. 10 D3
Portage, U.S.A. 54 D10
Portage La Prairie, Canada 51 D9
Portageville, U.S.A. 55 G10
Portalegre, Portugal 15 C2
Portales, U.S.A. 55 H3
Portbou, Spain 15 A7
Porter L., N.W.T., Canada 51 A7
Porter L., Sask., Canada 51 B7
Porterville, U.S.A. 57 H4
Porthcawl, U.K. 9 F4
Porthill, U.S.A. 56 B5
Porthmadog, U.K. 8 E3
Portile de Fier, Europe 13 F12
Portimão, Portugal 15 D1
Portishead, U.K. 9 F5
Portland, N.S.W., Australia 43 E5
Portland, Vic., Australia 43 F3
Portland, Maine, U.S.A. 47 D12
Portland, Mich., U.S.A. 52 D3
Portland, Oreg., U.S.A. 56 D2
Portland, Tex., U.S.A. 55 M6
Portland, I. of, U.K. 9 G5
Portland B., Australia 43 F3
Portland Bill, U.K. 9 G5
Portland Canal, U.S.A. 50 B2
Portmadoc = Porthmadog, U.K. 8 E3
Porto, Portugal 15 B1
Pôrto Alegre, Brazil 64 C6
Porto Amboim = Gunza, Angola 36 G2
Pôrto de Móz, Brazil 63 D8
Porto Empédocle, Italy 16 F5
Pôrto Esperança, Brazil 62 G7
Pôrto Franco, Brazil 63 E9
Porto Mendes, Brazil 64 A6
Pôrto Murtinho, Brazil 62 H7
Pôrto Nacional, Brazil 63 F9
Porto-Novo, Benin 34 G6
Porto Santo, Madeira 34 B2
Pôrto Seguro, Brazil 63 G11
Porto Tórres, Italy 16 D3
Pôrto União, Brazil 64 B6
Pôrto Válter, Brazil 62 E4
Porto-Vecchio, France 14 F8
Pôrto Velho, Brazil 62 E6
Portobelo, Panama 60 E4
Portoferráio, Italy 16 C4
Portola, U.S.A. 56 G3
Portoscuso, Italy 16 E3
Portoviejo, Ecuador 62 D2
Portree, U.K. 10 C3
Portsmouth, Domin. 61 C7
Portsmouth, U.K. 9 G6
Portsmouth, N.H., U.S.A. 53 D10
Portsmouth, Ohio, U.S.A. 52 F4
Portsmouth, Va., U.S.A. 52 G7
Portsmouth □, U.K. 9 G6
Porttipahtan tekojärvi, Finland 6 B22
Portugal ■, Europe 15 C1
Porvenir, Chile 64 G2
Porvoo, Finland 7 F21
Posadas, Argentina 64 B5
Posht-e-Badam, Iran 31 C7
Poso, Indonesia 27 E6
Posse, Brazil 63 F9
Possession I., Antarctica 5 D11
Possum Kingdom L., U.S.A. 55 J5
Post, U.S.A. 55 J4
Post Falls, U.S.A. 56 C5
Postavy = Pastavy, Belarus 7 J22
Poste-de-la-Baleine = Kuujjuarapik, Canada 48 A4
Postmasburg, S. Africa 37 K4
Postojna, Slovenia 12 F8
Postville, Canada 49 B8
Potchefstroom, S. Africa 37 K5
Poteau, U.S.A. 55 H7
Poteet, U.S.A. 55 L5
Potenza, Italy 16 D6
Poteriteri, L., N.Z. 39 M1
Potgietersrus, S. Africa 37 J5
Poti, Georgia 19 F7
Potiskum, Nigeria 35 F8
Potomac →, U.S.A. 52 G7
Potosí, Bolivia 62 G5
Pototan, Phil. 27 B6
Potrerillos, Chile 64 B3
Potsdam, Germany 12 B7
Potsdam, U.S.A. 52 C8
Pottstown, U.S.A. 52 E8
Pottsville, U.S.A. 52 E7
Pottuvil, Sri Lanka 28 R12
Pouce Coupé, Canada 50 B4
Poughkeepsie, U.S.A. 52 E9
Poulsbo, U.S.A. 56 C2
Poulton-le-Fylde, U.K. 8 D5
Pouthisat, Cambodia 26 B2
Považská Bystrica, Slovak Rep. 13 D10
Povenets, Russia 18 B5
Poverty B., N.Z. 39 H7
Póvoa de Varzim, Portugal 15 B1
Povungnituk = Puvirnituq, Canada 47 B12
Powassan, Canada 48 C4
Powder →, U.S.A. 54 B2
Powder River, U.S.A. 56 E10
Powell, U.S.A. 56 D9
Powell, L., U.S.A. 57 H8
Powell River, Canada 50 D4
Powers, U.S.A. 52 C2
Powys □, U.K. 9 E4
Poyang Hu, China 25 D6
Poyarkovo, Russia 21 E13
Poza Rica, Mexico 59 C5
Požarevac, Serbia, Yug. 17 B9
Poznań, Poland 13 B9
Pozo Almonte, Chile 62 H5
Pozoblanco, Spain 15 C3
Pozzuoli, Italy 16 D6
Prachuap Khiri Khan, Thailand 26 B1
Prado, Brazil 63 G11
Prague = Praha, Czech Rep. 12 C8
Praha, Czech Rep. 12 C8
Prainha, Amazonas, Brazil 62 E6
Prainha, Pará, Brazil 63 D8
Prairie, Australia 42 C3
Prairie City, U.S.A. 56 D4
Prairie Dog Town Fork →, U.S.A. 55 H5
Prairie du Chien, U.S.A. 54 D9
Prairies, L. of the, Canada 51 C8
Prapat, Indonesia 26 D1
Prata, Brazil 63 G9
Prato, Italy 16 C4
Pratt, U.S.A. 55 G5
Prattville, U.S.A. 53 J2
Pravia, Spain 15 A2
Praya, Indonesia 26 F5

Preeceville, *Canada* ... 51 C8
Preiļi, *Latvia* 7 H22
Premont, *U.S.A.* 55 M5
Prentice, *U.S.A.* 54 C9
Preobrazheniye, *Russia* 22 C6
Preparis North Channel,
  Ind. Oc. 29 M18
Preparis South Channel,
  Ind. Oc. 29 M18
Přerov, *Czech Rep.* 13 D9
Prescott, *Canada* 48 D4
Prescott, *Ariz., U.S.A.* . 57 J7
Prescott, *Ark., U.S.A.* . 55 J8
Prescott Valley, *U.S.A.* . 57 J7
Preservation Inlet, *N.Z.* 39 M1
Presho, *U.S.A.* 54 D4
Presidencia Roque
  Saenz Peña, *Argentina* 64 B4
Presidente Epitácio,
  Brazil 63 H8
Presidente Prudente,
  Brazil 63 H8
Presidio, *Mexico* 58 B4
Presidio, *U.S.A.* 55 L2
Prešov, *Slovak Rep.* ... 13 D11
Prespa, L. = Prespansko
  Jezero, *Macedonia* 17 D9
Prespansko Jezero,
  Macedonia 17 D9
Presque Isle, *U.S.A.* ... 53 B12
Prestatyn, *U.K.* 8 D4
Presteigne, *U.K.* 9 E5
Preston, *U.K.* 8 D5
Preston, *Idaho, U.S.A.* . 56 E8
Preston, *Minn., U.S.A.* . 54 D8
Preston, *Nev., U.S.A.* .. 57 G6
Preston, C., *Australia* .. 40 D2
Prestonburg, *U.S.A.* 52 G4
Pretoria, *S. Africa* 37 K5
Préveza, *Greece* 17 E9
Prey Veng, *Cambodia* .. 26 B3
Pribilof Is., *U.S.A.* 46 C2
Příbram, *Czech Rep.* .. 12 D8
Price, *U.S.A.* 56 G8
Price I., *Canada* 50 C3
Prichard, *U.S.A.* 53 K1
Priekule, *Latvia* 7 H19
Priekuļi, *Australia* 42 G4
Prienai, *Lithuania* 7 J20
Prieska, *S. Africa* 37 K4
Priest L., *U.S.A.* 56 B5
Priest River, *U.S.A.* ... 56 B5
Prievidza, *Slovak Rep.* . 13 D10
Prikaspiyskaya
  Nizmennost =
  Caspian Depression,
  Eurasia 19 E8
Prilep, *Macedonia* 17 D9
Priluki = Pryluky,
  Ukraine 19 D5
Prime Seal I., *Australia* 42 G4
Primrose L., *Canada* .. 51 C7
Prince Albert, *Canada* . 51 C7
Prince Albert Mts.,
  Antarctica 5 D11
Prince Albert Nat. Park,
  Canada 51 C7
Prince Albert Pen.,
  Canada 46 A8
Prince Albert Sd.,
  Canada 46 A8
Prince Alfred, C.,
  Canada 4 B1
Prince Charles I.,
  Canada 47 B12
Prince Charles Mts.,
  Antarctica 5 D6
Prince Edward I. □,
  Canada 49 C7
Prince Edward Is.,
  Ind. Oc. 3 G11
Prince George, *Canada* 50 C4
Prince of Wales I.,
  Australia 42 A3
Prince of Wales I.,
  Canada 46 A10
Prince of Wales I.,
  U.S.A. 46 C6
Prince Patrick I., *Canada* 4 B2
Prince Regent Inlet,
  Canada 4 B3
Prince Rupert, *Canada* . 50 C2
Princess Charlotte B.,
  Australia 42 A3
Princess May Ranges,
  Australia 40 C4
Princess Royal I.,
  Canada 50 C3
Princeton, *Canada* 50 D4
Princeton, *Ill., U.S.A.* . 54 E10
Princeton, *Ind., U.S.A.* 52 F2
Princeton, *Ky., U.S.A.* . 52 G2
Princeton, *Mo., U.S.A.* 54 E8
Princeton, *N.J., U.S.A.* 52 E8
Princeton, *W. Va.,*
  U.S.A. 52 G5
Principe, I. de, *Atl. Oc.* . 3 D10
Principe, I. de, *Atl. Oc.* . 3 D10
Principe da Beira, *Brazil* 62 F6
Prineville, *U.S.A.* 56 D3
Prins Harald Kyst,
  Antarctica 5 D4
Prinsesse Astrid Kyst,
  Antarctica 5 D3
Prinsesse Ragnhild Kyst,
  Antarctica 5 D4

Prinzapolca, *Nic.* 60 D3
Priozersk, *Russia* 18 B5
Pripet = Prypyat →,
  Europe 13 C16
Pripet Marshes, *Europe* 13 B15
Pripyats = Prypyat →,
  Pripet Marshes,
  Europe 13 B15
Pripyats = Prypyat →,
  Europe 13 C16
Prishtina, *Kosovo, Yug.* 17 C9
Privas, *France* 14 D6
Privolzhskaya
  Vozvyshennost,
  Russia 19 D8
Prizren, *Kosovo, Yug.* . 17 C9
Probolinggo, *Indonesia* 27 G15
Proddatur, *India* 28 M11
Profondeville, *Belgium* 11 D4
Progreso, *Coahuila,*
  Mexico 58 B4
Progreso, *Yucatán,*
  Mexico 59 C7
Prokopyevsk, *Russia* .. 20 D9
Prokuplje, *Serbia, Yug.* 17 C9
Prome = Pyè, *Burma* .. 29 K19
Prophet →, *Canada* ... 50 B4
Prophet River, *Canada* . 50 B4
Propriá, *Brazil* 63 F11
Proserpine, *Australia* .. 42 C4
Prosna →, *Poland* 13 B9
Prosser, *U.S.A.* 56 C4
Prostějov, *Czech Rep.* . 13 D9
Proston, *Australia* 43 D5
Provence, *France* 14 E6
Providence, *Ky., U.S.A.* 52 G2
Providence, *R.I., U.S.A.* 52 E10
Providence Bay, *Canada* 48 C3
Providencia, I. de,
  Colombia 60 D3
Provideniya, *Russia* ... 21 C19
Provins, *France* 14 B5
Provo, *U.S.A.* 56 F8
Provost, *Canada* 51 C6
Prudhoe Bay, *U.S.A.* .. 46 A5
Prudhoe I., *Australia* .. 42 C4
Prud'homme, *Canada* . 51 C7
Pruszków, *Poland* 13 B11
Prut →, *Romania* 13 F15
Pruzhany, *Belarus* 13 B13
Prydz B., *Antarctica* ... 5 C6
Pryluky, *Ukraine* 19 D5
Pryor, *U.S.A.* 55 G7
Prypyat →, *Europe* 13 C16
Przemyśl, *Poland* 13 D12
Przhevalsk, *Kyrgyzstan* 20 E8
Psará, *Greece* 17 E11
Pskov, *Russia* 18 C4
Ptich = Ptsich →,
  Belarus 13 B15
Ptolemaís, *Greece* 17 D9
Ptsich →, *Belarus* 13 B15
Puán, *Argentina* 64 D4
Pucallpa, *Peru* 62 E4
Pudasjärvi, *Finland* ... 6 D22
Pudozh, *Russia* 18 B6
Pudukkottai, *India* 28 P11
Puebla, *Mexico* 59 D5
Puebla □, *Mexico* 59 D5
Pueblo, *U.S.A.* 54 F2
Puelches, *Argentina* .. 64 D3
Puente Alto, *Chile* 64 C2
Puente-Genil, *Spain* ... 15 D3
Puerco →, *U.S.A.* 57 J10
Puerto Aisén, *Chile* ... 64 F2
Puerto Ángel, *Mexico* . 59 D5
Puerto Arista, *Mexico* . 59 D6
Puerto Armuelles,
  Panama 60 E3
Puerto Ayacucho,
  Venezuela 62 B5
Puerto Barrios,
  Guatemala 60 C2
Puerto Bermúdez, *Peru* 62 F4
Puerto Bolívar, *Ecuador* 62 D3
Puerto Cabello,
  Venezuela 62 A5
Puerto Cabezas, *Nic.* .. 60 D3
Puerto Cabo Gracias á
  Dios, *Nic.* 60 D3
Puerto Carreño,
  Colombia 62 B5
Puerto Castilla,
  Honduras 60 C2
Puerto Chicama, *Peru* . 62 E3
Puerto Coig, *Argentina* 64 G3
Puerto Cortés,
  Costa Rica 60 E3
Puerto Cortés, *Honduras* 60 C2
Puerto Cumarebo,
  Venezuela 62 A5
Puerto Deseado,
  Argentina 64 F3
Puerto Escondido,
  Mexico 59 D5
Puerto Heath, *Bolivia* . 62 F5
Puerto Inírida, *Colombia* 62 C5
Puerto Juárez, *Mexico* . 59 C7
Puerto La Cruz,
  Venezuela 62 A6
Puerto Leguízamo,
  Colombia 62 D4
Puerto Limón, *Colombia* 62 C4
Puerto Lobos, *Argentina* 64 E3

Puerto Madryn,
  Argentina 64 E3
Puerto Maldonado, *Peru* 62 F5
Puerto Manotí, *Cuba* .. 60 B4
Puerto Montt, *Chile* ... 64 E2
Puerto Morazán, *Nic.* .. 60 D2
Puerto Morelos, *Mexico* 59 C7
Puerto Natales, *Chile* .. 64 G2
Puerto Padre, *Cuba* ... 60 B4
Puerto Páez, *Venezuela* 62 B5
Puerto Peñasco, *Mexico* 58 A2
Puerto Pinasco,
  Paraguay 62 H7
Puerto Plata, *Dom. Rep.* 61 C5
Puerto Princesa, *Phil.* .. 27 C5
Puerto Quepos,
  Costa Rica 60 E3
Puerto Rico ■, *W. Indies* 61 C6
Puerto Rico Trench,
  Atl. Oc. 61 C6
Puerto San Julián,
  Argentina 64 F3
Puerto Sastre, *Paraguay* 62 H7
Puerto Suárez, *Bolivia* . 62 G7
Puerto Vallarta, *Mexico* 58 C3
Puerto Wilches,
  Colombia 62 B4
Puertollano, *Spain* 15 C3
Pueyrredón, L.,
  Argentina 64 F2
Pugachev, *Russia* 18 D8
Puget Sound, *U.S.A.* ... 56 C2
Pügünzī, *Iran* 31 E8
Puigcerdà, *Spain* 15 A6
Pukaki L., *N.Z.* 39 L3
Pukapuka, *Cook Is.* ... 45 J11
Pukaskwa Nat. Park,
  Canada 48 C2
Pukekohe, *N.Z.* 39 G5
Pula, *Croatia* 12 F7
Pulacayo, *Bolivia* 62 H5
Pularumpi, *Australia* ... 40 B5
Pulaski, *N.Y., U.S.A.* .. 52 D7
Pulaski, *Tenn., U.S.A.* . 53 H2
Pulaski, *Va., U.S.A.* ... 52 G5
Pulau →, *Indonesia* ... 27 F9
Puławy, *Poland* 13 C11
Pulicat L., *India* 28 N12
Pullman, *U.S.A.* 56 C5
Pulo-Anna, *Pac. Oc.* .. 27 D8
Pulog, Mt., *Phil.* 27 A6
Puttusk, *Poland* 13 B11
Pumlumon Fawr, *U.K.* . 9 E4
Puná, I., *Ecuador* 62 D2
Punakha, *Bhutan* 29 F16
Punata, *Bolivia* 62 G5
Punch, *India* 28 C9
Pune, *India* 28 K8
Punjab □, *India* 28 D10
Punjab □, *Pakistan* ... 28 E9
Puno, *Peru* 62 G4
Punta Alta, *Argentina* . 64 D4
Punta Arenas, *Chile* ... 64 G2
Punta de Díaz, *Chile* .. 64 B2
Punta Gorda, *Belize* ... 59 D7
Punta Gorda, *U.S.A.* .. 53 M5
Punta Prieta, *Mexico* .. 58 B2
Puntarenas, *Costa Rica* 60 E3
Punto Fijo, *Venezuela* . 62 A4
Punxsutawney, *U.S.A.* . 52 E6
Puquio, *Peru* 62 F4
Pur →, *Russia* 20 C8
Purace, Vol., *Colombia* 62 C3
Puralia = Puruliya, *India* 29 H15
Purbeck, Isle of, *U.K.* .. 9 G6
Purcell, *U.S.A.* 55 H6
Purcell Mts., *Canada* .. 50 D5
Puri, *India* 29 K14
Purmerend, *Neths.* 11 B4
Purnia, *India* 29 G15
Pursat = Pouthisat,
  Cambodia 26 B2
Purukcahu, *Indonesia* . 26 E4
Puruliya, *India* 29 H15
Purus →, *Brazil* 62 D6
Purvis, *U.S.A.* 55 K10
Purwakarta, *Indonesia* 27 G12
Purwodadi, *Indonesia* . 27 G14
Purwokerto, *Indonesia* 27 G13
Pusan, *S. Korea* 25 C7
Pushkino, *Russia* 19 D8
Putahow L., *Canada* ... 51 B8
Putao, *Burma* 29 F20
Putaruru, *N.Z.* 39 H5
Putignano, *Italy* 16 D7
Puting, Tanjung,
  Indonesia 26 E4
Putorana, Gory, *Russia* 21 C10
Puttalam, *Sri Lanka* ... 28 Q11
Puttgarden, *Germany* . 12 A6
Putumayo →, *S. Amer.* 62 D5
Putussibau, *Indonesia* . 26 D4
Puvirnituq, *Canada* 47 B12
Puy-de-Dôme, *France* . 14 D5
Puyallup, *U.S.A.* 56 C2
Püzeh Rīg, *Iran* 31 E8
Pwllheli, *U.K.* 8 E3
Pya-ozero, *Russia* 18 A5
Pyapon, *Burma* 29 L19
Pyasina →, *Russia* 21 B9
Pyatigorsk, *Russia* 19 F7
Pyè, *Burma* 29 K19
Pyetrikaw, *Belarus* 13 B15

Pyhäjoki, *Finland* 6 D21
Pyinmana, *Burma* 29 K20
P'yŏngyang, *N. Korea* . 25 C7
Pyote, *U.S.A.* 55 K3
Pyramid L., *U.S.A.* 56 G4
Pyrénées, *Europe* 14 E4
Pyu, *Burma* 29 K20

Qaanaaq, *Greenland* .. 4 B4
Qa'el Jafr, *Jordan* 33 E5
Qa'emābād, *Iran* 31 D9
Qā'emshahr, *Iran* 31 B7
Qahremānshahr =
  Bākhtarān, *Iran* 30 C5
Qaidam Pendi, *China* .. 24 C4
Qajarīyeh, *Iran* 31 D6
Qal'at al Akhḍar,
  Si. Arabia 30 E3
Qal'at Dīzah, *Iraq* 30 B5
Qal'at Ṣāliḥ, *Iraq* 30 D5
Qal'at Sukkar, *Iraq* 30 D5
Qamani'tuaq = Baker
  Lake, *Canada* 46 B10
Qamdo, *China* 24 C4
Qamruddin Karez,
  Pakistan 28 D6
Qandahār, *Afghan.* ... 28 D4
Qandahār □, *Afghan.* . 28 D4
Qapān, *Iran* 31 B7
Qapshaghay, *Kazakstan* 20 E8
Qaqortoq, *Greenland* . 4 C5
Qarabutaq, *Kazakstan* . 20 E7
Qaraghandy, *Kazakstan* 20 E8
Qārah, *Si. Arabia* 30 D4
Qaratau, *Kazakstan* ... 20 E8
Qareh →, *Iran* 30 B5
Qareh Tekān, *Iran* 31 B6
Qarqan He →, *China* .. 24 C3
Qarqaraly, *Kazakstan* .. 20 E8
Qarshi, *Uzbekistan* ... 20 F7
Qartabā, *Lebanon* 33 A4
Qaryat al Gharab, *Iraq* 30 D5
Qaryat al 'Ulyā,
  Si. Arabia 30 E5
Qasr 'Amra, *Jordan* ... 30 D3
Qaṣr-e Qand, *Iran* 31 E9
Qasr Farāfra, *Egypt* ... 35 C11
Qatanā, *Syria* 33 B5
Qatar ■, *Asia* 31 E6
Qatlīsh, *Iran* 31 B8
Qattâra, Munkhafed el,
  Egypt 35 C11
Qawām al Ḥamzah, *Iraq* 30 D5
Qāyen, *Iran* 31 C8
Qazaqstan =
  Kazakstan ■, *Asia* .. 20 E7
Qazimämmäd,
  Azerbaijan 31 A6
Qazvin, *Iran* 31 B6
Qena, *Egypt* 35 C12
Qeqertarsuaq,
  Greenland 4 C5
Qeqertarsuaq,
  Greenland 4 C5
Qeshlāq, *Iran* 30 C5
Qeshm, *Iran* 31 E8
Qeys, *Iran* 31 E7
Qezel Owzen →, *Iran* . 31 B6
Qezi'ot, *Israel* 33 E3
Qibā', *Si. Arabia* 30 E5
Qikiqtarjuaq, *Canada* . 47 B13
Qila Safed, *Pakistan* .. 28 E3
Qila Saifullāh, *Pakistan* 28 D6
Qilian Shan, *China* 24 C4
Qingdao, *China* 25 C7
Qinghai □, *China* 24 C4
Qinghai Hu, *China* 24 C5
Qingjiang = Huaiyin,
  China 25 C6
Qinhuangdao, *China* .. 25 C6
Qinzhou, *China* 24 D5
Qiqihar, *China* 21 E13
Qiraïya, W. →, *Egypt* .. 33 E3
Qiryat Ata, *Israel* 33 C4
Qiryat Gat, *Israel* 33 D3
Qiryat Mal'akhi, *Israel* . 33 D3
Qiryat Shemona, *Israel* 33 B4
Qiryat Yam, *Israel* 33 C4
Qitai, *China* 24 B3
Qızılağac Körfäzi,
  Azerbaijan 31 B6
Qojūr, *Iran* 30 B5
Qom, *Iran* 31 C6
Qomolangma Feng =
  Everest, Mt., *Nepal* . 29 E15
Qomsheh, *Iran* 31 D6
Qostanay, *Kazakstan* .. 20 D7
Qou'ân, Jazā'ir, *Egypt* . 30 E2
Quairading, *Australia* .. 41 F2
Qualicum Beach,
  Canada 50 D4
Quambatook, *Australia* 43 F3
Quambone, *Australia* .. 43 E4
Quamby, *Australia* 42 C3
Quan Long = Ca Mau,
  Vietnam 26 C3
Quanah, *U.S.A.* 55 H5
Quang Ngai, *Vietnam* .. 26 A3
Quang Tri, *Vietnam* ... 26 A3
Quantock Hills, *U.K.* .. 9 F4
Quanzhou, *China* 25 D6

Qu'Appelle, *Canada* ... 51 C8
Quaqtaq, *Canada* 47 B13
Quartu Sant'Elena, *Italy* 16 E3
Quartzsite, *U.S.A.* 57 K6
Quatsino Sd., *Canada* . 50 C3
Quba, *Azerbaijan* 19 F8
Qūchān, *Iran* 31 B8
Queanbeyan, *Australia* 43 F4
Québec, *Canada* 49 C5
Québec □, *Canada* ... 49 C6
Queen Alexandra Ra.,
  Antarctica 5 E11
Queen Charlotte City,
  Canada 50 C2
Queen Charlotte Is.,
  Canada 50 C2
Queen Charlotte Sd.,
  Canada 50 C3
Queen Charlotte Strait,
  Canada 50 C3
Queen Elizabeth Is.,
  Canada 2 A5
Queen Mary Land,
  Antarctica 5 D7
Queen Maud G., *Canada* 46 B9
Queen Maud Land,
  Antarctica 5 D3
Queen Maud Mts.,
  Antarctica 5 E13
Queens Chan., *Australia* 40 C4
Queenscliff, *Australia* .. 43 F3
Queensland □, *Australia* 42 C3
Queenstown, *Australia* 42 G4
Queenstown, *N.Z.* 39 L2
Queenstown, *S. Africa* . 37 L5
Queimadas, *Brazil* 63 F11
Quelimane, *Mozam.* .. 37 H7
Quellón, *Chile* 64 E2
Quelpart = Cheju do,
  S. Korea 25 C7
Quemado, *N. Mex.,*
  U.S.A. 57 J9
Quemado, *Tex., U.S.A.* 55 L4
Querétaro, *Mexico* 58 C4
Querétaro □, *Mexico* . 58 C5
Quesnel, *Canada* 50 C4
Quesnel →, *Canada* .. 50 C4
Quesnel L., *Canada* ... 50 C4
Questa, *U.S.A.* 57 H11
Quetico Prov. Park,
  Canada 48 C1
Quetta, *Pakistan* 28 D5
Quezaltenango,
  Guatemala 60 D1
Quezon City, *Phil.* 27 B6
Qui Nhon, *Vietnam* ... 26 B3
Quibaxe, *Angola* 36 F2
Quibdo, *Colombia* 62 B3
Quiberon, *France* 14 C2
Quiet L., *Canada* 50 A2
Quila, *Mexico* 58 C3
Quilán, C., *Chile* 64 E2
Quilengues, *Angola* ... 37 G2
Quillabamba, *Peru* 62 F4
Quillagua, *Chile* 62 H5
Quillota, *Chile* 64 C2
Quilon, *India* 28 Q10
Quilpie, *Australia* 43 D3
Quimilí, *Argentina* 64 B3
Quimper, *France* 14 B1
Quimperlé, *France* 14 C2
Quincy, *Calif., U.S.A.* .. 56 G3
Quincy, *Fla., U.S.A.* ... 53 K3
Quincy, *Ill., U.S.A.* 54 F9
Quincy, *Mass., U.S.A.* . 52 D10
Quincy, *Wash., U.S.A.* . 56 C4
Quines, *Argentina* 64 C3
Quinns Rocks, *Australia* 41 F2
Quintana Roo □, *Mexico* 59 D7
Quintanar de la Orden,
  Spain 15 C4
Quirindi, *Australia* 43 E5
Quirinópolis, *Brazil* ... 63 G8
Quissanga, *Mozam.* ... 37 G8
Quitman, *U.S.A.* 53 K4
Quito, *Ecuador* 62 D3
Quixadá, *Brazil* 63 D11
Quneitra, *Syria* 33 B4
Qünghirot, *Uzbekistan* 20 E6
Quoin I., *Australia* 40 B4
Quorn, *Australia* 43 E2
Qŭqon, *Uzbekistan* ... 20 E8
Qurnat as Sawdā',
  Lebanon 33 A5
Qûs, *Egypt* 35 C12
Qusaybah, *Iraq* 30 C4
Quşaybā', *Si. Arabia* .. 30 E4
Qūṭīābād, *Iran* 31 C6
Qüshchī, *Iran* 30 B5
Quzhou, *China* 25 D6
Qyzylorda, *Kazakstan* . 20 E7

Raahe, *Finland* 6 D21
Raalte, *Neths.* 11 B6
Raba, *Indonesia* 27 F5
Rába →, *Hungary* 13 E9
Rabat, *Malta* 16 G6
Rabat, *Morocco* 34 B4
Rabaul, *Papua N. G.* .. 38 B8
Rābigh, *Si. Arabia* 32 C2
Râbniţa, *Moldova* 13 E15

Rābor, *Iran* 31 D8
Race, C., *Canada* 49 C9
Rach Gia, *Vietnam* 26 B3
Rachid, *Mauritania* ... 34 E3
Raciborz, *Poland* 13 C10
Racine, *U.S.A.* 52 D2
Rădăuţi, *Romania* 13 E13
Radcliff, *U.S.A.* 52 G3
Radekhov = Radekhiv,
  Ukraine 13 C13
Radford, *U.S.A.* 52 G5
Radhwa, Jabal,
  Si. Arabia 30 E3
Radisson, *Qué., Canada* 48 B4
Radisson, *Sask., Canada* 51 C7
Radium Hot Springs,
  Canada 50 C5
Radnor Forest, *U.K.* ... 9 E4
Radom, *Poland* 13 C11
Radomsko, *Poland* 13 C10
Radomyshl, *Ukraine* .. 13 C15
Radstock, C., *Australia* . 43 E1
Radviliškis, *Lithuania* . 7 J20
Radville, *Canada* 51 D8
Rae, *Canada* 50 A5
Rae Bareli, *India* 29 F12
Rae Isthmus, *Canada* . 47 B11
Raeren, *Belgium* 11 D6
Raeside, L., *Australia* .. 41 E3
Raetihi, *N.Z.* 39 H5
Rafaela, *Argentina* 64 C4
Rafah, *Gaza Strip* 33 D3
Rafhā, *Si. Arabia* 30 D4
Rafsanjān, *Iran* 31 D8
Raft Pt., *Australia* 40 C3
Râgâ, *Sudan* 35 G11
Ragachow, *Belarus* 13 B16
Ragama, *Sri Lanka* 28 R11
Ragged, Mt., *Australia* . 41 F3
Raglan, *N.Z.* 39 G5
Ragusa, *Italy* 16 F6
Raha, *Indonesia* 27 E6
Rahaeng = Tak,
  Thailand 26 A1
Raḥimah, *Si. Arabia* .. 31 E6
Rahimyar Khan,
  Pakistan 28 E7
Rähjerd, *Iran* 31 C6
Raichur, *India* 28 L10
Raigarh, *India* 29 J13
Raijua, *Indonesia* 27 F6
Railton, *Australia* 42 G4
Rainbow Lake, *Canada* 50 B5
Rainier, *U.S.A.* 56 C2
Rainier, Mt., *U.S.A.* ... 56 C3
Rainy L., *Canada* 51 D10
Rainy River, *Canada* ... 51 D10
Raippaluoto, *Finland* .. 6 E19
Raipur, *India* 29 J12
Raisio, *Finland* 7 F20
Raj Nandgaon, *India* .. 29 J12
Raja, Ujung, *Indonesia* 26 D1
Raja Ampat, Kepulauan,
  Indonesia 27 E7
Rajahmundry, *India* ... 29 L12
Rajang →, *Malaysia* ... 26 D4
Rajapalaiyam, *India* ... 28 Q10
Rajasthan □, *India* 28 F8
Rajasthan Canal, *India* 28 E8
Rajgarh, *India* 28 G10
Rajkot, *India* 28 H7
Rajpipla, *India* 28 J8
Rajshahi, *Bangla.* 29 G16
Rajshahi □, *Bangla.* ... 29 G16
Rakaia, *N.Z.* 39 K4
Rakaia →, *N.Z.* 39 K4
Rakan, Ra's, *Qatar* 31 E6
Rakaposhi, *Pakistan* ... 28 A9
Rakata, Pulau, *Indonesia* 26 F3
Rakhiv, *Ukraine* 13 D13
Rakitnoye, *Russia* 22 B7
Rakvere, *Estonia* 7 G22
Raleigh, *U.S.A.* 53 H6
Ralls, *U.S.A.* 55 J4
Ram →, *Canada* 50 A4
Ram Allāh, *West Bank* . 33 D4
Ram Hd., *Australia* 43 F4
Rama, *Nic.* 60 D3
Ramanathapuram, *India* 28 Q11
Ramat Gan, *Israel* 33 C3
Rambipuji, *Indonesia* . 27 H15
Ramechhap, *Nepal* 29 F15
Ramgarh, *Bihar, India* . 29 H14
Ramgarh, *Raj., India* .. 28 F7
Rämhormoz, *Iran* 31 D6
Ramīān, *Iran* 31 B7
Ramingining, *Australia* 42 A2
Ramla, *Israel* 33 D3
Ramnad =
  Ramanathapuram,
  India 28 Q11
Râmnicu Sărat,
  Romania 13 F14
Râmnicu Vâlcea,
  Romania 13 F13
Ramona, *U.S.A.* 57 K5
Ramore, *Canada* 48 C3
Rampur, *India* 28 E11
Rampur Hat, *India* 29 G15
Ramree I., *Burma* 29 K19
Rāmsar, *Iran* 31 B6
Ramsey, *U.K.* 8 C3
Ramsey L., *Canada* ... 48 C3

Ramsgate, *U.K.* 9 F9
Ramtek, *India* 28 J11
Ranaghat, *India* 29 H16
Ranau, *Malaysia* 26 C5
Rancagua, *Chile* 64 C2
Rancheria →, *Canada* 50 A3
Ranchester, *U.S.A.* ... 56 D10
Ranchi, *India* 29 H14
Randers, *Denmark* 7 H14
Randolph, *Utah, U.S.A.* 56 F8
Randolph, *Vt., U.S.A.* .. 52 D9
Råne älv →, *Sweden* .. 6 D20
Rangaunu B., *N.Z.* ... 39 F4
Rangeley, *U.S.A.* 52 C10
Rangely, *U.S.A.* 56 F9
Ranger, *U.S.A.* 55 J5
Rangia, *India* 29 F17
Rangiora, *N.Z.* 39 K4
Rangitaiki →, *N.Z.* ... 39 G6
Rangitata →, *N.Z.* ... 39 K3
Rangkasbitung,
  Indonesia 27 G12
Rangon →, *Burma* ... 29 L20
Rangoon, *Burma* 29 L20
Rangpur, *Bangla.* 29 G16
Ranibennur, *India* 28 M9
Raniganj, *India* 29 H15
Raniwara, *India* 28 G8
Rāniyah, *Iraq* 30 B5
Ranken →, *Australia* .. 42 C2
Rankin, *U.S.A.* 55 K4
Rankin Inlet, *Canada* .. 46 B10
Rankins Springs,
  Australia 43 E4
Ranohira, *Madag.* 37 J8
Ranong, *Thailand* 26 C1
Ränsa, *Iran* 31 C6
Ransiki, *Indonesia* ... 27 E8
Rantauprapat, *Indonesia* 26 D1
Rantemario, *Indonesia* 27 E5
Rantoul, *U.S.A.* 52 E1
Rapa, *Pac. Oc.* 45 K13
Rapallo, *Italy* 14 D8
Räpch, *Iran* 31 E8
Raper, C., *Canada* ... 47 B13
Rapid City, *U.S.A.* ... 54 D3
Rapid River, *U.S.A.* .. 52 C2
Rapla, *Estonia* 7 G21
Rarotonga, *Cook Is.* .. 45 K12
Ra's al 'Ayn, *Syria* .. 30 B4
Ra's al Khaymah, *U.A.E.* 31 E7
Raseiniai, *Lithuania* .. 7 J20
Rasht, *Iran* 31 B6
Rason L., *Australia* ... 41 E3
Rat Islands, *U.S.A.* .. 46 C1
Rat L., *Canada* 51 B9
Ratangarh, *India* 28 E9
Raţāwi, *Iraq* 30 D5
Ratcatchers L., *Australia* 43 E3
Rathenow, *Germany* .. 12 B7
Ratibor = Racibórz,
  Poland 13 C10
Ratlam, *India* 28 H9
Ratnagiri, *India* 28 L8
Raton, *U.S.A.* 55 G2
Ratz, Mt., *Canada* ... 50 B2
Raudales de Malpaso,
  Mexico 59 D6
Raufarhöfn, *Iceland* .. 6 C6
Raufoss, *Norway* 7 F14
Raukumara Ra., *N.Z.* 39 H6
Rauma, *Finland* 7 F19
Raurkela, *India* 29 H14
Rausu-Dake, *Japan* .. 22 B12
Rava-Ruska, *Poland* .. 13 C12
Rava Russkaya = Rava-
  Ruska, *Poland* 13 C12
Ravalli, *U.S.A.* 56 C6
Ravänsar, *Iran* 30 C5
Rävar, *Iran* 31 D8
Ravenna, *Italy* 16 B5
Ravenna, *U.S.A.* 54 E5
Ravensburg, *Germany* . 12 E5
Ravenshoe, *Australia* . 42 B4
Ravensthorpe, *Australia* 41 F3
Ravenswood, *Australia* 42 C4
Ravenswood, *U.S.A.* . 52 F5
Ravi →, *Pakistan* 28 D7
Rawalpindi, *Pakistan* . 28 C8
Rawene, *N.Z.* 39 F4
Rawlinna, *Australia* .. 41 F4
Rawlins, *U.S.A.* 56 F10
Rawlinson Ra., *Australia* 41 D4
Rawson, *Argentina* ... 64 E3
Ray, *U.S.A.* 54 A3
Ray, C., *Canada* 49 C8
Rayadurg, *India* 28 M10
Rayagada, *India* 29 K13
Raychikhinsk, *Russia* . 21 E13
Räyen, *Iran* 31 D8
Rayleigh, *U.K.* 9 F8
Raymond, *Canada* ... 50 D6
Raymond, *U.S.A.* 56 C2
Raymond Terrace,
  Australia 43 E5
Raymore, *Canada* 51 C8
Rayón, *Mexico* 58 B2
Rayong, *Thailand* 26 B2
Rayville, *U.S.A.* 55 J9
Raz, Pte. du, *France* .. 14 C1
Razan, *Iran* 31 C6
Razdel'naya = Rozdilna,
  Ukraine 13 E16

Razdolnoye, *Russia* .. 22 C5
Razeh, *Iran* 31 C6
Razgrad, *Bulgaria* ... 17 C12
Razim, Lacul, *Romania* 13 F15
Ré, Î. de, *France* 14 C3
Reading, *U.K.* 9 F7
Reading, *U.S.A.* 52 E8
Reading □, *U.K.* 9 F7
Realicó, *Argentina* ... 64 D4
Reata, *Mexico* 58 B4
Rebi, *Indonesia* 27 F8
Rebiana, *Libya* 35 D10
Rebun-Tō, *Japan* 22 B10
Recherche, Arch. of the,
  Australia 41 F3
Rechytsa, *Belarus* ... 13 B16
Recife, *Brazil* 63 E12
Recklinghausen,
  Germany 11 C7
Reconquista, *Argentina* 64 B5
Recreo, *Argentina* ... 64 B3
Red →, *La., U.S.A.* .. 55 K9
Red →, *N. Dak., U.S.A.* 46 C10
Red Bay, *Canada* 49 B8
Red Bluff, *U.S.A.* 56 F2
Red Bluff L., *U.S.A.* .. 55 K3
Red Cliffs, *Australia* .. 43 E3
Red Cloud, *U.S.A.* ... 54 E5
Red Deer, *Canada* ... 50 C6
Red Deer →, *Alta.,
  Canada* 51 C7
Red Deer →, *Man.,
  Canada* 51 C8
Red Deer L., *Canada* . 51 C8
Red Indian L., *Canada* 49 C8
Red L., *Canada* 51 C10
Red Lake, *Canada* ... 51 C10
Red Lake Falls, *U.S.A.* 54 B6
Red Lake Road, *Canada* 51 C10
Red Lodge, *U.S.A.* ... 56 D9
Red Oak, *U.S.A.* 54 E7
Red Rock, *Canada* ... 48 C2
Red Rock, L., *U.S.A.* . 54 E8
Red Rocks Pt., *Australia* 41 F4
Red Sea, *Asia* 32 C2
Red Sucker L., *Canada* 48 B1
Red Tower Pass =
  Turnu Roşu, P.,
  Romania 13 F13
Red Wing, *U.S.A.* ... 54 C8
Redang, *Malaysia* ... 26 C2
Redange, *Lux.* 11 E5
Redcar, *U.K.* 8 C6
Redcar & Cleveland □,
  U.K. 8 C7
Redcliff, *Canada* 51 C6
Redcliffe, *Australia* .. 43 D5
Redcliffe, Mt., *Australia* 41 E3
Redding, *U.S.A.* 56 F2
Redditch, *U.K.* 9 E6
Redfield, *U.S.A.* 54 C5
Redmond, *U.S.A.* 56 D3
Redon, *France* 14 C2
Redonda, *Antigua* ... 61 C7
Redondela, *Spain* ... 15 A1
Redruth, *U.K.* 9 G2
Redvers, *Canada* 51 D8
Redwater, *Canada* ... 50 C6
Redwood City, *U.S.A.* 57 H2
Redwood Falls, *U.S.A.* 54 C7
Redwood National Park,
  U.S.A. 56 F1
Ree, L., *Ireland* 10 E3
Reed, L., *Canada* 51 C8
Reed City, *U.S.A.* 52 D3
Reedley, *U.S.A.* 57 H4
Reedsburg, *U.S.A.* ... 54 D9
Reedsport, *U.S.A.* ... 56 E1
Reefton, *N.Z.* 39 K3
Reese →, *U.S.A.* 56 F5
Refugio, *U.S.A.* 55 L6
Regensburg, *Germany* 12 D7
Réggio di Calábria, *Italy* 16 E6
Réggio nell'Emília, *Italy* 16 B4
Reghin, *Romania* 13 E13
Regina, *Canada* 51 C8
Regina Beach, *Canada* . 51 C8
Registro, *Brazil* 64 A7
Rehoboth, *Namibia* .. 37 J3
Rehovot, *Israel* 33 D3
Reichenbach, *Germany* 12 C7
Reid, *Australia* 41 F4
Reidsville, *U.S.A.* 53 G6
Reigate, *U.K.* 9 F7
Reims, *France* 14 B6
Reina Adelaida, Arch.,
  Chile 64 G2
Reindeer →, *Canada* . 51 B8
Reindeer I., *Canada* .. 51 C9
Reindeer L., *Canada* . 51 B8
Reinga, C., *N.Z.* 39 F4
Reinosa, *Spain* 15 A3
Reliance, *Canada* 51 A7
Remarkable, Mt.,
  Australia 43 E2
Rembang, *Indonesia* . 27 G14
Remedios, *Panama* .. 60 E3
Remeshk, *Iran* 31 E8
Remich, *Lux.* 11 E6
Remscheid, *Germany* . 11 C7
Remsdburg, *Germany* . 12 A5
Renfrew, *Canada* 48 C4
Rengat, *Indonesia* ... 26 E2
Reni, *Ukraine* 13 F15

Renmark, *Australia* .. 43 E3
Rennell Sd., *Canada* . 50 C2
Renner Springs,
  Australia 42 B1
Rennes, *France* 14 B3
Rennie L., *Canada* ... 51 A7
Reno, *U.S.A.* 56 G4
Reno →, *Italy* 16 B5
Rensselaer, *U.S.A.* .. 52 E2
Renton, *U.S.A.* 56 C2
Republic, *Mo., U.S.A.* 55 G8
Republic, *Wash., U.S.A.* 56 B4
Republican →, *U.S.A.* 54 F6
Repulse Bay, *Canada* . 47 B11
Requena, *Peru* 62 E4
Requena, *Spain* 15 C5
Reşadiye = Datça,
  Turkey 17 F12
Reserve, *U.S.A.* 57 K9
Resht = Rasht, *Iran* . 31 B6
Resistencia, *Argentina* 64 B5
Reşiţa, *Romania* 13 F11
Resolution I., *Canada* . 47 B13
Resolution I., *N.Z.* ... 39 L1
Reston, *Canada* 51 D8
Retalhuleu, *Guatemala* 60 D1
Retford, *U.K.* 8 D7
Réthímnon, *Greece* .. 17 G11
Réunion ■, *Ind. Oc.* . 3 F12
Reus, *Spain* 15 B6
Reutlingen, *Germany* . 12 D5
Reval = Tallinn, *Estonia* 7 G21
Revda, *Russia* 18 C10
Revelstoke, *Canada* .. 50 C5
Reventazón, *Peru* ... 62 E2
Revillagigedo, Is. de,
  Pac. Oc. 58 D2
Rewa, *India* 29 G12
Rewari, *India* 28 E10
Rexburg, *U.S.A.* 56 E8
Rey, *Iran* 31 C6
Rey, I. del, *Panama* . 60 E4
Rey Malabo, *Eq. Guin.* 36 D1
Reyðarfjörður, *Iceland* . 6 D6
Reykjahlið, *Iceland* ... 6 D5
Reykjanes, *Iceland* ... 6 D2
Reykjavík, *Iceland* ... 6 D3
Reynolds Ra., *Australia* 40 D5
Reynosa, *Mexico* 59 B5
Rēzekne, *Latvia* 7 H22
Rezvän, *Iran* 31 E8
Rhayader, *U.K.* 9 E4
Rhein →, *Europe* 11 C6
Rhein-Main-Donau-
  Kanal, *Germany* 12 D6
Rheine, *Germany* 12 B4
Rheinland-Pfalz □,
  Germany 12 C4
Rhin = Rhein →,
  Europe 11 C6
Rhine = Rhein →,
  Europe 11 C6
Rhineland-Palatinate =
  Rheinland-Pfalz □,
  Germany 12 C4
Rhinelander, *U.S.A.* . 54 C10
Rhir, Cap, *Morocco* .. 34 B4
Rhode Island □, *U.S.A.* 52 E10
Rhodes = Ródhos,
  Greece 17 F13
Rhodesia =
  Zimbabwe ■, *Africa* . 37 H5
Rhodope Mts. =
  Rhodopi Planina,
  Bulgaria 17 D11
Rhodopi Planina,
  Bulgaria 17 D11
Rhön, *Germany* 12 C5
Rhondda, *U.K.* 9 F4
Rhondda Cynon Taff □,
  U.K. 9 F4
Rhône →, *France* 14 E6
Rhum, *U.K.* 10 C3
Rhyl, *U.K.* 8 D4
Riachão, *Brazil* 63 E9
Riasi, *India* 28 C9
Riau □, *Indonesia* ... 26 D2
Riau, Kepulauan,
  Indonesia 26 D2
Riau Arch. = Riau,
  Kepulauan, *Indonesia* 26 D2
Ribadeo, *Spain* 15 A2
Ribas do Rio Pardo,
  Brazil 63 H8
Ribble →, *U.K.* 8 D5
Ribe, *Denmark* 7 J13
Ribeirão Prêto, *Brazil* . 63 H9
Riberalta, *Bolivia* 62 F5
Riccarton, *N.Z.* 39 K4
Rice Lake, *U.S.A.* ... 54 C9
Richards Bay, *S. Africa* 37 K6
Richardson →, *Canada* 51 B6
Richardson Lakes,
  U.S.A. 52 C10
Riche, C., *Australia* .. 41 F2
Richey, *U.S.A.* 54 B2
Richfield, *U.S.A.* 57 G8
Richibucto, *Canada* .. 49 C7
Richland, *Ga., U.S.A.* 53 J3
Richland, *Wash., U.S.A.* 56 C4
Richland Center, *U.S.A.* 54 D9
Richlands, *U.S.A.* ... 52 G5
Richmond, *Australia* . 42 C3

Richmond, *N.Z.* 39 J4
Richmond, *U.K.* 8 C6
Richmond, *Calif., U.S.A.* 56 H2
Richmond, *Ind., U.S.A.* 52 F3
Richmond, *Ky., U.S.A.* 52 G3
Richmond, *Mo., U.S.A.* 54 F8
Richmond, *Tex., U.S.A.* 55 L7
Richmond, *Utah, U.S.A.* 56 F8
Richmond, *Va., U.S.A.* 52 G7
Richmond Ra., *Australia* 43 D5
Richwood, *U.S.A.* ... 52 F5
Ridder = Leninogorsk,
  Kazakstan 20 D9
Ridgecrest, *U.S.A.* .. 57 J5
Ridgeland, *U.S.A.* ... 53 J5
Ridgetown, *Canada* .. 48 D3
Ridgway, *U.S.A.* 52 E6
Riding Mountain Nat.
  Park, *Canada* 51 C9
Ridley, Mt., *Australia* 41 F3
Ried, *Austria* 12 D7
Riesa, *Germany* 12 C7
Rieti, *Italy* 16 C5
Rifle, *U.S.A.* 56 G10
Riga, *Latvia* 7 H21
Riga, G. of, *Latvia* .. 7 H20
Rīgān, *Iran* 31 D8
Rigby, *U.S.A.* 56 E8
Rigestān, *Afghan.* ... 28 D4
Riggins, *U.S.A.* 56 D5
Rigolet, *Canada* 49 B8
Riihimäki, *Finland* ... 7 F21
Riiser-Larsen-halvøya,
  Antarctica 5 C4
Rijeka, *Croatia* 12 F8
Rijssen, *Neths.* 11 B6
Rikuzentakada, *Japan* . 22 E10
Riley, *U.S.A.* 56 E4
Rimah, Wadi ar →,
  Si. Arabia 30 E4
Rimbey, *Canada* 50 C6
Rímini, *Italy* 16 B5
Rimouski, *Canada* ... 49 C6
Rinca, *Indonesia* 27 F5
Rincón de Romos,
  Mexico 58 C4
Rinconada, *Argentina* . 62 H5
Ringkøbing, *Denmark* . 7 H13
Ringvassøy, *Norway* . 6 B18
Rinjani, *Indonesia* ... 26 F5
Rio Branco, *Brazil* ... 62 E5
Río Branco, *Uruguay* : 64 C6
Río Bravo del Norte →,
  Mexico 59 B5
Río Claro, *Brazil* 64 A6
Río Claro, *Trin. & Tob.* 61 D7
Río Colorado, *Argentina* 64 D4
Río Cuarto, *Argentina* . 64 C4
Rio de Janeiro, *Brazil* . 63 H10
Rio de Janeiro □, *Brazil* 63 H10
Rio do Sul, *Brazil* ... 64 B7
Río Gallegos, *Argentina* 64 G3
Rio Grande = Grande,
  Rio →, *U.S.A.* 55 N6
Río Grande, *Argentina* 64 G3
Rio Grande, *Brazil* ... 64 C6
Río Grande, *Mexico* . 58 C4
Río Grande, *Nic.* 60 D3
Rio Grande City, *U.S.A.* 55 M5
Rio Grande de
  Santiago →, *Mexico* 58 C3
Rio Grande do Norte □,
  Brazil 63 E11
Rio Grande do Sul □,
  Brazil 64 C6
Río Hato, *Panama* ... 60 E3
Río Lagartos, *Mexico* . 59 C7
Rio Largo, *Brazil* 63 E11
Rio Mulatos, *Bolivia* . 62 G5
Río Muni = Mbini □,
  Eq. Guin. 36 D2
Rio Negro, *Brazil* 64 B7
Rio Rancho, *U.S.A.* .. 57 J10
Rio Verde, *Brazil* 63 G8
Río Verde, *Mexico* ... 59 C5
Riobamba, *Ecuador* .. 62 D3
Riohacha, *Colombia* .. 62 A4
Riosucio, *Colombia* .. 62 B3
Riou L., *Canada* 51 B7
Ripley, *Tenn., U.S.A.* 55 H10
Ripley, *W. Va., U.S.A.* 52 F5
Ripon, *U.K.* 8 C6
Ripon, *U.S.A.* 52 D1
Rishā', W. ar →,
  Si. Arabia 30 E5
Rishiri-Tō, *Japan* 22 B10
Rishon le Ziyyon, *Israel* 33 D3
Rison, *U.S.A.* 55 J8
Risør, *Norway* 7 G13
Rita Blanca Cr. →,
  U.S.A. 55 H3
Ritzville, *U.S.A.* 56 C4
Riva del Garda, *Italy* . 16 B4
Rivadavia, *Chile* 64 B2
Rivas, *Nic.* 60 D2
Rivera, *Uruguay* 64 C5
River Cess, *Liberia* ... 34 G4
Riverhurst, *Canada* .. 51 C7
Rivers, *Canada* 51 C8
Rivers Inlet, *Canada* . 50 C3

Riverside, *U.S.A.* 57 K5
Riverton, *Australia* ... 43 E2
Riverton, *Canada* 51 C9
Riverton, *N.Z.* 39 M2
Riverton, *U.S.A.* 56 E9
Riviera di Levante, *Italy* 14 D8
Riviera di Ponente, *Italy* 14 D8
Rivière-au-Renard,
  Canada 49 C7
Rivière-du-Loup, *Canada* 49 C6
Rivière-Pentecôte,
  Canada 49 C6
Rivière-Pilote,
  Martinique 61 D7
Rivière St. Paul, *Canada* 49 B8
Rivne, *Ukraine* 13 C14
Rívoli, *Italy* 14 D7
Rivoli B., *Australia* ... 43 F3
Riyadh = Ar Riyāḍ,
  Si. Arabia 30 E5
Rize, *Turkey* 19 F7
Rizzuto, C., *Italy* 16 E7
Rjukan, *Norway* 7 G13
Road Town, *Virgin Is.* 61 C7
Roan Plateau, *U.S.A.* . 56 G9
Roanne, *France* 14 C6
Roanoke, *Ala., U.S.A.* 53 J3
Roanoke, *Va., U.S.A.* 52 G6
Roanoke →, *U.S.A.* . 53 H7
Roanoke I., *U.S.A.* .. 53 H8
Roanoke Rapids, *U.S.A.* 53 G7
Roatán, *Honduras* ... 60 C2
Robāt Sang, *Iran* 31 C8
Robbins I., *Australia* . 42 G4
Robe →, *Australia* ... 40 D2
Robe, *Australia* 43 F2
Robert Lee, *U.S.A.* .. 55 K4
Robertson I., *Antarctica* 5 C18
Robertson Ra., *Australia* 40 D3
Robertstown, *Australia* 43 E2
Roberval, *Canada* ... 49 C5
Robeson Chan.,
  Greenland 4 A4
Robinson, *U.S.A.* 52 F2
Robinson →, *Australia* 42 B2
Robinson Ra., *Australia* 41 E2
Robinvale, *Australia* .. 43 E3
Roblin, *Canada* 51 C8
Roboré, *Bolivia* 62 G7
Robson, *Canada* 50 D5
Robson, Mt., *Canada* . 50 C5
Robstown, *U.S.A.* ... 55 M6
Roca, C. da, *Portugal* . 15 C1
Rocas, I., *Brazil* 63 D12
Rocha, *Uruguay* 64 C6
Rochefort, *Belgium* .. 11 D5
Rochefort, *France* ... 14 D3
Rocher River, *Canada* 50 A6
Rochester, *U.K.* 9 F8
Rochester, *Ind., U.S.A.* 52 E2
Rochester, *Minn., U.S.A.* 54 C8
Rochester, *N.H., U.S.A.* 52 D10
Rochester, *N.Y., U.S.A.* 52 D7
Rock →, *Canada* 50 A3
Rock Falls, *U.S.A.* ... 54 E10
Rock Hill, *U.S.A.* 53 H5
Rock Island, *U.S.A.* .. 54 E9
Rock Rapids, *U.S.A.* . 54 D6
Rock Sound, *Bahamas* 60 B4
Rock Springs, *Mont.,
  U.S.A.* 56 C10
Rock Springs, *Wyo.,
  U.S.A.* 56 F9
Rock Valley, *U.S.A.* .. 54 D6
Rockdale, *U.S.A.* 55 K6
Rockefeller Plateau,
  Antarctica 5 E14
Rockford, *U.S.A.* 54 D10
Rockglen, *Canada* ... 51 D7
Rockhampton, *Australia* 42 C5
Rockingham, *Australia* 41 F2
Rockingham, *U.S.A.* . 53 H6
Rockingham B.,
  Australia 42 B4
Rocklake, *U.S.A.* 54 A5
Rockland, *Idaho, U.S.A.* 56 E7
Rockland, *Maine, U.S.A.* 53 C11
Rockland, *Mich., U.S.A.* 54 B10
Rockmart, *U.S.A.* ... 53 H3
Rockport, *Mo., U.S.A.* 54 E7
Rockport, *Tex., U.S.A.* 55 L6
Rocksprings, *U.S.A.* . 55 K4
Rockville, *U.S.A.* 52 F7
Rockwall, *U.S.A.* 55 J6
Rockwell City, *U.S.A.* 54 D7
Rockwood, *Maine,
  U.S.A.* 53 C11
Rockwood, *Tenn.,
  U.S.A.* 53 H3
Rocky Ford, *U.S.A.* .. 54 F3
Rocky Gully, *Australia* 41 F2
Rocky Harbour, *Canada* 49 C8
Rocky Island L., *Canada* 48 C3
Rocky Lane, *Canada* . 50 B5
Rocky Mount, *U.S.A.* 53 H7
Rocky Mountain House,
  Canada 50 C6
Rocky Mountain
  National Park, *U.S.A.* 56 F11
Rocky Mts., *N. Amer.* 56 G10
Rod, *Pakistan* 28 E3

Rødbyhavn, *Denmark* . 7 J14
Roddickton, *Canada* .. 49 B8
Rodez, *France* 14 D5
Ródhos, *Greece* 17 F13
Rodney, C., *N.Z.* 39 G5
Rodriguez, *Ind. Oc.* .. 3 E13
Roebourne, *Australia* . 40 D2
Roebuck B., *Australia* . 40 C3
Roermond, *Neths.* ... 11 D3
Roes Welcome Sd.,
  Canada 47 B11
Roeselare, *Belgium* .. 11 D3
Rogachev = Ragachow,
  Belarus 13 B16
Rogagua, L., *Bolivia* . 62 F5
Rogatyn, *Ukraine* ... 13 D13
Rogers, *U.S.A.* 55 G7
Rogers City, *U.S.A.* .. 52 C4
Rogersville, *Canada* .. 49 C6
Roggan, *Canada* 48 B4
Roggan L., *Canada* .. 48 B4
Rogoaguado, L., *Bolivia* 62 F5
Rogue →, *U.S.A.* 56 E1
Rohri, *Pakistan* 28 F6
Rohtak, *India* 28 E10
Roi Et, *Thailand* 26 A2
Roja, *Latvia* 7 H20
Rojo, C., *Mexico* 59 C5
Rokan →, *Indonesia* . 26 D2
Rokiškis, *Lithuania* .. 7 J21
Rolândia, *Brazil* 64 A6
Rolla, *U.S.A.* 55 G9
Rolleston, *Australia* .. 42 C4
Rollingstone, *Australia* 42 B4
Roma, *Australia* 43 D4
Roma, *Italy* 16 D5
Roma, *Sweden* 7 H18
Romain C., *U.S.A.* ... 53 J6
Romaine, *Canada* ... 49 B7
Romaine →, *Canada* . 49 B7
Roman, *Romania* 13 E14
Romang, *Indonesia* .. 27 F7
Români, *Egypt* 33 E1
Romania ■, *Europe* . 13 F12
Romano, Cayo, *Cuba* . 60 B4
Romanovka =
  Basarabeasca,
  Moldova 13 E15
Romans-sur-Isère,
  France 14 D6
Romblon, *Phil.* 27 B6
Rome = Roma, *Italy* . 16 D5
Rome, *Ga., U.S.A.* .. 53 H3
Rome, *N.Y., U.S.A.* .. 52 D8
Romney, *U.S.A.* 52 F6
Romney Marsh, *U.K.* . 9 F8
Rømø, *Denmark* 7 J13
Romorantin-Lanthenay,
  France 14 C4
Romsdalen, *Norway* . 7 E12
Romsey, *U.K.* 9 G6
Ronan, *U.S.A.* 56 C6
Roncador, Cayos,
  Caribbean 60 D3
Roncador, Serra do,
  Brazil 63 F8
Ronda, *Spain* 15 D3
Rondane, *Norway* ... 7 F13
Rondônia □, *Brazil* .. 62 F6
Rondonópolis, *Brazil* . 63 G8
Ronge, L. la, *Canada* . 51 B7
Rønne, *Denmark* 7 J16
Ronne Ice Shelf,
  Antarctica 5 D18
Ronsard, C., *Australia* 41 D1
Ronse, *Belgium* 11 D3
Roof Butte, *U.S.A.* ... 57 H9
Roorkee, *India* 28 E10
Roosendaal, *Neths.* .. 11 C4
Roosevelt, *U.S.A.* ... 56 F8
Roosevelt →, *Brazil* . 62 E6
Roosevelt, Mt., *Canada* 50 B3
Roosevelt I., *Antarctica* 5 D12
Roper →, *Australia* .. 42 A2
Roper Bar, *Australia* . 42 A1
Roquetas de Mar, *Spain* 15 D4
Roraima □, *Brazil* ... 62 C6
Roraima, Mt., *Venezuela* 62 B6
Røros, *Norway* 7 E14
Rosa, L., *Bahamas* .. 61 B5
Rosa, Monte, *Europe* . 11 D7
Rosalia, *U.S.A.* 56 C5
Rosario, *Argentina* ... 64 C4
Rosário, *Brazil* 63 D10
Rosario, *Baja Calif.,
  Mexico* 58 B1
Rosario, *Sinaloa,
  Mexico* 58 C3
Rosario, *Paraguay* ... 64 A5
Rosario de la Frontera,
  Argentina 64 B4
Rosário do Sul, *Brazil* 64 C6
Roscommon, *Ireland* . 10 E2
Roscommon □, *Ireland* 10 E2
Rose →, *Australia* ... 42 A2
Rose Blanche, *Canada* 49 C8
Rose Pt., *Canada* 50 C2
Rose Valley, *Canada* . 51 C8
Roseau, *Domin.* 61 C7
Roseau, *U.S.A.* 54 A7
Rosebery, *Australia* .. 42 G4
Rosebud, *S. Dak., U.S.A.* 54 D4
Rosebud, *Tex., U.S.A.* 55 K6
Roseburg, *U.S.A.* 56 E2

Rosedale, U.S.A. 55 J9
Rosemary, Canada 50 C6
Rosenberg, U.S.A. 55 L7
Rosenheim, Germany . . 12 E7
Roses, G. de, Spain . . . 15 A7
Rosetown, Canada 51 C7
Roseville, U.S.A. 56 G3
Rosewood, Australia . . . 43 D5
Roshkhvār, Iran 31 C8
Rosignano Maríttimo,
Italy 16 C4
Rosignol, Guyana 62 B7
Roșiori de Vede,
Romania 13 F13
Roskilde, Denmark 7 J15
Roslavl, Russia 18 D5
Ross, Australia 42 G4
Ross, N.Z. 39 K3
Ross I., Antarctica 5 D11
Ross Ice Shelf,
Antarctica 5 E12
Ross L., U.S.A. 56 B3
Ross-on-Wye, U.K. 9 F5
Ross River, Australia . . 42 C1
Ross River, Canada . . . 50 A2
Ross Sea, Antarctica . . 5 D11
Rossall Pt., U.K. 8 D4
Rossano, Italy 16 E7
Rossburn, Canada 51 C8
Rossignol, L., Canada . . 48 B5
Rossignol Res., Canada 49 D6
Rossland, Canada 50 D5
Rosslare, Ireland 10 E3
Rosso, Mauritania 34 E2
Rossosh, Russia 19 E6
Røssvatnet, Norway . . . 6 D16
Røst, Norway 6 C15
Rosthern, Canada 51 C7
Rostock, Germany 12 A7
Rostov, Don, Russia . . . 19 E6
Rostov, Yaroslavl,
Russia 18 C6
Roswell, Ga., U.S.A. . . . 53 H3
Roswell, N. Mex., U.S.A. 55 J2
Rotan, U.S.A. 55 J4
Rother →, U.K. 9 G8
Rotherham, U.K. 8 D6
Rothesay, Canada 49 C6
Roti, Indonesia 27 F6
Roto, Australia 43 E4
Rotondo Mte., France . . 14 E8
Rotorua, L., N.Z. 39 J4
Rotorua, N.Z. 39 H6
Rotorua, L., N.Z. 39 H6
Rotterdam, Neths. 11 C4
Rottnest I., Australia . . 41 F2
Rottumeroog, Neths. . . 11 A6
Rottweil, Germany 12 D5
Rotuma, Fiji 38 C10
Roubaix, France 14 A5
Rouen, France 14 B4
Rouleau, Canada 51 C8
Round Mountain, U.S.A. 56 G5
Round Mt., Australia . . 43 E5
Round Rock, U.S.A. . . . 55 K6
Roundup, U.S.A. 56 C9
Roussillon, France 14 E5
Rouyn-Noranda, Canada 48 C4
Rovaniemi, Finland . . . 6 C21
Rovereto, Italy 16 B4
Rovigo, Italy 16 B4
Rovinj, Croatia 12 F7
Rovno = Rivne, Ukraine 13 C14
Rovuma = Ruvuma →,
Tanzania 36 G8
Row'ān, Iran 31 C6
Rowena, Australia 43 D4
Rowley Shoals,
Australia 40 C2
Roxas, Phil. 27 B6
Roxboro, U.S.A. 53 G6
Roxburgh, N.Z. 39 L2
Roy, Mont., U.S.A. 56 C9
Roy, N. Mex., U.S.A. . . . 55 H2
Roy, Utah, U.S.A. 56 F7
Royal Leamington Spa,
U.K. 9 E6
Royal Tunbridge Wells,
U.K. 9 F8
Royan, France 14 D3
Royston, U.K. 9 E7
Rozdilna, Ukraine 13 E16
Rozhyshche, Ukraine . . 13 C13
Rtishchevo, Russia . . . 18 C7
Ruahine Ra., N.Z. 39 H6
Ruapehu, N.Z. 39 H5
Ruapuke I., N.Z. 39 M2
Ruâq, W. →, Egypt . . . 33 F2
Rub' al Khālī, Si. Arabia 32 D4
Rubio, Venezuela 62 B4
Rubtsovsk, Russia 20 D9
Ruby L., U.S.A. 56 F6
Ruby Mts., U.S.A. 56 F6
Rubyvale, Australia . . . 42 C4
Rüd Sar, Iran 31 B6
Rudall, Australia 43 E2
Rudall →, Australia . . . 40 D3
Rudnyy, Kazakstan . . . 20 D7
Rudolfa, Ostrov, Russia 20 A6
Rudyard, U.S.A. 52 B3
Rufiji →, Tanzania 36 F7
Rufino, Argentina 64 C4
Rugby, U.K. 9 E6
Rugby, U.S.A. 54 A5

Rügen, Germany 12 A7
Ruhnu, Estonia 7 H20
Ruhr →, Germany 12 C4
Ruidoso, U.S.A. 57 K11
Rujm Tal'at al Jamā'ah,
Jordan 33 E4
Ruki →, Dem. Rep. of
the Congo 36 E3
Rukwa, L., Tanzania . . . 36 F6
Rulhieres, C., Australia 40 B4
Rum = Rhum, U.K. . . . 10 C3
Rum Cay, Bahamas . . . 61 B5
Rum Jungle, Australia . 40 B5
Rumāḥ, Si. Arabia 30 E5
Rumania = Romania ■,
Europe 13 F12
Rumaylah, Iraq 30 D5
Rumbêk, Sudan 35 G11
Rumford, U.S.A. 53 C10
Rumia, Poland 13 A10
Rumoi, Japan 22 C10
Runanga, N.Z. 39 K3
Runaway, C., N.Z. 39 G6
Runcorn, U.K. 8 D5
Rundu, Namibia 37 H3
Rungwe, Mt., Tanzania 36 F6
Runton Ra., Australia . . 40 D3
Ruoqiang, China 24 C3
Rupa, India 29 F18
Rupat, Indonesia 26 D2
Rupert, U.S.A. 56 E7
Rupert →, Canada 48 B4
Rupert B., Canada 48 B4
Rupert House =
Waskaganish, Canada 48 B4
Rurrenabaque, Bolivia . 62 F5
Ruschuk = Ruse,
Bulgaria 17 C12
Ruse, Bulgaria 17 C12
Rushden, U.K. 9 E7
Rushmore, Mt., U.S.A. . 54 D3
Rushville, Ill., U.S.A. . . 54 E9
Rushville, Ind., U.S.A. . 52 F3
Rushville, Nebr., U.S.A. 54 D3
Russas, Brazil 63 D11
Russell, Canada 51 C8
Russell, U.S.A. 54 F5
Russell L., Man., Canada 51 B8
Russell L., N.W.T.,
Canada 50 A5
Russellkonda, India . . . 29 K14
Russellville, Ala., U.S.A. 53 H2
Russellville, Ark., U.S.A. 55 H8
Russellville, Ky., U.S.A. 53 G2
Russia ■, Eurasia 21 C11
Russkoye Ustie, Russia 4 B15
Rustavi, Georgia 19 F8
Rustenburg, S. Africa . . 37 K5
Ruston, U.S.A. 55 J8
Ruteng, Indonesia 27 F6
Rutland, U.S.A. 52 D9
Rutland □, U.K. 9 E7
Rutland Water, U.K. . . . 9 E7
Rutledge →, Canada . . 51 A6
Rutledge L., Canada . . 51 A6
Ruvuma →, Tanzania . . 36 G8
Ruwais, U.A.E. 31 E7
Ruwenzori, Africa 36 D5
Ružomberok,
Slovak Rep. 13 D10
Rwanda ■, Africa 36 E5
Ryazan, Russia 18 D6
Ryazhsk, Russia 18 D7
Rybache = Rybachye,
Kazakstan 20 E9
Rybachiy Poluostrov,
Russia 18 A5
Rybachye, Kazakstan . . 20 E9
Rybinsk, Russia 18 C6
Rybinskoye Vdkhr.,
Russia 18 C6
Rybnitsa = Râbniţa,
Moldova 13 E15
Rycroft, Canada 50 B5
Ryde, U.K. 9 G6
Rye, U.K. 9 G8
Rye →, U.K. 8 C7
Rye Bay, U.K. 9 G8
Rye Patch Reservoir,
U.S.A. 56 F4
Ryegate, U.S.A. 56 C9
Ryley, Canada 50 C6
Rylstone, Australia . . . 43 E4
Rypin, Poland 13 B10
Ryōtsu, Japan 22 E9
Ryūgasaki, Japan 23 G10
Ryūkyū Is. = Ryūkyū-
rettō, Japan 23 M3
Ryūkyū-rettō, Japan . . 23 M3
Rzeszów, Poland 13 C11
Rzhev, Russia 18 C5

Sa Dec, Vietnam 26 B3
Sa'ādatābād, Fārs, Iran 31 D7
Sa'ādatābād,
Hormozgān, Iran . . . 31 D7
Sa'ādatābād, Kermān,
Iran 31 D7
Saale →, Germany . . . 12 C6
Saalfeld, Germany . . . 12 C6
Saar →, Europe 14 B7
Saarbrücken, Germany 12 D4
Saaremaa, Estonia . . . 7 G20

Saarijärvi, Finland . . . 7 E21
Saariselkä, Finland . . . 6 B23
Sab 'Ābar, Syria 30 C3
Šabac, Serbia, Yug. . . . 17 B8
Sabadell, Spain 15 B7
Sabah □, Malaysia . . . 26 C5
Sabalān, Kūhhā-ye, Iran 30 B5
Sabalana, Kepulauan,
Indonesia 27 F5
Sábana de la Mar,
Dom. Rep. 61 C6
Sábanalarga, Colombia 62 A4
Sabang, Indonesia . . . 26 C1
Sabará, Brazil 63 G10
Saberania, Indonesia . . 27 E9
Sabhah, Libya 35 C8
Sabinal, Mexico 58 A3
Sabinal, U.S.A. 55 L5
Sabinas, Mexico 58 B4
Sabinas →, Mexico . . . 58 B4
Sabinas Hidalgo,
Mexico 58 B4
Sabine →, U.S.A. 55 L8
Sabine L., U.S.A. 55 L8
Sabine Pass, U.S.A. . . . 55 L8
Sabkhet el Bardawîl,
Egypt 33 D2
Sablayan, Phil. 27 B6
Sable, Canada 49 A6
Sable, C., Canada 49 D6
Sable, C., U.S.A. 60 A3
Sable I., Canada 49 D8
Sabrina Coast,
Antarctica 5 C9
Sabulubbek, Indonesia 26 E1
Sabzevār, Iran 31 B8
Sabzvārān, Iran 31 D8
Sac City, U.S.A. 54 D7
Sachigo →, Canada . . . 48 A2
Sachigo, L., Canada . . 48 B1
Sachsen □, Germany . . 12 C7
Sachsen-Anhalt □,
Germany 12 C7
Sackville, Canada 49 C7
Saco, Maine, U.S.A. . . . 53 D10
Saco, Mont., U.S.A. . . . 56 B10
Sacramento, U.S.A. . . . 56 G3
Sacramento →, U.S.A. . 56 G3
Sacramento Mts., U.S.A. 57 K11
Sada-Misaki, Japan . . . 23 H6
Sadd el Aali, Egypt . . . 35 D12
Sado, Japan 22 F9
Sado □, Japan 22 F9
Sadon, Burma 29 G20
Sæby, Denmark 7 H14
Şafājah, Si. Arabia . . . 30 E3
Säffle, Sweden 7 G15
Safford, U.S.A. 57 K9
Saffron Walden, U.K. . . 9 E8
Safi, Morocco 34 B4
Şafiābād, Iran 31 B8
Safid Dasht, Iran 31 C6
Safid Kūh, Afghan. . . . 28 B3
Safid Rūd →, Iran 31 B6
Safwān, Iraq 30 D5
Saga, Japan 23 H5
Saga □, Japan 23 H5
Sagae, Japan 22 E10
Sagar, India 28 M9
Saginaw, U.S.A. 52 D4
Saginaw →, U.S.A. . . . 52 D4
Saginaw B., U.S.A. . . . 52 D4
Saglouc = Salluit,
Canada 47 B12
Sagua la Grande, Cuba 60 B3
Saguache, U.S.A. 57 G10
Saguaro Nat. Park,
U.S.A. 57 K8
Saguenay →, Canada . 49 C5
Sagunt, Spain 15 C5
Sagunto = Sagunt,
Spain 15 C5
Sahagún, Spain 15 A3
Saham al Jawlān, Syria 33 C4
Sahand, Kūh-e, Iran . . 30 B5
Sahara, Africa 34 D6
Saharan Atlas =
Saharien, Atlas,
Algeria 34 B6
Saharanpur, India 28 E10
Saharien, Atlas, Algeria 34 B6
Sahel, Africa 34 E5
Sāḥiliyah, Iran 30 C4
Sahiwal, Pakistan 28 D8
Şahneh, Iran 30 C5
Sahuaripa, Mexico . . . 58 B3
Sahuarita, U.S.A. 57 L8
Sahuayo, Mexico 58 C4
Sa'id Bundās, Sudan . . 35 G10
Sa'īdābād, Kermān, Iran 31 D7
Sa'īdābād, Semnān, Iran 31 B7
Sa'īdīyeh, Iran 31 B6
Saidpur, Bangla. 29 G16
Saidu, Pakistan 28 B8
Saigon = Thanh Pho Ho
Chi Minh, Vietnam . . 26 B3
Saijō, Japan 23 H6
Saikhoa Ghat, India . . 29 F19
Saiki, Japan 23 H5
Sailolof, Indonesia . . . 27 E8
Saimaa, Finland 7 F23
St. Abb's Head, U.K. . . 10 F6
St. Alban's, Canada . . 49 C8

St. Albans, U.K. 9 F7
St. Albans, Vt., U.S.A. . 52 C9
St. Albans, W. Va.,
U.S.A. 52 F5
St. Alban's Head, U.K. . 9 G5
St. Albert, Canada . . . 50 C6
St. Andrew's, Canada . 49 C8
St. Andrews, U.K. 10 C5
St. Ann B., Canada . . . 49 C7
St. Ann's Bay, Jamaica 60 C4
St. Anthony, Canada . . 49 B8
St. Anthony, U.S.A. . . . 56 E8
St. Antoine, Canada . . 49 C7
St. Arnaud, Australia . . 43 F3
St-Augustin →,
Canada 49 B8
St-Augustin-Saguenay,
Canada 49 B8
St. Augustine, U.S.A. . . 53 L5
St. Austell, U.K. 9 G3
St. Barbe, Canada 49 B8
St-Barthélemy,
W. Indies 61 C7
St. Bees Hd., U.K. 8 C4
St. Bride's, Canada . . . 49 C9
St. Brides B., U.K. 9 F2
St-Brieuc, France 14 B2
St. Catharines, Canada 48 D4
St. Catherines I., U.S.A. 53 K5
St. Catherine's Pt., U.K. 9 G6
St-Chamond, France . . 14 D6
St. Charles, Ill., U.S.A. . 52 E1
St. Charles, Mo., U.S.A. 54 F9
St. Charles, Va., U.S.A. 52 F7
St. Christopher-Nevis =
St. Kitts & Nevis ■,
W. Indies 61 C7
St. Clair, L., Canada . . 48 D3
St. Claude, Canada . . . 51 D9
St. Cloud, Fla., U.S.A. . 53 L5
St. Cloud, Minn., U.S.A. 54 C7
St. Cricq, C., Australia . 41 E1
St. Croix, Virgin Is. . . . 61 C7
St. Croix →, U.S.A. . . . 54 C8
St. Croix Falls, U.S.A. . 54 C8
St. David's, Canada . . . 49 C8
St. David's, U.K. 9 F2
St. David's Head, U.K. . 9 F2
St-Denis, France 14 B5
St-Dizier, France 14 B6
St. Elias, Mt., U.S.A. . . 46 B5
St. Elias Mts., Canada . 50 A1
St. Elias Mts., U.S.A. . . 46 C6
St-Étienne, France . . . 14 D6
St. Eustatius, W. Indies 61 C7
St-Félicien, Canada . . . 48 C5
St-Flour, France 14 D5
St. Francis, U.S.A. 54 F4
St. Francis →, U.S.A. . . 55 H9
St. Francisville, U.S.A. . 55 K9
St-Gabriel, Canada . . . 48 C5
St. Gallen = Sankt
Gallen, Switz. 14 C8
St-Gaudens, France . . 14 E4
St. George, Australia . . 43 D4
St. George, Canada . . . 49 C6
St. George, S.C., U.S.A. 53 J5
St. George, Utah, U.S.A. 57 H7
St. George, C., Canada 49 C8
St. George, C., U.S.A. . 53 L3
St. George Ra., Australia 40 C4
St. George's, Canada . . 49 C8
St-Georges, Canada . . 49 C5
St. George's, Grenada . 62 A6
St. George's B., Canada 49 C8
St. Georges Basin,
N.S.W., Australia . . . 43 F5
St. Georges Basin,
W. Austral., Australia 40 C4
St. George's Channel,
Europe 10 F3
St. Georges Hd.,
Australia 43 F5
St. Gotthard, P. del = San
Gottardo, P. del,
Switz. 14 C8
St. Helena ■, Atl. Oc. . . 2 E9
St. Helena B., S. Africa 37 L3
St. Helens, Australia . . 42 G4
St. Helens, U.K. 8 D5
St. Helens, U.S.A. 56 D2
St. Helens, Mt., U.S.A. . 56 C2
St. Helier, U.K. 9 H5
St-Hubert, Belgium . . . 11 D5
St-Hyacinthe, Canada . 48 C5
St. Ignace, U.S.A. 52 C3
St. Ignace I., Canada . . 48 C2
St. Ignatius, U.S.A. . . . 56 C6
St. Ives, U.K. 9 G2
St. James, U.S.A. 54 D7
St-Jean →, Canada . . . 49 B7
St-Jean, L., Canada . . . 49 C5
St-Jean-Port-Joli,
Canada 49 C5
St-Jean-sur-Richelieu,
Canada 48 C5
St-Jérôme, Canada . . . 48 C5
St. John, U.S.A. 55 G5
St. John →, U.S.A. . . . 53 C12
St. John, C., Canada . . 49 C8
St. John's, Antigua . . . 61 C7
St. John's, Canada . . . 49 C9

St. Johns, Ariz., U.S.A. 57 J9
St. Johns, Mich., U.S.A. 52 D3
St. Johns →, U.S.A. . . 53 K5
St. Johnsbury, U.S.A. . . 52 C9
St. Joseph, La., U.S.A. . 55 K9
St. Joseph, Mo., U.S.A. 54 F7
St. Joseph →, U.S.A. . . 52 D2
St. Joseph, I., Canada . 48 C3
St. Joseph, L., Canada . 48 B1
St-Jovite, Canada 48 C5
St. Kilda, U.K. 10 C2
St. Kitts & Nevis ■,
W. Indies 61 C7
St. Laurent, Canada . . 51 C9
St. Lawrence, Australia 42 C4
St. Lawrence, Canada . 49 C8
St. Lawrence →,
Canada 49 C6
St. Lawrence, Gulf of,
Canada 49 C7
St. Lawrence I., U.S.A. . 46 C6
St. Leonard, Canada . . 49 C6
St-Léonard, Canada . . 49 B8
St-Lô, France 14 B3
St. Louis, Senegal 34 E2
St. Louis, U.S.A. 54 F9
St. Louis →, U.S.A. . . . 54 B8
St. Lucia ■, W. Indies . 61 D7
St. Lucia Channel,
W. Indies 61 D7
St. Maarten, W. Indies . 61 C7
St-Malo, France 14 B2
St-Marc, Haiti 61 C5
St. Maries, U.S.A. 56 C5
St-Martin, W. Indies . . 61 C7
St. Martin, L., Canada . 51 C9
St. Mary Pk., Australia 43 E2
St. Marys, Australia . . 42 G4
St. Marys, U.K. 9 H1
St. Marys, Ga., U.S.A. . 53 K5
St. Marys, Pa., U.S.A. . 52 E6
St. Mary's, C., Canada . 49 C9
St. Mary's B., Canada . 49 C9
St. Marys Bay, Canada 49 D6
St-Mathieu, Pte., France 14 B1
St. Matthew I., U.S.A. . 46 B2
St. Matthews, I. =
Zadetkyi Kyun, Burma 26 C1
St-Maurice →, Canada 48 C5
St-Nazaire, France . . . 14 C2
St. Neots, U.K. 9 E7
St-Niklaas, Belgium . . 11 C4
St-Omer, France 14 A5
St-Pamphile, Canada . . 49 C6
St. Pascal, Canada . . . 49 C6
St. Paul, Canada 50 C6
St. Paul, Minn., U.S.A. . 54 C8
St. Paul, Nebr., U.S.A. . 54 E5
St-Paul →, Canada . . . 49 B8
St. Paul, I., Ind. Oc. . . 3 F13
St. Paul I., Canada . . . 49 C7
St. Peter, U.S.A. 54 C8
St. Peter Port, U.K. . . . 9 H5
St. Peters, N.S., Canada 49 C7
St. Peters, P.E.I., Canada 49 C7
St. Petersburg = Sankt-
Peterburg, Russia . . 18 C5
St. Petersburg, U.S.A. . 53 M4
St-Pierre, St- P. & M. . . 49 C8
St-Pierre et Miquelon □,
St- P. & M. 49 C8
St. Quentin, Canada . . 49 C6
St-Quentin, France . . . 14 B5
St. Regis, U.S.A. 56 C6
St-Siméon, Canada . . . 49 C6
St. Simons I., U.S.A. . . 53 K5
St. Simons Island,
U.S.A. 53 K5
St. Stephen, Canada . . 49 C6
St. Thomas, Canada . . 48 D3
St. Thomas I., Virgin Is. 61 C7
St-Tite, Canada 48 C5
St-Tropez, France 14 E7
St. Troud = St. Truiden,
Belgium 11 D5
St. Truiden, Belgium . . 11 D5
St. Vincent, G., Australia 43 F2
St. Vincent & the
Grenadines ■,
W. Indies 61 D7
St. Vincent Passage,
W. Indies 61 D7
St-Vith, Belgium 11 D6
St. Walburg, Canada . . 51 C7
Ste-Agathe-des-Monts,
Canada 48 C5
Ste-Anne, L., Canada . 49 B6
Ste-Anne-des-Monts,
Canada 49 C6
Ste. Genevieve, U.S.A. 54 G9
Ste-Marguerite →,
Canada 49 B6
Ste-Marie, Martinique . 61 D7
Ste-Marie de la
Madeleine, Canada . 49 C5
Ste-Rose, Guadeloupe . 61 C7
Ste. Rose du Lac,
Canada 51 C9
Saintes, France 14 D3
Saintes, I. des,
Guadeloupe 61 C7
Saintonge, France . . . 14 D3
Saipan, Pac. Oc. 44 F6

St. Johns, Ariz., U.S.A. 57 J9
Sairang, India 29 H18
Saitama □, Japan 23 F9
Sajama, Bolivia 62 G5
Sajószentpéter, Hungary 13 D11
Sakai, Japan 23 G7
Sakaide, Japan 23 G6
Sakaiminato, Japan . . . 23 G6
Sakākah, Si. Arabia . . . 30 D4
Sakakawea, L., U.S.A. . 54 B4
Sakami →, Canada . . . 48 B4
Sakami, L., Canada . . . 48 B4
Sakarya, Turkey 19 F5
Sakashima-Guntō,
Japan 23 M2
Sakata, Japan 22 E9
Sakha □, Russia 21 C13
Sakhalin, Russia 21 D15
Sakhalinskiy Zaliv,
Russia 21 D15
Šakiai, Lithuania 7 J20
Sakon Nakhon, Thailand 26 A2
Sakuma, Japan 23 G8
Sakurai, Japan 23 G7
Sala, Sweden 7 G17
Sala Consilina, Italy . . 16 D6
Sala-y-Gómez, Pac. Oc. 45 K17
Salaberry-de-Valleyfield,
Canada 48 C5
Saladillo, Argentina . . 64 D5
Salado →,
Buenos Aires,
Argentina 64 D5
Salado →, La Pampa,
Argentina 64 D3
Salado →, Santa Fe,
Argentina 64 C4
Salado →, Mexico . . . 55 M5
Salaga, Ghana 34 G5
Şalāh, Syria 33 C5
Salālah, Oman 32 D5
Salamanca, Chile 64 C2
Salamanca, Spain 15 B3
Salamanca, U.S.A. . . . 52 D6
Salāmatābād, Iran . . . 30 C5
Salamís, Greece 17 F10
Salar de Uyuni, Bolivia 62 H5
Salatiga, Indonesia . . . 27 G14
Salavat, Russia 18 D10
Salaverry, Peru 62 E3
Salawati, Indonesia . . 27 E8
Salayar, Indonesia . . . 27 F6
Salcombe, U.K. 9 G4
Saldanha, S. Africa . . . 37 L3
Saldus, Latvia 7 H20
Sale, Australia 43 F4
Salé, Morocco 34 B4
Sale, U.K. 8 D5
Salekhard, Russia 20 C7
Salem, India 28 P11
Salem, Ill., U.S.A. 52 F1
Salem, Ind., U.S.A. . . . 52 F2
Salem, Mass., U.S.A. . . 52 D10
Salem, Mo., U.S.A. . . . 55 G9
Salem, N.J., U.S.A. . . . 52 F8
Salem, Ohio, U.S.A. . . 52 E5
Salem, Oreg., U.S.A. . . 56 D2
Salem, S. Dak., U.S.A. 54 D6
Salem, Va., U.S.A. 52 G5
Salerno, Italy 16 D6
Salford, U.K. 8 D5
Salgótarján, Hungary . 13 D10
Salgueiro, Brazil 63 E11
Salibabu, Indonesia . . 27 D7
Salihli, Turkey 17 E13
Salihorsk, Belarus . . . 13 B14
Salima, Malawi 37 G6
Salina, Italy 16 E6
Salina, Kans., U.S.A. . . 54 F6
Salina, Utah, U.S.A. . . 57 G8
Salina Cruz, Mexico . . 59 D5
Salinas, Brazil 63 G10
Salinas, Ecuador 62 D2
Salinas, U.S.A. 57 H3
Salinas →, Guatemala 59 D6
Salinas →, U.S.A. 57 H3
Salinas, B. de, Nic. . . . 60 D2
Salinas de Hidalgo,
Mexico 58 C4
Salinas Grandes,
Argentina 64 C4
Saline →, Ark., U.S.A. 55 J8
Saline →, Kans.,
U.S.A. 54 F6
Salinópolis, Brazil 63 D9
Salisbury = Harare,
Zimbabwe 37 H6
Salisbury, U.K. 9 F6
Salisbury, Md., U.S.A. . 52 F8
Salisbury, N.C., U.S.A. 53 H5
Salisbury I., Canada . . 47 B12
Salisbury Plain, U.K. . . 9 F6
Şalkhad, Syria 33 C5
Salla, Finland 6 C23
Salliq, Canada 47 B11
Sallisaw, U.S.A. 55 H7
Salluit, Canada 47 B12
Salmās, Iran 30 B5
Salmo, Canada 50 D5
Salmon, U.S.A. 56 D7
Salmon →, Canada . . . 50 C4
Salmon →, U.S.A. 56 D5
Salmon Arm, Canada . . 50 C5
Salmon Gums, Australia 41 F3
Salmon River Mts.,
U.S.A. 56 D6

Salo, *Finland* 7 F20
Salome, *U.S.A.* 57 K7
Salon-de-Provence,
France 14 E6
Salonica = Thessaloníki,
Greece 17 D10
Salonta, *Romania* 13 E11
Salpausselkä, *Finland* . 7 F22
Salsk, *Russia* 19 E7
Salso →, *Italy* 16 F5
Salt →, *Canada* 50 B6
Salt →, *U.S.A.* 57 K7
Salt Lake City, *U.S.A.* . 56 F8
Salta, *Argentina* 64 A3
Saltash, *U.K.* 9 G3
Saltburn by the Sea,
U.K. 8 C7
Saltfjellet, *Norway* . . 6 C16
Saltfjorden, *Norway* . . 6 C16
Saltillo, *Mexico* 58 B4
Salto →, *Italy* 16 C5
Salto del Guairá,
Paraguay 64 A6
Salton Sea, *U.S.A.* . . . 57 K6
Saluda →, *U.S.A.* . . . 53 J5
Salûm, *Egypt* 35 B11
Salur, *India* 29 K13
Salvador, *Brazil* 63 F11
Salvador, *Canada* . . . 51 C7
Salvador, L., *U.S.A.* . . 55 L9
Salween →, *Burma* . . 29 L20
Salyan, *Azerbaijan* . . 19 G8
Salzach →, *Austria* . . 12 D7
Salzburg, *Austria* . . . 12 E7
Salzgitter, *Germany* . . 12 B6
Salzwedel, *Germany* . . 12 B6
Sam Rayburn Reservoir,
U.S.A. 55 K7
Sama de Langreo =
Langreo, *Spain* . . . 15 A3
Samagaltay, *Russia* . . 21 D10
Samales Group, *Phil.* . . 27 C6
Samaná □, *Dom. Rep.* . 61 C6
Samana Cay, *Bahamas* 61 B5
Samani, *Japan* 22 C11
Samar, *Phil.* 27 B7
Samara, *Russia* 18 D9
Samaria = Shōmrōn,
West Bank 33 C4
Samarinda, *Indonesia* . 26 E5
Samarkand =
Samarqand,
Uzbekistan 20 F7
Samarqand, *Uzbekistan* 20 F7
Sāmarrā, *Iraq* 30 C4
Sambalpur, *India* . . . 29 J14
Sambar, Tanjung,
Indonesia 26 E4
Sambas, *Indonesia* . . 26 D3
Sambhal, *India* 28 E11
Sambhar, *India* 28 F9
Sambiase, *Italy* 16 E7
Sambir, *Ukraine* . . . 13 D12
Samnah, *Si. Arabia* . . 30 E3
Samoa ■, *Pac. Oc.* . . 39 B13
Samokov, *Bulgaria* . . 17 C10
Sámos, *Greece* 17 F12
Samothráki = Mathráki,
Greece 17 E8
Samothráki, *Greece* . . 17 D11
Sampang, *Indonesia* . . 27 G15
Sampit, *Indonesia* . . . 26 E4
Sampit, Teluk, *Indonesia* 26 E4
Samsø, *Denmark* . . . 7 J14
Samsun, *Turkey* 19 F6
Samui, Ko, *Thailand* . . 26 C2
Samut Prakan, *Thailand* 26 B2
Samut Songkhram →,
Thailand 26 B1
San, *Mali* 34 F5
San →, *Cambodia* . . 26 B3
San →, *Poland* 13 C11
San Agustin, C., *Phil.* . 27 C7
San Ambrosio, *Pac. Oc.* 45 K20
San Andreas, *U.S.A.* . 56 G3
San Andrés, I. de,
Caribbean 60 D3
San Andres Mts., *U.S.A.* 57 K10
San Andrés Tuxtla,
Mexico 59 D5
San Angelo, *U.S.A.* . . 55 K4
San Antonio, *Belize* . . 59 D7
San Antonio, *Chile* . . 64 C2
San Antonio, N. Mex.,
U.S.A. 57 K10
San Antonio, Tex.,
U.S.A. 55 L5
San Antonio →, *U.S.A.* 55 L6
San Antonio, C.,
Argentina 64 D5
San Antonio, C., *Cuba* . 60 B3
San Antonio de los
Baños, *Cuba* 60 B3
San Antonio de los
Cobres, *Argentina* . . 64 A3
San Antonio Oeste,
Argentina 64 E4
San Augustine, *U.S.A.* . 55 K7
San Benedetto del
Tronto, *Italy* 16 C5
San Benedicto, I.,
Mexico 58 D2
San Benito, *U.S.A.* . . . 55 M6
San Bernardino, *U.S.A.* 57 J5

San Bernardino Str.,
Phil. 27 B6
San Bernardo, *Chile* . . 64 C2
San Bernardo, I. de,
Colombia 62 B3
San Blas, *Mexico* . . . 58 B3
San Blas, Arch. de,
Panama 60 E4
San Blas, C., *U.S.A.* . . 53 L3
San Borja, *Bolivia* . . . 62 F5
San Buenaventura,
Mexico 58 B4
San Carlos, *Argentina* . 64 C3
San Carlos, *Chile* . . . 64 D2
San Carlos,
Baja Calif. S., Mexico 58 C2
San Carlos, Coahuila,
Mexico 58 B4
San Carlos, *Nic.* 60 D3
San Carlos, *Phil.* 27 B6
San Carlos, *Uruguay* . . 64 C6
San Carlos, *U.S.A.* . . . 57 K8
San Carlos, *Venezuela* . 62 B5
San Carlos de Bariloche,
Argentina 64 E2
San Carlos de Bolívar,
Argentina 64 D4
San Carlos del Zulia,
Venezuela 62 B4
San Carlos L., *U.S.A.* . . 57 K8
San Clemente, *U.S.A.* . 57 M5
San Clemente I., *U.S.A.* 57 K4
San Cristóbal, *Argentina* 64 C4
San Cristóbal,
Dom. Rep. 61 C5
San Cristóbal,
Solomon Is. 38 C9
San Cristóbal,
Venezuela 62 B4
San Cristóbal de la
Casas, *Mexico* 59 D6
San Diego, Calif., *U.S.A.* 57 K5
San Diego, Tex., *U.S.A.* 55 M5
San Diego, C., *Argentina* 64 G3
San Diego de la Unión,
Mexico 58 C4
San Felipe, *Chile* 64 C2
San Felipe, *Mexico* . . . 58 A2
San Felipe, *Venezuela* . 62 A5
San Félix, *Pac. Oc.* . . 45 K20
San Fernando, *Chile* . . 64 C2
San Fernando,
Baja Calif., Mexico . . 58 B1
San Fernando,
Tamaulipas, Mexico . 59 C5
San Fernando,
La Union, Phil. 27 A6
San Fernando,
Pampanga, Phil. . . . 27 A6
San Fernando, *Spain* . . 15 D2
San Fernando,
Trin. & Tob. 62 A6
San Fernando de Apure,
Venezuela 62 B5
San Fernando de
Atabapo, *Venezuela* . 62 C5
San Francisco,
Argentina 64 C4
San Francisco, *U.S.A.* . 57 H2
San Francisco →,
U.S.A. 57 K9
San Francisco de
Macorís, *Dom. Rep.* . 61 C5
San Francisco del Oro,
Mexico 58 B3
San Gottardo, P. del,
Switz. 14 C8
San Ignacio, *Belize* . . . 59 D7
San Ignacio, *Bolivia* . . 62 G6
San Ignacio, *Mexico* . . 58 B2
San Ignacio, *Paraguay* . 60 C2
San Ignacio, L., *Mexico* 58 B2
San Ildefonso, C., *Phil.* 27 A6
San Javier, *Bolivia* . . . 62 G6
San Jeronimo Taviche,
Mexico 59 D5
San Joaquín →, *U.S.A.* 56 G5
San Jon, *U.S.A.* 55 H3
San Jorge, *Argentina* . 64 C4
San Jorge, B. de,
Mexico 58 A2
San Jorge, G.,
Argentina 64 F3
San José, *Costa Rica* . . 60 D3
San José, *Guatemala* . . 60 D1
San José, *Mexico* 58 C2
San Jose, Mind. Occ.,
Phil. 27 B6
San Jose, Nueva Ecija,
Phil. 27 A6
San Jose, *U.S.A.* 57 H3
San Jose →, *U.S.A.* . . 57 J10
San Jose de Buenavista,
Phil. 27 B6
San José de Chiquitos,
Bolivia 62 G6
San José de Jáchal,
Argentina 64 C3
San José de Mayo,
Uruguay 64 C5
San José del Cabo,
Mexico 58 C3
San José del Guaviare,
Colombia 62 C4

San Juan, *Argentina* . . 64 C3
San Juan, *Mexico* . . . 58 C4
San Juan, *Puerto Rico* . 61 C6
San Juan □, *Dom. Rep.* 61 C5
San Juan →, *Nic.* . . . 60 D3
San Juan →, *U.S.A.* . . 57 H8
San Juan Bautista Valle
Nacional, *Mexico* . . . 59 D5
San Juan de Guadalupe,
Mexico 58 C4
San Juan de la Costa,
Mexico 58 C2
San Juan de los Morros,
Venezuela 62 B5
San Juan del Norte, *Nic.* 60 D3
San Juan del Norte, B.
de, *Nic.* 60 D3
San Juan del Río,
Mexico 59 C5
San Juan del Sur, *Nic.* . 60 D2
San Juan Mts., *U.S.A.* . 57 H10
San Justo, *Argentina* . 64 C4
San Lázaro, C., *Mexico* 58 C2
San Lázaro, Sa., *Mexico* 58 C3
San Lorenzo, *Ecuador* . 62 C3
San Lorenzo →,
Mexico 58 C3
San Lorenzo, I., *Mexico* 58 B2
San Lorenzo, Mte.,
Argentina 64 F2
San Lucas, *Bolivia* . . . 62 H5
San Lucas,
Baja Calif. S., Mexico 58 C3
San Lucas,
Baja Calif. S., Mexico 58 B2
San Lucas, C., *Mexico* . 58 C3
San Luis, *Argentina* . . 64 C3
San Luis, *Cuba* 60 B3
San Luis, *Guatemala* . . 60 C2
San Luis, Ariz., *U.S.A.* . 57 K6
San Luis, Colo., *U.S.A.* 57 H11
San Luis □, *Argentina* . 58 B2
San Luis de la Paz,
Mexico 58 C4
San Luis Obispo, *U.S.A.* 57 J3
San Luis Potosí, *Mexico* 58 C4
San Luis Potosí □,
Mexico 58 C4
San Luis Río Colorado,
Mexico 58 A2
San Manuel, *U.S.A.* . . 57 K8
San Marcos, *Guatemala* 60 D1
San Marcos, *Mexico* . . 58 B2
San Marcos, *U.S.A.* . . 55 L6
San Marino, *San Marino* 12 G7
San Marino ■, *Europe* 16 C5
San Martín →, *Bolivia* 62 F6
San Martin, L.,
Argentina 64 F2
San Martín de los
Andes, *Argentina* . . 64 E2
San Mateo, *U.S.A.* . . . 57 H2
San Matías, *Bolivia* . . 62 G7
San Matías, G.,
Argentina 64 E4
San Miguel, *El Salv.* . . 60 D2
San Miguel, *Panama* . . 60 E4
San Miguel, *U.S.A.* . . . 57 J3
San Miguel →, *Bolivia* 62 F6
San Miguel de
Tucumán, *Argentina* 64 B3
San Miguel I., *U.S.A.* . 57 J3
San Nicolás de los
Arroyos, *Argentina* . . 64 C4
San Nicolas I., *U.S.A.* . 57 K4
San Pédro, *Ivory C.* . . 34 H4
San Pedro, *Mexico* . . . 58 C2
San Pedro →,
Chihuahua, Mexico . . 58 B3
San Pedro →, Nayarit,
Mexico 58 C3
San Pedro →, *U.S.A.* . 57 K8
San Pedro de las
Colonias, *Mexico* . . . 58 B4
San Pedro de Macorís,
Dom. Rep. 61 C6
San Pedro del Norte,
Nic. 60 D3
San Pedro del Paraná,
Paraguay 64 B5
San Pedro Mártir,
Sierra, *Mexico* 58 A1
San Pedro Mixtepec,
Mexico 59 D5
San Pedro Ocampo =
Melchor Ocampo,
Mexico 58 C4
San Pedro Sula,
Honduras 60 C2
San Pietro, *Italy* 16 E3
San Quintín, *Mexico* . . 58 A1
San Rafael, *Argentina* . 64 C3
San Rafael, Calif., *U.S.A.* 56 H2
San Rafael, N. Mex.,
U.S.A. 57 J10
San Remo, *Italy* 14 E7
San Roque, *Argentina* . 64 B5
San Roque, *Spain* . . . 15 D3
San Rosendo, *Chile* . . 64 D2
San Saba, *U.S.A.* 55 K5
San Salvador, *El Salv.* . 60 D2
San Salvador de Jujuy,
Argentina 64 A4
San Salvador I.,
Bahamas 61 B5

San Sebastián =
Donostia-San
Sebastián, *Spain* . . 15 A5
San Severo, *Italy* 16 D6
San Simon, *U.S.A.* . . . 57 K9
San Telmo, *Mexico* . . . 58 A1
San Tiburcio, *Mexico* . 58 C4
San Valentin, Mte., *Chile* 64 F2
San Vicente de la
Barquera, *Spain* . . . 15 A3
San Vito, *Costa Rica* . . 60 E3
Sana', *Yemen* 32 D3
Sana →, *Bos.-H.* 12 F9
Sanaga →, *Cameroon* 36 D1
Sanaloa, Presa, *Mexico* 58 C3
Sanana, *Indonesia* . . . 27 E7
Sanandaj, *Iran* 30 C5
Sánchez, *Dom. Rep.* . . 61 C6
Sancti Spíritus, *Cuba* . 60 B4
Sancy, Puy de, *France* . 14 D5
Sand Hills, *U.S.A.* 54 D4
Sand Springs, *U.S.A.* . 55 G6
Sanda, *Japan* 23 G7
Sandakan, *Malaysia* . . 26 C5
Sandanski, *Bulgaria* . . 17 D10
Sanday, *U.K.* 10 B5
Sanders, *U.S.A.* 57 J9
Sanderson, *U.S.A.* . . . 55 K3
Sandersville, *U.S.A.* . . 53 J4
Sandfire Roadhouse,
Australia 40 C3
Sandfly L., *Canada* . . . 51 B7
Sandía, *Peru* 62 F5
Sandnes, *Norway* . . . 7 G11
Sandnessjøen, *Norway* 6 C15
Sandoa, Dem. Rep. of
the Congo 36 F4
Sandomierz, *Poland* . . 13 C11
Sandover →, *Australia* 42 C2
Sandoway, *Burma* . . . 29 K19
Sandoy, *Færoe Is.* . . . 6 F9
Sandpoint, *U.S.A.* . . . 56 B5
Sandringham, *U.K.* . . . 8 E8
Sandstone, *Australia* . 41 E2
Sandusky, Mich., *U.S.A.* 52 D4
Sandusky, Ohio, *U.S.A.* 52 E4
Sandviken, *Sweden* . . 7 F17
Sandwich, C., *Australia* 42 B4
Sandwich B., *Canada* . 49 B8
Sandy, *U.S.A.* 56 F8
Sandy Bay, *Canada* . . 51 B8
Sandy Bight, *Australia* . 41 F3
Sandy C., Queens.,
Australia 42 C5
Sandy C., Tas., *Australia* 42 G3
Sandy Cay, *Bahamas* . 61 B4
Sandy Cr. →, *U.S.A.* . 56 F9
Sandy L., *Canada* . . . 48 B1
Sandy Lake, *Canada* . . 57 J3
Sanford, Fla., *U.S.A.* . . 53 L5
Sanford, Maine, *U.S.A.* 53 D10
Sanford, N.C., *U.S.A.* . 53 H6
Sanford →, *Australia* . 41 E2
Sanford, Mt., *U.S.A.* . . 46 B5
Sanga →, *Congo* 36 E3
Sangamner, *India* . . . 28 K9
Sangar, *Russia* 21 C13
Sangay, *Ecuador* 62 D3
Sangeang, *Indonesia* . 27 F5
Sanger, *U.S.A.* 57 H4
Sangerhausen,
Germany 12 C6
Sanggau, *Indonesia* . . 26 D4
Sanghe, Kepulauan,
Indonesia 27 D7
Sangihe, Pulau,
Indonesia 27 D7
Sangkapura, *Indonesia* 26 F4
Sangkulirang, *Indonesia* 26 D5
Sangli, *India* 28 L9
Sangmélima, *Cameroon* 36 D2
Sangre de Cristo Mts.,
U.S.A. 55 G2
Sangudo, *Canada* . . . 50 C6
Sangue →, *Brazil* . . . 62 F7
Sanibel, *U.S.A.* 53 M4
Sanirajak, *Canada* . . . 47 B11
Sanjo, *Japan* 22 F9
Sankt Moritz, *Switz.* . . 14 C8
Sankt-Peterburg, *Russia* 18 C5
Sankt Pölten, *Austria* . 12 D8
Sankuru →, Dem. Rep.
of the Congo 36 E4
Sanliurfa, *Turkey* 19 G6
Sanlúcar de Barrameda,
Spain 15 D2
Sanmenxia, *China* . . . 25 C6
Sanming, *China* 25 D6
Sannicandro Gargánico,
Italy 16 D6
Sânnicolau Mare,
Romania 13 E11
Sannieguellie, *Liberia* . 34 G4
Sanok, *Poland* 13 D12
Sant Antoni Abat, *Spain* 15 C6
Sant Feliu de Guíxols,
Spain 15 B7
Sant Jordi, G. de, *Spain* 15 B6
Santa Ana, *Bolivia* . . . 62 F5

Santa Ana, *El Salv.* . . . 60 D2
Santa Ana, *Mexico* . . . 58 A2
Santa Ana, *U.S.A.* . . . 57 K5
Sant' Antíoco, *Italy* . . 16 E3
Santa Barbara,
Honduras 60 D2
Santa Bárbara, *Mexico* 58 B3
Santa Barbara, *U.S.A.* . 57 J4
Santa Catalina, Gulf of,
U.S.A. 57 K5
Santa Catalina, I.,
Mexico 58 B2
Santa Catalina I., *U.S.A.* 57 K4
Santa Catarina □, *Brazil* 64 B7
Santa Clara, *Cuba* . . . 60 B4
Santa Clara, *U.S.A.* . . . 57 H7
Santa Clara, El Golfo de,
Mexico 58 A2
Santa Clotilde, *Peru* . . 62 D4
Santa Coloma de
Gramenet, *Spain* . . 15 B7
Santa Cruz, *Argentina* . 64 G3
Santa Cruz, *Bolivia* . . 62 G6
Santa Cruz, *Costa Rica* 60 D2
Santa Cruz, *Phil.* 27 B6
Santa Cruz, *U.S.A.* . . . 57 H2
Santa Cruz →,
Argentina 64 G3
Santa Cruz de Tenerife,
Canary Is. 34 C2
Santa Cruz del Norte,
Cuba 60 B3
Santa Cruz del Sur,
Cuba 60 B4
Santa Cruz do Sul,
Brazil 64 B6
Santa Cruz I., *U.S.A.* . . 57 K4
Santa Cruz Is.,
Solomon Is. 38 C9
Santa Domingo, Cay,
Bahamas 60 B4
Santa Elena, C.,
Costa Rica 60 D2
Santa Fe, *Argentina* . . 64 C4
Santa Fe, *U.S.A.* 57 J11
Santa Fé do Sul, *Brazil* 63 H8
Santa Filomena, *Brazil* . 63 E9
Santa Inês, *Brazil* . . . 63 F11
Santa Inés, I., *Chile* . . 64 G2
Santa Isabel = Rey
Malabo, *Eq. Guin.* . . 36 D1
Santa Isabel, *Argentina* 64 D3
Santa Isabel do Morro,
Brazil 63 F8
Santa Lucia Range,
U.S.A. 57 J3
Santa Magdalena, I.,
Mexico 58 C2
Santa Margarita, I.,
Mexico 58 C2
Santa Maria, *Brazil* . . 64 B6
Santa Maria, *U.S.A.* . . 57 J3
Santa Maria →,
Mexico 58 A3
Santa Maria, B. de,
Mexico 58 B3
Santa Maria da Vitória,
Brazil 63 F10
Santa Maria di Léuca,
C., *Italy* 17 E8
Santa Marta, *Colombia* 62 A4
Santa Marta, Sierra
Nevada de, *Colombia* 62 A4
Santa Maura = Levkás,
Greece 17 E9
Santa Monica, *U.S.A.* . 57 K4
Santa Rita, *U.S.A.* . . . 57 K10
Santa Rosa, La Pampa,
Argentina 64 D4
Santa Rosa, San Luis,
Argentina 64 C3
Santa Rosa, *Brazil* . . . 64 B6
Santa Rosa, Calif.,
U.S.A. 56 G2
Santa Rosa, N. Mex.,
U.S.A. 55 H2
Santa Rosa de Copán,
Honduras 60 D2
Santa Rosa del Sara,
Bolivia 62 G6
Santa Rosa I., Calif.,
U.S.A. 57 K3
Santa Rosa I., Fla.,
U.S.A. 53 K2
Santa Rosa Range,
U.S.A. 56 F5
Santa Rosalía, *Mexico* . 58 B2
Santa Tecla = Nueva
San Salvador, *El Salv.* 60 D2
Santa Teresa, *Australia* 42 C1
Santa Teresa, *Mexico* . 59 B5
Santa Vitória do Palmar,
Brazil 64 C6
Santai, *China* 24 C5
Santana, Coxilha de,
Brazil 64 C5
Santana do Livramento,
Brazil 64 C5
Santander, *Spain* 15 A4
Santander Jiménez,
Mexico 59 C5
Santaquin, *U.S.A.* . . . 56 G8
Santarém, *Brazil* 63 D8
Santarém, *Portugal* . . 15 C1

Santaren Channel,
W. Indies 60 B4
Santee →, *U.S.A.* . . . 53 J6
Santiago, *Brazil* 64 B6
Santiago, *Chile* 64 C2
Santiago, *Panama* . . . 60 E3
Santiago →, *Peru* . . . 62 D3
Santiago de
Compostela, *Spain* . 15 A1
Santiago de Cuba, *Cuba* 60 C4
Santiago de los
Cabelleros, *Dom. Rep.* 61 C5
Santiago del Estero,
Argentina 64 B4
Santiago Ixcuintla,
Mexico 58 C3
Santiago Papasquiaro,
Mexico 58 C3
Santiaguillo, L. de,
Mexico 58 C4
Santo Amaro, *Brazil* . . 63 F11
Santo Ângelo, *Brazil* . 64 B6
Santo Antônio do Içá,
Brazil 62 D5
Santo Antônio do
Leverger, *Brazil* . . . 63 G7
Santo Domingo,
Dom. Rep. 61 C6
Santo Domingo,
Baja Calif., Mexico . . 58 A1
Santo Domingo,
Baja Calif. S., Mexico 58 B2
Santo Domingo, *Nic.* . 60 D3
Santo Domingo de los
Colorados, *Ecuador* . 62 D3
Santo Domingo Pueblo,
U.S.A. 57 J10
Santo Tomás, *Mexico* . 58 A1
Santo Tomás, *Peru* . . 62 F4
Santo Tomé, *Argentina* 64 B5
Santo Tomé de
Guayana = Ciudad
Guayana, *Venezuela* . 62 B6
Santoña, *Spain* 15 A4
Santoríni = Thíra,
Greece 17 F11
Santos, *Brazil* 64 A7
São Bernardo do
Campo, *Brazil* 64 A7
São Borja, *Brazil* 64 B5
São Carlos, *Brazil* . . . 63 H9
São Cristóvão, *Brazil* . 63 F11
São Domingos, *Brazil* . 63 F9
São Francisco, *Brazil* . 63 G10
São Francisco →,
Brazil 63 F11
São Francisco do Sul,
Brazil 64 B7
São Gabriel, *Brazil* . . . 64 C6
São João da Madeira,
Portugal 15 B1
São João del Rei, *Brazil* 63 H10
São João do Araguaia,
Brazil 63 E9
São João do Piauí,
Brazil 63 E10
São José do Rio Prêto,
Brazil 63 H9
São Leopoldo, *Brazil* . 64 B6
São Lourenço, *Brazil* . 63 H9
São Lourenço →,
Brazil 63 G7
São Luís, *Brazil* 63 D10
São Marcos →, *Brazil* 63 G9
São Marcos, B. de,
Brazil 63 D10
São Mateus, *Brazil* . . 63 G11
São Paulo, *Brazil* . . . 64 A7
São Paulo □, *Brazil* . . 63 H8
São Paulo, I., *Atl. Oc.* . 2 D8
São Paulo de Olivença,
Brazil 62 D5
São Roque, C. de, *Brazil* 63 E11
São Sebastião, I. de,
Brazil 64 A7
São Tomé & Príncipe ■,
Africa 3 D10
São Vicente, C. de,
Portugal 15 D1
Saona, I., *Dom. Rep.* . 61 C6
Saône →, *France* . . . 14 D6
Saonek, *Indonesia* . . . 27 E8
Saparua, *Indonesia* . . 27 E7
Sapele, *Nigeria* 34 G7
Sapelo I., *U.S.A.* 53 K5
Saposoa, *Peru* 62 E3
Sapphire, *Australia* . . 42 C4
Sapporo, *Japan* 22 C10
Sapulpa, *U.S.A.* 55 H6
Saqqez, *Iran* 30 B5
Sar Dasht, *Iran* 31 D6
Sar Gachineh, *Iran* . . . 31 D6
Sar Planina, *Macedonia* 17 C9
Sara Buri = Saraburi,
Thailand 26 B2
Sarāb, *Iran* 30 B5
Sarabadi, *Iraq* 30 C5
Saraburi, *Thailand* . . . 26 B2
Saragossa = Zaragoza,
Spain 15 B5
Saraguro, *Ecuador* . . . 62 D3
Sarajevo, *Bos.-H.* . . . 17 C8
Sarakhs, *Turkmenistan* 31 B9
Saran, Gunung,
Indonesia 26 E4

Saranac Lake, U.S.A. . . 52 C8
Sarangani B., Phil. . . . 27 C7
Sarangani Is., Phil. . . . 27 C7
Sarangarh, India 29 J13
Saransk, Russia 18 D8
Sarapul, Russia 18 C9
Sarasota, U.S.A. 53 M4
Saratoga, U.S.A. 56 F10
Saratoga Springs,
    U.S.A. 52 D9
Saratok, Malaysia 26 D4
Saratov, Russia 19 D8
Saravane, Laos 26 A3
Sarawak □, Malaysia . . 26 D4
Saray, Turkey 17 D12
Sarayköy, Turkey 17 F13
Sarbāz, Iran 31 E9
Sarbīsheh, Iran 31 C8
Sarda →, India 29 F12
Sardarshahr, India 28 E6
Sarda →, India 29 F12
Sardarshahr, India 28 E6
Sardegna □, Italy 16 D3
Sardinia = Sardegna □,
    Italy 16 D3
Sardis, Turkey 17 E12
Sārdūīyeh = Dar Mazār,
    Iran 31 D8
Sarera, G. of, Indonesia 38 B6
Sargasso Sea, Atl. Oc. . 45 D20
Sargodha, Pakistan . . . 28 C8
Sarh, Chad 35 G9
Sārī, Iran 31 B7
Sangöl, Turkey 17 E13
Sarikei, Malaysia 26 D4
Sarina, Australia 42 C4
Sarita, U.S.A. 55 M6
Sark, U.K. 9 H5
Şarköy, Turkey 17 D12
Sarlat-la-Canéda, France 14 D4
Sarmi, Indonesia 27 E9
Sarmiento, Argentina . . 64 F3
Särna, Sweden 7 F15
Sarnia, Canada 48 D3
Sarolangun, Indonesia . 26 E2
Saronikós Kólpos,
    Greece 17 F10
Saros Körfezi, Turkey . . 17 D12
Sarpsborg, Norway . . . 7 G14
Sarre = Saar →,
    Europe 14 B7
Sarreguemines, France . 14 B7
Sarthe →, France 14 C3
Sarvestān, Iran 31 D7
Sary-Tash, Kyrgyzstan . 20 F8
Saryshagan, Kazakstan . 20 E8
Sasaram, India 29 G14
Sasebo, Japan 23 H4
Saser, India 28 B10
Saskatchewan □,
    Canada 51 C7
Saskatchewan →,
    Canada 51 C7
Saskatoon, Canada . . . 51 C7
Saskylakh, Russia 21 B12
Sasovo, Russia 18 D7
Sassandra, Ivory C. . . . 34 H4
Sassandra →, Ivory C. . 34 H4
Sássari, Italy 16 D3
Sassnitz, Germany 12 A7
Sassuolo, Italy 16 B4
Sasyk, Ozero, Ukraine . 13 F15
Sata-Misaki, Japan . . . 23 J5
Satadougou, Mali 34 F3
Satakunta, Finland 7 F20
Satara, India 28 L8
Satevó, Mexico 58 B3
Satilla →, U.S.A. 53 K5
Sotka, Russia 18 C10
Satmala Hills, India . . . 28 J9
Satna, India 29 G12
Sátoraljaújhely, Hungary 13 D11
Satpura Ra., India 28 J10
Satsuna-Shotō, Japan . 23 K5
Sattahip, Thailand 26 B2
Satu Mare, Romania . . 13 E12
Satui, Indonesia 26 E5
Satun, Thailand 26 C2
Saturnina →, Brazil . . 62 F7
Sauceda, Mexico 58 B4
Saucillo, Mexico 58 B3
Sauda, Norway 7 G12
Sauðárkrókur, Iceland . . 6 D4
Saudi Arabia ■, Asia . . 30 B3
Sauerland, Germany . . 12 C4
Saugerties, U.S.A. 52 D9
Sauk Centre, U.S.A. . . . 54 C7
Sauk Rapids, U.S.A. . . . 54 C7
Sault Ste. Marie,
    Canada 48 C3
Sault Ste. Marie, U.S.A. 47 D11
Saumlaki, Indonesia . . 27 F8
Saumur, France 14 C3
Saunders C., N.Z. 39 L3
Saunders I., Antarctica . 5 B1
Saunders Point,
    Australia 41 E4
Saurimo, Angola 36 F4
Savá, Honduras 60 C2
Sava →, Serbia, Yug. . 17 B9
Savage, U.S.A. 54 B2
Savage I. = Niue,
    Cook Is. 45 J11
Savage River, Australia 42 G4
Savai'i, Samoa 39 A12
Savalou, Benin 34 G6

Savanna, U.S.A. 54 D9
Savanna-la-Mar,
    Jamaica 60 C4
Savannah, Ga., U.S.A. . 53 J5
Savannah, Mo., U.S.A. . 54 F7
Savannah, Tenn., U.S.A. 53 H1
Savannah →, U.S.A. . . 53 J5
Savannakhet, Laos . . . 26 A2
Savant L., Canada 48 B1
Savant Lake, Canada . . 48 B1
Save →, Mozam. 37 J6
Sāveh, Iran 31 C6
Savelugu, Ghana 34 G5
Savo, Finland 6 E22
Savoie □, France 14 D7
Savona, Italy 14 D8
Savonlinna, Finland . . . 18 B4
Savoy = Savoie □,
    France 14 D7
Savur, Turkey 30 B4
Sawahlunto, Indonesia . 26 E2
Sawai, Indonesia 27 E7
Sawai Madhopur, India 28 G10
Sawankhalok, Thailand . 26 A1
Sawara, Japan 23 G10
Sawatch Range, U.S.A. 57 G10
Sawtooth Range, U.S.A. 56 E6
Sawu, Indonesia 27 F6
Sawu Sea, Indonesia . . 27 F6
Saxby →, Australia . . . 42 B3
Saxmundham, U.K. . . . 9 E9
Saxony = Sachsen □,
    Germany 12 C7
Saxony, Lower =
    Niedersachsen □,
    Germany 12 B5
Sayabec, Canada 49 C6
Sayán, Peru 62 F3
Sayan, Vostochnyy,
    Russia 21 D10
Sayan, Zapadnyy,
    Russia 21 D10
Saydā, Lebanon 33 B4
Sayḥūt, Yemen 32 D5
Saynshand, Mongolia . 25 B6
Sayre, Okla., U.S.A. . . . 55 H5
Sayre, Pa., U.S.A. 52 E7
Sayula, Mexico 58 D4
Sayward, Canada 50 C3
Sazanit, Albania 17 D8
Sázava →, Czech Rep. . 12 D8
Sazin, Pakistan 28 B8
Scafell Pike, U.K. 8 C4
Scandia, Canada 50 C6
Scandicci, Italy 16 C4
Scandinavia, Europe . . 6 E16
Scandinavia, Europe . . 6 E16
Scarborough,
    Trin. & Tob. 62 A6
Scarborough, U.K. 8 C7
Scebeli, Wabi →,
    Somali Rep. 32 G3
Schaffhausen, Switz. . . 14 C8
Schagen, Neths. 11 B4
Schefferville, Canada . . 49 B6
Schelde →, Belgium . . 11 C4
Schell Creek Ra., U.S.A. 56 G6
Schenectady, U.S.A. . . . 52 D9
Schiedam, Neths. 11 C4
Schiermonnikoog,
    Neths. 11 A6
Schio, Italy 16 B4
Schleswig, Germany . . 12 A5
Schleswig-Holstein □,
    Germany 12 A5
Schouten I., Australia . . 42 G4
Schouten Is. = Supiori,
    Indonesia 27 E9
Schouwen, Neths. 11 C3
Schreiber, Canada 48 C2
Schuler, Canada 51 C6
Schumacher, Canada . . 48 C3
Schurz, U.S.A. 56 G4
Schuyler, U.S.A. 54 E6
Schwäbische Alb,
    Germany 12 D5
Schwaner, Pegunungan,
    Indonesia 26 E4
Schwarzwald, Germany 12 D5
Schwedt, Germany . . . 12 B8
Schweinfurt, Germany . 12 C6
Schweningen =
    Villingen-
    Schwenningen,
    Germany 12 D5
Schwerin, Germany . . . 12 B6
Schwyz, Switz. 14 C8
Sciacca, Italy 16 F5
Scilla, Italy 16 E6
Scilly, Isles of, U.K. . . . 9 H1
Scioto →, U.S.A. 52 F4
Scobey, U.S.A. 54 A2
Scone, Australia 43 E5
Scoresbysund =
    Illoqqortoormiit,
    Greenland 4 B6
Scotia, U.S.A. 56 F1
Scotia Sea, Antarctica . 5 B18
Scotland □, U.K. 10 C5
Scott, C., Canada 40 B4
Scott City, U.S.A. 54 F4
Scott Glacier, Antarctica 5 C8
Scott I., Antarctica 5 C11
Scott Is., Canada 50 C3

Scott L., Canada 51 B7
Scott Reef, Australia . . 40 B3
Scottsbluff, U.S.A. 54 E3
Scottsboro, U.S.A. 53 H3
Scottsburg, U.S.A. 52 F3
Scottsdale, Australia . . 42 G4
Scottsdale, U.S.A. 57 K7
Scottsville, U.S.A. 53 G2
Scottville, U.S.A. 52 D2
Scranton, U.S.A. 52 E8
Scunthorpe, U.K. 8 D7
Seabrook, L., Australia . 41 F2
Seaford, U.K. 9 G8
Seaford, U.S.A. 52 F8
Seaforth, Australia . . . 42 C4
Seagraves, U.S.A. 55 J3
Seaham, U.K. 8 C6
Seal →, Canada 51 B10
Seal L., Canada 49 B7
Sealy, U.S.A. 55 L6
Searchlight, U.S.A. 57 J6
Searcy, U.S.A. 55 H9
Searles L., U.S.A. 57 J5
Seascale, U.K. 8 C4
Seaside, Calif., U.S.A. . 57 G3
Seaside, Oreg., U.S.A. . 56 D2
Seaspray, Australia . . . 43 F4
Seattle, U.S.A. 56 C2
Seaview Ra., Australia . 42 B4
Sebastián Vizcaíno, B.,
    Mexico 58 B2
Sebastopol =
    Sevastopol, Ukraine . 19 F5
Sebewaing, U.S.A. 52 D4
Sebha = Sabhah, Libya 35 C8
Şebinkarahisar, Turkey . 19 F6
Sebring, U.S.A. 53 M5
Sebta = Ceuta, N. Afr. . 15 E3
Sebuku, Indonesia 26 E5
Sebuku, Teluk, Malaysia 26 D5
Sechelt, Canada 50 D4
Sechura, Desierto de,
    Peru 62 E2
Secretary I., N.Z. 39 L1
Secunderabad, India . . 28 L11
Security-Widefield,
    U.S.A. 54 F2
Sedalia, U.S.A. 54 F8
Sedan, France 14 B6
Sedan, U.S.A. 55 G6
Seddon, N.Z. 39 J5
Seddonville, N.Z. 39 J4
Sedé Boqér, Israel 33 E3
Sedeh, Fārs, Iran 31 D7
Sedeh, Khorāsān, Iran . 31 C8
Sederot, Israel 33 D3
Sédhiou, Senegal 34 F2
Sedley, Canada 51 C8
Sedona, U.S.A. 57 J8
Sedova, Pik, Russia . . . 20 B6
Sedro Woolley, U.S.A. . 56 B2
Seferihisar, Turkey 17 E12
Seg-ozero, Russia 18 B5
Segamat, Malaysia . . . 26 D2
Segesta, Italy 16 F5
Seget, Indonesia 27 E8
Segezha, Russia 18 B5
Ségou, Mali 34 F4
Segovia = Coco →,
    Cent. Amer. 60 D3
Segovia, Spain 15 B3
Segre →, Spain 15 B6
Séguéla, Ivory C. 34 G4
Seguin, U.S.A. 55 L6
Segura →, Spain 15 C5
Seh Konj, Kūh-e, Iran . 31 D8
Seh Qal'eh, Iran 31 C8
Sehore, India 28 H10
Seiland, Norway 6 A20
Seiling, U.S.A. 55 G5
Seinäjoki, Finland 7 E20
Seine →, France 14 B4
Seistan = Sīstān, Asia . 31 D9
Seistan, Daryācheh-ye =
    Sīstān, Daryācheh-ye,
    Iran 31 D9
Sekayu, Indonesia 26 E2
Sekondi-Takoradi,
    Ghana 34 H5
Selah, U.S.A. 56 C3
Selaru, Indonesia 27 F8
Selby, U.K. 8 D6
Selby, U.S.A. 54 C4
Selçuk, Turkey 17 F12
Selden, U.S.A. 54 F4
Sele →, Italy 16 D6
Selebi-Pikwe, Botswana 37 J5
Selemdzha →, Russia . 21 D13
Selenga = Selenge
    Mörön →, Asia 24 A5
Selenge Mörön →,
    Asia 24 A5
Seletan, Tanjung,
    Indonesia 26 E4
Sélibabi, Mauritania . . 34 E3
Seligman, U.S.A. 57 J7
Selîma, El Wâhât el,
    Sudan 35 D11
Selinda Spillway,
    Botswana 37 H4
Selkirk, Canada 51 C9
Selkirk I., Canada 51 C9
Selkirk Mts., Canada . . 46 C8
Sells, U.S.A. 57 L8
Selma, Ala., U.S.A. . . . 53 J2
Selma, Calif., U.S.A. . . 57 H4

Selma, N.C., U.S.A. . . . 53 H6
Selmer, U.S.A. 53 H1
Selpele, Indonesia 27 E8
Selsey Bill, U.K. 9 G7
Seltso, Russia 18 D5
Selu, Indonesia 27 F8
Selva, Argentina 64 B4
Selvas, Brazil 62 E5
Selwyn L., Canada 51 B8
Selwyn Mts., Canada . . 46 B6
Selwyn Ra., Australia . . 42 C3
Seman →, Albania . . . 17 D8
Semani =
    Seman →, Albania . 17 D8
Semarang, Indonesia . . 27 G14
Semeru, Indonesia . . . 27 H15
Semey, Kazakstan 20 D9
Seminoe Reservoir,
    U.S.A. 56 F10
Seminole, Okla., U.S.A. 55 H6
Seminole, Tex., U.S.A. . 55 J3
Seminole Draw →,
    U.S.A. 55 J3
Semipalatinsk = Semey,
    Kazakstan 20 D9
Semirara Is., Phil. 27 B6
Semitau, Indonesia . . . 26 D4
Semiyarka, Kazakstan . 20 D8
Semiyarskoye =
    Semiyarka, Kazakstan 20 D8
Semmering P., Austria . 12 E8
Semnän, Iran 31 C7
Semnän □, Iran 31 C7
Semporna, Malaysia . . 27 D5
Semuda, Indonesia . . . 26 E4
Sen →, Cambodia 26 B3
Senā, Iran 31 D6
Sena Madureira, Brazil 62 E5
Senador Pompeu, Brazil 63 E11
Senanga, Zambia 37 H4
Senatobia, U.S.A. 55 H10
Sendai, Kagoshima,
    Japan 23 J5
Sendai, Miyagi, Japan . 22 E10
Sendai-Wan, Japan . . . 22 E10
Seneca, U.S.A. 53 H4
Seneca Falls, U.S.A. . . . 52 D7
Seneca L., U.S.A. 52 D7
Senegal ■, W. Afr. . . . 34 F3
Sénégal →, W. Afr. . . . 34 E2
Senge Khambab =
    Indus →, Pakistan . 28 G5
Senhor-do-Bonfim,
    Brazil 63 F10
Senigállia, Italy 16 C5
Senj, Croatia 12 F8
Senja, Norway 6 B17
Senkaku-Shotō, Japan . 23 L1
Senlis, France 14 B5
Senmonorom,
    Cambodia 26 B3
Sennetere, Canada . . . 48 C4
Sens, France 14 B5
Senta, Serbia, Yug. . . . 17 B9
Sentani, Indonesia . . . 27 E10
Sentinel, U.S.A. 57 K7
Seo de Urgel = La Seu
    d'Urgell, Spain 15 A6
Seoul = Sŏul, S. Korea 25 C7
Sepīdān, Iran 31 D7
Sept-Îles, Canada 49 B6
Sequim, U.S.A. 56 B2
Sequoia National Park,
    U.S.A. 57 H4
Seraing, Belgium 11 D5
Seram, Indonesia 27 E7
Seram Sea, Indonesia . 27 E7
Serang, Indonesia 27 G12
Serasan, Indonesia . . . 26 D3
Serbia □, Yugoslavia . . 17 C9
Serdobsk, Russia 18 D7
Seremban, Malaysia . . 26 D2
Sereth = Siret →,
    Romania 13 F14
Sergino, Russia 20 C7
Sergipe □, Brazil 63 F11
Sergiyev Posad, Russia 18 C6
Seria, Brunei 26 D4
Serian, Malaysia 26 D4
Seribu, Kepulauan,
    Indonesia 26 F3
Sérifos, Greece 17 F11
Sérigny →, Canada . . . 49 A6
Seringapatam Reef,
    Australia 40 B3
Sermata, Indonesia . . . 27 F7
Serov, Russia 18 C11
Serowe, Botswana . . . 37 J5
Serpentine Lakes,
    Australia 41 E4
Serpukhov, Russia 18 D6
Serra do Navio, Brazil . 63 C8
Sérrai, Greece 17 D10
Serrinha, Brazil 63 F11
Serua, Indonesia 27 F8
Serui, Indonesia 27 E9
Sesepe, Indonesia 27 E7
Setana, Japan 22 C9
Sète, France 14 E5
Sète Lagôas, Brazil . . . 63 G10
Sétif, Algeria 34 A7
Seto, Japan 23 G8
Setonaikai, Japan 23 G6
Settat, Morocco 34 B4

Setting L., Canada 51 C9
Settle, U.K. 8 C5
Settlement Pt., Bahamas 53 M6
Setúbal, Portugal 15 C1
Setúbal, B. de, Portugal 15 C1
Seul, Lac, Canada 46 C10
Sevan, Ozero = Sevana
    Lich, Armenia 19 F8
Sevana Lich, Armenia . 19 F8
Sevastopol, Ukraine . . 19 F5
Seven Sisters, Canada . 50 C3
Severn →, Canada . . . 48 A2
Severn →, U.K. 9 F5
Severn L., Canada 48 B1
Severnaya Zemlya,
    Russia 21 B10
Severnyye Uvaly, Russia 18 C8
Severo-Kurilsk, Russia . 21 D16
Severo-Yeniseyskiy,
    Russia 21 C10
Severodvinsk, Russia . . 18 B6
Severomorsk, Russia . . 18 A5
Severouralsk, Russia . . 18 B10
Sevier, U.S.A. 57 G7
Sevier →, U.S.A. 57 G7
Sevier Desert, U.S.A. . . 56 G7
Sevier L., U.S.A. 56 G7
Sevilla, Spain 15 D2
Seville = Sevilla, Spain 15 D2
Sevlievo, Bulgaria 17 C11
Seward, Alaska, U.S.A. . 46 B5
Seward, Nebr., U.S.A. . 54 E6
Seward Peninsula,
    U.S.A. 46 B3
Sewer, Indonesia 27 F8
Sexsmith, Canada 50 B5
Seychelles ■, Ind. Oc. . 3 E12
Seyðisfjörður, Iceland . 6 D6
Seydişehir, Turkey 19 G5
Seydvān, Iran 30 B5
Seyhan →, Turkey 30 B2
Seym →, Ukraine 19 D5
Seymour, Australia . . . 43 F4
Seymour, Ind., U.S.A. . 52 F3
Seymour, Tex., U.S.A. . 55 J5
Sfântu Gheorghe,
    Romania 13 F13
Sfax, Tunisia 35 B8
Shaanxi □, China 25 C5
Shaba = Katanga □,
    Dem. Rep. of
    the Congo 36 F4
Shabogamo L., Canada 49 B6
Shache, China 24 C2
Shackleton Ice Shelf,
    Antarctica 5 C8
Shackleton Inlet,
    Antarctica 5 E11
Shādegān, Iran 31 D6
Shadrinsk, Russia 20 D7
Shafter, U.S.A. 57 J4
Shaftesbury, U.K. 9 F5
Shahba, Syria 33 C5
Shahdād, Iran 31 D8
Shahdād, Namakzār-e,
    Iran 31 D8
Shahdadkot, Pakistan . 28 F5
Shahgarh, India 28 F6
Shahjahanpur, India . . 28 F11
Shahr-e Bābak, Iran . . 31 D7
Shahr-e Kord, Iran 31 C6
Shāhrakht, Iran 31 C9
Shahrig, Pakistan 28 D5
Shajapur, India 28 H10
Shakhty, Russia 19 E7
Shakhunya, Russia . . . 18 C8
Shaki, Nigeria 34 G6
Shalqar, Kazakstan . . . 20 E6
Shaluli Shan, China . . . 24 C4
Shām, Iran 31 E8
Shām, Bādiyat ash, Asia 30 C3
Shamattawa, Canada . 48 A1
Shamattawa →,
    Canada 48 A2
Shamīl, Iran 31 E8
Shāmkūh, Iran 31 C8
Shammar, Jabal,
    Si. Arabia 30 E4
Shamo = Gobi, Asia . . 25 B5
Shamo, L., Ethiopia . . . 32 F2
Shamokin, U.S.A. 52 E7
Shan □, Burma 29 J21
Shāndak, Iran 31 D9
Shandong □, China . . . 25 C6
Shanga, Nigeria 34 F6
Shangani →,
    Zimbabwe 37 H5
Shanghai, China 25 C7
Shangqiu, China 25 C6
Shangrao, China 25 D6
Shangshui, China 25 C6
Shannon, N.Z. 39 J5
Shannon →, Ireland . . 10 E2
Shansi = Shanxi □,
    China 25 C6
Shantar, Ostrov
    Bolshoy, Russia 21 D14
Shantou, China 25 D6
Shantung =
    Shandong □, China . 25 C6
Shaoguan, China 25 D6
Shaoxing, China 25 D7

Shaoyang, China 25 D6
Shap, U.K. 8 C5
Shaqra', Si. Arabia 30 E5
Shaqrā', Yemen 32 E4
Sharafkhāneh, Iran . . . 30 B5
Shari, Japan 22 C12
Sharjah = Ash
    Shāriqah, U.A.E. . . . 31 E7
Shark B., Australia 41 E1
Sharon, U.S.A. 52 E5
Sharon Springs, U.S.A. 54 F4
Sharp Pt., Australia . . . 42 A3
Sharpe L., Canada 48 B1
Sharya, Russia 18 C8
Shashemene, Ethiopia . 32 F2
Shashi, China 25 C6
Shasta, Mt., U.S.A. . . . 56 F2
Shasta L., U.S.A. 56 F2
Shatt al Arab = Arab,
    Shatt al →, Asia . . . 31 D6
Shaunavon, Canada . . 51 D7
Shaw →, Australia . . . 40 D2
Shaw I., Australia 42 C4
Shawano, U.S.A. 52 C1
Shawinigan, Canada . . 48 C5
Shawnee, U.S.A. 55 H6
Shay Gap, Australia . . 40 D3
Shaybārā, Si. Arabia . . 30 E3
Shaykh, J. ash, Lebanon 33 B4
Shaykh Miskīn, Syria . . 33 C5
Shaykh Sa'īd, Iraq 30 C5
Shcherbakov = Rybinsk,
    Russia 18 C6
Shchuchinsk, Kazakstan 20 D8
Shebele = Scebeli,
    Wabi →,
    Somali Rep. 32 G3
Sheboygan, U.S.A. 52 D2
Shediac, Canada 49 C7
Sheerness, U.K. 9 F8
Sheet Harbour, Canada 49 D7
Sheffield, U.K. 8 D6
Sheffield, U.S.A. 53 H2
Shekhupura, Pakistan . 28 D8
Shelburne, N.S., Canada 49 D6
Shelburne, Ont., Canada 48 D3
Shelburne B., Australia 42 A3
Shelby, Mich., U.S.A. . . 52 D2
Shelby, Miss., U.S.A. . . 55 J9
Shelby, Mont., U.S.A. . 56 B8
Shelby, N.C., U.S.A. . . . 53 H5
Shelbyville, Ill., U.S.A. . 54 F10
Shelbyville, Ind., U.S.A. 52 F3
Shelbyville, Ky., U.S.A. 52 F3
Shelbyville, Tenn.,
    U.S.A. 53 H2
Sheldon, U.S.A. 54 D7
Sheldrake, Canada . . . 49 B7
Shelikhova, Zaliv,
    Russia 21 D16
Shell Lakes, Australia . 41 E4
Shellbrook, Canada . . . 51 C7
Shellharbour, Australia 43 E5
Shelton, U.S.A. 56 C2
Shenandoah, Iowa,
    U.S.A. 54 E7
Shenandoah, Pa., U.S.A. 52 E7
Shenandoah, Va., U.S.A. 52 F6
Shenandoah →, U.S.A. 52 F7
Shenandoah National
    Park, U.S.A. 52 F6
Shendam, Nigeria 34 G7
Shendî, Sudan 35 E12
Shensi = Shaanxi □,
    China 25 C5
Shenyang, China 25 B7
Sheopur Kalan, India . . 28 G10
Shepetivka, Ukraine . . 13 C14
Shepetovka =
    Shepetivka, Ukraine . 13 C14
Shepparton, Australia . 43 F4
Sheppey, I. of, U.K. . . . 9 F8
Shepton Mallet, U.K. . . 9 F5
Sherborne, U.K. 9 G5
Sherbro I., S. Leone . . . 34 G3
Sherbrooke, N.S.,
    Canada 49 C7
Sherbrooke, Qué.,
    Canada 49 C5
Sheridan, Ark., U.S.A. . 55 H8
Sheridan, Wyo., U.S.A. 56 D10
Sheringham, U.K. 8 E9
Sherman, U.S.A. 55 J6
Sherridon, Canada . . . 51 B8
Sherwood Forest, U.K. . 8 D6
Sherwood Park, Canada 50 C6
Sheslay →, Canada . . . 50 B2
Shethanei L., Canada . 51 B9
Shetland □, U.K. 10 A6
Sheyenne →, U.S.A. . . 54 B6
Shibām, Yemen 32 D4
Shibata, Japan 22 F9
Shibecha, Japan 22 C12
Shibetsu, Japan 22 B11
Shibogama L., Canada . 48 B2
Shibushi, Japan 23 J5
Shickshock Mts. = Chic-
    Chocs, Mts., Canada 49 C6
Shido, Japan 23 G7
Shield, C., Australia . . . 42 A2
Shiga □, Japan 23 G8
Shihchiachuangi =
    Shijiazhuang, China . 25 C6
Shijiazhuang, China . . 25 C6

Shikarpur, *Pakistan* ... 28 F6
Shikoku □, *Japan* 23 H6
Shikoku-Sanchi, *Japan* 23 H6
Shiliguri, *India* 29 F16
Shilka, *Russia* 21 D12
Shilka →, *Russia* 21 D13
Shillong, *India* 29 G17
Shilo, *West Bank* 33 C4
Shimabara, *Japan* ... 23 H5
Shimada, *Japan* 23 G9
Shimane □, *Japan* ... 23 G6
Shimanovsk, *Russia* .. 21 D13
Shimizu, *Japan* 23 G9
Shimodate, *Japan* ... 23 F9
Shimoga, *India* 28 N9
Shimonoseki, *Japan* .. 23 H5
Shinano-Gawa →,
  Japan 23 F9
Shināş, *Oman* 31 E8
Shindand, *Afghan.* 28 C3
Shingū, *Japan* 23 H7
Shinjō, *Japan* 22 E10
Shinshār, *Syria* 33 A5
Shinyanga, *Tanzania* .. 36 E6
Shio-no-Misaki, *Japan* . 23 H7
Shiogama, *Japan* 22 E10
Shiojiri, *Japan* 23 F8
Shipchenski Prokhod,
  Bulgaria 17 C11
Shiping, *China* 24 D5
Shippegan, *Canada* .. 49 C7
Shippensburg, *U.S.A.* . 52 E7
Shiprock, *U.S.A.* 57 H9
Shiqma, N. →, *Israel* . 33 D3
Shiquan He =
  Indus →, *Pakistan* . 28 G5
Shīr Kūh, *Iran* 31 D7
Shiragami-Misaki, *Japan* 22 D10
Shirakawa, *Fukushima,*
  Japan 23 F10
Shirakawa, *Gifu, Japan* 23 F8
Shirane-San, *Gumma,*
  Japan 23 F9
Shirane-San,
  Yamanashi, Japan . 23 G9
Shiraoi, *Japan* 22 C10
Shīrāz, *Iran* 31 D7
Shire →, *Africa* 37 H7
Shiretoko-Misaki, *Japan* 22 B12
Shiriya-Zaki, *Japan* .. 22 D10
Shiroishi, *Japan* 22 F10
Shīrvān, *Iran* 31 B8
Shirwa, L. = Chilwa, L.,
  Malawi 37 H7
Shivpuri, *India* 28 G10
Shizuoka, *Japan* 23 G9
Shizuoka □, *Japan* ... 23 G9
Shklov = Shklow,
  Belarus 13 A16
Shklow, *Belarus* 13 A16
Shkoder = Shkodër,
  Albania 17 C8
Shkodër, *Albania* ... 17 C8
Shkodra = Shkodër,
  Albania 17 C8
Shkumbini →, *Albania* 17 D8
Shmidta, Ostrov, *Russia* 21 A10
Shō-Gawa →, *Japan* . 23 F8
Shoal L., *Canada* 51 D9
Shoal Lake, *Canada* . 51 C8
Shōdo-Shima, *Japan* .. 23 G7
Sholapur = Solapur,
  India 28 L9
Shologontsy, *Russia* .. 21 C12
Shōmrōn, *West Bank* . 33 C4
Shoreham by Sea, *U.K.* 9 G7
Shoshone, *U.S.A.* 56 N6
Shoshone L., *U.S.A.* .. 56 D8
Shoshone Mts., *U.S.A.* 56 G5
Shoshoni, *U.S.A.* 56 E9
Show Low, *U.S.A.* 57 J9
Shreveport, *U.S.A.* ... 55 J8
Shrewsbury, *U.K.* 9 E5
Shrirampur, *India* 29 H16
Shropshire □, *U.K.* 9 E5
Shu, *Kazakstan* 20 E8
Shuangliao, *China* ... 25 B7
Shuangyashan, *China* . 25 B8
Shule, *China* 24 C2
Shumagin Is., *U.S.A.* .. 46 C4
Shumen, *Bulgaria* 17 C12
Shumikha, *Russia* 18 D7
Shūr →, *Fārs, Iran* .. 31 D7
Shūr →, *Kermān, Iran* 31 D8
Shūr →, *Yazd, Iran* .. 31 D7
Shūr Āb, *Iran* 31 C6
Shūr Gaz, *Iran* 31 D8
Shūrāb, *Iran* 31 C8
Shūrjestān, *Iran* 31 D7
Shurugwi, *Zimbabwe* . 37 H6
Shūsf, *Iran* 31 D9
Shūshtar, *Iran* 31 D6
Shuswap L., *Canada* .. 50 C5
Shūzū, *Iran* 31 D7
Shwebo, *Burma* 29 H19
Shwegu, *Burma* 29 G20
Shweli →, *Burma* ... 29 H20
Shymkent, *Kazakstan* . 20 E7
Shyok, *India* 28 B11
Shyok →, *Pakistan* .. 28 B8
Si Kiang = Xi Jiang →,
  China 25 D6
Si-ngan = Xi'an, *China* 25 C5
Siahan Range, *Pakistan* 28 F4

Siaksriindrapura,
  Indonesia 26 D2
Sialkot, *Pakistan* 28 C9
Siam = Thailand ■,
  Asia 26 A2
Sian = Xi'an, *China* .. 25 C5
Siantan, *Indonesia* ... 26 D3
Siāreh, *Iran* 31 D9
Siargao I., *Phil.* 27 C7
Siasi, *Phil.* 27 C6
Siau, *Indonesia* 27 D7
Šiauliai, *Lithuania* 7 J20
Sibâi, Gebel el, *Egypt* . 30 E2
Sibay, *Russia* 18 D10
Šibenik, *Croatia* 16 C6
Siberia, *Russia* 4 D13
Siberut, *Indonesia* ... 26 E1
Sibi, *Pakistan* 28 E5
Sibil = Oksibil,
  Indonesia 27 E10
Sibiti, *Congo* 36 E2
Sibiu, *Romania* 13 F13
Sibley, *U.S.A.* 54 D7
Sibolga, *Indonesia* ... 26 D1
Sibsagar, *India* 29 F19
Sibu, *Malaysia* 26 D4
Sibuco, *Phil.* 27 C6
Sibuguey B., *Phil.* 27 C6
Sibut, *C.A.R.* 36 C3
Sibutu, *Phil.* 27 D5
Sibutu Passage,
  E. Indies 27 D5
Sibuyan I., *Phil.* 27 B6
Sibuyan Sea, *Phil.* ... 27 B6
Sicamous, *Canada* ... 50 C5
Siccus →, *Australia* .. 43 E2
Sichuan □, *China* 24 C5
Sicilia, *Italy* 16 F6
Sicily = Sicilia, *Italy* .. 16 F6
Sicuani, *Peru* 62 F4
Siddipet, *India* 28 K11
Sidi-bel-Abbès, *Algeria* 34 A5
Sidley, Mt., *Antarctica* . 5 D14
Sidmouth, *U.K.* 9 G4
Sidmouth, C., *Australia* 42 A3
Sidney, *Canada* 50 D4
Sidney, *Mont., U.S.A.* . 54 B2
Sidney, *N.Y., U.S.A.* .. 52 D8
Sidney, *Nebr., U.S.A.* . 54 E3
Sidney, *Ohio, U.S.A.* .. 52 E3
Sidney Lanier, L., *U.S.A.* 53 H4
Sidoarjo, *Indonesia* .. 27 G15
Sidon = Saydā,
  Lebanon 33 B4
Sidra, G. of = Surt,
  Khalīj, *Libya* 35 B9
Siedlce, *Poland* 13 B12
Sieg →, *Germany* ... 12 C4
Siegen, *Germany* 12 C5
Siem Reap = Siemreab,
  Cambodia 26 B2
Siemreab, *Cambodia* . 26 B2
Siena, *Italy* 16 C4
Sieradz, *Poland* 13 C10
Sierra Blanca, *U.S.A.* . 57 L11
Sierra Blanca Peak,
  U.S.A. 57 K11
Sierra Colorada,
  Argentina 64 E3
Sierra Gorda, *Chile* .. 62 H5
Sierra Leone ■, *W. Afr.* 34 G3
Sierra Madre, *Mexico* . 59 D6
Sierra Mojada, *Mexico* 58 B4
Sierra Vista, *U.S.A.* ... 57 L8
Sifnos, *Greece* 17 F11
Sifton, *Canada* 51 C8
Sifton Pass, *Canada* .. 50 B3
Sighetu-Marmaţiei,
  Romania 13 E12
Sighişoara, *Romania* . 13 E13
Sigli, *Indonesia* 26 C1
Siglufjörður, *Iceland* .. 6 C4
Sigsig, *Ecuador* 62 D3
Sigüenza, *Spain* 15 B4
Siguiri, *Guinea* 34 F4
Sigulda, *Latvia* 7 H21
Sihanoukville =
  Kampong Saom,
  Cambodia 26 B2
Siikajoki →, *Finland* .. 6 D21
Siilinjärvi, *Finland* 6 E22
Sikar, *India* 28 F9
Sikasso, *Mali* 34 F4
Sikeston, *U.S.A.* 55 G10
Sikhote Alin, Khrebet,
  Russia 21 E14
Sikhote Alin Ra. =
  Sikhote Alin, Khrebet,
  Russia 21 E14
Síkinos, *Greece* 17 F11
Sikkani Chief →,
  Canada 50 B4
Sikkim □, *India* 29 F16
Sikotu-Ko, *Japan* 22 C10
Sil →, *Spain* 15 A2
Silacayoapan, *Mexico* 59 D5
Silchar, *India* 29 G18
Siler City, *U.S.A.* 53 H6
Silesia = Śląsk, *Poland* 12 C9
Silgarhi Doti, *Nepal* .. 29 E12
Silghat, *India* 29 F18
Silifke, *Turkey* 19 G5
Siliguri = Shiliguri,
  India 29 F16

Siling Co, *China* 24 C3
Silistra, *Bulgaria* 17 B12
Silivri, *Turkey* 17 D13
Siljan, *Sweden* 7 F16
Silkeborg, *Denmark* .. 7 H13
Sillajhuay, Cordillera,
  Chile 62 G5
Sillamäe, *Estonia* 7 G22
Silloth, *U.K.* 8 C4
Siloam Springs, *U.S.A.* 55 G7
Silsbee, *U.S.A.* 55 K7
Silva Porto = Kuito,
  Angola 37 G3
Silver City, *U.S.A.* 57 K9
Silver Cr. →, *U.S.A.* .. 56 E4
Silver Lake, *U.S.A.* ... 56 E3
Silverton, *Colo., U.S.A.* 57 H10
Silverton, *Tex., U.S.A.* 55 H4
Silvies →, *U.S.A.* 56 E4
Simanggang = Bandar
  Sri Aman, *Malaysia* . 26 D4
Simard, L., *Canada* ... 48 C4
Simav, *Turkey* 17 E13
Simbirsk, *Russia* 18 D8
Simcoe, *Canada* 48 D3
Simcoe, L., *Canada* .. 48 D4
Simeria, *Romania* 13 F12
Simeulue, *Indonesia* .. 26 D1
Simferopol, *Ukraine* .. 19 F5
Sími, *Greece* 17 F12
Simi Valley, *U.S.A.* ... 57 J4
Simikot, *Nepal* 29 E12
Simla, *India* 28 D10
Simmie, *Canada* 51 D7
Simojärvi, *Finland* ... 6 C22
Simojovel, *Mexico* ... 59 D6
Simonette →, *Canada* 50 B5
Simplonpass, *Switz.* .. 14 C8
Simpson Desert,
  Australia 42 D2
Simpson Pen., *Canada* 47 B11
Simrishamn, *Sweden* . 7 J16
Simushir, Ostrov, *Russia* 21 E16
Sin Cowe I.,
  S. China Sea 26 C4
Sinabang, *Indonesia* .. 26 D1
Sinadogo, *Somali Rep.* 32 F4
Sinai = Es Sînâ', *Egypt* 33 F3
Sinai, Mt. = Mûsa,
  Gebel, *Egypt* 30 D2
Sinai Peninsula, *Egypt* . 33 F3
Sinaloa □, *Mexico* ... 58 C3
Sinaloa de Leyva,
  Mexico 58 B3
Sincelejo, *Colombia* .. 62 B3
Sinclair, *U.S.A.* 56 F10
Sinclair Mills, *Canada* . 50 C4
Sincorá, Serra do, *Brazil* 63 F10
Sind □, *Pakistan* 28 G6
Sind Sagar Doab,
  Pakistan 28 D7
Sindangan, *Phil.* 27 C6
Sindangbarang,
  Indonesia 27 G12
Sines, *Portugal* 15 D1
Sines, C. de, *Portugal* . 15 D1
Singa, *Sudan* 35 F12
Singapore ■, *Asia* ... 26 D2
Singaraja, *Indonesia* .. 26 F5
Singida, *Tanzania* 36 E6
Singitikós Kólpos,
  Greece 17 D11
Singkaling Hkamti,
  Burma 29 G19
Singkang, *Indonesia* .. 27 E6
Singkawang, *Indonesia* 26 D3
Singkep, *Indonesia* ... 26 E2
Singleton, *Australia* .. 43 E5
Singleton, Mt., *N. Terr.,*
  Australia 40 D5
Singleton, Mt.,
  W. Austral., Australia 41 E2
Singora = Songkhla,
  Thailand 26 C2
Sinî □, *Egypt* 33 F3
Sinjai, *Indonesia* 27 F6
Sinjar, *Iraq* 30 B4
Sinkat, *Sudan* 35 E13
Sinkiang Uighur =
  Xinjiang Uygur
  Zizhiqu □, *China* .. 24 C3
Sinmak, *Korea* 25 C14
Sinnamary, *Fr. Guiana* 63 B8
Sinni →, *Italy* 16 D7
Sinop, *Turkey* 19 F6
Sinsk, *Russia* 21 C13
Sintang, *Indonesia* ... 26 D4
Sinton, *U.S.A.* 55 L6
Sintra, *Portugal* 15 C1
Siocon, *Phil.* 27 C6
Siófok, *Hungary* 13 E10
Sion, *Switz.* 14 C7
Sioux City, *U.S.A.* 54 D6
Sioux Falls, *U.S.A.* ... 54 D6
Sioux Lookout, *Canada* 48 B1
Sioux Narrows, *Canada* 51 D10
Siping, *China* 25 B7
Sipiwesk L., *Canada* .. 51 B9
Sipura, *Indonesia* 26 E1
Siquia →, *Nic.* 60 D3
Siquijor, *Phil.* 27 C6
Siquirres, *Costa Rica* . 60 D3
Şir Banī Yās, *U.A.E.* ... 31 E7

Sir Edward Pellew
  Group, *Australia* ... 42 B2
Sir Graham Moore Is.,
  Australia 40 B4
Sir James MacBrien,
  Mt., *Canada* 46 B7
Sira →, *Norway* 7 G12
Siracusa, *Italy* 16 F6
Sirajganj, *Bangla.* 29 G16
Sīrdān, *Iran* 31 B6
Sirdaryo =
  Syrdarya →,
  Kazakstan 20 E7
Siren, *U.S.A.* 54 C8
Siret →, *Romania* ... 13 F14
Sirghāyā, *Syria* 33 B5
Sirohi, *India* 28 G8
Sironj, *India* 28 G10
Síros, *Greece* 17 F11
Sirri, *Iran* 31 E7
Sirsa, *India* 28 E9
Sisak, *Croatia* 12 F9
Sisaket, *Thailand* 26 A2
Sisipuk L., *Canada* ... 51 B8
Sisophon, *Cambodia* . 26 B2
Sisseton, *U.S.A.* 54 C6
Sīstān, *Asia* 31 D9
Sīstān, Daryācheh-ye,
  Iran 31 D9
Sīstān va
  Balūchestān □, *Iran* . 31 E9
Sisters, *U.S.A.* 56 D3
Sitapur, *India* 29 F12
Sitges, *Spain* 15 B6
Sitía, *Greece* 17 G12
Sitka, *U.S.A.* 50 B1
Sittang Myit →, *Burma* 29 L20
Sittard, *Neths.* 11 C5
Sittingbourne, *U.K.* ... 9 F8
Sittoung = Sittang
  Myit →, *Burma* ... 29 L20
Sittwe, *Burma* 29 J18
Situbondo, *Indonesia* . 27 G16
Siuna, *Nic.* 60 D3
Siuri, *India* 29 H15
Sivand, *Iran* 31 D7
Sivas, *Turkey* 19 G6
Siverek, *Turkey* 30 B3
Sivomaskinskiy, *Russia* 18 A11
Sivrihisar, *Turkey* 19 G5
Sîwa, *Egypt* 35 C11
Siwalik Range, *Nepal* . 29 F13
Siwan, *India* 29 F14
Sixth Cataract, *Sudan* . 35 E12
Sjælland, *Denmark* ... 7 J14
Sjumen = Shumen,
  Bulgaria 17 C12
Skadarsko Jezero,
  Montenegro, Yug. .. 17 C8
Skaftafell, *Iceland* ... 6 D5
Skagafjörður, *Iceland* . 6 D4
Skagastølstindane,
  Norway 7 F12
Skagaströnd, *Iceland* . 6 D3
Skagen, *Denmark* ... 7 H14
Skagerrak, *Denmark* . 7 H13
Skagway, *U.S.A.* 50 B1
Skala-Podilska, *Ukraine* 13 D14
Skala Podolskaya =
  Skala-Podilska,
  Ukraine 13 D14
Skalat, *Ukraine* 13 D13
Skåne, *Sweden* 7 J15
Skara, *Sweden* 7 G15
Skardu, *Pakistan* 28 B9
Skarżysko-Kamienna,
  Poland 13 C11
Skeena →, *Canada* .. 50 C2
Skeena Mts., *Canada* . 50 B3
Skegness, *U.K.* 8 D8
Skeldon, *Guyana* 62 B7
Skellefte älv →,
  Sweden 6 D19
Skellefteå, *Sweden* ... 6 D19
Skelleftehamn, *Sweden* 6 D19
Skerries, The, *U.K.* ... 8 D3
Ski, *Norway* 7 G14
Skíathos, *Greece* 17 E10
Skiddaw, *U.K.* 8 C4
Skidegate, *Canada* ... 50 C2
Skien, *Norway* 7 G13
Skierniewice, *Poland* . 13 C11
Skikda, *Algeria* 34 A7
Skipton, *U.K.* 8 D5
Skirmish Pt., *Australia* . 42 A1
Skíros, *Greece* 17 E11
Skive, *Denmark* 7 H13
Skjálfandafljót →,
  Iceland 6 D5
Skjálfandi, *Iceland* ... 6 C5
Skoghall, *Sweden* 7 G15
Skole, *Ukraine* 13 D12
Skópelos, *Greece* 17 E10
Skopje, *Macedonia* .. 17 C9
Skövde, *Sweden* 7 G15
Skovorodino, *Russia* .. 21 D13
Skowhegan, *U.S.A.* .. 53 C11
Skunk →, *U.S.A.* 54 E9
Skuodas, *Lithuania* .. 7 H19
Skvyra, *Ukraine* 13 D15
Skykomish, *U.S.A.* ... 56 C3
Skyros = Skíros, *Greece* 17 E11
Slættaratindur, *Færoe Is.* 6 E9

Slagelse, *Denmark* ... 7 J14
Slamet, *Indonesia* ... 27 G13
Śląsk, *Poland* 12 C9
Slate Is., *Canada* 48 C2
Slatina, *Romania* 13 F13
Slaton, *U.S.A.* 55 J4
Slave →, *Canada* 50 A6
Slave Coast, *W. Afr.* .. 34 G6
Slave Lake, *Canada* .. 50 B6
Slave Pt., *Canada* 50 A5
Slavgorod, *Russia* ... 20 D8
Slavonski Brod, *Croatia* 17 B8
Slavuta, *Ukraine* 13 C14
Slavyanka, *Russia* ... 22 C5
Slavyansk = Slovyansk,
  Ukraine 19 E6
Slawharad, *Belarus* .. 13 B16
Sleaford, *U.K.* 8 D7
Sleaford B., *Australia* . 43 E2
Sleeper Is., *Canada* .. 47 C11
Sleepy Eye, *U.S.A.* ... 54 C7
Slemon L., *Canada* .. 50 A5
Slidell, *U.S.A.* 55 K10
Sligeach = Sligo,
  Ireland 10 D2
Sligo, *Ireland* 10 D2
Slite, *Sweden* 7 H18
Sliven, *Bulgaria* 17 C12
Slobodskoy, *Russia* .. 18 C9
Slobozia, *Romania* ... 13 F14
Slocan, *Canada* 50 D5
Slonim, *Belarus* 13 B13
Slough, *U.K.* 9 F7
Slough □, *U.K.* 9 F7
Slovak Rep. ■, *Europe* 13 D10
Slovakia = Slovak
  Rep. ■, *Europe* 13 D10
Slovakian Ore Mts. =
  Slovenské Rudohorie,
  Slovak Rep. 13 D10
Slovenia ■, *Europe* .. 12 F8
Slovenija = Slovenia ■,
  Europe 12 F8
Slovenské Rudohorie,
  Slovak Rep. 13 D10
Slovyansk, *Ukraine* .. 19 E6
Sluch →, *Ukraine* ... 13 C14
Sluis, *Neths.* 11 C3
Słupsk, *Poland* 13 A9
Slurry, *Belarus* 13 B14
Slyudyanka, *Russia* .. 21 D11
Småland, *Sweden* ... 7 H16
Smalltree L., *Canada* . 51 A8
Smallwood Res.,
  Canada 49 B7
Smara, *Morocco* 34 B4
Smeaton, *Canada* 51 C8
Smederevo,
  Serbia, Yug. 17 B9
Smidovich, *Russia* ... 21 E14
Smith, *Canada* 50 B6
Smith Center, *U.S.A.* . 54 F5
Smith Sund, *Greenland* 4 B4
Smithburne →,
  Australia 42 B3
Smithers, *Canada* ... 50 C3
Smithfield, *N.C., U.S.A.* 53 H6
Smithfield, *Utah, U.S.A.* 56 F8
Smiths Falls, *Canada* . 48 D4
Smithton, *Australia* .. 42 G4
Smithville, *U.S.A.* 55 K6
Smoky →, *Canada* ... 50 B5
Smoky Bay, *Australia* . 43 E1
Smoky Hill →, *U.S.A.* 54 F6
Smoky Hills, *U.S.A.* .. 54 F5
Smoky Lake, *Canada* . 50 C6
Smøla, *Norway* 6 E13
Smolensk, *Russia* 18 D5
Smolikas, Óros, *Greece* 17 D9
Smolyan, *Bulgaria* ... 17 D11
Smooth Rock Falls,
  Canada 48 C3
Smoothstone L., *Canada* 51 C7
Smorgon = Smarhon,
  Belarus 13 A14
Smyrna = İzmir, *Turkey* 17 E12
Smyrna, *U.S.A.* 52 F8
Snæfell, *Iceland* 6 D6
Snaefell, *U.K.* 8 C3
Snæfellsjökull, *Iceland* . 6 D2
Snake →, *U.S.A.* 56 C4
Snake I., *Australia* 43 F4
Snake Range, *U.S.A.* . 56 G6
Snake River Plain,
  U.S.A. 56 E7
Snåsavatnet, *Norway* . 6 D14
Sneek, *Neths.* 11 A5
Snežka, *Europe* 12 C8
Snøhetta, *Norway* ... 7 E13
Snohomish, *U.S.A.* .. 56 C2
Snow Hill, *U.S.A.* 52 F8
Snow Lake, *Canada* .. 51 C8
Snowbird L., *Canada* . 51 A8
Snowdon, *U.K.* 8 D3
Snowdrift →, *Canada* 51 A6
Snowflake, *U.S.A.* ... 57 J8
Snowshoe Pk., *U.S.A.* 56 B6
Snowtown, *Australia* . 43 E2
Snowville, *U.S.A.* 56 F7
Snowy →, *Australia* .. 43 F4
Snowy Mts., *Australia* . 43 F4
Snug Corner, *Bahamas* 61 B5
Snyatyn, *Ukraine* 13 D13

Snyder, *Okla., U.S.A.* . 55 H5
Snyder, *Tex., U.S.A.* .. 55 J4
Sobat, Nahr →, *Sudan* 35 G12
Sobradinho, Reprêsa de,
  Brazil 63 E10
Sobral, *Brazil* 63 D10
Soc Trang, *Vietnam* .. 26 C3
Soch'e = Shache, *China* 24 C2
Sochi, *Russia* 19 F6
Société, Is. de la,
  Pac. Oc. 45 J12
Society Is. = Société, Is.
  de la, *Pac. Oc.* 45 J12
Socompa, Portezuelo
  de, *Chile* 64 A3
Socorro, *N. Mex., U.S.A.* 57 J10
Socorro, *Tex., U.S.A.* . 57 L10
Socorro, I., *Mexico* ... 58 D2
Socotra, *Ind. Oc.* 32 E5
Soda L., *U.S.A.* 57 J5
Soda Springs, *U.S.A.* . 56 E8
Sodankylä, *Finland* ... 6 C22
Söderhamn, *Sweden* . 7 F17
Söderköping, *Sweden* . 7 G17
Södermanland, *Sweden* 7 G17
Södertälje, *Sweden* .. 7 G17
Sodiri, *Sudan* 35 F11
Soest, *Neths.* 11 B5
Sofia = Sofiya, *Bulgaria* 17 C10
Sofia →, *Madag.* ... 37 H9
Sofiya, *Bulgaria* 17 C10
Sōfu-Gan, *Japan* 23 K10
Sogamoso, *Colombia* . 62 B4
Sogār, *Iran* 31 E8
Sogndalsfjøra, *Norway* 7 F12
Søgne, *Norway* 7 G12
Sognefjorden, *Norway* 7 F11
Soh, *Iran* 31 C6
Sohâg, *Egypt* 35 C12
Soignies, *Belgium* 11 D4
Soissons, *France* 14 B5
Sōja, *Japan* 23 G6
Sokal, *Ukraine* 13 C13
Söke, *Turkey* 17 F12
Sokhumi, *Georgia* ... 19 F7
Sokodé, *Togo* 34 G6
Sokol, *Russia* 18 C7
Sokółka, *Poland* 13 B12
Sokołów Podlaski,
  Poland 13 B12
Sokoto, *Nigeria* 34 F7
Sol Iletsk, *Russia* 18 D10
Solano, *Phil.* 27 A6
Solapur, *India* 28 L9
Soldotna, *U.S.A.* 46 B4
Soledad, *Colombia* ... 62 A4
Soledad, *U.S.A.* 57 H3
Soledad, *Venezuela* .. 62 B6
Solent, The, *U.K.* 9 G6
Solfonn, *Norway* 7 F12
Solhan, *Turkey* 30 B4
Soligalich, *Russia* 18 C7
Soligorsk = Salihorsk,
  Belarus 13 B14
Solihull, *U.K.* 9 E6
Solikamsk, *Russia* ... 18 C10
Solimões =
  Amazonas →,
  S. Amer. 63 D9
Solingen, *Germany* .. 12 C4
Sollefteå, *Sweden* ... 6 E17
Sóller, *Spain* 15 C7
Solo →, *Indonesia* .. 27 G15
Sologne, *France* 14 C4
Solok, *Indonesia* 26 E2
Sololá, *Guatemala* ... 60 D1
Solomon, N. Fork →,
  U.S.A. 54 F5
Solomon, S. Fork →,
  U.S.A. 54 F5
Solomon Is. ■, *Pac. Oc.* 38 B8
Solon, *China* 25 B7
Solon Springs, *U.S.A.* . 54 B9
Solor, *Indonesia* 27 F6
Solothurn, *Switz.* 14 C7
Šolta, *Croatia* 16 C7
Solţānābād, *Khorāsān,*
  Iran 31 C8
Solţānābād, *Khorāsān,*
  Iran 31 B8
Solunska Glava,
  Macedonia 17 D9
Solvang, *U.S.A.* 57 J3
Solvay, *U.S.A.* 52 D7
Sölvesborg, *Sweden* . 7 H16
Solvychegodsk, *Russia* 18 B8
Solway Firth, *U.K.* ... 8 C4
Solwezi, *Zambia* 37 G5
Sōma, *Japan* 22 F10
Soma, *Turkey* 17 E12
Somali Rep. ■, *Africa* . 32 F4
Somalia = Somali
  Rep. ■, *Africa* 32 F4
Sombor, *Serbia, Yug.* . 17 B8
Sombrerete, *Mexico* . 58 C4
Sombrero, *Anguilla* .. 61 C7
Somers, *U.S.A.* 56 B6
Somerset, *Ky., U.S.A.* . 52 G3
Somerset, *Pa., U.S.A.* . 52 E6
Somerset □, *U.K.* 9 F5
Somerset I., *Canada* .. 46 A10
Somerton, *U.S.A.* ... 57 K6

Someş →, Romania . . . 13 D12
Somme →, France . . . 14 A4
Somosierra, Puerto de,
  Spain 15 B4
Somoto, Nic. 60 D2
Somport, Puerto de,
  Spain 14 E3
Soná, Panama 60 E3
Sønderborg, Denmark . 7 J13
Sóndrio, Italy 14 C8
Sonepur, India 29 J13
Song Cau, Vietnam . . 26 B3
Songea, Tanzania . . 36 G7
Songhua Jiang →,
  China 25 B8
Songkhla, Thailand . . 26 C2
Songo, Mozam. 37 H6
Songo, Sudan 35 G10
Songpan, China 24 C5
Sonipat, India 28 E10
Sonmiani, Pakistan . . 28 G5
Sono →, Brazil 63 E9
Sonora, Calif., U.S.A. . 57 H3
Sonora, Tex., U.S.A. . 55 K4
Sonora □, Mexico . . 58 B2
Sonora →, Mexico . . 58 B2
Sonoran Desert, U.S.A. 57 K6
Sonoyta, Mexico 58 A2
Sonsonate, El Salv. . . 60 D2
Sonsorol Is., Pac. Oc. . 27 C8
Soochow = Suzhou,
  China 25 C7
Sopi, Indonesia 27 D7
Sopot, Poland 13 A10
Sopron, Hungary . . . 13 E9
Sør-Rondane, Antarctica 5 D4
Sorel, Canada 48 C5
Sórgono, Italy 16 D3
Soria, Spain 15 B4
Sorkh, Kuh-e, Iran . . 31 C8
Soroca, Moldova . . . 13 D15
Sorocaba, Brazil . . . 64 A7
Sorochinsk, Russia . . 18 D9
Soroki = Soroca,
  Moldova 13 D15
Sorong, Indonesia . . 27 E8
Soroti, Uganda 36 D6
Sørøya, Norway 6 A20
Sørøysundet, Norway . 6 A20
Sorrell, Australia . . . 42 G4
Sorsele, Sweden 6 D17
Sorsogon, Phil. 27 B6
Sortavala, Russia . . . 18 B5
Sortland, Norway . . . 6 B16
Soscumica, L., Canada 48 B4
Sosnogorsk, Russia . . 18 B9
Sosnowiec, Poland . . 13 C10
Sotkamo, Finland . . . 6 D23
Soto la Marina →,
  Mexico 59 C5
Sotuta, Mexico 59 C7
Souanké, Congo 36 D2
Soúdhas, Kólpos,
  Greece 17 G11
Soufrière, St. Lucia . . 61 D7
Sŏul, S. Korea 25 C7
Sound, The, U.K. . . . 9 G3
Sources, Mt. aux,
  Lesotho 37 K5
Soure, Brazil 63 D9
Souris, Man., Canada . 51 D8
Souris, P.E.I., Canada . 49 C7
Souris →, Canada . . 51 D9
Sousa, Brazil 63 E11
Sousse, Tunisia 35 A8
South Africa ■, Africa . 37 L4
South Aulatsivik I.,
  Canada 49 A7
South Australia □,
  Australia 43 E2
South Baldy, U.S.A. . . 57 J10
South Bend, U.S.A. . . 52 E2
South Boston, U.S.A. . 53 G6
South Branch, Canada . 49 C8
South Brook, Canada . 49 C8
South C., Australia . . . 38 F7
South Carolina □,
  U.S.A. 53 J5
South Charleston,
  U.S.A. 52 F5
South China Sea, Asia . 26 C4
South Dakota □, U.S.A. 54 C5
South Downs, U.K. . . 9 G7
South East C., Australia 42 G4
South East Is., Australia 41 F3
South Foreland, U.K. . 9 F9
South Fork Grand →,
  U.S.A. 54 C3
South Fork
  Republican →,
  U.S.A. 54 E4
South Georgia,
  Antarctica 64 G9
South
  Gloucestershire □,
  U.K. 9 F5
South Haven, U.S.A. . 52 D2
South Henik, L., Canada 51 A9
South Honshu Ridge,
  Pac. Oc. 44 E6
South Horr, Kenya . . 36 D7
South I., N.Z. 39 L3
South Indian Lake,
  Canada 51 B9

South Invercargill, N.Z. 39 M2
South Knife →,
  Canada 51 B10
South Korea ■, Asia . 25 C7
South Lake Tahoe,
  U.S.A. 56 G3
South Loup →, U.S.A. 54 E5
South Magnetic Pole,
  Antarctica 5 C9
South Milwaukee,
  U.S.A. 52 D2
South Molton, U.K. . . 9 F4
South Moose L., Canada 51 C8
South Nahanni →,
  Canada 50 A4
South Natuna Is. =
  Natuna Selatan,
  Kepulauan, Indonesia 26 D3
South Negril Pt.,
  Jamaica 60 C4
South Orkney Is.,
  Antarctica 5 C18
South Ossetia □,
  Georgia 19 F7
South Pagai, I. = Pagai
  Selatan, Pulau,
  Indonesia 26 E2
South Pittsburg, U.S.A. 53 H3
South Platte →, U.S.A. 54 E4
South Pole, Antarctica . 5 E
South Porcupine,
  Canada 48 C3
South Portland, U.S.A. 53 D10
South River, Canada . . 48 C4
South Ronaldsay, U.K. . 10 B5
South Sandwich Is.,
  Antarctica 5 B1
South
  Saskatchewan →,
  Canada 51 C7
South Seal →, Canada 51 B9
South Shetland Is.,
  Antarctica 5 C18
South Shields, U.K. . . 8 C6
South Sioux City, U.S.A. 54 D6
South Taranaki Bight,
  N.Z. 39 H5
South Thompson →,
  Canada 50 C4
South Twin I., Canada . 48 B4
South Tyne →, U.K. . . 8 C5
South Uist, U.K. 10 C3
South West Africa =
  Namibia ■, Africa . . 37 J3
South West C., Australia 42 G4
South West Rocks,
  Australia 43 E5
South Yorkshire □, U.K. 8 D6
Southampton, Canada . 48 D3
Southampton, U.K. . . 9 G6
Southampton, U.S.A. . 52 E9
Southampton □, U.K. . 9 G6
Southampton I., Canada 47 B11
Southaven, U.S.A. . . 55 H9
Southbank, Canada . . 50 C3
Southbridge, N.Z. . . . 39 K4
Southend, Canada . . . 51 B8
Southend-on-Sea, U.K. 9 F8
Southend-on-Sea □,
  U.K. 9 F8
Southern Alps, N.Z. . . 39 K3
Southern Cross,
  Australia 41 F2
Southern Indian L.,
  Canada 51 B9
Southern Ocean,
  Antarctica 5 C6
Southern Pines, U.S.A. 53 H6
Southern Uplands, U.K. 10 D5
Southland □, N.Z. . . . 39 L1
Southport, Australia . . 43 D5
Southport, U.K. 8 D4
Southport, U.S.A. . . . 53 K3
Southwest C., N.Z. . . 39 M1
Southwold, U.K. 9 E9
Sovetsk, Kaliningd.,
  Russia 7 J19
Sovetsk, Kirov, Russia . 18 C8
Sovetskaya Gavan =
  Vanino, Russia . . . 21 E15
Soweto, S. Africa . . . 37 K5
Sōya-Kaikyō = La
  Perouse Str., Asia . . 22 B11
Sōya-Misaki, Japan . . 22 B10
Sozh →, Belarus . . . 13 B16
Spa, Belgium 11 D5
Spain ■, Europe . . . 15 B4
Spalding, Australia . . 43 E2
Spalding, U.K. 8 E7
Spanish, Canada . . . 48 C3
Spanish Fork, U.S.A. . 56 F8
Spanish Town, Jamaica 60 C4
Sparks, U.S.A. 56 G4
Sparta = Spárti, Greece 17 F10
Sparta, Mich., U.S.A. . 52 D3
Sparta, Wis., U.S.A. . 54 D9
Spartanburg, U.S.A. . 53 H5
Spárti, Greece 17 F10
Spartivento, C.,
  Calabria, Italy . . . 16 F7
Spartivento, C., Sard.,
  Italy 16 E3
Sparwood, Canada . . 50 D6
Spassk Dalniy, Russia . 21 E14

Spátha, Ákra, Greece . 17 G10
Spatsizi →, Canada . . 50 B3
Spatsizi Plateau
  Wilderness Park,
  Canada 50 B3
Spearfish, U.S.A. . . . 54 C3
Spearman, U.S.A. . . . 55 G4
Speightstown, Barbados 61 D8
Spencer, Idaho, U.S.A. 56 D7
Spencer, Iowa, U.S.A. 54 D7
Spencer, Nebr., U.S.A. 54 D5
Spencer, C., Australia . 43 F2
Spencer G., Australia . 43 E2
Spences Bridge, Canada 50 C4
Spennymoor, U.K. . . 8 C6
Spenser Mts., N.Z. . . 39 K4
Spey →, U.K. 10 C5
Speyer, Germany . . . 12 D5
Spirit River, Canada . . 50 B5
Spiritwood, Canada . . 51 C7
Spithead, U.K. 9 G6
Spitzbergen = Svalbard,
  Arctic 4 B8
Spjelkavik, Norway . . 7 E12
Split, Croatia 16 C7
Split L., Canada 51 B9
Split Lake, Canada . . 51 B9
Spofford, U.S.A. . . . 55 L4
Spokane, U.S.A. . . . 56 C5
Spoleto, Italy 16 C5
Spooner, U.S.A. 54 C9
Sporyy Navolok, Mys,
  Russia 20 B7
Sprague, U.S.A. 56 C5
Spratly I., S. China Sea 26 C4
Spratly Is., S. China Sea 26 C4
Spray, U.S.A. 56 D4
Spree →, Germany . . 12 B7
Sprengisandur, Iceland 6 D5
Spring Creek, U.S.A. . 56 F6
Spring Hill, U.S.A. . . 53 L4
Spring Mts., U.S.A. . . 57 H6
Springbok, Canada . . 49 C8
Springbok, S. Africa . . 37 K3
Springdale, Canada . . 49 C8
Springdale, U.S.A. . . 55 G7
Springer, U.S.A. 55 G2
Springerville, U.S.A. . 57 J9
Springfield, N.Z. . . . 39 K3
Springfield, Colo.,
  U.S.A. 55 G3
Springfield, Ill., U.S.A. 54 F10
Springfield, Mass.,
  U.S.A. 52 D9
Springfield, Mo., U.S.A. 55 G8
Springfield, Ohio, U.S.A. 52 F4
Springfield, Oreg.,
  U.S.A. 56 D2
Springfield, Tenn.,
  U.S.A. 53 G2
Springfield, Vt., U.S.A. 52 D9
Springhill, Canada . . 49 C7
Springhill, U.S.A. . . . 55 J8
Springhouse, Canada . 50 C4
Springs, S. Africa . . . 37 K5
Springsure, Australia . 42 C4
Springville, U.S.A. . . 56 F8
Spur, U.S.A. 55 J4
Spurn Hd., U.K. 8 D8
Spuzzum, Canada . . . 50 D4
Squamish, Canada . . 50 D4
Square Islands, Canada 49 B8
Squires, Mt., Australia . 41 E4
Srbija = Serbia □,
  Yugoslavia 17 C9
Sre Ambel, Cambodia . 26 B2
Sre Umbell = Sre
  Ambel, Cambodia . . 26 B2
Srebrenica, Bos.-H. . . 17 B8
Sredinny Ra. =
  Sredinnyy Khrebet,
  Russia 21 D16
Sredinnyy Khrebet,
  Russia 21 D16
Srednekolymsk, Russia 21 C16
Śrem, Poland 13 B9
Sremska Mitrovica,
  Serbia, Yug. 17 B8
Srepok →, Cambodia . 26 B3
Sretensk, Russia 21 D12
Sri Lanka ■, Asia . . . 28 R12
Srikakulam, India . . . 29 K13
Srinagar, India 28 B9
Staaten →, Australia . 42 B3
Stade, Germany 12 B5
Stadskanaal, Neths. . . 11 A6
Stafford, U.K. 8 E5
Stafford, U.S.A. 55 G5
Staffordshire □, U.K. . 8 E5
Staines, U.K. 9 F7
Stakhanov, Ukraine . . 19 E6
Stalingrad = Volgograd,
  Russia 19 E7
Staliniri = Tskhinvali,
  Georgia 19 F7
Stalino = Donetsk,
  Ukraine 19 E6
Stalinogorsk =
  Novomoskovsk,
  Russia 18 D6
Stalowa Wola, Poland . 13 C12
Stalybridge, U.K. . . . 8 D5
Stamford, Australia . . 42 C3
Stamford, U.K. 9 E7
Stamford, Conn., U.S.A. 52 E9
Stamford, Tex., U.S.A. 55 J5

Stamps, U.S.A. 55 J8
Standish, U.S.A. 52 D4
Stanford, U.S.A. . . . 56 C8
Stanislav = Ivano-
  Frankivsk, Ukraine . 13 D13
Stanke Dimitrov,
  Bulgaria 17 C10
Stanley, Australia . . . 42 G4
Stanley, Canada 51 B8
Stanley, Falk. Is. . . . 64 G5
Stanley, U.K. 8 C6
Stanley, Idaho, U.S.A. . 56 D6
Stanley, N. Dak., U.S.A. 54 A3
Stanovoy Khrebet,
  Russia 21 D13
Stanovoy Ra. =
  Stanovoy Khrebet,
  Russia 21 D13
Stansmore Ra.,
  Australia 40 D4
Stanthorpe, Australia . 43 D5
Stanton, U.S.A. 55 J4
Staples, U.S.A. 54 B7
Star City, Canada . . . 51 C8
Stara Planina, Bulgaria 17 C10
Stara Zagora, Bulgaria 17 C11
Starachowice, Poland . 13 C11
Staraya Russa, Russia . 18 C5
Starbuck I., Kiribati . . 45 H12
Stargard Szczeciński,
  Poland 12 B8
Staritsa, Russia 18 C5
Starke, U.S.A. 53 L4
Starogard Gdański,
  Poland 13 B10
Starokonstantinov =
  Starokonstyantyniv,
  Ukraine 13 D14
Starokonstyantyniv,
  Ukraine 13 D14
Start Pt., U.K. 9 G4
Staryy Chartoriysk,
  Ukraine 13 C13
Staryy Oskol, Russia . 19 D6
State College, U.S.A. . 52 E7
Staten, I. = Estados, I.
  de los, Argentina . . 64 G4
Statesboro, U.S.A. . . 53 J5
Statesville, U.S.A. . . 53 H5
Staunton, Ill., U.S.A. . 54 F10
Staunton, Va., U.S.A. . 52 F6
Stavanger, Norway . . 7 G11
Staveley, N.Z. 39 K3
Stavelot, Belgium . . . 11 D5
Stavern, Norway . . . 7 G14
Stavoren, Neths. . . . 11 B5
Stavropol, Russia . . . 19 E7
Stawell, Australia . . . 42 F3
Stawell →, Australia . 42 C3
Stayton, U.S.A. 56 D2
Steamboat Springs,
  U.S.A. 56 F10
Steele, U.S.A. 54 B5
Steelton, U.S.A. 52 E7
Steen River, Canada . 50 B5
Steenkool = Bintuni,
  Indonesia 27 E8
Steens Mt., U.S.A. . . 56 E4
Steenwijk, Neths. . . . 11 B6
Steep Pt., Australia . . 41 E1
Steep Rock, Canada . 51 C9
Stefanie L. = Chew
  Bahir, Ethiopia . . . 32 G2
Stefansson Bay,
  Antarctica 5 C5
Steiermark □, Austria . 12 E8
Steinbach, Canada . . 51 D9
Steinkjer, Norway . . . 6 D14
Steinkopf, S. Africa . . 37 K3
Stellarton, Canada . . 49 C7
Stendal, Germany . . . 12 B6
Steornabhaigh =
  Stornoway, U.K. . . 10 B3
Stepanakert =
  Xankändi, Azerbaijan 19 G8
Stephens Creek,
  Australia 43 E3
Stephens I., Canada . . 50 C2
Stephens L., Canada . 51 B9
Stephenville, Canada . 49 C8
Stephenville, U.S.A. . 55 J5
Stepnoi = Elista, Russia 19 E7
Sterling, Colo., U.S.A. 54 E3
Sterling, Ill., U.S.A. . . 54 E10
Sterling, Kans., U.S.A. 54 F5
Sterling City, U.S.A. . 55 K4
Sterling Heights, U.S.A. 52 D4
Sterlitamak, Russia . . 18 D10
Stettin = Szczecin,
  Poland 12 B8
Stettiner Haff, Germany 12 B8
Stettler, Canada 50 C6
Steubenville, U.S.A. . 52 E5
Stevenage, U.K. . . . 9 F7
Stevens Point, U.S.A. . 54 C10
Stevenson L., Canada . 51 C9
Stevensville, U.S.A. . . 56 C6
Stewart, B.C., Canada . 50 B3
Stewart, N.W.T., Canada 46 B6
Stewart →, Canada . . 46 B2
Stewart, C., Australia . 42 A1
Stewart, I., Chile . . . 64 G2
Stewart, I., N.Z. 39 M1
Stewartville, U.S.A. . . 54 D8
Stewiacke, Canada . . 49 C7
Steyr, Austria 12 D8

Stigler, U.S.A. 55 H7
Stikine →, Canada . . 50 B2
Stillwater, N.Z. 39 K3
Stillwater, Minn., U.S.A. 54 C8
Stillwater, Okla., U.S.A. 55 G6
Stillwater Range, U.S.A. 56 G4
Stilwell, U.S.A. 55 H7
Stip, Macedonia 17 D10
Stirling, U.K. 10 C5
Stirling Ra., Australia . 41 F2
Stjernøya, Norway . . 6 A20
Stjørdalshalsen, Norway 6 E14
Stockerau, Austria . . 12 D9
Stockholm, Sweden . . 7 G18
Stockport, U.K. 8 D5
Stocksbridge, U.K. . . 8 D6
Stockton, Calif., U.S.A. 57 H3
Stockton, Kans., U.S.A. 54 F5
Stockton, Mo., U.S.A. . 55 G8
Stockton-on-Tees, U.K. 8 C6
Stockton-on-Tees □,
  U.K. 8 C6
Stockton Plateau, U.S.A. 55 K3
Stoke-on-Trent, U.K. . 8 D5
Stoke-on-Trent □, U.K. 8 D5
Stokes Pt., Australia . . 42 G3
Stokes Ra., Australia . 40 C5
Stokksnes, Iceland . . 6 D6
Stokmarknes, Norway . 6 B16
Stolac, Bos.-H. 17 C7
Stolbovoy, Ostrov,
  Russia 21 B14
Stolbtsy = Stowbtsy,
  Belarus 13 B14
Stolin, Belarus 13 C14
Stone, U.K. 8 E5
Stonehaven, U.K. . . . 10 C5
Stonehenge, Australia . 42 C3
Stonehenge, U.K. . . . 9 F6
Stonewall, Canada . . 51 C9
Stony L., Canada . . . 51 B9
Stony Rapids, Canada . 51 B7
Stony Tunguska =
  Podkamennaya
  Tunguska →,
  Russia 21 C10
Stora Lulevatten,
  Sweden 6 C18
Storavan, Sweden . . . 6 D18
Stord, Norway 7 G11
Store Bælt, Denmark . 7 J14
Støren, Norway 6 E14
Storm B., Australia . . 42 G4
Storm Lake, U.S.A. . . 54 D7
Stormberge, S. Africa . 37 L5
Stornoway, U.K. 10 B3
Storozhinets =
  Storozhynets, Ukraine 13 D13
Storozhynets, Ukraine . 13 D13
Storsjön, Sweden . . . 6 E16
Storuman, Sweden . . 6 D17
Storuman, sjö, Sweden 6 D17
Stoughton, Canada . . 51 D8
Stour →, Dorset, U.K. . 9 G5
Stour →, Kent, U.K. . . 9 F9
Stour →, Suffolk, U.K. 9 F9
Stourbridge, U.K. . . . 9 E5
Stout L., Canada . . . 51 C10
Stowbtsy, Belarus . . . 13 B14
Stowmarket, U.K. . . . 9 E9
Strahan, Australia . . . 42 G4
Stralsund, Germany . . 12 A7
Stranda,
  Møre og Romsdal,
  Norway 7 E12
Stranda,
  Nord-Trøndelag,
  Norway 6 E14
Stranraer, U.K. 10 D4
Strasbourg, Canada . . 51 C8
Strasbourg, France . . 14 B7
Stratford, Canada . . . 48 D3
Stratford, N.Z. 39 H5
Stratford, U.S.A. . . . 55 G3
Stratford-upon-Avon,
  U.K. 9 E6
Strathalbyn, Australia . 43 F2
Strathcona Prov. Park,
  Canada 50 D3
Strathmore, Canada . 50 C6
Strathnaver, Canada . 50 C4
Strathroy, Canada . . 48 D3
Straubing, Germany . . 12 D7
Straumnes, Iceland . . 6 C2
Strawberry →, U.S.A. 56 F8
Streaky B., Australia . 43 E1
Streaky Bay, Australia . 43 E1
Streator, U.S.A. 54 E10
Strelka, Russia 21 D10
Streymoy, Færoe Is. . . 6 E9
Strezhevoy, Russia . . 20 C8
Strimón →, Greece . . 17 D10
Strimonikós Kólpos,
  Greece 17 D11
Strómboli, Italy 16 E6
Stromsburg, U.S.A. . . 54 E6
Strömstad, Sweden . . 7 G14
Strömsund, Sweden . . 6 E16
Stronsay, U.K. 10 B5
Stroud, U.K. 9 F5
Stroud Road, Australia 43 E5
Struer, Denmark . . . 7 H13
Strumica, Macedonia . 17 D10

Struthers, Canada . . . 48 C2
Stryker, U.S.A. 56 B6
Stryy, Ukraine 13 D12
Strzelecki Cr. →,
  Australia 43 D2
Stuart, Fla., U.S.A. . . 53 M5
Stuart, Nebr., U.S.A. . 54 D5
Stuart →, Canada . . 50 C4
Stuart Bluff Ra.,
  Australia 40 D5
Stuart L., Canada . . . 50 C4
Stuart Ra., Australia . . 43 D1
Stull L., Canada 48 B1
Stung Treng = Stoeng
  Treng, Cambodia . . 26 B3
Stupart →, Canada . . 48 A1
Sturgeon B., Canada . 51 C9
Sturgeon Bay, U.S.A. . 52 C2
Sturgeon Falls, Canada 48 C4
Sturgeon L., Alta.,
  Canada 50 B5
Sturgeon L., Ont.,
  Canada 48 C1
Sturgis, Canada 51 C8
Sturgis, Mich., U.S.A. . 52 E3
Sturgis, S. Dak., U.S.A. 54 C3
Sturt Cr. →, Australia . 40 C4
Stuttgart, Germany . . 12 D5
Stuttgart, U.S.A. . . . 55 H9
Stykkishólmur, Iceland 6 D2
Styria = Steiermark □,
  Austria 12 E8
Suakin, Sudan 35 E13
Suaqui, Mexico 58 B3
Subang, Indonesia . . 27 G12
Subansiri →, India . . 29 F18
Subayhah, Si. Arabia . 30 D3
Subi, Indonesia 26 D3
Subotica, Serbia, Yug. 17 A8
Suceava, Romania . . 13 E14
Suchan, Russia 22 C6
Suchitoto, El Salv. . . 60 D2
Suchou = Suzhou,
  China 25 C7
Süchow = Xuzhou,
  China 25 C6
Sucre, Bolivia 62 G5
Sucuriú →, Brazil . . . 63 H8
Sud, Pte. du, Canada . 49 C7
Sud-Ouest, Pte. du,
  Canada 49 C7
Sudan, U.S.A. 55 H3
Sudan ■, Africa 35 E11
Sudbury, Canada . . . 48 C3
Sudbury, U.K. 9 E8
Südd, Sudan 35 G12
Sudeten Mts. = Sudety,
  Europe 13 C9
Sudety, Europe 13 C9
Suðuroy, Færoe Is. . . 6 F9
Sudirman, Pegunungan,
  Indonesia 27 E9
Sueca, Spain 15 C5
Suemez I., U.S.A. . . . 50 B2
Suez = El Suweis, Egypt 35 C12
Suez, G. of = Suweis,
  Khalig el, Egypt . . . 35 C12
Suez Canal = Suweis,
  Qanâ es, Egypt . . . 35 B12
Suffield, Canada . . . 50 C6
Suffolk, U.S.A. 52 G7
Suffolk □, U.K. 9 E9
Sugluk = Salluit,
  Canada 47 B12
Şuhār, Oman 31 E8
Suhl, Germany 12 C6
Suihua, China 25 B7
Sukabumi, Indonesia . 27 G12
Sukadana, Indonesia . 26 E3
Sukagawa, Japan . . . 23 F10
Sukaraja, Indonesia . 26 E4
Sukarnapura =
  Jayapura, Indonesia . 27 E10
Sukhona →, Russia . . 18 C6
Sukhumi = Sokhumi,
  Georgia 19 F7
Sukkur, Pakistan . . . 28 F6
Sukkur Barrage,
  Pakistan 28 F6
Sukumo, Japan 23 H6
Sukunka →, Canada . 50 B4
Sula, Kepulauan,
  Indonesia 27 E7
Sulaco →, Honduras . 60 C2
Sulaiman Range,
  Pakistan 28 D6
Sülär, Iran 31 D6
Sulawesi □, Indonesia . 27 E6
Sulawesi □, Indonesia . 27 E6
Sulawesi Sea = Celebes
  Sea, Indonesia . . . 27 D6
Sulawesi Selatan □,
  Indonesia 27 E6
Sulawesi Utara □,
  Indonesia 27 D6
Sulima, S. Leone . . . 34 G3
Sulina, Romania . . . 13 F15
Sulitjelma, Norway . . 6 C17
Sullana, Peru 62 D2
Sullivan, Ill., U.S.A. . . 54 F10
Sullivan, Ind., U.S.A. . 52 F2
Sullivan, Mo., U.S.A. . 54 F9
Sullivan Bay, Canada . 50 C3
Sullivan I. = Lambi
  Kyun, Burma 26 B1

Sulphur, La., U.S.A. 55 K8
Sulphur, Okla., U.S.A. .. 55 H6
Sulphur Pt., Canada 50 A6
Sulphur Springs, U.S.A. 55 J7
Sultan, Canada 48 C3
Sultanpur, India 29 F13
Sulu Arch., Phil. 27 C6
Sulu Sea, E. Indies 27 C6
Suluq, Libya 35 B10
Sulzberger Ice Shelf,
  Antarctica 5 D10
Sumalata, Indonesia .. 27 D6
Sumatera, Indonesia 26 D2
Sumatera Barat □,
  Indonesia 26 E2
Sumatera Utara □,
  Indonesia 26 D1
Sumatra = Sumatera □,
  Indonesia 26 D2
Sumba, Indonesia 27 F5
Sumba, Selat, Indonesia 27 F5
Sumbawa, Indonesia .. 26 F5
Sumbawa Besar,
  Indonesia 26 F5
Sumbawanga □,
  Tanzania 36 F6
Sumbe, Angola 36 G2
Sumedang, Indonesia . 27 G12
Šumen = Shumen,
  Bulgaria 17 C12
Sumenep, Indonesia .. 27 G15
Sumgait = Sumqayıt,
  Azerbaijan 19 F8
Summer L., U.S.A. ... 56 E3
Summerland, Canada . 50 D5
Summerside, Canada . 49 C7
Summersville, U.S.A. . 52 F5
Summerville, Ga.,
  U.S.A. 53 H3
Summerville, S.C.,
  U.S.A. 53 J5
Summit Lake, Canada . 50 C4
Summit Peak, U.S.A. . 57 H10
Sumner, U.S.A. 54 D8
Sumoto, Japan 23 G7
Šumperk, Czech Rep. . 13 D9
Sumqayıt, Azerbaijan . 19 F8
Sumter, U.S.A. 53 J5
Sumy, Ukraine 19 D5
Sun City, U.S.A. 57 K7
Sun City Center, U.S.A. 53 M4
Sun Lakes, U.S.A. 57 K8
Sun Valley, U.S.A. 56 E6
Sunagawa, Japan 22 C10
Sunburst, U.S.A. 56 B8
Sunbury, Australia 43 F3
Sunbury, U.S.A. 52 E7
Sunda, Selat, Indonesia 26 F3
Sunda Is., Indonesia . 44 H2
Sunda Str. = Sunda,
  Selat, Indonesia ... 26 F3
Sundance, Canada ... 51 B10
Sundance, U.S.A. 54 C2
Sundarbans, The, Asia 29 J16
Sundargarh, India ... 29 H14
Sunderland, U.K. 8 C6
Sundre, Canada 50 C6
Sundsvall, Sweden ... 7 E17
Sungai Petani, Malaysia 26 C2
Sungaigerong,
  Indonesia 26 E2
Sungailiat, Indonesia . 26 E3
Sungaipenuh, Indonesia 26 E2
Sungari = Songhua
  Jiang →, China 25 B8
Sunghua Chiang =
  Songhua Jiang →,
  China 25 B8
Sunland Park, U.S.A. . 57 L10
Sunndalsøra, Norway . 7 E13
Sunnyside, U.S.A. 56 C3
Sunnyvale, U.S.A. 57 H2
Suntar, Russia 21 C12
Suomenselkä, Finland . 6 E21
Suomussalmi, Finland . 6 D23
Suoyarvi, Russia 18 B5
Supai, U.S.A. 57 H7
Supaul, India 29 F15
Superior, Ariz., U.S.A. . 57 K8
Superior, Mont., U.S.A. 56 C6
Superior, Nebr., U.S.A. 54 E5
Superior, Wis., U.S.A. . 54 B8
Superior, L., N. Amer. . 48 C2
Suphan Dağı, Turkey .. 30 B4
Supiori, Indonesia ... 27 E9
Süq Suwayq, Si. Arabia 30 E3
Sür, Lebanon 33 B4
Sür, Oman 32 C6
Sur, Pt., U.S.A. 57 H3
Sura →, Russia 18 C8
Surabaja = Surabaya,
  Indonesia 27 G15
Surabaya, Indonesia . 27 G15
Surakarta, Indonesia . 27 G14
Surat, Australia 43 D4
Surat, India 28 J8
Surat Thani, Thailand . 26 C1
Suratgarh, India 28 E8
Surgut, Russia 20 C8
Suriapet, India 28 L11
Surigao, Phil. 27 C7
Surinam ■, S. Amer. . 63 C7
Suriname = Surinam ■,
  S. Amer. 63 C7

Suriname →, Surinam 63 B7
Sürmaq, Iran 31 D7
Surrey □, U.K. 9 F7
Surt, Libya 35 B9
Surt, Khalīj, Libya 35 B9
Surtsey, Iceland 6 E3
Suruga-Wan, Japan .. 23 G9
Susaki, Japan 23 H6
Susangerd, Iran 31 D6
Susanville, U.S.A. ... 56 F3
Susquehanna →,
  U.S.A. 52 F7
Susques, Argentina .. 64 A3
Sussex, Canada 49 C6
Sussex, E. □, U.K. ... 9 G8
Sussex, W. □, U.K. ... 9 G7
Sustut →, Canada .. 50 B3
Susuman, Russia ... 21 C15
Susunu, Indonesia ... 27 E8
Susurluk, Turkey ... 17 E13
Sutherland, S. Africa . 37 L4
Sutherland, U.S.A. ... 54 E4
Sutherland Falls, N.Z. . 39 L1
Sutherlin, U.S.A. 56 E2
Sutlej →, Pakistan .. 28 E7
Sutton, Nebr., U.S.A. . 54 E6
Sutton, W. Va., U.S.A. . 52 F5
Sutton →, Canada .. 48 A3
Sutton Coldfield, U.K. . 9 E6
Sutton in Ashfield, U.K. 8 D6
Sutton L., Canada ... 48 B3
Suttor →, Australia .. 42 C4
Suttsu, Japan 22 C10
Suva, Fiji 39 D8
Suva Planina,
  Serbia, Yug. 17 C10
Suvorov Is. = Suwarrow
  Is., Cook Is. 45 J11
Suwałki, Poland 13 A12
Suwannee →, U.S.A. 53 L4
Suwanose-Jima, Japan 23 K4
Suwarrow Is., Cook Is. 45 J11
Suwayq aş Şuqban, Iraq 30 D5
Suweis, Khalīg el, Egypt 35 C12
Suweis, Qanâ es, Egypt 35 B12
Suzdal, Russia 18 C7
Suzhou, China 25 C7
Suzu, Japan 23 F8
Suzu-Misaki, Japan .. 23 F8
Suzuka, Japan 23 G8
Svalbard, Arctic 4 B8
Svappavaara, Sweden . 6 C19
Svartisen, Norway ... 6 C15
Svay Rieng, Cambodia 26 B3
Svealand □, Sweden . 7 F16
Sveg, Sweden 7 E16
Svendborg, Denmark . 7 J14
Sverdlovsk =
  Yekaterinburg, Russia 20 D7
Sverdrup Is., Canada . 4 B3
Svetlaya, Russia 22 A9
Svetlogorsk =
  Svyetlahorsk, Belarus 13 B15
Svir →, Russia 18 B5
Svishtov, Bulgaria ... 17 C11
Svislach, Belarus ... 13 B13
Svobodnyy, Russia .. 21 D13
Svolvær, Norway 6 B16
Svyetlahorsk, Belarus . 13 B15
Swabian Alps =
  Schwäbische Alb,
  Germany 12 D5
Swainsboro, U.S.A. .. 53 J4
Swakopmund, Namibia 37 J2
Swale →, U.K. 8 C6
Swan →, Australia ... 41 F2
Swan →, Canada ... 51 C8
Swan Hill, Australia .. 43 F3
Swan Hills, Canada .. 50 C5
Swan Is., W. Indies .. 60 C3
Swan L., Canada 51 C8
Swan Peak, U.S.A. ... 56 C7
Swan Ra., U.S.A. 56 C7
Swan Reach, Australia 43 E2
Swan River, Canada . 51 C8
Swanage, U.K. 9 G6
Swansea, Australia .. 42 G4
Swansea, U.K. 9 F4
Swansea □, U.K. 9 F4
Swastika, Canada ... 48 C3
Swatow = Shantou,
  China 25 D6
Swaziland ■, Africa . 37 K6
Sweden ■, Europe .. 7 E16
Sweet Home, U.S.A. . 56 D2
Sweetgrass, U.S.A. .. 56 B8
Sweetwater, Tenn.,
  U.S.A. 53 H3
Sweetwater, Tex.,
  U.S.A. 55 J4
Sweetwater →, U.S.A. 56 E10
Swellendam, S. Africa 37 L4
Świdnica, Poland 13 C9
Świdnik, Poland 13 C12
Świebodzin, Poland . 12 B8
Świecie, Poland 13 B10
Swift Current, Canada 51 C7
Swiftcurrent →,
  Canada 51 C7
Swindon, U.K. 9 F6
Swindon □, U.K. 9 F6
Swinemünde =
  Świnoujście, Poland . 12 B8
Świnoujście, Poland . 12 B8

Switzerland ■, Europe 14 C8
Sydney, Australia 43 E5
Sydney, Canada 49 C7
Sydney L., Canada .. 51 C10
Sydney Mines, Canada 49 C7
Sydprøven = Alluitsup
  Paa, Greenland 4 C5
Sydra, G. of = Surt,
  Khalīj, Libya 35 B9
Syktyvkar, Russia 18 B9
Sylacauga, U.S.A. ... 53 J2
Sylarna, Sweden 6 E15
Sylhet, Bangla. 29 G17
Sylt, Germany 12 A5
Sylvania, U.S.A. 53 J5
Sylvan Lake, Canada . 50 C6
Sylvester, U.S.A. 53 K4
Sym, Russia 20 C9
Symón, Mexico 58 C4
Synnott Ra., Australia . 40 C4
Syracuse, Kans., U.S.A. 55 G4
Syracuse, N.Y., U.S.A. . 52 D7
Syracuse, Nebr., U.S.A. 54 E6
Syrdarya →, Kazakstan 20 E7
Syria ■, Asia 30 C3
Syrian Desert = Shām,
  Bādiyat ash, Asia .. 30 C3
Syzran, Russia 18 D8
Szczecin, Poland 12 B8
Szczecinek, Poland .. 13 B9
Szczeciński, Zalew =
  Stettiner Haff,
  Germany 12 B8
Szczytno, Poland 13 B11
Szechwan = Sichuan □,
  China 24 C5
Szeged, Hungary 13 E11
Székesfehérvár,
  Hungary 13 E10
Szekszárd, Hungary .. 13 E10
Szentes, Hungary 13 E11
Szolnok, Hungary ... 13 E11
Szombathely, Hungary 13 E9

Tabacal, Argentina ... 64 A4
Tabaco, Phil. 27 B6
Ṭābah, Si. Arabia 30 E4
Ṭabas, Khorāsān, Iran . 31 C9
Ṭabas, Khorāsān, Iran . 31 C8
Tabasará, Serranía de,
  Panama 60 E3
Tabasco □, Mexico .. 59 D6
Tabāsīn, Iran 31 D8
Tabatinga, Serra da,
  Brazil 63 F10
Taber, Canada 50 D6
Tablas I., Phil. 27 B6
Table B. = Tafelbaai,
  S. Africa 37 L3
Table B., Canada 49 B8
Table Mt., S. Africa ... 37 L3
Table Rock L., U.S.A. . 55 G8
Tabletop, Mt., Australia 42 C4
Tábor, Czech Rep. ... 12 D8
Tabora, Tanzania 36 F6
Tabou, Ivory C. 34 H4
Tabrīz, Iran 30 B5
Tabuaeran, Pac. Oc. .. 45 G12
Tabūk, Si. Arabia 30 D3
Tacámbaro de Codallos,
  Mexico 58 D4
Tacheng, China 24 B3
Tacloban, Phil. 27 B6
Tacna, Peru 62 G4
Tacoma, U.S.A. 56 C2
Tacuarembó, Uruguay . 64 C5
Tademaït, Plateau du,
  Algeria 34 C6
Tadjoura, Djibouti ... 32 E3
Tadmor, N.Z. 39 J4
Tadoule L., Canada .. 51 B9
Tadoussac, Canada .. 49 C6
Tadzhikistan =
  Tajikistan ■, Asia .. 20 F8
Taegu, S. Korea 25 C7
Taejŏn, S. Korea 25 C7
Tafalla, Spain 15 A5
Tafelbaai, S. Africa ... 37 L3
Tafermaar, Indonesia . 27 F8
Tafiḥān, Iran 31 D7
Tafresh, Iran 31 C6
Taft, Iran 31 D7
Taft, Phil. 27 B7
Taft, U.S.A. 57 J4
Taftān, Kūh-e, Iran ... 31 D9
Taga Dzong, Bhutan . 29 F16
Taganrog, Russia 19 E6
Tagbilaran, Phil. 27 C6
Tagish, Canada 50 A2
Tagish L., Canada ... 50 A2
Tagliamento →, Italy . 16 B5
Taguatinga, Brazil ... 63 F10
Tagum, Phil. 27 C7
Tagus = Tejo →,
  Europe 15 C1
Tahakopa, N.Z. 39 M2
Tahan, Gunong,
  Malaysia 26 D2
Tahat, Algeria 34 D7
Tāherī, Iran 31 E7
Tahiti, Pac. Oc. 45 J13
Tahlequah, U.S.A. ... 55 H7
Tahoe, L., U.S.A. 56 G3

Tahoe City, U.S.A. ... 56 G3
Tahoka, U.S.A. 55 J4
Tahoua, Niger 34 F7
Tahrūd, Iran 31 D8
Tahsis, Canada 50 D3
Tahta, Egypt 35 C12
Tahulandang, Indonesia 27 D7
Tahuna, Indonesia ... 27 D7
Taibei = T'aipei, Taiwan 25 D7
T'aichung, Taiwan ... 25 D7
Taieri →, N.Z. 39 M3
Taihape, N.Z. 39 H5
Tailem Bend, Australia 43 F2
Taimyr Peninsula =
  Taymyr, Poluostrov,
  Russia 21 B11
Tain, U.K. 10 C4
T'ainan, Taiwan 25 D7
Taínaron, Ákra, Greece 17 F10
T'aipei, Taiwan 25 D7
Taiping, Malaysia ... 26 D2
Taitao, Pen. de, Chile . 64 F2
T'aitung, Taiwan 25 D7
Taivalkoski, Finland .. 6 D23
Taiwan ■, Asia 25 D7
Taïyetos Óros, Greece . 17 F10
Taiyiba, Israel 33 C4
Taiyuan, China 25 C6
Taizhong = T'aichung,
  Taiwan 25 D7
Ta'izz, Yemen 32 E3
Tājābād, Iran 31 D7
Tajikistan ■, Asia ... 20 F8
Tajima, Japan 23 F9
Tajo →, Europe 15 C1
Tajrīsh, Iran 31 C6
Tak, Thailand 26 A1
Takāb, Iran 30 B5
Takachiho, Japan 23 H5
Takada, Japan 23 F9
Takahagi, Japan 23 F10
Takaka, N.Z. 39 J4
Takamatsu, Japan ... 23 G7
Takaoka, Japan 23 F8
Takapuna, N.Z. 39 G5
Takasaki, Japan 23 F9
Takatsuki, Japan 23 G7
Takayama, Japan 23 F8
Take-Shima, Japan .. 23 J5
Takefu, Japan 23 G8
Takengon, Indonesia . 26 D1
Takeo, Japan 23 H5
Taketa, Japan 23 H5
Takev, Cambodia ... 26 B2
Takikawa, Japan ... 22 C10
Takla L., Canada 50 B3
Takla Landing, Canada 50 B3
Takla Makan =
  Taklamakan Shamo,
  China 24 C3
Taklamakan Shamo,
  China 24 C3
Taku →, Canada 50 B2
Tal Halāl, Iran 31 D7
Talamanca, Cordillera
  de, Cent. Amer. ... 60 E3
Talara, Peru 62 D2
Talas, Kyrgyzstan ... 20 E8
Talâta, Egypt 33 E1
Talaud, Kepulauan,
  Indonesia 27 D7
Talaud Is. = Talaud,
  Kepulauan, Indonesia 27 D7
Talavera de la Reina,
  Spain 15 C3
Talayan, Phil. 27 C6
Talbot, C., Australia .. 40 B4
Talbragar →, Australia 43 E4
Talca, Chile 64 D2
Talcahuano, Chile ... 64 D2
Talcher, India 29 J14
Taldy Kurgan =
  Taldyqorghan,
  Kazakstan 20 E8
Taldyqorghan,
  Kazakstan 20 E8
Tālesh, Iran 31 B6
Tālesh, Kūhhā-ye, Iran . 31 B6
Tali Post, Sudan ... 35 G12
Taliabu, Indonesia ... 27 E6
Talibon, Phil. 27 B6
Talihina, U.S.A. 55 H7
Taliwang, Indonesia . 26 F5
Tall 'Afar, Iraq 30 B4
Tall Kalakh, Syria 33 A5
Talladega, U.S.A. 53 J2
Talladega, U.S.A. 53 J2
Tallangatta, Australia . 43 F4
Tallering Pk., Australia 41 E2
Tallinn, Estonia 7 G21
Tallulah, U.S.A. 55 J9
Taloyoak, Canada ... 46 B10
Talpa de Allende,
  Mexico 58 C4
Taltal, Chile 64 B2
Taltson →, Canada .. 50 A6
Talurqjuak = Taloyoak,
  Canada 46 B10
Talwood, Australia ... 43 D4
Talyawalka →,
  Australia 43 E3

Tamale, Ghana 34 G5
Tamano, Japan 23 G6
Tamanrasset, Algeria . 34 D7
Tamar →, U.K. 9 G3
Tamaulipas □, Mexico 59 C5
Tamaulipas, Sierra de,
  Mexico 59 C5
Tamazula, Mexico ... 58 C3
Tamazunchale, Mexico 59 C5
Tambacounda, Senegal 34 F3
Tambelan, Kepulauan,
  Indonesia 26 D3
Tambellup, Australia . 41 F2
Tambo, Australia 42 C4
Tambo de Mora, Peru 62 F3
Tambora, Indonesia .. 26 F5
Tambov, Russia 18 D7
Tambuku, Indonesia . 27 G15
Tâmega →, Portugal . 15 B1
Tamenglong, India .. 29 G18
Tamiahua, L. de, Mexico 59 C5
Tamil Nadu □, India . 28 P10
Tammerfors =
  Tampere, Finland ... 7 F20
Tammisaari, Finland . 7 F20
Tamo Abu,
  Pegunungan,
  Malaysia 26 D5
Tampa, U.S.A. 53 M4
Tampa B., U.S.A. 53 M4
Tampere, Finland ... 7 F20
Tampico, Mexico ... 59 C5
Tamu, Burma 29 G19
Tamworth, Australia . 43 E5
Tamworth, U.K. 9 E6
Tan-Tan, Morocco ... 34 C3
Tana →, Kenya 36 E8
Tana →, Norway 6 A23
Tana, L., Ethiopia ... 32 E2
Tanabe, Japan 23 H7
Tanafjorden, Norway . 6 A23
Tanahbala, Indonesia . 26 E1
Tanahgrogot, Indonesia 26 E5
Tanahjampea, Indonesia 27 F6
Tanahmasa, Indonesia 26 E1
Tanahmerah, Indonesia 27 F10
Tanakura, Japan 23 F10
Tanami, Australia ... 40 C4
Tanami Desert, Australia 40 C5
Tanana, U.S.A. 46 B4
Tananarive =
  Antananarivo, Madag. 37 H9
Tánaro →, Italy 14 D8
Tandag, Phil. 27 C7
Tandil, Argentina ... 64 D5
Tando Adam, Pakistan 28 G6
Tandou L., Australia . 43 E3
Tane-ga-Shima, Japan 23 J5
Taneatua, N.Z. 39 H6
Tanen Tong Dan, Burma 29 L21
Tanezrouft, Algeria .. 34 D6
Tang, Ra's-e, Iran ... 31 E8
Tanga, Tanzania 36 F7
Tanganyika, L., Africa . 36 F6
Tanger = Tangier,
  Morocco 34 A4
Tangerang, Indonesia . 27 G12
Tanggula Shan, China . 24 C4
Tangier, Morocco 34 A4
Tangorin, Australia .. 42 C3
Tangshan, China 25 C6
Tanimbar, Kepulauan,
  Indonesia 27 F8
Tanimbar Is. =
  Tanimbar, Kepulauan,
  Indonesia 27 F8
Tanjay, Phil. 27 C6
Tanjore = Thanjavur,
  India 28 P11
Tanjung, Indonesia .. 26 E5
Tanjungbalai, Indonesia 26 D1
Tanjungbatu, Indonesia 26 D5
Tanjungkarang
  Telukbetung,
  Indonesia 26 F3
Tanjungpandan,
  Indonesia 26 E3
Tanjungpinang,
  Indonesia 26 D2
Tanjungredeb,
  Indonesia 26 D5
Tanjungselor, Indonesia 26 D5
Tannu-Ola, Russia .. 21 D10
Tannum Sands,
  Australia 42 C5
Tanout, Niger 34 F7
Tanta, Egypt 35 B12
Tantoyuca, Mexico .. 59 C5
Tantung = Dandong,
  China 25 B7
Tanunda, Australia .. 43 E2
Tanzania ■, Africa .. 36 F6
Tanzilla →, Canada . 50 B2
Taolanaro, Madag. .. 37 K9
Taos, U.S.A. 57 H11
Taoudenni, Mali 34 D5
Tapa, Estonia 7 G21
Tapa Shan = Daba
  Shan, China 25 C5
Tapachula, Mexico .. 59 E6
Tapaktuan, Indonesia . 26 D1

Tapanui, N.Z. 39 L2
Tapauá →, Brazil ... 62 E6
Tapeta, Liberia 34 G4
Tapi →, India 28 J8
Tapirapecó, Serra,
  Venezuela 62 C6
Tapuaenuku, Mt., N.Z. 39 K4
Tapul Group, Phil. ... 27 C6
Tapurucuará, Brazil .. 62 D5
Taqtaq, Iraq 30 C5
Taquari →, Brazil ... 62 G7
Tara, Australia 43 D5
Tara, Russia 20 D8
Tara →,
  Montenegro, Yug. .. 17 C8
Tarabagatay, Khrebet,
  Kazakstan 20 E9
Ṭarābulus, Lebanon . 33 A4
Ṭarābulus, Libya 35 B8
Tarakan, Indonesia .. 26 D5
Tarama-Jima, Japan . 23 M2
Taran, Mys, Russia ... 7 J18
Taranaki □, N.Z. 39 H5
Taranaki, Mt., N.Z. .. 39 H5
Tarancón, Spain 15 B4
Táranto, Italy 16 D7
Táranto, G. di, Italy .. 16 D7
Tarapacá, Colombia . 62 D5
Tarapoto, Peru 62 E3
Tararua Ra., N.Z. 39 J5
Tarashcha, Ukraine . 13 D16
Tarauacá, Brazil 62 E4
Tarauacá →, Brazil . 62 E5
Tarawa, Kiribati 44 G9
Tarawera, N.Z. 39 H6
Tarawera L., N.Z. ... 39 H6
Tarazona, Spain 15 B5
Tarbela Dam, Pakistan 28 B8
Tarbes, France 14 E4
Tarboro, U.S.A. 53 H7
Tarcoola, Australia .. 43 E1
Tarcoon, Australia .. 43 E4
Taree, Australia 43 E5
Tarfaya, Morocco 34 C3
Târgovişte, Romania . 13 F13
Târgu-Jiu, Romania .. 13 F12
Târgu Mureş, Romania 13 E13
Tarif, U.A.E. 31 E7
Tarifa, Spain 15 D3
Tarija, Bolivia 62 H6
Tariku →, Indonesia . 27 E9
Tarim Basin = Tarim
  Pendi, China 24 C3
Tarim He →, China .. 24 C3
Tarim Pendi, China .. 24 C3
Taritatu →, Indonesia 27 E9
Tarkhankut, Mys,
  Ukraine 19 E5
Tarko Sale, Russia ... 20 C8
Tarkwa, Ghana 34 G5
Tarlac, Phil. 27 A6
Tarma, Peru 62 F3
Tarn →, France 14 E4
Târnăveni, Romania . 13 E13
Tarnobrzeg, Poland . 13 C11
Tarnów, Poland 13 C11
Tarnowskie Góry,
  Poland 13 C10
Ṭārom, Iran 31 D7
Taroom, Australia ... 43 D4
Taroudannt, Morocco . 34 B4
Tarpon Springs, U.S.A. 53 L4
Tarragona, Spain ... 15 B6
Tarraleah, Australia . 42 G4
Tarrasa = Terrassa,
  Spain 15 B7
Tarshiha = Me'ona,
  Israel 33 B4
Tarso Emissi, Chad .. 35 D9
Tarsus, Turkey 19 G5
Tartagal, Argentina .. 62 H6
Tartu, Estonia 7 G22
Ṭarṭūs, Syria 30 C2
Tarumizu, Japan 23 J5
Tarutao, Ko, Thailand . 26 C1
Tarutung, Indonesia . 26 D1
Taseko →, Canada .. 50 C4
Tash-Kömür, Kyrgyzstan 20 E8
Tash-Kumyr = Tash-
  Kömür, Kyrgyzstan .. 20 E8
Tashauz = Dashhowuz,
  Turkmenistan 20 E6
Tashi Chho Dzong =
  Thimphu, Bhutan . 29 F16
Tashk, Daryācheh-ye,
  Iran 31 D7
Tashkent = Toshkent,
  Uzbekistan 20 E7
Tashtagol, Russia ... 20 D9
Tasiilaq, Greenland .. 4 C6
Tasikmalaya, Indonesia 27 G13
Täsjön, Sweden 6 D16
Taşköprü, Russia ... 21 C16
Tasman B., N.Z. 39 J4
Tasman Mts., N.Z. ... 39 J4
Tasman Pen., Australia 42 G4
Tasman Sea, Pac. Oc. . 38 E9
Tasmania □, Australia 42 G4
Tassili n'Ajjer, Algeria 34 C7
Tastahouine, Tunisia . 35 B8
Tatabánya, Hungary . 13 E10
Tatar Republic =
  Tatarstan □, Russia . 18 C9
Tatarbunary, Ukraine . 13 F15

Tatarsk, *Russia* 20 D8
Tatarstan □, *Russia* ... 18 C9
Tateyama, *Japan* 23 G9
Tathlina L., *Canada* 50 A5
Tathra, *Australia* 43 F4
Tatinnai L., *Canada* 51 A9
Tatla L., *Canada* 50 C4
Tatnam, C., *Canada* 51 B10
Tatra = Tatry,
  Slovak Rep. 13 D11
Tatry, *Slovak Rep.* 13 D11
Tatshenshini →,
  Canada 50 B1
Tatsuno, *Japan* 23 G7
Tatta, *Pakistan* 28 G5
Tatum, *U.S.A.* 55 J3
Tat'ung = Datong,
  China 25 B6
Tatvan, *Turkey* 19 G7
Taubaté, *Brazil* 64 A7
Tauern, *Austria* 12 E7
Taumarunui, *N.Z.* 39 H5
Taumaturgo, *Brazil* 62 E4
Taungdwingyi, *Burma* . 29 J19
Taunggyi, *Burma* 29 J20
Taungup, *Burma* 29 K19
Taungup Taunggya,
  Burma 29 K18
Taunton, *U.K.* 9 F4
Taunton, *U.S.A.* 52 E10
Taunus, *Germany* 12 C5
Taupo, *N.Z.* 39 H6
Taupo, L., *N.Z.* 39 H5
Tauragė, *Lithuania* ... 7 J20
Tauranga, *N.Z.* 39 G6
Tauranga Harb., *N.Z.* . 39 G6
Taureau, Rés., *Canada* . 48 C5
Taurianova, *Italy* 16 E7
Taurus Mts. = Toros
  Dağları, *Turkey* ... 19 G5
Tavda, *Russia* 20 D7
Tavda →, *Russia* 20 D7
Taveuni, *Fiji* 39 C9
Tavira, *Portugal* 15 D2
Tavistock, *U.K.* 9 G3
Tavoy = Dawei, *Burma* 26 B1
Taw →, *U.K.* 9 F4
Tawas City, *U.S.A.* ... 52 C4
Tawau, *Malaysia* 26 D5
Tawitawi, *Phil.* 27 B6
Taxco de Alarcón,
  Mexico 59 D5
Tay →, *U.K.* 10 C5
Tay, L., *Australia* 41 F3
Tayabamba, *Peru* 62 E3
Taylakova, *Russia* ... 20 D8
Taylakovy = Taylakova,
  Russia 20 D8
Taylor, *Canada* 50 B4
Taylor, *Nebr., U.S.A.* . 54 E5
Taylor, *Tex., U.S.A.* . 55 K6
Taylor, Mt., *U.S.A.* .. 57 J10
Taylorville, *U.S.A.* .. 54 F10
Taymā, *Si. Arabia* ... 30 E3
Taymyr, Oz., *Russia* .. 21 B11
Taymyr, Poluostrov,
  Russia 21 B11
Tayshet, *Russia* 21 D10
Taytay, *Phil.* 27 B5
Taz →, *Russia* 20 C8
Taza, *Morocco* 34 B5
Tāzah Khurmātū, *Iraq* . 30 C5
Tazawa-Ko, *Japan* ... 22 E10
Tazin, *Canada* 51 B7
Tazin L., *Canada* 51 B7
Tazovskiy, *Russia* ... 20 C8
Tbilisi, *Georgia* 19 F7
Tchad = Chad ■, *Africa* 35 E9
Tchad, L., *Chad* 35 F8
Tch'eng-tou = Chengdu,
  China 24 C5
Tchentlo L., *Canada* .. 50 B4
Tchibanga, *Gabon* ... 36 E2
Tch'ong-k'ing =
  Chongqing, *China* .. 24 D5
Tczew, *Poland* 13 A10
Te Anau, *N.Z.* 39 L1
Te Anau, L., *N.Z.* ... 39 L1
Te Aroha, *N.Z.* 39 G5
Te Awamutu, *N.Z.* ... 39 H5
Te Kuiti, *N.Z.* 39 H5
Te Puke, *N.Z.* 39 G6
Te Waewae B., *N.Z.* .. 39 M1
Teague, *U.S.A.* 55 K6
Teapa, *Mexico* 59 D6
Tebakang, *Malaysia* .. 26 D4
Tébessa, *Algeria* 34 A7
Tebicuary →, *Paraguay* 64 B5
Tebingtinggi, *Indonesia* 26 D1
Tebintingii, *Indonesia* . 26 E2
Tecate, *Mexico* 58 A1
Tecka, *Argentina* 64 E2
Tecomán, *Mexico* 58 D4
Tecoripa, *Mexico* 58 B3
Tecuala, *Mexico* 58 C3
Tecuci, *Romania* 13 F14
Tecumseh, *Mich., U.S.A.* 52 D4
Tecumseh, *Okla., U.S.A.* 55 H6
Tedzhen = Tejen,
  Turkmenistan 20 F7
Tees →, *U.K.* 8 C6
Tees B., *U.K.* 8 C6
Tefé, *Brazil* 62 D6
Tegal, *Indonesia* 27 G13

Tegid, L. = Bala, L., *U.K.* 8 E4
Tegucigalpa, *Honduras* 60 D2
Tehachapi, *U.S.A.* ... 57 J4
Tehachapi Mts., *U.S.A.* 57 J4
Tehoru, *Indonesia* ... 27 E7
Tehrān, *Iran* 31 C6
Tehuacán, *Mexico* ... 59 D5
Tehuantepec, *Mexico* . 59 D5
Tehuantepec, G. de,
  Mexico 59 D5
Tehuantepec, Istmo de,
  Mexico 59 D6
Teifi →, *U.K.* 9 E3
Teign →, *U.K.* 9 G4
Teignmouth, *U.K.* ... 9 G4
Tejen, *Turkmenistan* . 20 F7
Tejen →, *Turkmenistan* 31 B9
Tejo →, *Europe* 15 C1
Tekamah, *U.S.A.* 54 E6
Tekapo, L., *N.Z.* 39 K3
Tekax, *Mexico* 59 C7
Tekeli, *Kazakstan* ... 20 E8
Tekirdağ, *Turkey* 17 D12
Tekkali, *India* 29 K14
Tekoa, *U.S.A.* 56 C5
Tel Aviv-Yafo, *Israel* . 33 C3
Tel Lakhish, *Israel* .. 33 D3
Tel Megiddo, *Israel* .. 33 C4
Tela, *Honduras* 60 C2
Telanaipura = Jambi,
  Indonesia 26 E2
Telavi, *Georgia* 19 F8
Telegraph Creek,
  Canada 50 B2
Telekhany =
  Tsyelyakhany, *Belarus* 13 B13
Telemark, *Norway* ... 7 G12
Teleng, *Iran* 31 E9
Teles Pires →, *Brazil* . 62 E7
Telescope Pk., *U.S.A.* . 57 H5
Telfer Mine, *Australia* . 40 C3
Telford, *U.K.* 9 E5
Telford and Wrekin □,
  U.K. 8 E5
Telkwa, *Canada* 50 C3
Tell City, *U.S.A.* 52 G2
Tellicherry, *India* ... 28 P9
Telluride, *U.S.A.* ... 57 H10
Teloloapán, *Mexico* .. 59 D5
Telpos Iz, *Russia* ... 18 B10
Telsen, *Argentina* ... 64 E3
Telšiai, *Lithuania* ... 7 H20
Teluk Anson = Teluk
  Intan, *Malaysia* 26 D2
Teluk Betung =
  Tanjungkarang
  Telukbetung,
  Indonesia 26 F3
Teluk Intan, *Malaysia* . 26 D2
Telukbutun, *Indonesia* . 26 D3
Telukdalem, *Indonesia* 26 D1
Tema, *Ghana* 34 G5
Temax, *Mexico* 59 C7
Tembagapura,
  Indonesia 27 E9
Teme →, *U.K.* 9 E5
Temecula, *U.S.A.* ... 57 K5
Temerloh, *Malaysia* .. 26 D2
Teminabuan, *Indonesia* 27 E8
Temir, *Kazakstan* 19 E10
Temirtau, *Kazakstan* . 20 D8
Temirtau, *Russia* 20 D9
Temiscamie →,
  Canada 49 B5
Témiscaming, *Canada* . 48 C4
Témiscamingue, L.,
  Canada 48 C4
Temosachic, *Mexico* .. 58 B3
Tempe, *U.S.A.* 57 K8
Temple, *U.S.A.* 55 K6
Temple B., *Australia* .. 42 A3
Templeton →,
  Australia 42 C2
Tempoal, *Mexico* 59 C5
Temuco, *Chile* 64 D2
Temuka, *N.Z.* 39 L3
Tenabo, *Mexico* 59 C6
Tenaha, *U.S.A.* 55 K7
Tenakee Springs, *U.S.A.* 50 B1
Tenali, *India* 29 L12
Tenancingo, *Mexico* .. 59 D5
Tenango, *Mexico* 59 D5
Tenasserim, *Burma* .. 26 B1
Tenby, *U.K.* 9 F3
Tenda, Colle di, *France* 14 D7
Tendaho, *Ethiopia* ... 32 E3
Ténéré, *Niger* 34 E7
Tenerife, *Canary Is.* . 34 C2
Teng Xian, *China* 25 G9
Tengah □, *Indonesia* . 27 E6
Tengah, Kepulauan,
  Indonesia 26 F5
Tengchong, *China* ... 24 D4
Tenggara □, *Indonesia* 27 E6
Tenggarong, *Indonesia* 26 E5
Tenggol, Pulau,
  Malaysia 26 D2
Tengiz, Ozero,
  Kazakstan 20 D7
Tenkasi, *India* 28 Q10
Tennant Creek, *Australia* 42 B1
Tennessee □, *U.S.A.* . 53 H2
Tennessee →, *U.S.A.* . 52 G1
Tenom, *Malaysia* 26 C5
Tenosique, *Mexico* .. 59 D6

Tenryū-Gawa →,
  Japan 23 G8
Tenterden, *U.K.* 9 F8
Tenterfield, *Australia* . 43 D5
Teófilo Otoni, *Brazil* . 63 G10
Tepa, *Indonesia* 27 F7
Tepalcatepec →,
  Mexico 58 D4
Tepehuanes, *Mexico* . 58 B3
Tepetongo, *Mexico* .. 58 C4
Tepic, *Mexico* 58 C4
Teplice, *Czech Rep.* .. 12 C7
Tepoca, C., *Mexico* .. 58 A2
Tequila, *Mexico* 58 C4
Ter →, *Spain* 15 A7
Ter Apel, *Neths.* 11 B7
Teraina, *Kiribati* 45 G11
Téramo, *Italy* 16 C5
Terang, *Australia* ... 43 F3
Terebovlya, *Ukraine* . 13 D13
Terek →, *Russia* 19 F8
Teresina, *Brazil* 63 E10
Terewah, L., *Australia* . 43 D4
Teridgerie Cr. →,
  Australia 43 E4
Termez = Termiz,
  Uzbekistan 20 F7
Términi Imerese, *Italy* . 16 F5
Términos, L. de, *Mexico* 59 D6
Termiz, *Uzbekistan* .. 20 F7
Térmoli, *Italy* 16 C6
Ternate, *Indonesia* ... 27 D7
Terneuzen, *Neths.* ... 11 C3
Terney, *Russia* 21 E14
Terni, *Italy* 16 C5
Ternopil, *Ukraine* ... 13 D13
Ternopol = Ternopil,
  Ukraine 13 D13
Terowie, *Australia* ... 43 E2
Terra Nova Nat. Park,
  Canada 49 C9
Terrace, *Canada* 50 C3
Terrace Bay, *Canada* . 48 C2
Terracina, *Italy* 16 D5
Terralba, *Italy* 16 E3
Terranova = Ólbia, *Italy* 16 D3
Terrassa, *Spain* 15 B7
Terre Haute, *U.S.A.* .. 52 F2
Terrebonne B., *U.S.A.* 55 L9
Terrell, *U.S.A.* 55 J6
Terrenceville, *Canada* . 49 C9
Terry, *U.S.A.* 54 B2
Terschelling, *Neths.* . 11 A5
Teruel, *Spain* 15 B5
Tervola, *Finland* 6 C21
Teryaweyna L., *Australia* 43 E3
Teshio, *Japan* 22 B10
Teshio-Gawa →, *Japan* 22 B10
Tesiyn Gol →,
  Mongolia 24 A4
Teslin, *Canada* 50 A2
Teslin →, *Canada* ... 50 A2
Teslin L., *Canada* 50 A2
Tessalit, *Mali* 34 D6
Test →, *U.K.* 9 G6
Testigos, Is. Las,
  Venezuela 61 D7
Tetachuck L., *Canada* . 50 C3
Tetas, Pta., *Chile* ... 64 A2
Tete, *Mozam.* 37 H6
Teterev →, *Ukraine* . 13 C16
Teteven, *Bulgaria* ... 17 C11
Tethul →, *Canada* ... 50 A6
Tetiyev, *Ukraine* 13 D15
Teton →, *U.S.A.* 56 C8
Tétouan, *Morocco* ... 34 A4
Tetovo, *Macedonia* .. 17 C9
Teuco →, *Argentina* . 64 B4
Teulon, *Canada* 51 C9
Teun, *Indonesia* 27 F7
Teutoburger Wald,
  Germany 12 B5
Tevere →, *Italy* 16 D5
Teverya, *Israel* 33 C4
Tewantin, *Australia* .. 43 D5
Tewkesbury, *U.K.* ... 9 F5
Texada I., *Canada* ... 50 D4
Texarkana, *Ark., U.S.A.* 55 J8
Texarkana, *Tex., U.S.A.* 55 J7
Texas, *Australia* 43 D5
Texas □, *U.S.A.* 55 K5
Texas City, *U.S.A.* .. 55 L7
Texel, *Neths.* 11 A4
Texline, *U.S.A.* 55 G3
Texoma, L., *U.S.A.* .. 55 J6
Teziutlán, *Mexico* ... 59 D5
Tezpur, *India* 29 F18
Tezzeron L., *Canada* . 50 C4
Tha-anne →, *Canada* . 51 A10
Thabana Ntlenyana,
  Lesotho 37 K5
Thabazimbi, *S. Africa* . 37 J5
Thādiq, *Si. Arabia* .. 30 E5
Thailand ■, *Asia* 26 A2
Thailand, G. of, *Asia* . 26 B2
Thakhek, *Laos* 26 A2
Thal, *Pakistan* 28 C7
Thala La = Hkakabo
  Razi, *Burma* 29 E20
Thallon, *Australia* ... 43 D4
Thames →, *Canada* . 48 D3
Thames, *N.Z.* 39 G5
Thames →, *U.K.* 9 F8
Thames Estuary, *U.K.* . 9 F8

Thane, *India* 28 K8
Thanet, I. of, *U.K.* .. 9 F9
Thangool, *Australia* .. 42 C5
Thanh Pho Ho Chi Minh,
  Vietnam 26 B3
Thanjavur, *India* 28 P11
Thaolinta L., *Canada* . 51 A9
Thar Desert, *India* ... 28 F8
Tharad, *India* 28 G7
Thargomindah,
  Australia 43 D3
Tharrawaddy, *Burma* . 29 L19
Tharthār, Mileh, *Iraq* . 30 C4
Tharthār, W. ath →,
  Iraq 30 C4
Thásos, *Greece* 17 D11
Thatcher, *Ariz., U.S.A.* 57 K9
Thatcher, *Colo., U.S.A.* 55 G2
Thaton, *Burma* 29 L20
Thaungdut, *Burma* .. 29 G19
Thayer, *U.S.A.* 55 G9
Thayetmyo, *Burma* .. 29 K19
Thazi, *Burma* 29 J20
The Alberga →,
  Australia 43 D2
The Bight, *Bahamas* .. 61 B4
The Coorong, *Australia* 43 F2
The Dalles, *U.S.A.* .. 56 D3
The English Company's
  Is., *Australia* 42 A2
The Frome →,
  Australia 43 D2
The Great Divide =
  Great Dividing Ra.,
  Australia 42 C4
The Hague = 's-
  Gravenhage, *Neths.* . 11 B4
The Hamilton →,
  Australia 43 D2
The Macumba →,
  Australia 43 D2
The Neales →,
  Australia 43 D2
The Officer →,
  Australia 41 E5
The Pas, *Canada* 51 C8
The Rock, *Australia* .. 43 F4
The Salt L., *Australia* . 43 E3
The Stevenson →,
  Australia 43 D2
The Warburton →,
  Australia 43 D2
The Woodlands, *U.S.A.* 55 K7
Thebes = Thívai, *Greece* 17 E10
Thebes, *Egypt* 35 C12
Thedford, *U.S.A.* 54 E4
Theebine, *Australia* .. 43 D5
Thekulthili L., *Canada* . 51 A7
Thelon →, *Canada* .. 51 A8
Theodore, *Australia* . 42 C5
Theodore, *Canada* ... 51 C8
Theodore, *U.S.A.* ... 53 K1
Theodore Roosevelt
  National Memorial
  Park, *U.S.A.* 54 B3
Theodore Roosevelt
  Res., *U.S.A.* 57 K8
Thermaïkós Kólpos,
  Greece 17 D10
Thermopolis, *U.S.A.* . 56 E9
Thermopylae P., *Greece* 17 E10
Thessalía □, *Greece* . 17 E10
Thessalon, *Canada* .. 48 C3
Thessaloníki, *Greece* . 17 D10
Thessaloníki, Gulf of =
  Thermaïkós Kólpos,
  Greece 17 D10
Thetford, *U.K.* 9 E8
Thetford Mines, *Canada* 49 C5
Thevenard, *Australia* . 43 E1
Thibodaux, *U.S.A.* ... 55 L9
Thicket Portage, *Canada* 51 B9
Thief River Falls, *U.S.A.* 54 A6
Thiel Mts., *Antarctica* . 5 E16
Thiers, *France* 14 D5
Thiès, *Senegal* 34 F2
Thika, *Kenya* 36 E7
Thikombia, *Fiji* 39 B9
Thimphu, *Bhutan* ... 29 F16
Thingvallavatn, *Iceland* 6 D3
Thionville, *France* ... 14 B7
Thíra, *Greece* 17 F11
Third Cataract, *Sudan* . 35 E12
Thirsk, *U.K.* 8 C6
Thisted, *Denmark* ... 7 H13
Thistle I., *Australia* .. 43 F2
Thívai, *Greece* 17 E10
Thjórsá →, *Iceland* .. 6 E3
Thlewiaza →, *Man.,*
  Canada 51 B8
Thlewiaza →, *N.W.T.,*
  Canada 51 A10
Thoa →, *Canada* 51 A7
Thoen, *Thailand* 26 A1
Thohoyandou, *S. Africa* 37 J6
Thomas, *U.S.A.* 55 H5
Thomas, L., *Australia* . 43 D2
Thomaston, *U.S.A.* .. 53 J3
Thomasville, *Ala.,*
  U.S.A. 53 K2
Thomasville, *Ga., U.S.A.* 53 K4
Thomasville, *N.C.,*
  U.S.A. 53 H5
Thompson, *Canada* .. 51 B9
Thompson, *U.S.A.* ... 57 G9
Thompson →, *Canada* 50 C4

Thompson →, *U.S.A.* 54 F8
Thompson Falls, *U.S.A.* 56 C6
Thompson Pk., *U.S.A.* . 56 F2
Thompson Springs,
  U.S.A. 57 G9
Thomson, *U.S.A.* ... 53 J4
Thomson →, *Australia* 42 C3
Thomson's Falls =
  Nyahururu, *Kenya* . 36 D7
Thórisvatn, *Iceland* .. 6 D4
Thornaby on Tees, *U.K.* 8 C6
Thorne, *U.K.* 8 D7
Thornhill, *Canada* ... 50 C3
Thórshöfn, *Iceland* .. 6 C6
Thouin, C., *Australia* . 40 D2
Thrace, *Turkey* 17 D12
Three Forks, *U.S.A.* .. 56 D8
Three Hills, *Canada* .. 50 C6
Three Hummock I.,
  Australia 42 G3
Three Points, C., *Ghana* 34 H5
Three Rivers, *U.S.A.* . 55 L5
Three Sisters, *U.S.A.* . 56 D3
Three Springs, *Australia* 41 E2
Throssell, L., *Australia* . 41 E3
Throssell Ra., *Australia* 40 D3
Thubun Lakes, *Canada* 51 A6
Thuin, *Belgium* 11 D4
Thule = Qaanaaq,
  Greenland 4 B4
Thun, *Switz.* 14 C7
Thunder B., *U.S.A.* .. 52 C4
Thunder Bay, *Canada* . 48 C2
Thung Song, *Thailand* . 26 C1
Thunkar, *Bhutan* 29 F17
Thüringer Wald,
  Germany 12 C6
Thurles, *Ireland* 10 E3
Thurrock □, *U.K.* ... 9 F8
Thursday I., *Australia* . 42 A3
Thurso, *Canada* 48 C4
Thurso, *U.K.* 10 B5
Thurston I., *Antarctica* . 5 D16
Thutade L., *Canada* .. 50 B3
Thysville = Mbanza
  Ngungu, *Dem. Rep. of*
  the Congo 36 F2
Ti Tree, *Australia* ... 42 C1
Tian Shan, *Asia* 24 C3
Tianjin, *China* 25 C6
Tianshui, *China* 24 C5
Tiaret, *Algeria* 34 A6
Tiber = Tevere →,
  Italy 16 D5
Tiberias = Teverya,
  Israel 33 C4
Tiberias, L. = Yam
  Kinneret, *Israel* ... 33 C4
Tibesti, *Chad* 35 D9
Tibet = Xizang
  Zizhiqu □, *China* .. 24 C3
Tibnī, *Syria* 30 C3
Tibooburra, *Australia* . 43 D3
Tiburón, I., *Mexico* .. 58 B2
Ticino →, *Italy* 14 D8
Ticonderoga, *U.S.A.* . 52 D9
Ticul, *Mexico* 59 C7
Tidaholm, *Sweden* ... 7 G15
Tiddim, *Burma* 29 H18
Tidjikja, *Mauritania* . 34 E3
Tidore, *Indonesia* ... 27 D7
Tiel, *Neths.* 11 C5
Tielt, *Belgium* 11 C3
Tien Shan = Tian Shan,
  Asia 24 B3
Tien-tsin = Tianjin,
  China 25 C6
T'ienching = Tianjin,
  China 25 C6
Tienen, *Belgium* 11 D4
Tientsin = Tianjin,
  China 25 C6
Tieri, *Australia* 42 C4
Tierra Amarilla, *U.S.A.* 57 H10
Tierra Colorada, *Mexico* 59 D5
Tierra de Campos,
  Spain 15 A3
Tierra del Fuego, I. Gr.
  de, *Argentina* 64 G3
Tiétar →, *Spain* 15 C3
Tiffin, *U.S.A.* 52 E4
Tiflis = Tbilisi, *Georgia* 19 F7
Tifton, *U.S.A.* 53 K4
Tifu, *Indonesia* 27 E7
Tighina, *Moldova* ... 13 E15
Tigil, *Russia* 21 D16
Tignish, *Canada* 49 C7
Tigre →, *Peru* 62 D4
Tigre →, *Venezuela* . 62 B6
Tigris = Dijlah,
  Nahr →, *Asia* 30 D5
Tigyaing, *Burma* 29 H20
Tijuana, *Mexico* 58 A1
Tikal, *Guatemala* 60 C2
Tikamgarh, *India* 28 G11
Tikhoretsk, *Russia* .. 19 E7
Tikhvin, *Russia* 18 C5
Tikrīt, *Iraq* 30 C4
Tiksi, *Russia* 21 B13
Tilamuta, *Indonesia* . 27 D6
Tilburg, *Neths.* 11 C5
Tilbury, *Canada* 48 D3
Tilbury, *U.K.* 9 F8
Tilden, *U.S.A.* 54 D6

Tilichiki, *Russia* 21 C17
Till →, *U.K.* 8 B5
Tillamook, *U.S.A.* ... 56 D2
Tillsonburg, *Canada* . 48 D3
Tilos, *Greece* 17 F12
Tilpa, *Australia* 43 E3
Timagami, L., *Canada* . 48 C3
Timanskiy Kryazh,
  Russia 18 A9
Timaru, *N.Z.* 39 L3
Timber Creek, *Australia* 40 C5
Timber Lake, *U.S.A.* . 54 C4
Timbuktu =
  Tombouctou, *Mali* . 34 E5
Timimoun, *Algeria* .. 34 C6
Timiris, Râs, *Mauritania* 34 E2
Timișoara, *Romania* . 13 F11
Timmins, *Canada* ... 48 C3
Timok →, *Serbia, Yug.* 17 B10
Timor, *Indonesia* ... 27 F7
Timor Sea, *Ind. Oc.* . 40 B4
Timor Timur □,
  Indonesia 27 F7
Tin Can Bay, *Australia* 43 D5
Tinaca Pt., *Phil.* 27 C7
Tindal, *Australia* 40 B5
Tindouf, *Algeria* 34 C4
Tingo Maria, *Peru* ... 62 E3
Tingrela, *Ivory C.* ... 34 F4
Tinnevelly = Tirunelveli,
  India 28 Q10
Tinogasta, *Argentina* . 64 B3
Tínos, *Greece* 17 F11
Tintinara, *Australia* . 43 F3
Tioga, *U.S.A.* 54 A3
Tioman, Pulau, *Malaysia* 26 D2
Tipongpani, *India* ... 29 F19
Tipperary, *Ireland* ... 10 E2
Tipton, *U.S.A.* 54 E9
Tiptonville, *U.S.A.* .. 55 G10
Tīrān, *Iran* 31 C6
Tirana = Tiranë, *Albania* 17 D8
Tiranë, *Albania* 17 D8
Tiraspol, *Moldova* ... 13 E15
Tire, *Turkey* 17 E12
Tirebolu, *Turkey* 19 F6
Tiree, *U.K.* 10 C3
Tîrgovişte = Târgovişte,
  Romania 13 F13
Tîrgu-Jiu = Târgu-Jiu,
  Romania 13 F12
Tîrgu Mureş = Târgu
  Mureş, *Romania* .. 13 E13
Tirich Mir, *Pakistan* . 28 A7
Tírnavos, *Greece* 17 E10
Tirodi, *India* 28 J11
Tirol □, *Austria* 12 E6
Tirso →, *Italy* 16 E3
Tiruchchirappalli, *India* 28 P11
Tirunelveli, *India* ... 28 Q10
Tirupati, *India* 28 N11
Tiruppur, *India* 28 P10
Tiruvannamalai, *India* . 28 N11
Tisa →, *Serbia, Yug.* . 17 B9
Tisdale, *Canada* 51 C8
Tishomingo, *U.S.A.* .. 55 H6
Tisza = Tisa →,
  Serbia, Yug. 17 B9
Tit-Ary, *Russia* 21 B13
Titicaca, L., *S. Amer.* . 62 G5
Titograd = Podgorica,
  Montenegro, Yug. . 17 C8
Titule, *Dem. Rep. of*
  the Congo 36 D5
Titusville, *Fla., U.S.A.* 53 L5
Titusville, *Pa., U.S.A.* . 52 E5
Tivaouane, *Senegal* .. 34 F2
Tiverton, *U.K.* 9 G4
Tívoli, *Italy* 16 D5
Tizi-Ouzou, *Algeria* .. 34 A6
Tizimín, *Mexico* 59 C7
Tjeggelvas, *Sweden* . 6 C17
Tjirebon = Cirebon,
  Indonesia 27 G13
Tjörn, *Sweden* 7 G14
Tlacotalpan, *Mexico* . 59 D5
Tlahualilo, *Mexico* .. 58 B4
Tlaquepaque, *Mexico* . 58 C4
Tlaxcala, *Mexico* 59 D5
Tlaxcala □, *Mexico* .. 59 D5
Tlaxiaco, *Mexico* 59 D5
Tlemcen, *Algeria* 34 B5
Toad →, *Canada* 50 B4
Toad River, *Canada* .. 50 B3
Toamasina, *Madag.* .. 37 H9
Toay, *Argentina* 64 D4
Toba, *Japan* 23 G8
Toba, Danau, *Indonesia* 26 D1
Toba Kakar, *Pakistan* . 28 D6
Tobago, *W. Indies* ... 62 A6
Tobelo, *Indonesia* ... 27 D7
Tobermory, *Canada* .. 48 C3
Tobermory, *U.K.* 10 C3
Tobi, *Pac. Oc.* 27 D8
Tobin, *Australia* 40 D4
Tobin L., *Canada* 51 C8
Toboali, *Indonesia* .. 26 E3
Toboli, *Indonesia* ... 27 E6
Tobol = Tobyl →,
  Russia 20 D7
Tobruk = Tubruq, *Libya* 35 B10
Tobyl = Tobol →,
  Russia 20 D7

107

Tocantinópolis, Brazil . 63 E9
Tocantins □, Brazil 63 F9
Tocantins →, Brazil 63 D9
Toccoa, U.S.A. 53 H4
Tochigi, Japan 23 F9
Tochigi □, Japan 23 F9
Tocopilla, Chile 62 H4
Tocumwal, Australia .. 43 F4
Tocuyo →, Venezuela 62 A5
Todeli, Indonesia 27 E6
Todos os Santos, B. de,
  Brazil 63 F11
Todos Santos, Mexico . 58 C2
Tofield, Canada 50 C6
Tofino, Canada 50 D3
Tofua, Tonga 39 D11
Tōgane, Japan 23 G10
Togian, Kepulauan,
  Indonesia 27 E6
Togliatti, Russia 18 D8
Togo ■, W. Afr. 34 G6
Tōhoku □, Japan 22 E10
Toinya, Sudan 35 G11
Toiyabe Range, U.S.A. 56 G5
Tojikiston =
  Tajikistan ■, Asia .. 20 F8
Tojo, Indonesia 27 E6
Tōjō, Japan 23 G6
Tok, U.S.A. 46 B5
Tok-do, Japan 23 F5
Tokachi-Dake, Japan .. 22 C11
Tokachi-Gawa →,
  Japan 22 C11
Tokala, Indonesia 27 E6
Tōkamachi, Japan 23 F9
Tokanui, N.Z. 39 M2
Tokara-Rettō, Japan .. 23 K4
Tokarahi, N.Z. 39 L3
Tokashiki-Shima, Japan 23 L3
Tokat □, Turkey 19 F6
Tokelau Is., Pac. Oc. .. 44 H10
Tokmak, Kyrgyzstan .. 20 E8
Toko Ra., Australia .. 42 C2
Tokoro-Gawa →,
  Japan 22 B12
Tokuno-Shima, Japan . 23 L4
Tokushima, Japan 23 G7
Tokushima □, Japan .. 23 H7
Tokuyama, Japan 23 G5
Tōkyō, Japan 23 G9
Tolaga Bay, N.Z. 39 H7
Tolbukhin = Dobrich,
  Bulgaria 17 C12
Toledo, Spain 15 C3
Toledo, Ohio, U.S.A. .. 52 E4
Toledo, Oreg., U.S.A. .. 56 D2
Toledo, Wash., U.S.A. . 56 C2
Toledo, Montes de,
  Spain 15 C3
Toledo Bend Reservoir,
  U.S.A. 55 K8
Tolga, Australia 42 B4
Toliara, Madag. 37 J8
Tolima, Colombia 62 C3
Tolitoli, Indonesia 27 D6
Tolo, Teluk, Indonesia . 27 E6
Toluca, Mexico 59 D5
Tom Price, Australia . 40 D2
Tomah, U.S.A. 54 D9
Tomahawk, U.S.A. ... 54 C10
Tomakomai, Japan ... 22 C10
Tomar, Portugal 15 C1
Tomaszów Mazowiecki,
  Poland 13 C10
Tomatlán, Mexico 58 D3
Tombador, Serra do,
  Brazil 62 F7
Tombigbee →, U.S.A. 53 K2
Tombouctou, Mali ... 34 E5
Tombstone, U.S.A. ... 57 L8
Tombua, Angola 37 H2
Tomelloso, Spain 15 C4
Tomini, Indonesia 27 D6
Tomini, Teluk, Indonesia 27 E6
Tomkinson Ranges,
  Australia 41 E4
Tommot, Russia 21 D13
Tomo →, Colombia .. 62 B5
Tomsk, Russia 20 D9
Tonalá, Mexico 59 D6
Tonantins, Brazil 62 D5
Tonasket, U.S.A. 56 B4
Tonbridge, U.K. 9 F8
Tondano, Indonesia .. 27 D6
Tone →, Australia ... 41 F2
Tone-Gawa →, Japan 23 F9
Tonekābon, Iran 31 B6
Tonga ■, Pac. Oc. ... 39 D11
Tonga Trench, Pac. Oc. 44 J10
Tongareva, Cook Is. .. 45 H12
Tongatapu, Tonga ... 39 E12
Tongchuan, China ... 25 C5
Tongeren, Belgium .. 11 D5
Tonghua, China 25 B7
Tongoy, Chile 64 C2
Tongres = Tongeren,
  Belgium 11 D5
Tongsa Dzong, Bhutan 29 F17
Tongue →, U.S.A. ... 54 B2
Tonj, Sudan 35 G11

Tonk, India 28 F9
Tonkawa, U.S.A. 55 G6
Tonkin, G. of, Asia 24 E5
Tonle Sap, Cambodia . 26 B2
Tono, Japan 22 E10
Tonopah, U.S.A. 57 G5
Tonosi, Panama 60 E3
Tønsberg, Norway ... 7 G14
Toobanna, Australia .. 42 B4
Toodyay, Australia .. 41 F2
Tooele, U.S.A. 56 F7
Toompine, Australia . 43 D3
Toora, Australia 43 F4
Toora-Khem, Russia .. 21 D10
Top-ozero, Russia ... 18 A5
Top Springs, Australia . 40 C5
Topeka, U.S.A. 54 F7
Topley, Canada 50 C3
Topock, U.S.A. 57 J6
Topol'čany, Slovak Rep. 13 D10
Topolobampo, Mexico 58 B3
Toppenish, U.S.A. ... 56 C3
Torata, Peru 62 G4
Torbalı, Turkey 17 E12
Torbat-e Heydārīyeh,
  Iran 31 C8
Torbat-e Jām, Iran ... 31 C9
Torbay, Canada 49 C9
Torbay □, U.K. 9 G4
Tordesillas, Spain ... 15 B3
Torfaen □, U.K. 9 F4
Torgau, Germany ... 12 C7
Torhout, Belgium ... 11 C3
Tori-Shima, Japan ... 23 J10
Torin, Mexico 58 B2
Torino, Italy 14 D7
Torit, Sudan 35 H12
Torkamān, Iran 30 B5
Tormes →, Spain ... 15 B2
Tornado Mt., Canada . 50 D6
Torne älv →, Sweden 6 D21
Torneå = Tornio,
  Finland 6 D21
Torneträsk, Sweden .. 6 B18
Tornio, Finland 6 D21
Tornionjoki →, Finland 6 D21
Tornquist, Argentina . 64 D4
Toro, Cerro del, Chile . 64 B3
Toroníios Kólpos,
  Greece 17 D10
Toronto, Canada 48 D4
Toronto, U.S.A. 52 E5
Toropets, Russia 18 C5
Tororo, Uganda 36 D6
Toros Dağları, Turkey . 19 G5
Torquay, Australia .. 43 F3
Torquay, U.K. 9 G4
Torre de Moncorvo,
  Portugal 15 B2
Torre del Greco, Italy . 16 D6
Torrejón de Ardoz,
  Spain 15 B4
Torrelavega, Spain ... 15 A3
Torremolinos, Spain . 15 D3
Torrens, L., Australia . 43 E2
Torrens Cr. →,
  Australia 42 C4
Torrens Creek, Australia 42 C4
Torrent, Spain 15 C5
Torreón, Mexico 58 B4
Torres, Mexico 58 B2
Torres Strait, Australia 38 B7
Torres Vedras, Portugal 15 C1
Torrevieja, Spain ... 15 D5
Torrey, U.S.A. 57 G8
Torridge →, U.K. ... 9 G3
Torrington, U.S.A. .. 54 D2
Tórshavn, Færoe Is. . 6 E9
Tortola, Virgin Is. ... 61 C7
Tortosa, Spain 15 B6
Tortosa, C., Spain ... 15 B6
Tortue, I. de la, Haiti . 61 B5
Torūd, Iran 31 C7
Toruń, Poland 13 B10
Tosa, Japan 23 H6
Tosa-Shimizu, Japan . 23 H6
Tosa-Wan, Japan ... 23 H6
Toscana □, Italy 16 C4
Toshkent, Uzbekistan . 20 E7
Tostado, Argentina .. 64 B4
Tosu, Japan 23 H5
Totma, Russia 18 C7
Totnes, U.K. 9 G4
Totness, Surinam ... 63 B7
Totonicapán, Guatemala 60 D1
Totten Glacier,
  Antarctica 5 C8
Tottenham, Australia . 43 E4
Tottori, Japan 23 G7
Tottori □, Japan 23 G7
Toubkal, Djebel,
  Morocco 34 B4
Tougan, Burkina Faso . 34 F5
Touggourt, Algeria .. 34 B7
Toul, France 14 B6
Toulon, France 14 E6
Toulouse, France ... 14 E4
Toummo, Niger 35 D8
Toungoo, Burma 29 K20
Touraine, France ... 14 C4
Tourane = Da Nang,
  Vietnam 26 A3
Tourcoing, France .. 14 A5

Touriñán, C., Spain .. 15 A1
Tournai, Belgium 11 D3
Tournon-sur-Rhône,
  France 14 D6
Tours, France 14 C4
Tousidé, Pic, Chad ... 35 D9
Toussora, Mt., C.A.R. . 36 C4
Towada, Japan 22 D10
Towada-Ko, Japan ... 22 D10
Towanda, U.S.A. 52 E7
Towang, India 29 F17
Tower, U.S.A. 54 B8
Towerhill Cr. →,
  Australia 42 C3
Towner, U.S.A. 54 A4
Townsend, U.S.A. ... 56 C8
Townshend I., Australia 42 C5
Townsville, Australia . 42 B4
Towson, U.S.A. 52 F7
Towuti, Danau,
  Indonesia 27 E6
Toya-Ko, Japan 22 C10
Toyama, Japan 23 F8
Toyama □, Japan ... 23 F8
Toyama-Wan, Japan . 23 F8
Toyohashi, Japan ... 23 G8
Toyokawa, Japan ... 23 G8
Toyonaka, Japan ... 23 G7
Toyooka, Japan 23 G7
Toyota, Japan 23 G8
Tozeur, Tunisia 34 B7
Trá Li = Tralee, Ireland 10 E2
Trabzon, Turkey 19 F6
Tracadie, Canada ... 49 C7
Tracy, Calif., U.S.A. .. 57 H3
Tracy, Minn., U.S.A. .. 54 C7
Trafalgar, C., Spain .. 15 D2
Trail, Canada 50 D5
Trainor L., Canada .. 50 A4
Tralee, Ireland 10 E2
Tranås, Sweden 7 G16
Trancas, Argentina .. 64 B3
Trang, Thailand 26 C1
Trangan, Indonesia .. 27 F8
Trangie, Australia ... 43 E4
Trani, Italy 16 D7
Transantarctic Mts.,
  Antarctica 5 E12
Transilvania, Romania . 13 E12
Transilvanian Alps =
  Carpații Meridionali,
  Romania 13 F13
Transvaal, S. Africa .. 37 K5
Transylvania =
  Transilvania, Romania 13 E12
Trápani, Italy 16 E5
Trapper Pk., U.S.A. .. 56 D6
Traralgon, Australia . 43 F4
Trasimeno, L., Italy .. 16 C5
Trat, Thailand 26 B2
Traun, Austria 12 D8
Travellers L., Australia . 43 E3
Travemünde, Germany 12 B6
Travers, Mt., N.Z. ... 39 K4
Traverse City, U.S.A. . 52 C3
Travis, L., U.S.A. 55 K5
Travnik, Bos.-H. 17 B7
Trébbia →, Italy 14 D8
Třebíč, Czech Rep. .. 12 D8
Trebinje, Bos.-H. 17 C8
Trebonne, Australia . 42 B4
Tregaron, U.K. 9 E4
Tregrosse Is., Australia 42 B5
Treherne, Canada ... 51 D9
Treinta y Tres, Uruguay 64 C6
Trelew, Argentina ... 64 E3
Trelleborg, Sweden .. 7 J15
Tremadog Bay, U.K. . 8 E3
Tremonton, U.S.A. .. 56 F7
Tremp, Spain 15 A6
Trenche →, Canada . 48 C5
Trenčín, Slovak Rep. . 13 D10
Trenggalek, Indonesia . 27 H14
Trenque Lauquen,
  Argentina 64 D4
Trent →, U.K. 8 D7
Trento, Italy 16 A4
Trenton, Canada 48 D4
Trenton, Mo., U.S.A. . 54 E8
Trenton, N.J., U.S.A. . 52 E8
Trenton, Nebr., U.S.A. 54 E4
Trepassey, Canada .. 49 C9
Tres Arroyos, Argentina 64 D4
Três Corações, Brazil . 64 A7
Três Lagoas, Brazil .. 63 H8
Tres Marías, Islas,
  Mexico 58 C3
Tres Montes, C., Chile . 64 F1
Tres Puntas, C.,
  Argentina 64 F3
Três Rios, Brazil 63 H10
Tres Valles, Mexico .. 59 D5
Tresco, U.K. 9 H1
Treviso, Italy 16 B5
Triabunna, Australia . 42 G4
Tribulation, C., Australia 42 B4
Tribune, U.S.A. 54 F4
Trichinopoly =
  Tiruchchirappalli,
  India 28 P11
Trichur, India 28 P10
Trida, Australia 43 E4
Trier, Germany 12 D4
Trieste, Italy 16 B5

Triglav, Slovenia 12 E7
Trikkala, Greece 17 E9
Trikora, Puncak,
  Indonesia 27 E9
Trincomalee, Sri Lanka 28 Q12
Trindade, Brazil 63 G9
Trindade, I., Atl. Oc. . 2 F8
Trinidad, Bolivia 62 F6
Trinidad, Cuba 60 B4
Trinidad, Uruguay ... 64 C5
Trinidad, U.S.A. 55 G2
Trinidad, W. Indies .. 61 D7
Trinidad →, Mexico . 59 D5
Trinidad & Tobago ■,
  W. Indies 62 A6
Trinity, Canada 49 C9
Trinity →, Calif., U.S.A. 56 F2
Trinity →, Tex., U.S.A. 55 L7
Trinity B., Canada ... 49 C9
Trinity Is., U.S.A. ... 46 C4
Trinity Range, U.S.A. . 56 F4
Trinkitat, Sudan 35 E13
Tripoli = Tarābulus,
  Lebanon 33 A4
Tripoli = Tarābulus,
  Libya 35 B8
Tripolis, Greece 17 F10
Tripolitania, N. Afr. .. 35 B8
Tripura □, India 29 H18
Tristan da Cunha,
  Atl. Oc. 2 F9
Trivandrum, India ... 28 Q10
Trnava, Slovak Rep. . 13 D9
Trochu, Canada 50 C6
Trodely I., Canada .. 48 B4
Troglav, Croatia 16 C7
Troilus, L., Canada .. 48 B5
Trois-Pistoles, Canada . 49 C6
Trois-Rivières, Canada . 48 C5
Troitsk, Russia 20 D7
Troitsko Pechorsk,
  Russia 18 B10
Trölladyngja, Iceland . 6 D5
Trollhättan, Sweden . 7 G15
Trollheimen, Norway . 6 E13
Trombetas →, Brazil . 63 D7
Tromsø, Norway 6 B18
Tronador, Mte.,
  Argentina 64 E2
Trøndelag, Norway .. 6 D14
Trondheim, Norway . 6 E14
Trondheimsfjorden,
  Norway 6 E14
Tropic, U.S.A. 57 H7
Trout →, Canada ... 50 A5
Trout L., N.W.T., Canada 50 A4
Trout L., Ont., Canada 51 C10
Trout Lake, Canada .. 50 B6
Trout River, Canada . 49 C8
Trouville-sur-Mer,
  France 14 B4
Trowbridge, U.K. ... 9 F5
Troy, Turkey 17 E12
Troy, Ala., U.S.A. ... 53 K3
Troy, Kans., U.S.A. .. 54 F7
Troy, Mo., U.S.A. ... 54 F9
Troy, Mont., U.S.A. . 56 B6
Troy, N.Y., U.S.A. ... 52 D9
Troy, Ohio, U.S.A. .. 52 E3
Troyes, France 14 B6
Truchas Peak, U.S.A. . 55 H2
Trucial States = United
  Arab Emirates ■, Asia 31 F7
Truckee, U.S.A. 56 G3
Trudovoye, Russia .. 22 C6
Trujillo, Honduras .. 60 C2
Trujillo, Peru 62 E3
Trujillo, Spain 15 C3
Trujillo, U.S.A. 55 H2
Trujillo, Venezuela .. 62 B4
Truk, Micronesia ... 44 G7
Trumann, U.S.A. ... 55 H9
Trumbull, Mt., U.S.A. 57 H7
Trundle, Australia ... 43 E4
Truro, Canada 49 C7
Truro, U.K. 9 G2
Truskavets, Ukraine . 13 D12
Trutch, Canada 50 B4
Truth or Consequences,
  U.S.A. 57 K10
Trutnov, Czech Rep. . 12 C8
Tsaratanana, Madag. . 37 G9
Tsarevo = Michurin,
  Bulgaria 17 C12
Tselinograd = Astana,
  Kazakstan 20 D8
Tsetserleg, Mongolia . 24 B5
Tshabong, Botswana . 37 K4
Tshane, Botswana ... 37 J4
Tshela, Dem. Rep. of
  the Congo 36 E2
Tshikapa, Dem. Rep. of
  the Congo 36 F4
Tsiigehtchic, Canada . 46 B6
Tsimlyansk Res. =
  Tsimlyanskoye Vdkhr.,
  Russia 19 E7
Tsimlyanskoye Vdkhr.,
  Russia 19 E7
Tsinan = Jinan, China . 25 C6
Tsinghai = Qinghai □,
  China 24 C4
Tsingtao = Qingdao,
  China 25 C7

Tskhinvali, Georgia .. 19 F7
Tsna →, Russia 18 D7
Tsu, Japan 23 G8
Tsu L., Canada 50 A6
Tsuchiura, Japan ... 23 F10
Tsugaru-Kaikyō, Japan 22 D10
Tsumeb, Namibia ... 37 H3
Tsuruga, Japan 23 G8
Tsurugi-San, Japan .. 23 H7
Tsuruoka, Japan 22 E9
Tsushima, Gifu, Japan 23 G8
Tsushima, Nagasaki,
  Japan 23 G4
Tsuyama, Japan 23 G7
Tsyelyakhany, Belarus . 13 B13
Tual, Indonesia 27 F8
Tuamotu Arch. =
  Tuamotu Is., Pac. Oc. 45 J13
Tuamotu Is., Pac. Oc. . 45 J13
Tuamotu Ridge, Pac. Oc. 45 K14
Tuao, Phil. 27 A6
Tuapse, Russia 19 F6
Tuatapere, N.Z. 39 M1
Tuba City, U.S.A. ... 57 H8
Tuban, Indonesia ... 27 G15
Tubarão, Brazil 64 B7
Tūbās, West Bank ... 33 C4
Tübingen, Germany . 12 D5
Tubruq, Libya 35 B10
Tubuai Is., Pac. Oc. . 45 K13
Tucacas, Venezuela .. 62 A5
Tuchodi →, Canada . 50 B4
Tuckanarra, Australia . 41 E2
Tucson, U.S.A. 57 K8
Tucumcari, U.S.A. .. 55 H3
Tucupita, Venezuela . 62 B6
Tucuruí, Brazil 63 D9
Tucuruí, Reprêsa de,
  Brazil 63 D9
Tudela, Spain 15 A5
Tudmur, Syria 30 C3
Tudor, L., Canada ... 49 A6
Tuguegarao, Phil. ... 27 A6
Tugur, Russia 21 D14
Tui →, Spain 15 A1
Tukangbesi, Kepulauan,
  Indonesia 27 F6
Tukarak I., Canada .. 48 A4
Tukayyid, Iraq 30 D5
Tuktoyaktuk, Canada . 46 B6
Tukums, Latvia 7 H20
Tukuyu, Tanzania ... 36 F6
Tula, Hidalgo, Mexico . 59 C5
Tula, Tamaulipas,
  Mexico 59 C5
Tula, Russia 18 D6
Tulancingo, Mexico . 59 C5
Tulare, U.S.A. 57 H4
Tulare Lake Bed, U.S.A. 57 J4
Tularosa, U.S.A. 57 K10
Tulcán, Ecuador 62 C3
Tulcea, Romania 13 F15
Tulchyn, Ukraine ... 13 D15
Tūleh, Iran 31 C7
Tulemalu L., Canada . 51 A9
Tulia, U.S.A. 55 H4
Tulita, Canada 46 B7
Tülkarm, West Bank . 33 C4
Tullahoma, U.S.A. .. 53 H2
Tullamore, Australia . 43 E4
Tullamore, Ireland .. 10 E3
Tulle, France 14 D4
Tully, Australia 42 B4
Tulsa, U.S.A. 55 G7
Tulsequah, Canada .. 50 B2
Tulua, Colombia 62 C3
Tulun, Russia 21 D11
Tulungagung, Indonesia 27 H14
Tuma →, Nic. 60 D3
Tumaco, Colombia .. 62 C3
Tumatumari, Guyana . 62 B7
Tumba, Sweden 7 G17
Tumba, L., Dem. Rep. of
  the Congo 36 E3
Tumbarumba, Australia 43 F4
Tumbes, Peru 62 D2
Tumby Bay, Australia . 43 E2
Tumeremo, Venezuela 62 B6
Tumkur, India 28 N10
Tump, Pakistan 28 F3
Tumpat, Malaysia ... 26 C2
Tumu, Ghana 34 F5
Tumucumaque, Serra,
  Brazil 63 C8
Tumut, Australia ... 43 F4
Tumwater, U.S.A. .. 56 C2
Tunas de Zaza, Cuba . 60 B4
Tunbridge Wells =
  Royal Tunbridge
  Wells, U.K. 9 F8
Tuncurry-Forster,
  Australia 43 E5
Tundzha →, Bulgaria . 17 C11
Tungabhadra →, India 28 M11
Tungla, Nic. 60 D3
Tungsten, Canada .. 50 A3
Tunguska,
  Nizhnyaya →, Russia 21 C9
Tunguska,
  Podkamennaya →,
  Russia 21 C10
Tunica, U.S.A. 55 H9
Tunis, Tunisia 35 A8
Tunisia ■, Africa ... 35 A7

Tunja, Colombia 62 B4
Tunnsjøen, Norway .. 6 D15
Tunungayualok I.,
  Canada 49 A7
Tununirusiq = Arctic
  Bay, Canada 47 A11
Tunuyán →, Argentina 64 C3
Tūp Āghāj, Iran 30 B5
Tupelo, U.S.A. 53 H1
Tupinambaranas, Brazil 62 D7
Tupiza, Bolivia 62 H5
Tupper, Canada 50 B4
Tupper Lake, U.S.A. . 52 C8
Tupungato, Cerro,
  S. Amer. 64 C3
Túquerres, Colombia . 62 C3
Tura, Russia 21 C11
Turabah, Si. Arabia .. 30 D4
Tūrān, Iran 31 C8
Turan, Russia 21 D10
Turayf, Si. Arabia ... 30 D3
Turda, Romania 13 E12
Turek, Poland 13 B10
Turen, Venezuela ... 62 B5
Turfan = Turpan, China 24 B3
Turgeon →, Canada . 48 C4
Türgovishte, Bulgaria . 17 C12
Turgutlu, Turkey ... 17 E12
Turia →, Spain 15 C5
Turiaçu, Brazil 63 D9
Turiaçu →, Brazil ... 63 D9
Turin = Torino, Italy . 14 D7
Turkestan = Türkistan,
  Kazakstan 20 E7
Turkey ■, Eurasia .. 19 G6
Turkey Creek, Australia 40 C4
Türkistan, Kazakstan . 20 E7
Türkmenbashi,
  Turkmenistan 19 G9
Türkmenistan ■, Asia . 20 F6
Turks & Caicos Is. ■,
  W. Indies 61 B5
Turks Island Passage,
  W. Indies 61 B5
Turku, Finland 7 F20
Turlock, U.S.A. 57 H3
Turnagain →, Canada 50 B3
Turnagain, C., N.Z. .. 39 J6
Turneffe Is., Belize .. 59 D7
Turner, U.S.A. 56 B9
Turner Pt., Australia . 42 A1
Turner Valley, Canada . 50 C6
Turnhout, Belgium .. 11 C4
Turnor L., Canada ... 51 B7
Türnovo = Veliko
  Tŭrnovo, Bulgaria .. 17 C11
Turnu Măgurele,
  Romania 13 G13
Turnu Roşu, P.,
  Romania 13 F13
Turpan, China 24 B3
Tursāq, Iraq 30 C5
Turtle Head I., Australia 42 A3
Turtle L., Canada ... 51 C7
Turtle Lake, U.S.A. .. 54 B4
Turtleford, Canada .. 51 C7
Turukhansk, Russia . 21 C9
Tuscaloosa, U.S.A. .. 53 J2
Tuscany = Toscana □,
  Italy 16 C4
Tuscola, Ill., U.S.A. .. 52 F1
Tuscola, Tex., U.S.A. . 55 J5
Tuscumbia, U.S.A. .. 53 H2
Tuskegee, U.S.A. ... 53 J3
Tuticorin, India 28 Q11
Tutóia, Brazil 63 D10
Tutong, Brunei 26 D4
Tutrakan, Bulgaria .. 17 B12
Tuttle Creek L., U.S.A. 54 F6
Tuttlingen, Germany . 12 E5
Tutuala, Indonesia .. 27 F7
Tutuila, Amer. Samoa . 39 B13
Tutume, Botswana .. 37 J5
Tututepec, Mexico .. 59 D5
Tuva □, Russia 21 D10
Tuvalu ■, Pac. Oc. .. 38 B10
Tuxpan, Mexico 59 C5
Tuxtla Gutiérrez, Mexico 59 D6
Tuy = Tui, Spain 15 A1
Tuya L., Canada 50 B2
Tüysarkān, Iran 31 C6
Tuz Gölü, Turkey ... 19 G5
Tūz Khurmātū, Iraq . 30 C5
Tuzla, Bos.-H. 17 B8
Tver, Russia 18 C6
Tweed Heads, Australia 43 D5
Tweedsmuir Prov. Park,
  Canada 50 C3
Twentynine Palms,
  U.S.A. 57 J5
Twillingate, Canada . 49 C9
Twin Bridges, U.S.A. . 56 D7
Twin Falls, Canada .. 49 B7
Twin Falls, U.S.A. ... 56 E6
Twin Valley, U.S.A. .. 54 B6
Two Harbors, U.S.A. . 54 B9
Two Hills, Canada .. 50 C6
Two Rivers, U.S.A. .. 52 C2
Two Rocks, Australia . 41 F2
Twofold B., Australia . 43 F4
Tyachiv, Ukraine ... 13 D12
Tychy, Poland 13 C10
Tyler, Minn., U.S.A. . 54 C6

Vermilion

Tyler, Tex., U.S.A. 55 J7
Tynda, Russia 21 D13
Tyndall, U.S.A. 54 D6
Tyne →, U.K. 8 C6
Tyne & Wear □, U.K. 8 B6
Tynemouth, U.K. 8 B6
Tyre = Sūr, Lebanon 33 B4
Tyrifjorden, Norway 7 F14
Tyrol = Tirol □, Austria 12 E6
Tyrrell →, Australia 43 F3
Tyrrell, L., Australia 43 F3
Tyrrell L., Canada 51 A7
Tyrrhenian Sea, Medit. S. 16 E5
Tysfjorden, Norway 6 B17
Tyulgan, Russia 18 D10
Tyumen, Russia 20 D7
Tywi →, U.K. 9 F3
Tywyn, U.K. 9 E3
Tzaneen, S. Africa 37 J6
Tzukong = Zigong, China 24 D5

U.S.A. = United States of America ■, N. Amer. 2 B4
Uatumã →, Brazil 62 D7
Uaupés, Brazil 62 D5
Uaupés →, Brazil 62 C5
Uaxactún, Guatemala 60 C2
Ubá, Brazil 63 H10
Ubaitaba, Brazil 63 F11
Ubangi = Oubangi →, Dem. Rep. of the Congo 36 E3
Ubauro, Pakistan 28 E6
Ubayyiḍ, W. al →, Iraq 30 C4
Ube, Japan 23 H5
Úbeda, Spain 15 C4
Uberaba, Brazil 63 G9
Uberlândia, Brazil 63 G9
Ubon Ratchathani, Thailand 26 A2
Ubort →, Belarus 13 B15
Ubundu, Dem. Rep. of the Congo 36 E5
Ucayali →, Peru 62 D4
Uchiura-Wan, Japan 22 C10
Uchquduq, Uzbekistan 20 E7
Uchur →, Russia 21 D14
Ucluelet, Canada 50 D3
Uda →, Russia 21 D14
Udagamandalam, India 28 P10
Udaipur, India 28 G8
Udaipur Garhi, Nepal 29 F15
Uddevalla, Sweden 7 G14
Uddjaur, Sweden 6 D17
Uden, Neths. 11 C5
Udgir, India 28 K10
Udhampur, India 28 C9
Údine, Italy 16 A5
Udmurtia □, Russia 18 C9
Udon Thani, Thailand 26 A2
Udupi, India 28 N9
Ueda, Japan 23 F9
Uedineniya, Os., Russia 4 B12
Uele →, Dem. Rep. of the Congo 36 D4
Uelen, Russia 21 C19
Uelzen, Germany 12 B6
Ufa, Russia 18 D10
Ufa →, Russia 18 D10
Ugab →, Namibia 37 J2
Ugalla →, Tanzania 36 F6
Uganda ■, Africa 36 D6
Uglegorsk, Russia 21 E15
Ugljan, Croatia 12 F8
Uhrichsville, U.S.A. 52 E5
Uibhist a Deas = South Uist, U.K. 10 C3
Uibhist a Tuath = North Uist, U.K. 10 C3
Uíge, Angola 36 F2
Uinta Mts., U.S.A. 56 F8
Uitenhage, S. Africa 37 L5
Uithuizen, Neths. 11 A6
Uji-guntō, Japan 23 J4
Ujjain, India 28 H9
Ujung Pandang, Indonesia 27 F5
Uka, Russia 21 D17
Uke-Shima, Japan 23 K4
Ukhrul, India 29 G19
Ukhta, Russia 18 B9
Ukiah, U.S.A. 56 G2
Ukmergė, Lithuania 7 J21
Ukraine ■, Europe 19 E5
Ulaanbaatar, Mongolia 21 E11
Ulaangom, Mongolia 24 A4
Ulaanjirem, Mongolia 24 B5
Ulan Bator = Ulaanbaatar, Mongolia 21 E11
Ulan Ude, Russia 21 D11
Ulcinj, Montenegro, Yug. 17 D8
Ulefoss, Norway 7 G13
Ulhasnagar, India 28 K8
Uliastay, Mongolia 24 B4
Ulithi Atoll, Pac. Oc. 27 B9
Ulladulla, Australia 43 F5
Ullapool, U.K. 10 C4
Ullswater, U.K. 8 C5
Ullŭng-do, S. Korea 23 F5
Ulm, Germany 12 D5
Ulmarra, Australia 43 D5
Ulricehamn, Sweden 7 H15
Ulster □, U.K. 10 D3
Ulubat Gölü, Turkey 17 D13
Uludağ, Turkey 17 D13
Ulungur He →, China 24 B3
Uluru = Ayers Rock, Australia 41 E5
Uluru Nat. Park, Australia 41 E5
Ulutau, Kazakstan 20 E7
Ulverston, U.K. 8 C4
Ulverstone, Australia 42 G4
Ulya, Russia 21 D15
Ulyanovsk = Simbirsk, Russia 18 D8
Ulyasutay = Uliastay, Mongolia 24 B4
Ulysses, U.S.A. 55 G4
Umala, Bolivia 62 G5
Uman, Ukraine 13 D16
Umaria, India 29 H12
Umarkot, Pakistan 28 G6
Umatilla, U.S.A. 56 D4
Umba, Russia 18 A5
Umbakumba, Australia 42 A2
Umbrella Mts., N.Z. 39 L2
Ume älv →, Sweden 6 E19
Umeå, Sweden 6 E19
Umera, Indonesia 27 E7
Umlazi, S. Africa 37 L6
Umm ad Daraj, J., Jordan 33 C4
Umm al Qaywayn, U.A.E. 31 E7
Umm al Qittayn, Jordan 33 C5
Umm Bāb, Qatar 31 E6
Umm el Fahm, Israel 33 C4
Umm Keddada, Sudan 35 F11
Umm Lajj, Si. Arabia 30 E3
Umm Ruwaba, Sudan 35 F12
Umnak I., U.S.A. 46 C3
Umniati →, Zimbabwe 37 H5
Umpqua →, U.S.A. 56 E1
Umtata, S. Africa 37 L5
Umuarama, Brazil 64 A6
Umzimvubu, S. Africa 37 L5
Una →, Bos.-H. 12 F9
Unalakleet, U.S.A. 46 B3
Unalaska, U.S.A. 46 C3
Unalaska I., U.S.A. 46 C3
'Unayzah, Si. Arabia 30 E4
'Unāzah, J., Asia 30 C3
Uncía, Bolivia 62 G5
Uncompahgre Peak, U.S.A. 57 G10
Uncompahgre Plateau, U.S.A. 57 G9
Underbool, Australia 43 F3
Ungarie, Australia 43 E4
Ungarra, Australia 43 E2
Ungava, Pén. d', Canada 47 C12
Ungava B., Canada 47 C13
Ungeny = Ungheni, Moldova 13 E14
Ungheni, Moldova 13 E14
União da Vitória, Brazil 64 B6
Unimak I., U.S.A. 46 C3
Union, Miss., U.S.A. 55 J10
Union, Mo., U.S.A. 54 F9
Union, S.C., U.S.A. 53 H5
Union City, Pa., U.S.A. 52 E6
Union City, Tenn., U.S.A. 55 G10
Union Gap, U.S.A. 56 C3
Union Springs, U.S.A. 53 J3
Uniontown, U.S.A. 52 F6
Unionville, U.S.A. 54 E8
United Arab Emirates ■, Asia 31 F7
United Kingdom ■, Europe 10 E6
United States of America ■, N. Amer. 2 B4
United States of America ■, N. Amer. 2 B4
Unity, Canada 51 C7
University Park, U.S.A. 57 K10
Unnao, India 29 F12
Unst, U.K. 10 A6
Unuk →, Canada 50 B2
Uozu, Japan 23 F8
Upata, Venezuela 62 B6
Upemba, L., Dem. Rep. of the Congo 36 F5
Upernavik, Greenland 4 B5
Upington, S. Africa 37 K4
Upolu, Samoa 39 A13
Upper Alkali L., U.S.A. 56 F3
Upper Arrow L., Canada 50 C5
Upper Foster L., Canada 51 B7
Upper Hutt, N.Z. 39 J5
Upper Klamath L., U.S.A. 56 E3
Upper Lake, U.S.A. 56 G2
Upper Musquodoboit, Canada 49 C7
Upper Red L., U.S.A. 54 A7
Upper Sandusky, U.S.A. 52 E4
Upper Volta = Burkina Faso ■, Africa 34 F5
Uppland, Sweden 7 F17
Uppsala, Sweden 7 G17
Upstart, C., Australia 42 B4
Upton, U.S.A. 54 C2
Ur, Iraq 30 D5
Urakawa, Japan 22 C11
Ural = Zhayyq →, Kazakstan 19 E9
Ural, Australia 43 E4
Ural Mts. = Uralskie Gory, Eurasia 18 C10
Uralla, Australia 43 E5
Uralsk = Oral, Kazakstan 19 D9
Uralskie Gory, Eurasia 18 C10
Urambo, Tanzania 36 F6
Urana, Australia 43 F4
Urandangi, Australia 42 C2
Uranium City, Canada 51 B7
Uraricoera →, Brazil 62 C6
Urawa, Japan 23 G9
Uray, Russia 20 C7
'Uray'irah, Si. Arabia 31 E6
Urbana, Ill., U.S.A. 52 E1
Urbana, Ohio, U.S.A. 52 E4
Urbino, Italy 16 C5
Urbión, Picos de, Spain 15 A4
Urcos, Peru 62 F4
Urdzhar, Kazakstan 20 E9
Ure →, U.K. 8 C6
Ures, Mexico 58 B2
Urfa = Sanliurfa, Turkey 19 G6
Urganch, Uzbekistan 20 E7
Urgench = Urganch, Uzbekistan 20 E7
Ürgüp, Turkey 30 B2
Uribia, Colombia 62 A4
Urique, Mexico 58 B3
Urique →, Mexico 58 B3
Urk, Neths. 11 B5
Urla, Turkey 17 E12
Urmia = Orūmīyeh, Iran 30 B5
Urmia, L. = Orūmīyeh, Daryācheh-ye, Iran 30 B5
Uroševac, Kosovo, Yug. 17 C9
Uruaçu, Brazil 63 F9
Uruapan, Mexico 58 D4
Urubamba →, Peru 62 F4
Uruçara, Brazil 62 D7
Uruçuí, Brazil 63 E10
Uruguai →, Brazil 64 B6
Uruguaiana, Brazil 64 B5
Uruguay ■, S. Amer. 64 C5
Uruguay →, S. Amer. 64 C5
Urumchi = Ürümqi, China 20 E9
Ürümqi, China 20 E9
Urup, Ostrov, Russia 21 E16
Usa →, Russia 18 A10
Uşak, Turkey 19 G4
Usakos, Namibia 37 J3
Usedom, Germany 12 B8
Useless Loop, Australia 41 E1
Ush-Tobe, Kazakstan 20 E8
Ushakova, Ostrov, Russia 4 A12
Ushant = Ouessant, Î. d', France 14 B1
Ushibuka, Japan 23 H5
Ushuaia, Argentina 64 G3
Ushumun, Russia 21 D13
Usk, Canada 50 C3
Usk →, U.K. 9 F5
Usman, Russia 18 D6
Usolye Sibirskoye, Russia 21 D11
Uspallata, P. de, Argentina 64 C3
Uspenskiy, Kazakstan 20 E8
Ussuri →, Asia 22 A7
Ussuriysk, Russia 21 E14
Ussurka, Russia 22 B6
Ust-Aldan = Batamay, Russia 21 C13
Ust-Amginskoye = Khandyga, Russia 21 C14
Ust-Bolsheretsk, Russia 21 D16
Ust-Chaun, Russia 21 C18
Ust-Ilimpeya = Yukta, Russia 21 C11
Ust-Ilimsk, Russia 21 D11
Ust-Ishim, Russia 20 D8
Ust-Kamchatsk, Russia 21 D17
Ust-Kamenogorsk = Öskemen, Kazakstan 20 E9
Ust-Khayryuzovo, Russia 21 D16
Ust-Kut, Russia 21 D11
Ust-Kuyga, Russia 21 B14
Ust-Maya, Russia 21 C14
Ust-Mil, Russia 21 D14
Ust-Nera, Russia 21 C15
Ust-Nyukzha, Russia 21 D13
Ust-Olenek, Russia 21 B12
Ust-Omchug, Russia 21 C15
Ust-Port, Russia 20 C9
Ust-Tsilma, Russia 18 A9
Ust Urt = Ustyurt Plateau, Asia 20 E6
Ust-Usa, Russia 18 A10
Ust-Vorkuta, Russia 18 A11
Ústí nad Labem, Czech Rep. 12 C8
Ústica, Italy 16 E5
Ustinov = Izhevsk, Russia 18 C9
Ustyurt Plateau, Asia 20 E6
Usu, China 24 B3
Usuki, Japan 23 H5
Usulután, El Salv. 60 D2
Usumacinta →, Mexico 59 D6
Usumbura = Bujumbura, Burundi 36 E5
Uta, Indonesia 27 E9
Utah □, U.S.A. 56 G8
Utah L., U.S.A. 56 F8
Utatlan, Guatemala 60 C1
Ute Creek →, U.S.A. 55 H3
Utena, Lithuania 7 J21
Utiariti, Brazil 62 F7
Utica, U.S.A. 52 D8
Utikuma L., Canada 50 B5
Utopia, Australia 42 C1
Utrecht, Neths. 11 B5
Utrecht □, Neths. 11 B5
Utrera, Spain 15 D3
Utsjoki, Finland 6 B22
Utsunomiya, Japan 23 F9
Uttar Pradesh □, India 28 F12
Uttaradit, Thailand 26 A2
Uttoxeter, U.K. 8 E6
Uummannarsuaq = Nunap Isua, Greenland 4 D5
Uusikaarlepyy, Finland 6 E20
Uusikaupunki, Finland 7 F19
Uva, Russia 18 C9
Uvalde, U.S.A. 55 L5
Uvat, Russia 20 D7
Uvinza, Tanzania 36 F6
Uvira, Dem. Rep. of the Congo 36 E5
Uvs Nuur, Mongolia 24 A4
'Uwairidh, Ḥarrat al, Si. Arabia 30 E3
Uwajima, Japan 23 H6
Uweinat, Jebel, Sudan 35 D10
Uxmal, Mexico 59 C7
Uyo, Nigeria 34 G7
Uyûn Mûsa, Egypt 33 F1
Uyuni, Bolivia 62 H5
Uzbekistan ■, Asia 20 E7
Uzen, Kazakstan 19 F9
Uzen, Mal →, Kazakstan 19 E8
Uzerche, France 14 D4
Uzh →, Ukraine 13 C16
Uzhgorod = Uzhhorod, Ukraine 13 D12
Uzhhorod, Ukraine 13 D12
Užice, Serbia, Yug. 17 C8
Uzunköprü, Turkey 17 D12

Vaal →, S. Africa 37 K4
Vaasa, Finland 6 E19
Vác, Hungary 13 E10
Vacaville, U.S.A. 56 G3
Vach = Vakh →, Russia 20 C8
Vache, Î. à, Haiti 61 C5
Vadodara, India 28 H8
Vadsø, Norway 6 A23
Vaduz, Liech. 14 C8
Værøy, Norway 6 C15
Vágar, Færoe Is. 6 E9
Vågsfjorden, Norway 6 B17
Váh →, Slovak Rep. 13 D9
Vahsel B., Antarctica 5 D1
Vaigach, Russia 20 B6
Vakh →, Russia 20 C8
Val-d'Or, Canada 48 C4
Val Marie, Canada 51 D7
Valahia, Romania 13 F13
Valandovo, Macedonia 17 D10
Valcheta, Argentina 64 E3
Valdayskaya Vozvyshennost, Russia 18 C5
Valdepeñas, Spain 15 C4
Valdés, Pen., Argentina 64 E4
Valdez, U.S.A. 46 B5
Valdivia, Chile 64 D2
Valdosta, U.S.A. 53 K4
Valdres, Norway 7 F13
Vale, U.S.A. 56 E5
Vale of Glamorgan □, U.K. 9 F4
Valemount, Canada 50 C5
Valença, Brazil 63 F11
Valença do Piauí, Brazil 63 E10
Valence, France 14 D6
Valencia, Spain 15 C5
Valencia, U.S.A. 57 J10
Valencia, Venezuela 62 A5
Valencia □, Spain 15 C5
Valencia, G. de, Spain 15 C6
Valencia de Alcántara, Spain 15 C2
Valencia I., Ireland 10 F1
Valenciennes, France 14 A5
Valentim, Sa. do, Brazil 63 E10
Valentin, Russia 22 C7
Valentine, U.S.A. 55 K2
Valera, Venezuela 62 B4
Valga, Estonia 7 H22
Valier, U.S.A. 56 B7
Valjevo, Serbia, Yug. 17 B8
Valka, Latvia 7 H21
Valkeakoski, Finland 7 F20
Valkenswaard, Neths. 11 C5
Vall de Uxó = La Vall d'Uixó, Spain 15 C5
Valladolid, Mexico 59 C7
Valladolid, Spain 15 B3
Valle de la Pascua, Venezuela 62 B5
Valle de Santiago, Mexico 58 C4
Valle de Suchil, Mexico 58 C4
Valle de Zaragoza, Mexico 58 B3
Valle Hermoso, Mexico 59 B5
Valledupar, Colombia 62 A4
Vallejo, U.S.A. 56 G2
Vallenar, Chile 64 B2
Valletta, Malta 16 G6
Valley City, U.S.A. 54 B6
Valley Falls, U.S.A. 56 E3
Valleyview, Canada 50 B5
Valls, Spain 15 B6
Valmiera, Latvia 7 H21
Valognes, France 14 B3
Valona = Vlorë, Albania 17 D8
Valozhyn, Belarus 13 A14
Valparaíso, Chile 64 C2
Valparaíso, Mexico 58 C4
Valparaiso, U.S.A. 52 E2
Vals, Tanjung, Indonesia 27 F9
Valsad, India 28 J8
Valverde del Camino, Spain 15 D2
Vammala, Finland 7 F20
Van, Turkey 19 G7
Van, L. = Van Gölü, Turkey 19 G7
Van Alstyne, U.S.A. 55 J6
Van Blommestein Meer, Surinam 63 C7
Van Buren, Canada 49 C6
Van Buren, Ark., U.S.A. 55 H7
Van Buren, Maine, U.S.A. 53 B11
Van Buren, Mo., U.S.A. 55 G9
Van Diemen, C., N. Terr., Australia 40 B5
Van Diemen, C., Queens., Australia 42 B2
Van Diemen G., Australia 40 B5
Van Gölü, Turkey 19 G7
Van Horn, U.S.A. 55 K2
Van Rees, Pegunungan, Indonesia 27 E9
Van Wert, U.S.A. 52 E3
Vanadzor, Armenia 19 F7
Vanavara, Russia 21 C11
Vancouver, Canada 50 D4
Vancouver, U.S.A. 56 D2
Vancouver, C., Australia 41 G2
Vancouver I., Canada 50 D3
Vandalia, Ill., U.S.A. 54 F10
Vandalia, Mo., U.S.A. 54 F9
Vanderhoof, Canada 50 C4
Vanderlin I., Australia 42 B2
Vänern, Sweden 7 G15
Vänersborg, Sweden 7 G15
Vangaindrano, Madag. 37 J9
Vanguard, Canada 51 D7
Vanino, Russia 21 E15
Vanna, Norway 6 A18
Vännäs, Sweden 6 E18
Vannes, France 14 C2
Vanrhynsdorp, S. Africa 37 L3
Vansbro, Sweden 7 F16
Vansittart B., Australia 40 B4
Vantaa, Finland 7 F21
Vanua Levu, Fiji 39 C8
Vanua Mbalavu, Fiji 39 C9
Vanuatu ■, Pac. Oc. 38 C9
Vapnyarka, Ukraine 13 D15
Varanasi, India 29 G13
Varanger-halvøya, Norway 6 A23
Varangerfjorden, Norway 6 A23
Varaždin, Croatia 12 E9
Varberg, Sweden 7 H15
Vardar = Axiós →, Greece 17 D10
Varde, Denmark 7 J13
Vardø, Norway 6 A24
Varėna, Lithuania 7 J21
Varese, Italy 14 D8
Varkaus, Finland 7 E22
Varna, Bulgaria 17 C12
Värnamo, Sweden 7 H16
Varzaneh, Iran 31 C7
Vasa Barris →, Brazil 63 F11
Vascongadas = País Vasco □, Spain 15 A4
Vasht = Khāsh, Iran 28 E2
Vasilevichi, Belarus 13 B15
Vasilkov = Vasylkiv, Ukraine 13 C16
Vaslui, Romania 13 E14
Vassar, Canada 51 D9
Vassar, U.S.A. 52 D4
Västerås, Sweden 7 G17
Västerbotten, Sweden 6 D18
Västerdalälven →, Sweden 7 F16
Västervik, Sweden 7 H17
Västmanland, Sweden 7 G16
Vasto, Italy 16 C6
Vasylkiv, Ukraine 13 C16
Vatican City ■, Europe 16 D5
Vatnajökull, Iceland 6 D5
Vatoa, Fiji 39 D9
Vatra-Dornei, Romania 13 E13
Vättern, Sweden 7 G16
Vaughn, Mont., U.S.A. 56 C8
Vaughn, N. Mex., U.S.A. 57 J11
Vaujours L., Canada 48 A5
Vaupés = Uaupés →, Brazil 62 C5
Vaupes □, Colombia 62 C4
Vauxhall, Canada 50 C6
Vava'u, Tonga 39 D12
Vawkavysk, Belarus 13 B13
Växjö, Sweden 7 H16
Vaygach, Ostrov, Russia 20 C6
Vechte →, Neths. 11 B6
Vedea →, Romania 13 G13
Veendam, Neths. 11 A6
Veenendaal, Neths. 11 B5
Vefsna →, Norway 6 D15
Vega, Norway 6 D14
Vega, U.S.A. 55 H3
Vegreville, Canada 50 C6
Vejer de la Frontera, Spain 15 D3
Vejle, Denmark 7 J13
Velas, C., Costa Rica 60 D2
Velebit Planina, Croatia 12 F8
Veles, Macedonia 17 D9
Vélez-Málaga, Spain 15 D3
Vélez Rubio, Spain 15 D4
Velhas →, Brazil 63 G10
Velika Kapela, Croatia 12 F8
Velikaya →, Russia 18 C4
Velikaya Kema, Russia 22 B8
Veliki Ustyug, Russia 18 B8
Velikiye Luki, Russia 18 C5
Veliko Tŭrnovo, Bulgaria 17 C11
Velikonda Range, India 28 M11
Velletri, Italy 16 D5
Vellore, India 28 N11
Velsk, Russia 18 B7
Velva, U.S.A. 54 A4
Venado Tuerto, Argentina 64 C4
Vendée □, France 14 C3
Vendôme, France 14 C4
Venézia, Italy 16 B5
Venézia, G. di, Italy 16 B5
Venezuela ■, S. Amer. 62 B5
Venezuela, G. de, Venezuela 62 A4
Vengurla, India 28 M8
Venice = Venézia, Italy 16 B5
Venice, U.S.A. 53 M4
Venkatapuram, India 29 K12
Venlo, Neths. 11 C6
Vennesla, Norway 7 G12
Venray, Neths. 11 C6
Ventana, Punta de la, Mexico 58 C3
Ventnor, U.K. 9 G6
Ventoténe, Italy 16 D5
Ventoux, Mt., France 14 D6
Ventspils, Latvia 7 H19
Ventuarí →, Venezuela 62 C5
Ventura, U.S.A. 57 J4
Venus B., Australia 43 F4
Vera, Argentina 64 B4
Vera, Spain 15 D5
Veracruz, Mexico 59 D5
Veracruz □, Mexico 59 D5
Veraval, India 28 J7
Verbánia, Italy 14 D8
Vercelli, Italy 14 D8
Verdalsøra, Norway 6 E14
Verde →, Argentina 64 E3
Verde →, Goiás, Brazil 63 G8
Verde →, Mato Grosso do Sul, Brazil 63 H8
Verde →, Chihuahua, Mexico 58 B3
Verde →, Oaxaca, Mexico 59 D5
Verde →, Veracruz, Mexico 58 C4
Verde, Cay, Bahamas 60 B4
Verden, Germany 12 B5
Verdun, France 14 B6
Vereeniging, S. Africa 37 K5
Verga, C., Guinea 34 F3
Vergemont Cr. →, Australia 42 C3
Verín, Spain 15 B2
Verkhnevilyuysk, Russia 21 C13
Verkhniy Baskunchak, Russia 19 E8
Verkhoyansk, Russia 21 C14
Verkhoyansk Ra. = Verkhoyanskiy Khrebet, Russia 21 C13
Verkhoyanskiy Khrebet, Russia 21 C13
Vermilion, Canada 51 C6
Vermilion →, Alta., Canada 51 C6
Vermilion →, Qué., Canada 48 C5

Vermilion, B., U.S.A. ... 55 L9
Vermilion Bay, Canada 51 D10
Vermilion L., U.S.A. 54 B8
Vermillion, U.S.A. 54 D6
Vermont □, U.S.A. 52 D9
Vernal, U.S.A. 56 F9
Verner, Canada 48 C3
Vernon, Canada 50 C5
Vernon, U.S.A. 55 H5
Vero Beach, U.S.A. ... 53 M5
Véroia, Greece 17 D10
Verona, Italy 16 B4
Verona, U.S.A. 54 D10
Versailles, France 14 B5
Vert, C., Senegal 34 F2
Verviers, Belgium 11 D5
Veselovskoye Vdkhr.,
    Russia 19 E7
Vesoul, France 14 C7
Vesterålen, Norway ... 6 B16
Vestfjorden, Norway ... 6 C15
Vestmannaeyjar, Iceland 6 E3
Vestspitsbergen,
    Svalbard 4 B8
Vestvågøy, Norway ... 6 B15
Vesuvio, Italy 16 D6
Vesuvius, Mt. =
    Vesuvio, Italy 16 D6
Veszprém, Hungary ... 13 E9
Vetlanda, Sweden 7 H16
Vetlugu →, Russia ... 18 C8
Vettore, Mte., Italy ... 16 C5
Veurne, Belgium 11 C2
Veys, Iran 31 D6
Vezhen, Bulgaria 17 C11
Viacha, Bolivia 62 G5
Viamão, Brazil 64 C6
Viana, Brazil 63 D10
Viana do Alentejo,
    Portugal 15 C2
Viana do Castelo,
    Portugal 15 B1
Vianden, Lux. 11 E6
Vianópolis, Brazil ... 63 G9
Viaréggio, Italy 16 C4
Vibo Valéntia, Italy ... 16 E7
Viborg, Denmark 7 H13
Vic, Spain 15 B7
Vicenza, Italy 16 B4
Vich = Vic, Spain 15 B7
Vichada →, Colombia 62 C5
Vichy, France 14 C5
Vicksburg, U.S.A. ... 55 J9
Victor, India 28 J7
Victor Harbor, Australia 43 F2
Victoria = Labuan,
    Malaysia 26 C5
Victoria, Canada 50 D4
Victoria, Chile 64 D2
Victoria, Kans., U.S.A. 54 F5
Victoria, Tex., U.S.A. . 55 L6
Victoria □, Australia . 43 F3
Victoria →, Australia . 40 C4
Victoria, Grand L.,
    Canada 48 C4
Victoria, L., Africa ... 36 E6
Victoria, L., Australia . 43 E3
Victoria Beach, Canada 51 C9
Victoria de Durango =
    Durango, Mexico .. 58 C4
Victoria de las Tunas,
    Cuba 60 B4
Victoria Falls, Zimbabwe 37 H5
Victoria I., Canada ... 46 A8
Victoria L., Canada ... 49 C8
Victoria L., Antarctica . 5 D11
Victoria River, Australia 40 C5
Victoria Str., Canada . 46 B9
Victoria Taungdeik,
    Burma 29 J18
Victoriaville, Canada . 49 C5
Victorica, Argentina . 64 D3
Victorville, U.S.A. ... 57 J5
Vicuña, Chile 64 C2
Vidalia, U.S.A. 53 J4
Vidin, Bulgaria 17 C10
Vidisha, India 28 H10
Vidzy, Belarus 7 J22
Viedma, Argentina ... 64 E4
Viedma, L., Argentina 64 F2
Vielsalm, Belgium ... 11 D5
Vienna = Wien, Austria 12 D9
Vienna, Ill., U.S.A. ... 55 G10
Vienna, Mo., U.S.A. . 54 F9
Vienne, France 14 D6
Vienne →, France ... 14 C4
Vientiane, Laos 26 A2
Vientiane, Laos 26 A2
Vientos, Paso de los,
    Caribbean 61 C5
Vierzon, France 14 C5
Vietnam ■, Asia 26 A3
Vigan, Phil. 27 A6
Vigévano, Italy 14 D8
Vigia, Brazil 63 D9
Vigia Chico, Mexico . 59 D7
Vigo, Spain 15 A1
Vijayawada, India ... 29 L12
Vijosë →, Albania ... 17 D8
Vík, Iceland 6 E4
Vikeke, Indonesia ... 27 F7
Viking, Canada 50 C6
Vikna, Norway 6 D14

Vila do Bispo, Portugal 15 D1
Vila Franca de Xira,
    Portugal 15 C1
Vila Nova de Gaia,
    Portugal 15 B1
Vila Real, Portugal ... 15 B2
Vila Real de los Infantes,
    Spain 15 C5
Vila Real de Santo
    António, Portugal .. 15 D2
Vila Velha, Brazil 63 H10
Vilagarcía de Arousa,
    Spain 15 A1
Vilaine →, France ... 14 C2
Vilanculos, Mozam. .. 37 J7
Vilanova i la Geltrú,
    Spain 15 B6
Vileyka, Belarus 13 A14
Vilhelmina, Sweden .. 6 D17
Vilhena, Brazil 62 F6
Viliga, Russia 21 C16
Viljandi, Estonia 7 G21
Viliya →, Lithuania .. 7 J21
Vilkitskogo, Proliv,
    Russia 21 B11
Vilkovo = Vylkove,
    Ukraine 13 F15
Villa Ahumada, Mexico 58 A3
Villa Ángela, Argentina 64 B4
Villa Bella, Bolivia ... 62 F5
Villa Bens = Tarfaya,
    Morocco 34 C3
Villa Cisneros = Dakhla,
    W. Sahara 34 D2
Villa de María,
    Argentina 64 B4
Villa Dolores, Argentina 64 C3
Villa Frontera, Mexico 58 B4
Villa Hayes, Paraguay 64 B5
Villa Juárez, Mexico . 58 B4
Villa María, Argentina 64 C4
Villa Mazán, Argentina 64 B3
Villa Montes, Bolivia . 62 H6
Villa Ocampo, Argentina 64 B5
Villa Ocampo, Mexico 58 B3
Villa Unión, Mexico .. 58 C3
Villacarrillo, Spain ... 15 C4
Villach, Austria 12 E7
Villagrán, Mexico ... 59 C5
Villaguay, Argentina . 64 C5
Villahermosa, Mexico 59 D6
Villajoyosa, Spain ... 15 C5
Villalba, Spain 15 A2
Villanueva, U.S.A. ... 55 H2
Villanueva de la Serena,
    Spain 15 C3
Villanueva y Geltrú =
    Vilanova i la Geltrú,
    Spain 15 B6
Villarreal = Vila-real de
    los Infantes, Spain . 15 C5
Villarrica, Chile 64 D2
Villarrica, Paraguay . 64 B5
Villarrobledo, Spain . 15 C4
Villavicencio, Colombia 62 C4
Villaviciosa, Spain ... 15 A3
Villazón, Bolivia 62 H5
Ville-Marie, Canada . 48 C4
Ville Platte, U.S.A. ... 55 K8
Villena, Spain 15 C5
Villeneuve-d'Ascq,
    France 14 A5
Villeneuve-sur-Lot,
    France 14 D4
Villingen-
    Schwenningen,
    Germany 12 D5
Vilna, Canada 50 C6
Vilnius, Lithuania ... 7 J21
Vilvoorde, Belgium .. 11 D4
Vilyuy →, Russia ... 21 C13
Vilyuysk, Russia 21 C13
Viña del Mar, Chile .. 64 C2
Vinarós, Spain 15 B6
Vincennes, U.S.A. ... 52 F2
Vindelälven →,
    Sweden 6 E18
Vindeln, Sweden 6 D18
Vindhya Ra., India .. 28 H10
Vineland, U.S.A. 52 F8
Vinita, U.S.A. 55 G7
Vinkovci, Croatia ... 17 B8
Vinnitsa = Vinnytsya,
    Ukraine 13 D15
Vinnytsya, Ukraine .. 13 D15
Vinton, Iowa, U.S.A. . 54 D8
Vinton, La., U.S.A. ... 55 K8
Virac, Phil. 27 B6
Virago Sd., Canada .. 50 C2
Viramgam, India 28 H8
Virananşehir, Turkey . 30 B3
Virden, Canada 51 D8
Vire, France 14 B3
Virgenes, C., Argentina 64 G3
Virgin →, U.S.A. ... 57 H6
Virgin Gorda, Virgin Is. 61 C7
Virgin Is. (British) ■,
    W. Indies 61 C7
Virgin Is. (U.S.) ■,
    W. Indies 61 C7
Virginia, S. Africa ... 37 K5
Virginia, U.S.A. 54 B8
Virginia □, U.S.A. ... 52 G7
Virginia Beach, U.S.A. 52 G8

Virginia City, Mont.,
    U.S.A. 56 D8
Virginia City, Nev.,
    U.S.A. 56 G4
Virginia Falls, Canada 50 A3
Virginiatown, Canada 48 C4
Viroqua, U.S.A. 54 D9
Virovitica, Croatia ... 16 B7
Virton, Belgium 11 E5
Virudunagar, India .. 28 Q10
Vis, Croatia 16 C7
Visalia, U.S.A. 57 H4
Visayan Sea, Phil. ... 27 B6
Viscount Melville Sd.,
    Canada 4 B2
Visé, Belgium 11 D5
Viseu, Brazil 63 D9
Viseu, Portugal 15 B2
Vishakhapatnam, India 29 L13
Viso, Mte., Italy 14 D7
Visokoi I., Antarctica . 5 B1
Vistula = Wisła →,
    Poland 13 A10
Vitebsk = Vitsyebsk,
    Belarus 18 C5
Viterbo, Italy 16 C5
Viti Levu, Fiji 39 C7
Vitigudino, Spain ... 15 B2
Vitim, Russia 21 D12
Vitim →, Russia 21 D12
Vitória, Brazil 63 H10
Vitória da Conquista,
    Brazil 63 F10
Vitória de São Antão,
    Brazil 63 E11
Vitoria-Gasteiz, Spain 15 A4
Vitória Véneto, Italy .. 16 B5
Viveiro, Spain 15 A2
Vivian, U.S.A. 55 J8
Vizcaíno, Desierto de,
    Mexico 58 B2
Vizcaíno, Sierra, Mexico 58 B2
Vizianagaram, India . 29 K13
Vjosa = Vijosë →,
    Albania 17 D8
Vlaardingen, Neths. . 11 C4
Vladikavkaz, Russia . 19 F7
Vladimir, Russia 18 C7
Vladimir Volynskiy =
    Volodymyr-Volynskyy,
    Ukraine 13 C13
Vladivostok, Russia .. 21 E14
Vlieland, Neths. 11 A4
Vlissingen, Neths. ... 11 C3
Vlóra = Vlorë, Albania 17 D8
Vlorë, Albania 17 D8
Vltava →, Czech Rep. 12 D8
Vogelkop = Doberai,
    Jazirah, Indonesia . 27 E8
Vogelsberg, Germany 12 C5
Voghera, Italy 14 D8
Vohimarina = Iharana,
    Madag. 37 G10
Vohimena, Tanjon' i,
    Madag. 37 K9
Voi, Kenya 36 E7
Voiron, France 14 D6
Voisey B., Canada ... 49 A7
Vojmsjön, Sweden .. 6 D17
Vojvodina □,
    Serbia, Yug. 17 B9
Volborg, U.S.A. 54 C2
Volcano Is. = Kazan-
    Rettō, Pac. Oc. ... 44 E6
Volda, Norway 7 E12
Volga →, Russia ... 19 E8
Volga Hts. =
    Privolzhskaya
    Vozvyshennost,
    Russia 19 D8
Volgodonsk, Russia . 19 E7
Volgograd, Russia .. 19 E7
Volgogradskoye Vdkhr.,
    Russia 19 D8
Volkhov →, Russia . 18 B5
Volkovysk = Vawkavysk,
    Belarus 13 B13
Volochanka, Russia . 21 B10
Volodymyr-Volynskyy,
    Ukraine 13 C13
Vologda, Russia 18 C6
Vólos, Greece 17 E10
Volovets, Ukraine ... 13 D12
Volozhin = Valozhyn,
    Belarus 13 A14
Volsk, Russia 18 D8
Volta →, Ghana 34 G6
Volta Redonda, Brazil 63 H10
Voltaire, C., Australia 40 B4
Volterra, Italy 16 C4
Volturno →, Italy ... 16 D5
Volzhskiy, Russia ... 19 E7
Vopnafjörður, Iceland 6 D6
Vóriai Sporádhes,
    Greece 17 E10
Vorkuta, Russia 18 A11
Vormsi, Estonia 7 G20
Voronezh, Russia ... 19 D6
Voroshilovgrad =
    Luhansk, Ukraine .. 19 E6

Voroshilovsk =
    Alchevsk, Ukraine . 19 E6
Võrts Järv, Estonia .. 7 G22
Võru, Estonia 7 H22
Vosges, France 14 B7
Voss, Norway 7 F12
Vostok I., Kiribati ... 45 J12
Votkinsk, Russia 18 C9
Votkinskoye Vdkhr.,
    Russia 18 C10
Votsuri-Shima, Japan 23 M1
Vouga →, Portugal . 15 B1
Vozhe, Ozero, Russia 18 B6
Voznesensk, Ukraine 19 E5
Voznesenye, Russia . 18 B6
Vrangelya, Ostrov,
    Russia 21 B19
Vranje, Serbia, Yug. . 17 C9
Vransko, Bos.-H. ... 17 C8
Vratsa, Bulgaria 17 C10
Vrbas, Serbia, Yug. .. 16 B7
Vršac, Serbia, Yug. .. 17 B9
Vryburg, S. Africa .. 37 K4
Vryheid, S. Africa .. 37 K6
Vukovar, Croatia 17 B8
Vulcan, Canada 50 C6
Vulcan, Romania 13 F12
Vulcănești, Moldova 13 F15
Vulcano, Italy 16 E6
Vulkaneshty =
    Vulcănești, Moldova 13 F15
Vung Tau, Vietnam .. 26 B3
Vyatka = Kirov, Russia 18 C8
Vyatka →, Russia ... 18 C9
Vyatskiye Polyany,
    Russia 18 C9
Vyazemskiy, Russia . 21 E14
Vyazma, Russia 18 C5
Vyborg, Russia 18 B4
Vychegda →, Russia 18 B8
Vychodné Beskydy,
    Europe 13 D11
Vyg-ozero, Russia .. 18 B5
Vylkove, Ukraine ... 13 F15
Vynohradiv, Ukraine 13 D12
Vyrnwy, L., U.K. 8 E4
Vyshniy Volochek,
    Russia 18 C5
Vyshza = imeni 26
    Bakinskikh
    Komissarov,
    Turkmenistan 31 B7
Vyškov, Czech Rep. . 13 D9
Vytegra, Russia 18 B6

W.A.C. Bennett Dam,
    Canada 50 B4
Waal →, Neths. 11 C5
Waalwijk, Neths. 11 C5
Wabana, Canada 49 C9
Wabasca →, Canada . 50 B5
Wabasca-Desmarais,
    Canada 50 B6
Wabash, U.S.A. 52 E3
Wabash →, U.S.A. . 52 G1
Wabigoon L., Canada 51 D10
Wabowden, Canada . 51 C9
Wabuk Pt., Canada .. 48 A2
Wabush, Canada 49 B6
Waco, U.S.A. 55 K6
Waconichi, L., Canada 48 B5
Wad Hamid, Sudan . 35 E12
Wad Medanî, Sudan . 35 F12
Wadayama, Japan .. 23 G7
Waddeneilanden, Neths. 11 A5
Waddenzee, Neths. .. 11 A5
Waddington, Mt.,
    Canada 50 C3
Waddy Pt., Australia . 43 C5
Wadebridge, U.K. ... 9 G3
Wadena, Canada 51 C8
Wadena, U.S.A. 54 B7
Wadeye, Australia .. 40 B4
Wadhams, Canada .. 50 C3
Wādī as Sīr, Jordan . 33 D4
Wadi Halfa, Sudan .. 35 D12
Wadsworth, U.S.A. . 56 G4
Wafrah, Si. Arabia .. 30 D5
Wageningen, Neths. . 11 C5
Wager B., Canada ... 47 B11
Wagga Wagga,
    Australia 43 F4
Waghete, Indonesia . 27 E9
Wagin, Australia 41 F2
Wagner, U.S.A. 54 D5
Wagon Mound, U.S.A. 55 G2
Wagoner, U.S.A. 55 H7
Wah, Pakistan 28 C8
Wahai, Indonesia ... 27 E7
Wâhid, Egypt 33 E1
Wahoo, U.S.A. 54 E6
Wahpeton, U.S.A. .. 54 B6
Waiau →, N.Z. 39 K4
Waibeem, Indonesia 27 E8
Waigeo, Indonesia .. 27 E8
Waihi, N.Z. 39 G5
Waihou →, N.Z. 39 G5
Waika, Dem. Rep. of
    the Congo 36 C5
Waikabubak, Indonesia 27 F5
Waikari, N.Z. 39 K4
Waikato →, N.Z. ... 39 G5
Waikerie, Australia .. 43 E3
Waikokopu, N.Z. 39 H6
Waikouaiti, N.Z. 39 L3
Waimakariri →, N.Z. 39 K4

Waimate, N.Z. 39 L3
Wainganga →, India 28 K11
Waingapu, Indonesia 27 F6
Waini →, Guyana .. 62 B7
Wainwright, Canada . 51 C6
Waiouru, N.Z. 39 H5
Waipara, N.Z. 39 K4
Waipawa, N.Z. 39 H6
Waipiro, N.Z. 39 H7
Waipu, N.Z. 39 F5
Waipukurau, N.Z. ... 39 J6
Wairakei, N.Z. 39 H6
Wairarapa, L., N.Z. . 39 J5
Wairoa, N.Z. 39 H6
Waitaki →, N.Z. 39 L3
Waitara, N.Z. 39 H5
Waitsburg, U.S.A. ... 56 C5
Waiuku, N.Z. 39 G5
Wajima, Japan 23 F8
Wajir, Kenya 36 D8
Wakasa, Japan 23 G7
Wakasa-Wan, Japan . 23 G7
Wakatipu, L., N.Z. .. 39 L2
Wakaw, Canada 51 C7
Wakayama, Japan .. 23 G7
Wakayama □, Japan . 23 H7
Wake Forest, U.S.A. . 53 H6
Wake I., Pac. Oc. ... 44 F8
WaKeeney, U.S.A. .. 54 F5
Wakefield, N.Z. 39 J4
Wakefield, U.K. 8 D6
Wakefield, U.S.A. ... 54 B10
Wakkanai, Japan .. 22 B10
Wakool, Australia .. 43 F3
Wakool →, Australia 43 F3
Wakre, Indonesia ... 27 E8
Wakuach, L., Canada 49 A6
Walbrzych, Poland .. 12 C9
Walbury Hill, U.K. .. 9 F6
Walcha, Australia ... 43 E5
Walcheren, Neths. .. 11 C3
Walcott, U.S.A. 56 F10
Walden, U.S.A. 56 F10
Waldport, U.S.A. ... 56 D1
Waldron, U.S.A. 55 H7
Walebing, Australia . 41 F2
Wales □, U.K. 9 E3
Walgett, Australia .. 43 E4
Walgreen Coast,
    Antarctica 5 D15
Walker, U.S.A. 54 B7
Walker, L., Canada .. 49 B6
Walker L., Canada .. 51 C9
Walker L., U.S.A. ... 56 G4
Walkerston, Australia 42 C4
Walkerton, Canada .. 48 D3
Wall, U.S.A. 54 D3
Walla Walla, U.S.A. . 56 C4
Wallabadah, Australia 42 B3
Wallace, Idaho, U.S.A. 56 C6
Wallace, N.C., U.S.A. 53 H7
Wallaceburg, Canada 48 D3
Wallachia = Valahia,
    Romania 13 F13
Wallal, Australia 43 D4
Wallam Cr. →,
    Australia 43 D4
Wallambin, L., Australia 41 F2
Wallan, Australia ... 43 F3
Wallangarra, Australia 43 D5
Wallaroo, Australia . 43 E2
Wallis & Futuna, Is.,
    Pac. Oc. 38 C11
Wallowa, U.S.A. 56 D5
Wallowa Mts., U.S.A. 56 D5
Wallula, U.S.A. 56 C4
Wallumbilla, Australia 43 D4
Walmsley, L., Canada 51 A7
Walney, I. of, U.K. .. 8 C4
Walnut Ridge, U.S.A. 55 G9
Walpole, Australia .. 41 F2
Walsall, U.K. 9 E6
Walsenburg, U.S.A. . 55 G2
Walsh, U.S.A. 55 G3
Walsh →, Australia . 42 B3
Walterboro, U.S.A. .. 53 J5
Walters, U.S.A. 55 H5
Waltman, U.S.A. 56 E10
Walton-on-the-Naze,
    U.K. 9 F9
Walvis Bay, Namibia 37 J2
Walvisbaai = Walvis
    Bay, Namibia 37 J2
Wamba, Dem. Rep. of
    the Congo 36 D5
Wamego, U.S.A. 54 F6
Wamena, Indonesia . 27 E9
Wamsutter, U.S.A. .. 56 F9
Wamulan, Indonesia 27 E7
Wana, Pakistan 28 C6
Wanaaring, Australia 43 D3
Wanaka, N.Z. 39 L2
Wanaka, L., N.Z. ... 39 L2
Wanapitei L., Canada 48 C3
Wandel Sea = McKinley
    Sea, Arctic 4 A7
Wandoan, Australia . 43 D4
Wang →, Thailand . 26 A1
Wangal, Indonesia .. 27 F8
Wanganella, Australia 43 F3
Wanganui, N.Z. 39 H5
Wangaratta, Australia 43 F4
Wangary, Australia . 43 E2

Wangerooge, Germany 12 B4
Wangiwangi, Indonesia 27 F6
Wanless, Canada 51 C8
Wantage, U.K. 9 F6
Wapakoneta, U.S.A. 52 E3
Wapato, U.S.A. 56 C3
Wapawekka L., Canada 51 C8
Wapikopa L., Canada 48 B2
Wapiti →, Canada . 50 B5
Wapsipinicon →,
    U.S.A. 54 E9
Warangal, India 28 L11
Waratah, Australia .. 42 G4
Waratah B., Australia 43 F4
Warburton, Vic.,
    Australia 43 F4
Warburton, W. Austral.,
    Australia 41 E4
Warburton Ra., Australia 41 E4
Ward, N.Z. 39 J5
Ward →, Australia . 43 D4
Wardha, India 28 J11
Wardha →, India .. 28 K11
Ware, Canada 50 B3
Waregem, Belgium . 11 D3
Waremme, Belgium . 11 D5
Warialda, Australia . 43 D5
Wariap, Indonesia .. 27 E8
Warkopi, Indonesia . 27 E8
Warm Springs, U.S.A. 57 G5
Warman, Canada ... 51 C7
Warminster, U.K. ... 9 F5
Warner Mts., U.S.A. . 56 F3
Warner Robins, U.S.A. 53 J4
Waroona, Australia . 41 F2
Warracknabeal,
    Australia 43 F3
Warragul, Australia . 43 F4
Warrego →, Australia 43 E4
Warrego Ra., Australia 42 C4
Warren, Australia ... 43 E4
Warren, Ark., U.S.A. 55 J8
Warren, Mich., U.S.A. 52 D4
Warren, Minn., U.S.A. 54 A6
Warren, Ohio, U.S.A. 52 E5
Warren, Pa., U.S.A. . 52 E6
Warrensburg, U.S.A. 54 F8
Warrenton, U.S.A. .. 56 C2
Warri, Nigeria 34 G7
Warrina, Australia .. 43 D2
Warrington, U.K. ... 8 D5
Warrington, U.S.A. . 53 K2
Warrington □, U.K. . 8 D5
Warrnambool, Australia 43 F3
Warroad, U.S.A. 54 A7
Warruwi, Australia .. 42 A1
Warsa, Indonesia ... 27 E9
Warsaw = Warszawa,
    Poland 13 B11
Warsaw, U.S.A. 52 E3
Warszawa, Poland .. 13 B11
Warta →, Poland .. 12 B8
Warthe = Warta →,
    Poland 12 B8
Waru, Indonesia 27 E8
Warwick, Australia .. 43 D5
Warwick, U.K. 9 E6
Warwick, U.S.A. 52 E10
Warwickshire □, U.K. 9 E6
Wasagaming, Canada 51 C9
Wasatch Ra., U.S.A. 56 F8
Wasco, Calif., U.S.A. 57 J4
Wasco, Oreg., U.S.A. 56 D3
Waseca, U.S.A. 54 C8
Wasekamio L., Canada 51 B7
Wash, The, U.K. 8 E8
Washburn, N. Dak.,
    U.S.A. 54 B4
Washburn, Wis., U.S.A. 54 B9
Washim, India 28 J10
Washington, D.C.,
    U.S.A. 52 F7
Washington, Ga., U.S.A. 53 J4
Washington, Ind., U.S.A. 52 F2
Washington, Iowa,
    U.S.A. 54 E9
Washington, Mo., U.S.A. 54 F9
Washington, N.C.,
    U.S.A. 53 H7
Washington, Pa., U.S.A. 52 E5
Washington, Utah,
    U.S.A. 57 H7
Washington □, U.S.A. 56 C3
Washington, Mt., U.S.A. 52 C10
Washington Court
    House, U.S.A. 52 F4
Washington I., U.S.A. 52 C2
Wasian, Indonesia .. 27 E8
Wasilla, U.S.A. 46 B5
Wasior, Indonesia .. 27 E8
Waskaganish, Canada 48 B4
Waskaiowaka, L.,
    Canada 51 B9
Waskesiu Lake, Canada 51 C7
Wasserkuppe, Germany 12 C5
Waswanipi, Canada . 48 C4
Waswanipi, L., Canada 48 C4
Watampone, Indonesia 27 E6
Water Park Pt., Australia 42 C5
Water Valley, U.S.A. 55 H10
Waterbury, U.S.A. .. 52 E9
Waterbury L., Canada 51 B8
Waterford, Ireland .. 10 E3

Waterhen L., *Canada* .. 51 C9
Waterloo, *Belgium* 11 D4
Waterloo, *Canada* 48 D3
Waterloo, *Ill., U.S.A.* .. 54 F9
Waterloo, *Iowa, U.S.A.* 54 D8
Watersmeet, *U.S.A.* .. 54 B10
Waterton Lakes Nat.
  Park, *U.S.A.* 56 B7
Watertown, *N.Y., U.S.A.* 52 D8
Watertown, *S. Dak.,*
  U.S.A. 54 C6
Watertown, *Wis., U.S.A.* 54 D10
Waterville, *Maine,*
  U.S.A. 53 C11
Waterville, *Wash.,*
  U.S.A. 56 C3
Wates, *Indonesia* 27 G14
Watford, *U.K.* 9 F7
Watford City, *U.S.A.* .. 54 B3
Wathaman →, *Canada* 51 B8
Wathaman L., *Canada* 51 B8
Watheroo, *Australia* .. 41 F2
Watkins Glen, *U.S.A.* .. 52 D7
Watling I. = San
  Salvador I., *Bahamas* 61 B5
Watonga, *U.S.A.* 55 H5
Watrous, *Canada* 51 C7
Watrous, *U.S.A.* 55 H2
Watsa, *Dem. Rep. of*
  the Congo 36 D5
Watseka, *U.S.A.* 52 E2
Watson, *Australia* 41 F5
Watson, *Canada* 51 C8
Watson Lake, *Canada* . 50 A3
Watsonville, *U.S.A.* ... 57 H3
Wattiwarriganna
  Cr. →, *Australia* .. 43 D2
Watuata = Batuata,
  Indonesia 27 F6
Watubela, Kepulauan,
  Indonesia 27 E8
Watubela Is. =
  Watubela, Kepulauan,
  Indonesia 27 E8
Wau = Wâw, *Sudan* .. 35 G11
Waubay, *U.S.A.* 54 C6
Wauchope, *N.S.W.,*
  Australia 43 E5
Wauchope, *N. Terr.,*
  Australia 42 C1
Wauchula, *U.S.A.* 53 M5
Waukarlycarly, L.,
  Australia 40 D3
Waukegan, *U.S.A.* 52 D2
Waukesha, *U.S.A.* 52 D1
Waukon, *U.S.A.* 54 D9
Waupaca, *U.S.A.* 54 C10
Waupun, *U.S.A.* 54 D10
Waurika, *U.S.A.* 55 H6
Wausau, *U.S.A.* 54 C10
Wautoma, *U.S.A.* 54 C10
Wauwatosa, *U.S.A.* .. 52 D2
Waveney →, *U.K.* ... 9 E9
Waverley, *N.Z.* 39 H5
Waverly, *Iowa, U.S.A.* . 54 D8
Waverly, *N.Y., U.S.A.* . 52 E7
Wavre, *Belgium* 11 D4
Wâw, *Sudan* 35 G11
Wâw al Kabîr, *Libya* .. 35 C9
Wawa, *Canada* 48 C3
Wawanesa, *Canada* .. 51 D9
Waxahachie, *U.S.A.* .. 55 J6
Way, L., *Australia* 41 E3
Waycross, *U.S.A.* 53 K4
Wayne, *Nebr., U.S.A.* . 54 D6
Wayne, *W. Va., U.S.A.* 52 F4
Waynesboro, *Ga.,*
  U.S.A. 53 J4
Waynesboro, *Miss.,*
  U.S.A. 53 K1
Waynesboro, *Pa., U.S.A.* 52 F7
Waynesboro, *Va., U.S.A.* 52 F6
Waynesburg, *U.S.A.* .. 52 F5
Waynesville, *U.S.A.* .. 53 H4
Waynoka, *U.S.A.* 55 G5
Wazirabad, *Pakistan* .. 28 C9
We, *Indonesia* 26 C1
Weald, The, *U.K.* 9 F8
Wear →, *U.K.* 8 C6
Weatherford, *Okla.,*
  U.S.A. 55 H5
Weatherford, *Tex.,*
  U.S.A. 55 J6
Weaverville, *U.S.A.* ... 56 F2
Webb City, *U.S.A.* ... 55 G7
Webequie, *Canada* ... 48 B2
Webster, *U.S.A.* 54 C6
Webster City, *U.S.A.* . 54 D8
Webster Springs, *U.S.A.* 52 F5
Weda, *Indonesia* 27 D7
Weda, Teluk, *Indonesia* 27 D7
Weddell I., *Falk. Is.* .. 64 G4
Weddell Sea, *Antarctica* 5 D1
Wedderburn, *Australia* 43 F3
Wedgeport, *Canada* .. 49 D6
Wee Waa, *Australia* .. 43 E4
Weed, *U.S.A.* 56 F2
Weert, *Neths.* 11 C5
Weiden, *Germany* ... 12 D7
Weifang, *China* 25 C6
Weimar, *Germany* ... 12 C6
Weipa, *Australia* 42 A3
Weir →, *Australia* ... 43 D4
Weir →, *Canada* 51 B10

Weir River, *Canada* ... 51 B10
Weirton, *U.S.A.* 52 E5
Weiser, *U.S.A.* 56 D5
Wejherowo, *Poland* .. 13 A10
Wekusko L., *Canada* . 51 C9
Welch, *U.S.A.* 52 G5
Welkom, *S. Africa* 37 K5
Welland, *Canada* 48 D4
Welland →, *U.K.* 9 E7
Wellesley Is., *Australia* 42 B2
Wellingborough, *U.K.* . 9 E7
Wellington, *Australia* .. 43 E4
Wellington, *Canada* .. 48 D4
Wellington, *N.Z.* 39 J5
Wellington, *Somst., U.K.* 9 G4
Wellington,
  Telford & Wrekin, U.K. 9 E5
Wellington, *Colo.,*
  U.S.A. 54 E2
Wellington, *Kans.,*
  U.S.A. 55 G6
Wellington, *Tex., U.S.A.* 55 H4
Wellington, *I., Chile* .. 64 F2
Wellington, *L., Australia* 43 F4
Wells, *U.K.* 9 F5
Wells, *U.S.A.* 56 F6
Wells, *L., Australia* ... 41 E3
Wells, *Mt., Australia* .. 40 C4
Wells Gray Prov. Park,
  Canada 50 C4
Wells-next-the-Sea, *U.K.* 8 E8
Wellsboro, *U.S.A.* 52 E7
Wellsville, *N.Y., U.S.A.* 52 D7
Wellsville, *Utah, U.S.A.* 56 F8
Wellton, *U.S.A.* 57 K6
Wels, *Austria* 12 D8
Welshpool, *U.K.* 9 E4
Welwyn Garden City,
  U.K. 9 F7
Wem, *U.K.* 8 E5
Wemindji, *Canada* ... 48 B4
Wenatchee, *U.S.A.* ... 56 C3
Wenchi, *Ghana* 34 G5
Wenchow = Wenzhou,
  China 25 D7
Wendesi, *Indonesia* .. 27 E8
Wendover, *U.S.A.* ... 56 F6
Wenlock →, *Australia* 42 A3
Wenshan, *China* 24 D5
Wensleydale, *U.K.* ... 8 C6
Wensu, *China* 24 B3
Wensum →, *U.K.* ... 8 E9
Wentworth, *Australia* .. 43 E3
Wenut, *Indonesia* ... 27 E8
Wenzhou, *China* 25 D7
Weott, *U.S.A.* 56 F2
Werda, *Indonesia* 27 E8
Werra →, *Germany* . 12 C5
Werrimull, *Australia* .. 43 E3
Werris Creek, *Australia* 43 E5
Weser →, *Germany* . 12 B5
Wesiri, *Indonesia* 27 F7
Wesleyville, *Canada* .. 49 C9
Wessel, C., *Australia* .. 42 A2
Wessel Is., *Australia* .. 42 A2
Wessington Springs,
  U.S.A. 54 C5
West, *U.S.A.* 55 K6
West Baines →,
  Australia 40 C4
West Bank □, *Asia* .. 33 C4
West Bend, *U.S.A.* ... 52 D1
West Bengal □, *India* . 29 H16
West Berkshire □, *U.K.* 9 F6
West Beskids =
  Západné Beskydy,
  Europe 13 D10
West Branch, *U.S.A.* .. 52 C3
West Bromwich, *U.K.* . 9 E6
West Cape Howe,
  Australia 41 G2
West Chester, *U.S.A.* . 52 F8
West Columbia, *U.S.A.* 55 L7
West Des Moines,
  U.S.A. 54 E8
West End, *Bahamas* .. 60 A4
West Falkland, *Falk. Is.* 64 G5
West Fargo, *U.S.A.* ... 54 B6
West Fjord =
  Vestfjorden, *Norway* 6 C15
West Fork Trinity →,
  U.S.A. 55 J6
West Frankfort, *U.S.A.* 54 G10
West Helena, *U.S.A.* .. 55 H9
West Ice Shelf,
  Antarctica 5 C7
West Indies,
  Cent. Amer. 61 D7
West Jordan, *U.S.A.* .. 56 F8
West Memphis, *U.S.A.* 55 H9
West Midlands □, *U.K.* 9 E6
West Monroe, *U.S.A.* . 55 J8
West Palm Beach,
  U.S.A. 53 M5
West Plains, *U.S.A.* .. 55 G9
West Point, *Nebr.,*
  U.S.A. 54 E6
West Point, *Va., U.S.A.* 52 G7
West Pt. = Ouest, Pte.
  de l', *Canada* 49 C7
West Pt., *Australia* 43 F2
West Road →, *Canada* 50 C4
West Schelde =
  Westerschelde →,
  Neths. 11 C3

West Seneca, *U.S.A.* .. 52 D6
West Sussex □, *U.K.* . 9 G7
West-Terschelling,
  Neths. 11 A5
West Valley City, *U.S.A.* 56 F8
West Virginia □, *U.S.A.* 52 F5
West-Vlaanderen □,
  Belgium 11 D2
West Wyalong, *Australia* 43 E4
West Yellowstone,
  U.S.A. 56 D8
West Yorkshire □, *U.K.* 8 D6
Westall Pt., *Australia* .. 43 E1
Westbrook, *U.S.A.* ... 53 D10
Westbury, *Australia* .. 42 G4
Westby, *U.S.A.* 54 A2
Westerland, *Germany* . 7 J13
Western Australia □,
  Australia 41 E2
Western Dvina =
  Daugava →, *Latvia* . 7 H21
Western Ghats, *India* .. 28 N9
Western Sahara ■,
  Africa 34 D3
Western Samoa =
  Samoa ■, *Pac. Oc.* . 39 B13
Westernport, *U.S.A.* .. 52 F6
Westerschelde →,
  Neths. 11 C3
Westerwald, *Germany* . 12 C4
Westhope, *U.S.A.* 54 A4
Westland Bight, *N.Z.* .. 39 K3
Westlock, *Canada* ... 50 C6
Westmar, *Australia* ... 43 D4
Westminster, *U.S.A.* .. 52 F7
Westmorland, *U.S.A.* . 57 K6
Weston, *Oreg., U.S.A.* 56 D4
Weston, *W. Va., U.S.A.* 52 F5
Weston I., *Canada* ... 48 B4
Weston-super-Mare,
  U.K. 9 F5
Westport, *Ireland* 10 E2
Westport, *N.Z.* 39 J3
Westport, *U.S.A.* 56 C1
Westray, *Canada* 51 C8
Westray, *U.K.* 10 B5
Westree, *Canada* 48 C3
Westwood, *U.S.A.* ... 56 F3
Wetar, *Indonesia* 27 F7
Wetaskiwin, *Canada* .. 50 C6
Wete, *Tanzania* 36 F7
Wetherby, *U.K.* 8 D6
Wetteren, *Belgium* ... 11 D3
Wetzlar, *Germany* ... 12 C5
Wewoka, *U.S.A.* 55 H6
Wexford, *Ireland* 10 E3
Weyburn, *Canada* ... 51 D8
Weymouth, *Canada* .. 49 D6
Weymouth, *U.K.* 9 G5
Weymouth, *C., Australia* 42 A3
Wha Ti, *Canada* 50 B8
Whakatane, *N.Z.* 39 G6
Whale →, *Canada* .. 49 A6
Whale Cove, *Canada* . 51 A10
Whales, B. of, *Antarctica* 5 D12
Whangamomona, *N.Z.* 39 H5
Whangarei, *N.Z.* 39 F5
Whangarei Harb., *N.Z.* 39 F5
Wharfe →, *U.K.* 8 D6
Wharfedale, *U.K.* 8 C5
Wharton, *U.S.A.* 55 L6
Wheatland, *U.S.A.* ... 54 D2
Wheaton, *Md., U.S.A.* 52 F7
Wheaton, *Minn., U.S.A.* 54 C6
Wheeler, *Oreg., U.S.A.* 56 D2
Wheeler, *Tex., U.S.A.* . 55 H4
Wheeler →, *Canada* . 49 A6
Wheeler L., *U.S.A.* ... 53 H2
Wheeler Pk., *N. Mex.,*
  U.S.A. 57 H11
Wheeler Pk., *Nev.,*
  U.S.A. 57 G6
Wheeling, *U.S.A.* 52 E5
Whernside, *U.K.* 8 C5
Whiskey Jack L., *Canada* 51 B8
Whistleduck Cr. →,
  Australia 42 C2
Whistler, *Canada* 50 C4
Whitby, *U.K.* 8 C7
White →, *Ark., U.S.A.* 55 J9
White →, *Ind., U.S.A.* 52 F2
White →, *S. Dak.,*
  U.S.A. 54 D5
White →, *Tex., U.S.A.* 55 J4
White →, *Utah, U.S.A.* 56 F9
White, L., *Australia* ... 40 D4
White B., *Canada* ... 49 C8
White Bird, *U.S.A.* ... 56 D5
White Butte, *U.S.A.* .. 54 B3
White City, *U.S.A.* ... 56 E2
White Cliffs, *Australia* . 43 E3
White Hall, *U.S.A.* ... 54 F9
White Horse, Vale of,
  U.K. 9 F6
White I., *N.Z.* 39 G6
White L., *U.S.A.* 55 L8
White Mountain Peak,
  U.S.A. 57 H4
White Mts., *Calif., U.S.A.* 57 H4
White Mts., *N.H., U.S.A.* 52 C10
White Nile = Nîl el
  Abyad →, *Sudan* .. 35 E12
White Otter L., *Canada* 48 C1
White River, *Canada* .. 48 C2

White River, *U.S.A.* ... 54 D4
White Russia =
  Belarus ■, *Europe* . 13 B14
White Sea = Beloye
  More, *Russia* 18 A6
White Sulphur Springs,
  Mont., U.S.A. 56 C8
White Sulphur Springs,
  W. Va., U.S.A. 52 G5
Whitecliffs, *N.Z.* 39 K3
Whitecourt, *Canada* .. 50 C5
Whitefish, *U.S.A.* 56 B6
Whitefish L., *Canada* . 51 A7
Whitefish Point, *U.S.A.* 52 B3
Whitegull, L., *Canada* . 49 A7
Whitehall, *Mich., U.S.A.* 52 D2
Whitehall, *Mont., U.S.A.* 56 D7
Whitehall, *N.Y., U.S.A.* 52 D9
Whitehall, *Wis., U.S.A.* 54 C9
Whitehaven, *U.K.* 8 C4
Whitehorse, *Canada* .. 50 A1
Whitemark, *Australia* . 42 G4
Whiteriver, *U.S.A.* ... 57 K9
Whitesand →, *Canada* 50 A5
Whitesboro, *U.S.A.* .. 55 J6
Whiteshell Prov. Park,
  Canada 51 D9
Whiteville, *U.S.A.* 53 H6
Whitewater, *U.S.A.* .. 52 D1
Whitewater Baldy,
  U.S.A. 57 K9
Whitewater L., *Canada* 48 B2
Whitewood, *Australia* . 42 C3
Whitewood, *Canada* .. 51 C8
Whitianga, *N.Z.* 39 G5
Whitney, *Canada* 48 C4
Whitney, *Mt., U.S.A.* .. 57 H4
Whitstable, *U.K.* 9 F9
Whitsunday I., *Australia* 42 C4
Whittlesea, *Australia* . 43 F4
Wholdaia L., *Canada* . 51 A8
Whyalla, *Australia* ... 43 E2
Wiarton, *Canada* 48 D3
Wibaux, *U.S.A.* 54 B2
Wichita, *U.S.A.* 55 G6
Wichita Falls, *U.S.A.* .. 55 J5
Wick, *U.K.* 10 B5
Wickenburg, *U.S.A.* .. 57 K7
Wickepin, *Australia* .. 41 F2
Wickham, *Australia* .. 40 D2
Wickham, *C., Australia* 42 F3
Wicklow Mts., *Ireland* . 10 E3
Widgeegoara Cr. →,
  Australia 43 D4
Widgiemooltha,
  Australia 41 F3
Widnes, *U.K.* 8 D5
Wieluń, *Poland* 13 C10
Wien, *Austria* 12 D9
Wiener Neustadt,
  Austria 12 E9
Wiesbaden, *Germany* . 12 C5
Wigan, *U.K.* 8 D5
Wiggins, *Colo., U.S.A.* 54 E2
Wiggins, *Miss., U.S.A.* 55 K10
Wight, I. of □, *U.K.* .. 9 G6
Wigston, *U.K.* 9 E6
Wigton, *U.K.* 8 C4
Wilber, *U.S.A.* 54 E6
Wilberforce, C.,
  Australia 42 A2
Wilburton, *U.S.A.* ... 55 H7
Wilcannia, *Australia* .. 43 E3
Wildspitze, *Austria* ... 12 E4
Wilhelm II Coast,
  Antarctica 5 C7
Wilhelmshaven,
  Germany 12 B5
Wilkes-Barre, *U.S.A.* . 52 E8
Wilkie, *Canada* 51 C7
Wilkinson Lakes,
  Australia 41 E5
Willandra Creek →,
  Australia 43 E4
Willapa B., *U.S.A.* ... 56 C2
Willcox, *U.S.A.* 57 K9
Willemstad, *Neth. Ant.* 62 A5
William →, *Canada* .. 51 B7
William 'Bill' Dannely
  Res., *U.S.A.* 53 J2
William Creek, *Australia* 43 D2
Williams, *Australia* ... 41 F2
Williams, *U.S.A.* 57 J7
Williams Harbour,
  Canada 49 B8
Williams Lake, *Canada* 50 C4
Williamsburg, *Ky.,*
  U.S.A. 53 G3
Williamsburg, *Va.,*
  U.S.A. 52 G7
Williamson, *U.S.A.* ... 52 G4
Williamsport, *U.S.A.* . 52 E7
Williamston, *U.S.A.* .. 53 H7
Williamstown, *Australia* 43 F3
Williamstown, *U.S.A.* . 52 F2
Willingboro, *U.S.A.* .. 52 E8
Willis Group, *Australia* 42 B5
Williston, *Fla., U.S.A.* . 53 L4
Williston, *N. Dak.,*
  U.S.A. 54 A3
Williston L., *Canada* .. 50 B4
Willits, *U.S.A.* 56 G2
Willmar, *U.S.A.* 54 C7
Willow Bunch, *Canada* 51 D7
Willow L., *Canada* ... 50 A5

Willowlake →, *Canada* 50 A4
Willows, *U.S.A.* 56 G2
Wills, L., *Australia* ... 40 D4
Wills Cr. →, *Australia* 42 C3
Willunga, *Australia* ... 43 F2
Wilmette, *U.S.A.* 52 D2
Wilmington, *Australia* . 43 E2
Wilmington, *Del., U.S.A.* 52 F8
Wilmington, *N.C., U.S.A.* 53 H7
Wilmington, *Ohio,*
  U.S.A. 52 F4
Wilmslow, *U.K.* 8 D5
Wilpena →, *Australia* 43 E2
Wilsall, *U.S.A.* 56 D8
Wilson, *U.S.A.* 53 H7
Wilson →, *Australia* . 40 C4
Wilson Bluff, *Australia* . 41 F4
Wilson Inlet, *Australia* . 41 G2
Wilsons Promontory,
  Australia 43 F4
Wilton, *U.S.A.* 54 B4
Wilton →, *Australia* . 42 A1
Wiltshire □, *U.K.* 9 F6
Wiltz, *Lux.* 11 E5
Wiluna, *Australia* 41 E3
Wimborne Minster, *U.K.* 9 G6
Wimmera →, *Australia* 43 F3
Winchester, *U.K.* 9 F6
Winchester, *Idaho,*
  U.S.A. 56 C5
Winchester, *Ind., U.S.A.* 52 E3
Winchester, *Ky., U.S.A.* 52 G3
Winchester, *Tenn.,*
  U.S.A. 53 H2
Winchester, *Va., U.S.A.* 52 F6
Wind →, *U.S.A.* 56 E9
Wind River Range,
  U.S.A. 56 E9
Windau = Ventspils,
  Latvia 7 H19
Winder, *U.S.A.* 53 J4
Windermere, *U.K.* ... 8 C5
Windhoek, *Namibia* .. 37 J3
Windom, *U.S.A.* 54 D7
Windorah, *Australia* .. 42 D3
Window Rock, *U.S.A.* . 57 J9
Windrush →, *U.K.* .. 9 F6
Windsor, *Australia* ... 43 E5
Windsor, *N.S., Canada* 49 D7
Windsor, *Ont., Canada* 48 D3
Windsor, *U.K.* 9 F7
Windsor, *Colo., U.S.A.* 54 E2
Windsor, *Mo., U.S.A.* . 54 F8
Windsor, *Vt., U.S.A.* .. 52 D9
Windsor &
  Maidenhead □, *U.K.* 9 F7
Windward Is., *W. Indies* 61 D7
Windward Passage =
  Vientos, Paso de los,
  Caribbean 61 C5
Winefred L., *Canada* . 51 B6
Winfield, *U.S.A.* 55 G6
Wingate Mts., *Australia* 40 B5
Wingham, *Australia* .. 43 E5
Wingham, *Canada* ... 48 D3
Winisk, *Canada* 48 A2
Winisk →, *Canada* .. 48 A2
Winisk L., *Canada* ... 48 B2
Wink, *U.S.A.* 55 K3
Winkler, *Canada* 51 D9
Winnebago, L., *U.S.A.* 52 D1
Winnecke Cr. →,
  Australia 40 C5
Winnemucca, *U.S.A.* . 56 F5
Winnemucca L., *U.S.A.* 56 F4
Winnett, *U.S.A.* 56 C9
Winnfield, *U.S.A.* 55 K8
Winnibigoshish, L.,
  U.S.A. 54 B7
Winnipeg, *Canada* ... 51 D9
Winnipeg →, *Canada* 51 C9
Winnipeg, L., *Canada* . 51 C9
Winnipeg Beach,
  Canada 51 C9
Winnipegosis, *Canada* 51 C9
Winnipegosis L., *Canada* 51 C9
Winnsboro, *La., U.S.A.* 55 J9
Winnsboro, *S.C., U.S.A.* 53 H5
Winnsboro, *Tex., U.S.A.* 55 J7
Winokapau, L., *Canada* 49 B7
Winona, *Minn., U.S.A.* 54 C9
Winona, *Miss., U.S.A.* 55 J10
Winooski, *U.S.A.* 52 C9
Winschoten, *Neths.* .. 11 A7
Winsford, *U.K.* 8 D5
Winslow, *U.S.A.* 57 J8
Winston-Salem, *U.S.A.* 53 G5
Winter Garden, *U.S.A.* 53 L5
Winter Haven, *U.S.A.* . 53 M5
Winter Park, *U.S.A.* .. 53 L5
Winterswijk, *Neths.* .. 11 C6
Winterthur, *Switz.* ... 14 C8
Winthrop, *U.S.A.* 56 B3
Winton, *Australia* 42 C3
Winton, *N.Z.* 39 M2
Wirrulla, *Australia* ... 43 E1
Wisbech, *U.K.* 9 E8
Wisconsin □, *U.S.A.* . 54 C10
Wisconsin →, *U.S.A.* 54 D9
Wisconsin Rapids,
  U.S.A. 54 C10
Wisdom, *U.S.A.* 56 D7
Wishek, *U.S.A.* 54 B5
Wisła →, *Poland* ... 13 A10
Wismar, *Germany* ... 12 B6

Wisner, *U.S.A.* 54 E6
Witbank, *S. Africa* 37 K5
Witham, *U.K.* 9 F8
Witham →, *U.K.* 8 E7
Withernsea, *U.K.* 8 D8
Witney, *U.K.* 9 F6
Wittenberge, *Germany* 12 B6
Wittenoom, *Australia* . 40 D2
Wkra →, *Poland* ... 13 B11
Wlingi, *Indonesia* ... 27 H15
Włocławek, *Poland* .. 13 B10
Włodawa, *Poland* ... 13 C12
Wokam, *Indonesia* ... 27 F8
Woking, *U.K.* 9 F7
Wokingham □, *U.K.* .. 9 F7
Wolf →, *Canada* 50 A2
Wolf Creek, *U.S.A.* ... 56 C7
Wolf L., *Canada* 50 A2
Wolf Point, *U.S.A.* ... 54 A2
Wolfe I., *Canada* 48 D4
Wolfsberg, *Austria* ... 12 E8
Wolfsburg, *Germany* . 12 B6
Wolin, *Poland* 12 B8
Wollaston, Is., *Chile* .. 64 H3
Wollaston L., *Canada* . 51 B8
Wollaston Lake, *Canada* 51 B8
Wollaston Pen., *Canada* 46 B8
Wollongong, *Australia* 43 E5
Wolsey, *U.S.A.* 54 C5
Wolvega, *Neths.* 11 B6
Wolverhampton, *U.K.* . 9 E5
Wondai, *Australia* ... 43 D5
Wongalarroo L.,
  Australia 43 E3
Wongan Hills, *Australia* 41 F2
Wonosari, *Indonesia* . 27 G14
Wonosobo, *Indonesia* . 27 G13
Wonowon, *Canada* ... 50 B4
Wŏnsan, *N. Korea* ... 25 C7
Wonthaggi, *Australia* . 43 F4
Wood Buffalo Nat. Park,
  Canada 50 B6
Wood Is., *Australia* ... 40 C3
Wood L., *Canada* 51 B8
Woodah I., *Australia* .. 42 A2
Woodbridge, *U.K.* ... 9 E9
Woodburn, *U.S.A.* ... 56 D2
Woodenbong, *Australia* 43 D5
Woodend, *Australia* .. 43 F3
Woodford, *Australia* .. 43 D5
Woodland, *Calif., U.S.A.* 56 G3
Woodland, *Maine,*
  U.S.A. 53 C12
Woodland Caribou Prov.
  Park, *Canada* 51 C10
Woodridge, *Canada* .. 51 D9
Woodroffe, Mt.,
  Australia 41 E5
Woods, L., *Australia* .. 42 B1
Woods, L. of the,
  Canada 51 D10
Woodside, *Australia* .. 43 F4
Woodstock, *Australia* . 42 B4
Woodstock, *N.B.,*
  Canada 49 C6
Woodstock, *Ont.,*
  Canada 48 D3
Woodstock, *U.K.* 9 F6
Woodstock, *U.S.A.* .. 54 D10
Woodsville, *U.S.A.* .. 52 C10
Woodville, *N.Z.* 39 J5
Woodville, *Miss., U.S.A.* 55 K9
Woodville, *Tex., U.S.A.* 55 K7
Woodward, *U.S.A.* ... 55 G5
Woody →, *Canada* .. 51 C8
Woolamai, C., *Australia* 43 F4
Wooler, *U.K.* 8 B5
Woolgoolga, *Australia* 43 E5
Woomera, *Australia* .. 43 E2
Woonsocket, *R.I., U.S.A.* 52 E10
Woonsocket, *S. Dak.,*
  U.S.A. 54 C5
Wooramel →,
  Australia 41 E1
Wooramel Roadhouse,
  Australia 41 E1
Wooster, *U.S.A.* 52 E5
Worcester, *S. Africa* .. 37 L3
Worcester, *U.K.* 9 E5
Worcester, *U.S.A.* ... 52 D10
Worcestershire □, *U.K.* 9 E5
Workington, *U.K.* ... 8 C4
Worksop, *U.K.* 8 D6
Workum, *Neths.* 11 B5
Worland, *U.S.A.* 56 D10
Worms, *Germany* ... 12 D5
Worsley, *Canada* 50 B5
Wortham, *U.S.A.* 55 K6
Worthing, *U.K.* 9 G7
Worthington, *U.S.A.* . 54 D7
Wosi, *Indonesia* 27 E7
Wou-han = Wuhan,
  China 25 C6
Wousi = Wuxi, *China* . 25 C7
Wowoni, *Indonesia* .. 27 E6
Wrangel I. = Vrangelya,
  Ostrov, *Russia* 21 B19
Wrangell, *U.S.A.* 50 B2
Wrangell Mts., *U.S.A.* . 46 B5
Wrath, C., *U.K.* 10 B4
Wray, *U.S.A.* 54 E3
Wrens, *U.S.A.* 53 J4
Wrexham, *U.K.* 8 D4
Wrexham □, *U.K.* ... 8 D5

Wright, U.S.A. 54 D2
Wrightson Mt., U.S.A. . 57 L8
Wrigley, Canada 46 B7
Wrocław, Poland 13 C9
Września, Poland 13 B9
Wu Jiang ➤, China .. 24 D5
Wubin, Australia 41 F2
Wudinna, Australia ... 43 E2
Wuhan, China 25 C6
Wuhsi = Wuxi, China . 25 C7
Wuhu, China 25 C6
Wukari, Nigeria 34 G7
Wuliaru, Indonesia ... 27 F8
Wuluk'omushih Ling, China 24 C3
Wulumuchi = Ürümqi, China 20 E9
Wundowie, Australia .. 41 F2
Wunnummin L., Canada 48 B2
Wuntho, Burma ... 29 H19
Wuppertal, Germany .. 12 C4
Würzburg, Germany .. 12 D5
Wusuli Jiang = Ussuri ➤, Asia 22 A7
Wutongqiao, China ... 24 D5
Wuwei, China 24 C5
Wuxi, China 25 C7
Wuzhou, China 25 D6
Wyaaba Cr. ➤, Australia 42 B3
Wyalkatchem, Australia 41 F2
Wyandra, Australia ... 43 D4
Wyangala Res., Australia 43 E4
Wyara, L., Australia .. 43 D3
Wycheproof, Australia . 43 F3
Wye ➤, U.K. 9 F5
Wyemandoo, Australia 41 E2
Wymondham, U.K. ... 9 E9
Wymore, U.S.A. 54 E6
Wyndham, Australia .. 40 C4
Wyndham, N.Z. 39 M2
Wynne, U.S.A. 55 H9
Wynyard, Australia ... 42 G4
Wynyard, Canada ... 51 C8
Wyola L., Australia ... 41 E5
Wyoming □, U.S.A. .. 56 E10
Wyong, Australia 43 E5
Wytheville, U.S.A. .. 52 G5

Xaçmaz, Azerbaijan ... 19 F8
Xai-Xai, Mozam. 37 K6
Xainza, China 24 C3
Xangongo, Angola 37 H3
Xankändi, Azerbaijan .. 19 G8
Xánthi, Greece 17 D11
Xapuri, Brazil 62 F5
Xátiva, Spain 15 C5
Xenia, U.S.A. 52 F4
Xi ➤, China 25 D6
Xiaguan, China 24 D5
Xiamen, China 25 D6
Xi'an, China 25 C5
Xiang Jiang ➤, China . 25 D6
Xiangfan, China 25 C6
Xianggang = Hong Kong □, China . 25 D6
Xiangquan He = Sutlej ➤, Pakistan . 28 E7
Xiangtan, China 25 D6
Xianyang, China 25 C5
Xiao Hinggan Ling, China 25 B7
Xichang, China 24 D5
Xigazê, China 24 D3
Xing'an, China 25 D6
Xingu ➤, Brazil ... 63 D8
Xining, China 24 C5
Xinjiang Uygur Zizhiqu □, China .. 24 C3
Xinxiang, China 25 C6
Xique-Xique, Brazil ... 63 F10
Xisha Qundao = Paracel Is., S. China Sea . 26 A4
Xixabangma Feng, China 29 E14
Xizang Zizhiqu □, China 24 C3
Xuanhua, China 25 B6
Xúquer ➤, Spain ... 15 C5
Xuzhou, China 25 C6

Yaamba, Australia ... 42 C5
Yaapeet, Australia ... 43 F3
Yablonovy Ra. = Yablonovyy Khrebet, Russia 21 D12
Yablonovyy Khrebet, Russia 21 D12
Yabrūd, Syria 33 B5
Yacheng, China 25 E5
Yacuiba, Bolivia 62 H6
Yacuma ➤, Bolivia .. 62 F5
Yadgir, India 28 L10
Yadkin ➤, U.S.A. ... 53 H5
Yaeyama-Rettō, Japan 23 M1
Yagodnoye, Russia ... 21 C15
Yahk, Canada 50 D5
Yahuma, Dem. Rep. of the Congo 36 D4
Yaita, Japan 23 F9

Yakima, U.S.A. 56 C3
Yakima ➤, U.S.A. 56 C3
Yakobi I., U.S.A. 50 B1
Yakovlevka, Russia ... 22 B6
Yaku-Shima, Japan ... 23 J5
Yakumo, Japan 22 C10
Yakutat, U.S.A. 46 C6
Yakutia = Sakha □, Russia 21 C13
Yakutsk, Russia 21 C13
Yala, Thailand 26 C2
Yalgoo, Australia 41 E2
Yalinga, C.A.R. 36 C4
Yalkubul, Punta, Mexico 59 C7
Yalleroi, Australia ... 42 C4
Yalobusha ➤, U.S.A. . 55 J10
Yalong Jiang ➤, China 24 D5
Yalova, Turkey 17 D13
Yalta, Ukraine 19 F5
Yam Zhol = Dead Sea, Asia 33 D4
Yam Kinneret, Israel . 33 C4
Yamada, Japan 23 H5
Yamagata, Japan ... 22 E10
Yamagata □, Japan .. 22 E10
Yamaguchi, Japan ... 23 G5
Yamaguchi □, Japan .. 23 G5
Yamal, Poluostrov, Russia 20 B8
Yamal Pen. = Yamal, Poluostrov, Russia .. 20 B8
Yamanashi □, Japan .. 23 G9
Yamantau, Gora, Russia 18 D10
Yamba, Australia 43 D5
Yambarran Ra., Australia 40 C5
Yâmbiô, Sudan 35 H11
Yambol, Bulgaria ... 17 C12
Yamdena, Indonesia .. 27 F8
Yame, Japan 23 H5
Yamethin, Burma ... 29 J20
Yamma-Yamma, L., Australia 43 D3
Yamoussoukro, Ivory C. 34 G4
Yampa ➤, U.S.A. ... 56 F9
Yampi Sd., Australia .. 40 C3
Yampil, Moldova ... 13 D15
Yampol = Yampil, Moldova 13 D15
Yamuna ➤, India .. 29 G12
Yamzho Yumco, China 24 D4
Yana ➤, Russia 21 B14
Yanagawa, Japan ... 23 H5
Yanaul, Russia 18 C10
Yanbu 'al Baḥr, Si. Arabia 30 F3
Yanchep Beach, Australia 41 F2
Yanco, Australia 43 E4
Yanco Cr. ➤, Australia 43 F4
Yandoon, Burma ... 29 L19
Yangambi, Dem. Rep. of the Congo 36 D4
Yangch'ü = Taiyuan, China 25 C6
Yangon = Rangoon, Burma 29 L20
Yangquan, China 25 C6
Yangtse = Chang Jiang ➤, China . 25 C7
Yangtze Kiang = Chang Jiang ➤, China . 25 C7
Yangzhou, China 25 C6
Yanji, China 25 B7
Yankton, U.S.A. 54 D6
Yanqi, China 24 B3
Yantabulla, Australia .. 43 D4
Yantai, China 25 C7
Yaoundé, Cameroon .. 36 D2
Yap I., Pac. Oc. 44 G5
Yapen, Indonesia 27 E9
Yapen, Selat, Indonesia 27 E9
Yapero, Indonesia ... 27 E9
Yappar ➤, Australia .. 42 B3
Yaqui ➤, Mexico ... 58 B2
Yar-Sale, Russia 20 C8
Yaraka, Australia ... 42 C3
Yaransk, Russia 18 C8
Yare ➤, U.K. 9 E9
Yaremcha, Ukraine .. 13 D13
Yarensk, Russia 18 B8
Yarí ➤, Colombia ... 62 D4
Yarkand = Shache, China 24 C2
Yarkhun ➤, Pakistan . 28 A8
Yarmouth, Canada .. 49 D6
Yarmūk ➤, Syria ... 33 C4
Yaroslavl, Russia 18 C6
Yarqa, W. ➤, Egypt . 33 F2
Yarra Yarra Lakes, Australia 41 E2
Yarram, Australia ... 43 F4
Yarraman, Australia .. 43 D5
Yarras, Australia 43 E5
Yartsevo, Russia 21 C10
Yasawa Group, Fiji .. 39 C7
Yaselda, Belarus ... 13 B14
Yasinski, L., Canada .. 48 B4
Yasinya, Ukraine ... 13 D13
Yass, Australia 43 E4
Yatağan, Turkey ... 17 F13
Yates Center, U.S.A. . 55 G7
Yathkyed L., Canada . 51 A9

Yatsushiro, Japan 23 H5
Yavari ➤, Peru 62 D4
Yávaros, Mexico 58 B3
Yavatmal, India 28 J11
Yavne, Israel 33 D3
Yavoriv, Ukraine ... 13 D12
Yavorov = Yavoriv, Ukraine 13 D12
Yawatahama, Japan .. 23 H6
Yazd, Iran 31 D7
Yazd □, Iran 31 D7
Yazd-e Khvāst, Iran .. 31 D7
Yazoo ➤, U.S.A. ... 55 J9
Yazoo City, U.S.A. .. 55 J9
Yding Skovhøj, Denmark 7 J13
Ye Xian = Laizhou, China 25 C6
Yebyu, Burma 29 M21
Yecla, Spain 15 C5
Yécora, Mexico 58 B3
Yedintsy = Edineț, Moldova 13 D14
Yegros, Paraguay ... 64 B5
Yehuda, Midbar, Israel 33 D4
Yei, Sudan 35 H12
Yekaterinburg, Russia . 20 D7
Yekaterinodar = Krasnodar, Russia .. 19 E6
Yelarbon, Australia .. 43 D5
Yelets, Russia 18 D6
Yelizavetgrad = Kirovohrad, Ukraine . 19 E5
Yell, U.K. 10 A6
Yellow Sea, China ... 25 C7
Yellowhead Pass, Canada 50 C5
Yellowknife, Canada .. 50 A6
Yellowknife ➤, Canada 50 A6
Yellowstone ➤, U.S.A. 54 B3
Yellowstone L., U.S.A. 56 D8
Yellowstone National Park, U.S.A. 56 D9
Yelsk, Belarus 13 C15
Yemen ■, Asia 32 E3
Yenangyaung, Burma . 29 J19
Yenbo = Yanbu 'al Baḥr, Si. Arabia 30 F3
Yenda, Australia ... 43 E4
Yenice, Turkey 17 E12
Yenisey ➤, Russia .. 20 B9
Yeniseysk, Russia ... 21 D10
Yeniseyskiy Zaliv, Russia 20 B9
Yenyuka, Russia ... 21 D13
Yeo ➤, U.K. 9 G5
Yeo, L., Australia ... 41 E3
Yeola, India 28 J9
Yeovil, U.K. 9 G5
Yeppoon, Australia .. 42 C5
Yerbent, Turkmenistan 28 F6
Yerbogachen, Russia . 21 C11
Yerevan, Armenia ... 19 F7
Yerington, U.S.A. ... 56 G4
Yermak, Kazakstan .. 20 D8
Yermo, U.S.A. 57 J5
Yeropol, Russia ... 21 C17
Yershov, Russia 19 D8
Yerushalayim = Jerusalem, Israel .. 33 D4
Yes Tor, U.K. 9 G4
Yeso, U.S.A. 55 H2
Yessey, Russia 21 C11
Yetman, Australia ... 43 D5
Yeu, Î. d', France .. 14 C2
Yevpatoriya, Ukraine . 19 E5
Yeysk, Russia 19 E6
Yezd = Yazd, Iran .. 31 D7
Yi 'Allaq, G., Egypt .. 33 E2
Yiannitsa, Greece ... 17 D10
Yibin, China 24 D5
Yichang, China 25 C6
Yichun, China 25 B7
Yıldız Dağları, Turkey . 17 D12
Yilehuli Shan, China .. 25 A7
Yinchuan, China 24 C5
Yindarlgooda, L., Australia 41 F3
Yingkou, China 25 B7
Yining, China 20 E9
Yinmabin, Burma .. 29 H19
Yirga Alem, Ethiopia . 32 F2
Yirrkala, Australia ... 42 A2
Yishan, China 24 D5
Yíthion, Greece ... 17 F10
Yiyang, China 25 D6
Yli-Kitka, Finland ... 6 C23
Ylitornio, Finland ... 6 C20
Ylivieska, Finland ... 6 D21
Yoakum, U.S.A. ... 55 L6
Yog Pt., Phil. 27 B6
Yogyakarta, Indonesia 27 G14
Yoho Nat. Park, Canada 50 C5
Yojoa, L. de, Honduras 60 D2
Yokadouma, Cameroon 36 D2
Yokkaichi, Japan ... 23 G8
Yoko, Cameroon ... 36 C2
Yokohama, Japan ... 23 G9
Yokosuka, Japan ... 23 G9
Yola, Nigeria 35 G8
Yolaina, Cordillera de, Nic. 60 D3
Yoloten, Turkmenistan 31 B9
Yom ➤, Thailand .. 26 A2
Yonago, Japan 23 G6

Yonaguni-Jima, Japan 23 M1
Yonezawa, Japan ... 22 F10
Yonibana, S. Leone .. 34 G3
Yonkers, U.S.A. ... 52 E9
Yonne ➤, France .. 14 B5
York, Australia 41 F2
York, U.K. 8 D6
York, Ala., U.S.A. .. 55 J10
York, Nebr., U.S.A. .. 54 E6
York, Pa., U.S.A. .. 52 F7
York, C., Australia .. 42 A3
York, City of □, U.K. . 8 D6
York, Kap, Greenland . 4 B4
York, Vale of, U.K. .. 8 C6
York Sd., Australia .. 40 C4
Yorke Pen., Australia . 43 E2
Yorketown, Australia . 43 F2
Yorkshire Wolds, U.K. . 8 C7
Yorkton, Canada ... 51 C8
Yoro, Honduras ... 60 C2
Yoron-Jima, Japan .. 23 L4
Yos Sudarso, Pulau = Dolak, Pulau, Indonesia 27 F9
Yosemite National Park, U.S.A. 57 H4
Yoshkar Ola, Russia .. 18 C8
Yotvata, Israel 33 F4
Youghal, Ireland ... 10 F3
Young, Australia ... 43 E4
Young, Canada 51 C7
Younghusband, L., Australia 43 E2
Younghusband Pen., Australia 43 F2
Youngstown, Canada . 50 C6
Youngstown, U.S.A. . 52 E5
Yozgat, Turkey 19 G5
Ypres = Ieper, Belgium 11 D2
Yreka, U.S.A. 56 F2
Ystad, Sweden 7 J15
Ysyk-Köl, Ozero, Kyrgyzstan 20 E8
Ytyk Kyuyel, Russia .. 21 C14
Yu Jiang ➤, China .. 25 D6
Yuan Jiang ➤, China . 25 D6
Yuba City, U.S.A. .. 56 G3
Yūbari, Japan 22 C10
Yūbetsu, Japan ... 22 B11
Yucatán □, Mexico .. 59 C7
Yucatán, Canal de, Caribbean 60 B2
Yucatan Str. = Yucatán, Canal de, Caribbean . 60 B2
Yucca, U.S.A. 57 J6
Yuci, China 25 C6
Yuendumu, Australia . 40 D5
Yugoslavia ■, Europe . 17 B9
Yukon □, U.S.A. .. 46 B3
Yukon Territory □, Canada 46 B6
Yukta, Russia 21 C11
Yukuhashi, Japan ... 23 H5
Yulara, Australia ... 41 E5
Yule ➤, Australia ... 40 D2
Yuleba, Australia ... 43 D4
Yuma, Ariz., U.S.A. . 57 K6
Yuma, Colo., U.S.A. . 54 E3
Yuma, B. de, Dom. Rep. 61 C6
Yumen, China 24 C4
Yuna, Australia ... 41 E2
Yungas, Bolivia 62 G5
Yunnan □, China .. 24 D5
Yunta, Australia ... 43 E2
Yurga, Russia 20 D9
Yurimaguas, Peru ... 62 E3
Yuryung Kaya, Russia . 21 B12
Yuscarán, Honduras . 60 D2
Yushu, China 24 C4
Yuxan Qarabağ = Nagorno-Karabakh, Azerbaijan 19 F8
Yuxi, China 24 D5
Yuzawa, Japan ... 22 E10
Yuzhno-Sakhalinsk, Russia 21 E15
Yvetot, France 14 B4

Zaanstad, Neths. ... 11 B4
Zāb al Kabīr ➤, Iraq . 30 C4
Zāb aş Şaḡīr ➤, Iraq . 30 C4
Zabaykalsk, Russia ... 21 E12
Zābol, Iran 31 D9
Zābol □, Iran 31 E9
Zabrze, Poland 13 C10
Zacapa, Guatemala .. 60 D2
Zacapu, Mexico 58 D4
Zacatecas, Mexico ... 58 C4
Zacatecas □, Mexico . 58 C4
Zacatecoluca, El Salv. . 60 D2
Zachary, U.S.A. ... 55 K9
Zacoalco, Mexico ... 58 C4
Zacualtipán, Mexico .. 59 C5
Zadar, Croatia 12 F8
Zadetkyi Kyun, Burma 26 C1
Zafarqand, Iran 31 C7
Zafra, Spain 15 C2
Żagań, Poland 12 C8
Zagazig, Egypt 35 B12
Zāgheh, Iran 31 C6
Zagorsk = Sergiyev Posad, Russia 18 C6
Zagreb, Croatia ... 12 F9

Zāgros, Kūhhā-ye, Iran 31 C6
Zagros Mts. = Zāgros, Kūhhā-ye, Iran .. 31 C6
Zāhedān, Fārs, Iran .. 31 D7
Zāhedān, Sīstān va Balūchestān, Iran 31 D9
Zahlah, Lebanon ... 33 B4
Zaïre = Congo ➤, Africa 36 F2
Zaječar, Serbia, Yug. . 17 C10
Zakamensk, Russia .. 21 D11
Zakhodnaya Dzvina = Daugava ➤, Latvia . 7 H21
Zākhū, Iraq 30 B4
Zákinthos, Greece .. 17 F9
Zakopane, Poland ... 13 D10
Zalaegerszeg, Hungary 13 E9
Zalău, Romania ... 13 E12
Zaleshchiki = Zalishchyky, Ukraine 13 D13
Zalew Wiślany, Poland 13 A10
Zalingei, Sudan ... 35 F10
Zalishchyky, Ukraine . 13 D13
Zambeze ➤, Africa .. 37 H7
Zambezi = Zambeze ➤, Africa ... 37 H7
Zambezi, Zambia ... 37 G4
Zambia ■, Africa ... 37 G5
Zamboanga, Phil. ... 27 C6
Zamora, Mexico 58 D4
Zamora, Spain 15 B3
Zamość, Poland ... 13 C12
Zandvoort, Neths. .. 11 B4
Zanesville, U.S.A. .. 52 F4
Zangābād, Iran 30 B5
Zanjān, Iran 31 B6
Zanjān □, Iran 31 B6
Zanjān ➤, Iran 31 B6
Zante = Zákinthos, Greece 17 F9
Zanthus, Australia .. 41 F3
Zanzibar, Tanzania .. 36 F7
Zaouiet El-Kala = Bordj Omar Driss, Algeria . 34 C7
Zaouiet Reggane, Algeria 34 C6
Zap Suyu = Zāb al Kabīr ➤, Iraq ... 30 C4
Zapadnaya Dvina = Daugava ➤, Latvia . 7 H21
Západné Beskydy, Europe 13 D10
Zapala, Argentina ... 64 D2
Zapata, U.S.A. 55 M5
Zapolyarnyy, Russia .. 18 A5
Zaporizhzhya, Ukraine 19 E6
Zaporozhye = Zaporizhzhya, Ukraine 19 E6
Zara, Turkey 30 B3
Zaragoza, Coahuila, Mexico 58 B4
Zaragoza, Nuevo León, Mexico 59 C5
Zaragoza, Spain ... 15 B5
Zarand, Kermān, Iran . 31 D8
Zarand, Markazī, Iran . 31 C6
Zaranj, Afghan. 28 D2
Zarasai, Lithuania .. 7 J22
Zárate, Argentina ... 64 C5
Zard, Kūh-e, Iran ... 31 C6
Zāreh, Iran 31 C6
Zaria, Nigeria 34 F7
Zarneh, Iran 30 C5
Zarqā', Nahr az ➤, Jordan 33 C4
Zarrīn, Iran 31 C7
Zaruma, Ecuador ... 62 D3
Żary, Poland 12 C8
Zarzis, Tunisia 35 B8
Zaskar Mts., India .. 28 C10
Zastron, S. Africa .. 37 K5
Zavāreh, Iran 31 C7
Zavitinsk, Russia ... 21 D13
Zavodovski, I., Antarctica 5 B1
Zawiercie, Poland ... 13 C10
Zāwiyat al Bayḍā = Al Bayḍā, Libya ... 35 B10
Zāyā, Iraq 30 C5
Zāyandeh ➤, Iran .. 31 C7
Zaysan, Kazakstan .. 20 E9
Zaysan, Oz., Kazakstan 20 E9
Zayü, China 24 D4
Zāzūr, Iran 31 C6
Zbarazh, Ukraine ... 13 D13
Zdolbuniv, Ukraine .. 13 C14
Zduńska Wola, Poland 13 C10
Zeballos, Canada ... 50 D3
Zeebrugge, Belgium . 11 C3
Zeehan, Australia ... 42 G4
Zeeland □, Neths. .. 11 C3
Zefat, Israel 33 C4
Zeil, Mt., Australia .. 40 D5
Zeila, Somali Rep. .. 32 E3
Zeitz, Germany 12 C7
Zelenograd, Russia .. 18 C6
Zelenogradsk, Russia . 7 J19
Zémio, C.A.R. 36 D5
Zemun, Serbia, Yug. . 17 B9
Zenica, Bos.-H. ... 17 B7
Žepče, Bos.-H. ... 17 B8
Zeya, Russia 21 D13
Zeya ➤, Russia 21 D13

Zghartā, Lebanon ... 33 A4
Zgorzelec, Poland ... 12 C8
Zhabinka, Belarus .. 13 B13
Zhailma, Kazakstan .. 20 D7
Zhambyl, Kazakstan .. 20 E8
Zhangaqazaly, Kazakstan 20 E7
Zhangjiakou, China .. 25 B6
Zhangye, China 24 C5
Zhangzhou, China ... 25 D6
Zhanjiang, China ... 25 D6
Zhannetty, Ostrov, Russia 21 B16
Zhanyi, China 24 D5
Zhaotong, China ... 24 D5
Zhashkiv, Ukraine ... 13 D16
Zhayyq ➤, Kazakstan 19 E9
Zhdanov = Mariupol, Ukraine 19 E6
Zhejiang □, China .. 25 D7
Zheleznodorozhnyy, Russia 18 B9
Zheleznogorsk-Ilimskiy, Russia 21 D11
Zhengzhou, China .. 25 C6
Zhetiqara, Kazakstan . 20 D7
Zhezqazghan, Kazakstan 20 E7
Zhigansk, Russia ... 21 C13
Zhilinda, Russia ... 21 C12
Zhitomir = Zhytomyr, Ukraine 13 C15
Zhlobin, Belarus ... 13 B16
Zhmerinka = Zhmerynka, Ukraine . 13 D15
Zhmerynka, Ukraine . 13 D15
Zhob, Pakistan 28 D6
Zhodino = Zhodzina, Belarus 13 A15
Zhodzina, Belarus .. 13 A15
Zhokhova, Ostrov, Russia 21 B16
Zhongdian, China ... 24 D4
Zhumadian, China .. 25 C6
Zhytomyr, Ukraine .. 13 C15
Ziārān, Iran 31 B6
Zibo, China 25 C6
Zielona Góra, Poland . 12 C8
Zierikzee, Neths. ... 11 C3
Zigey, Chad 35 F9
Zigong, China 24 D5
Ziguinchor, Senegal . 34 F2
Zihuatanejo, Mexico . 58 D4
Žilina, Slovak Rep. .. 13 D10
Zillah, Libya 35 C9
Zima, Russia 21 D11
Zimapán, Mexico ... 59 C5
Zimbabwe ■, Africa . 37 H5
Zimnicea, Romania .. 13 G13
Zinder, Niger 34 F7
Zion National Park, U.S.A. 57 H7
Zirreh, Gowd-e, Afghan. 28 E3
Zitácuaro, Mexico ... 58 D4
Ziway, L., Ethiopia .. 32 F2
Zlatograd, Bulgaria .. 17 D11
Zlatoust, Russia ... 18 C10
Zlin, Czech Rep. ... 13 D9
Zmeinogorsk, Kazakstan 20 D9
Znojmo, Czech Rep. . 12 D9
Zobeyrī, Iran 30 C5
Zoetermeer, Neths. .. 11 B4
Zolochev = Zolochiv, Ukraine 13 D13
Zolochiv, Ukraine ... 13 D13
Zomba, Malawi 37 H7
Zongo, Dem. Rep. of the Congo 36 D3
Zonguldak, Turkey .. 19 F5
Zorritos, Peru 62 D2
Zouar, Chad 35 D9
Zouérate = Zouîrât, Mauritania 34 D3
Zouîrât, Mauritania .. 34 D3
Zoutkamp, Neths. .. 11 A6
Zrenjanin, Serbia, Yug. 17 B9
Zufār, Oman 32 D5
Zug, Switz. 14 C8
Zugspitze, Germany .. 12 E6
Zuid-Holland □, Neths. 11 C4
Zuidbeveland, Neths. . 11 C3
Zuidhorn, Neths. ... 11 A6
Zula, Eritrea 32 D2
Zumbo, Mozam. ... 37 H6
Zumpango, Mexico .. 59 D5
Zunhua, U.S.A. 57 J9
Zunyi, China 24 D5
Zurbāţīyah, Iraq ... 30 C5
Zürich, Switz. 14 C8
Zutphen, Neths. ... 11 B6
Zūzan, Iran 31 C8
Zverinogolovskoye, Russia 20 D7
Zvishavane, Zimbabwe 37 J6
Zvolen, Slovak Rep. .. 13 D10
Zwettl, Austria 12 D8
Zwickau, Germany .. 12 C7
Zwolle, Neths. 11 B6
Zwolle, U.S.A. 55 K8
Żyrardów, Poland ... 13 B11
Zyryan, Kazakstan .. 20 E9
Zyryanovsk = Zyryan, Kazakstan 20 E9
Żywiec, Poland 13 D10